COAL IN VICTORIAN BRITAIN

CONTENTS OF THE EDITION

COAL IN VICTORIAN BRITAIN

GENERAL EDITOR
John Benson

Part I: Coal in the Victorian Economy

Volume 1
Useful Knowledge

Edited by
Quentin Outram

Routledge
Taylor & Francis Group
LONDON AND NEW YORK

First published 2012 by Pickering & Chatto (Publishers) Limited

Published 2016 by Routledge
2 Park Square, Milton Park, Abingdon, Oxon OX14 4RN
711 Third Avenue, New York, NY 10017, USA

Routledge is an imprint of the Taylor & Francis Group, an informa business

BRITISH LIBRARY CATALOGUING IN PUBLICATION DATA

Coal in Victorian Britain.
Part 1, Volumes 1–3.
1. Coal trade – Great Britain – History – 19th century – Sources. 2. Coal mines and mining – Great Britain – History – 19th century – Sources. 3. Coal – Environmental aspects – Great Britain – History – 19th century – Sources. 4. Coal mine accidents – Great Britain – History – 19th century – Sources. 5. Coal miners – Great Britain – Social conditions – 19th century – Sources. 6. Coal miners – Labor unions – Great Britain – History – 19th century – Sources. I. Benson, John, 1945 July 23– II. Outram, Quentin.
338.2'724'0941'09034–dc22

ISBN-13: 978-1-84893-060-5 (set)

Typeset by Pickering & Chatto (Publishers) Limited

CONTENTS

GENERAL INTRODUCTION

Scale and Significance

It is almost impossible to exaggerate the role that the coal industry played in Victorian (and Edwardian) Britain.[1] Coal, along with cotton, was the driving force of the British industrial revolution, and had an impact, directly and indirectly, upon the lives of everybody in the country. The bare statistics alone attest to the vitality and success of this key sector of the economy. Between 1800 and 1913, the industry's output of coal increased from ten million tons to over 287 million tons, its exports from less than a million tons to more than 73 million tons, and its workforce from 40,000 to in excess of 1.1 million. By the time the First World War broke out in 1914, nearly two-thirds of all the coal entering world trade was mined in Britain, and coal mining accounted for one in ten of Great Britain's entire occupied male population.[2] Coal, explains B. R. Mitchell, 'had come to be an essential input for all the main productive activities of the country except agriculture, and – what was perhaps the most strategically important for the economy as a whole – for the main means of transport both within the country and for its overseas trade.'[3] According to the chairman of the coal owners' association, the Mining Association of Great Britain, the nineteenth and early twentieth-century industry had 'a great record of progress and expansion ... It was private enterprise, real private enterprise, and in 1913 it led the world.'[4]

The expansion of coal mining had a profound impact not just upon the British economy but upon the social, cultural, religious, industrial and political life of the country.[5] The success of the industry came, in particular, at the cost of the health and well-being of those employed in it. Whether or not the coal owners were the uncaring and neglectful despots of popular imagination or were motivated, some of them at least, by care and consideration for their employees, the industry was a killer.[6] 'The most painful feature of the coal-mining industry', it was stressed in 1920, remained 'the heavy toll it takes on human life by accidents causing death or injury [or disease].'[7] It is not easy to appreciate the impact of such a cull. Accidents alone exerted a terrible toll: 'Between 1868 and 1919, a miner was killed at work every six hours, seriously injured every two hours, and injured badly enough to need a week off work every two or three minutes.'[8]

The success of the industry also meant, explains Roy Church, that the employers were able 'to externalise the social costs of coalmining by disfiguring the landscape and indirectly by damaging the national health'. He cites an 1842 description of a rural area transformed by the winning of new collieries: the 'dense volumes of rolling smoke – the funeral colour imparted to the district – are surely sufficient to untenant the seats of the wealthy'.[9] When Sir Arthur Redmayne (who went on to become Chief Inspector of Mines) recalled the eight-and-a-half years he had spent in the Durham mining village of Hetton-le-Hole during the 1880s, he remembered 'the discomfort and inconvenience of the dwellings provided for the miners in those days – a lack of adequate water supply, one outside tap shared between several householders, communal ash-bins close to the cottage doors, bad roads and a dreary outlook'.[10]

The industry's activities had an impact far beyond the coalfield towns and villages that extracted the nation's fuel. There have been the stirrings of interest in environmental (or 'green') history. All over the country, the pollution produced when coal was burned, whether in factories, on trains or in people's homes, exacerbated – when it did not cause – the heart and lung complaints that exercised such a deleterious effect upon nineteenth- and early twentieth-century health.[11] In big cities such as Manchester and London, winter fogs had consequences both physical and psychological. During a week of heavy fog in London in 1873, for instance, many people were 'thrown so much out of health that they did not recover for some weeks'. Indeed, there were apparently 700 more deaths than would normally have been expected in the capital at that time of year.[12] Just over a quarter of a century later, the Inter-Departmental Committee on Physical Deterioration, which was set up in the wake of the revelations of working-class failing uncovered by the Boer War, condemned air pollution as one of the major causes of the country's poor health.[13]

The scale and success of coal mining had other ramifications besides. 'The national economic importance of this labour-intensive industry', Church goes on, 'found a parallel in the central role played by the miners in British industrial and political life.' The concentration of miners in certain parts of the country (along with the industry's increasing concentration of production, the nature of mining work and all that went with it) enabled them to play a leading role in the trade union movement, and thus in labour politics as a whole. Between 1889 and 1914, the Miners' Federation of Great Britain consolidated its position as the largest bargaining organization not just in the coalfields, but in the country as a whole. By 1908, it represented 60 per cent of all miners – and a remarkable 25 per cent of all trade unionists.[14]

The Federation used every means at is disposal to secure its two principal aims: a minimum wage and an eight-hour day for all underground workers. It fought two enormous set-piece battles during this period. The 1893 lock-out, for example, lasted from July until November, involved 300,000 men, resulted in the loss of 21 million working days, and was settled only by the intervention of the government. This was the point, according to B. J. McCormick, at which 'the state became a party to industrial matters and voluntary collective bargaining started to decline.[15] The Federation also did its best to secure a body of sympathizers and supporters to represent the miners' interests in Parliament. It was a slow process, but in 1906 it managed to return eleven of its candidates as MPs. In 1910, fifteen were elected. The result was, claims Roy Gregory, that by 1918 the miners 'had become the Praetorian guard of an explicitly socialist Labour Party.'[16]

It really is difficult to overstate the importance of coal in Victorian and Edwardian Britain. Indeed, Roy Church opens his magisterial study of the industry by noting that whereas the economic historian Sir John Clapham labelled the second quarter of the nineteenth century 'The Railway Age', Britain's foremost locomotive engineer, George Stephenson, took an altogether different view. The strength of Britain, he concluded 'lies in her iron and coal beds ... The Lord Chancellor now sits upon a bag of wool; but wool has long since ceased to be emblematical of the staple commodity of England. He ought rather to sit upon a bag of coal.'[17]

Homogeneity and Continuity

The editors of the volumes in this collection have kept coal mining's broad reach – its scale and its significance – constantly in mind. We have also taken account of recent developments in the historiography of the industry. On the one hand, the study of coal mining has remained untouched by – and often seemingly unaware of – intellectual developments such as structuralism and poststructuralism, modernism and postmodernism. On the other hand, it is no exaggeration to say that our understanding of the nineteenth- and early twentieth-century industry has been transformed over the past twenty-five to thirty years.

One enduring difficulty is that stereotyping has been more common in coal mining historiography than in almost any other branch of British business, social and labour history. Some views of the industry remain almost entirely unchallenged. The coal owners have been regarded, and not just by trade unionists and trade union historians, as the epitome of capitalist selfishness and intransigence.[18] As the Conservative cabinet minister Lord Birkenhead remarked at the time of the 1926 general strike, 'it would be possible to say without exaggeration of the miners' leaders that they were the stupidest men in England if we had not had frequent occasion to meet the owners'. According to Quentin Outram, the leading authority on British coal owners (and editor of the first three volumes in this collection), this was a group of employers which was 'widely regarded, and not merely by their employees, as obdurate, stubborn, intransigent, uncompromising, aggressive, vengeful, greedy, tight-fisted, flint-hearted, short-sighted, hide-bound, arrogant and incompetent'.[19]

The charge sheet against the coal owners was – and is – long, varied and persuasive. The owners failed to mechanize, it is said, in the face of declining labour productivity. Although a number of coal-cutting machines were patented during the second half of the century, few employers chose to adopt them. The result was, as Carolyn Baylies explained in 1993, that 'Only 3¼ million tons was cut by machinery in the UK in the early years of the twentieth century, as opposed to 52 million tons in the US, though total output was roughly the same in both.'[20] The owners were just as culpable, it is claimed, when it came to the industry's appalling strike record. Indeed, as Roy Church and Quentin Outram pointed out in 1998, 'the perception that coalowners, or at least their leaders, have been bulwarks in the defence of *laissez-faire* capitalism seems unchallenged.'[21] Moreover, the owners were indifferent, it is generally believed, to the appalling toll that the industry took upon its workforce.[22] Well into the 1920s and 30s, concludes Arthur McIvor, they took advantage, where and when they could, in order to 'skimp on safety and health'.[23] Victor Allen's language is more unusual than his conclusion.

> The coal owners did virtually as they liked with their mines, constrained only by geological conditions and the collective reactions of miners. They strutted about the coal scene intent on making profit, with local authorities, Government politicians, the police and the armed forces in their wake, supporting and preserving the conditions which made the maximization of profit possible.[24]

Another perception of the coal industry that remained more or less unchallenged until relatively recently concerned the character and behaviour of the workforce. The men tended to be seen – at best – as rough and ready. 'The typical coal miner is not always an attractive individual on the outside,' explained one industry expert in 1920, 'but an uncouth and unprepossessing exterior often hides a strong and resolute character and a kindly disposition.'[25] It was many years before such views were challenged in any serious way. Indeed, the trade union historians who began to study the industry during the 1960s and 70s were inclined to perpetuate a similarly disparaging view of the miners, their families and their capacity for self-improvement. 'In many places' in the first half of the century, claimed Ray Challinor and Brian Ripley, 'miners lived a life of barbaric isolation in hovels far worse than those any other section of the community would tolerate.'[26] According to J. E. Williams, 'The basic needs of the miner and his family were easily satisfied in the 'sixties. His pint of beer was comparatively cheap and beyond that his pleasures were few and simple.'[27] These were not isolated voices.

> The brutalized conditions of the miner were reflected in the dirt, neglect and habitual drunkenness prevailing in many mining villages ... violence was never far away from the miner's life, either at work or leisure. His basic needs remained simple and his tastes were largely customary, hence the increase in absenteeism during booms ... Habitual drunkenness led to 'irregular habits' and drained the miner's meagre income, impairing his ability to create and sustain trade unionism.[28]

It is not difficult to see, of course, that such views sit uneasily alongside another, much noted characteristic of coalfield life, the miner's supposed tendency towards industrial militancy. Indeed, some historians of the industry and its unions seemed to see developments primarily in terms of strikes, lockouts and play-days. The trade union sponsors of the miners' histories published in the decades following the Second World War were clear that this was the approach which they wanted. 'Who will read these pages and will fail to realise the mighty debt this nation owes to its miners?', demanded the president, vice-president and secretary of the National Union of Mineworkers in their 1949 foreword to the first volume of R. Page Arnot's history of the Miners' Federation of Great Britain. 'Yet even as that is recognised the thought is borne in on us, as the various events unfold themselves, what a bitter struggle these men had to wage to rise from oppression and want to their outstanding place as the vanguard of the British working class.'[29]

Subsequent generations of trade union historians were less inclined than one might imagine to distance themselves from such commitment, to move beyond the dominant heroic, and often hagiographic, perspective on the working-class past.[30] Assuming rather too readily that the history of the union was synonymous with the history of the workforce and the history of the wider community, they produced a series of detailed institutional studies – what has been dubbed by one hostile commentator as 'the boring bureaucracy of trade unions and proletarian parties'.[31] It was a genre which both reflected and reinforced the 'long standing tradition in which the miner or collier is seen as the original and quintessential proletarian'.[32]

It was but a short step from historical accounts of individual strikes and trade unions to sociological attempts to construct ideal models of mining militancy and the mining communities from which such solidarities emerged.[33] By the mid-1970s, there were three – sometimes overlapping – models of mining community designed to explain the workforce's legendary solidarity and readiness to strike. The first was the 'archetypal proletarian' community, hinted at above, in which, it is said, miners reacted with an unusual degree of unity and determination to the extreme capitalist exploitation which they confronted. The second model was that of the 'occupational' community, in which miners' kinship, neighbourhood, industrial and political ties can be understood, it is claimed, only in terms of their common relationship to the workplace.[34] The third, and most influential, was the 'isolated mass' model of community life. Miners' propensity to strike was explicable, this suggested, by the tendency of miners to live in isolated, homogeneous industrial communities, where shared grievances encourage the workforce to develop the 'habit of solidarity'. Indeed, Clark Kerr and Abraham Siegel suggested as long ago as 1954 that in such homogeneous environments, strikes were 'a kind of colonial revolt against far-removed authority, an outlet for accumulated tensions, and a substitute for occupational and social mobility'.[35]

It is clear then that for many years, the study of the nineteenth- and early twentieth-century coal industry, its owners, its workers, its communities and its industrial relations practices was characterized by a readiness to generalize, and a tendency in particular to regard the industry – in its broadest sense – as fundamentally monolithic and unchanging. This is not to deny, of course, the value either of the empirical research which was conducted or of the theoretical modelling which was undertaken by historians and sociologists (and others) in the years following the Second World War. But the essentialism underlying so much of this scholarly work made it difficult to move beyond the assumptions with which, and the paradigms within which, those interested in the industry were working.

Hetrogeneity and Change

Each generation reinterprets the past anew, and the last thirty to forty years have seen major challenges to the orthodoxies of British coal mining history. What was once implicit has been made explicit, what was once accepted has been challenged. This was an industry, it is now widely recognized, in which powerful centrifugal and centripetal pressures were at play. As A. J. Taylor observed in 1976, 'the twin forces of geology and geography have determined the course of mining development; and because of this the history of coal mining is to be approached as much at the regional as at the national level.'[36] The heterogeneity of coal and its markets, the trade cycle and the different trajectories of growth (and decline) in different parts of the country make all generalization about the owners, the industry, its workers, its communities and its industrial relations hazardous in the extreme.[37]

Research undertaken since the 1970s shows, for example, that the coal owners were rather less short-sighted than conventional stereotyping suggests. This work reveals too that miners and their families did not necessarily live bleakly narrow lives in featureless, single-industry communities cut off from the remainder of society. Moreover, this new scholarship makes clear, just as radically, that it is no longer possible to think of the nineteenth- and early twentieth-century industry in terms simply of an unending – and unchanging – confrontation between grasping owners and militant miners, locked together in an unending stream of toxic strikes and debilitating lockouts. Heterogeneity, it now seems clear, was as important as homogeneity, and change as significant as continuity.

There is still not much sympathy for the coal owners.[38] But whatever the attractions of stereotyping and demonization, such a stance, it is now seen, is unlikely to prove very helpful in unravelling the complex history of this once great industry. It has been shown, for instance, that while some owners were almost wilfully blind to the possible benefits of coal-face mechanization, the majority were far less Luddite than their critics allowed. In the main, the owners mechanized, it is now suggested, where and when they deemed it sensible to do so. Rhodri Walters argues, for example, that the reason for the employers' failure to adopt mechanized coal cutting in South Wales 'was certainly not lack of interest in new techniques, but rather the difficulty of using cutters in most Welsh coalmines and the dubious saving of costs that resulted.'[39] Roy Church defends the owners more generally from accusations of inertia and lack of initiative. He believes that 'only between one-quarter and one-third of coal mined in 1913 was geologically suitable for mechanised cutting'. If this is true, he points out, it 'places the 8.6 per cent mined in this way in 1913 into a different perspective from that which assumes that 100 per cent of coal could have been cut by machinery'.[40] The owners' reluctance to mechanize, a growing body of opinion now agrees, was based less on prejudice and complacency than upon a reasoned assessment of the risks and benefits likely to accrue from such large-scale investment.[41]

Nor is it possible any longer to accept unquestioningly the characterization of nineteenth- and early twentieth-century coal mining communities as patriarchal, dreary backwaters, cut off physically and culturally from the rest of society, and bereft of all amenities bar the chapel, the co-op and the ubiquitous public house. Such stereotyping, it is now apparent, is not very helpful: it both simplifies the gender relations in, and exaggerates the isolation of, many, if not most, mining communities.[42]

Not all intellectual innovations have passed mining history by. We know much more than we used to about the lives of the women (and children) living in the coalfields. In her pioneering study of 'pit bow lasses' published in 1980, Angela John took issue with existing accounts of mining communities which had 'not only forgotten the single woman and the widow' but had also 'internalised the male miner's "eye-view"'. Her aim, she explained, was 'to depict the pit brow lasses not just as crucial members of the family in an industry where familial support was extremely important, but to show them as women and as part of a working class involved in production'.[43] John's lead has been followed, but not with the enthusiasm that one might have expected. There has been a vigorous debate, it is true, about the health of children in coal mining communities.[44] There has been other interesting work besides. Dot Jones's research enhances our understanding of women's lives in the Rhondda,[45] and Griselda Carr's study of *Coal Communities in Northern England in the Early Twentieth Century* considers issues such as the socialization of girls, women's networks and the impact of industrial struggle on women's lives. She is at pains to reassert the historiography of solidarity. 'Once persuaded in family discussions of the justice of the union's fight against cuts in wages or the lengthening of the working day, most women were as stalwart as their men, whatever the degree of hardship imposed upon them during the struggle.'[46]

We now know more about the health (and ill-health) of mining work. The oral evidence collected by Arthur McIvor and Ronald Johnston for their book, *Miners' Lung: A History of Dust Disease in British Coal Mining* during the late nineteenth and early to mid twentieth centuries, 'sheds significant insights', they explain, 'into the damage accrued to workers' bodies from the interface between a productionist managerial ethos in a period of contraction for deep coal mining and the persistence of a *machismo*, high-risk work culture'.[47] We also have a clearer understanding of the isolation (and integration) of mining communities. It is clear, for instance that few, if any colliery villages were more than a few miles from a non-mining settlement, and during the second half of the century the railways broke down still more the isolation of all but the most remote villages. Indeed, it is easily overlooked that miners all over the country lived in large towns and cities. It was common for Yorkshire miners to commute to work from places like Bradford, Barnsley, Leeds, Castleford and Wakefield; and by 1911, over a third of all Lancashire mineworkers lived in towns and cities such as Burnley, Bolton, Blackburn, Oldham, Wigan, St Helens and Manchester.[48]

Moreover, the conventional characterization of mining communities sits oddly with another widely recognized feature of coalfield life, the support which miners and their families offered to movements such as co-operation, trade unionism and Methodism.[49] It is true that there was often a time lag between the establishment of colliery settlements and the provision of the amenities needed by their growing, often youthful populations.[50] However, by the end of the century, many pit villages had developed a wide-ranging, and often sophisticated, variety of spiritual, commercial, cultural and leisure facilities. Hywel Francis and David Smith open their monumental study of the 'Fed', the South Wales Miners' Federation, with a chapter examining 'The Union in its Society'. In most early twentieth-century valley towns, they stress, 'there existed embryonic chain-stores, cavernous emporia positively dripping with hardware of one sort or another. This was a society concerned about its appearance, anxious about its watch-chains and fobs, queuing for haircuts and shaves on Saturday nights'.[51]

However, we know most by far about Northumberland and Durham.[52] James Jaffe examines miners' attitudes towards the market;[53] Robert Moore and Robert Lee subject Methodism and the Church of England to new, sophisticated levels of analysis;[54] while Bill Williamson uses the life of his grandfather, Northumberland miner James Brown, to produce what he describes as 'a biographical study of social change in mining'.[55] Meanwhile, Robert Colls has produced two substantial studies of song, work, culture and protest in the north-east during the first half of the nineteenth century.[56] Huw Beynon and Terry Austrin adopt a similarly broad approach in their examination of working-class politics in County Durham between the early nineteenth century and the mid-twentieth century. Believing that 'history and sociology were dominated by identical concerns', they did their best to understand 'how the social is constructed'.[57] Their book included, as might be expected, chapters on 'Durham Mining Villages', 'Rough Cavils' and 'Community and Association'. Dealing with the latter, they placed great importance on the role played by the chapel, the co-operative store – and the working men's club. Although the Club and Institute Union was founded in London in 1862, there were no clubs registered in Durham until the very end of the century. Thereafter, however, the movement grew apace. By the time representatives of the association met at Prudhoe in 1919 to discuss the establishment of their own brewery, 'there were 220 clubs registered across the Durham coalfield, all of them administered by committees of workmen – most usually miners'.[58]

The research undertaken in recent decades also challenges widely held views concerning the strike propensity and thus the militancy of the coal mining work force. Peter Ackers explores the attitudes and behaviour of one overlooked group, the colliery deputies.[59] Carolyn Baylies examines the history of the Yorkshire miners between 1881 and 1918. Her book, she explains, 'is concerned with the fortunes of the miners in Yorkshire, their union and, to a lesser extent, the broader mining communities in which they lived during the Yorkshire Miners' Association's first decades.' But she is careful to point to the perils of generalization, distinguishing carefully between what went on at national level, at district level and at branch level – and indeed between what went on at different branches. 'The number and substance of local grievances and the level of satisfaction gained in dealings with management varied considerably from one branch to the next. Some were relatively trouble free over long periods. Others were hotbeds of agitation, with frequent complaints over management activities.'[60] It is an approach which distinguishes her work – despite the familiar format in which it appears – from many, if not most, earlier trade union commissioned histories.

However, it is comparative history which has been fundamental to the reassessment of militancy and strike propensity. Alan Campbell, for instance, compares developments in two mid-nineteenth-century Lanarkshire communities, Coatbridge and Larkhall, in order to identify the factors influencing the direction and pace of labour organization. On the one hand, 'trade union organisation and with it the tradition of the colliers' independence was crushed in Coatbridge by a series of inter-related factors. The ironmasters were able to impose their rigid discipline and social control upon a workforce that was fractured along lines of 'nationality, religion and craft jealousy under conditions, generally of a labour surplus'. On the other hand, in Larkhill, 'greater resilience amid the lesser numbers of Irishmen, a more stable community, and less determined and powerful employers ... clearly sustained the men of that district in their union struggles'.[61]

International, as well as intra-national, comparison has become increasingly fashionable in recent years. Spurred on no doubt by the International Congress for Mining History, whose first conference was held at Melbourne in 1985, historians of the industry have met with colleagues from around the world to discuss, and subsequently publish, the results of their research. Although much of this work, it must be said, confines itself to identifying developments in individual countries, it paves the way for the rigorous comparison most likely to advance our understanding of life in coalfield communities.[62]

Roger Fagge and Leighton James show what can be achieved. Fagge contrasts South Wales with Virginia, James compares South Wales and the Ruhr.[63] Why was it, wonders James, that mining trade unionism was more united in South Wales than it was in the Ruhr? Focusing upon organizational identities, he argues that, 'In the period between 1890 and 1926, south Wales exhibited a working-class political development, whereby a single union, the SWMF [South Wales Miners' Federation], and one party, the Labour Party, were able gradually to overcome sectionalist loyalties, dominate worker politics and enable a broad-based working-class identity to emerge. In the Ruhr region, by contrast, unions and parties representing working-class interests became increasingly fragmented.'[64]

It is Roy Church and Quentin Outram, once again, who provide the most detailed, most sophisticated and most though-provoking contribution to the reappraisal of strike propensity, employee militancy and industrial relations. Their research reveals, for instance, that between 1893 and 1913 – and indeed between 1914 and 1940 – 'South Wales and Scotland emerge as consistently more strike-prone than the industry in the country as a whole.' Indeed, they show that 'between 42 and 53 per cent of officially recorded local and district strikes occurred in only thirty-five places' (and this at a time when here were more – and sometimes many more – than 2,700 collieries operating in the country).[65] This means, to put it another way, that between 42 and 53 per cent of all local and district strikes took place in fewer than 1.3 per cent of all collieries. It is difficult to overstate the importance of this research. It shows, of course, that coal mining's strike record and industrial relations history was no more homogeneous – and no more predictable – than the employers' attitudes towards coal face mechanization or their employees' enthusiasm for trade-union organization.

Church and Outram's work demonstrates something too of the direction in which, and the extent to which, the study of nineteenth- and early twentieth-century British coal mining has been moving in recent years. It is easy, of course, to adopt a Whiggish complacency when reviewing the developing historiography of a subject in which one is interested. But in this case there truly is cause for satisfaction.

Coal, History and the Future

Coal mining in Britain is virtually dead. But concerns about global warming and the security of energy supplies combined with the expansion of the industry in other parts of the world may well herald – indeed are already beginning to herald – a revival of scholarly interest in coal, its workers and its communities.[66] So just as our generation refers so often to the nineteenth and early twentieth centuries, economic, social, cultural and political historians of the future may well look back to the early twenty-first century in their attempts to understand, and learn from, the lessons of the past. It is a development which, we hope of course, will be both fostered and facilitated by the six volumes that make up this collection.

John Benson

Acknowledgements

I am grateful for the advice of Daire Carr, Keith Gildart, James Jaffe and, in particular, of Peter Ackers and Quentin Outram.

Notes

1. The standard guide remains J. Benson, R. G. Neville and C. H. Thompson, *Bibliography of the British Coal Industry: Secondary Literature, Parliamentary and Departmental Papers, Mineral Maps and Plans and a Guide to Sources* (Oxford: Oxford University Press, 1981). The standard history is R. Church, *The History of the British Coal Industry Volume 3 1830–1913: Victorian Pre-eminence* (Oxford: Clarendon Press, 1986). For the years preceding and following the Victorian (and Edwardian) period, see M. W. Flinn, *The History of the British Coal Industry Volume 2 1700–1830: The Industrial Revolution* (Oxford: Clarendon Press, 1984) and B. Supple, *The History of the British Coal Industry Volume 4 1913–1946: The Political Economicy of Decline* (Oxford: Clarendon Press, 1987).
2. J. Benson, *British Coalminers in the Nineteenth Century: A Social History* (Dublin: Gill and Macmillan, 1980), ch. 1; Church, *Coal Industry*, ch. 9.
3. B. R. Mitchell, *Economic Development of the British Coal Industry 1800–1914* (Cambridge: Cambridge University Press, 1984), p. 1. Cf. G. Clark and D. Jacks, 'Coal and the Industrial Revolution, 1700–1869', *European Review of Economic History*, 11 (2007), pp. 39–72.

4. W. A. Lee, *Thirty Years in Coal 1917–1947: A Review of the Coal Mining Industry under Private Enterprise* (London: Mining Association of Great Britain, 1954), pp. 9–10.
5. See, for example, F. Gorman, *Banner Bright: An Illustrated History of the Banners of the British Trade Union Movement* (London: Allen Lane, 1973); *Coal: British Mining in Art 1680–1980* (London: Arts Council of Great Britain, 1982); D. Weinbrein, 'The Good Samaritan, Friendly Societies and the Gift Economy', *Social History*, 31 (2006), pp. 319–36; W. Jackson (ed.), *A Pitman' Anthology: Compiled by William Maurice 1872–1951* (London: James & James, 2004).
6. P. W. J. Bartrip and S. B. Burman, *The Wounded Soldiers of Industry: Industrial Compensation Policy 1833–1897* (Oxford: Clarendon Press, 1983); J. Benson, 'Myopia, Intransigence and Indifference? The British Coalowners, 1850–1914', in A. Westermann and E. Westermann (ed.), *Streik im Revier: Unruhe, Protest und Ausstand vom 8. bis 20. Jahrhundert* (St Katharinen: Scripta Mercaturae Verlag, 2007).
7. H. F. Bulman, *Coal Mining and the Coal Miner* (London: Methuen, 1920), p. 61.
8. Benson, *British Coalminers*, p. 43.
9. Church, *Coal Industry*, p. 780.
10. Benson, *British Coalminers*, p. 82.
11. J. Benson, *Affluence and Authority: A Social History of Twentieth-Century Britain* (London: Hodder Arnold, 2005), ch. 3.
12. P. Brimblecombe, *The Big Smoke: A History of Air Pollution in London since Medieval Times* (London: Routledge, 1987), pp. 122–3. See also S. Mosley, *The Chimney of the World: A History of Smoke Pollution in Victorian and Edwardian Manchester* (Cambridge: White Horse Press, 2001); P. Thorsheim, *Inventing Pollution: Coal, Smoke, and Culture in Britain since 1800* (Athens, GA: Ohio University Press, 2006). Cf. A. E. Dingle, '"The Monster Nuisance of All": Landowners, Alkali Manufacturers, and Air Pollution, 1828–64', *Economic History Review*, 35 (1982), pp. 529–48.
13. Church, *Coal Industry*, pp. 781–2. See also D. Stradling and P. Thorsheim, 'The Smoke of Great Cities: British and American Efforts to Control Air Pollution, 1860–1914', *Environmental History*, 4 (1999), pp. 6–31; B. Luckin, '"The Heart and Home of Horror": The Great London Fogs of the Late Nineteenth Century', *Social History*, 28 (2003), pp. 31–48.
14. Scotland, South Wales and Northumberland and Durham remained outside the Federation. J. Benson, 'Coalmining', in C. J. Wrigley (ed.), *A History of British Industrial Relations 1875–1914* (Brighton: Harvester Press, 1982), pp. 17–208, at p. 198.
15. B. J. McCormick, *Industrial Relations in the Coal Industry* (London: Macmillan, 1979), p. 21. Also T. Adams, 'Market and Institutional Forces in Industrial Relations: The Development of National Collective Bargaining, 1910–1920', *Economic History Review*, 50 (1997), pp. 506–30.
16. R. Gregory, *The Miners and British Politics 1906–1914* (Oxford: Oxford University Press, 1968), p. 178. Also Benson, 'Coalmining'.
17. Church, *Coal Industry*, p. 1. Also G. Orwell, *The Road to Wigan Pier* (London: Penguin, 1962), p. 18.
18. R. Church and Q. Outram, *Strikes and Solidarity: Coalfield Conflict in Britain 1889–1966* (Cambridge: Cambridge University Press, 1998), p. 60. See also R. Church, 'Employers, Trade Unions and the State, 1889–1987: The Origins and Decline of Tripartism in the British Coal Industry', in G. D. Feldman and K. Tenfelde (ed.), *Workers, Owners and Politics in Coal Mining: An International Comparison in Industrial Relations* (Oxford: Berg, 1990).

19. Q. Outram, '"The Stupidest Men in England"? The Industrial Relations Strategy of the Coalowners between the Lockouts, 1923–1924', *Historical Studies in Industrial Relations*, 4 (1997), pp. 65–6. Also Q. Outram, 'Class Warriors: The Coalowners', in J. McIlroy, A. Campbell and K. Gildart (ed.), *Industrial Politics and the 1926 Mining Lockout* (Cardiff: University of Wales Press, 2004), pp. 107–35.
20. C. Baylies, *The History of the Yorkshire Miners 1881–1918* (London: Routledge, 1993), pp. 200–1.
21. Church and Outram, *Strikes and Solidarity*, p. 60.
22. Benson, *Coal Miners*, p. 37. Some, of course, have stressed the paternalism of aristocratic owners. See, for example, G. Mee, *Aristocratic Enterprise: The Fitzwilliam Industrial Undertakings 1795–1857* (Glasgow: Blackie, 1975).
23. A. J. McIvor, *A History of Work in Britain, 1880–1950* (Basingstoke: Palgrave, 2001), p. 138.
24. V. L. Allen, *The Militancy of British Miners* (Shipley: Moor Press, 1981), p. 30.
25. Bulman, *Coal Mining*, p. 2.
26. R. Challinor and B. Ripley, *The Miners' Assocation: A Trade Union in the Age of the Chartists* (London: Lawrence and Wishart, 1968), p. 50.
27. J. E. Willams, *The Derbyshire Miners: A Study in Industrial and Social History* (London: Allen and Unwin, 1962), p. 61.
28. K. Burgess, *The Origins of British Industrial Relations: The Nineteenth Century Experience* (London: Croom Helm, 1975). See also D. Anderson, *The Orrell Coalfield, Lancashire 1740–1850* (Buxton: Moorland Publishing, 1975), p. 141.
29. R. Page Arnot, *The Miners: A History of the Miners' Federation of Great Britain 1889–1910* (London: Allen & Unwin, 1949), p. 5. See also his volumes, *A History of the Scottish Miners from the Earliest Times* (London: Allen & Unwin, 1955); *South Wales Miners Glowyr de Cymru: A History of the South Wales Miners' Federation (1898–1914)* (London: Allen & Unwin, 1967).
30. See, for example, Baylies, *Yorkshire Miners*, p. xii.
31. Mining histories probably displayed a stronger sense of community and society than most trade union histories. H. Perkin, 'Social History in Britain', *Journal of Social History*, 10 (1976), pp. 129–43 at p. 133.
32. R. Harrison, 'Introduction', in R. Harrison (ed.), *Independent Collier: The Coal Miner as Archetypal Proletarian Reconsidered* (Hassocks: Harvester Press, 1978), p. 3.
33. For a convenient summary, see R. Fagge, *Power, Culture and Conflict in the Coalfields: West Virginia and South Wales, 1900–1922* (Manchester: Manchester University Press, 1996), pp. 1–3.
34. Church and Outram, *Strikes and Solidarity*, pp. 138–9.
35. Ibid., p. 139. Also M. Bulmer, 'Social Structures and Social Change in the Twentieth-Century', in M. Bulmer (ed.), *Mining and Social Change in the Twentieth Century* (London: Croom Helm, 1978). The classic statement remains N. Dennis, F. Henriques and C. Slaughter, *Coal is our Life: An Analysis of a Yorkshire Mining Community* (London: Tavistock, 1969).
36. A. J. Taylor, 'Foreword', in J. Benson and R.G. Neville (ed.), *Studies in the Yorkshire Coal Industry* (Manchester: Manchester University Press, 1976).
37. Benson, *British Coalminers*, p. 9.
38. For a study of twentieth-century paternalism, see R. J. Waller, *The Dukeries Transformed: The Social and Political Development of a Twentieth-Century Coalfield* (Oxford: Clarendon Press, 1983).

39. R. Walters, 'Labour Productivity in the South Wales Steam-Coal Industry, 1870–1914', *Economic History Review*, 23 (1975), pp. 280–99 at p. 296.
40. Church, *Coal Industry*, p. 357.
41. See also D. Greasley, 'Fifty Years of Coal-Mining Productivity: The Record of the British Coal Industry before 1939', *Journal of Economic History*, 50 (1990), pp. 877–902.
42. A recent contribution is R. Thompson, 'A Breed Apart? Class and Community in a Somerset Coal-Mining Parish, *c.* 1750–1850', *Rural History*, 16 (2005), pp. 137–59.
43. A. John, *By the Sweat of their Brow: Women Workers at Victorian Coal Mines* (London: Croom Helm, 1980), p. 15. See also J. Humphries, 'Protective Legislation, the Capitalist State, and Working Class Men: The Case of the 1842 Mines Regulation Act', *Feminist Review*, 7 (1981), pp. 1–33.
44. P. Kirby, 'Causes of Short Stature among Coal-Mining Children, 1823–1850', *Economic History Review*, 48 (1995), pp. 687–99; J. Humphries, 'Short Stature among Coal-Mining Children: A Comment', *Economic History Review*, 50 (1997), pp. 531–7 at p. 531.
45. L. J. Williams and D. Jones, 'Women at Work in Nineteenth-Century Wales', *Llafur*, 3 (1982); D. Jones, 'Self-Help in Nineteenth-Century Wales: The Rise and Fall of the Female Friendly Society', *Llafur*, 4 (1984), pp. 14–26.
46. G. Carr, *Pit Women: Coal Communities in Northern England in the Early Twentieth Century* (London: Merlin Press, 2001), p. 153.
47. A. McIvor and R. Johnston, *Miners' Lung: A History of Dust Disease in British Coal Mining* (London: Ashgate, 2007). To place this outstanding contribution in its context, see McIvor, *Work*, ch. 5.
48. Benson, *British Coalminers*, p. 83.
49. For instance, P. Ackers, 'West End Chapel, Back Street Bethel: Labour and Capital in the Wigan Churches of Christ *c.* 1845–1945', *Journal of Ecclesiastical History*, 47 (1996), pp. 298–329.
50. Benson, *British Coalminers*, p. 88.
51. H. Francis and D. Smith, *The Fed: A History of the South Wales Miners in the Twentieth Century* (London: Lawrence and Wishart, 1980), p. 3.
52. For example, D. Douglass, 'The Durham Pitman' and 'Pit Talk in County Durham', in R. Samuel (ed.), *Miners, Quarrymen and Saltworkers* (London: Routledge & Kegan Paul, 1977), pp. 205–348; V. G. Hall, 'The Anatomy of a Changing Consciousness: The Miners of Northumberland, 1898–1914', *Labour History Review*, 66 (2001), pp. 165–86.
53. J. A. Jaffe, *The Struggle for Market Power: Industrial Relations in the British Coal Industry, 1800–1840* (Cambridge: Cambridge University Press, 1991). Also J. A. Jaffe, *Striking a Bargain: Work and Industrial Relations in England 1815–1865* (Manchester: Manchester University Press, 2000).
54. R. Moore, *Pit-Men, Preachers & Politics: The Effects of Methodism in a Durham Mining Community* (Cambridge: Cambridge University Press, 1974; R. Lee, *The Church of England and the Durham Coalfield, 1810–1926* (Woodbridge: Boydell & Brewer, 2007).
55. B. Williamson, *Class, Culture and Community: A Biographical Study of Social Change in Mining* (London: Routledge & Kegan Paul, 1982).
56. R. Colls, *The Collier's Rant: Song and Culture in the Industrial Village* (London: Croom Helm, 1977); R. Colls, *The Pitmen of the Northern Coalfield: Work, Culture, and Protest, 1790–1850* (Manchester: Manchester University Press, 1987).
57. H. Beynon and T. Austrin, *Masters and Servants: Class and Patronage in the Making of a Labour Organisation: The Durham Miners and the English Political Tradition* (London: Rivers Oram Press, 1994), pp. 198–9.

58. Ibid., pp. 198–9.
59. P. Ackers, 'Colliery Deputies in the British Coal Industry before Nationalization', *International Review of Social History*, 39 (1994), pp. 383–414.
60. Baylies, *Yorkshire Miners*, pp. ix, 175.
61. A. Campbell, 'Honourable Men and Degraded Slaves: A Comparative Study of Trade Unionism in two Lanarkshire Mining Communities, *c.* 1830–1874', in Harrison (ed.), *Independent Collier*, pp. 75–113 at p. 102. See, by the same author, *The Lanarkshire Miners: A Social History of their Trade Unions, 1775–1974* (Edinburgh: Donald, 1979). Also M. J. Daunton, 'Down the Pit: Work in the Great Northern and South Wales Coalfields, 1870–1914', *Economic History Review*, 34 (1981), pp. 578–97; D. Gilbert, *Class, Community and Collective Action: Social Change in Two British Coalfields, 1850–1926* (Oxford: Clarendon Press, 1992); D. Warwick and G. Littlejohn, *Coal, Capital and Culture: A Sociological Analysis of Mining Communities in West Yorkshire* (London: Routledge, 1992), ch. 3; J. Benson, 'Coalminers and Consumption: The Cannock Chase Coalfield, 1893 and 1926', in A. Knotter, B. Altena and D. Damsma (ed.), *Labour, Social Policy, and the Welfare State* (Amsterdam: Stichting beheer IISG, 1997), pp. 57–69.
62. See, for example, G. D. Feldman and K. Tenfelde (ed.), *Workers, Owners and Politics*; K. Tenfelde (ed.), *Towards a Social History of Mining in the 19th and 20th Centuries* (Munich: Verlag C.H. Beck, 1992).
63. Fagge, *Power, Culture and Conflict*.
64. L. S. James, *The Politics of Identity and Civil Society in Britain and Germany: Miners in the Ruhr and South Wales 1890–1926* (Manchester: Manchester University Press, 2008). On identities, see also K. Gildart, 'Mining Memories: Reading Coalfield Autobiographies', *Labor History*, 50 (2009), pp. 139–61.
65. Church and Outram, *Strikes and Solidarity*, pp. 81, 87, 388.
66. C. Flavin and S. Dunn, 'A New Energy Paradigm for the 21st Century', *Journal of International Affairs*, 53 (1999); J. Harris, 'Emerging Third World Powers: China, India and Brazil', *Race & Class*, 46 (2005), pp. 7–27. For China, see R. Bin Wong, *China Transformed: Historical Change and the Limits of European Experience* (Ithaca, NY: Cornell University Press, 1997); K. Anderson and C. Y. Peng, 'Feeding and Fueling China in the 21st Century', *World Development*, 26 (1998), pp. 1413–29; K. Pomeranz, *The Great Divergence: China, Europe and the Making of the Modern World Economy* (Princeton, NJ: Princeton University Press, 2000); P. Crompton and Y. Wu, 'Energy Consumption in China: Past Trends and Future Directions', *Energy Economics*, 27 (2005), pp. 195–208.

SELECT BIBLIOGRAPHY

Ackers, P., 'Colliery Deputies in the British Coal Industry before Nationalization', *International Review of Social History*, 39 (1994), pp. 383–414.

—, 'West End Chapel, Back Street Bethel: Labour and Capital in the Wigan Churches of Christ *c.* 1845–1945', *Journal of Ecclesiastical History*, 47 (1996), pp. 298–329.

Adams, T., 'Market and Institutional Forces in Industrial Relations: The Development of National Collective Bargaining, 1910–1920', *Economic History Review*, 50 (1997), pp. 506–30.

Allen, V. L., *The Militancy of British Miners* (Shipley: Moor Press, 1981).

Anderson, D., *The Orrell Coalfield, Lancashire 1740–1850* (Buxton: Moorland Publishing, 1975).

Anderson, K., and C. Y. Peng, 'Feeding and Fueling China in the 21st Century', *World Development*, 26 (1998), pp. 1413–29.

Bartrip, P. W. J., and S. B. Burman, *The Wounded Soldiers of Industry: Industrial Compensation Policy 1833–1897* (Oxford: Clarendon Press, 1983).

Baylies, C., *The History of the Yorkshire Miners 1881–1918* (London: Routledge, 1993).

Benson, J., *British Coalminers in the Nineteenth Century: A Social History* (Dublin: Gill and Macmillan, 1980).

—, 'Coalmining', in C. J. Wrigley (ed.), *A History of British Industrial Relations 1875–1914* (Brighton: Harvester Press, 1982), pp. 187–208.

—, 'Coalminers and Consumption: The Cannock Chase Coalfield, 1893 and 1926', in A. Knotter, B. Altena and D. Damsma (eds), *Labour, Social Policy, and the Welfare State* (Amsterdam: Stichting beheer IISG, 1997), pp. 57–69.

—, *Affluence and Authority: A Social History of Twentieth-Century Britain* (London: Hodder Arnold, 2005).

—, 'Myopia, Intransigence and Indifference? The British Coalowners, 1850–1914', in A. Westermann and E. Westermann (eds), *Streik im Revier: Unruhe, Protest und Ausstand vom 8. bis 20. Jahrhundert* (St Katharinen: Scripta Mercaturae Verlag, 2007), pp. 317–33.

Benson, J., R. G. Neville and C. H. Thompson, *Bibliography of the British Coal Industry: Secondary Literature, Parliamentary and Departmental Papers, Mineral Maps and Plans and a Guide to Sources* (Oxford: Oxford University Press, 1981).

Beynon, H., and T. Austrin, *Masters and Servants: Class and Patronage in the Making of a Labour Organisation: The Durham Miners and the English Political Tradition* (London: Rivers Oram Press, 1994).

Bin Wong, R., *China Transformed: Historical Change and the Limits of European Experience* (Ithaca, NY: Cornell University Press, 1997).

Brimblecombe, P., *The Big Smoke: A History of Air Pollution in London since Medieval Times* (London: Routledge, 1987).

Bulman, H. F., *Coal Mining and the Coal Miner* (London: Methuen, 1920).

Bulmer, M., 'Social Structures and Social Change in the Twentieth-Century', in M. Bulmer (ed.), *Mining and Social Change in the Twentieth Century* (London: Croom Helm, 1978), pp. 15–48.

Burgess, K., *The Origins of British Industrial Relations: The Nineteenth Century Experience* (London: Croom Helm, 1975).

Campbell, A., 'Honourable Men and Degraded Slaves: A Comparative Study of Trade Unionism in two Lanarkshire Mining Communities, c. 1830–1874', in R. Harrison (ed.), *Independent Collier: The Coal Miner as Archetypal Proletarian Reconsidered* (Hassocks: Harvester Press, 1978), pp. 75–113.

—, *The Lanarkshire Miners: A Social History of their Trade Unions, 1775–1974* (Edinburgh: Donald, 1979).

Carr, G., *Pit Women: Coal Communities in Northern England in the Early Twentieth Century* (London: Merlin Press, 2001).

Challinor, R., and B. Ripley, *The Miners' Association: A Trade Union in the Age of the Chartists* (London: Lawrence and Wishart, 1968).

Church, R., *The History of the British Coal Industry Volume 3 1830–1913: Victorian Pre-eminence* (Oxford: Clarendon Press, 1986).

—, 'Employers, Trade Unions and the State, 1889–1987: The Origins and Decline of Tripartism in the British Coal Industry', in G. D. Feldman and K. Tenfelde (eds), *Workers, Owners and Politics in Coal Mining: An International Comparison in Industrial Relations* (Oxford: Berg, 1990), pp. 12–73.

Church, R., and Q. Outram, *Strikes and Solidarity: Coalfield Conflict in Britain 1889–1966* (Cambridge: Cambridge University Press, 1998).

Clark, G., and D. Jacks, 'Coal and the Industrial Revolution, 1700–1869', *European Review of Economic History*, 11 (2007), pp. 39–72.

Coal: British Mining in Art 1680–1980 (London: Arts Council of Great Britain, 1982).

Colls, R., *The Collier's Rant: Song and Culture in the Industrial Village* (London: Croom Helm, 1977).

—, *The Pitmen of the Northern Coalfield: Work, Culture, and Protest, 1790–1850* (Manchester: Manchester University Press, 1987).

Crompton, P., and Y. Wu, 'Energy Consumption in China: Past Trends and Future Directions', *Energy Economics*, 27 (2005), pp. 195–208.

Daunton, M. J., 'Down the Pit: Work in the Great Northern and South Wales Coalfields, 1870–1914', *Economic History Review*, 34 (1981), pp. 578–97.

Dennis, N., F. Henriques and C. Slaughter, *Coal is our Life: An Analysis of a Yorkshire Mining Community* (London: Tavistock, 1969).

Dingle, A.E., '"The Monster Nuisance of All": Landowners, Alkali Manufacturers, and Air Pollution, 1828–64', *Economic History Review*, 35 (1982), pp. 529–48.

Douglass, D., 'The Durham Pitman' and 'Pit Talk in County Durham', in R. Samuel (ed.), *Miners, Quarrymen and Saltworkers* (London: Routledge & Kegan Paul, 1977), pp. 205–348.

Fagge, R., *Power, Culture and Conflict in the Coalfields: West Virginia and South Wales, 1900–1922* (Manchester: Manchester University Press, 1996).

Flavin, C., and S. Dunn, 'A New Energy Paradigm for the 21st Century', *Journal of International Affairs*, 53 (1999), pp. 167–90.

Flinn, M. W., *The History of the British Coal Industry Volume 2 1700–1830: The Industrial Revolution* (Oxford: Clarendon Press, 1984).

Francis, H., and D. Smith, *The Fed: A History of the South Wales Miners in the Twentieth Century* (London: Lawrence and Wishart, 1980).

Gilbert, D., *Class, Community and Collective Action: Social Change in Two British Coalfields, 1850–1926* (Oxford: Clarendon Press, 1992).

Gildart, K., 'Mining Memories: Reading Coalfield Autobiographies', *Labor History*, 50 (2009), pp. 139–61.

Gorman, F., *Banner Bright: An Illustrated History of the Banners of the British Trade Union Movement* (London: Allen Lane, 1973).

Greasley, D., 'Fifty Years of Coal-Mining Productivity: The Record of the British Coal Industry before 1939', *Journal of Economic History*, 50 (1990), pp. 877–902.

Gregory, R., *The Miners and British Politics 1906–1914* (Oxford: Oxford University Press, 1968).

Hall, V. G., 'The Anatomy of a Changing Consciousness: The Miners of Northumberland, 1898–1914', *Labour History Review*, 66 (2001), pp. 165–86.

Harris, J. 'Emerging Third World Powers: China, India and Brazil', *Race & Class*, 46 (2005), pp. 7–27.

Harrison, R., 'Introduction', in R. Harrison (ed.), *Independent Collier: The Coal Miner as Archetypal Proletarian Reconsidered* (Hassocks: Harvester Press, 1978). pp. 1–16.

Humphries, J., 'Protective Legislation, the Capitalist State, and Working Class Men: The Case of the 1842 Mines Regulation Act', *Feminist Review*, 7 (1981), pp. 1–33.

—, 'Short Stature among Coal-Mining Children: A Comment', *Economic History Review*, l (1997), pp. 531–7.

Jackson, W. (ed.), *A Pitman's Anthology: Compiled by William Maurice 1872–1951* (London: James & James, 2004).

Jaffe, J. A., *The Struggle for Market Power: Industrial Relations in the British Coal Industry,1800–1840* (Cambridge: Cambridge University Press, 1991).

—, *Striking a Bargain: Work and Industrial Relations in England 1815–1865* (Manchester: Manchester University Press, 2000).

James, L. S., *The Politics of Identity and Civil Society in Britain and Germany: Miners in the Ruhr and South Wales 1890–1926* (Manchester: Manchester University Press, 2008).

John, A., *By the Sweat of their Brow: Women Workers at Victorian Coal Mines* (London: Croom Helm, 1980).

Jones, D., 'Self-Help in Nineteenth-Century Wales: The Rise and Fall of the Female Friendly Society', *Llafur*, 4 (1984), pp. 14–26.

Kirby, P., 'Causes of Short Stature among Coal-Mining Children, 1823–1850', *Economic History Review*, 48 (1995), pp. 687–99.

Lee, R., *The Church of England and the Durham Coalfield, 1810–1926* (Woodbridge: Boydell & Brewer, 2007).

Lee, W. A., *Thirty Years in Coal 1917–1947: A Review of the Coal Mining Industry under Private Enterprise* (London: Mining Association of Great Britain, 1954).

Luckin, B., '"The Heart and Home of Horror": The Great London Fogs of the Late Nineteenth Century', *Social History*, 28 (2003), pp. 31–48.

McCormick, B. J., *Industrial Relations in the Coal Industry* (London: Macmillan, 1979).

McIvor, A. J., *A History of Work in Britain, 1880–1950* (Basingstoke: Palgrave, 2001).

McIvor, A., and R. Johnston, *Miners' Lung: A History of Dust Disease in British Coal Mining* (Aldershot: Ashgate, 2007).

Mee, G., *Aristocratic Enterprise: The Fitzwilliam Industrial Undertakings 1795–1857* (Glasgow: Blackie, 1975).

Mitchell, B. R., *Economic Development of the British Coal Industry 1800–1914* (Cambridge: Cambridge University Press, 1984).

Moore, R., *Pit-Men, Preachers & Politics: The Effects of Methodism in a Durham Mining Community* (Cambridge: Cambridge University Press, 1974).

Mosley, S., *The Chimney of the World: A History of Smoke Pollution in Victorian and Edwardian Manchester* (Cambridge: White Horse Press, 2001).

Outram, Q., '"The Stupidest Men in England"? The Industrial Relations Strategy of the Coalowners between the Lockouts, 1923–1924', *Historical Studies in Industrial Relations*, 4 (1997), pp. 65–95.

—, 'Class Warriors: The Coalowners', in J. McIlroy, A. Campbell and K. Gildart (eds), *Industrial Politics and the 1926 Mining Lockout* (Cardiff: University of Wales Press, 2004), pp. 107–35.

Page Arnot, R., *The Miners: A History of the Miners' Federation of Great Britain 1889–1910* (London: Allen & Unwin, 1949).

—, *A History of the Scottish Miners from the Earliest Times* (London: Allen & Unwin, 1955).

—, *South Wales Miners Glowyr de Cymru: A History of the South Wales Miners' Federation (1898–1914)* (London: Allen & Unwin, 1967).

Perkin, H., 'Social History in Britain', *Journal of Social History*, 10 (1976), pp 129–43.

Pomeranz, K., *The Great Divergence: China, Europe and the Making of the Modern World Economy* (Princeton, NJ: Princeton University Press, 2000).

Stradling, D. and P. Thorsheim, 'The Smoke of Great Cities: British and American Efforts to Control Air Pollution, 1860–1914, *Environmental History*, 4 (1999), pp. 6–31.

Supple, B., *The History of the British Coal Industry Volume 4 1913–1946: The Political Economy of Decline* (Oxford: Clarendon Press, 1987).

Taylor, A. J., 'Foreword' in J. Benson and R. G. Neville (eds), *Studies in the Yorkshire Coal Industry* (Manchester: Manchester University Press, 1976), p. vii.

Tenfelde, K. (ed.), *Towards a Social History of Mining in the 19th and 20th Centuries* (Munich: Verlag C. H. Beck,1992).

Thompson, R., 'A Breed Apart? Class and Community in a Somerset Coal-Mining Parish, *c.* 1750–1850', *Rural History*, 16 (2005), pp. 137–59.

Thorsheim, P., *Inventing Pollution: Coal, Smoke, and Culture in Britain Since 1800* (Athens, GA: Ohio University Press, 2006).

Walters, R., 'Labour Productivity in the South Wales Steam-Coal Industry, 1870–1914', *Economic History Review*, 38 (1975), pp. 280–99.

Warwick, D., and G. Littlejohn, *Coal, Capital and Culture: A Sociological Analysis of Mining Communities in West Yorkshire* (London: Routledge, 1992).

Weinbrein, D., 'The Good Samaritan, Friendly Societies and the Gift Economy', *Social History*, 31 (2006), pp. 319–36.

Willams, J. E., *The Derbyshire Miners: A Study in Industrial and Social History* (London: Allen & Unwin, 1962).

Williams, L. J., and D. Jones, 'Women at Work in Nineteenth-Century Wales', *Llafur*, 3 (1982), pp. 20–32.

Williamson, B., *Class, Culture and Community: A Biographical Study of Social Change in Mining* (London: Routledge & Kegan Paul, 1982).

INTRODUCTION TO VOLUME 1: USEFUL KNOWLEDGE

The value of a resource depends on knowing how to use it. If you do not know that a lump of coal will burn, it is only a black rock. How valuable a resource is will depend on the uses to which it can be put and whether there are alternative and cheaper ways of achieving the same ends. If you know only that a lump of coal will burn, the demand for it is limited to those uses that require only heat: warming houses and cooking food. If you discover that coal can be transformed into coke and coke can be used to smelt iron, the demand for coal will increase, if, that is, coke is cheaper than charcoal. If you know that coal can be made to emit a gas which can be collected and burned to provide light, the demand for coal will rise again, if gaslight is cheaper than oil-light. If you know that coal can be distilled and from the distillates dyes, aromas, pharmaceuticals, explosives, indeed an entire array of organic chemicals can be constructed, the demand for coal will rise again, unless there are cheaper sources of these outputs.

Knowledge accumulates but it does not do so randomly. To find out one thing, one has to know other things first. There is a sequence to the accumulation of knowledge. To plot the position of Pluto, one has to know about gravity; to know enough about gravity, one has to understand some mathematics, to understand mathematics, one has to understand what numbers are. One finds that coal can be made to produce steam from water and steam can be used in a machine to generate motion in various directions: the linear movement of a piston in a cylinder, transformed into the circular movement of a wheel or a propeller and, again the linear movement of a locomotive or a ship. Then we find that electricity can be generated from a dynamo. How do we make the dynamo go round? The answer is now obvious because we know all about making wheels and propellers go round: design a reciprocating steam engine to turn the dynamo. Hence one's demand for a resource may be dependent on achieving prior advances in technology. If we are to understand the contemporary demand for coal we must first understand contemporary knowledge of the uses of coal.[1] After the contemporary Introduction provided by pp. 1–20, this volume turns to the uses of coal.

Coal is mixed with labour, capital equipment and other raw materials to produce something valuable. But in the course of producing something valuable, something valueless, unwanted or injurious is typically produced as well: colliery spoil tips, for example, and polluted rivers. If the injury is sustained wholly by the person who acquires the output of value, they will discount the value of the output by the value of the injury. Once again, knowledge is crucial. A person who wrongly believes that coal can be mined under their house without the house sustaining damage may make a poor decision about whether or not to mine the coal. But frequently the injuries sustained in producing and using coal have been sustained by people other than the coal producers and users and the injured have not been compensated by them or have been compensated only partially. The costs are born externally and there is a 'market failure'. In these circumstances the production of coal is not restrained by the injuries inflicted by the producers and users and too much coal is produced. The next section (pp. 179–239) documents the contemporary understanding of the injuries involved in producing and using coal.

Pages 21–239 are concerned with the demand for coal. The supply of coal is of course intimately bound up with the contemporary understanding of how to produce it, that is the technology of coal production. So much would be true of any commodity but there is a special problem with coal: not only does it need to be produced, it must first be found. Exploration and production technology are the subjects of the next three sections. Pp. 241–67 document the extent of geological knowledge and the techniques used to find coal at the start of the nineteenth century. We return to the topic and see some of the developments of the century in Volume 3 (pp. 195–257) which deals with the duration of the coal. This Volume then turns to colliery engineering (pp. 269–373). This was a complex area and one which refused to conform to the mental model of production held by Victorian economists and engineers alike. According to this model, raw material was processed by a machine to produce an output. So, for example, cotton yarn was supplied to a weaving machine and out came a strip of cloth; clay was fed into a brick-making machine and out came bricks; paper and ink were fed into a printing machine and out came a newspaper. In such processes, accessing the raw material, controlling the environment in which production took place and transporting the product around the site of production were minor matters. But in coal mining they were major matters; in comparison, the extraction of coal from the coal face is a matter of little difficulty. This section therefore treats of many topics of which there was no parallel in manufacturing industry: boring to explore for coal; the sinking of pits to access the coal; pumping water to stop the pit from flooding, ventilating the colliery atmosphere to stop mine gasses from exploding, lighting the mine so that colliers could see what they were doing, arranging methods of communication so that workers could cooperate with each other, and methods of moving the coal hewn from the face to the surface. The selected extracts give snapshots of the knowledge of these processes at various times. These are followed by the reflections of Thomas Lindsay Galloway in the late 1870s on the progress of colliery engineering knowledge up to his time.

The following section (pp. 375–94) turns to two topics rarely considered then or later: the care and management of colliery horses and ponies and the impact of the working environment on the ability of miners to work. David Edgerton has pointed out that throughout the 'age of steam' horses remained the mainstay of urban transport and the use of horses in transport in the UK peaked not at some point in the early nineteenth century but at some point in the early twentieth.[2] Similarly in the mines, the use of ponies for haulage away from the main roads was not a hangover from earlier centuries but was a practice introduced in County Durham in the mid-1840s in the wake of the exclusion of women and young children from the mines by the 1842 Mines Act. The employment of ponies and horses spread throughout the country and in 1913 most face haulage was still pony work.[3] Despite this, few colliery managers gave much thought to the care and management of this part of their capital stock and the extract given on pp. 393–4 is from a rare example of a paper on the topic to be read before a society of mine engineers. Similarly, despite the labour intensivity of the industry and despite the obviously difficult and wearing working conditions, few colliery managers or mine engineers gave thought to facilitating the work of their colliers by optimizing their working environment. The extract given is from one of the very earliest papers to treat the problem; it was published in 1914.

The last section (pp. 399–429) concludes the volume by considering the institutions created to produce and disseminate knowledge on the supply side of the industry. The main fact to face the historian is that, apart from the institutes of mine engineering, there were few such institutions. The first two extracts are chosen to illustrate the difficulties in establishing a college of mine engineering of a standard equivalent or superior to those on the continent of Europe and, at a later period, in the USA. The 1872 Coal Mines Regulation Act[4] had, for the first time, required every mine subject to its provisions to be under the control and supervision of a certificated manager. The final extract illustrates the democratization of mine engineering knowledge brought about by the increased demand for qualified colliery managers consequent upon this and subsequent legislation and the supply of many such managers from the ranks of working miners. Increasingly as the century progressed, working miners were able to study for their qualifications at night schools provided by local authorities. Eventually, as the extract shows, some local authorities in colliery areas introduced lessons on coal mining in primary schools. By the end of the nineteenth century a working miner, whose great-grandfather at the start of the century may well have been ignorant, uncouth and unlettered, could reasonably aspire to learn the letters, the law, and the geology, physics, chemistry and arithmetic required to take responsibility for the safety of many hundreds of men working in a mine under his management.

Notes

1. Joel Mokyr has emphasized the importance of knowledge to economic development in a number of works: J. Mokyr, *The Lever of Riches: Technological Creativity and Economic Progress* (New York: Oxford University Press, 1990); J. Mokyr, *The Enlightened Economy: An Economic History of Britain 1700–1850* (New Haven, CT: Yale University Press, 2009); J. Mokyr, *The Gifts of Athena: Historical Origins of the Knowledge Economy* (Princeton, NJ: Princeton University Press, 2002)
2. D. Edgerton, *The Shock of the Old: Technology and Global History Since 1800* (London: Profile, 2006), pp. 32–3.
3. Church, *History*, p. 365.
4. 35 & 36 Vict. c. 76.

A SURVEY

The Society for the Diffusion of Useful Knowledge was founded in London in 1827 by Henry Brougham (1778–1868), first Baron Brougham and Vaux, a campaigner for slave emancipation, popular education and law reform, a prominent lawyer and Lord Chancellor (1830–4).[1] Brougham's collaborators in the Society included James Mill, Zachary Macaulay, the abolitionist and father of Thomas Babington Macaulay, and George Birkbeck the founder of the London Mechanics' Institution which evolved into the university college that still bears his name. The Society, as its name suggests, was utilitarian; it was also secular. It was profoundly middle-class and sought to 'diffuse' knowledge from where it thought it resided – in the middle classes – to where it thought it was needed – the working classes.

The *Penny Magazine* was first issued in 1832 under the editorship of the Society's publisher Charles Knight (1791–1873) who became 'the very symbol of the cheap book movement'.[2] While the *Penny Magazine* was intended to bring knowledge to the working man (there is little to suggest that the editor wished to reach working women) it made heavy demands on the reader's literacy and general knowledge and for this reason it has usually been assumed that it was read largely by the middle classes. Altick commented that 'at best' it 'was never light reading' and is scathing in his criticism of its style and subject matter. Nevertheless it sold well, reaching a peak circulation of 200,000 in the first few years of publication and Patricia Anderson has argued that it had a substantial working-class readership.[3] It ceased publication in 1845.

The *Penny Magazine* was, doubtless unwittingly, written from a London viewpoint, distant from the coalfields of the north and west. Features of the coalfields which caused little local remark appeared strange, wonderful and sometimes disconcerting to the *Penny Magazine*'s London writers and editor as will be apparent from the text given here.

Notes

1. For Brougham's life see R. Stewart, *Henry Brougham: 1778–1868: His Public Career* (London: Bodley Head, 1986) or R. K. Huch, *Henry, Lord Brougham: The Later Years: 1830–1868: The 'Great Actor'* (Lewiston, NY: Mellen, 1993).
2. For his autobiography see C. Knight, *Passages of a Working Life during Half a Century*, 3 vols (London: Bradbury & Evans, 1864–5). The most recent study is V. Gray, *Charles Knight: Educator, Publisher, Writer* (Aldershot: Ashgate, 2006).
3. P. J. Anderson, *The Printed Image and the Transformation of Popular Culture, 1790–1860* (Oxford: Clarendon Press, 1991), ch. 5.

'The Collieries', *Penny Magazine* (1835)

'The Collieries. – No. I.', *Monthly Supplement of the Penny Magazine of the Society for the Diffusion of Useful Knowledge*, 28 February–31 March 1835, pp. 121–8 and 'The Collieries. – No. II.', idem, 31 March–30 April 1835, pp. 161–8.

THE COLLIERIES. – No. I.

NOT WITHSTANDING the variety and abundance of the productions which nature offers for our use in this country, and which we have with so much enterprize and skill made subservient to our comfort and wealth, they would have been of comparatively little utility to us at the present time, if we had been deprived of that one by which alone we obtain from others their most valuable properties. Without coal, in what manner could we now carry on our vast operations in every department of industry? In what way could we employ hundreds and thousands of our large population in fashioning those implements which so effectively aid us in extending our domain over the natural world? It is true that this mineral was not extensively used at a period when our manufactures were not altogether unimportant, although of very trifling extent when compared with the enlarged scale on which they are at present conducted; but, in those times, the woods which were spread over the country had not yielded to the encroachments of an increasing population; and as long as they existed, the fuel which they furnished was obtained at a cheaper rate than coal, which could only be extracted by the union of considerable capital and skill. In the mention which early writers make of our iron-works, fears are generally expressed respecting the decay into which it was imagined they must gradually fall by the disappearance of the native forests. These old smelting-works necessarily existed on a confined scale. It is not a hundred years since the iron ore in the Staffordshire mining district was carried, by a train of pack-horses form the pits, to be smelted. The employment of coal in the process of smelting was then unknown; and its successful application was a great relief to those whose fears had led them to regard the native iron-trade as doomed to extinction. While the forests flourished, it would have been altogether unprofitable to resort to an expensive mode of procuring fuel from the bowels of the earth, even if there had existed a sufficient amount of mechanical skill to have done so in any extensive manner. The moment when by agricultural improvements and the successive clearing of the land, wood became scarce, the question was soon decided as to the advantage of making the necessary exertion to obtain coal.

It is not clear at what precise period this necessity sprung up. It is argued, that the Romans continued unacquainted, if not with the existence of coal, at least with its useful properties during the four centuries in which they held this country in their possession; and this opinion is maintained on the ground that no word is found for coal in the Latin language, although *carbo*, for charcoal, is not unfrequently met with. The use of coal was, however, well known to our Saxon ancestors, although its consumption was limited by the causes to which we have alluded; and it is not improbable that at the same period several of the northern nations were equally familiar with its properties. Several terms in use among miners in England, Germany, and other countries of the north, have a striking resemblance to each other. The French word for coal is *houille*, which is very similar to the Saxon word *hulla*, although its more frequent designation in France is *charbon de terre*, or charcoal of the earth. The name by which coal is designated in Germany is *steinkohlen*, or stone-coal; by the Dutch it is called *steenkoolen*; by the Danes *steenkull*; by the Swedes *stenkol*. The Italians and Spaniards, having no familiar term for coal, employ a modification of its scientific name, *carbo fossilis*.

The progress which England made in the first 200 years after the Conquest prepared the way for the introduction of coal as an article of commerce. In the year 1239 Henry III. granted a charter for digging coal. Forty years afterwards Newcastle was celebrated for its coal-trade. In 1306 its use was prohibited in London, on account of the supposed effect which it had in rendering the air impure and unwholesome. But this prejudice was either soon dissipated, or the cheapness and excellence of the material, as an article of fuel, became so apparent, that the prohibition was not very effective, and probably was soon abolished. In 1325 coal was exported to France. In 1379 a duty of 6*d*. per ton was charged on ships coming to London from Newcastle with coals. At this period, also, a duty was levied on such ships by the Corporation of Newcastle, on their clearing out at that port. In 1384 Richard II., out of regard and reverence to the tutelary saint of Durham,[1] exempted the coal-owners of the Wear from the above corporation duty. Pope Pius II.[2] visited this island previous to his elevation to the papal chair, during the former part of the fifteenth century; and he remarked that the poor of Scotland received for alms pieces of stone which they burnt instead of wood. The earliest mention of coal-mines being worked in Scotland occurs in a charter granted in 1291 to the monks of Dunfermline, conferring upon them the privilege of digging for coal in the neighbourhood of their monastery. In the sixteenth century 'sea-coal'was the general term applied to this mineral, which proves (as there were inland collieries worked at the time), that the state of the roads and means of communication were so imperfect, that the quantity which they furnished was trifling, and that the market depended almost entirely on the supply of sea-borne coals.

Two hundred and sixty years ago, Camden,[3] who travelled in various parts of England, previous to the publication of his 'Britannia,' said in that work, when speaking of the now active district of North Stafford-shire, – 'The north part of Staffordshire hath coles digged out of the earth, and mines of iron. But whether more for their commoditie[4] or hinderance I leave others to determine who doe or shall better understand it.' It will be curious to contrast the commercial importance of our mines at the present day with their state in the sixteenth century; and when we arrive at this part of the subject, the opinion of Camden may be referred to with some interest.

England is by far the richest country in the world as it respects her coal-mines. They have been the source of greater wealth to her than ever the gold mines of Peru were to Spain, because they are a means whereby man obtains a direct increase of power over materials which minister to his comfort. If he knows not how to use these materials, he remains in a state of comparative barbarism; or if he possesses that imperfect skill which only enables him to effect this in an inefficient and expensive manner, he cannot, under certain circumstances, rise above a state of comparative poverty.

The different coal districts of England and Wales are arranged in the following manner by Messrs. Conybeare and Phillips:–[5]

1. *Coal district north of Trent*, or grand Penine chain. – 1. Northumberland and Durham; 2. North of Yorkshire; 3. South York, Nottingham, and Derby; 4. South of Derby; 5. North Stafford; 6. South Lancashire; 7. North Lancashire; 8. Cumberland and Whitehaven; 9. Foot of Crossfell.[6]
2. *Central Coal district*. – 1. Ashby de la Zouch, 2. Warwickshire; 3. South Stafford or Dudley, 4. Indications near the Lickey Hill, &c.
3. *Western Coal district*, divided into, 1. *North Western* or *North Welch*. – 1. Isle of Anglesea; 2. Flintshire.
4. *Middle Western or Shropshire*. – 1. Plain of Shrewsbury; 2. Colebrokedale; 3. The Clee Hills and South Shropshire; 4. Near the Abberley Hill.
5. *South Western*. – 1. South Wales; 2. Forest of Dean; 3. South Gloucester and Somerset.

Considerable beds of coal exist in Scotland; and it has been found in seventeen counties in Ireland. The largest coal field on the continent is in Belgium; there are smaller ones in several parts of Germany. Coal abounds in the United States; and is more or less found in a line which sweeps round the globe from the north-east to the south-west. It is impossible to regard this extensive provision of so valuable a substance, which in some places has been in a course of consumption for some centuries, and in others yet offers almost inexhaustible stores, without a strong desire to know something of the history of its formation. For this knowledge we must refer to the 'Penny Magazine,' Nos. 100, 102, 105, 108, 109, 110, and 111, in which, under the head 'Mineral Kingdom,'[7] the subject is treated under its appropriate divisions. It may, however, be desirable to state in this place that the formation of coal is attributed to trees and vegetables being carried down the rivers of the primeval world, and deposited in the bed of the sea, in an age of which we have obtained some definite conceptions by the most interesting science of geology. The probable process of the formation is accounted for in the Numbers of this Magazine to which we have already referred. The irregularity of the coal seams is occasioned by subsequent convulsions to which the earth has been subjected. These have produced what the miners call faults or dykes, which often interrupt the labours of the pit, by affording a passage to the water. A fault or dike is in fact a fissure or rent, which appears to have been effected by some tremendous power. A district in which mines are found is called a coal-field. Coal-measures is the term which miners give to the successive strata which are found alternating with beds of coal, such as slate-clay, freestone, &c.

The traveller who visits for the first time an extensive coal district will be struck by the vast canopies of smoke continually rolling their sluggish course in the direction of the wind. This smoke arises from the engine fires and from the small coal burnt at the mouth of the pit. On the clearest day these fires impart a cloudy aspect to the landscape. If a visit to the great northern coal district be the object of the traveller's journey, he will find on the road from Newcastle to Durham, which is on elevated and rising ground, a series of magnificent views successively burst upon him, almost unequalled in any part of England. At intervals, as he ascends, a wider horizon spreads out before him, the hills are bold and picturesque, and occasionally exhibit in their sweeping outlines combinations of unusual grandeur. When he at length reaches the coal-fields, he will find the face of the country black and blasted; and this appearance, united with the perpetual clatter of the waggon trains, may fill him with somewhat gloomy feelings. When the first impressions of the traveller have subsided, and he looks more narrowly at surrounding objects, he cannot fail to be strongly impressed with the vastness and extent of the commercial enterprize of the district. On every side rise extensive buildings, and in the centre of each, one more lofty than the rest contains that mighty power which has created by its effects more than one-half of this sphere of human activity. These buildings are the works connected with the collieries. In the neighbourhood of the northern coal-fields the landscape is studded with a number of mansions, situated in the midst of extensive grounds, in which the coal-owners and capitalists whose property is connected with the collieries reside. In the present paper we shall confine our description to the northern collieries: those of the central coal district will be more properly connected with some future account of our iron-works.

Many years ago, before the science of geology had assumed so positive a character, much capital was, almost literally speaking, sunk in the attempt to discover coal. It has since been found that many of the indications which were then looked upon as a proof of its existence beneath the surface were often geologically erroneous, and necessarily led to disappointment. At present, when speculations of this kind are conducted on safer foundations, the greater part of the collieries are leased for a term of years. As property of this description cannot be insured from the risks either of fire or water, to which they are alike liable; and as large properties are required to ensure all the operations connected with the works being at once perfect and economical, the combination of a number of men of capital is doubtless an advantageous arrangement.

The animated parts of the scene in a northern coal district are not less peculiar than the other characteristic objects which strike the eye. Occasionally bands of 'pitmen,' as black as sweeps, each man carrying a safety-lamp suspended at his belt, are seen traversing the dingy lanes on their return from an eight-hours' 'shift' of labour. The physiognomy of the miners is not of course of a very intellectual cast; but from the nature of their occupation, and from living, as they do, in a great measure apart from other classes of the community, its peculiarities are strongly marked. These have been transmitted from one generation to another, owing to the unions which they form being almost exclusively confined to families whose pursuit is similar to their own, and consist of high cheek bones, great width of the middle part of the face, and an angular form of its lowest portion. In these respects they are quite a distinct race from the neighbouring peasantry. The colliers who work in mines where the seam of coal is of sufficient thickness to permit the free use of muscular action, are erect and of good figure; while in others where the seam is of smaller dimensions, the miners have the spine permanently curved, and the legs frequently bowed. Their complexion, when it can be seen in its own hue, is generally sallow and unhealthy. Owing to the unusual light by which they pursue their occupations, the eyelids often become swollen, and the eyes assume a diminutive appearance. The strong light of day occasions them to experience a somewhat painful sensation.[8] The dress of the colliers is necessarily characteristic. Their working clothes consist of a tunic or short frock, and trowsers of coarse flannel. Their holiday clothes are generally of velveteen, decorated with a profusion of shining metal buttons.

In the neighbourhood of an extensive coal-work in the north, there is usually a village exclusively inhabited by the pitmen and other persons connected with the colliery. These places have a singularly unpicturesque appearance. The houses consist each of one room, with a wash-house behind, and a chamber over the whole, access being obtained to the latter by means of a ladder. About two hundred such abodes, ranged at irregular intervals alongside the road, constitute one of these hamlets. Heaps of ashes and other refuse are suffered to accumulate before the front and back-doors; and upon these, during fine weather, a number of robust and half-clothed children, of an age too young to be employed at the works, are too often suffered to idle away the day. In front of every fifth or sixth house stands a bake-house for common use, which contains a large brick-built oven. Early in the morning the wife and daughters of a pitman may be seen assembled there with sundry old gossips, to bake a week's bread for the family; and to a person who has no previous idea of the sharpness and extent of a pitman's appetite, the size of the loaves may perhaps be a matter of some astonishment. Before the front window of each tenement stands a pile of small coal, which is replenished every week by a gratuitous cart-load from the pit. The fires are consequently large; and to the rapid ventilation thereby produced the general good health of the household is to be attributed, in spite of their too frequent disregard of habits of cleanliness.

If a new colliery is opened in a part of the country where such a work had not previously existed, the colliery village springs up in necessary connexion with it, and a previously dreary and uninhabited district becomes full of life and activity. South Hetton may be mentioned as an example of this rapid growth of a community. Five years ago it was a barren spot of ground, from which the nearest habitation was two miles distant. Now it is covered with buildings, and contains a population of 2000 persons, who are exclusively connected with the coal-works. As an enumeration of their various occupations, and the number of persons connected with each, affords no bad idea of the distribution of labour which this branch of industry calls forth, we have procured an accurate census of the male working population of South Hetton, which we subjoin:–

Officers.	
Manager*	1
Viewer*	1
First Engineer*	1
Second Engineer*	1
Surgeon	1
Clerks	4
Workmen above Pit.	
Joiners and Sawyers. (These men keep the works in repair.)	13
Engine-Wrights. (Repair and make the machinery.)	7
Engine-Men. (Keep the machinery in action.)	8
Firemen. (Attend the boilers.)	9
Smiths. (Prepare the iron-work in the rough.)	18
Masons	8
Labourers to do.	6

Cartmen	11
Horsemen	9
Saddler	1
Waggonway-Wrights. (Lay down and mend the rails on the rail-roads, &c.)	6
Waggon-Riders. (Conductors of the waggons, of which there is one to each train.)	11
Staithmen. (Attend at the staith to empty the waggons of their coals into the ships.)	4
Banksmen, who deliver the corves	8
Waggon-Fillers and Screeners	12
Wailers. (Boys who pick out the stones and otherwise clean the coals.)	9
Corvers or Basket-makers	4
Heap-keeper. (Looks after the quality of the clean coals.)	1
Store-keeper. (This man presides over a vast magazine of stores, which he delivers to the men as they are wanted.)	1
Attendants on Railway, including Engineers and Furnacemen	8
Trimmers. (Men who fill up the holds of vessels with the coal discharged into them from the staiths.)	8
Boys for sundry purposes	39
Carry over /	210
Brought forward	210
WORKMEN IN THE PIT.	
Hewers. (Miners who "hew" out and blast the coal.)	140
Putters, who "put" the corves on the trains; Dragmen and Foals, who draw them to the bottom of the shaft; Helpers-up and Trappers, who manage the ventilating doors	140
Deputies or Foremen; Ventilators, Shifters, or Pit-Masons, &c.	36
TOTAL	526

* [Commonly called Agents.]

In passing through the northern colliery-villages, it is curious to remark how strikingly the character of each family is indicated by the appearance of their respective dwellings. The residence of a steady and industrious workman is distinguished by a neatly white-washed door-stead;[9] the windows are furnished with curtains, and contain a few choice plants in bright red pots; and not unfrequently a written or painted notice announces that the good housewife prepares herbwaters,[10] or exercises her industry in some other way for the advantage of her family. In the interior of the cottage may be seen a good and decent four-post bedstead, an eight-day clock,[11] a venerable oak-table, and perhaps a few books.[12] In melancholy contrast with such gratifying indications, a little further on stands a cottage destitute of the commonest household conveniences, and marked by a dirty, comfortless, and neglected appearance. In the middle of the floor, in rainy weather, it is not uncommon to see perhaps half-a-dozen children playing with what they call a 'cuddy,' or, in other words, an ass, introduced in this unsuitable place, with a careless disregard to comfort and propriety.[13] The only inhabitants of these villages, besides the work-people and colliery agents, are, the butcher, the general chandler, and the publican. Of butchers and chandlers there is seldom more than one each, but of publicans there are generally six or seven. To the practice of indulging at the public-houses is to be attributed the degradation of some of the pitmen, and the misery of their families.

As the influence of the great coal owners and lessees can be exercised in so direct a manner on the large population whose industry is sustained by means of their capital, it is to be regretted that it is not more generally employed in calling forth an improved state of moral feeling among them, and exciting some relish for pleasures less debasing than those in which they are now too much habituated to indulge. The collier's cottage might, under due regulations, be provided with a garden; and a love for the simple pleasures which it would afford might perhaps be more easily fostered than any other.

The terms by which the colliers are connected with their employers, are usually an engagement for twelve months at a fixed sum, generally 14*s*. or 15*s*. a-week. This they receive whether employed or not; and it does not unfrequently happen that they are in the receipt of it for many weeks, when it is not possible to carry on the works, owning to the drowning of the pit, or the occurrence of some other unexpected impediment. Besides this, they are paid by the piece. The employers provide a house, and supply the family with coal gratuitously, or in some cases the small sum of 3*d*. per week is paid for these advantages. The bond, containing the terms of agreement, stipulates all the conditions into which the parties mutually enter. A bounty or increase of wages is commonly given to the workmen to induce them to break the coal as little as possible. When work is abundant, and there is not too great a number of hands, the best workmen have been known to obtain, at a particular description of work, from 10*s*. to 12*s*. a-day. Their earnings are of course much lower on an average, and may be taken at from 15*s*. to 20*s*. per week, from which, it should be recollected, there is no outgoing for rent or fuel. At times, when work has been less abundant, and the supply of hands unusually great, wages have sometimes been as low as 8*s*. or 10*s*. a-week. Some decrease has taken place in the average amount of wages during the last twenty years; but the reduction is not so great as that which has taken place in the cost of all the first necessaries of life. The men generally work from eight to ten hours a day, and they are in the mine at a very early hour in the morning. In extensive works there are different sets or shifts of men, so that the operations are carried on unremittingly. Boys are found useful at a very early age, – so early as seven,[14] – and are employed in opening trap-doors, driving horses, propelling trucks, &c.

It is gratifying to remark that, in spite of the obstacles which may operate against the formation of provident habits among the colliers, the deposits in the Savings' Banks of the two northern counties, in which the coal-trade is the most active and predominant branch of industry, are such as not only prove the existence of considerable prosperity, but indicate a wider prevalence of economy and foresight than we could have anticipated.

Having thus endeavoured to present a picture of the general condition and economy of a colliery village, we shall now attempt to explain the operations connected with the working of a colliery. The coal-works of Colonel Breddyl,[15] at South Hetton, near Durham, are perhaps better calculated than any other to display all the operations of a colliery in the highest degree of perfection, owing to their very recent establishment. The machinery is all new, and of the most improved and scientific construction, and the whole of the arrangements are on an extensive scale. The various operations may be divided into five series:–

1. *Winning the Coal.* – The first thing to be done in establishing a colliery is to survey the ground which it is proposed to open, which is done by an individual called a *viewer*, who ought to possess not only scientific attainments, but extensive practical knowledge, as his task is one of great importance and responsibility. Not less than 50,000*l.* have been sometimes expended to no purpose in endeavouring to procure coal; and the useless consumption of so much capital has been frequently occasioned by the erroneous judgment of the viewer. Cases of this description are, however, now of rare occurrence. The expense of sinking a pit varies from 10,000*l.* to 150,000*l.*

The average expense incurred in the operation, including the steam-engine and its apparatus, is about 30,000*l.* The site being determined upon, the sinking of the shaft is commenced, and a steam-engine is erected on the spot to work a set of pumps for drawing off the water which the 'sinkers' encounter in their descent, and also to raise to the surface the excavated earth and other materials. While the sinking is proceeding, every part of the process is carefully noted in a journal kept for the purpose. The volume of water which is met with is accurately measured in vessels containing fifty or sixty gallons, and the time which each takes in filling observed. Means are then used to stop the apertures by which the pit is inundated, and this is done by what is called cribbing or tubbing. The shaft is cased with strong boarding or brick-work, which is progressively done as the work advances. In the South Helton Pit the shaft is 1080 feet deep, the 'low main-coal,' which is the best and thickest in the field, lying at this depth. The labour of sinking such a shaft is immense, and the danger of suffocation imminent, from the irruption of water, the disengagement of pernicious gases, or the falling in of materials. The inflammable air or gases, found in the strata, would, if allowed to accumulate, affect the safety of all engaged in the works. The proper ventilation of the mine is therefore a point of immense importance, and rarefication[16] is usually produced by means of a fire constantly kept up for the purpose, which creates a powerful draught from below. The deepest pit in the northern coal-field, and probably in England, descends to a depth of 360 yards.

The average depth is somewhat under 150 yards. In some cases the workmen carry on their labours beneath the bed of the sea. Commercial considerations prevent coal-pits being carried to a lower depth, as the impediments which are then met with can only be overcome by great additional outlays of capital. The shallowest of the northern pits is forty-six yards deep, but it only furnishes an inferior description of coal. The strata successively passed through by the sinkers affords matter of curious speculation to the geologist. We have been favoured by Mr. Buddle, one of the most experienced coal-viewers in England, with a very accurate statement of the series of strata met with in sinking the Eppleton Jane Pit,[17] from which the following abstract has been prepared:–

After passing through four different strata, consisting of the alluvial cover, sand and gravel, limestone, and yellow sand, water was reached which produced 360 gallons an hour. In the next eight yards, seven other strata occurred, and the influx of water now increased to about 4200 gallons an hour. At sixteen yards ten inches below the surface, the first coal-measure was met with. The whole of the water was stopped by 'cribbing.' The progress of the work, from the commencement to its termination, was as follows:– 12 strata to the first coal-measure; 10 strata to the second; 6 strata to the third; 5 strata to the fourth; 6 strata to the fifth; 7 strata to the sixth; 7 strata to the seventh; 4 strata to the eighth; 5 strata to the ninth, or 'three-quarter coal-seam,' with about 20 inches of coarse top coal and coarse coal at bottom; 6 strata to the tenth coal-measure; 2 strata to the eleventh; 3 strata to the twelfth; 10 strata to the thirteenth, 'coal high main,' at a depth of 296 yards: a stratum of 'blue metal, very mild,'[18] was found below this, when the 'low main of coal' was reached, containing 5 feet 6 inches of good coal, 3 inches black swad,[19] and 1 foot 10 inches of bottom coal. Beneath this, 3 strata were passed to a measure of splinty coal;[20] 5 strata to another measure 10 inches deep; 6 strata to another measure; and 11 strata to the 'Hetton coal-seam,' the depth from the mouth of the pit to the thill[21] of this seam being 348 yards 11 feet 2 1/2 inches. Excavations were made 6 yards 5 feet 4 inches deeper, making the total depth of the pit 356 yards 2 feet 3½ inches, in the course of which 132 strata, including the various coal-measures, were cut through.

While the shaft is sinking, the necessary buildings are in course of erection, and the machinery and apparatus for 'winning the coal' are got into a state of readiness. A platform is laid down round the mouth of the pit, about twelve feet above the level of the ground, called a 'bank,' or 'bank-top,' upon which the coal is landed. A more powerful and complete winding apparatus is affixed to two or more steam-engines for raising the coal; larger pumps are added to the engine for drawing off the water; supplementary boilers are erected for the generation of more copious supplies of steam; ventilating fires and draught-doors are prepared for exhausting the foul air of the pit, and supplying it with a current of fresh air; rail-roads for the conveyance of the coal to the nearest harbour are laid down;

houses are built for the accommodation of the work-people; and when all these subordinate arrangements are finished, and all the ingenious combinations to accomplish the great object in view are brought into a state of efficient order under the superintendence of the principal agent and engineers, a day is fixed for bringing the first 'coal to bank.' The whole 'country side' assemble on the occasion; and the opening of the pit, the winning of the coal, and the starting of the first train of waggons, is celebrated with the most lively joy.

2. *Pumping and Winding.* – The pumping of water from coal-mines was at one period performed by men or horses. This mode was of course only practised in an early era of mining operations, and was necessarily so ineffectual, that both the depth of the pit, and the extent to which it could be worked, were in consequence very limited. The hydraulic engine, or water-wheel, with cranks and vibrating beams, appears to have been introduced in colliery works in the year 1680, and into Scotland about the year 1712. About 100 years ago this mode was superseded by Newcomen's steam-engine; but even that was not of much value in pits which were as deep as 120 yards. The pumping is now effected in pits of much greater depth by the powerful and splendid engines of the present day. At South Hetton, at the back of the shaft, a noble engine-house is erected of massive stone, which contains an engine of 300-horse power. This engine is the most powerful one in the district, and its magnificent action may be seen to great advantage from three galleries which surround the interior of the engine-house. The sole business of this engine is to pump up the constantly accumulating waters of the pit, which it discharges into an adjacent reservoir from which the boilers are supplied. The constant and steady exertion of its power is as necessary as the beating of the heart to the continuation of animal life. Any impediment to its operations would be attended with disastrous consequences, and on it goes, day and night, from one year's end to another, until accident, or the wear and tear of some of its parts, bring both itself and the industry of the pit to a stand.

Adjoining the above engine, in buildings erected for the purpose, are three winding engines of ninety-horse power each, for drawing up or bringing to bank the tubs, buckets, or corves containing coal, and for enabling the workmen to descend the shaft. This is accomplished by two sets of ropes, each weighing thirty-eight cwts., which are coiled or uncoiled from two large drum wheels, as the ascending or descending motion is required. The day is chosen as the most convenient time for bringing up coal, and the night for sending down provender for the horses and the various stores.

The engine which keeps the pumps in action is furnished with four enormous boilers, and the smaller ones with two each, of proportionate dimensions. Two supernumerary boilers are kept, in order to be ready, should those in use sustain any injury. The fact that the power of 570 horses is constantly exerted in effecting the two simple operations of pumping, and drawing up the coal, affords a striking illustration of the magnitude of the operations connected with first-rate colliery works.

3. *Mining.* – We must beg the reader to imagine himself in a gloomy excavation or subterranean passage about eight feet high and fourteen feet wide. This is one of the 'ways' of a coal-pit, the bottom of which is called by the miners the thill, and the top the roof. Here and there along the walls of this passage a safety-lamp is suspended; and when the intense darkness of the place is occasionally illuminated by the slight ignition of the fire-damp, the whole scene presents an extraordinary appearance. The generation of inflammable air is frequently so great from the solid coal that the miners dare not proceed onward above a few feet from the current of fresh air. The light afforded by the safety-lamps seems to possess an unusual illuminating power; but though the visitor can see perfectly well, he still feels encompassed by pitchy and midnight darkness. In these galleries the miners or hewers, as they are called, carry on their work, in pairs, each taking about twelve feet of the side wall to excavate, and leaving between each such space an interval of the same width on which the roof may securely rest. The first process is to form what is denominated a 'bord,'[22] which is done by digging out the coal from the bottom with a pick ... to a depth of three or four feet. The 'bord' being completed has next to be formed into a 'judd': this is effected by picking away the sides, as had previously been done with the thill; and when finished, it forms a projecting mass of coal measuring on its surface about eleven feet by six. Into this judd a deep sloping hole is then bored, which is filled with gunpowder and fired by a train, when the judd is shivered into large fragments and scattered over the floor. In this way much labour is saved, and a larger and more profitable sized coal is secured for the market.

The coal seams of Yorkshire average from one and a half to nine feet in thickness, while in the more northern coal-fields they run from two and a half to seven feet. Near Dudley, in Staffordshire, is a seam of coal known by the name of the ten-yard coal, from its extraordinary thickness. This remarkable bed is about seven miles long and four broad. Seams of coal have been worked as thin as eighteen inches, and instances have occurred of seams being wrought only twelve inches in thickness. Young men and boys are employed under such circumstances. The differences of thickness sometimes admit the erect posture, and sometimes oblige the men to sit, recline, or bend the body to an extreme degree. They often work almost naked, either for the convenience of motion, or from the effect of the atmosphere, which is always at a high temperature in coal-pits.

On the coal being detached in the manner above described, a corve, tub, or basket, is then brought to the spot on a four-wheeled train, by a man and boy, technically called a 'dragsman and foal,' and when filled with the scattered fragments, it is dragged to the bottom of the shaft, hooked to the end of the rope, and drawn to the top in about three minutes. When the corves are made of iron they are called tubs, and the labours of the dragsman and his assistant are then performed by horses. When the corve arrives at the mouth of the pit it is received by the banksman, by whom it is landed. It is his duty to see that it is properly filled, and that the coal-owner gets his proper measure from the pitmen. He also keeps an account of the quantity drawn up, for which service he is paid three farthings per London chaldron.[23]

Plot,[24] in his 'History of Staffordshire,' written about 150 years ago, says that about Dudley, Wednesbury, and Sedgley, or within a circuit of ten miles, 'there are usually twelve or fifteen collieries in work, and as many out of work. Some of these afford 2000 tons of coal yearly; others 3000, 4000, or 5000 tons.' This was in the very centre of the richest part of the Staffordshire coal-field, which now ranks the fourth in the kingdom for the extent of its supplies; and at that time coal was not consumed for domestic purposes only, but likewise in many manufactures. The amount raised annually was probably about 60,000 tons. About one-half the collieries were out of work, owing most likely to the impediments which occurred in them being of a nature which the mechanical powers of the machinery then employed could not overcome. In the same district alluded to by Plot, there is now used, not reckoning that employed in the general manufactures which are so extensively carried on in that quarter, and excluding the quantity consumed for domestic purposes, 1,725,000 tons of coal annually, in rendering iron fit for the processes which it has to pass through in its conversion into articles of utility. For this one purpose alone the consumption is now thirty times greater than it was in the year 1680, when applied to a multiplicity of uses. In eighteen hours the South Hetton pit sometimes sends to bank as great a quantity of coal as would fill thirty of the Thames barges, or above 600 tons, while in Plot's day, the whole of the collieries situated in a most productive district did not in the same time supply one-third of this quantity.

We need not wonder at the striking contrast here displayed, when it is considered that so much of the work of a colliery was then carried on by human labour. We have seen that, previous to the introduction of Newcomen's steam-engine, there existed no means of drawing out the water from pits above forty or fifty yards deep; but that on its introduction this was accomplished in those which were twice that depth, and thus a greater quantity of coal was brought within reach, and rendered serviceable whenever it might be required; and that now pits above 300 yards deep are brought into a proper state for working by means of further improvements in the application of the power of steam. If the calling of a collier is now considered repulsive by many, it was much more so a century or two ago, when the most slavish labour of the mines was performed by men, and even women, instead of by steam-engines. The lowest part of some of the earliest mines was reached by inclined planes, along which women carried the coal from the depths of the pit to the surface in baskets which they bore on their backs. The women employed in this degrading occupation were termed bearers, and each carried a weight of from one to two cwts.; sometimes they carried three cwts. Even after the period when the coals were drawn up a perpendicular shaft by machinery, women were employed in carrying the coal from distant parts of the pit to the bottom of the shaft; and in some collieries 60,000 tons have annually been carried in this way. It is only within the last half-century that women have been relieved[25] from such unsuitable employment.

4. *Screening*. – When the corve is received by the banksman, it is conveyed, either by a train or a new suspensory apparatus, to one of a series of trap-doors in the bank-floor, through which the coal is teemed,[26] and in its descent rolls down a long sloping sieve or screen to a stage below. The large and small coal is thus separated, and the latter is collected for inferior purposes. All the large coal for the London market is so carefully sifted that, on leaving the pit, it is perfectly free from dust and small particles. In its subsequent progress to the consumer the breakage which occurs is of course inevitable.

All coal which passes over a sieve whose meshes are five-eights of an inch asunder without falling through, is called 'Wallsend'; and the same coal teemed over a three-eighth screen is vended as 'second coal,' and sold to the shipowner at about 4*s*. per Newcastle chaldron less than the best Wallsend.[27] A third sort, called 'nuts,' is obtained from that which had fallen through the screen in procuring the Wallsend and seconds; and a fourth termed the 'dead small,'[28] from that which falls through in the preparation of the nuts.

The screened coal is collected on a wooden stage, and shovelled into the waggons which are brought underneath, and which are each made to contain exactly fifty-three hundred weight. While this is doing, several men and boys pick out any stones, slate, or other refuse with which the coal may happen to be intermixed.

The best coal for domestic consumption is the worst for a blacksmith or a founder. It sometimes happens that the produce of a pit containing inferior coal is selling in the market for a higher price than the best coal, in consequence of an increase in the demand of that required for manufacturing purposes.

In a subsequent Number we shall follow the further progress of the coal on its passage to the consumer, and enter into some particulars showing the commercial importance of the coal-trade.

THE COLLIERIES. – No. II.

WE explained in the preceding Supplement the process of obtaining coal, and the manner in which it is prepared for the market. When this is accomplished, it has next to be transported to the ships employed in the coal-trade. For this purpose a road is constructed (generally a rail-road) leading from the mouth of the pit directly to the nearest harbour or river.

Nature has intersected the northern coal-field by three considerable rivers, in consequence of which the whole district possesses an easy, cheap, and expeditious mode by which its produce may find its way into the general market. These three rivers are the Tyne, the Wear, and the Tees, each of which is admirably adapted, both by its volume of water, its tides, and harbour-room, for the purposes in question.

The Tyne is the most important of the northern coal-rivers, and, as it possesses all the excellencies of the others, we shall confine our description to it. It originates from two small streams called the North and South Tyne, which unite a little above the ancient town of Hexham, at about thirty miles distance from the sea, where it becomes navigable for small craft. From Hexham it flows through a fine hilly country to New-castle, where it is sufficiently wide and deep for vessels of large burden, and where its office as a coal-river may be said properly to commence. Its course from Newcastle to the sea, at Tynemouth, presents scenes full of activity and enterprize. Nowhere is capital seen in fuller or more beneficial employment. Heedless alike of the obstructions of hills and valleys, it has created hundreds of railways, which, commencing at the mouths of the different pits, terminate at some convenient place on the banks of the river. On these thousands of waggons convey with rapidity the produce of the mines to the vessels lying at anchor in the river, which, as they complete their freight, are towed out and depart with every favourable wind for their several destinations.

The large collieries in the vicinity of the rivers have each a railway running in the most direct line to their banks. Upon these railways the waggons move in trains of from ten to thirty or more in number, according to the extent of the works or the existing demand for coal. The nature of the power which puts them in motion depends in some measure on the distance they have to travel, and the inclination or other peculiarities of the surface. On those which are perfectly level, a locomotive steam-engine generally heads the train, and drags it to its destination with startling rapidity. On other railroads, which have a regular descent the whole way, the waggons are impelled by their own gravity, and, by the aid of a long rope and a series of pulleys, drag up the empty train, which, in its turn, when again descending with a load, draws the other to the pit in like manner. When the railroad is carried up an ascending piece of ground, the train is drawn up the ascent by a winding-engine placed at the summit. In many small establishments, and in some which are situated very near one of the rivers or the coast, horses are employed to draw the train of coal-waggons; and, in others, a combination of all these methods is practised. Those collieries which are situated several miles from either the rivers or coast have frequently to pay sums amounting to 400*l*. or 500*l*. a-year for the right of carrying their communications through private property which intervenes between the pits and the place of loading.

At the end of the railway, and overhanging the river, a large platform of wood is erected, which is called a staith. Upon this the waggons laden with coal are brought to a stand previous to the discharge of their contents into the holds of the ships which lie at anchor underneath. Each waggon contains about 2½ tons (53 cwts.) of coal, and when the number of waggons has been entered by a clerk appointed for that purpose, they are placed, one at a time, on a square open frame, which, on the withdrawal of a bolt, is immediately moved from the staith by machinery until it is suspended over the main-hatchway of the vessel. A man who descends with it then unfastens a latch at the bottom of the waggon, which, being made to turn upon hinges like a door, immediately opens, and the whole of the coal in the waggon is cleanly poured into the hold. To facilitate this operation the sides of the waggons converge towards the bottom, and are lined with smooth iron-plates. Attached to the suspending machinery are two counterpoising weights, which, being less heavy than the waggon when laden with coal, do not impede but add steadiness to its descent; but, the moment the coal is discharged, their gravity draws up the waggon to the staith. This mode of loading the vessels is both complete and ingenious. In an excursion on the Tyne, between Newcastle and Shields, the perpetual ascent and descent of the waggons in the manner above described forms a very novel and curious spectacle to a stranger.

In situations where, owing to the height of the cliffs, the above mode of emptying the waggons would be inconvenient or impracticable, a large spout is used, and the vessel is brought under the aperture at the lower end; so that the coal emptied at the top passes along the spout, and is discharged into the ship's hold. The height of the staith at Seaham is perhaps forty feet above the deck of the vessel, and to diminish the force with which the coal would descend the spout from such a height, there is a trap-door at the lower end, by which the force of its descent is diminished, and it reaches the hold without injury to the vessels. …

One of these two methods [waggon-by-waggon or spout] is invariably pursued wherever there is a sufficient depth of water to allow the vessel to come alongside the staith; but as this is not always the case, whenever an impediment exists, some other mode becomes necessary. There are many coal-works in which, owing to local obstacles and the intersection of private property, a right of way cannot always be obtained. The greatest obstacle of all, and one which is coeval with the coal-trade itself, is the bridge which crosses the Tyne at Newcastle, which effectually bars the passage of coal-vessels above the town. Those owners, therefore, whose pits lie 'above bridge' are compelled, in addition to the railway and staith, to employ a number of light barges called 'keels,' for the purpose of conveying their coal to the ships. This mode of conveyance is the most ancient, and was universal before the invention of the staith and its mechanical apparatus.

A keel is built sharp at both ends, and is capable of containing about 16½ London chaldrons of coal (about 21 tons), has a sort of quarter-deck for the convenience of the keelmen, and a footway or gangway along the sides. The collier, waiting to receive the cargo of the keel, lies at anchor in a convenient part of the river, and generally a keel is lashed on each side of her. The coal is shovelled through her ports, or into a large tub, which, when filled, is drawn up, turned over, and the coal emptied into the hold. But this method occasions the breakage of the coal to such an extent as to deteriorate its value in the market.

By the vessel receiving her cargo from the staith, without the intervention of the keel, a saving of about 9*d.* per London chaldron is effected in keel dues. The employment of keelmen is therefore dispensed with wherever it is possible. Still their wages are tolerably constant, and are higher than those received by pitmen, and considerably higher than the wages of an agricultural labourer. They average from 18*s.* to 21*s.* per week, and occasionally they obtain, under certain circumstances, from 30*s.* to 40*s.* They are paid by the tide, voyage, or trip.

We feel much pleasure in recording a circumstance in the history of the keelmen, which does great credit to their foresight, and is worthy of imitation by all classes of our industrious population. Warned many years ago by the sentiment expressed in the northern proverb –

> "Did youth but know what age would crave,
> Many a penny it would save,"

they raised a sum by subscription among themselves, with which they founded an extensive establishment in Newcastle, known by the name of the 'Keelman's Hospital.' In this quiet retreat fifty-two aged men and women find a comfortable asylum during their latter years. We believe that this is the only hospital in the kingdom built and supported by the working classes for their own members. The keelmen meet once a-year to celebrate the establishment of this institution, perambulating the town with bands of music, playing the lively Northern air – 'Weel may the keel row.'

A stranger who visits the banks of the Tyne will not fail to be struck by the immense heaps of sand which are to be seen, some of them being from 100 to 200 feet in height. The colliers, after discharging their cargoes, take in a quantity of sand as ballast, and on their return to the river, it is discharged on its banks. It is afterwards removed to the top of these 'ballast hills,' which is often a tedious and expensive process. Sometimes a steam-engine and an 'endless train' of ascending and descending buckets is necessary.

Newcastle, the metropolis of this district, has doubled its population within the last thirty years. It has been enriched by the coal-trade, which attracts vessels from all parts of the world to discharge their merchandize upon its quays. By the exchanges which follow these transactions, a multitude of trades are called into activity, which in their turn give employment and wealth to industrious thousands, who, spreading over the neighbourhood, form new and flourishing communities. In this way North and South Shields, at the mouth of the Tyne, and many intermediate villages on its banks, have sprung up within the memory of persons yet living. Of the coal annually consumed in London, one-half, amounting to more than 1,000,000 tons, is shipped at Newcastle. The foreign export of coal from Newcastle amounted, in 1833, to 233,448 tons, being above a third of the whole quantity sent abroad. Vessels do not enter or clear at North and South Shields, but at Newcastle, of which those places are the out-stations. The number of ships registered at Newcastle is above 1,100, and their tonnage amounts to 221,276 tons. A collier makes on an average nine or ten, and sometimes more, voyages to London in a year; and the number of arrivals in the Tyne annually is not less than 13,000 or 14,000, – 10,000 of which are on account of the coal-trade.

Five-and-thirty years since, Colquhoun,[29] who wrote a treatise containing an historical view of the commerce of the port of London, says, in that part of it which relates to the coal-trade, that this branch of our enterprise 'exceeds the foreign commerce in the number of ships annually discharged; and requires double the number of craft which is required for the whole import and export trade of the Thames.' In 1799, the number of colliers which arrived in the Thames was 3279; in 1818, there were 5239; and in 1833, 7077.

THE USES OF COAL

In the introduction to this Volume, I pointed out that the demand for a commodity depended on the possession of knowledge about how the commodity might be used. This section documents that knowledge as it existed at various points in the Victorian era.

Before turning to this point it is useful to note that the uses of coal were many. This multiplicity of uses arose partly because coal was not only a source of energy but was also useful because of its physical properties and chemical constituents. But it is also notable that as a source of energy it much more adaptable than previous sources. In comparison with human and animal muscle it was possible to use coal to provide heat and, through the agency of the steam engine, much greater power at a point than could be conveniently generated by human or animal agency. Because coal was transportable, power could be provided in places where water- and wind-power were unavailable. As a source of town gas, coal could provide light on a scale previously impossible with candles and other light sources. Later in the century, coal as a power source for electricity generators made the energy it provided more adaptable still.

The main competitor with coal throughout the nineteenth century was wood, burnt as a fuel. In many applications it was a viable source of energy. It continued to be used as a source of domestic heat and as a cooking fuel in continental Europe and North America throughout the nineteenth century.[1] It was used to power steam locomotives and other steam engines. But it had technical disadvantages which encouraged the transition to coal whenever it was easily available. It was bulky in comparison to the amount of heat generated in its combustion; in other words it was not as 'energy dense' as coal. This was a major consideration in the use of wood as a fuel where space was at a premium: on board ship and for locomotives. It also raised transport costs. Secondly, it produced large quantities of ash. These problems could be reduced by the use of charcoal which had perhaps double the energy density of wood[2] and produced insignificant amounts of ash but charcoal had technical problems of its own, principally its fragility and tendency to disintegrate.

On top of these problems, wood and charcoal had become expensive to produce in England in comparison with coal. Data for the south east of England suggest that wood fuel had been a relatively expensive source of energy since about 1550. At this point both wood fuel and coal cost perhaps £200 per ton of oil equivalent in 2000 prices. Both coal and wood fuel prices fluctuated alarmingly from year to year but after a fall in coal prices from about 1550 to about 1600, the trend of prices for both coal and wood fuel was clearly upwards from about 1600 to about 1750. The trend for wood fuel was steeper, however, so that by about 1750 coal prices were only back to the level of 1550 whereas wood fuel prices had more than doubled to over £400 per ton of oil equivalent.[3] Although wood fuel prices fell back after this peak, it remained a relatively costly source of energy.

The physical properties of coal are crucial in metal manufacture. The burning of coal in a blast furnace provides heat throughout a three-dimensional space rather than at a point, along a line, or over a surface. In other words, it is useful and of importance in some contexts that coal is a solid, not a liquid or a gas, and a solid that may be broken to allow the passage of the air or oxygen needed for combustion around the broken pieces.

Coal also has chemical properties. The discovery of these properties, initially through the distillation of coal, had hardly begun at the beginning of the nineteenth century. It was known early that a flammable gas could be produced from coal and that it could be used to produce light, as pp. 105–9 in this section show, but knowledge about coal tar, its constituents, and their uses was very limited at the start of the nineteenth century, as pp. 167–8 demonstrate. It was only after mid-century that the surprising, fascinating and valuable properties of the organic chemicals derived from coal, including the coal tar dyes and saccharine, began to be discovered.

This takes us back to the main point of this section, that usefulness and value depend on knowledge. Such is obvious in the case of the organic chemicals derived from coal, only slightly less so in the case of the gas and electricity derived from coal and the use of steam generated by coal fuel in machinery of all kinds. But it is also the case with the elementary uses of coal to provide heat for human warmth and for cooking. It is not obvious that the black rock called coal will burn; after all, few rocks do, and it can be quite hard to set coal, especially anthracite, alight. It is thus possible for coal resources to have been ignored for millennia. An anonymous author wrote for the magazine the *Leisure Hour* in December 1863:

> At this season, when the blazing fire in our grates receives a large proportion of our attention, and the thoughts of many a housewife stray naturally to the coal-cellar and its supply, it may not be amiss to look into one of the great coal-cellars of our globe, and speculate on what we find there. English consumers are perhaps never likely to

burn a block from its countless tons of fuel, for they are stowed away in a certain county of Pennsylvania: and instead of being accumulated in the deep places of the earth, they lie heaped, as though in a profusion which had exhausted underground storage, in a mountain summit far above the level of the sea.

In the year 1792, a man walking over this summit saw, thrust out of the green ground, the angle of a rock of coal. He examined further, and found that the grass was merely a carpet over a flooring of such coal: he informed General Weiss, owner of the land, of the value which lay beneath his soil. The General, being ill-advised, sold the whole crest of the mountain next year to the Lehigh Coal Company, so called from the little river which they hoped to make their channel of traffic ... [Eventually a mining settlement grew up called Mauch Chunk, a Native American name] signifying the Bear's Mountain: a reminiscence of the olden forest times when as yet the country was verily 'Penn's Sylvain,' or woodland, and the red men hunting the savage denizens of the wilderness new nothing of the grand civilizing agent – the coal – beneath their tread.[4]

Thus began the Pennsylvania coal industry: when the coal was seen, one can hardly say, 'discovered', by someone who knew what it was.[5]

***

The collection begins with the elementary uses of coal: heating and cooking. The articles on pp. 41–5 and pp. 51–2 are from the anonymous *Practical Economy: Or, The Application of Modern Discoveries to the Purposes of Domestic Life* of 1821 (no further editions were included after the one reproduced here). It is an advice manual and one that attempts to be 'scientific'; it uses the term 'caloric' from Lavoisier's theory of heat and refers to Count Rumford's experiments without, unfortunately, noting that the latter tended to disprove the former. It suggests that while the knowledge that coal burns and produces heat was of course widespread in early nineteenth-century Britain, beyond this there was widespread ignorance, particularly over methods of achieving fuel efficiency and reducing atmospheric pollution.[6] It is noticeable, for example, that the author of this manual fails to articulate in plain terms the fact that visible smoke is unburnt coal. Further hints suggestive of a general ignorance much later in the century are contained in an article in the series 'The Doctor in the Kitchen' published by the *British Medical Journal* in 1879. A 'number of correspondents' had asked Ernest Hart, the author, about the economy of fuel that might be attained by using 'furnaces such as those employed in French kitchens or such as the American stoves and ranges'. In response, Hart wrote:

[B]y way of example I may say I ascertained the ordinary cost for kitchen fuel in a house in Paris, where the usual continental routine was followed of *café-au-lait* at 8, with a roll; a *déjeûner* of the usual three or four dishes at 12, and dinner at 6, for a household of twelve persons; and I found that the total annual cost there was £5.

> This was easy to calculate, because the fuel used is always of a special kind, viz., coke and compressed peat, coal being little or not at all used in French kitchens.
>
> In an English household of which I have the particulars before me, I find, on the other hand, with a very careful and intelligent cook, skilful and yet economical, that for this household of two persons and five servants the annual expenditure for fuel in the kitchen is £12; but this does not include the gas used in the gas-cooking apparatus, which is a good deal employed during the summer, and as a supplemental stove at other times.[7]

Hart continued that coke in the past year, as used in the English household as well as the French, had been less than half the price in London that it was in Paris. Therefore, the expenditure in the Parisian kitchen should be halved in sterling, and the conclusion drawn that cooking in this household was effected at a quarter of the cost of the English kitchen.[8]

A review from the 1850s (pp. 47–50), suggests that by this time Rumford's ideas were better understood. But it also suggests that domestic coal-fired heating in Britain at that time was not only inefficient but also to a large extent ineffective, failing to achieve the desired level of warmth at all, not merely failing to achieve that warmth for the minimum quantity of coal or at minimum cost:

> faces are scorched while feet are freezing, and, except for those in the immediate vicinity of the hearth, there is little warmth or comfort in many a room which bears the outward semblance of both in its cheerful open fire.

The typical method of heating the Victorian home remained the open grate. Badly designed heating and ventilation arrangements based on the open grate could, by increasing the volume of cold air entering a room from outside and allowing it, once heated, to move rapidly up the chimney, actually reduce the temperature in the room below what it had been before the fire was lit.

Central heating did not become common in Britain, except in institutional contexts, until the 1960s.[9] The *Colliery Guardian* carried a report in 1889, relayed from the *Manchester Guardian*, stating that 'a movement was on foot to establish a house-to-house heating supply similar to that of gas and water' based on the provision of water at a temperature of 400°F (about 200° Celsius) and a pressure of 250 psi through a domestically located reducing valve 'which permits the water to resolve itself into steam'.[10] Nothing appears to have come of this scheme which we now recognize as 'district' or 'neighbourhood' heating. Similar schemes were later advocated by radicals as a method of reducing the burden of housework on women but such schemes remained confined to a small number of visionary twentieth-century housing projects.[11] Eventually, the conversion of increasing numbers of homes to alternative fuels after the Second World War diminished the need for such innovations.[12]

'The Centenary of the Steam Engine of Watt' (pp. 53–6) moves us on to the most well-known of all the uses of coal in Victorian Britain, to generate steam. The Victorians were themselves in absolutely no doubt of the importance of the steam engine and the centenary of Boulton and Watt's steam engine was widely celebrated by addresses such as the one extracted here by Sir William Armstrong, one of the most prominent of the manufacturing engineers of his day. Armstrong tells the story as it had become mythologized by the mid-Victorian period. A simple catalogue of the adjectives and similar parts of speech deployed in this address to describe Watt and his invention is telling. Armstrong first uses 'illustrious', 'greatest', 'sagacity', 'tenacity', then, as the narrative arc develops, 'vain attempts', 'ailing health', 'narrow pecuniary means', 'inclining to despondency', 'unfitted', and then, as triumph follows adversity, 'persevering', 'attractive character', 'fine intellect', 'severe discouragement', 'irresistible impulse', 'succeeded', 'genius' and 'brilliant'.

The main point I wish to draw attention to is a different one, however. In his reflections on Watt's history, Armstrong comments on two aspects of the technological advances of the previous hundred years. The first comment is about how easy the process of invention had become in the century since the invention of the Boulton and Watt engine. The century had seen an advance in engineering techniques towards precision and reliability; the struggle that Watt endured to achieve a steam-tight piston and cylinder was a thing of the past. Moreover, a myriad of devices had been invented, perfected and made familiar to the extent that invention within the confines of steam technology had become, it sometimes seemed, merely a matter of assembling the requisite combination of devices and fitting them together:

> In the present day, every contrivance is practicable in a constructive point of view, and the vast variety of devices used in modern mechanism, and applicable to new mechanical combinations, are made known to inventors, in minute detail, by the press (p. 54).

It is sometimes said that the most important feature of western technological progress is not the invention of any particular technology but the invention of invention itself.[13] Here, Armstrong makes a similar, though less fundamental point: once an appropriate suite of techniques and devices within a particular technology has been established, invention becomes almost routine.[14] And of course, the ease of invention within such a technology tends to bias invention towards that technology.

Armstrong's second point is that technical knowledge is cumulative. His address turns towards the then-recent success, after a number of costly failures, in laying the first Atlantic telegraph, 'one of the very greatest and most honourable achievements of man'. It would have been impossible, reflects Armstrong, without 'a steam-ship of such gigantic size [Brunel's *SS Great Eastern*][15] as to be itself one of the greatest wonders of modern engineering':

> Thus it is that one great invention hangs upon another. First came the Steam Engine, then followed the great Steam Ship, and finally the Atlantic Cable, which, without the aid of steam, could never have been laid (p. 55).

Armstrong goes on to reflect on the Suez Canal. He points out the enormous scale of the excavations – impossible without steam dredgers and comments:

> In contemplating this undertaking, we are naturally led to compare it with the great neighbouring relics of Egyptian antiquity. In quantity of material moved, the Suez Canal is far more vast than the great Pyramid (p. 56).

This introduces a further theme emerging from this sequence of texts: scale. Armstrong was astonished (as doubtless were his listeners) at the scale of Brunel's ship, at the vastness of the excavations forming the Suez Canal. Without steam, he implies, industry would have remained at the scale set by the eighteenth century, when the largest industrial objects, sailing ships, registered no more than a few thousand tons.[16]

The next text (pp. 57–62) turns to one of the earliest industrial uses of the steam engine, to pump water. Rather than a text concerned with pumping water from mines, I have, in order to emphasize the width of application of the new technology, chosen one concerned with pumping sewage. It is the report by Sir Joseph William Bazalgette to the Metropolitan Board of Works on the completion of the London Main Drainage in 1875. Again the huge scale of the undertaking is at the forefront of the text and quantified at every opportunity. The scale was truly extraordinary. The London Main Drainage conveyed the sewage of 3.5 million people from an area of 117 square miles. It did this with only four pumping stations but these contained 21 engines, working 42 pumps, capable of lifting half a billion gallons a day. The steam engines employed at the Western Pumping Station were titanic: cylinders of 3 feet 1 inch diameter (almost a metre) and 8 feet stroke (2.4 m); they consumed the steam generated by eight Cornish boilers, each 22 feet (6.6 m) long.

The knowledge required to make use of coal covered a broad field. This is perhaps most clear in the texts on steam navigation and steam locomotion (pp. 63–85). In both cases considerable prior accumulations of knowledge were required to make use of the coal. In the case of steam navigation, knowledge of shipbuilding, navigation and geography as well as the mechanical engineering knowledge required to apply steam technology to ships; in the case of steam locomotion, not only the metallurgical and mechanical engineering knowledge required to construct the engine but also the civil engineering skills required to construct the railway.[17]

The application of steam engines increased transport speeds. That the 20 miles per hour achieved by the early Liverpool and Manchester Railway or the 36 miles per hour achieved by the Grand Junction Railway between Liverpool and Birmingham was regarded as a speed of god-like or mythological swiftness is well known. 'It is quite a just remark', wrote Lord Shaftesbury in 1839, 'that the Devil, if he travelled, would go by train'.[18] Similarly, shipping speeds increased markedly, a development which in the opinion of the anonymous author of 'Steam Communication with India' (1842) was 'far more extraordinary than any of the changes wrought by the railways'.

> Sixty years ago the voyage from London to Calcutta usually occupied five and six months, and to China seven months, and the 'course of post' with India was calculated at little less than twelve months (p. 63).

The author goes on to relate that now the mails from India were despatched from Bombay (now Mumbai) on the 1st of each month and the steamer carrying them usually arrived at Suez about the 20th. The mail was then put on board a Mediterranean steamer at Alexandria on the 22nd, reaching Marseilles on the 30th. The 740 miles from Marseilles to London were then covered by special couriers in four days, reaching London less than five weeks after the departure from Bombay. The steamship had brought the journey from Bombay to London down from five months to five weeks. The ship on the Bombay–Suez leg could make the return trip perhaps six times a year instead of once, demonstrating the dramatic increases in capital productivity enabled by the higher speeds themselves enabled by steam technology. It is a mistake to assume it was solely a labour-saving suite of innovations.

'A Day at a Cotton Factory' from 1843 (pp. 87–103) treats the foremost industrial sector of the time. The narrative provided by this text emphasizes another feature of the technological knowledge of the time which favoured the early adoption of steam engines as power sources and thus added to the demand for coal. This was the pre-existing water-powered technology. Water-powered mills had been built since the 1770s and, by the time this piece was written, factories housing substantial quantities of machinery were, if still capable of shocking those unfamiliar with them, no longer new. In them power was transmitted from a rotating water wheel; what could be simpler than to replace the water wheel with a reciprocating steam engine?

Not that this was the route to making the most of coal-fired steam technology. Falling water as a power source had substantial disadvantages. It tied water-powered mills to water-courses which were found almost entirely in 'country districts', far from adequate supplies of labour. Hence the grim story of the wholesale use, one might almost say 'purchase', of pauper apprentices in the early mills, transported in batches from the workhouses of London and the south to the mill towns and villages of the north.[19] This was not the only disadvantage. The necessity of siting a water-powered mill on a stream or a river, the limited number of sites where this could be accomplished, and the limited power available from the river at any given site acted to keep mills, mill towns and villages small and often separated them from one another. Transportable coal enabled cotton masters to site their steam-powered factories nearer to supplies of labour, or nearer to supplies of raw material, or nearer to output markets, and enabled them to build on a scale unconfined by limited power resources. In the event, the cotton masters sought the economies of agglomeration or in Marshall's terms, the 'external economies of scale', of a location within easy reach of Manchester.[20] Coal thus enabled the transfer of industry from the countryside to the city and the conurbation, and led to the growth of the industrial city to the scales with which the world has now become familiar.

This is well expressed in the text. The unknown author was clearly impressed not only by the scale of individual factories but by the scale of the towns around Manchester and of Manchester itself. 'In 1760', he or she writes, 'not more than forty thousand persons are supposed to have been employed in this manufacture' (p. 87). There were now, in 1843, 'in all its various branches, considerably above a million' (p. 87). He or she continues:

> Ashton in 1775 contained five thousand inhabitants; in 1831 it contained more than thirty thousand. Stayley Bridge in 1748 contained forty-eight houses and one hundred and forty people; it has now twenty thousand inhabitants. Hyde in 1770 contained one dwelling-house and one chapel, while Duckinfield was at the same time designated as a 'pleasant country spot;' now they contain some of the largest factories in the whole district, and an extensive population (p. 93).

And later:

> The population of the township of Hyde increased *ninefold* between 1801 and 1831! (p. 93)

The astonishment expressed at the Manchester factories is occasioned not only by their physical scale and their cost but by the number of people set to work in a single building:

> the scene which is presented when the operatives leave these factories to go to their meals is one of the most striking that can be conceived; the busy hive pours forth in a stream from each building, some of which employ more than a thousand hands (p. 90).

The impact of steam on production was thus complex. It was not a simple increase in labour or capital productivity and a reduction in costs. It enabled a complete reorganization of production. By relocating, cotton masters were enabled to take advantage of lower costs in input markets and external economies of scale. The ability of coal-powered technology to supply almost unlimited power at a given point allowed full advantage to be taken of internal economies of scale. The result was industrial urbanization and the emergence of industrial conurbations in Lancashire, Yorkshire, the west Midlands, the north east, and around Glasgow. The dramatic reduction in ocean transport speeds enabled by the steam-ship and the steam-dredged Suez Canal began the Victorian phase of the globalization of industrial production.

The collection now moves on to gas and electricity. To those most familiar with Victorian England through its fiction, it will be surprising to see how early the gas industry began. 'Gaslight', like Michael Sadleir's period novel, *Fanny by Gaslight*,[21] is something the reader of Victorian and Edwardian novels associates with the end of the nineteenth century and the start of the next: it is the world of Arthur Conan Doyle and Arnold Bennett, not the world of Scott, Thackeray or Dickens.[22] Nevertheless, as Murdock's 'An Account of the Application of the Gas from Coal to Œconomical Purposes ... Read before the Royal Society' (1808, pp. 105–9) demonstrates, the industry had its beginnings in the eighteenth century and by the end of the Napoleonic Wars, the Gas Light and Coke Company had received the charter which allowed it to lay gas pipes throughout London and Westminster. By 1822 the capacity of the London gasometers, only 14,000 cubic feet (not quite 400 m^3) in 1814, was nearly 310,000 cubic feet (over 8,750 m^3). In the latter year they supplied an average of 10,660 private lights, 2,248 street lamps and 3,894 theatre lamps.[23]

At this time, the demand for gas as almost entirely for lighting and a large part of this demand was from public authorities, commerce, services and industry as the following account of events as darkness fell over the London streets indicates:

> The lamplighter is seen busily hastening from lamp to lamp, placing his slight ladder against the street-irons, and kindling the flames which give to our streets no small share of their evening attractions; the shopkeeper begins to illuminate his wares, with one blaze if he be an humble dealer, with a dozen if his house be a 'gin-palace,' with a score or two if he sells 'unparalleled bargains' in linen-drapery; the theatres, the club-houses, the evening exhibition rooms – all begin to display a blaze of light...[24]

The use of gaslight in ordinary domestic premises is notable by its absence from this account. The use of gas as 'the modern domestic fuel' for cooking, heating water and warming rooms remained unusual until at least the 1890s, despite the invention of many varieties of 'gas-cookery apparatus' many decades before.[25] 'Public education in this important matter', wrote an anonymous contributor to the *British Medical Journal* in 1893,

> has been greatly facilitated by the various gas companies and corporations throughout the kingdom hiring to their consumers at small rentals stoves of approved construction and design. That the public have appreciated this enterprising and wise policy of the companies is abundantly proved by the enormous number of stoves applied for.[26]

This suggests that the key constraint was risk and access to credit, rather than knowledge. Dickens had told the story in 1853 of what must have been a wealthy 'establishment in the west of London, consisting of a large number of persons, who make a very observable impression on several large joints of meat every day.' But the 'expenditure of coal' was 'awful'. They decided to replace their cast-iron coal-fired cooking range with a 'gas-cooking apparatus' at a cost of 100 guineas or £105, then equivalent to two year's wages for a building labourer or a governess. But they were dissatisfied with the way it cooked their meat: 'all the food seemed sodden, and neither baked, nor roasted, nor boiled properly'. They ripped out the gas-cooking apparatus and replaced the coal-fired cooking range.[27]

They had taken a risk; it had turned out badly. Being wealthy, they presumably had no need to borrow the 100 guineas, but for other families, the imperfection of credit markets and their consequent inability to borrow such sums on acceptable terms or any terms at all would have prevented the project.[28] Its riskiness would have lessened their desire to pursue it. The 'enterprising and wise policy' of the late nineteenth-century gas companies addressed these problems with a rare display of imagination. Nevertheless, gas for domestic cooking and heating was still being advertised as a novelty in 1913[29] and Harry Jones's remark in 1916 concerning 'the very large increase in the use of gas by the lower classes of the population for domestic purposes on the slot system', suggests that there had been another problem preventing the diffusion of gas consumption, contractual terms for gas supply which were unacceptable to customers living from week to week, or from day to day, or from hand to mouth.[30]

That 'all the food seemed sodden' would have seemed an advantage to Stevenson Macadam, the author of the next piece (pp. 111–19). This confirmed that cooking by gas was indeed safe and presented the reduced loss of moisture from food baked in a gas oven relative to that lost in a coal-fired range as an advantage. One wonders whether tastes had changed since Dickens wrote in the 1850s or whether Macadam was carried away by his enthusiasm for the gas cooking stove.

The next three texts reflect the rise of electricity. Once again, the importance of the rise of knowledge in understanding the uses of electricity and thus the uses of coal and the demand for it is clear. Early uses, for telegraphy, did not lead to substantial derived demands for coal. It was long expected that, one day, it would be possible to use electricity for lighting, not only in special uses and circumstances such as in the maritime lighthouses mentioned frequently in

'Electricity as a Light Producer' (pp. 131–5) but also in private and public buildings and, not least, as we shall see in the next section, in the mines. Nevertheless the technical problems and the paucity of the resources devoted to solving them, prevented progress towards the incandescent light bulb for much of the century. The 'Age of Electricity' had, indeed, been anticipated for many years before it could have been said to have arrived.[31]

In the van of progress towards this new age was, rather surprisingly, Lord Salisbury. This scion of an ancient family and 'titan' of late Victorian Conservatism electrified his estate at Hatfield in 1887 and installed little fewer than 2,000 Swan lamps. He was, it is true, not quite the pioneer of such developments. In 1870 Sir William Armstrong, the author of the 'Centenary of the Steam Engine of Watt' (pp. 53–6), installed an electric dynamo in Cragside, his country house. It was powered by water from one of the lakes on the estate and the electricity was used to power an arc lamp from 1878 until this was replaced with incandescent Swan lamps in 1880. This was thought to be the first domestic installation of electric lighting using incandescent light bulbs.[32]

Nevertheless, whatever the boost to electrification given by these noble and celebrated examples, A. T. Stewart, writing in *Chambers's Journal* twenty years after the installation at Cragside in 1900, had to admit that 'electricity as an illuminant' was 'only in its infancy'.[33] The cost was admitted to be a problem. The advantages over gas were largely limited to its 'hygienic advantages':

> No longer need we inhale air impregnated with the noxious fumes produced by the combustion of coal-gas, nor be disgusted by the offensive smell of the oil which exhales from the imperfect lamp.[34]

The ignorance of other possible uses is indicated by the way Stewart wrote of them. 'To many', we read, 'the very idea of electricity heating seems almost a paradox. Electricity has of late been chiefly associated in the public mind with lighting; and, in the opinion of many, one of its principal advantages over gas has been the absence of heat'.[35] On electricity as a power source, he wrote

> To some people the information may seem quite a revelation that the same current which gives light when switched on to an electric lamp causes an electric motor to revolve rapidly when it is switched on in an equally simple manner.[36]

But there was also a lack of imagination about the possible uses of electric power in the home. There was no hint of its future use for powering record players, radios, televisions or other domestic media, of course. But other lacunae seem likely to spring from the unfamiliarity of almost all male middle-class writers and researchers on the topic with the diverse drudgeries and difficulties of housework. Stewart did not suggest that electric power might one day be used to power mechanized devices for cleaning laundry, washing dishes or for sweeping floors. It seemed to occur to no one in the nineteenth century that an electrically powered device for keeping food cool might not only reduce the labour involved in marketing and the waste of food in the domestic preparation of meals but might also enable significant advances in infant and child health and survival.[37] This was despite the fact that industrial refrigeration plants had, by 1900, a relatively long history. Instead, Stewart thought the power suitable for 'numerous domestic purposes such as organ and harmonium playing, the turning of knife-cleaning machines, butter churns, mangles, boot-polishing machines, [and] ventilating fans'.[38]

We turn now to uses of coal which depended on its characteristics as matter not simply as a store of energy. The texts on pp. 141–56 are concerned with metal manufacture, pp. 141–51 with the manufacture of coke, largely for the purpose of manufacturing iron and steel, and pp. 153–6 with the smelting of iron. The use of coke in the manufacture of iron is perhaps the most well-known example of demand determined by knowledge. Galloway described the substitution of coal for charcoal in the smelting of metalliferous ores and manufacture of iron as 'the most important as well as the most difficult industrial problem of the seventeenth century'.[39] By the end of that century coal was being used to smelt lead, tin and copper, and according to one source, iron. It was not until Abraham Darby succeeded in smelting iron ore with coke from about 1713 that iron was manufactured with coke on any extensive scale, however. The advance in knowledge marked by this development was necessary if the transition to coke was to be made but it was not sufficient. Charcoal prices were insufficiently high relative to coal prices to force the change to coke before the 1750s.[40] From that point, what had been a demand for charcoal became a demand for coke; a demand for coke was a demand for coal – and lots of it.

Techniques of coke production in use in the later eighteenth and early nineteenth centuries made a profligate use of coal. Steavenson is not as clear as he might be on this point and it is helpful to consider the following account, from 1831:

> The method of coking in Wales is not remarkable for that economy to which it may and will probably be brought when coal is of more value than it is at present. The general system is to place the coal in long open heaps, containing 30 or 40 tons, laying the pieces of coal as loose and open as possible, to allow of their swelling, and covering the whole with smaller pieces so as to give the external surface a tolerably level appearance. The heap is then set on fire in different places, and suffered to burn till the whole surface is completely ignited. When this is the case, the coker covers it entirely over with the dust and ashes of former fires, to exclude the air and prevent waste, and it is left to burn out, or rather to cool gradually, till it is in a proper state to be uncovered and carried to the tunnel head of the furnace ...
>
> By the system of open fires much of the coal must be reduced to ashes before the air is excluded. This is more particularly the case when the wind is high, as it not

> infrequently is in those mountainous and exposed situations. On a stormy night, the unremitting exertions of a double set of cokers are perhaps required on the coke hearth to keep the fires tolerably covered; and in an extensive work, probably sixty or a hundred tons of coal may be wasted in one night in spite of all their labour.[41]

As the nineteenth century progressed, as we pointed out in the introduction to these three volumes, economies in the production of coke from coal were found and for this and other reasons coal requirements per ton of iron fell from 5 to 8 tons in 1850 to 2 tons or less by the end of the 1930s.

Finally we come to the uses of coal based solely on its chemical characteristics. The text on pp. 157–65 is designed as a non-specialist introduction to coal chemistry and is taken from a small book, *The Story of a Piece of Coal* published in 1896. This was designed for juvenile readers but, as was the way with many works allegedly designed for the young at this time, it made few concessions to whatever defects there might have been in the reader's knowledge and understanding. It finishes with a useful 'genealogical' chart, reproduced here, showing the distillation products of coal.

'Some Account of Tar and its Properties' (pp. 167–8) goes back to 1809 and demonstrates how little of the knowledge accumulated by 1896 and available to every bright schoolboy and girl with parents rich enough to buy them books had been available ninety years before. 'What can you do with coal-tar?' someone had asked the readers of *The Tradesman, or Commercial Magazine*. 'Not much', replied a correspondent, 'You can use it to preserve wood at sea and on land'. The myriad uses found for the distillates of coal and briefly noticed in *The Story of a Piece Coal* were unsuspected.

That such was the case is hardly surprising. As the anonymous author of 'Colour in the Coal-Scuttle' (pp. 169–74) wrote:

> Who would have dreamed, ten years ago [in 1853], that the black, evil-smelling substance [coal-tar], that we hastily passed in the street, holding our breath the while, for fear of inhaling its loathsome vapour, would produce delicious scents, vying with the rose and violet in delicacy of odour, and colours that rival in brilliancy of hue the lovely tints of these queens of the garden? Yet so it is.

The quantities of coal needed to produce the colours, aromas and other substances created from coal distillates were not enormous but neither were they entirely insignificant. Henry Roscoe in 'Saccharin' stated that a ton of Lancashire coal would yield 12 gallons (55 litres) of coal tar. That in turn would yield a little over a pound (about 0.5 kg) of aniline. In turn, that would yield colours that would dye 500 yards of flannel magenta; 3,800 yards of flannel naphthol yellow; 120 yards aurin (orange); and so on. The derived demand for coal from the organic chemical industry was useful, nothing more. The real significance of these products of coal for the coal industry is to remind us that it was not only an energy industry and an adjunct of a metallurgical industry but also the foundation of the Victorian production of organic chemicals.

***

In nineteenth-century Britain the development of science revealed by these texts was rapid and impressive in chemistry, physics and, as we shall see later, in geology. The development of technology appears to show significant biases, however, and the most obvious is against the domestic technologies of heating and cooking. After the investigations of Benjamin Franklin and Count Rumford in the late eighteenth century, noticed in the texts on pp. 41–50, there was very little research into these domestic technologies until the invention of the gas stove in the 1890s.[42] The review of 1854 extracted on pp. 47–50 considers work which appears amateurish and elementary in comparison to that typical of the extra-domestic fields surveyed on pp. 53–177. While there were prestigious professional institutes for civil, mechanical and mining engineers by 1860 and another for electrical engineers was established soon after the introduction of electrical technologies in the 1870s,[43] the Institution of Heating and Ventilating Engineers was not founded until 1897. Although it published papers and proceedings from 1901 it never achieved the status of the civil engineers or the influence of the mine engineers.[44] Researchers in the field preferred to associate themselves with more prestigious groups and publish their work in the *Proceedings* of the Institution of Civil Engineers, other engineering and architectural journals or in the medical press.[45] In 1920 the government's Committee on Smoke and Noxious Vapours Abatement concluded:

> With regard to the question of domestic heating in general, we are struck by the absence of full and scientific knowledge. We think that the whole subject of hygienic and scientific heating deserves a very much greater measure of public attention than it has hitherto received.[46]

Although the relative absence of research from this field is notable, the lack of innovation was not solely due to the lack of research. The superiority of the continental closed heating stove over the British open fire, both in terms of fuel efficiency and atmospheric pollution, was well understood throughout the later nineteenth century.[47] The survival of the latter was often put down to its 'cheerfulness'.[48] The wide availability of cheap coal and cheap domestic servants will also have played its part, as will the refusal of the state to insist on domestic fuel economy. These circumstances must, in turn, have diminished the attractions of research in these fields. They became and have remained 'Cinderella' topics.

Notes

1. See, for example, 'Consumption of Fuel in France and England', *Penny Magazine*, 5:298 (26 November 1836), pp. 462–4, which comments on the continued prevalence of wood as a domestic fuel in France.
2. Although 'energy density' is the usual term in the social and environmental sciences, engineers refer to this concept as the Heating Value of a fuel and distinguish between the Higher Heating Value (HHV), which is measured by techniques which bring all the products of combustion back to the original temperature, condensing any vapour produced, and the Lower Heating Value which is measured by techniques which do not. The HHV of coal varies from about 15 MJ/kg for lignite to about 30 MJ/kg for anthracite, where MJ denotes a megajoule. Air dry wood has an HHV of about 15 MJ/kg, charcoal about 30 MJ/kg (US Department of Energy, *Biomass Energy Data Book*, available at http://cta.ornl.gov/bedb/appendix_a.shtml (accessed 21 April 2011)).
3. Again, in the prices of 2000. See Fouquet, *Heat, Power and Light*, pp. 52–4, and fig. 4.1. As Fouquet argues, the debate about whether there was, or was not, an Elizabethan wood fuel crisis appears largely settled in favour of the sceptics, since on the whole, wood fuel prices did not rise in real terms in the last half of the sixteenth century. The crisis, if a period of over half a century can be so termed, was a century later, from 1640 till the end of the seventeenth century.
4. 'A Mountain of Coal', *Leisure Hour*, 626 (December 1863) pp. 827–8, at p. 827.
5. The industry's development also had to wait until relative prices were right. Because of the easy availability of wood 'before 1821 scarce a thousand tons of the treasure had been sold'. Ibid., p. 827. Similar points to those made here in respect of American coal can be made with regard to rubber, discovered by Mesoamericans before 1600 BC but used by them almost solely to make rubber balls for use in the 'Mesoamerican Ball Game' and not used, of course, to waterproof raincoats, manufacture pencil erasers, hydraulic tubing or car tyres, or to insulate electric cables. See D. Hosler, S. Burkett and M. Tarkanian, 'Prehistoric Polymers: Rubber Processing in Ancient Mesoamerica', *Science* (1999), pp. 1988–91; L. F. Nadal, 'Rubber and Rubber Balls in Mesoamerica', in E. M. Whittington (ed.), *The Sport of Life and Death: The Mesoamerican Ballgame* (London: Thames and Hudson, 2001), pp. 20–31; J. S. Day, 'Performing on the B+Court', in Whittington (ed.), *Sport of Life and Death*, pp. 64–77; M. J. Tarkanian and D. Hosler, 'An Ancient Tradition Continued: Modern Rubber Processing in Mexico', in Whittington (ed.), *Sport of Life and Death*, pp. 116–21.
6. This view is also implicit in C. Dickens, 'Pot and Kettle Philosophy', *Household Words*, 8:193 (3 December 1853), pp. 333–6.
7. E. Hart, 'A Doctor in the Kitchen', *British Medical Journal*, 2:982 (25 October 1879), pp. 671–3 at p. 672.
8. This suggests that Hart used market exchange rates to attain his previous comparison of £5 in Paris and £12 in London. Hart's sample size renders his results merely suggestive of course, and his English household with its five servants for two persons sounds far too wealthy to be typical of even the upper middle classes of England, but his subsequent technical critique of English cooking ranges gives plausibility to his comparison.
9. Central heating was described as 'a system not in general use in private houses in this country [the UK], but widely employed on the Continent and in America' by a government committee in 1920. It went on to describe the advantages of a coke-fuelled central heating system installed by the Austin Motor Company at its village of Northfield near

Birmingham in 1917 (Ministry of Health, Departmental Committee on Smoke and Noxious Vapours Abatement, *Interim Report* (Cmd. 755), 1920, pp. xxv, 253, paras 38–43, quotation from para. 38). Progress remained slow, however, with the National Coal Board feeling it necessary to point out that 'central heating is not just for rich people' as late as 1962 ('Central heating for all [Display Advertising]', *The Times*, 29 October 1962). It was not until 1971 that more than a third of UK houses and flats had central heating installed (Government Statistical Service, *Social Trends*, 3 (London: HMSO, 1972), table 106).

10. 'A New Method of Heating Houses', *Colliery Guardian*, 20 September 1889, p. 422. The principles of such a system were clearly set out in an article in the *Penny Magazine* in 1842 which notes that 'many of our large public buildings are thus heated by steam' ('The Minor Uses of Steam', *Penny Magazine*, 11:682 (19 November 1842), pp. 455–6, at p. 455).
11. European projects were reviewed by Sydney Bryan Donkin, 'Industrial, Agricultural, and Domestic Heating, with Electricity as a By-product', *Journal of the Institution of Civil Engineers*, 1:3 (January 1936), pp. 378–400 and 'Discussion', pp. 400–24. The most well known of the British schemes was the Pimlico scheme built in a blitzed area of London and formally opened in 1951; see B. Donkin, A. E. Margolis and C. G. Carrothers, 'The Pimlico District Heating Undertaking', *ICE Proceedings*, 3:3 (May 1954), pp. 259–85.
12. C. Black, *A New Way of Housekeeping* (London: W. Collins, 1918).
13. J. Rae, 'The Invention of Invention', in M. Kranzberg and C. W. Pursell, Jr (eds), *Technology in Western Civilization*, vol. 1 (New York: Oxford University Press, 1967), pp. 325–36.
14. A similar point was made by Harry E. Jones in a 1916 retrospective of the last century of the gas industry. Noting the 'entire absence' of 'skilled and experienced contractors' in the early days of the industry and the poor transport infrastructure with which the early engineers had had to contend, he continued 'To-day, plant, implements, and machinery of the most microscopic delicacy and efficiency are found everywhere, while even the largest of the enormous constructions necessary are well within the scope of the average practical builder and contractor' (H. E. Jones, 'Thomas Hawksley Lecture: The Gas Engineer of the Last Century', *Proceedings of the Institution of Mechanical Engineers*, 91 (1916), pp. 631–74 and plate V, at p. 631).
15. Isambard Kingdom Brunel (1806–59), one of the greatest heroes of Victorian engineering, widely known and admired in twenty-first-century Britain, less well known overseas. The standard biography remains L. T. C. Rolt's *Isambard Kingdom Brunel* (London: Longmans, Green, 1957) despite the publication of more recent competitors. The SS *Great Eastern*, built in 1858, was 680 feet long. Typical Atlantic liners of the 1880s were 500 or 600 feet (150 to 180 m) in length (e.g. the 1881 *City of Rome*, 546 feet; the 1888–9 *City of New York* and *City of Paris*, 560 feet; and the 1889–90 *Teutonic* and *Majestic*, 582 feet). The *Great Eastern* was not surpassed until the building of the *RMS Oceanic* by Harland and Wolff of Belfast in 1899 and then described as the largest ship in the world; it was 704 feet (211 m) long (*Engineering*, 4 December 1891; 'Inspection of the Oceanic', *Liverpool Mercury*, 31 August 1899, p. 8e).
16. The largest sailing ships were constructed not in the eighteenth but in the late nineteenth century, another example of David Edgerton's *Shock of the Old*. *La France*, a five-master built in 1890–1 and regarded as 'colossal' by contemporaries, had a displacement of 8,800 tons. The steel hulled *Marie Rickmers* built for Messrs Rickmers of Bremen by Russell & Co of Port Glasgow in 1891–2, and thought to be the biggest sailing ship

in the world on her launch, could spread no less that 56,500 square feet (5,250 square metres) of sail and was 375 feet (m) long but was of only 5,700 tons deadweight('The Biggest Sailing Ship', *Tuapeka Times* [New Zealand], 2 March 1892, p. 5).

17. The point may seem obvious but it has frequently been ignored, not least in 'technology transfer' development projects and in policies designed to encourage foreign direct investment (FDI). Such projects and policies have tended to fail to generate the benefits expected where the 'absorptive capacity' of the country has been low. In other words it has been difficult to benefit from small pieces of technological knowledge in a context of wider technological ignorance. See B. M. Hoekman, K. E. Maskus and K. Saggi, 'Transfer of Technology to Developing Countries: Unilateral and Multilateral Policy Options', *World Development*, 33:10 (2005), pp. 1587–1602 and N. Crespo and M. Paula Fontoura, 'Determinant Factors of FDI Spillovers –What do we Really Know?', *World Development*, 35:3 (2007) pp. 410–25.
18. See the extracts gathered by Humphrey Jennings in his *Pandæmonium: The Coming of the Machine as Seen by Contemporary Observers* (André Deutsch, 1985; London: Macmillan, 1995), especially numbers 187, 'The Steam-Carriages' of 1833; 211, 'From an Old Journal' of 1839; 214, 'Faust's Flight' from the same year; and 242 'Dombey in the Train' in which Dickens compares the 'power that forced itself upon its iron way' to the 'triumphant monster, Death!' The quotation from Shaftesbury is from number 213 'The Devil' which Jennings took from Shaftesbury's journal as quoted by Edwin Hodder in his 1888 *Life and Work of the Seventh Earl of Shaftesbury*.
19. The classic account remains J. L. Hammond and B. Hammond, *The Town Labourer 1760–1832: The New Civilisation* (London: Longmans, Green, and Co., 1919), ch. 8.
20. Alfred Marshall, *Principles of Economics*, 9th (Variorum) edn (London: Macmillan for the Royal Economic Society, 1961), ch. 10 'The Concentration of Specialized Industries in Particular Localities', pp. 267–77.
21. M. Sadleir, *Fanny by Gaslight* (London: Constable, 1940), set in the London of the 1870s; filmed by Gainsborough Pictures in 1944.
22. Indeed, Scott (1771–1832) installed gas lighting at his home, Abbotsford House, and became a director of his local gas company (H. Barty-King, *New Flame* (Tavistock: Graphmitre, 1984), p. 41).
23. 'A Day at the Westminster Gas-Works', *Penny Magazine*, 11:635 (26 February 1842), pp. 81–8 at p. 88.
24. Ibid., p. 86.
25. See, for example, Dickens, 'Pot and Kettle', p. 335.
26. 'Cooking and Heating by Gas', *British Medical Journal*, 2:1718 (2 December 1893), pp. 1241–2 at p. 1241.
27. Dickens, 'Pot and Kettle'.
28. Ibid., p. 335. I regret my precis rather destroys the literary quality of the original.
29. The British Commercial Gas Association, 'The Modern Domestic Fuel [display advertisement]', *The Times*, 1 December 1913.
30. Harry Jones, 'Hawksley Lecture', p. 651. The 'slot system' was a pre-payment system using coin-operated supply meters located in the home by means of which gas could be purchased in small quantities at a time.
31. See, for example the series of articles by William Henry Preece, F. R. S. 'The Age of Electricity', *Time* [London], 7:37 (April 1882), pp. 80–90; 7:38 (May 1882), pp. 193–205; 7:39 (June 1882), pp. 291–305; 7:40 (July 1882), pp. 440–52; and 7:41 (August 1882), pp. 528–35.

32. G. A. Irlam, 'William Armstrong's Hydraulic Engine and Pumps at Cragside', *Industrial Archaeology Review*, 11 (1988), pp. 68–74; G. A. Irlam, 'Electricity Supply at Cragside', *Industrial Archaeology Review*, 11 (1989), pp. 187–95, later published together as *Domestic Engineering at Cragside* (Coventry: National Trust, 1991). The installation was described in 'Swan's electric light at Cragside', *Graphic*, 2 April 1881, p. 327.
33. A. T. Stewart, 'The Application of Electricity for Domestic Purposes', *Chambers's Journal*, 6th series, 3:146 (15 September 1900) pp. 657–60, at p. 657.
34. Stewart, 'The Application', p. 657.
35. Ibid., p. 659.
36. Ibid., p. 659.
37. A domestic electric refrigerator, the 'Domelre', was first produced in Chicago 1913. The first to be widely marketed in Britain, although only to the wealthy, was the 'Frigidaire', introduced in 1923. Harrods first advertised one in *The Times* in 1925 ('Harrods [Display Advertising]', *The Times*, 21 May 1925, p. 9f). The historiography begins with Oscar E. Anderson, *Refrigeration in America: A History of a New Technology and its Impact* (Princeton, NJ: Princeton University Press for the University of Cincinnati, 1953). More recent work includes W. R. Woolrich, *The Men who Created Cold: A History of Refrigeration* (New York: Exposition Press, 1967), R. Thévenot, *A History of Refrigeration Throughout the World*, J. C. Fidler (Paris: International Institute of Refrigeration, 1979) and A. J. Cooper, *The World Below Zero: A History of Refrigeration in the UK* (Aylesbury: ACR Today & Battlepress, 1997).
38. Stewart, 'The Application', p. 659.
39. Galloway, *A History of Coal Mining in Great Britain*, p. 39.
40. The researches of Charles K. Hyde appear conclusive on this point. His explanation for Darby's success with the then high-cost coke technology was that it produced iron which was more fluid at given temperatures which could therefore be used to manufacture thin castings without the holes, cracks and other defects of charcoal iron. He was thus able to manufacture, for example, a gallon pot that weighed only 3 kg, half the usual weight, which could be sold for a higher price, despite the fact that it contained less iron (C. K. Hyde, 'The Adoption of Coke-Smelting by the British Iron Industry, 1709–1790', *Explorations in Economic History*, 10:4 (1973), pp. 397–418).
41. Society for the Diffusion of Useful Knowledge, *Manufacture of Iron* (Library of Useful Knowledge) (London: Society for the Diffusion of Useful Knowledge, 1831), p.6. E. Rogers, 'On the Manufacture of Charcoal and Coke', *Proceedings of the Institution of Mechanical Engineers*, 8 (1857), pp. 25–35 and 'Discussion', pp. 35–40 and plates 100–103, has useful illustrations of charcoal and coke heaps and the coke ovens that superseded them.
42. This is not to say that invention and research completely ceased. John Buddle, Jr, the colliery viewer, patented 'a fire grate or stove' in 1814. There were two works by civil engineers: Robert Stuart Meikleham's *Theory and Practice of Warming and Ventilating Public Buildings, Dwelling-houses, and Conservatories ...* (London: Thomas and George Underwood, 1825), and Charles Hood's *Practical Treatise on Warming Buildings by Hot Water, on Ventilation, and the Various Methods of Distributing Artificial Heat, and their Effects on Animal and Vegetable Physiology: To Which are Added, an Inquiry into the Laws of Radiant and Conducted Heat, the Chemical Constitution of Coal, and the Combustion of Smoke* (London: Whittaker, 1844) which went into its fifth edition in 1879. Nevertheless, Rumford's ideas were still being presented as the acme of domestic efficiency more than fifty years after his death. See, for example, F. Edwards, *On the Extravagant*

use of Fuel in Cooking Operations: With a Short Account of Benjamin Count of Rumford, and his Economical Systems and Numerous Practical Suggestions Adapted for Domestic Use (London: Longman's Green & Co., 1869). The principles of the Rumford fireplace are explained by Jim Buckley, 'Reviving Rumford', *Journal of Light Construction* (March 1994).

43. The Society of Telegraph Engineers was founded in 1871. It changed its name in 1880 to the Society of Telegraph Engineers and Electricians and again, in 1889, to the Institution of Electrical Engineers. It received a Royal Charter in 1921. It is now the Institution of Engineering and Technology.
44. The Institution of Heating and Ventilating Engineers and the Illuminating Engineering Society (founded in 1909) merged in 1976 and formed the Chartered Institution of Building Services, adding the word 'Engineers' to its title in 1985.
45. For example, E. R. Dolby, 'Some Methods of Heating Adopted in Hospitals and Asylums Recently Built', *Institution of Civil Engineers Minutes of the Proceedings*, 174 (1908), pp. 91–130 and plate and 'Discussion', pp. 131–40; and W. Eassie, 'Reports on Sanitary Engineering in Houses, Hospitals, and Public Institutions', *British Medical Journal*, 1:682 (24 January 1874), pp. 119–21, respectively.
46. Ministry of Health, Departmental Committee on Smoke and Noxious Vapours Abatement, *Interim Report* (Cmd. 755), 1920, xxv, 253, para. 63.
47. See, for example, 'Art[icle]. V.—[A Review of] 1. The Coal Question: An Inquiry Concerning the Progress of the Nation, and the Probable Exhaustion of our Coal-Mines [and other works]', *Quarterly Review*, 119 (April 1866), pp. 435–72, esp. pp. 451–6.
48. 'The Open Grate: Its Virtues and Failings', *The Times*, 1 December 1913, p. 27c. See also J. E. Crowley, *The Invention of Comfort: Sensibilities and Design in Early Modern Britain and Early America* (Baltimore, MD: Johns Hopkins University Press, 2004), pp. 182–90 and L. Wright, *Home Fires Burning: The History of Domestic Heating and Cooking* (London: Routledge and Kegan Paul, 1964).

Practical Economy: Or, The Application of Modern Discoveries to the Purposes of Domestic Life (1821)

Practical Economy: Or, The Application of Modern Discoveries to the Purposes of Domestic Life, 2nd edn (London: Henry Colburn, 1822), pp. 220–8.

STORE OFFICES.

COAL CELLAR – *Management of Coals – Qualities of Coals – Economic Management of Heat. ...*

COAL CELLAR

THERE is no part of domestic economy which every body professes to understand better than the management of a fire, and yet there is no branch in the household arrangement where there is a greater proportional and unnecessary waste, than arises from ignorance and mismanagement in this article. It is an old adage, that we must stir no man's fire until we have known him seven years; but we might find it equally prudent if we were careful as to the stirring of our own. Any body, indeed, can take up a poker and toss the coals about; but that is not *stirring a fire!* /

In short, the use of a poker applies solely to two particular points – the opening of a dying fire, so as to admit the free passage of the air *into* it, and sometimes, but not always, *through* it – or else approximating the remains of a half-burned fire, so as to concentrate the heat, whilst the parts still ignited are opened to the atmosphere.

The same observation may apply to the use of a pair of bellows, the mere blowing of which, at random, nine times out of ten will fail; the force of the current of air sometimes blowing out the fire, as it is called, that is, carrying off the caloric[1] too rapidly, and at others, directing the warmed current from the unignited fuel, instead of into it. To prove this, let any person sit down with a pair of bellows, to a fire only partially ignited, or partially extinguished; let him blow, at first, not into the burning part, but into the dead coals close to it, so that the air may partly extend to the burning coal. After a few blasts let the bellows blow into the burning fuel, but directing the stream partly towards the dead coal; when it will be found that the ignition will extend much more rapidly than under the common method of blowing furiously into the flame at random.

The reason of this, both in regard to the poker and the bellows, is, that fire cannot exist without the presence of atmospheric air, seventeen parts in one hundred of which are pure oxygen, which forms the *pabulum* or food of fire, in addition to its own combustible qualities. It is on the same principle that water is thrown on the forge fire, in order that the existing heat shall produce decomposition; when its component particles, oxygen and hydrogen, both become combustible, and increase the ignition; just as a little water sprinkled on a parlour fire appears to increase the smoke, whilst it unites the small coals, / and prevents the atmospheric air, from the draught of the apartment, from passing through, before its oxygen has been decomposed by the fire, adding its own oxygen and hydrogen to the amount, as well as its own caloric, which is by no means inconsiderable.

With these principles in view, we may now proceed to a more practical illustration of the subject, the first point being the qualities of the material, of which there is a great choice in the London market; amounting to upwards of sixty species, from the mere bituminous slate, up to the brilliant Cannel[2] coal. For common use, in London, however, we recommend the best of the sea coal, which is generally supposed to be from the Walls-end Colliery, which comes by the Newcastle ships, and contains a sufficient quantity of bitumen, mixed with purer materials than any other species, thus affording heat and possessing durability. According to the present system, indeed, the consumer is quite at the mercy of the coal merchant, but a little management may remedy even that. If the consumer, instead of ordering a large supply at once, will, at first, content himself with a sample, he may with very little trouble ascertain who will deal fairly with him; and, if he wisely pays ready money, he will be independent of his coal merchant; a situation, which few families, even in genteel life, can boast of. Indeed we cannot too often repeat the truth, that to deal for ready money only, in all the departments of domestic arrangement, is the truest economy. Ready money will always command the best and cheapest of every article of consumption, if expended with judgment; and the dealer, who means to act fairly, will always prefer it. Trust not him who seems more anxious to give credit, than to receive cash. / The former hopes to secure custom by having a hold upon you in his books; and continues always to make up for his advance, either by an advanced price, or an inferior article; whilst the latter knows that your custom can only be secured by fair dealing. On this point, however, every ones experience may convince him; we therefore proceed to the more practical management of the subject in question.

There is, likewise, another consideration, as far as economy is concerned, which is not only to buy with ready money, but to buy at proper seasons; for there is with every article a cheap season, and a dear one; and with none more than coals; insomuch, that the master of a family, who fills his coal cellar in the middle of the summer, rather than the beginning of the winter, will find it filled at half the expense it would otherwise cost him; and will be enabled to see December's snows falling, without feeling his enjoyment of his fire-side lessened, by the consideration that the cheerful blaze is supplied at twice the rate that it need have done, if he had exercised a little more foresight.

We must now call to the recollection of our readers, that chimnies often smoke, and that coals are often wasted by throwing too much fuel at once upon a fire. To prove this observation, it is only necessary to remove the superfluous coal from the top of the grate, when the smoking instantly ceases; as to the waste, that evidently proceeds from the frequent intemperate and injudicious use of the poker, which not only throws a great portion of the small coals among the cinders, but often extinguishes the fire it was intended to foster.

The philosophy of the matter is simply this. When the heat begins to operate, the gas is extricated, and carrying some of the grosser particles / along with it, a heavy smoke is thrown up, which will not rise in the chimney, and by its own gravity is forced back into the room, on which the warm air of the apartment, being lighter than what comes in, instantly ascends towards the ceiling, and the lower part becomes cool. But if a portion of the fuel is taken off, then the small quantity of active caloric acts with greater force on the unconsumed coal, brings out its latent heat more rapidly, and thereby producing a quicker decomposition of the gases by the increasing combustion, the smoke becomes thinner and lighter, and though it carries up certainly more caloric with it, proportionally than before, yet the quantity of radiant heat is greater, and the general temperature of the apartment is more equalized.

Taking off the superabundant fuel has also the advantage of permitting a freer draught through the fire, and of course presents a greater quantity of atmospheric oxygen as food for combustion, rendering a poker almost useless. In short a few minutes patience will do more for a fire, than stirring and knocking the coals about for half an hour. The true secret is that stirring a fire is only necessary to keep the bottom clear, except when the top absolutely requires breaking, or rather perforation only.

Attention to these hints will save nearly one-third of the coal expenditure; certainly an important object not only in London house-keeping, but in all parts of the Empire.

We may add that although a well acting chimney carries up a greater portion of caloric than a smoky one in the same period of time, yet it does not diminish the active heat of the fire, but rather increases it; for as a smaller quantity of coals is in the grate, so a greater proportion of that quantity / is in active combustion, throwing out more radiant heat, and burning until nothing is left but a mere *caput mortuum*.[3] 'Tis true that there will be fewer cinders, and that these will be less serviceable than under other circumstances; but then the quantity of coals consumed will be much less in proportion. According to this method too, the warm air of the apartment is prevented from rushing up the chimney before it has passed through the fire; an arrangement which we attempt to produce artificially by the application of a tin blower, or register.

These hints apply both to parlour and kitchen fires; but with respect to the latter, if it were facile to make cooks practical philosophers, it ought to be explained to them that when water is once made to boil, all that is further necessary, is just to keep the water at that temperature, which Count Rumford[4] has proved by repeated experiments to require a very minute, though frequent addition of fuel. Meat will thus be as well boiled, and in the same time; with this advantage that a smaller quantity of the water will be evaporated: and less additional water to fill up, being thus required, consequently the fire will not so often demand copious additions of fuel – to say nothing of the injury done to the meat by the frequent dashing in of cold water.

It has been ascertained that 100lbs. of beef may be kept boiling hot for three hours, by means of 2½lbs. of pit coal in a confined place, so prepared as to prevent the radiating of the heat, except in the direction required, and at an expense of about three farthings, when coals are £4 per chaldron.

When fuel was comparatively cheap, this saving might not be considered as of high importance; nor is it easily practicable in England to make great savings in fuel, whilst rounds and sirloins are boiled and roasted. But in small families there / is less economy in cooking a large joint in one day to last for seven, than there would be in smaller dishes, cooked as in the warmer climates, in both the East and West Indies, and even in Spain and Italy; where, according to the national mode of cooking, less fire is consumed in dressing a large dinner than an English cook-maid will require to boil a tea-kettle. Even in both the Indies, the native cooks contrive to dress English dinners with a smaller consumption of fuel, than beef steaks for half a dozen can be cooked at home.

The steam cooking is also another important saving in domestic economy; though, at first the preparatory expense is considerable. With many indeed there exist strong prejudices against meat thus dressed; but that may be obviated in large establishments, when by a very simple process the steam may be applied, not to the meat itself, but to the warming of the water in which the meat is boiled. The practice of heating water in this manner by steam is now becoming general in breweries and in large manufactories, such as dyeing houses, &c., and even on a small scale might be made convenient for private families at a moderate expense; requiring, indeed, rather more patience and attention than English cooks are disposed to bestow upon economical practices.

But even without this, much may be done to prevent an extravagant and unnecessary waste of heat, by attention to the preparation of the general cooking apparatus.

On turning over the various philosophical repositories of the present day, we find that many attempts have been made of late to preserve a uniform temperature in breweries and distilleries, by confining the warmth to substances which are bad conductors of heat. The cement invented for / this purpose by Mr. Kurten,[5] the architect at Wiesbaden, has been highly commended. It is stated to have the property of concentrating in stoves, and especially the economic stoves, almost all the heat, so that it is expended only upon the things to be heated, and never in vain. The Polytechnic Society at Munich, which has lately analysed this cement, finds that it is indeed useful, but however, not so advantageous as the inventor supposed. According to the analysis of this Society, Mr. Kurten's cement consists of earthy marle, sand, and ochre, and though not perfectly adequate to the purpose, may yet be applied judiciously, until better means are found to produce the desired effect.

We may here conclude, by hinting that much saving would take place from paying more attention to the sifting of cinders and mixing them, for use, with small coal. A patent has lately been obtained for an improved apparatus for this purpose. It consists of a bin, or box, containing a sieve suspended upon swinging pivots: this is moved in a manner similar to the sieves of winnowing machines, by the intervention of a crank connected with the handle, and its motion may be regulated by a flywheel. There is a contrivance, by means of a sliding lever and handle, to discharge the contents of the sieve after it has been sifted, into a scuttle placed beneath; and by this means the operator is protected from all the dust which naturally arises. We would also recommend to the attention of the public the mode practised by the people in Wales, in preparing their coal for the hearth, by which the quantity is doubly increased, besides the durability of the fire, which lasts thrice as long as it would if made of coal alone. It is as follows:– To every bushel of small coal (the smaller the / better,) add one bushel of clay or river mud, mix them intimately together with some water to soften the clay, then form this mass into small balls, about twice the size of a hen's egg. According to the state of the weather, the balls are fit for use in from six to twelve hours. A fire made with these balls throws out a regular, ardent, intense heat, and if made with clay will burn eighteen hours, but if with mud about twelve hours; so that by this mode of preparation, a bushel of coal will last as long as four, consumed in the usual way. There is another advantage, as small coal, the very refuse of the coal-hole, answers best: this, it is presumed, may be purchased at a lower price than coal in general. /

'On Warming and Ventilating', *Quarterly Review* (1854)

'Art[icle]. VI. [A Review of] On Warming and Ventilating ... By Neil Arnott ... [and other works]', *Quarterly Review*, 96:191 (December 1854), pp. 145–76, pp. 145–6, 152–3, 159–60 and 160–1.

т. VI. – 1. *On Warming and Ventilating; with Directions for Making and Using the Thermometer Stove, or Self-Regulating Fire, and other New Apparatus.* By Neil Arnott,[1] M.D., F.R.S., &c. London, 1838.

2. *Journal of the Society of Arts*, Vol. II. No. 77. *On a new Smoke-Consuming and Fuel-Saving Fireplace, with Accessaries insuring the healthful Warming and Ventilation of Houses.* By Neil Arnott, M.D., F.R.S., &c. 10th May, 1854.

3. *A Rudimentary Treatise on Warming and Ventilation, being a concise Exposition of the General Principles of the Art of Warming and Ventilating Domestic and Public Buildings, Mines, Lighthouses, Ships, &c.* By Charles Tomlinson.[2] Published in Weale's 'Rudimentary Series.' London, 1850.

4. *Practical Remarks on the Warming, Ventilation, and Humidity of Rooms.* By Francis Lloyd.[3] London, 1854.

5. *Some Account of Domestic Architecture in England from the Conquest to the end of the Thirteenth Century.* By T. Hudson Turner.[4] Oxford, 1851. *And from the time of Edward I. to Richard II.* By the Editor of the 'Glossary of Architecture.' Oxford, 1853.

IT is mid-winter: cold, dark, and dreary without; warm and cheerful within. Seated by the side of the family hearth, the lover of home pleasures may now for the first time enjoy the luxury of an open fire without its usually-attendant inconveniences. This result, which is due to the inventions of a scientific physician of our own day, forms a successful supplement to the labours of ingenious men of past ages, who have devoted their talents to improving the domestic comfort of their fellow-creatures, and thus diminishing or cutting off some of the numerous sources of disease. And if the use of fire may in itself be considered as the distinguishing physical characteristic of man (the most savage nations being adepts in the use of the 'fire-stick,' while animals, until domesticated, have a dread of flame), then must we also consider in the light of benefactors all those who enhance the value of the gift, by bringing it more completely under our dominion, whether for the requirements of the arts, science, and commerce, or for the not less needful purposes of home comfort and healthful enjoyment.

> 'Now stir the fire, and close the shutters fast,
> Let fall the curtains, wheel the sofa round,
> And while the bubbling and loud hissing urn
> Throws up a steamy column, and the cups
> That cheer but not inebriate, wait on each,
> So let us welcome peaceful evening in.' /

This passage, from Cowper's[5] 'Task,'* owes its popularity to the delightful associations it calls up. Convert 'the fire' into a dull, dry, irradiant stove, and the charm is dissolved. We may heat our public buildings and churches with steam or with hot water, but we must leave to the German or the Russ the pleasurable ideas connected with such sullen warmth in living apartments. The enjoyment of the open fire is even too deeply seated among Englishmen to be greatly disturbed by its ordinary defects. Every house has its annual chapter of accidents or annoyances: fuel is wasted, chimneys smoke, dust is increased, soot accumulates, perhaps takes fire, property is destroyed, children are burnt to death; while it cannot be denied that rooms are unequally warmed and badly ventilated, faces are scorched while feet are freezing, and, except for those in the immediate vicinity of the hearth, there is little warmth or comfort in many a room which bears the outward semblance of both in its cheerful open fire. /

The quantity of air contained in a room 30 feet long, 28 feet wide, and 19 feet high, equals 15,960 cubic feet (30 x 28 x 19 = 15,960), and as 13 cubic feet of air weigh nearly one pound, the total weight of air in such a room is about 1220 pounds, or rather more than half a ton. Four-fifths of this air consist of nitrogen, which supports neither animal life nor combustion; one-fifth only consists of oxygen or vital air, without which no animal could live, no fire could burn. The very processes, however, of living and burning convert this oxygen into carbonic acid gas,[6] an enemy both to life and to combustion. We occupy such a room for many hours together, and exert our ingenuity in excluding cold air: windows and doors are *listed*,[7] sand-bags are placed over the junction of the sash-frames, a thick mat is laid at the bottom of the door, and even the keyhole is closed by a little falling shutter. Under these circumstances the inmates suffer from head-

* One of the most beautiful gift-books which has appeared this season – one of the most beautiful, indeed, that has ever appeared in any season – is a new edition of 'The Task' of Cowper, richly illustrated by Birkett Forster./

ache and nervous sensations, but the most obvious source of annoyance to them is that the fire will not burn or that the chimney smokes. The freer the room is from draughts the greater is the evil, for air is the *pabulum vitæ*[8] to the fire as well as to ourselves, and if it is not admitted to have a passage through the room, it comes down the chimney, and brings the smoke with it. In truth we do wrong to leave the supply to chance crevices. Nearly 150 years ago Gauger[9] devised a remedy for the inconvenience, by making a channel under the floor, one end passing through the outer wall of the house and the other opening in the centre of the hearth. Dr. Franklin's[10] method of ascertaining in a rough way how much air is required to be admitted per minute, was to set the door ajar until the fire burnt properly, and gradually close it again until smoke began to appear; he then opened it a little wider, and if the width of the crevice was half an inch in a door 8 feet high, the room would need an aperture equal to 48 square inches, or a hole 6 inches by 8. Six inches square would probably be sufficient for the wants of most chimneys. But where to form this aperture is a difficult question. If made in the door, it admits a cold current to the back and feet of persons sitting near the fire, and also interferes with the privacy of the room: if made in the window, it brings down a cataract of untempered[11] air upon the head. A plan which has come of late into pretty general use, is to have the opening nearly on a level with the top of / the room at the corner furthest from the chimney-place, and to shield it on the inside with a board sloping upwards. This directs the atmospheric current which enters from without against the ceiling, along which it streams, and coming in contact with the hot ascending air of the apartment, mingles therewith and partakes of its warmth. /

The most successful of all the modern attempts to improve grates and economise fuel was that of Count Rumford,[12] at the close of the last century. His labours were more generally received than those of his predecessors, and the Rumford stove soon became and still continues a favourite. When he began his reform of domestic fireplaces, the common construction (in spite of all that had been advanced by Gauger and others) was to make the back of the fireplace as wide as the opening in front, with the sides perpendicular to it, and parallel to each other. The space above the fire was also of large dimensions, and there was a metal plate or cover in use, which sloped upwards towards the *back* of the chimney, and tended to draw up the warm air instead of reflecting the heat into the apartment.

In order to increase the warming effect of the fire, Count Rumford brought the grate forward, that the rays of heat which had formerly struck against its perpendicular jambs might be available in the room. It thus became necessary to build up a new / back to the grate, which now stood detached from the original chimney-back, and this gave him an opportunity of effecting his second great improvement, which was to diminish the throat of the chimney to the smallest possible size that would suffice for the transmission of the smoke.

To the other beneficial changes was added the diminution of the size of the grate by filling up the back and sides with pieces of firestone, till the width of the cavity was reduced to six or eight inches. Under the old construction the Count calculated that 14-15ths of the heat escaped up the chimney and was lost.* Any attempt to maintain a small fire was ineffectual, on account of the great mass of metal of the grate, and the air rushing into it, cooling down the fire below the point necessary for combustion, as a live coal which falls upon the hearth soon ceases to be red-hot from the cooling effect of the surrounding atmosphere and the cold material on which it falls. /

Such is a brief statement of Count Rumford's important additions to domestic comfort, derived from his verbose Essay,[13] which possesses the charm which is communicated by earnestness of purpose. He is constantly returning to points which have been already demonstrated; and, lest there should be any mistake, after giving, at the end of his Essay, 'Directions for laying out the work,' he has a second supplement consisting of wood-engravings with separate descriptions. He also names many of the nobility and gentry who have adopted his plans with success, and gives references to the workpeople who executed them. With the honest pride of an inventor, he refers to at least five hundred smoky chimneys which he has conquered, and says, 'I have never been obliged, except in one single instance, to have recourse to any other method of cure than merely reducing the fireplace and the throat of the chimney to a proper form and just dimensions.' He remarks that the alterations involve very little expense, requiring only a few bricks and some mortar, or a few pieces of firestone; that they are adapted to any kind of grate or stove, and that they have effected a saving of fuel equal to one-half, and frequently two-thirds, of the quantity previously consumed. He requests the public, tradesmen, and manufacturers to observe that as he had no intention of patenting any inventions of his which might be of public utility, all persons were at full liberty to imitate them, and vend them for their own emolument; 'and those who wish for further information will receive *gratis* the information they require by applying to the author, who will take pleasure in giving them every assistance in his power.' /

* Dr. Arnott estimates the loss at seven-eighths, of which one half is lost in the smoke as it issues from the burning mass; two-eighths are carried off by the current of the warmed air of the room, which is constantly entering the chimney between the fire and the mantelpiece, and mixing with the smoke; and the rest is lost from about an eighth of the combustibles passing away, as soot or unburned fuel. /

Practical Economy: Or, The Application of Modern Discoveries to the Purposes of Domestic Life (1821)

Practical Economy: Or, The Application of Modern Discoveries to the Purposes of Domestic Life, 2nd edn (London: Henry Colburn, 1821), pp. 146–8.

DOMESTIC OFFICES.

KITCHEN – *Culinary Heat – Water – Furniture – Boiling and Stewing. ...*

KITCHEN.

IF all books of cookery were treatises on economy, our labours in this department would be short indeed; but even now we shall not trespass far upon the secrets of these Plutonian regions, whose Empress[1] will bear no rival near her throne. The three-headed dog,[2] who guarded the poetic hell, might be entitled, ex officio, to a sop; but the unlucky critical dog, who should dare to enter this modern / *Hades* in hopes of a sop in the pan, might chance to have his head broken, had he as many as Cerberus himself. The 'secrets of this prison-house,'[3] then we shall not dare unfold, but proceed to notice some improvements which may be judiciously adopted, even in addition to the convenient arrangements of the Rumford[4] plans which have already, in a considerable degree, superseded the use of the immense long ranges, that burned as much fuel in one day as might suffice for a week. Of the extraordinary quantity of caloric,[5] or of radiant heat, emitted from those long ranges, it is almost impossible to account for the consumption, except in the belief that a great portion was wasted, beyond what was absorbed by the dressed meat, and by the cook; of which wasted portion, some went up the chimney, whilst the remainder united with the surrounding air.

To remedy this, much was done by Rumford: but further philosophic principles have been elicited, and applied to practice, by means of which a kitchen may be fitted so as to require less labour and attention; rendering the food more wholesome and agreeable, and preventing that offensive smell, which makes a kitchen, on the old construction, so great a domestic nuisance even whilst it is most useful.

Many beneficial effects were produced on the Rumford plan, by means of hot steam; but the new principle is founded upon the application of *hot air*, requiring so little alteration as scarcely to be called a new arrangement, consisting solely of a stone hearth, a small fire-place on the Rumford plan, and a roaster for large dishes, serving also for an oven, together with a steaming apparatus.

The roaster is also supplied with a current of warm air, sufficient to have a great effect on the substances to be baked or roasted; contributing to / the formation of that crusty brown so generally liked in roast meats, and removing completely that disagreeable smell which meat is apt to acquire in a common oven.

In a fire-place of this construction the steaming apparatus occupies a recess in the wall similar to that used for the common stew-hearth; and the vessels which hold the substances to be steamed are generally of tin, perforated with holes like a cullender, in order to admit the steam of hot air freely on every side.

This arrangement may also be made to supply the scullery at all times with warm water, heated by the surplus steam from the fire-place.

That fitting up a kitchen, on these principles, will be expensive in the first instance, cannot be denied; but the saving, particularly on a large establishment, will amply repay it in a year or two. The saving in coals will be considerable; and we must not forget the saving in cooks, and in all broils but those intended for alimentary refection.[6] /

Sir William Armstrong, 'Centenary of the Steam Engine of Watt' (1869)

Sir William Armstrong,[1] 'Centenary of the Steam Engine of Watt', *Address of Sir William Armstrong, C.B., LL.D., F.R.S., &c. as President of the Institution of Mechanical Engineers: Newcastle Meeting 1869* (Newcastle-Upon-Tyne: J. M. Carr, printer, 1869), pp. 3–6.

TO THE MEMBERS OF THE INSTITUTION OF MECHANICAL ENGINEERS.

THIS year is the centenary of the Steam Engine of Watt,[2] and I am glad that it has fallen to the lot of Newcastle-upon-Tyne to receive, on so auspicious an occasion, a Society which must regard Watt, more than any other man, as the father of their calling. First, then, I shall discharge my duty as your President, by paying a tribute of respect to the memory of the illustrious man who, in the corresponding year of the last century, completed and set to work the greatest of mechanical inventions.

In 1765, the authorities of Glasgow College, little thinking of the momentous step they were taking, entrusted a model of a Newcomen Engine,[3] to James Watt, a maker of mathematical instruments, for repair. The sagacity of Watt enabled him, by an inspection of the model, to detect a radical defect in the principle of the Engine. He saw that the condensation effected within the cylinder reduced its temperature, and rendered restoration of the wasted heat necessary at every stroke. He perceived that the steam ought to act in a vessel always hot, and be condensed in a vessel always cold. He thus conceived the idea of separate condensation. With a quiet tenacity of purpose he set to work, under great disadvantages, to realize his idea of a more economical Steam Engine. His design was soon matured, but the difficulty of execution long remained a barrier to practical success. In the Newcomen Engine, the weight of the atmosphere, acting against a vacuum, was the moving power, and leakage of air past the piston was prevented by water resting on the upper side. An unbored cylinder, made in separate parts, sufficed for this arrangement, but in Watt's design, steam instead of air, / acted on the piston; a water packing was inapplicable; and leakage could only be prevented by the more accurate fit of the piston in the cylinder. A moderately steam-tight cylinder and piston were, however, more than the workshops of the day could produce, and we read of his vain attempts to correct by pasteboard and cork, inaccuracies of workmanship, such as in our time have no existence. With ailing health, narrow pecuniary means, and a temperament inclining to despondency, he was, in many respects, unfitted for a struggle with difficulty; but he was a man whose mind was taken captive by an idea, and he could not help persevering. His attractive character and fine intellect had attached to him many valuable friends, superior in station to himself, and his letters to some of those friends, written during his struggles, exhibit at once his severe discouragement and his irresistible impulse to proceed. In 1768, he had succeeded in producing a condenser with its necessary appendage of an air-pump, but it was not until the following year 1769, – exactly a century ago, – that his first complete Steam Engine was finished and put in motion. The first trial was made by Watt, in a secluded glen, behind the house of his friend, Dr. Roebuck,[4] near Linlithgow. The Engine was not a mere working model, but a machine of considerable power. It had a cylinder of 18 inches in diameter, and a stroke of 5 feet; but the cylinder and piston, which were described as the best the Carron Iron Works could produce, were still so inaccurately made as to defeat, in a great measure, the anticipated success. The Engine, however, afforded a practical demonstration of the value of the invention sufficient to lead eventually to the happy alliance of the capital of Boulton,[5] with the genius of Watt. In 1773, the Engine was removed to Mr. Boulton's works, at Soho, and was fitted with a new cast-iron cylinder, the casting and boring of which were deemed no small achievements in those primitive days of mechanical engineering. This first Engine of Watt was, like that of Newcomen, only applicable to pumping, but Watt quickly saw by what modifications it could be rendered available for rotative motion. By a succession of brilliant inventions, comprising, amongst others, his Parallel Motion[6] and his Ball Governor,[7] he advanced to the final conception of the double-acting rotative Engine, which became applicable to every purpose requiring motive power, and continues to this day, in nearly its original form, to be the chief moving agent employed by man. /

To do full justice to the genius of Watt, we must consider the disadvantages under which he laboured. In the present day, every contrivance is practicable in a constructive point of view, and the vast variety of devices used in modern mechanism, and applicable to new mechanical combinations, are made known to inventors, in minute detail, by the press. But Watt had no such facilities. He had to draw from his own mind what we can now choose from pre-accomplished invention, and his choice of means was restricted to the narrow limits of what was practicable in the rude workshops of the period. If we give due weight to these considerations, we shall be able to appreciate the remarkable originality of his mind, and the sagacity displayed in his inventions.

Watt lived to see his Steam Engine bear fruit in marvellous utility to the human race, but he could have had no idea of the results it was destined to realize before the expiration of the first century of its existence. It is impossible to contemplate these results without feelings of enthusiasm. To appreciate how much we owe to the Steam Engine, we need only consider, for a moment, what our position would be if we were deprived of its agency. The factories which clothe all the nations of the earth would be almost extinguished. The deep mines which supply nearly all our mineral wealth would be abandoned. The manufacture of iron would shrink into comparative insignificance. Horses and sailing ships would again become our only means of transit. All great engineering works would cease, and mankind would relapse into that condition of slow and torpid progress, which preceded the subjugation of steam by Watt.

Having thus, in honour of an inventor, whose name will grow greater as the world grows older, referred, in general terms, to engineering progress during the last hundred years, I need but glance at some of the more recent achievements in mechanical and constructive art, in order to shew that the extraordinary advance of the century continues unabated. That such is the fact, will at once be apparent, when I remind you that during the short period of eleven years, which has elapsed since the Institution of Mechanical Engineers last held their annual meeting, in this town, the Atlantic Telegraph Cables, the Suez Canal, and the great Railway across the American Continent, exceeding in length the sea passage from Europe to America, have been added to the engineering triumphs / of the century. Of these, there is but one of which England can claim the glory, and that is the first successful Atlantic Telegraph. The recondite science involved in that undertaking, the boldness of the enterprise, the perseverance displayed after the first failure, and the moral effects, as yet but partially developed, of its ultimate success, justify us in regarding the first Atlantic Telegraph as one of the very greatest and most honourable achievements of man. But Englishmen may feel additional pride in reflecting that the successful laying of that cable, as well as of the subsequent French one, just now completed, was chiefly due to the fact that there had been previously completed in this country, a steam-ship of such gigantic size[8] as to be itself one of the greatest wonders of modern engineering. Thus it is that one great invention hangs upon another. First came the Steam Engine, then followed the great Steam Ship, and finally[9] the Atlantic Cable, which, without the aid of steam, could never have been laid.

The Suez Canal presents another example of the direct application of the Steam Engine to the execution of one of the most remarkable of modern works, the chief part of the Canal having been executed by Steam Dredgers, of which an interesting description was received by this Institution at the Paris Meeting. In contemplating this undertaking, we are naturally led to compare it with the great neighbouring relics of Egyptian antiquity. In quantity of material moved, the Suez Canal is far more vast than the great Pyramid. In its moral and intellectual aspect, it is immeasurably superior. The ancient work is a useless monument of the idle vanity of a tyrant; the modern work will bear witness to the practical science and utilitarian spirit of our better times. Surely the world improves as the dominion of mind over matter is extended. /

The Engineer, 'Report to the Metropolitan Board of Works' (1875)

The Engineer, 'Appendix No. 1' to the *Report of the Metropolitan Board of Works Pursuant to the Act of Parliament of 18th and 19th Victoria, Cap. 120, Sec. 200.* (London: Metropolitan Board of Works,[1] 1875), pp. 113–17.

APPENDIX No. 1.

Engineer's Department,
Spring Gardens, S.W.,
31st December, 1875.

GENTLEMEN, – I beg to submit this, my twentieth, Annual Report on the principal works executed, and the general business transacted, by this department during the year 1875.

MAIN DRAINAGE.

At the date of my last Annual Report the only portions of the Main Drainage system which had not been wholly completed and in operation for several years, were the permanent Western Pumping Station then in course of erection near the Chelsea Suspension Bridge; the part of the Northern Low Level Sewer extending thence, westward, to the temporary pumping station at Cremorne, a length of about 8,230 feet; and the interception of the sewage from small areas in the City and Pimlico, from a part of Wapping, and from North Woolwich. Within the past year the Western Pumping Station, and such portions (about 800 feet) of the length of Low Level Sewer above referred to, as were unfinished at the commencement of the year, have been completed, and the works of intercepting from the river certain local sewers and drains in the neighbourhood of Upper Thames Street, and at Wapping, have been in progress, as hereinafter described. The works of the *Western Pumping Station* were, with slight exceptions, wholly completed by Thursday, the 5th August last, and on that date the station was formally opened by the Chairman of the Board, Lieutenant-Colonel

Sir J. M. Hogg,[2] K.C.B., M.P. The following descriptive account of the work was prepared for the occasion –

'The opening of the Pumping Station at Pimlico completes the system of Metropolitan Main Drainage, which conveys away the sewage of about three and a half millions of people, from an area of 117 square miles, at a total cost of about four and a half millions.

'Its history may be thus shortly recapitulated: Prior to 1815 it was penal to discharge house drainage into sewers, and it was carefully stored under the houses in cesspools, till at last the ground became so saturated with sewage that disease and death were the result. In 1847, the law required the destruction of cesspools, and the draining of all houses into sewers. The house drainage was consequently turned into the culverts, which had previously taken only surface drainage, and was conveyed by them into the natural watercourses, which discharged their contents into the Thames in London. The Metropolis had suffered severely from cholera in 1831–2, and again in 1848–9, and, lastly, in 1853–4, and the Thames at last became so polluted that no one, willingly, approached its banks, and the removal of the House of Commons to some point more distant from the river, was seriously contemplated. /

'The Metropolitan Board of Works were constituted in 1856, and power given to them to grapple with these evils. They eventually determined to divert all sewage from the Thames near London, and convey it to Barking and Crossness, 14 miles below London Bridge, and, with this object, they commenced the Main Drainage works in 1859. Under this arrangement the bulk of the sewage is carried away by gravitation, but, from the low districts, it has to be pumped in order to effect its discharge at Barking Creek or Crossness at the period of high water, so that it may be carried still further away by the ebbing tide. An Act of Parliament was obtained in 1865, to enable a Company to convey the sewage of the north side of the Metropolis from Barking Creek to the sea on the Essex Coast, and to irrigate and fertilize the Maplin Sands, but the Company have hitherto failed to complete the project, and in the meantime the volume and scour of the river at Crossness is such that it dilutes, disintegrates, and sweeps away the sewage to an extent which was originally hardly anticipated, and so as to cause little or no deposit in the river.

'There are now four pumping stations at work, containing 21 engines, working 42 pumps, with an aggregate of 2,616 nominal horse-power, capable of lifting about 500,000,000 gallons per diem.

'The Pumping Station at Pimlico, which is now to be opened, is the last of these stations, and will complete the lifting power requisite to relieve the low districts of stagnant sewage. A temporary substitute for this permanent station has been in operation for several years delivering the sewage of the western area into the river at Cremorne, but the permanent arrangements will convey the sewage to the reservoirs at the outfall at Barking Creek.

'The localities of Chelsea, Fulham, Brompton, Kensington, Shepherd's Bush, Wormwood Scrubs, Notting Hill, and Hammersmith, covering an area of about 14½ square miles, are now drained by a main sewer under the Chelsea Embankment, which conveys the sewage to the new pumping station. Here the engines are capable of lifting 54,720,000 gallons per diem to a height of 18 feet into the Low Level Sewer, through which the sewage will flow to the Abbey Mills Pumping Station, and be again lifted to a height of 36 feet into the Outfall Sewer, which will ultimately convey it to the general outlet for the sewage of the North side of the Metropolis at Barking Creek, after having travelled about 12½ miles.

'The engine power of the Western Station is divided amongst four engines, each of 90 H.P., or a total of 360 H.P., all being placed in one rectangular building, two at either end. The pump well, which occupies the entire basement of the building, is divided into two compartments, one under each pair of engines. These compartments communicate with each other, but means are provided for separating them, and there is a separate inlet into each from the sewer, so that each pair of engines and their corresponding pumping machinery, can be worked separately. Each inlet sewer is provided with a penstock[3] near its entrance to the pump-well for opening and closing the communication between the sewers and wells, and also with moveable gratings or cages to intercept any solid substance which might interfere with the action of the pumps, and which will be lifted at intervals, and the accumulated matter removed from them into a covered gallery above the penstock chamber, for ultimate disposal. A second cage is also provided to each inlet, which is lowered in front of the sewer during the process of cleansing before the first is raised.

'The engines employed are high pressure condensing beam engines, worked expansively, the steam cylinder being placed at one end of the / beam and the fly wheel at the other, the pumps being placed at either side of the main bearing, half way between the centre and the ends, so that the stroke of the pumps is only half that of the steam piston. The cylinders are 3 feet 1 inch diameter, with a stroke of 8 feet, the pumps being 5 feet 3½ inches in diameter, and having a stroke of 4 feet. The engines are double acting, the steam being admitted at both ends of the cylinder, but the pumps are single acting plunger pumps, delivering only on the down stroke, but as there are two pumps, one ascending while the other is descending, the flow of the discharge is continuous. The suction valves are placed horizontally in the pump case, and are hinged clack valves, but the discharge valves are Porter's patent, placed vertically, or nearly so, on the pump case, and they deliver into circular cast-iron culverts, 5 feet in diameter. The culverts are placed in the centre of the building, parallel to its longer side, and at their mid-distance are connected with a similar circular cast-iron culvert, but 6 feet 9 inches in diameter, placed at right angles to the smaller culverts. This larger culvert is extended at one end into the river, and at the other under the boiler-house to the Low Level Sewer leading to Abbey Mills. Two engines discharge into the smaller culvert on either side of the larger one, and there are valves in the larger culvert to turn the sewage at will, either into the Low Level Sewer or into the river, the latter to be used in case of accident or during storms of rain. There are also valves to shut off either end of the small culvert from the main, and further means for isolating the discharge valves of each pump from the culvert into which it delivers, so as to enable the pump valves of any one engine to be examined or repaired without throwing a second engine out of work.

'The steam is supplied from eight Cornish boilers,[4] each 6 feet 9 inches in diameter and 22 feet long, and having two furnaces with internal flues, 2 feet 7 inches in diameter. The boilers are fixed in a house at the back or land side of the engine-house, in a line parallel to its longer side. The stoke-hole floor is adjacent to the engine-house, and 12 feet below the level of the engine-room floor, and on the same level as the floor of the coal vaults, from which a tram way is carried into and along the stoke-hole, to facilitate the delivery of fuel into the boiler-house. The steam pipes, as well as the feed pipes, are made continuous, and fitted with valves to enable any of the engines to be supplied from any one of the boilers independently of the others. The water for the boilers is brought from the hot wells attached to the condensers, the cold water for condensation being pumped from tanks placed under and at each end of the engine-room. These tanks are supplied from a reservoir placed under the coal-sheds at the west end of the engine-house. The water used for the purpose is tidal water, conveyed by pipes from the river in front of the Pumping Station; the water is not, however, conveyed direct from the river to the reservoir, but, in the first instance, to a large open reservoir or settling pond, situate in the grounds behind the boiler house, capable of containing about half a million gallons. This is divided into two compartments, to admit of the water depositing the mud held in suspension in the one, whilst the other is in use, the clear water being then conveyed to the covered reservoir under the coal-sheds. In order to ensure the purity of the water for the use of the boilers as far as possible, arrangements are made for conveying the water which has been used for condensing, from the cold water overflow into the tanks under the engine-room. Provision is also made for using the water from the hot well for the same purpose, by passing it, in its transmission to the reservoir, through a series of coiled / pipes situate in the pump well, where the heat is abstracted from it by being brought into contact with a large and ever-changing volume of sewage.

'The fuel for the boilers is stored in brick vaults over the covered reservoirs for water before referred to. The character of the subsoil rendered it necessary that the foundations for the coal-sheds should be carried down to a considerable depth, and the space below was on this account utilized as a store for condensing water. The floor of the coalvaults is level with the stoke-hole floor, and the coals will be conveyed from the store to the boilers in small trucks, running on tramways, which are laid on the floor of the coal-vaults, and extend thence into the boiler-house, and along the stoke-hole in front of the boilers. The tramways are continued on the same level from the boiler-house round the engine-house in a sunk area, and through a subway passing under the Grosvenor Road to a wharf alongside the river. The coals will be raised from the barges at the wharf into trucks, which will be sent on the tram to the coal-vaults, where the coals will either be delivered on the floor level, or again lifted by a crane on to the tramways on to the top of the vaults, into which they will be shot through openings, which are covered by sliding doors when not in use. It was originally intended to land the coals from the wharf alongside the Grosvenor Basin, which is adjacent to the coal-vaults, and in this case the coals would have been lifted by one operation from the barges to the trams on the top of the vaults. This arrangement, however, had to be abandoned, in consequence of difficulties with regard to the owner's claims, and the wharf formed alongside the river, to which access is given by the subway under the Grosvenor Road.

'The engine-house[5] is in the Italian style, and is constructed of bricks; its facade is parallel to the river and the Grosvenor Road, and is set back about 16 feet from the roadway. Its length is 116 feet, and depth 44 feet; its height from the ground to the springing of the roof is 50 feet, and to the ridge 71 feet. The lower storey, or engine-room floor, is faced with stone, rusticated, having a splayed and moulded plinth below, and moulded architrave above. The upper storey or beam floor is faced with brick, the dressings of the windows being of Portland stone. In the lower storey the principal entrance, which projects slightly from the general face, is flanked on either side by 3 square headed windows, the upper storey being pierced with eight windows, having segmental heads. The beam floor is surmounted by a bold cornice of Portland stone, from which rises a curved Mansard roof, with ornamental copper covering, pierced with hooded circular openings for ventilation. The boiler-house, situate at the rear of the engine-house, is a building of plain design, faced with stone, and rusticated to correspond with the lower storey of the engine-house.

'The chimney-shaft is a detached structure, standing on the northwest of the engine-house, with which it corresponds in style. It rises 172 feet in height above the ground level, where it is 21 feet in width, tapering to 15 feet under the cornice at the top. The shaft is of brick, corresponding with the beam floor of the engine-house, and each of its four sides is relieved by three recessed panels, arched over at a short distance below the cornice of Portland stone which surmounts the shaft. Above the cornice rises a pyramidal roof of iron, terminating in an ornamental cresting of wrought-iron. The shaft, on the exterior, is square on plan, but there is an internal circular shaft, 7 feet in diameter, / within the outer casing, the space between the two being occupied by a stone staircase, extending from the bottom to the top of the shaft. The foundations have been carried down of solid concrete to a depth of 50 feet below the surface.

'In order to provide for the contingency of a break down of the principal engines, an auxiliary engine has been erected in a separate building, situate at the rear of the principal buildings and adjacent to the Canal. This is a high pressure non-condensing engine of 120 H.P., and is supplied with steam by two boilers of the same dimensions as those in the main boiler house. It works two pumps, each four feet in diameter, placed in a separate well at one end of the auxiliary engine-house, and has inlet and outlet culverts distinct from those of the main engines. The flues from these boilers are connected with the main chimney-shaft.

'There are several other accessory buildings, erected at the rear of the principal buildings; these are all of brick and of simple elevation. They comprise repairing shops, stores, and dwelling houses for the staff and Superintendent in charge of the works. The plot of ground upon which the whole has been erected contains about four acres, lying between the Grosvenor Canal and the several lines of railway from the Victoria Station – a part of it was formerly the site of the Chelsea Waterworks, and the remainder was reclaimed from the river in 1858.

'The foundation-stone of these works was laid by William Newton, Esq.,[6] in July, 1873, and the whole of the works have been executed by Mr. William Webster, the contractor, at a total estimated cost of £183,739, of which £56,789 is for engines and pumping machinery, which have been supplied by the firm of Messrs. Watt and Co. The whole has been designed and erected under the superintendence of Sir J. W. Bazalgette, C.B.,[7] Engineer to the Metropolitan Board of Works, assisted by Mr. Thomas Lovick,[8] their Assistant Engineer.' /

'Steam Communication with India', *Penny Magazine* (1842)

'Steam Communication with India', *Penny Magazine of the Society for the Diffusion of Useful Knowledge*, 11:654 (11 June 1842) pp. 225–6 and 235–7.

STEAM COMMUNICATION WITH INDIA.

WHEN two places become connected by a railway, the change effected in their means of communication is striking in proportion to their distance from each other. London Bridge and Greenwich are some twenty minutes nearer to one another than they were before a railway linked them more closely; but the journey from London to Lancaster or Darlington is shortened by fourteen or fifteen hours, even on a comparison with the quick travelling of the mail-coaches, which were superseded by the railways when everything connected with them was carried to the utmost perfection. The improvements effected within the last seven years in the means of communication between England and India are far more extraordinary than any of the changes wrought by the railways in this country. Sixty years ago the voyage from London to Calcutta usually occupied five and six months, and to China seven months, and the 'course of post' with India was calculated at little less than twelve months. Intelligence from this distant quarter arrived only at uncertain intervals, and often through indirect channels. A Dutch or Danish East Indiaman left despatches for England at Lisbon, or Falmouth, or wherever it was most convenient to touch. The French received despatches from their establishments in India; and reports, originating in France, were often in circulation in London, which neither the East India Company, the government, nor any one could affirm or contradict, though they might relate to matters of the highest import and which called immediately for active measures. Occasionally despatches were received overland both in England and France, and by the Asiatic Company at Trieste; but these opportunities of communication were only available to the parties who received them, and led to vague rumours, or such reports as it happened to be for the interest of each to put into circulation. Overland despatches reached London in rather more than three months through Persia and Turkey, *viâ* Constantinople. Thirty or forty years ago, by improvements in nautical science, the voyage between England and India was reduced to about four months and a half; and within the last ten or fifteen years, further improvements of this nature, and a more accurate knowledge of the currents and winds experienced in the course traversed, reduced the average duration of the voyage to about three months and a half. A few voyages have been made in three months; but, taking the average, the saving effected was at least two months, the total saving in the 'course of post' being nearly five months. Within the last half-dozen years the means of communication with India have been still further quickened, as we shall presently show.

Until 1836 the intercourse between Europe and India was carried on by the Cape of Good Hope. The distance of Calcutta from London by this route is above sixteen thousand miles; and it is something like going from London to Herne Bay by Tunbridge, Dover and Ramsgate, the distance to India by the Red Sea being one-half shorter. This advantageous line of communication was not opened until after several years' active exertions both in England and India. In 1830 the Hugh Lindsay, a steamer of four hundred tons, with two engines each of eighty horse-power, made the first experimental voyage from Bombay to Suez at the expense of the Indian government. Depôts of coal were previously formed at Aden, Judda,[1] Cosseir,[2] and Suez. The steamer left Bombay on the 20th of March, and arrived at Suez on the 22nd of April. The mail consisted of three hundred and six letters, which might have reached England in sixty-one days from Bombay, if any arrangements had been made for forwarding them. The second voyage from Bombay to Suez was completed between the 5th and 27th of December in the same year. The third voyage was made in January, 1832, and though very unfavourable weather was experienced, the passage was completed in twenty-nine days and sixteen hours, the time actually occupied in steaming being twenty-one days and six hours. Seven hundred letters were in the mail-bags, and, but for the reason abovementioned, they could have been received in England in fifty-eight days. The Hugh Lindsay made a fourth experimental voyage in January, 1833, which was completed in thirty-three days, allowing above ten days for stoppages. In July, 1834, a select committee of the House of Commons on the subject of steam-navigation with India recommended the line by the / Red Sea, and a grant of twenty thousand pounds for the survey of the Euphrates; but this river was found to be impracticable, and the route by the Red Sea alone fixed the public attention. By this time its practicability for steam-navigation had been ascertained during the north-east monsoons, but not in those from the south-west. The latter, however, only prevail four months in the year, from June to September inclusive. Only a quarterly communication was thought of at this period, either by Lord William Bentinck,[3] then Governor-General of

India, or Mr. Waghorn,[4] whose services in improving the means of intercourse with India can scarcely be too highly praised.

In 1835 the line of communication by the Post-office steamers in the Mediterranean was extended to Alexandria, and this encouraged the exertions making in India to establish a regular communication by steamers between Bombay and Suez. Letters could now be transmitted from London to Alexandria, to the care of the British Consul, who despatched them whenever an opportunity presented itself, though they were often delayed several months. Only one-half of the line to India was yet opened. Mr. Waghorn proceeded to Egypt about this time, to remedy the defect in the transmission of Indian letters to and from Alexandria. He appointed an agency in London, where letters intended to be confided to him were registered and marked before being put into the Post-office. On the mails reaching Alexandria, these letters were forwarded immediately to Suez, and if no vessels were on the point of sailing, they were sent onward by janissaries[5] or by the country boats to Mocha[6] or Aden, where the opportunities of transmitting them to India were much more frequent. The letters which were not sent through Mr. Waghorn's agency, laid quietly at the British Consul's until they could be despatched direct from Suez. At this period, there was, strictly speaking, no regular conveyance between England and India. Ship-letter bags were made up at the Post-office in the same way as they now are for the Australian colonies, but no one on putting a letter into the Post-office of a country town knew when it would leave England, and those who had frequent occasion to write to friends in India often found it advantageous to transmit their letters to some agent in London, who knew what ships were likely to make the quickest passage, or to stop at the fewest intermediate points; and could send expresses to ships for India lying wind-bound in the Channel, while letters sent through the Post-office remained there until another ship sailed. In 1836, the Hugh Lindsay again left Bombay for Suez, with letters and passengers, and in consequence of the arrangements of Mr. Waghorn, and the extension of the packet service to Alexandria, the mail reached England in fifty days; but it was hoped that by various improvements the time might at a future period be reduced to about forty days. More than a year elapsed before the line of steamers between Suez and Bombay was completely established; but in this interval Mr. Waghorn accelerated the rate of communication by conveying the Indian letters through France, instead of sending them to Falmouth by the Mediterranean steamers, which stopped at Gibraltar and Lisbon. In 1839 the English Government concluded a convention with that of France, for the transmission of the India mails through Paris to Marseille.

The mails from India are now despatched from Bombay on the first day in every month, after the arrival of the steamer from Ceylon, and the inland post with the correspondence from Madras and Calcutta. About the 20th of the month the steamer lands the mails at Suez, and by the 22nd they are put on board the Mediterranean steamer at Alexandria, which reaches Malta on the 24th, and Marseille on the 30th. Its arrival is announced in Paris by telegraph on the same day, a distance of nearly five hundred miles, and the most important items of news are communicated by the same means. Early in the afternoon the intelligence is published by the ministerial evening journal, a copy of which is forwarded by an extraordinary express to London, where the news is re-published about twenty-four hours afterwards. It is however sometimes the practice of the French government not to announce the telegraphic news until the day after it is received, or later; but occasionally the arrival of the mail at Marseille, and the intelligence which it brings, is officially made known by an official placard at the Bourse. The exertions of the London newspapers do not end with the despatch of the express from Paris, which perhaps may just simply announce the arrival of the mail. As soon as possible special couriers (for on several occasions more than one has been despatched) start for London with packets for the principal morning papers. The distance is about seven hundred and forty miles, namely, from Marseille to Paris, four hundred and ninety-seven; Paris to Calais, one hundred and fifty; Calais to Dover, twenty-one; and Dover to London, seventy-two. The expense of each express is above 100*l*., and on the fourth day after the mail has reached Marseille the intelligence from India, China, and the East generally is published in London. The opening of the South-Eastern Railway will frequently have the effect of bringing the publication of this information within the usual hours of business at the great marts for East India and China produce. Railroads through France would shorten the route by a couple of days. The Post-office authorities in France have on several occasions interfered most vexatiously with the couriers conveying these despatches for the London journals, and they have several times been seized, on the pretence that they were not authorised to carry letters. In March last, one of these couriers was prosecuted by the Post-office and sentenced to pay certain fines. It was frivolously contended that they might convey the despatches in post-chaises, but not on horseback. The London journalists represented their case to the French Minister, through our ambassador at Paris, but it does not appear that they have obtained any security against future interruptions. On the day following the arrival of the newspaper expresses, the mails with the letters and newspapers are received at the Post-office. A week elapses, and the letters arrive which pay a lower rate of postage, and are not sent through France, but brought to Falmouth by the Mediterranean steamer.

WE have mentioned the number of letters transmitted by the Hugh Lindsay in 1836, and while that vessel was employed in making experimental voyages. In 1783, according to one of the daily newspapers of that date, an overland mail brought twenty private letters in addition to the public despatches. On an average of several years prior to 1836, the number of letters annually received and despatched from the several presidencies of India, and from Ceylon, was 300,000. With increased certainty, rapidity, and frequency of transmission, the number had risen to 616,796 in 1840, and to 840,070 in 1841. Mr. Rowland Hill[7] could scarcely desire a better illustration of his principles of Post-office philosophy; but in this instance the postage is high. The Hugh Lindsay in 1836 conveyed a few hundred newspapers, but the number sent from India to Europe last year is believed to have exceeded 80,000; above 250,000 were received there from Europe; and it is thought that the number both ways, for 1842, will amount to 400,000.* In this enumeration each cover is counted as one, though it may contain several newspapers.

Availing themselves of the certainty and regularity of communication, several of the principal newspapers of India publish a monthly summary for circulation in Europe, containing the news from all parts of the East up to the time of the steamer starting. There are such monthly newspapers at Calcutta, Madras, Bombay, and Ceylon, and altogether about five thousand are despatched to England by each steamer for Suez. They will be found extremely interesting to the English reader, and no news-room should be without one of these concise summaries of Indian intelligence. They will tend materially to strengthen the interest which is felt in England for all that affects that vast monument of English power and influence, which has grown gradually from the possession of a trading fort, to the dominion, more or less supreme, over a hundred and fifty millions of the human race, the administration of a system of finance which raises an annual revenue of 15,000,000*l.*, and the maintenance of an army of two hundred thousand men. Besides the large number of London and other newspapers circulated in India, four of the principal Indian newspapers supply their readers gratuitously with a monthly newspaper, carefully prepared in London at a considerable expense. There is, besides, a monthly newspaper for India prepared in London, which is unconnected with any of the Indian journals; and one is published in London for circulation in England, which gives a monthly summary of Indian news immediately after the arrival of the overland mall. Every one who has connections in the colonies which do not enjoy the means of regular and certain communication with the mother-country has experienced the pain and annoyance arising from this circumstance. Letters and newspapers occasionally arrive several weeks before others are received which were transmitted some time before. Under such a system, the strongest ties at length become weakened; while the colony and its interests remain comparatively unknown. A rapid intercourse, effected by a line of steamers, would bring these distant interests within the range of general

* 'Bombay Times,' April 1.

observation; and they would assume the distinctness and / prominence to which they are of right entitled. In the case of India, a great revolution has been effected in the character of those who now proceed to pass the best part of their lives in that country. The interests of home are not obliterated by the uncertainty and slowness of intercourse; and in the midst of the jungles, a man may be as well informed on the leading topics of the day in England as the daily frequenter of a news-room here. Besides newspapers, reviews and magazines, and new works generally, are also despatched in boxes of a certain size which will admit of their being slung on each side of a camel.

The mails for India are made up in London on the last day of the month, and on the 4th; the former being sent by the steamer from Falmouth, and the latter through France to Marseille, and onward to Malta, whence the Falmouth steamer conveys them to Alexandria. The arrival of the English mail at either of the three Presidencies[8] is usually by far the most interesting event of the month. The 'Bombay Times,' in its 'Monthly Summary' dated April 1st, has graphically described the scene which occurs at that place. At the extremity of one of the promontories of the island there is a lighthouse ninety feet high, and, with its elevated base, it has an altitude of one hundred and twenty feet. At a distance of twenty or twenty-five miles out at sea it is an interesting land-mark; and from its summit vessels may be descried at a great distance. As soon as they appear in the horizon, and their number can be ascertained, it is announced by signals at the lighthouse, which are repeated from a number of signal-posts, one or more of which are visible from nearly every house in the island. When the time for the arrival of the Suez steamer approaches, the lighthouse and signal-posts are watched with the greatest anxiety. A steamer is seen from the lighthouse, and the flag denoting that class of vessel is instantly hoisted; but there are steamers from the Indus, the Persian Gulf, and Surat,[9] and it is uncertain whether it is the steamer from Suez or one of these. The doubt cannot be solved for another hour; but if it be the one from Suez, an immense red flag, fifteen feet long, with three white crosses on it, is immediately hoisted. A couple of hours elapses, and the vessel is visible to every one; and now business is at a stand until she reaches the roadstead. Boats push off, and she is boarded by persons from the newspaper-offices, who obtain a list of the passengers, particulars of the voyage, &c. In ten or fifteen minutes after the mails are landed, the 'peons,' or messengers attached to the two newspaper establishments whose proprietors join in the expense of the publication, obtain from the Post-office the monthly newspaper prepared in London and sent wet from the press on the day the mails were made up. Copies are forwarded in separate packages through France, so that no delay may take place in their delivery at Bombay and the other Presidencies. Ten or a dozen native 'peons,' each under an 'havildar' or serjeant, are attached to each of the newspaper-offices. Their costume is novel, that of the 'havildar' being smarter than the rest. All carry an umbrella or Chinese 'chittery' as a protection either against the rain or the heat. As soon as the papers are folded, these newsmen are seen hurrying with them in all directions. About forty 'peons' are employed by the Bombay Post-office, and shortly afterwards they are also equally on the alert. The letters are enclosed in from fifty to sixty boxes, about two feet long by one and a half wide. Part of them are of wood lined with tin, but those which are transmitted through France are of tin entirely, and fastened by a spring in such a way that they cannot be opened except by force. Blacksmiths are in attendance at the Post-office to effect this. The editor of the 'Bombay Times' suggests that they should be of copper or zinc, with patent locks, which might be frequently changed; as the tin boxes become rusted, and papers are frequently injured. At Ceylon, Madras, and Calcutta, the arrival of the monthly mail from England excites the same degree of interest.

Bombay is at present the central point of communication between India and Europe. The communication between London and Calcutta is effected in six weeks, instead of as many months; and with Bombay in ten or twelve days less; and on one occasion (in August last) in thirty-one days and five hours. Powerful steamers will be established during the present year, by which the letters to Calcutta and Madras will be forwarded, instead of by dâk[10] across the peninsula. One of the North American steamers has just made the voyage from Halifax[11] to Liverpool in ten days and three hours, so that it is actually possible to traverse a portion of the globe between 63° 38' west longitude and 72° 57' east longitude in the space of six weeks, passing at the same time through Liverpool and London. As the Australian colonies increase in wealth and population, they will naturally become desirous of connecting themselves with the mother-country by the East India line of steam-navigation; and the Cape of Good Hope, with the Mauritius, might also be placed in connection with it. The system of steam communication in the Eastern hemisphere would be complete if Singapore, Ceylon, and the island of Socotra,[12] at the mouth of the Red Sea, were made grand points of rendezvous for steamers. Lines of steamers from Canton, the Eastern Archipelago, and the colonies of Australia would make Singapore their centre of European communication; those from Calcutta and Madras would for the same purpose be connected with Ceylon; and those from Bombay, the Cape, and the Mauritius would join the grand line at the island of Socotra. New Zealand might perhaps be more advantageously connected, *viâ* the Isthmus of Panama, with the line of steamers already established between England, the West Indies, and the ports on the Gulf of Mexico. Some time or other there is every probability that such a plan will be in active operation.

We have given in the previous part of this article a view of Suez from the sea. The town derives its sole importance from its situation at the head of the westernmost gulf or arm in which the northern extremity of the Red Sea terminates, which renders it the point of communication between India and Europe; and it is the port where a large concourse of pilgrims annually embark for Mecca. Suez is not of older date than the early part of the sixteenth century; but the importance of the situation as a place of transit has always caused the existence of a city in the neighbourhood. The population of Suez consists of about twelve hundred Mohammedans and a hundred and fifty Christians. The place is poorly built and destitute of fresh water, and there is no fertile land in the vicinity. A bazaar, or street of shops, is tolerably well supplied with goods from Cairo, and there are several Khans, or inns built around large courts; but the houses are generally of mean appearance. A commodious hotel has been established by Mr. Waghorn for the passengers to and from England and India. The town is surrounded by a poor wall on three sides, and there is a harbour and a good quay on the seaward side. It is about seventy miles from Cairo, between which place and Suez there are seven station-houses erected at the expense of the Bombay Steam Committee, and which are rented by Messrs. Hill and Co. of the Pacha[13] of Egypt. The journey is performed in two-wheeled vans, with a sort of tilt cover, carrying four persons each. An omnibus has been just started which carries / six persons in summer and eight in winter. A light sedan is also used, slung upon poles, and carried by two donkeys, one before and the other behind. Both horses and donkeys are used for the saddle; and camels and dromedaries are employed to transport the luggage. The number of passengers by each of the Bombay steamers varies from thirty to seventy each way.

'The Manchester and Liverpool Rail-Road', *Penny Magazine* (1833)

'The Manchester and Liverpool Rail-Road', *Monthly Supplement of The Penny Magazine of the Society for the Diffusion of Useful Knowledge*, 2:68 (27 April 1833) pp. 161–8.

THE MANCHESTER AND LIVERPOOL RAIL-ROAD.

THE increased rapidity of travelling is one of the most remarkable features of the present age. Remote places are, by this means, virtually brought near to each other; and thus, while intelligence is diffused, an impulse is given to commerce, each of which advantages most powerfully affects the condition of the people. The benefits of cheap and quick communication to a great commercial state are too evident to require to be enlarged upon. Time and money are thus most importantly saved: and the rapid and economical transit of goods, by lessening their cost, enables the humblest to partake of comforts which were formerly considered as luxuries only for the rich.

Of all the local improvements made with this object, in modern times, the Manchester and Liverpool Railway is the most remarkable. Its completion forms an epoch in the history and application of mechanical power. If only ten years back it had been said, that persons could pass, without inconvenience and without danger, over a distance of thirty-one miles in one hour, the tale would have been treated as one of those visionary stories which in former days were the amusements of the nursery.

The advantage of rail-roads over common roads consists in the great diminution of friction which they occasion, whereby given weights may be drawn through equal distances at a much less expense of power. Many experiments have been made in order to ascertain the economy of power which they produce. The most moderate calculations estimate the resistance on a level turnpike-road to be more than seven times as great as that on a level rail-road;* while, by some experi-

* Wood on Rail-roads,[1] p. 279.

ments, it has been found that the traction* of the wheels on a level road is to that on a good rail-road as twenty to one†.

It is at once evident, that a smooth wheel will roll along a smooth plane of iron much easier than it will roll along a plane covered with rough and loose stones; for in the latter case, it has either to be lifted over the inequalities, or it has to push them on one side as it passes, or to crush them. But the crushing of the rough material, or the pushing it aside, is so much / waste of power; and hence the great advantages of a smooth road.‡

Rail-roads on an extended scale are of very recent application; although for the last two centuries they have, with various modifications, been adopted in the collieries of Northumberland, where the expense of conveying so heavy an article as coals by ordinary methods first showed the necessity for discovering some plan by which the labour might be lessened. Up to the year 1600, it appears that coals were conveyed from the collieries in carts on common roads, and in some cases in baskets on the backs of horses. The precise period when any improved method of conveyance was first attempted is not ascertained, but this was certainly between the years 1602 and 1649. Rail-roads were about that time first adopted. They were then made of timber; and, though very rude in their construction, materially diminished the resistance, and therefore economised the power.

These wooden rails consisted of parallel oaken blocks placed tranversely on the road at intervals of from two to three feet, and fastened firmly into the ground; long thick pieces of wood of about six or seven inches in breadth were laid on these, securely fastened to them and joined together at the different lengths by pins, forming two continuous parallel lines on which the wheels of the waggon traversed. These roads were very imperfect and perishable. The timber was soon worn away by the attrition of the wheels, and repairs were constantly required; the holes made in the transverse blocks or sleepers became too

* The traction of the carriage is only *part* of the resistance offered. This resistance is distinguishable into two separate causes: that arising from the traction or attrition of the rubbing parts, and that of the obstruction to the rolling of the wheels upon the rails.

† Gordon's Practical Treatise upon Elemental Locomotion,[2] p. 150.

‡ Mr. Telford's Report[3] on the state of the Holyhead and Liverpool roads contains the result of some experiments on different roads, by which it is found that

	lbs.
On well-made pavement the draught is	33
On a broken stone surface, or old flint road	65
On a gravel road	147
On a broken stone road, upon a rough pavement foundation	46
On a broken stone surface, upon a bottoming of concrete formed of Parker's cement and gravel	46

large for the pins after these had been once or twice displaced in order to renew the rails; while the constant treading of the horses' feet weakened and ultimately destroyed the blocks in the middle, and they were in consequence soon made inefficient. To remedy this evil an improvement called the double rail-way was made. This consisted in laying other pieces of wood on the first, to which they were fastened by pins. These upper pieces could therefore be renewed when worn out without injury to the other parts; and as the rails were raised from the ground the sleepers could be covered and secured from the action of the horses feet. Such roads were still, however, of rude formation, and were liable to be constantly out of repair, notwithstanding which they were long used with little or no alteration at the collieries of Northumberland and Durham. The regular load of a horse with a cart along the common road was 17 cwt., while on this rail-road it was 42 cwt. The advantage so gained appears to have been thought quite sufficient, and no farther economy of power was for some time sought to be obtained. Where there were any acclivities[4] or abrupt curves, thin pieces of wrought iron were nailed over those parts of the rail to diminish the resistance opposed to the wheels; and so that one horse could draw 42 cwt., the required maximum of power, no farther effort was considered necessary.

Until within a very few years rail-roads have been considered as only supplementary to canals, – to be employed in short distances, or where the nature of the ground has precluded the application of inland navigation. Accordingly, while the attention of some of the most enterprising and highly gifted minds was turned to the consideration of the important point of inland water communication, the better construction of rail-roads was overlooked and neglected. This country is now every where traversed by canals, intersecting each other, which afford inland navigation between all parts of the kingdom. This very excellence for a long time seemed to preclude the necessity of any farther improvements in the facility of communication.

The superiority of rail-ways is however very great, where celerity of motion is required, as this cannot be obtained with the same economy on canals, through the employment of horse-power. When locomotive carriages are substituted on rail-roads, the difference is rendered still more striking. It has been found by experiment that at the rate of two miles an hour, a horse can drag three times as much weight in a boat on a canal as he can drag upon a carriage on a rail-road. At the rate of three miles and a half an hour, his power exerted on the rail-road, or in tracking on the side of a canal, is exactly the same. But at an increase of speed beyond this rate, the disproportion in favour of rail-roads becomes very great; so that at the rate of six miles an hour, owing to the resistance of the water, he can draw upon the railroad a weight three times heavier than he can draw in a boat on a canal. As the velocity is increased the difference becomes still greater.*

It is now between fifty and sixty years since iron has been gradually substituted for wood on rail-roads, and their construction has by degrees become better understood and executed. The date of the first introduction of cast and wrought iron rail-ways, is variously stated in different accounts: it is most probable that iron was substituted for wood in several places without any concert, and that the adoption of cast iron was not the result of any one discovery. From 1768 to 1776 is the period when the plate-rail-road (more generally known as the tram-road) was first used. This, with but slight modifications, is the same as the plate-rail of the present day. It consists of cast iron rails about four feet long, having a flange or upright ledge three inches high, to keep the wheel upon the horizontal part, which is about four inches wide and an inch thick, and another flange at the other side projecting downwards to strengthen the rail. These rails are fixed together and fastened securely to stone supports. At first they were made to rest on the transverse wooden blocks, already described, stretched across the whole breadth of the rail-road, or upon short square wooden sleepers: stone blocks are now mostly used. An improvement of the plate-rail is the edge-rail, which is now most generally adopted. The advantage of the edge over the plate-rail, is the diminution of friction. In this case the ledge is placed on the wheel instead of the rail, and it is found that a ledge of one inch depth is sufficient to keep it in its situation.

It has been found by experiment that on a well-constructed rail-road a horse will draw

10	tons at the rate of	2	miles an hour.
6½	. . . . .	3	. . .
5	. . . . .	4	. . .
4	. . . . .	5	. . .
3½	. . . . .	6	. . .

But it must be borne in mind that the great superiority of a rail-way over a common road can only exist on an exact level. Let there be an ascent so small as scarcely to attract observation, and this advantage is at once very materially diminished; while, at greater elevations, it is entirely lost. Since the traction of the wheels is so much less on rail-ways than on common roads, it follows that when the force of gravity is brought into operation by an ascending plane, this opposing force, being proportioned to the load, will be much greater than on a common road. It has been found by experiment, that if a locomotive engine draws, by the adhesion of its four wheels, 67.25 tons on a level, it will only draw, by the same adhesion, 15.21 up an inclination of / one in a hundred; at an inclination of one in fifty, it will draw scarcely any load; and at an inclination of one

* Wood on Rail-roads, p. 305.

in twelve, a locomotive engine will not ascend by itself on a rail-way, the force exerted causing the wheels to turn round on the same spot instead of advancing. Abrupt curves and sudden turnings increase resistance very much. The medium friction of a train of five waggons on a level rail-way was found by experiment to be nine pounds per ton; while on a curved part, with a radius of about eight hundred feet, it was eighteen pounds per ton.*

In the formation of rail-ways for the general purposes of traffic, it is therefore essential to their beneficial effect that they should be made as nearly as possible on a level straight line. Most of the rail-ways heretofore constructed have been for the conveyance of the products of the mines, – such as of coals from the pits to the river side; and since the weights were all to be carried in one direction, the road had an inclination downwards given to it, requiring no power but that of gravity to produce locomotion. Where the traffic is to and fro, this arrangement must of course be abandoned.

Since the close of the last century rail-ways have multiplied extremely in the neighbourhood of our collieries and other mining districts. In Glamorganshire alone it is estimated that there are three hundred miles of railways.† These are, however, all detached, isolated, and private undertakings, appropriated solely to the conveyance of mineral produce to those points where water communication is established.

The Stockton and Darlington Rail-way was the first laid down, by Act of Parliament, for the conveyance of general merchandize and passengers,[7] as well as of coals. This road was opened in the autumn of 1825. It is about twenty-five miles in length; and consists of only a single rail-way, having at intervals of every quarter of a mile 'sidings' to allow of the carriages passing each other.

The project of a rail-way between Liverpool and Manchester was first entertained in 1822. Before so great and novel an undertaking could be carried into execution, many preliminary measures were necessary, and much opposition was to be expected from those whose interest might possibly be affected by the successful issue of the project. A company was formed under the title of 'The Liverpool and Manchester Rail-road Company,' and their prospectus was issued in October, 1824. £400,000 was to be raised by shares of £100 each. It was found, subsequently, that this sum was inadequate to the purpose. A bill was brought into Parliament for the formation of the rail-way in 1825. The opposition made to the measure was so strenuous, however, that it was not till the ensuing session that the company succeeded in its application.

* Milne's Practical View of the Steam-engine[5] (Appendix). From the same authority it appears that the draught on a rail-road was one hundred and eight pounds per ton, at the rate of three miles an hour when the rails were dry, and only sixty-eight pounds when the rails were wet.

† Dupin,[6] vol. i. p. 207.

The peculiar connection between Liverpool and Manchester renders a rapid and cheap communication between these places a subject of national interest and importance. Liverpool is the port whence Manchester receives all her raw material, and to which she returns a large portion of her manufactured goods for shipment to all parts of the world. This constant and increasing interchange of merchandize, and, in consequence, the incessant intercourse of the inhabitants of the two towns, must in an eminent degree be promoted and facilitated by a quickness of transit hitherto supposed impossible. It is true, there is water communication between Liverpool and Manchester by two separate routes; namely, on the river Mersey, from Liverpool to Runcorn, a distance of sixteen or eighteen miles; and thence, either by the Duke of Bridgewater's canal, or by a navigation consisting alternately of canals and the rivers Mersey and Trivell. The whole distance by water is about fifty miles. The average length of passage by these conveyances is about thirty-six hours, varying according to the state of the wind and the tide. By the rail-road the transit of goods is effected in about two hours. The economy of time in transport is of the greatest importance in all large commercial operations; and certainty of delivery is an equally important element in the saving of capital. The cotton spinner is no longer required to keep large stocks of the raw material in his warehouse at Manchester. He buys at the hour when he finds it most advantageous to buy, assured that the delivery of the goods will immediately follow the completion of the contract. Manchester may now be considered as the great cotton factory of most parts of the globe; and the constantly increasing traffic between this place and Liverpool, could not be carried on by the canal establishments with sufficient despatch, regularity, and punctuality, at all periods and seasons. The different position of these towns in 1760, when first the Duke of Bridgewater's canal was projected, and in 1824, when the rail-road company was formed, shows the rapid increase of their commercial importance. In 1760 the population of Manchester was about 22,000; in 1824 it was 150,000. In 1790 the first steam-engine was used in Manchester; in 1824 more than two hundred steam-engines were at work, and nearly 30,000 power-looms. In 1760 the population of Liverpool was about 26,000; in 1824 the population was 125,000. In 1760 the number of vessels which paid dock-dues was 2,560; in 1824 this number amounted to 10,000. In 1784 eight bags of cotton were seized by the custom-house officers out of an American vessel arriving at Liverpool, under the conviction that they could not be the growth of America. In 1824 there were imported into Liverpool from America 409,670 bags of cotton.* The quantity of goods daily passing between Manchester and Liverpool was estimated in 1824 at 1,000 tons, but since that period it has much increased.

* These statistical facts are taken from Booth's Account of the Manchester and Liverpool Rail-way, p. 3.[8]

The legislature having concurred in the practicability and advantages of the rail-way, the undertaking was commenced in June, 1826, under the direction of Mr. George Stephenson. It was proposed to lay the railway as nearly as possible in a straight line between the two places. The nature of the country rendered this undertaking a task of no ordinary difficulty. Tunnels were to be made; eminences to be excavated, artificial mounds to be erected; and a moss (Chat Moss), four miles in extent, was to be drained and levelled in the centre and embanked at each end. This latter was a most arduous task, and the practicability of carrying it into execution was seriously questioned in the House of Commons; by some of the witnesses who were examined it was deemed impossible, and one asserted that it could not be accomplished at the cost of £200,000.* Chat Moss is a 'huge bog,' of so soft and spongy a texture, that cattle cannot walk over it. The bottom is composed of clay and sand, and above this, varying in depth from ten to thirty-five feet deep, is a mass of vegetable pulpy matter. This barren waste comprises an area of about twelve square miles; and, according to moderate calculation, contains at least sixty millions of tons of vegetable matter.

The first actual operations of the company were directed to the draining of this moss. Many difficulties occurred in the progress of the work, but they were all at length overcome. On the eastern border an embankment of about twenty feet had to be raised above the natural level. The weight of this embankment pressed down the surface of the moss, and / many thousand cubic yards gradually disappeared. Perseverance, however, at length succeeded in consolidating the moss, and giving to it an equable pressure. On the western side an embankment is formed of moss, nearly a mile in length, and from ten to twenty feet perpendicular height, at an inclination of rather less than forty-five degrees, which was found from experience to stand better than if at a greater angle. Sand and gravel, from two to three feet in depth, were laid over this; and on the whole so prepared, the permanent road,[9] consisting of a layer of broken stone and sand, was deposited.

At one part, about three-quarters of a mile from the western edge, distinguished as the 'Flow Moss,' the semi-fluid consistency of the moss required some farther contrivances to render it sufficiently firm. Hurdles were placed upon it, thickly interwoven with twisted heath, forming a platform on which sand and gravel are laid, and on which the wood sleepers which support the rails are placed. The quantity of moss required for the embankments, and which was dug from the neighbouring parts, amounted to five hundred and twenty thousand cubic yards.†

The rail-way enters Liverpool by means of a tunnel and inclined plane, thus effecting a communication with the docks without interfering with a single street, a passage being formed in fact underneath the town. The first shaft of

* In the general abstract of expenditure, the Chat Moss account is put down at £27,719. 11*s*. 10*d*.

† 'Companion to the Almanac for 1829,'[10] p. 228.

this tunnel was opened in September, 1826. Very little progress was made in this work for the first few months from its commencement, but during the whole of the ensuing year the operations were carried on with great perseverance and activity. This tunnel is twenty-two feet wide and sixteen feet high; the sides are perpendicular for five feet in height, surmounted by a semi-circular arch of twenty-two-feet diameter; the total length is two thousand two hundred and fifty yards. The entrance in the Company's yard in Wapping, is by an open cutting twenty-two feet deep and forty-six wide, affording space for four lines of rail-way. Between the lines are pillars. For the length of two hundred and eighty yards the railway is perfectly level, curving to the south-east. Over this part are the Company's warehouses, to which there are hatchways or trap-doors, allowing the waggons placed underneath to be readily loaded or unloaded. The inclined plane, which is a perfectly straight line, commences here: it is one thousand nine hundred and seventy yards in length, with a uniform rise of 1 in 48, the whole rise from Wapping to the tunnel-mouth at Edge-hill being one hundred and twenty-three feet. A considerable portion of this excavation was hewn through a solid rock, consisting of a fine red sand-stone, which forms in these parts a natural roof, requiring neither props nor artificial arching. But in some places the substance excavated was with difficulty supported till the masonry which formed the roof was erected. The construction of this tunnel was commenced in seven or eight separate lengths; upright shafts being opened in each of these places, communicating with the surface, and through which the substance excavated was conveyed away. The accuracy of the work rendered the joinings exact and perfect in every case. In the early part of September, 1828, the whole was completed at a cost of £34,791. The depth of the super-stratum of earth, from the roof of the tunnel to the open surface of the ground varies from five to seventy feet. The whole length of the tunnel is furnished with gas-lights, suspended from the centre of the arched roof, at distances of twenty-five yards apart; and the sides and roofs are white-washed, for the better reflection of the light. At the upper end of the inclined plane the tunnel terminates in a spacious area, forty feet below the surface of the ground, cut out of the solid rock, and surmounted on every side by walls and battlements. From this area there returns another small tunnel, quite distinct from the larger one, and communicating with the upper part of Liverpool. Its dimensions are two hundred and ninety yards in length, fifteen feet wide, and twelve feet high. It terminates in the Company's premises in Crown Street, which is the principal station for the rail-way coaches. Above this area on the surface of the ground two steam chimneys are erected of one hundred feet in height; / these are built in the form of columns, with handsome capitals. In the area below are two stationary engines, by which the loaded waggons are drawn up the inclined plane. Proceeding eastward from the two tunnels, the road passes through a Moorish arch-way, erected from a design of

Mr. Foster. This connects the two engine-houses, and forms the grand entrance to the Liverpool stations.

The road in this part curves slightly, but is perfectly level for one thousand yards; it then for the length of five miles and a half has a fall of only 1 in 1092, or of four feet in a mile, – a declivity so slight and uniform as not to be perceptible. This nearly level line was not obtained without much labour. A little beyond the perfect level the road has been formed in a deep excavation made through marl. Beyond this, about half a mile to the north of the village of Wavertree, is a passage cut through a steep eminence, called Olive Mount, the substance of which is entirely rocky. This deep and narrow ravine, formed in the solid rock, is more than two miles in extent, and in the deepest part is seventy feet below the surface of the ground; the road here is little more than sufficiently wide for two trains of carriages to pass each other. It winds gently round to the south-east, and the view is bounded by the perpendicular rock on either side. Four hundred and eighty thousand cubic yards of stone have been dug out of this excavation, and have been made available to the building of bridges and walls on this portion of the line. Over the marl and the Olive Mount excavations are several bridges to form the requisite communications between the roads and farms on the opposite sides of the rail-way. Emerging from the Olive Mount cutting, the road is thence artificially raised by the great Roby embankment, which is nearly three miles long, varying in height from fifteen to forty-five feet, and in breadth at the base from sixty to one hundred and thirty-five feet. This is formed of the materials dug out from the various excavations. The quantity employed was 550,000 cubic yards. After passing the Roby embankment the rail-way crosses, by means of a bridge, over the Huyton turnpike-road; and proceeds in a slightly curved direction to Whiston, between seven and eight miles from the station at Liverpool. Here the rail-road continues for a mile and a half in a straight line, having in this length an inclination of 1 in 96; at the top of this inclined plane the road runs nearly two miles on an exact level, produced by the excavation of 220,000 cubic yards. Over this part, called Rainhill level, the turnpike road between Liverpool and Manchester proceeds, crossing the line of rail-way at an acute angle of 34°, by means of a substantial stone bridge. At the other side of this two miles of level is the Sutton inclined plane, which is similar in extent and inclination to the Whiston plane, descending from Rainhill in the opposite direction. A little distance thence is Parr Moss, over which the road is carried. This Moss is twenty feet deep, and extends three-quarters of a mile in the line. The materials for the road which forms the rail-way on this unsubstantial matter was obtained from the excavations of the Sutton inclined plane, which produced 144,000 cubic yards of clay and stone. The heavy deposit sank to the bottom, and now forms with the moss a firm embankment, in reality twenty-five feet high, though only four or five feet above the surface of the other parts of the moss. Not very far from this, and about half way between Liverpool and Manchester, is the valley of the Sankey, at the bottom of which the canal flows. Over this valley, without interruption to its navigation, the rail-way is carried along a magnificent viaduct, supported on nine arches; each arch is fifty feet span, and varies from sixty to seventy feet in height; these are built principally of brick with stone facings; the width of the rail-way between the parapets is twenty-five feet. The *piling* for the foundation of the piers of this great viaduct was a business of much labour and cost, but indispensable for the security of the superstructure. About two hundred piles, varying from twenty to thirty feet in length, were driven hard into the foundation site of each of the ten piers.

The approach to this structure is by an embankment attaining to the height of sixty feet. This is formed / principally of clay dug out from the high lands on the borders of the valley. Not far from Sankey is Newton, near to which town the rail-way crosses a narrow valley by a short but lofty embankment, and by a handsome bridge of four arches, each having forty feet span. The turnpike-road from Newton to Warrington passes under one of these arches, and beneath another flows a small river. At Kenyon, a few miles beyond Newton, is an excavation of greater magnitude than any other on the line, 800,000 cubic yards of clay and sand having been dug out of it. Near the end of this cutting the Kenyon and Leigh Junction Rail-way joins the Liverpool and Manchester line by two branches, pointing to the two towns respectively. This rail-way joins the Bolton and Leigh line, and thus forms the connecting link between Bolton, Liverpool, and Manchester. After the Kenyon excavation is the Brosely embankment, and a little beyond that commences the Chat Moss. The difficulties overcome here have already been briefly described; and now, by the ingenuity and perseverance of man, trains of carriages of many tons weight are constantly passing and repassing over a bog, which originally would not allow of a person walking over it except in the driest weather. About a mile from the extremity of the moss the rail-way crosses the Duke of Bridgewater's canal, by a neat stone bridge of two arches. Some little distance beyond is the village of Eccles, four miles from Manchester. Through this extent is an excavation from which 295,000 cubic yards of earth have been dug out. At Manchester the rail-way crosses the river Irwell by a very handsome stone bridge, of two arches of sixty-five feet span, thirty feet from the water; and then over a series of twenty-two arches, and a bridge, to the Company's station in Water-street. The whole line of road is a distance of thirty-one miles.

It was a matter of some importance to determine whether cast or wrought iron rails should be used for this undertaking; each description had its advocates; but after deliberation and inquiry, those of wrought iron obtained the preference. These were made in lengths of five yards each, weighing thirty-five pounds per yard. The blocks, or sleepers, are some of stone and some of wood. Those of stone contain nearly four cubic feet each: they are laid along about eighteen miles. The wood sleepers are made of oak or larch; and are principally laid across the embankments, and across the two districts of moss, wherever it is expected that the road may subside a little. The stone blocks are let firmly into the permanent road, which consists of a layer of broken rock and sand about two feet thick, one foot of which is placed below the blocks, and one foot distributed between them, serving to keep them in their places. They are placed at intervals of three feet; in each block two holes six inches deep and an inch in diameter are drilled, and into these are driven oak plugs. The rails are supported at every three feet on cast-iron chairs or pedestals, into which they are immediately fitted and securely fastened; the chairs are placed on the blocks, and firmly spiked down to the plugs, the whole forming a work of great solidity and strength; the rails are about two inches in breadth, and rise about an inch above the surface; they are laid down with extreme correctness, and consist of four parallel rails four feet eight inches apart, allowing two trains of carriages to pass in opposite directions with perfect safety. Under the warehouses at Liverpool there are four distinct rail-ways for the greater convenience and facility of loading and unloading the wagons.

It may be observed, from the description given of this rail-road, how much the principle was acted upon of making it as far as practicable perfectly *level* and *straight*. With the exception of the two inclined planes at Rainhill, where the inclination is 1 in 96, there is no greater inclination than in the ratio of about 1 in 880. The surface of the rails at the top of the tunnel in Liverpool is forty-six feet above the rail-way at Manchester. Along the whole extent there are no abrupt curves; the curvature rarely exceeds a deviation from a straight line of more than four inches in twenty-two yards.

At the first projection of the rail-road it was by no means decided what kind of power should be employed for locomotion – whether horses or locomotive engines, or fixed engines drawing the load by means of ropes from one station to another. Each of these methods had been tried. The directors were not, however, at a loss to decide from the paucity of evidence brought before them; and the schemes offered by some projectors were of the most various and extravagant nature. Mature consideration, and the experience obtained in other undertakings, satisfied the directors that the employment of horses was entirely out of the question. At length it was determined, in April, 1829, to offer a premium of £500 for the most improved locomotive engine, subject to certain stipulations and conditions.

The trial of the different engines offered, in competition for the reward just mentioned, took place on the 6th of October, 1829, before competent judges, on the level portion of the rail-way at Rainhill. Four steam-carriages were entered on the lists to contend for the premium. The distance appointed to be run was seventy miles, and the engine, when fairly started, was to travel on the road at a speed of not less than ten miles an hour, drawing after it a gross weight of three tons for every ton of its own weight. This distance was to be accomplished by moving backwards and forwards on a level plane of one mile and three-quarters in length, by which arrangement the machine had to pass over the plane forty times, and make as many stoppages. The 'Rocket,' weighing four tons five hundred weight, performed the distance in less than six hours and a half, including stoppages. The speed at which it travelled was frequently eighteen miles per hour, and occasionally upwards of twenty. In this trial, half a ton of coke was consumed as fuel; coke being used instead of coal to prevent the annoyance of smoke. This engine was the only one which performed the stipulated task. The premium was awarded by the directors to Mr. Booth[11] and the Messrs. Stephenson. Engines similar to the 'Rocket' are those now used on the Manchester and Liverpool railway. The peculiarities of this engine could not be rendered intelligible without some previous knowledge of the construction of an ordinary steam-engine. The following cut [omitted here] exhibits its external appearance. /

We have now traced the steps of this important national work to the time when the engines were prepared, and in a fit state for being applied to useful purposes. The stupendous undertaking was finished in September, 1830, little more than three years having been consumed in the completion of a work in which difficulties of no ordinary kind presented themselves. A brief recapitulation of what was accomplished in the space of thirty-one miles will evince the skill, energy, and perseverance which were brought to the task. Two tunnels were excavated, six considerable eminences cut through, great part of which excavations were hewn out of the solid rock; upwards of three millions of cubic yards of stone, clay and soil, have been dug out of the different excavations. From these materials artificial mounds of great height and extent have been raised through valleys, and semi-fluid matter has been consolidated into strength and consistency. Along the whole line there are sixty-three bridges; under thirty of these the rail-way passes, on twenty-eight it passes over the common road, and on five it is conducted over the waters of the river Irwell, of canals, &c. Twenty-two of the bridges are composed of brick, seventeen of wood and brick, eleven of brick and stone, eleven of wood, and two of stone and wood. The weight of the double lines of rail laid down is 3847 tons, and of the cast iron pedestals on which they are fastened, 1428 tons. There are occasional lines of communication between the rail-ways, and additional side lines at the different depots.

The total sum expended in effecting this magnificent project, and putting the whole in a situation for active operation, including the cost of constructing warehouses, machinery, and carriages, is estimated at £820,000.

On the 15th of September, 1830, the rail-way was opened by the passage of eight locomotive engines, all built by Messrs. Stephenson and Co. To these were attached twenty-eight carriages of different forms and capacities, capable of containing altogether a company of six hundred persons. Preparations were made on a scale of great magnificence to render this a ceremony of no ordinary kind; and some of the most distinguished characters were invited and attended, to go first over that ground which is now become the scene of daily traffic. The Northumbrian, a steam-engine of fourteen-horse power, took the lead, having in its train three carriages. The performance of the engines was extremely satisfactory until they reached Parkfield, seventeen miles from Liverpool, when they were stopped to renew the feeders and to take in a fresh supply of fuel. Here several of the company alighted from the different carriages; on again starting, that fatal accident happened to Mr. Huskisson, which, after a few hours of extreme agony, terminated his life.[12]

On the following day the Northumbrian left Liverpool with one hundred and thirty passengers, and arrived at Manchester in one hour and fifty minutes. In the evening it returned with twenty-one passengers and three tons of luggage in one hour and forty-eight minutes; and on Friday, the 17th, six carriages commenced running regularly between the two towns, accomplishing the journey usually in much less than two hours. On the 23d of November, 1830, one of the engines went over the distance in the space of one hour, two minutes of which time was taken up in oiling and examining the machinery about midway. No carriages were attached to the engine, and it had only the additional weight of three persons. On the 4th of December following the 'Planet' locomotive engine took the first load of merchandise which passed along the rail-way between Liverpool and Manchester. Attached to the engine were eighteen waggons, containing two hundred barrels of flour, thirty-four sacks of malt, sixty-three bags of oat-meal, and a hundred and thirty-five bags and bales of cotton. The gross weight drawn, including the waggons and engine-tender, was about eighty tons. The speed over level ground was at the rate of twelve to fourteen miles per hour. The train was assisted up the Whiston inclined plane by another engine, at the rate of nine miles an hour; it descended the Sutton inclined plane at the rate of sixteen miles and a half an hour; and the average rate of the remaining part was twelve miles and a half an hour. The whole journey was performed in two hours and fifty-four minutes, including three stoppages, of five minutes each, for oiling, watering, and taking in fuel. This was the greatest performance heretofore accomplished by any locomotive power, but it was only the commencement of much greater speed. The Samson engine, on the 25th of February, 1831, started with a train of thirty wagons from Liverpool, the gross weight of the whole being 164½ tons, and with this enormous weight it averaged a speed of twenty miles an hour on level ground. It was assisted up the inclined plane by three other engines, and arrived in Manchester within two hours and thirty-four minutes from first starting; deducting thirteen minutes for stoppages employed in taking in water, &c., the net time of travelling was two hours and twenty-one minutes. The quantity of coke consumed by the engine in this journey was 1376 lbs. being not quite one-third of a pound per ton per mile. By taking the average speed throughout at thirteen miles an hour, the same work would have required seventy good horses.

From the first opening of the rail-way in September to the end of that year, more than 70,000 persons passed by it for various distances between Liverpool and Manchester, without personal injury to a single individual, except one person, who while mounting on the roof of one of the carriages had his leg severely bruised by coming in contact with another vehicle. The security and celerity of this mode of conveyance being thus clearly established, it has become the chief mode of personal communication between the two towns. In the second half year of 1832, however, the conveyance of passengers appears to have materially decreased. This, the directors in the last Report attribute to temporary causes. This Report contains some further interesting details, of which the following is the substance:-

> The company carried in the last half year of 1832, 86,842 tons of goods, and 39,940 tons of coal, showing an increase of 7,821 tons of goods, and 10,484 tons of coal, beyond the previous half year. The total number of passengers was 182,823, or 73,498 fewer than were carried in the first six months of 1832.

	£.	*s.*	*d.*
The total receipts for the half year were	80,902	2	10
Total disbursements (including maintenance of way, cost and repair of engines, expenses of establishments, interests on loans, &c.)	48,218	8	10
Leaving a net profit of .... for the half year ending Dec. 31, 1832.	32,623	14	0

The rate of profit on the transport of each ton of goods and coals appears to have materially increased during the same half year.

A very general opinion has been gaining ground, that the great expense attending the wear and tear of the locomotive engines would render the adoption of some other plan necessary. On this subject the directors admit that in this branch of their expenditure they have met with unexpected discouragement, and with difficulties which they have not yet been able to overcome. The principal items of excessive expenditure in this department have arisen from the frequent renewal of the tubes and fire-places, which, in most of the engines, have been found to burn very rapidly away. To this general result, however, there have been some exceptions; for the company have engines which have run between twenty and thirty thousand miles, with very inconsiderable repairs either to the fire-places or the tubes. /

According to the Report, the total amount of capital stock created from the commencement to the 31st December last, whether in shares or by loan, is £1,024,375, every farthing of which has been expended on the works.

The proprietors have divided out of the *net profits* of the concern up to the 30th June, 1832	£112,040	12	6
And the directors are about to recommend a further dividend for the half year ending 31st December last, of..................	£33,468	15	0
Making a total of realized profits out of the working of the concern, and altogether independent of the capital invested, of..	£145,509	7	6
being for a period of about two years and a quarter.			

A trip, as it is called, by this extraordinary road for the first time is an event which cannot readily be effaced by the recollections of more common modes of travelling. A pleasurable wonder takes possession of the mind, as we glide along at a speed equal to the gallop of the race-horse. It might be supposed that so great a speed would almost deprive the traveller of breath, and that he could not fail to be unpleasantly conscious of the velocity with which he cut through the air. The reverse is, however, the case; the motion is so uniform, and so entirely free from the shaking occasioned by the inequality or friction of common roads, that the passenger can scarcely credit he is really passing over the ground at such a rapid pace, and it is only when meeting another train, and passing it with instantaneous flight, that he is fully aware of the velocity of his career. The novelty of the scene is delightful: now, where the natural surface of the ground is at the highest, we travel embosomed in deep recesses, and then, where the ordinary course of the road would lead through a valley, we 'ride above the tops of the trees,' and look down upon the surrounding country. The reflecting traveller probably falls into a pleasing vision arising out of the triumph of human art. He sees the period fast approaching when the remotest parts of his own country shall be brought into easy and rapid communication; and he looks beyond this probable event of a few years, to the more distant day when other nations shall emulate these gigantic works of peace. He sees the evils arising out of the differences of language and soil, and climate, all vanishing before the desire of mankind for peaceful commercial intercourse; and as he knows that the prejudices and mistaken interests which separate one district of the same nation from another are broken down by such noble inventions as these, he feels that the same spirit of civilization which results from that exercise of our reason, which is bestowed by a beneficent Providence, will eventually render all men as brethren, and children of one great Father.

'A Day at a Cotton Factory', *Penny Magazine* (1843)

'A Day at a Cotton Factory', *Penny Magazine of the Society for the Diffusion of Useful Knowledge*, 12:721 (25 June 1843), pp. 241–8.

A DAY AT A COTTON-FACTORY.

IF we take the town of Manchester as a centre, and draw around it a circle of ten miles radius, we shall find within that circle the seat of the most extraordinary manufacture which the world has yet witnessed: extraordinary in relation to the annual amount of property produced, to the effects which that property has wrought on the social features of the district, and to the mechanical inventions whereby the manufacture has been founded. We allude, of course, to the COTTON manufacture. At a period which may be remembered by persons yet living, the quantity of raw cotton worked up in Britain was about three millions of pounds annually: it is now three hundred millions. At a period not very much earlier, it employed a spinner one year to produce as much yarn as he can now produce in about a day. In 1760 not more than forty thousand persons are supposed to have been employed in this manufacture: there are now, in all its various branches, considerably above a million. In 1760 there was, perhaps, not a single yard of cotton goods exported; whereas in recent years the exports of cotton have nearly equalled all our other exports put together. And, lastly, at the present day the population of the manufacturing district is four times as great as it was at the former period.

Should it be asked why this district is so distinguished as the seat of the cotton manufacture, we may perhaps be correct in saying that the circumstance is due to a number of different causes. For instance: five centuries ago, when Edward III. married the daughter of the Earl of Hainault, he invited a number of Flemish clothiers to come to England; and they, settling at Bolton, within the district which we have marked out, established the processes of spinning and weaving there. Again, when the revocation of the Edict of Nantes drove many weavers from France, in 1685, many of these settled at and near Bolton; and although both of these immigrations relate more to the history of the *wool-*

len than to the *cotton* manufacture, yet they laid a foundation for the modern improvements in both. Then, again, the physical character of the district presents marked facilities for such a manufacture: the hilly range which separates Lancashire from Yorkshire gives rise to numerous streams, which, before they reach the estuary of the river Mersey, give motive power to water-wheels, and a supply of water to bleach-works and dye-works, such as has no parallel for extent in any other country. It has been said that the Mersey and the Irwell are the two 'hardest-worked rivers in the world.' We may also adduce the existence of coal in abundance in the county, and iron in adjacent counties with which there is easy communication, as causes for the settlement of the cotton manufacture here. We must not forget, too, that Liverpool, one of the most admirably situated ports in the kingdom, is in the immediate vicinity of the cotton districts; serving at once as a depot for the imported raw material and for the exported finished goods. Lastly, we might be expected to mention the canals and railways which intersect this district in unparalleled abundance; but these are rather *consequences* than *causes* of the location of the manufacture.

We may regard this district as one huge town, almost as one huge factory; for there is such a connecting / link between Manchester as a centre, and Bolton, Bury, Rochdale, Oldham, Ashton, Stayley Bridge, Hyde, Stockport, &c. as branches, that we cannot properly appreciate the one without noticing the others. Let us, then, beginning at the centre, take a rapid glance at this wonderful scene of industry.

If we take our station in Market Street, Manchester, at the west end of which is the Exchange, we are immersed in the very heart of the whole system. We have around us the wholesale 'warehouses' and offices wherein is transacted all the business between the dealers, the manufacturers, the spinners, the bleachers, the calico-printers, &c., whether of Manchester or of any of the surrounding towns. One street especially, viz. Mosley Street, presents a curious index to the whole arrangement. Here almost every house is occupied in the way stated: no manufactures are carried on; no retail shops exhibit the manufactured goods; but every house, and almost every floor of every house, constitutes the business establishment for some large manufacturing firm. The houses were once small and humble; but the value of room in Manchester has increased so rapidly, that it has been a profitable speculation to rebuild nearly the whole of them in this street on a large and elegant scale. So thoroughly developed has the system become, that it is not found necessary to keep a large stock of manufactured goods at these places. A bargain is struck, say for ten thousand pieces of calico, as per sample; and this may be done in a small room, between the manufacturer and the dealer, while the goods are perhaps at that moment being manufactured at Bolton, or Ashton, or Stockport. Even the kitchens or cellars, as they would be termed in other places, are warehouses or counting-houses, and may be rented by a calico-printer, while the ground-floor constitutes the place of business for a fustian manufacturer, the first floor for a spinner, the second for a muslin manufacturer, and so on.

The admirable manner in which the wholesale Manchester business is now conducted, has been the growth of experience. Dr. Aikin,[1] fifty years ago, separated the history of Manchester, as regards the position of its manufacturers, into four epochs, and these will give us some insight into the gradual changes, in the agency of a mercantile system. The first epoch he places anterior to about the year 1690, when the manufacturers worked hard merely for a livelihood, without having accumulated any capital; and Aikin supposes that there were few or no manufacturers who had accumulated so much as 3000*l.* or 4000*l.* The second epoch began about the year just named, and lasted, say till 1730. The manufacturers during this epoch began to acquire little fortunes, but worked as hard and lived in as plain a manner as before, increasing their fortunes as well by economy as by moderate gains. They began to build modern brick houses, in place of those of wood and plaster. They confined their trade to the wholesale dealers of London, Bristol, Norwich, Newcastle, and Chester. Aikin says: – 'An eminent manufacturer of that age used to be in his warehouse before six in the morning, accompanied by his children and apprentices. At seven they all came in to breakfast, which consisted of one large dish of water-pottage, made of oatmeal, water, and a little salt, boiled thick, and poured into a dish: at the side was a pan or basin of milk, and the master and apprentices, each with a wooden spoon in his hand, without loss of time, dipped into the same dish, and thence into the milk-pan; and as soon as it was finished they all returned to their work. In George, I.'s reign, many country gentlemen began to send their sons apprentices to the Manchester manufacturers.'

Dr. Aikin's third epoch is from about 1730 to the era of Arkwright's inventions.[2] The marked feature of this epoch was the manner in which the manufacturers 'pushed' for orders. At first the chapmen or dealers used to keep gangs of pack-horses, and to drive them to the principal towns with goods in packs, which they opened and sold to shopkeepers; lodging what was unsold in small stores at the inns, and taking back sheep's wool to the manufacturing district. By degrees, however, turnpike-roads were improved waggons were laden, instead of pack-horses; and the chapmen only rode out for orders, carrying with them patterns in their bags. In the former epoch, country districts were supplied from the five or six large towns which received goods direct from Manchester, each acting as a centre to the surrounding counties: but now the manufacturers began to send their riders to every part of the kingdom soliciting orders.

The fourth epoch was consequent on the introduction of machinery into the manufacture. The trade became so large, that partners in commercial firms went to reside in London or on the Continent: foreigners and London merchants sent agents to reside permanently at Manchester; agents, factors, and brokers were established, some at Liverpool and some at Manchester, to manage the transactions between the Liverpool merchant and the Manchester manufacturer, both in respect to the raw cotton and to the manufactured goods; all the manufacturers around Manchester agreed to make that town their mart, and to appoint certain days of the week as 'market-days' with each other; and Manchester became, what it has ever since continued, one of the wealthiest towns in the empire.

When we depart from the mercantile focus of Manchester, and walk in any direction towards the suburbs, we come in sight of the cotton-factories, those enormous brick structures which excite such astonishment in the mind of a stranger. There are nearly two hundred of these vast piles in the immediate vicinity of the town. One or two canals pass through Manchester, and the factories are generally situated in convenient proximity to these canals. A first-rate cotton-factory, with its machinery, costs very little short of a hundred thousand pounds; and a slight guess may hence be made at the value of the whole. The division of the town near the Oldham Road is especially full of these large factories; and the scene which is presented when the operatives leave these factories to go to their meals is one of the most striking that can be conceived; the busy hive pours forth in a stream from each building, some of which employ more than a thousand hands; and in a few minutes all have reached their homes, in small streets near the factories.

Departing still farther from the centre, we see ample evidence of the commercial character of the district, in the numerous railway-stations which the outskirts of the town exhibit, each leading to some busy tributary to the giant depôt of manufactures. On the west, we have the station of the railway to Liverpool and Warrington; on the north-west, that of the railway to Bolton and Bury; on the north-east, that to Oldham, Rochdale, and Leeds; on the south-east, that to Ashton, Staley Bridge, and Sheffield; and finally, that to Stockport and London. A vast traffic is carried on by means of these lines of railway, especially from Manchester to the towns in its vicinity, both as respects passengers and goods.

If we next enlarge the radius of our visit, and pass from town to town of the 'cotton district,' we shall have the means more and more of appreciating the extent to which the system is carried. Say that we proceed north-westward, to Bolton, a distance of about ten miles. Here we come to a town which, in connection with the history of the cotton manufacture, is second to Manchester, and in some respects even takes precedence of it. Bolton was once the centre of the / district, as Manchester now is, and was noted for its textile fabrics many centuries ago. Leland,[3] writing in 1552, says:– 'Bolton upon Moore Market stondith most by cottons, and course yarne. Divers villages in the Moors about Bolton doe make cottons.' It is now known, however, that the goods which obtained the name of 'cottons' in those times, were really a kind of woollen; and that the first undoubted evidence we have of the real cotton manufacture in England dates back to the year 1641 only, just above two centuries ago. Bolton, in bygone times, had its warehouses, where dealers were wont to come from all the surrounding towns: a system which has been superseded by the concentration of the wholesale dealings at Manchester; but Bolton still holds its rank as one of the most important towns of the series. There were, in 1838, more than seventy cotton-factories in Bolton parish, and there are more than twenty large bleach-grounds within five miles of Bolton.

There is a pleasant walk of three or four miles northward from Bolton, which we will notice because it enables us to show that some of the factories, situated out of the dense mass at Manchester, are more favourably circumstanced than many readers are apt to suppose. In walking along the road from Bolton to Turton, which is a thoroughly open and country district, we arrive at a spot where a gentle range of hills separates the road from a valley through which a small river flows. On one of these eminences is a pretty church, recently built; and just beyond it is a small village of cottages; mostly new, almost wholly occupied by persons employed in a neighbouring cotton-factory. The factory is in the valley just spoken of, and the house of one of the proprietors is on a gentle eminence between it and the village. There is a school-house or room, supported partly by the proprietors of the factory, and there are chapels in the village for the principal denominations of Christian sects. The factory is bounded on every side by green fields; and being situated on the banks of the little stream, receives its motive-power from thence by means of a magnificent water-wheel sixty feet in diameter, the largest or nearly the largest in the kingdom. The employers and the employed live near each other, and all are located in a spot where there are as many green fields and as much blue sky, as pure rivulets and as pure air, as if no such place as a factory were near. In Manchester itself the factories are certainly and necessarily surrounded by smoke and bustle; but there are four times as many factories beyond the limits of Manchester as there are within those limits; and many of this larger number are analogous in their position to the one above described.

If, leaving Bolton, we direct our attention eastward, a distance of four or five miles brings us to Bury, another of the busy manufacturing towns. Nearly a hundred and twenty cotton-factories were, in 1838, enumerated in the parish of Bury, comprising the town and its environs. But Bury is perhaps still more celebrated for its print and bleach works than for its spinning and weaving factories. It was here that the first Sir Robert Peel,[4] father of the present premier, established several print-works (*i.e.* 'calico-printing' establishments), and laid the foundation for the fortune of his children; there are members of the Peel family yet residing there, although some of the works have passed into other hands.

Bolton and Bury, besides their present rank as manufacturing towns, have contributed their full share, and more than their share, to the inventions by which the manufacture has been enabled to attain its present vast extent. It was to John Kay,[5] of Bury, that the weavers are indebted for the 'fly-shuttle,' by which the weft-thread is thrown across the warp with so much more facility than by the old method. It was to his son, Robert Kay,[6] also of Bury, that we owe an ingenious contrivance by which three or four different coloured threads can be used in weaving with great facility. It was Whitehead,[7] of Bury, who introduced the plan of 'piecening,' by which much time is saved in spinning cotton. It was a Bolton barber, Richard Arkwright,[8] who was mainly instrumental in placing the manufacture in its present position, and the wealth of whose son[9] has recently so astonished the world. It was Crompton,[10] of Bolton, who invented the 'spinning-mule,' and whose house is still shown near that town, in which he used to work secretly in his garret, until inquisitive persons, by mounting ladders to look in at his window, discovered the secret of his machine, and robbed him of the fruit. It was also in this immediate neighbourhood that Hargreaves,[11] the inventor of the 'spinning-jenny,' endeavoured to introduce his machine, and experienced the fate which so often attends inventors, viz. persecution.

A little north-east of Bury lies Rochdale, another important member of the series. In the parish, including the town and environs, there are about a hundred factories, as well as extensive bleach and print works. Rochdale has, however, been remarkable rather for its woollens than its cottons.

From Rochdale we may turn southward, and we shall there find an immense amount of factory operations going on. Rochdale and Oldham are both approached from Manchester by way of the Manchester and Leeds Railway, and an easy and constant communication is thus kept up. Oldham parish, which is a large one, contains no fewer than two hundred cotton-factories, and carries on a large manufacture, not only in cottons, but also in woollens and in hats. Oldham is a place which retains many characteristics, such as in other places have been rubbed off by the friction of intercourse with larger towns. Among these the dress of the operatives is observable. The writer happened to be opposite to one of the factories of Oldham on a May evening, when the people were leaving work, and was struck with the universal use of *handkerchiefs*, instead of *bonnets*, as a head-covering for the women and girls; while both sexes, almost without exception among several hundreds, wore wooden clogs with brass buckles or clasps. Wooden clogs have been much worn in Lancashire ever since the Flemish clothiers located there, and appear to have become smarter than they were originally; but in most of the towns they are gradually giving way to the use of leather.

Proceeding a little farther southward, we come to that extraordinary knot of manufacturing towns, Ashton, Stayley Bridge, Duckinfield, and Hyde; a group which displays perhaps more remarkably than any others the effects of the progress of the cotton manufacture. We here come to the banks of the Mersey, that small but mighty river, which, separating Lancashire from Cheshire throughout its whole extent from hence to the sea, feeds more factories, perhaps, than any other river in any other country. At the extreme south-east corner of Lancashire, where it joins Cheshire and Yorkshire, lie these four towns, two on the Lancashire side, and two on the Cheshire side of the Mersey. Ashton in 1775 contained five thousand inhabitants; in 1831 it contained more than thirty thousand. Stayley Bridge in 1748 contained forty-eight houses and one hundred and forty people; it has now twenty thousand inhabitants. Hyde in 1770 contained one dwelling-house and one chapel, while Duckinfield was at the same time designated as a 'pleasant country spot;' now they contain some of the largest factories in the whole district, and an extensive population. These towns being, as has been / said, on the banks of the Mersey (or rather the Tame, for although the same river, it is not called the Mersey till it reaches Stockport), have water communication with Liverpool; while three canals in the neighbourhood connect them with Manchester, Huddersfield, and Derbyshire. At one of these towns, or rather manufacturing villages, viz. Hyde, there is a group of factories which were thus spoken of by Dr. J. P. Kay,[12] in a work on the 'Moral and Physical Condition of the Working Classes employed in the Cotton Manufacture in Manchester,' published a few years ago:– 'Twelve hundred persons are employed in the cotton factories of Mr. Thomas Ashton of Hyde.[13] This gentleman has erected commodious dwellings for his work-people, with each of which he has connected every convenience that can minister to comfort. He resides in the immediate vicinity, and has frequent opportunities of maintaining a cordial association with his operatives. Their houses are well furnished, clean, and their tenants exhibit every indication of health and happiness. Mr. Ashton has also built a school, where 640 children, chiefly belonging to his establishment, are instructed on Tuesday in reading, writing, arithmetic, &c. A library, connected with this school, is eagerly resorted to, and the people frequently read after the hours of labour have expired. An infant school is, during the week, attended by 280 children, and in the evenings others are instructed by masters selected for the purpose. The factories themselves are certainly excellent examples of the cleanliness and order which may be obtained by a systematic and persevering attention to the habits of the artizans.'

The population of the township of Hyde increased *ninefold* between 1801 and 1831!

We have not yet completed the circuit of this remarkable district. Following the course of the Mersey from Stayley Bridge and its neighbourhood, we soon arrive at Stockport, a town which at the present day ranks, after Manchester, as high perhaps as any other in the district in the extent of its factory arrangements. Being situated on the southern bank of the Mersey, the town itself is in Cheshire;

but its factories have gradually extended to the Lancashire side. Like all the other towns, it has intimate communication with Manchester by railway, the Manchester and Birmingham Railway passing through the town; while the Sheffield line places Ashton, Duckinfield, Stayley Bridge, and Hyde, within reach of the great cotton metropolis. An incident came under our own notice at Stockport, which, as it illustrates one of the features in the factory system, we will mention. A factory, built many years ago, on the plan then in vogue, was enlarged at a later period to meet the extended business of the proprietor; but the new portion was built on the fire-proof plan of modern factories, that is, having very little wood in its construction. The old portion of the building caught fire, on the occasion alluded to, and was utterly destroyed; while the new portion, contiguous to it, and filled with machinery moved by the same steam-engine, escaped almost entirely unhurt. The poor workpeople, standing on the opposite bank of the river, were witnessing the wreck which would infallibly throw half of them out of work for a time; and they had the best of all possible grounds for appreciating the new mode in which these large buildings are now constructed.

South-west of Stockport there are some large factories here and there, and also northward of the Mersey through Eccles towards Bolton; but we need not stop to mention these more particularly, after the details already given. Suffice it to say that all the towns which we have mentioned lie within about ten miles of Manchester, on every side, and form, with it, one great workshop for cotton goods. We also find the whole of this district chequered over with the lowly dwellings of the hand-loom weavers, those hard-working men who are competing with the steam-engine in the business of working up the spun-yarn into woven fabrics. The clack of the hand-loom is to be heard on many a road-side in the district. We do not, when speaking of cotton factories and weavers within a certain distance of Manchester, mean to imply that they are limited to this district: far from it; the remaining parts of Lancashire and of Cheshire, together with Yorkshire and Derbyshire, and especially the Glasgow district of Scotland, present a very considerable extent of cotton manufacture; but it is within the limits which we have chosen that the wonderful effects of the manufacture are most observable.

When we speak of a 'cotton-factory,' it means in most cases a factory for *spinning cotton-yarn,* afterwards to be used by the weaver, the stocking-maker, or the bobbin-net maker; but sometimes, and especially in the modern factories, *power-loom weaving* is combined with spinning, that is, the same steam-engines which work the spinning-machinery also work the looms which weave the yarn into cotton cloth. Hence the factories are distinguished as 'spinning,' or 'weaving,' or 'spinning and weaving' factories. But it does not follow that *all* kinds of cotton-cloth are either spun or woven in the same factory. In fact it is very far otherwise; each manufacturer confining his operations, generally to a small number of different kinds. The varieties of woven cottons are very large; but so far as regards a slight glance at the principles of the manufacture, all these varieties may be put out of view, and we may consider *spinning* and *weaving* as the two staple objects of the ten or twelve hundred cotton-factories which engirdle Manchester. If, then, we can glance at the interior arrangement of any one large factory wherein spinning and weaving are both carried on, we shall be able to form something like a judgment of them all. Many such are to be found, both in Manchester and in the towns by which it is surrounded; and it matters little where we make our choice, for the manufacturers of the district generally are liberally disposed to permit strangers to view the operations. We will give our description with reference to Mr. Orrell's factory[14] in the neighbourhood of Stockport, as being one of those which exhibit all the most important improvements in the engineering and mechanical arrangements of factories.

Stockport is itself in Cheshire, but the factory under notice, being on the north side of the river Mersey, is in Lancashire, and we must therefore rank it among the Lancashire factories. The intercourse now between Manchester and Stockport is mainly carried on per railway, and is very extensive; Manchester being as much the mart for Stockport cottons, as for those of Ashton, Oldham, or Bolton. The railway conveys us to the immediate vicinity of the factory, which we approach under one of the arches of the lofty viaduct over the Mersey. When we came within sight of the factory, its arrangement cannot appear otherwise than striking to a stranger; for the lofty chimney is separated from the factory itself by a public road, and stands isolated on a kind of rocky mount. Being a well-formed structure, this chimney (which, but for the smoke, looks more like an honorary column than anything else) presents a fine appearance. The furnaces, which supply heat to the boilers for four large steam-engines, are situated in a building at one end of the factory: and the smoke from these furnaces passes through a flue under the public road, into the chimney, which thus conveys it up into the atmosphere at a distance from the factory.

When we come in front of the factory itself, we find it speckled over with windows to an enormous amount. / The building extends, from end to end, nearly three hundred feet, having a centre and two projecting wings. There are six ranges of windows in height, each range giving light to one floor or story of workshops. There are nearly a hundred windows in each of these ranges, on the four sides of the building, so that the whole amount to not much fewer than six hundred. The perfect regularity with which the windows of modern factories are arranged, constitutes one of their most conspicuous features. The ground-floor is two hundred feet in depth from front to back, but the upper floors are much less than this.

With inside the building, the extraordinary scene and deafening noise presented by the operations conducted on the ground-floor are well calculated to bewilder a stranger: but of these more anon; we will at present confine our attention to the upper floors. There are staircases conveniently situated for gaining access to the various floors; but besides this there is a very ingenious arrangement for mounting to any floor without the least exertion on the part of the person ascending. There is a kind of square well, open from top to bottom of the factory, and measuring a few feet square. We place ourselves on a platform within this space, and by pulling a rope, place the platform in connection with certain moving machinery, by which it is carried up, supporting its load – animate or inanimate – safely. When we desire it to stop, on the level of any one of the floors, we have only to let go the rope, and the platform will stop. When we wish to descend, we pull another rope, which enables the machinery to give a reverse movement to the platform.

When, having ascended either by this piece of mechanism or by the staircase, we reach any of the upper floors, we find them to consist of very long rooms, lighted on all sides by windows, and filled with machinery so complicated and extensive that we may well wonder how all can receive their movement from steam-engines in a remote part of the building. Yet such is the case. There are two engines for the spinning-machinery, of eighty horse-power each; and two for the weaving-machinery, of forty horse-power each. These splendid engines are supplied from six boilers, the fires for which consume more than twenty tons of coal per day; and the main shaft from each engine is so connected with other shafts, both vertical and horizontal, as to convey motive-power to every floor, and to every machine in every floor.

Let us next see what are the most distinctive features in these processes of manufacture, and how each one is dependent on the others. The unprecedented train of inventions by which the present state of the manufacture was brought about, and the beauty and intricacy of the machinery by which it is effected, are subjects for a volume, rather than for half a dozen pages, and have indeed formed the subjects of volumes by Dr. Ure, Mr. Baines, Mr. Guest,[15] and other writers. But the broad principles of the operations by which the contents of a cotton-pod are converted into woven calico or muslin, may perhaps be made clear.

In the first place, then, we have to ask what this remarkable substance is. It is a downy substance contained in the pod of the cotton-tree, a plant cultivated extensively in India, America, and other countries. When the pods begin to open, women and children go through the plantations, and pluck the cotton and seeds, leaving the husks behind. The cotton and seeds thus gathered, are exposed to the action of the sun till quite dry, and are then passed through a machine called a 'gin,' by which the seeds are separated from the fibres of cotton. The cotton is not further prepared in the land of its growth, but is packed very tightly in bags, and in that state imported into England, the bags containing somewhere about three hundred pounds each on an average.

When these bags of cotton arrive at Liverpool, they are placed in warehouses; and cotton-brokers then negotiate dealings between the merchants of

Liverpool and the manufacturers of Manchester and its vicinity; consequent on which the cotton is forwarded by railway or canal to the towns where it is to be manufactured.

We will suppose bags of cotton, such as those above alluded to, to have arrived at the factory which is the object of our notice. They are classified according to their qualities, to suit the different kinds of yarn spun from them; and after being opened, the cotton is removed, preparatory to the manufacture. Although the fibres of cotton form very light locks or tufts when they have been cleaned from the seeds abroad, yet they are so powerfully pressed when being made up into packages, that the tufts get matted and entangled, and require opening before anything else can be done; because, in all the subsequent operations, each fibre must be combined, unbroken, with others, to form the collected group or thread. This opening of the matted cotton is effected by a large and powerful machine called a *willow*. This machine consists of an inner framework, capable of revolving with very great rapidity, and enclosed in an outer case. Upon the four edges of the inner frame are fixed a series of iron pins or pegs, which in their rotation pass between other similar pins fixed to the inner surface of the outer case. Now if a quantity of cotton be put in the receptacle between the inner and outer frames, and the inner one be made to rotate, it is not difficult to conceive what will follow. The clotted locks of cotton, tossed about within the machine, are caught by the various iron pins, and torn open fibre by fibre. All the dirt and other impurities which may have been mixed with the cotton are at the same time separated from it, and made to fall through a kind of grating into another receptacle. Various forms of the willow, or 'devil,' as it is sometimes called, are used; but all act on the principle of separating the fibres by revolving spikes, the revolutions amounting to five or six hundred in a minute.

The fibres are thus nearly separated one from another, and nearly cleansed from dust, but not quite; and therefore the next process is to complete the opening and cleansing thus begun. This process is called 'scutching,' or 'batting,' or 'blowing' (for all three terms seem to be in use), and is effected in various ways, but generally by some such arrangement as the following:– The cotton is laid upon a kind of endless apron, which by its movement conveys its burden to a fitting spot, where flat bars, carried rapidly round, strike the cotton violently as it exudes from between two rollers, and thus separates the fibres most thoroughly. There is also a particular kind of fan or vane, so arranged as to produce a most powerful draught, by which all the dirt and dust are carried up and conveyed away – not only out of the machine, but out of the room, and out of the factory itself; for so admirable are the arrangements of a modern factory, that the room in which a very dusty process is carried on is as free from floating dust as any part of the building.

The cotton is now in the form of a very clean, light, downy substance, consisting of short fibres thoroughly disentangled. But these fibres are not *parallel*; they lie across each other at every imaginable angle, and any attempt to combine them together in this state would be fruitless: they must be rendered parallel, and to effect this is the object of the beautiful operation of *carding*, one of those which have exercised such a large amount of inventive ingenuity. If we were to take two combs, and pass the teeth of one between / those of the other, we should have a rude idea of the process of carding, especially if we had a few fibres of cotton entangled among the teeth; for the movement of the two combs would tend to arrange the fibres in some degree parallel. A number of pieces of wire are inserted in a piece of wood or leather, so that all shall project to an equal distance and at an equal angle; and if two such pieces of apparatus were placed with their wires in contact, and moved in contrary directions, a few fibres of cotton placed on the lower one would be *combed out* by the upper one, and arranged parallel. In various stages of the history of the manufacture, the two cards have been arranged in different ways. Sometimes one was on a convex surface, and the other on a concave surface fitted to it: sometimes one was on a cylinder, and the other on a flat surface: sometimes both were on the surfaces of cylinders. But the principle of action is the same in all, and is nothing more nor less than a process of combing. In some arrangements the cotton is brought into the form of a 'lap,' or flat layer, by the scutching-machine, and in that state transferred to the carding-engine; while in other cases the latter is fed by hand with cotton.

The cotton leaves the carding-engine in the state of a delicate, flat, narrow strip or riband, called a *sliver*; and these slivers have now to be converted into *drawings* by being elongated, narrowed, and thinned to a still more delicate condition. This process is one to which Arkwright paid particular attention, as having an important influence on the quality of the spun cotton. In the first place the slivers are collected in tall cans, generally either four or six in number, on one side of the 'drawing-frame,' and are from thence carried upwards to two pair of rollers, the two rollers of each pair revolving in contact. Here all the slivers or cardings are collected into one group, and are drawn between the rollers by the rotation of the latter. Now if these rollers all revolved equally fast, the cotton would leave them with the same united thickness as when it entered; but the last pair revolve quicker than the first, so as to draw out the cotton into a more attenuated riband; because the more slowly-revolving rollers do not supply the material fast enough for the maintenance of the original thickness. This is perhaps the most important principle in the whole range of the cotton manufacture; for it is exhibited alike in the present process and in the next two which follow. All the four or six slivers are connected into one before being caught between the rollers; and after leaving the rollers, the united 'drawing' passes through a kind of trumpet-shaped funnel, and thence conducted into a tall can, round the interior of which it coils itself. One consequence of the drawing-process, if properly conducted, is that the drawing is perfectly equal in thickness in every part, and formed of parallel fibres; and in order to ensure this, the drawing is repeated more than once, each narrow riband being 'doubled' with others before each successive drawing.

The slender ribands thus produced next pass through the 'roving-machine,' where they are brought to the state of *rovings*. In many respects the process of roving is similar to that of drawing, inasmuch as it draws out the cotton to a state of still greater attenuation; but as the cotton, in its now reduced thickness, has scarcely cohesive strength enough to make the fibres hold together, the roving has a slight twist given to it, by which it is converted into a loose kind of thread or spongy cord. A remarkable degree of ingenuity has been shown in the invention of machines to effect this double operation. In the 'can-roving frame,' contrived by Arkwright, ... the cardings, coming from two cans, A [and] A, and passing between ... pairs of rollers, ... become elongated, and fall into the can B, which by its rotation lays the roving in a coil, and at the same time twists it slightly. This was followed by the 'Jack-roving frame,' in which the revolving can contained a bobbin whereon the roving was wound as fast as made. Next succeeded the 'bobbin-and-fly frame,' which, from the time of Arkwright to the present day, has undergone a greater number of improvements than most other machines in the cotton manufacture. This consists of a system of vertical spindles, on each of which is placed a reel or bobbin, and also a kind of fork called a 'fly,' still farther removed than the bobbin from the axis of the spindle. The drawing or delicate sliver of cotton is first drawn through or between rollers, and elongated to the state of a roving; then this roving passes down a tube in one prong of the fork or fly, and becomes twisted by the revolution of the fly round the bobbin, while at the same time the twisted roving becomes wound with great regularity upon the bobbin. The machine in fact performs three different and distinct operations: it first attenuates the 'drawing' to a state of still greater thinness and delicacy than it had before; it then gives to the 'roving' thus produced a slight twist, sufficient to enable the fibres to cohere; and lastly, it winds this twisted roving upon a bobbin, on which it is conveniently transferred to the spinning-machine. There is a variety of the apparatus employed in this process called the 'tube-roving frame,' which produces a much larger quantity of roving in a given time than the 'bobbin-and-fly frame;' but the roving produced is inferior, and only fitted for certain purposes.

We then come to the *spinning* process, that which has given a name to the whole series, and to the factories in which the whole are conducted. Indeed when we consider that this is the process which finally presents the cotton in a state fit for the weaver, and that all the others are preparatory to it, we may reasonably deem it the most important in the manufacture. Hargreaves' spinning-jenny, Arkwright's spinning-frame, and Crompton's mule-machine were all constructed expressly for the process of spinning. If we bear in mind the true nature of the process of spinning, we shall see that all the beautiful machines which have been invented within the last hundred years for the spinning of cotton are merely different contrivances for effecting these two objects, viz., the elongating of the roving till it contain in thickness exactly as many fibres as are necessary to produce the required size of yarns, and the twisting of these fibres into a compact thread.

James Hargreaves, in 1764, made such a notable improvement in the spinning-wheel, that he could spin / many threads at once, instead of a single thread upon the old plan. It is said that on one occasion a spinning-wheel happening to be overturned, Hargreaves observed that both the wheel and the spindle continued to revolve for a considerable period; and he conceived the idea of moving several spindles at once with one wheel. He contrived a frame, in one part of which he placed eight rovings in a row, and in another part a row of eight spindles. The rovings, when extended to the spindles, passed between a clasp which opened and shut, and thus loosened or held them. A certain length of roving being extended from the spindles to the clasp, the clasp was closed, and was then drawn along to a considerable distance from the spindles, by which the threads were lengthened and attenuated. This was done with the spinner's left hand, while the right hand turned a wheel which caused the spindles to revolve rapidly, and thus the roving was spun into yarn. By a further adjustment the yarn was wound on the spindle.

This was one of the great and notable applications of mechanism to spinning, and Arkwright's spinning or 'water-twist' frame was another. The name 'water-twist' arose from the circumstance that, whereas Hargreaves' machine was worked by hand, Arkwright's was worked by a water-wheel; and hence the yarn or twist which he produced was called '*water*-twist.' The principle of this machine bears much more resemblance to the 'bobbin-and-fly' frame than to the 'spinning-jenny.' The roving or loose cord, after it leaves the bobbin on which it is wound, passes between rollers whose velocity of rotation is regulated so as to elongate the roving; and the thinner roving thus produced is then twisted into yarn or thread by the revolution of a fork or fly round the spindle on to which the thread is wound. The horizontal rotation of the bobbins, combined with the vertical rotation of the fly, gives the twist.

At a later period Crompton made a peculiar modification of the 'spinning-jenny' and the 'water-twist frame,' so as to produce a kind of a combination of both, which he called a 'mule-jenny' – one among the many odd appellations which have been given to the machines in the cotton manufacture. It was found that though Arkwright's machine could produce strong yarn for the warp or long threads of cloth, it could not produce fine and delicate yarns; and Crompton sought to contrive a machine which should obviate this defect. Like the 'water-frame,' the 'mule-jenny' has a system of rollers to reduce the roving; and like the 'spinning-jenny,' it has spindles without bobbins to give the twist, and the thread is stretched and spun at the same time by the spindles after the rollers have ceased to give out the roving. The spindles in the mule travel to and fro in a carriage, whereas in both the former machines the spindles were fixed in position. The elongation was performed first partially by rollers, on Arkwright's principle, and then finished by the stretching action of a moveable carriage on Hargreaves' principle, and it was found that a finer and more delicate yarn could thus be produced.

The details above given will render us better understood when we say that in modern cotton-factories the spinning-machines partake generally of the character either of Arkwright's or of Crompton's machines. The roller principle, modified in a manner which is represented by the *throstle*-machine, is that by which the strong and hard yarns are produced; while the moveable carriage of Hargreaves and Crompton, made automatic in the *self-acting mule* of Mr. Roberts,[16] is the arrangement adopted for spinning the finer yarns. Some factories are fitted up only for throstle-spinning; others for mule-spinning: and these two terms have now got into such general use, as to imply at once what kind of machines are used – whether those for the stronger or those for the finer work; whether those which work by rollers and the bobbin-and-fly, or those which work by the travelling carriage; whether those for which Arkwright is to have the greater honour, or those for which honour is due to Crompton. Some factories, again, have both throstles and mules; and such is the case in the establishment whose interior arrangement we have described. Two or three of the ranges are entirely fitted up with mule-frames, whose appearance is very remarkable. There is a carriage which draws out five or six feet, bringing with it a large number of threads or yarns, which are stretched by this action, and at the same time are twisted by the revolution of the spindles to which they are attached. In the common mules this carriage is moved by the left hand of the spinner, but in the self-acting mule it is moved by machinery.

The yarn, produced by these two classes of machines, is appropriated to various purposes according to its fineness, strength, hardness, smoothness, and other qualities. Some is employed as *warp* or long threads for coarse goods; some for *weft* or cross-threads; some for printing-calicoes; some for fine muslins; some for cotton hosiery; some for bobbin-net; some for sewing-cotton. The owner of the spinning-factory either works up the yarn into woven goods or sells it to others, according to the nature of the business which he carries on; or he may perhaps combine both methods, by spinning all the yarn for one particular kind of goods which he weaves in the same building, and also spinning other kinds of yarn which he sells to other persons.

At the factory under our notice there are the enormous number of *thirteen hundred* power-looms, all employed in making one kind of cotton goods, of which there is an astonishing quantity produced every week. Wherever the weaving process is carried on, there are always many intermediate steps to be pursued after the spinning is completed; such as 'dressing,' 'beaming,' 'winding,' 'warping,' &c. At this factory these processes are conducted in the upper floors of the building. The dressing is a process by which either melted size or flour-paste is applied to the yarn, as a means of rendering it smooth and stiff. We had occasion to speak of the action of the admirable modern 'dressing-machines,' while describing the operations of a Sail-Cloth Factory, some months back,[17] and may here therefore merely remark that the threads of yarn, spread out in a parallel layer, after dipping into a trough of paste, are brushed by two reciprocating brushes, by which the paste is laid smoothly over the surface, and are then dried by passing over steam-heated cylinders or boxes. It was estimated ten years ago that there were 80,000 power-looms in Great Britain; that each power-loom required three pounds of flour weekly for the dressing of the yarn which it wove; and hence that there were 44,562 loads of flour consumed annually for this purpose only, valued at nearly 100.000*l*. This is one of those minor circumstances which tend quite as much as those of more obvious importance to show the gigantic extent of this manufacture.

Besides the dressing, there are several curious machines employed to prepare the yarn for the loom; by arranging the threads in a parallel layer, winding them on the warp-beam or roller of the loom, passing them through the 'harness' or loops and strings of the loom, and so on. Many of these operations are nearly alike in all the textile manufactures, whether of cotton, wool, linen, or silk.

When we descend from the upper rooms of the factory to the ground-floor, where the weaving takes place, the appearance is certainly more astonishing than anything else presented in the factory. Thirteen hundred looms, each one a distinct and complete piece of / mechanism, are here arranged in parallel rows, over a space of ground measuring probably two hundred and fifty feet by one hundred and fifty; having passages between the rows. Each loom is between three and four feet high, and perhaps five or six wide; and they are all so placed that one female can attend to two looms. Every loom receives its moving-power from mechanism near the ceiling, where shafts and wheels present almost as complex an assemblage as the looms beneath them. These shafts are connected with the main-shafts of the two smaller steam-engines, so as to receive their moving-power from thence.

In order to understand how this immense room is lighted, we must state that only half of it is under or in the main building itself: the other half extends to a great distance in the rear, having no other rooms over. A series of arches, in the wall of the main building, open a communication between the two halves of the weaving-room, so that numerous passages lead from one to the other. In the hinder half the roof is intersected at regular distances with skylights, running from end to end, and placed at such an angle as will throw down the light conveniently upon the looms below. At regular intervals openings can be made in the roof, as a means of ventilation, according to the temperature below.

Six hundred and fifty females are here engaged in attending the looms, two to each, and these comprise almost the only occupants of the weaving-room. The noise created by thirteen hundred machines, each consisting of a great number of distinct moving parts, and each producing what would in an ordinary-sized shop be considered a pretty vigorous din, is so stunning and confounding, that a stranger finds it almost utterly impossible to hear a person speak to him, even close at his elbow, or even to hear himself speak: he walks along the avenues which separate the rows of looms, and arrives one after another at looms all exactly alike; he sees these clattering, hard-working machines on all sides of him, with the heads of the six hundred and fifty females just visible above them; and he may not unreasonably marvel that the persons, exposed to this incessant uproar for ten or twelve hours a day, can appear indifferent to it. Yet such is the case; habit smooths away the inconvenience, and the work people seem to think light of it.

In these power-looms steam-power may be said to do everything. It unwinds the warp from the warp-beam; it lifts and depresses the treadles, by which the warp-threads are placed in the proper positions for receiving the weft-threads; it throws the shuttle from side to side, carrying the weft-thread with it; it moves the batten or lay by which the weft-thread is driven up close; and finally, it winds the woven cotton on the cloth-beam which is to receive it. The female who has to manage a pair of looms has merely to attend to a few minor adjustments, which altogether about occupy her time; such as mending one of the threads which may have been broken, removing an empty shuttle and replacing it with a full one, removing an empty warp-beam, or a filled cloth-beam, and replacing them with others fitted for continuing the process.

When the cloth has left the loom, whatever be its quality, it has to undergo certain finishing processes. In some cases it is drawn between heated rollers, which impart to it a smoothness and gloss; in other cases, such as are instanced by velvets and fustians, a nap or pile is raised by a very remarkable series of operations; while other varieties require a yet different mode of procedure. /

William Murdock, 'An Account of the Application of the Gas from Coal to Œconomical Purposes' (1808)

William Murdock, *An Account of the Application of the GAS from Coal to Œconomical purposes, by Mr. WILLIAM MURDOCK, read before the Royal Society, on the 25th February, 1808, and printed in the Philosophical Transactions for that year.*[1]

The facts and results intended to be communicated in this paper, are founded upon observations made during the present winter at the Cotton Manufactory of Messrs. Philips and Lee[2] at Manchester, where the light obtained by the combustion of the Gas from Coal is used upon a very large scale; the Apparatus for its production and application having been prepared by me[3] at the Works of Messrs. Boulton, Watt, and Co. at Soho.

The whole of the rooms of this Cotton Mill which is I believe, the most extensive in the united Kingdom, as well as its counting houses and store rooms, and the adjacent dwelling house of Mr. Lee, are lighted with the Gas from Coal. The total quantity of light used during the hours of burning, has been assertained by a comparison of shadows,[4] to be about equal to the light which 2500 mould candles,[5] of six in the pound, would give; each of the candles with which the comparison was made, consuming at the rate of 1/16 of an ounce, (175 grs.)[6] of tallow per hour.

The quantity of light is necessarily liable to some variation, from the difficulty of adjusting all the flames so as to be perfectly equal at all times. But the admirable precision and exactness with which the business of this Mill is conducted, afforded as excellent an opportunity of making the comparative trials I had in view, as is perhaps likely to be ever obtained in general practice. And the experiments being made upon so large a scale, and for a considerable period of time, may I think be assumed as a sufficiently accurate standard for determining the advantages / to be expected from the use of the Gas-lights under favourable circumstances.

It is not my intention in the present paper, to enter into a particular description of the Apparatus employed for producing the Gas. But I may observe generally, that the Coal is distilled in large iron retorts, which during the winter season are kept constantly at work, except during the intervals of charging; and that the Gas as it rises from them, is conveyed by iron pipes into large Reservoirs, or Gazometers, where it is washed and purified, previous to its being conveyed through mains to the Mill. These mains branch off into a variety of ramifications, (forming a total length of several miles) and diminish in size, as the quantity of Gas required to be passed through them becomes less. The Burners, where the Gas is consumed, are connected with the above pipes, or mains, by short tubes, each of which is furnished with a cock to regulate the admission of the Gas to each burner, and to shut it totally off when requisite. This latter operation may likewise be instantaneously performed throughout the whole of the burners in each room, by turning a cock with which each main is provided near its entrance into the room.

The burners are of two kinds: The one is upon the principle of the Argand Lamp,[7] and resembles it in appearance; the other is a small curved tube with a conical end, having three circular apertures, or perforations, of about a 30th of an inch in diameter, one at the point of the cone and two lateral ones, through which the Gas issues, forming three divergent jets of flame, somewhat like a fleur de lis. The shape and general appearance of this tube, has procured it among the workmen the name of the Cockspur burner.

The number of burners employed in all the buildings amounts to 271 argands and 633 cockspurs; each of the former giving a light equal to that of 4 candles of the description above mentioned; and each of the latter, a light / equal to 2¼ of the same candles; making therefore the total of the Gas light a little more than equal to that of 2500 candles.

When thus regulated, the whole of the above burners require an *hourly* supply of 1250 cubic feet of the Gas produced from Cannel Coal:[8] the superior quality and quantity of the Gas produced from that material, having given it a decided preference in this situation, over every other coal, notwithstanding its higher price.

The time during which the Gas light is used, may upon an average of the whole year, be stated at least at 2 hours per day of 24 hours. In some Mills where there is over work, it will be 3 hours; and in the few where night work is still continued, nearly 12 hours.

But taking 2 hours per day as the common average throughout the year, the consumption in Messrs. Philips and Lee's Mill will be 1250 x 2 = 2500 cubic feet of Gas per day; to produce which, 7 cwt. of cannel coal is required in the retort. The price of the best Wigan cannel, (the sort used) is 13½d per cwt. delivered at the Mill, or say about 8s for the 7 cwt. Multiplying by the number of working days in the year, (313) the annual consumption of cannel will be 110 tons, and its cost 125l.

About one third of the above quantity, or say 40 tons of good common coal: value 10s per ton, is required for fuel to heat the retorts; the annual amount of which is 20l.

The 110 tons of cannel coal when distilled, produce about 70 tons of good coke, which is sold upon the spot as 1s 4d per cwt. and will therefore amount annually to the sum of 93l.

The quantity of tar produced from each ton of cannel coal is from 11 to 12 ale gallons,[9] making a total annual produce of about 1250 ale gallons, which not having been yet sold, I cannot determine its value, but whenever it comes to be manufactured in large quantities, it cannot be / such as materially to influence the œconomical statement, unless indeed new applications of it should be discovered.

The quantity of aqueous fluid which came over in the course of the observations which I am now giving an account of, was not exactly ascertained, from some springs having got into the Reservoir; and as it has not been yet applied to any beneficial purpose, I may omit further notice of it in this statement.

The interest of the capital expended in the necessary apparatus and buildings, together with what is considered as an ample allowance for wear and tear, is stated by Mr. Lee at about 550l per annum: in which, some allowance is made for this apparatus being constructed upon a scale adequate to the supply of a still greater quantity of light than he has occasion to make use of.

He is of opinion, that the cost of attendance upon candles would be as much, if not more, than upon the Gas apparatus; so that in forming the comparison, nothing need be stated upon that score, on either side.

The œconomical statement for one year then stands thus,

Cost of 110 tons of cannel coal	125l.
Do. of 40 tons of common ditto	20l.
	145l.
Deduct value of 70 tons Coke	93l.
The annual expenditure in coal after deducting the value of the coke, and without allowing any thing for the tar, is therefore	52l.
And the interest of capital and wear and tear of apparatus	550l.

Making the total expence of the Gas apparatus about 600l. per annum.

That of candles to give the same light, would be about 2000l. For, each candle consuming at the rate of 1/16 of an ounce of tallow per hour, the 2500 candles burning upon an average of the year 2 hours per day, would at 1s. / per lb. the present price, amount to nearly the sum of money above mentioned.

If the comparison were made upon an average of *three* hours per day, the advantage would be still more in favour of the Gas-light; the interest of the capital and wear and tear of the apparatus containing nearly the same as in the former case. Thus 1250 x 3 = 3750 cubic feet of Gas per day, which would be produced by 10¾ cwt. of cannel; this multiplied by the number of working days, gives

168 tons per annum which valued as above, amounts to - -	188l.
And 60 tons common coal for burning under the retorts, will amount to	30l.
	218
Deduct 105 tons of coke at 26s 8d	140l.
Leaving the expenditure in coal after deduction of the coke, and without allowance for the tar, at	78l.

Adding to which, the interest and wear and tear of apparatus as before, the total annual cost will not be more than 650; whilst that of tallow, rated as before, will be 3000l.

It will readily occur, that the greater number of hours the Gas is burnt, the greater will be its comparative œconomy; although in extending it beyond three hours, an increase of some parts of the apparatus would be necessary.

If the œconomical comparison were made with oils, the advantages would be less than with tallow.

The introduction of this species of light into the establishment of Messrs. Philips and Lee, has been gradual; beginning, in the year 1805, with two rooms of the Mill, the counting houses and Mr. Lee's dwelling house. After which, it was extended through the whole manufactory as expeditiously as the apparatus could be prepared.

At first, some inconvenience was experienced from the smell of the unconsumed, or imperfectly purified Gas, which may, in great measure, be attributed to the introduction / of successive improvements in the construction of the apparatus, as the work proceeded. But since its completion, and since the persons to whose care it is confided, have become familiar with its management, this inconvenience has been obviated, not only in the Mill, but also in Mr. Lee's house, which is most brilliantly illuminated with it, to the exclusion of every other species of artificial light.

The peculiar softness and clearness of this light, with its almost unvarying intensity, have brought it into great favor with the work-people. And its being free from the inconvenience and danger resulting from the sparks and frequent snuffing of candles, is a circumstance of material importance, as tending to diminish the hazard of fire, to which Cotton Mills are known to be much exposed.

The above particulars, it is conceived, contain such information, as may tend to illustrate the general advantages attending the use of Gas-light; but nevertheless the Royal Society may perhaps not deem it uninteresting to be apprized of the circumstances which originally gave rise in my mind to its application as an œconomical substitute for Oils and Tallow.

It is now nearly sixteen years, since in the course of experiments I was making at Redruth, in Cornwall, upon the quantities and qualities of the Gas produced by distillation from different mineral and vegetable substances, I was induced by some observations I had previously made upon the burning of Coal, to try the combustible property of the Gases produced from it, as well as from Peat, Wood and other inflammable substances, and being struck with the great quantities of Gas which they afforded, as well as the brilliancy of the light, and the facility of its production, I instituted several experiments with a view of ascertaining the cost at which it might be obtained, compared with that of equal quantities of light, yielded by Oils and Tallow. /

My apparatus consisted of an iron retort, with tinned, iron and copper tubes, through which the Gas was conducted to a considerable distance: and there, as well as at intermediate points, was burnt through apertures of varied forms and dimensions. The experiments were made upon Coal of different qualities, which I procured from distant parts of the Kingdom, for the purpose of ascertaining which would give the most œconomical results. The Gas was also washed with water and other means were employed to purify it.

In the year 1798, I removed from Cornwall to Messrs. Boulton, Watt, and Co's. works for the manufactory of Steam Engines at the Soho Foundry, and there I constructed an apparatus upon a larger scale, which during many successive nights was applied to the lighting of their principal building, and various new methods were practised of washing and purifying the Gas.

The experiments were continued with some interruptions, until the peace of 1802,[10] when a public display of this light was made by me in the illumination of Mr. Boulton's manufactory at Soho, upon that occasion.

Since that period, I have, under the sanction of Messrs. Boulton, Watt, and Co. extended the apparatus at Soho Foundry, so as to give light to all the principal shops, where it is in regular use, to the exclusion of other artifical light. But I have preferred giving the results from Messrs. Philips and Lee's apparatus, both on account of its greater extent, and the greater uniformity of the lights, which rendered the comparison with candles less difficult.

At the time I commenced my experiments, I was entirely unacquainted with the circumstance of the Gas from Coal having been observed by others to be capable of combustion. But I am since informed, that the current of Gas escaping from Lord Dundonald's[11] Tar Ovens has been frequently fired; and I find that Dr. Clayton in a paper[12] in the 41st vol. of the Transactions of the Royal / Society, so long ago as the year 1739, gave an account of some observations and experiments made by him, which clearly manifest his knowledge of the inflammable property of the Gas, which he denominates 'the Spirit of Coals.' But the idea of applying it as an œconomical substitute for Oils and Tallow, does not appear to have occurred to this Gentleman, and I believe I may, without presuming too much, claim both the first idea of applying, and the first actual application of this Gas to œconomical purposes.

FINIS.

Stevenson Macadam, *The Sanitary Aspects of Cooking and Heating by Coal Gas* (1892)

Stevenson Macadam,[1] *The Sanitary Aspects of Cooking and Heating by Coal Gas* (London: Walter King for the Research and Investigation Committee of the North British Association of Gas Managers, 1892).

/

ON THE SANITARY ASPECTS OF COOKING AND HEATING BY COAL GAS.

The subject of the employment of coal gas in the cooking of food and for the heating of houses is one of great importance, and much has already been done to determine the power of gas to do the work. Specially in the Jury Report of the Exhibition[2] held by the Philosophical Society of Glasgow in 1880, two elaborate and instructive reports are given, one of which is on cooking by gas, and the other on heating by gas. The sanitary aspects of the question, however, have not received so much attention as they deserve; and, indeed, beyond a few skirmishes for and against flues, and bearing upon atmospheric pollution, little has been said. But whilst the sanitary aspects of heating by gas may be practically confined to the atmosphere, yet, in regard to cooking by gas, more detailed inquiry requires to be made as to the nature of the gaseous products evolved during the combustion of the coal gas, the effect of such on the meat undergoing the process of cooking, the wholesomeness of the cooked meat in retaining all its proper juices and elements, and in evolving all the vapours of a noxious nature produced during the cooking, as well as in the meat not absorbing noxious or deleterious elements, and in the keeping power and digestibility of the cooked material.

In approaching this subject, I resolved at the outset to devote special attention to proper cooking heats and their attainment in various stoves and to study the nature of the spent gases and the means provided for their escape. In order not to go over ground already well trodden, I took the Glasgow trials as the starting-point and resolved to experiment mainly with the three cooking-stoves which the Jury had placed first in the Glasgow Exhibition, and which had obtained certificates of merit, being the highest awards. These were Waddell and Main's (Glasgow) 'Universal Domestic', Wilson's (Leeds) 'Eclipse' Gas Kitchener,[3] and Wright's (Birmingham) Gas Cooker No. 492. On application to these firms, they at once agreed to place at my disposal stoves of the same size and pattern as those used in Glasgow, in order to enable me to experiment upon them in any way I might consider desirable. Many trials were made with these stoves, alike as to the necessary consumption of gas, the cooking temperature obtained in the ovens, and the nature of the spent gases. The results obtained may be summarized as follows:– /

Waddell and Main's 'Universal Domestic,' No. 3. – This stove stands 31 inches in height, has a top cooking space of 18¼ in. by 17 in., and an oven space of 18 in. by 14 in. and 14 in., being fully 2 cubic feet. The oven is lined with fire-brick both on the sides and the top; there are three boiling-rings on the top, and there is also a reflecting-ring within the top of the oven. Perforated fire-clay slabs are placed between the meat and pastry or bread. The fire-brick lining of the oven serves as an excellent non-conductor, and retains the heat within the oven. The interior of the oven is heated by a series of burners with small side jets which consume the gas with a white flame, as in ordinary house combustion; whilst the rings on the top of the stove are on the Bunsen principle,[4] and burn the gas with a blue non-luminous flame. Two of these upper / rings are used for heating pots or kettles; whilst the third is intended for grilling by deflection when covered with a plate, or for ordinary boiling purposes when the deflector is removed.

When using the oven alone, I found, with a consumption of gas ranging between 11.50 to 11.70 cubic feet per hour, that a cooking temperature of 340° Fahr.[5] was reached in 10 to 15 minutes; and that, keeping up the same quantity of gas, the temperature of 400° was obtained in an hour, which thereafter increased to nearly 500°.[6] As a temperature of 310° to 340° Fahr. is amply sufficient for the cooking of meat, such as joints, I made other trials which showed that after the oven had been heated to 340° Fahr. it could be retained at that temperature by an expenditure of 5.7 cubic feet of gas per hour. It therefore follows that, commencing to heat up the oven to roasting-point by using 12 cubic feet of gas per hour, you may in about 15 minutes reduce the consumption of gas to 6 cubic feet per hour, and still retain the proper heat for cooking a joint of meat. As the meat is well done in two hours, it follows that with a consumption of 14 cubic feet of gas the cooking of the joint may be accomplished. Moreover, pastry or a meat pie may be cooked at the same time within the same oven, and with no further expenditure of gas, except from the use of the browning ring within the top of the oven for 15 to 20 minutes at the close, so that a supply of gas decidedly under 20 cubic feet will amply suffice for the full cooking of joint and pastry, or joint and meat pie, or the whole contents of the oven. There remains the top cooking, where the vegetables – including soups, potatoes, &c. – are boiled. The upper rings consume about 12 cubic feet per hour; and 20 cubic feet in all would more than amply suffice for all possible contingencies, including even reasonable waste. It would thus appear that 40 cubic of gas would cover the cooking of a full dinner in an ordinary middle-class household;[7] and taking the price of the gas as 4s. 2d. per 1000 cubic feet, we have 2d. as the cost of the fuel required from first to last in the operation – being 1d. worth of gas for the two hours' work of the oven, and 1d. worth of gas for the boiling processes on the top of the oven. /

The proportions of gas and cost given for these three first-class gas cooking-stoves have been reckoned on the assumption that roasts were required to be cooked every day; but if a less pretentious dinner be only prepared on alternate days, dispensing probably with much of the oven or top cooking appliances, the quantity of gas consumed and cost of fuel would necessarily be less, and in the majority of middle-class houses it would probably be found that, for stewing, grilling, and boiling operations on these alternate days, about 20 cubic feet, or 1d. worth of gas, would suffice for the preparation of the dinner. So that for the sum of 3d. the dinner for two days would be cooked. In the preparation of breakfast, the employment of the upper rings for the making of porridge, boiling of the kettle, cooking of fish, ham, or a chop, the making of toast, the boiling of eggs, &c., would certainly not consume more than 10 cubic feet of gas in any of the three stoves already referred to; so that, for an expenditure / of ½d. in gas, a substantial family breakfast would be laid upon the table. A similar sum would amply cover the whole expenditure in gas fuel for all the heating operations required for tea and supper.

The foregoing experimental results have reference to stoves sufficiently large for the daily wants of middle-class families; but, where less cooking is required, smaller-sized stoves may be used. The various 'little cookers' and 'bachelor' stoves will suffice to do all the cooking for a plain breakfast, dinner, or tea, at an expenditure in gas of 6 to 10 cubic feet per hour, or about 1d. per day. When consuming 6 cubic feet per hour, these little stoves in 10 minutes get up a temperature in the brander[8] of from 330° to 430° Fahr., according as the brander is placed farther from or nearer to the gas-jets.

The above remarks apply to the use of the gas-stoves at temperatures within the proper range for cooking purposes. By increasing the consumption of gas in the larger stoves, it is easy to obtain a heat which goes up to 500° and even to 600° Fahr.; but such high temperatures are no more desirable in gas heating-stoves than in ordinary coal heating-ranges. /

The sanitary aspects of cooking by gas must depend greatly upon the nature of the gases and vapours produced during the combustion of the coal gas, and which impinge upon the meat. These gases or vapours are mainly carbonic acid, water vapour, and sulphurous acid, accompanied, when the gas is improperly burned, by traces of carbonic oxide, acetylene, and other oily hydrocarbons.[9] The carbonic acid is formed in large quantities, ranging from 80 to 90 per cent. of the volume of the gas consumed. In special experiments on the Edinburgh gas, I found that 100 volumes of the coal gas yielded from 85 to 90 volumes of carbonic acid; so that in round numbers we may regard the gas as evolving during combustion about its own volume of carbonic acid. Taking the specific gravity of the coal gas as 500, and that of carbonic acid as 1529 (air = 1000), a cubic foot of the coal gas will weigh 268 grains, whilst the cubic foot of carbonic acid will weigh 821 grains.[10] This amount of carbonic acid can also be obtained by the combustion of 224 grains of carbon, of 298 grains of coal, from 1½ hours' consumption of a tallow candle, and from a small house-jet of coal gas. The water vapour is also produced in large quantity during the combustion of the coal gas, and special experiments on the Edinburgh gas showed that one cubic foot of the gas yielded from 1.4 to 1.5 cubic feet of vapour. The sulphurous acid gas is always formed during the burning of the coal gas, but the quantity is small. In 100 cubic feet of gas, we may take 10 grains of sulphur as an average proportion; so that 1 cubic foot of gas will contain 0.1 grain of sulphur. During combustion the sulphur burns into double its weight of sulphurous acid gas, so that the cubic foot of coal gas weighing 268 grains will yield 0.2 grain of sulphurous acid gas, or 1-1340th of the weight of the coal gas. The proportion of sulphur in ordinary coal may be reckoned as 0.5 in 100 parts, or 1-200th of the weight of the coal, yielding during burning 1.0 of sulphurous acid, or 1-100th of the weight of the coal, being fully thirteen times the quantity of sulphurous acid gas evolved during the combustion of coal as compared with coal gas, weight for weight.

The other products of combustion of coal gas, such as carbonic oxide, acetylene, and other oily hydrocarbons, are only formed during the imperfect combustion of the gas, as when burners do not properly fit their sockets, or the lights strike back and burn more or less smoky. In none of my trials with the gas cooking-stoves, where the gas was properly attended to, were any of these products observable in the spent gases. Undoubtedly, were the gas consumed imperfectly, acetylene would specially be produced, and would tend to taint the meat; but such can as readily be avoided, with reasonable care, as the smoking of food from an imperfectly lighted coal fire in an ordinary coal cooking-range.

In any stove and with any system of burners the ventilation of the stove must be kept up, so as to ensure that the products of combustion and the gases and vapours evolved from the meat during the cooking are carried away. A deficiency of ventilation may lead to the imperfect combustion of the gas, and even to the partial extinguishment of the lights and the tainting of the meat; but, at the same time, there must not be too much ventilation, for such would conduce to the lowering of the temperature in the oven, and to the drying up of the meat during the progress of the cooking. / The three stoves specially experimented upon by me were fully equipped with ventilating pipes.

The cooking of meat in the gas-stoves yields a large return of cooked meat than in the ordinary coal-ranges. The loss in ordinary cooking with an open fire or in a coal-fire oven – under the best circumstances of having water in the pan underneath, and repeated basting of the joint or *gigot* – is about 40 per cent.; while in meat cooked in gas-stoves the loss is only about 25 per cent. To a large extent the difference of 15 per cent. is due to the meat being constantly surrounded by an aqueous vapour or watery atmosphere derived in great part from the water produced during the combustion of the gas itself; there being about 1½ cubic feet of water vapour formed during the burning of every cubic foot of gas. The influence upon the meat of this atmosphere saturated with moisture, will be not only to keep the meat more moist, but to hinder the escape and evaporation of the juices of the meat, and to retain the osmazome[11] or flavouring matter, so that the meat, when properly done, will be found to be more juicy and more palatable, and yet free from those alkaloidal bodies produced during the confined cooking of meat, and which are more or less hurtful and even poisonous. As the gas-cooked meat is more juicy, it will be more easily digested; but it will be less liable to keep, owing to its being more moist and juicy. Dry meat undoubtedly keeps longer than moist and juicy meat, and if the dryness is carried out till little moisture is left and the meat is hardened, the material can be kept for months without tending to give way, but such dried and hardened meat is more difficult of digestion. The more juicy and tasty gas-cooked meat is a step in the right direction; for we cook to eat, and we eat to digest, so as to impart ready and immediate strength to the animal frame.

The best cooking-stove is one which an ordinary domestic can least fail to keep in order, and where the gas-jets are least likely to go wrong and lead to the imperfect combustion of the gas. In ordinary cooking, the Bunsen jets are more liable to strike back and burn imperfectly, leading to the formation of acetylene and other oily hydrocarbon compounds; whilst the common lighting jets, in their various forms, are least liable to get out of order. Moreover, the Bunsen arrangements are more difficult to light; there being a tendency for explosions to take place, and the lights to be blown out, and when once the Bunsen jets get clogged up with grease they are also more difficult to clean out.

A good gas cooking-stove should be easily heated, easily regulated, and easily worked. All of these conditions were practically obtained in the three stoves under special trial; but I am bound to say that they are more thoroughly obtained in Waddell and Main's stove than in the others, on the following grounds:—(1) That the fire-clay lining, being an excellent non-conductor, retains the heat within the stove without exposing iron to rust. (2) That the jets of gas may be turned down to the smallest lights without striking back or burning imperfectly. (3) That the stove door may be opened and shut without risk of extinguishing the lights or rapidly cooling down the stove.

In the use of a gas cooking-stove the ventilating flue from the stove should be carried into an ordinary chimney, and it will be better that the whole stove should be placed within an ordinary / fireplace, so that the gases produced during the combustion of the upper gas-jets may be carried out of the room. In my opinion the best arrangement would be to place the gas-stove within the ordinary open fireplace without any special building or damper fittings, and to carry the flue from the gas-stove oven only about 3 feet high in the open chimney. The result will be that the short flue will ventilate the oven into the chimney, and at the same time cause a draught which will facilitate the gases from the upper cooking-rings being also carried up the chimney.

A word about the sanitary aspect of heating-stoves. These should never be placed in any room or part of a house without being connected with flues to carry away the spent gases. The statement that no noxious gases are evolved because no smell is observable is quite erroneous. No doubt the gases given off from a heating-stove are the same as those yielded by an ordinary gas-jet in a room, and the inference is sometimes drawn that the heating-stove is no more hurtful than the lighting-jet; but the gas-stove and the gas-bracket are not placed under the same circumstances. When the light-bracket is burning during the long sittings of the winter months, our fires are keeping the rooms well ventilated; and though the common fires may be off during the summer, yet that is the period when our light-bracket is burning during only a few hours, and window ventilation is indulged in. Even when gaslight is kept burning all night in sick-rooms, it is generally lowered, and the ventilation is often aided by a fire in the room. The use of the gas-stove in any room, without proper ventilation, is dangerous, and the spent stove gases should invariably be carried into a chimney. No doubt the stove might be placed in the room without any connection with the chimney, and the room itself be ventilated; but this constant renewal of the air would be a wasteful expenditure of heat, and it would be much more economical to use the connection with the chimney vent. The constant heating of an apartment by a gas-stove would be rather expensive as compared with coal; but where, as in an evening, for an hour or two, it is desired to have a room heated in a ready and serviceable manner, the gas will beat the coal, alike for facility of doing duty and for strict economy.

The wholesomeness of the meat cooked in the gas-stoves must be regarded as beyond doubt. The mere impinging of the spent gases produced during the combustion of the coal gas upon the meat, in the process of cooking, cannot lead to the impregnation of the meat with any noxious matter. These spent gases and vapours are simply carbonic acid and water vapour, with minute proportions of sulphurous acid, and are the same as those evolved from a common coal fire used for grilling a chop or steak, and such have never been challenged as being unhealthy because the spent gases from the coal fire impinged upon them. Indeed, from the quantity of coal consumed in an ordinary coal cooking fire, the proportions or carbonic acid and sulphurous acid evolved therefrom must be many times greater than the amounts yielded by the gas cooking range; and hence the coal-cooked grilled meat should be more influenced by the spent gases than the gas-cooked meat. Moreover, during the process of cooking, the meat is always exuding vapour from itself, and hence is not liable to absorb other vapours which may surround it; so that, independently of the relatively inert / nature of the spent gases, the meat is prevented from absorbing such, were they even noxious. As the best practical proof of the wholesome nature of the meat cooked by gas, and of the absolute want of taint about such, I may further state that for several years I have been officially connected with a large establishment where all the principal joints and dishes, including pastry, are cooked in a gas-range, and I have invariably found the meat, &c., to be thoroughly well done, to be exceedingly good to the taste, and decidedly wholesome. In fact, no better cooked meat and pastry could be prepared, and be more palatable and acceptable.

For cooking purposes, I am confident that gas is not only serviceable but is also economical, besides being cleanly and handy. The attention required by an ordinary coal-range is mainly occupied in the firing or heating operations, and not in the actual cooking process. Either the fire must be kept in night and day for service at only limited periods, or, if allowed to go out, preliminary processes of lighting up with paper and sticks and coal must be gone through for some time before the fire-range is available for service. On the other hand, the gas-stove and cooker is ever ready for work, and the mere turning of a cock and lighting of the gas at once places the gas-range in serviceable order for cooking purposes. Moreover, the coal fire or range is difficult to regulate – at times too hot, at times too cold – but the gas fire or range can, in a moment, be raised or lowered in heating power by the mere opening or closing of the stopcock; and, still further, the coal-range becomes clogged with ash *débris*, which must be removed now and again, leading to much dust and annoyance, while in the gas-range there are no residual products or ashes to remove.

Independently of the more cleanly and handy nature of gas heating-stoves over coal heating-ranges, there is the practical question of the relative cost of fuel. I have already given the detailed statements based upon experimental data, proving that any of our best gas-ranges may be thoroughly worked for all the necessary cooking connected with an ordinary middle-class family at an expense in gas not exceeding 4d. per day, and where more moderate roasting operations are carried on, on alternate days, for about 3d. a day. Taking the larger of these figures as representing use and probable waste, we have to contrast such with the cost of coal. Now I have determined, in two coal cooking-ranges connected with moderate-sized middle-class houses, that the amount of coal used in ordinary working, including actual cooking and keeping the fire in during the intervals, runs from ½ cwt. to 1 cwt. per day; and taking the average price of coal as laid down in house cellars as 16s. per ton, the cost of the coal used in the coal cooking-ranges would be from 8d. to 16d. per day, or an average of 1s. per day. Taking even the lower figure of 8d. per day, which is rather within the mark, we find that the cost of the fuel for a serviceable coal cooking-range is twice that of a gas cooking-range. Of course, the coal-range is always more or less on duty, whether required or not; whilst the gas-range is only on duty when absolutely required, but is always ready for work at a moment's notice. I admit that the coal-range also heats the kitchen, and probably also heats water in a boiler at the same time, and some allowance must be made for these extras, in the way, either of having a supplemental heating fire in winter or employing extra / gas for such purposes; as, indeed, has been done in some gas-stoves. But, taking everything into consideration, I am of opinion that gas cooking will beat coal cooking in cost of material, as well as in facilities of doing work; in cleanliness; and in efficiency.

Another and very important element in the question of economy is the respective yield of cooked meat from the coal and gas ranges, which in the case of the coal range is 60 per cent. of the raw material and of the gas-range 75 per cent.; which practically means this – that a joint or *gigot* weighing 10 lbs. as purchased from the butcher will come out of the coal-range in a cooked condition weighing 6 lbs., and out of the gas-range weighing 7½ lbs., being a difference of 1½ lbs. in favour of the gas-range. Now, granting that a part of this difference or saving is due to the retention of more water vapour in the meat, there can be no doubt that in the other part it is due to the meat juices being more thoroughly kept in the gas-cooked meat. The practical dietetic result is that the latter cuts out better and goes farther, in the proportion of 25 per cent. more, than the coal-cooked meat. Taking this excess of cooked meat alone into consideration, the saving is far more than ample to cover the whole cost of gas fuel, allowance for cost of stove, and even attendance thereon.

In smaller houses, where the little cooker and bachelor stove is sufficient, especially in summer, when no heating fire is required, the economy in using the gas-stoves must be very great. For an expenditure of 1d. in gas, the whole cooking can be accomplished for the day with comparatively no trouble in lighting the fire, carrying coals, and removing ashes. When required, the gas can be instantly lighted, and the stove is practically in use in a minute. When the cooking is done, the gas is turned off, and the expense instantly stopped. If the kettle requires to be kept hot, the water may simmer away for hours with a minute jet of gas, and the temperature be instantly raised when boiling water is wanted – no preliminary expenditure in sticks or lighters, and no delay or time wasted. Moreover, no smoky chimneys, no soot falling into pots, no cleaning up of fire-places, and no ash-dust diffused throughout the room. Sooty hands, blackened faces, and tarnished dresses reduced to a minimum.

Finally, my experiments on the gas-stoves have thoroughly satisfied me that Scotch gas or cannel gas,[12] as now supplied in Scotland, can be used with efficiency in the heating of gas-ranges, and that there is no necessity to reduce the quality of lighting gas to suit any supposed standard for heating gas. Economy, however, may necessitate that as coals of high-class quality fail or get scarce, we may require to use coals of lower-class quality; and if such be advisable for lighting purposes, then no harm will ensue for heating operations. The primary use of gas is for lighting, and I have every confidence that cooking will adapt itself to the lighting necessity of the time. /

‘Electricity and the Electric Telegraph’, *Cornhill Magazine* (1860)

‘Electricity and the Electric Telegraph’, *Cornhill Magazine*, 2:7 (July 1860), pp. 61–73.

Before entering on the question of the application of electricity to telegraphy, a brief recapitulation of the great physical facts on which every attempt of the kind has been based will render the subject more intelligible to the uninitiated. Frictional, or, as it is commonly termed, *statical* electricity, evolved by rubbing glass or kindred substances, is possessed of the property of attracting light substances, such as shreds of paper or pith balls. It also emits sparks, either in the process of evolution, or in its accumulated state, as in the discharge of Leyden jars.[1] Voltaic electricity, evolved by chemical change, chemical combination, and the contact of two dissimilar metals, causes a magnetic needle to deviate from its natural position; it confers magnetism on soft iron; and it also possesses the power of decomposing numerous chemical combinations in solution. Magneto-electricity, evolved by the approximation[2] of a bar of magnetized steel to a coil of wire, followed by its sudden withdrawal, produces effects precisely similar to those of voltaic electricity.

The question of the invention of the electric telegraph has long been a sorely vexed one. The honour has been claimed for America, for England, and for nearly every country on the continent. The scientific world is doubtless divided in its opinions as to the practicability of those early inventions which were worked by means of frictional electricity. But a series of experiments instituted in 1816, showed that the obstacles which had so frequently baffled preceding inventors, were partly of a pecuniary nature, and were not therefore absolutely insurmountable. The question, thus extricated from a labyrinth of prejudice, of conflicting claims, and of still more conflicting opinions, might therefore assume somewhat of the following historical development. One hundred and seven years ago, there appeared in the *Scots' Magazine* a remarkable letter dated from Renfrew, and headed, 'An Expeditious Method for Conveying Intelligence.'[3] Premising that electricity is transmissible through a short wire without any apparent diminution of intensity, the writer shows how, in his opinion, it may be turned to practical account. Extend wires, equal in number to the letters of the alphabet, between two distant places; support them at intervals on glass fixed to solid bodies; let each wire terminate in a ball; place beneath each ball, a shred of paper on which the corresponding letter of the alphabet has been printed. Bring the further end of the first wire into contact with an excited glass tube,[4] and the paper 'A' will instantly rise / to the first ball, in virtue of the principle of attraction. Thus the whole alphabet may be represented. A series of electrical bells, decreasing in tone from 'A' to 'Z,' may be employed instead of the paper. Possible objections are anticipated and met, by showing how the wires may be insulated throughout.

Such was the first electric telegraph invented in 1753; an instrument theoretically accurate in every detail, although rendered impracticable for any considerable distance by its cumbrous arrangement of wires. But the genius which was capable of contriving, was, no doubt, equal to the task of improving. Little is known of the inventor, beyond the fact that an elderly Scotch lady remembered a 'very clever man' of obscure position, named Charles Marshall, who could make 'lichtnin'[5] write an' speak;' and who could 'licht a room wi' coal-reek' (*Anglice*[6] – coal-smoke). However humble the sphere in which he moved, Marshall was clearly a man of no ordinary intellect. Mark the significance of his words, – '*An Expeditious Method for Conveying Intelligence!*' At a time when the very alphabet of the science was unformed, he saw what had not only escaped the acute intellect of Franklin, but what had evidently never been dreamt of by men who inherited the thrones of Newton, of Halley, and of Boyle. In describing the intellectual aspects of that half-century, which not only saw Reid and Smith, Hume and Robertson,[7] in the zenith of their fame, but gave birth to Burns, to Scott, and to Carlyle, some future Macaulay may adorn his 'pictured page' by stories of humble Scotchmen, who gave to civilization the steam-engine, the steam-ship, the electric telegraph, and the gas with which we light our houses and our streets.

In the year 1774, Le Sage, a Frenchman, resident in Geneva,[8] who has been hitherto recognized by many as the originator of electric communication, submitted a plan to Frederick of Prussia, which differed so slightly from that which we have just described, that an account of it might seem a *rifacimento9* of the letter of Charles Marshall. The next we read of, that of M. Lomond, appeared in 1787, and consisted of only one wire; the signals being indicated by the attraction and repulsion of pith balls. Arthur Young – who explains the *modus operandi* in his *Travels* – describes the inventor as a 'very ingenious and inventive mechanic.' 'As the length of the wire makes no difference in the effect,' says the clever and vivacious advocate of *la grande culture, 'a correspondence might be carried on at any distance*.'[10] Other projects followed, in some of which the active principle was that of the discharge of Leyden jars; the first suggestion of which was made so early as 1767, by a professor of natural philosophy in Rome, named Bozolus, and not by Cavallo,[11] as has been hitherto supposed. Each and all of those attempts may, however, be justly regarded as experiments, as it was not until 1816 that their practicability for a distance of eight or ten miles was satisfactorily demonstrated by Mr. Ronalds, of Hammersmith;[12] who, by the provision of perfect insulation, overcame, to some extent, the difficulties which had so frequently baffled his predecessors. About that period, however, the superiority of / Voltaic electricity over that of friction for such purposes became apparent. The former is regular, controllable, and easily held in its legitimate channel, whilst the latter is unsteady, and remarkable for its high tension, escaping easily from its conductors.

During the succeeding twenty years several inventions appeared, some of which were failures, whilst others were more or less successful on a limited scale. Still, grave doubts existed, even in the minds of some distinguished philosophers, as to the practicability of such schemes for great distances, until Professor Wheatstone[13] asserted, in 1834, that the velocity of electricity exceeded 280,000 miles in a second. Three years later, he, in conjunction with Mr. Cooke, patented an invention which, in one sense, deserves to be recognized in the same light as the first steam-engine of Watt; and which, after having undergone numerous improvements, ultimately assumed the form of that 'double-needle' instrument so common in this country. On the night of the 25th of June, 1837, this famous invention was subjected to trial in the presence of several distinguished men; – prominent among whom was the late Robert Stephenson. Wires stretching from Euston Square to Camden Town were connected with the instruments. At the one end stood the able and energetic Mr. Cooke, at the other his coadjutor, Professor Wheatstone. The experiment was successful. 'Never,' says one of the inventors, 'never did I feel such a tumultuous sensation before, as, when all alone in the still room, I heard the needles click; and as I spelled the words, I felt all the magnitude of the invention, now proved to be practicable beyond cavil or dispute.'[14]

Another instrument, most extensively employed, is the recording one, invented in the autumn of 1837, by Professor Morse.[15] In a letter addressed to the Secretary of the Treasury of the United States, written in September of that year, the inventor says:– 'About five years ago, on my voyage home from Europe, the electric experiment of Franklin upon a wire some four miles in length was casually recalled to my mind in a conversation with one of the passengers, in which experiment it was ascertained that the electricity travelled through the whole circuit in a time apparently instantaneous. It immediately occurred to me, that if the presence of electricity could be made visible in any part of this circuit, it would not be difficult to construct a system of signs, by which intelligence could be instantaneously transmitted. From the pressure of unavoidable duties, I was compelled to postpone my experiments, and was not able to test the whole plan, until within a few weeks. The result has realized my most sanguine expectations.'

In the following year Mr. Edward Davy[16] patented an electro-chemical recording instrument, which formed the basis of the 'printing' one of Bain, an obscure clockmaker from Watten in the 'far north,'[17] whose ingenuity gave a powerful impetus to the art of telegraphy in the earlier stages of its progress.

As the 'needle' instrument of Cooke and Wheatstone, the electromagnetic one of Morse, and the electro-chemical one of Bain, form the / grand types of the telegraphic system, and are more extensively used than any other, we shall proceed to explain the relation of their component parts – the battery, the instrument, and the conductor, – with their respective modes of operation.

A battery, in its simplest and most intelligible form, consists of three elements, namely, – two plates of dissimilar metals, such as zinc and copper, and a solution of sulphuric acid and water. The moment the plates are metallically united, electricity is generated. Originating, we shall say, at the zinc, it traverses the wire, then proceeding down the copper, passes through the solution to the point whence it started. An unbroken 'circuit' is thus formed, consisting of the zinc, the uniting wire, the copper, and the solution. Break the continuity of that circuit by snapping the wire, and no current can possibly be generated. Electricians have long differed in opinion as to the origin of the fluid.[18] Volta[19] had triumphantly shown that the mere contact of two dissimilar metals developed it, and his opinion still finds numerous advocates on the continent. The 'contact theory' was combated, however, so early as 1792, by Fabroni,[20] who, in a paper communicated to the Florentine Academy, attributed the fluid to chemical change. According to this theory, which has obtained universal assent in this country, it is the result of the union of the zinc with the oxygen of the water; the quantity of electricity being dependent on the amount of zinc oxydized. Thus chemical combination and chemical decomposition alike contribute to its generation.

To recur to our illustration. Make your uniting wire a hundred miles in length, instead of a few inches: the result, in rapidity of operation, and indeed in every respect, will be similar, save in the proportionate diminution of intensity, consequent on the greater length. Extend a wire from the zinc to a distance of one hundred miles, bury its further end in the ground, connect the copper by a short wire to the ground also, and the result will still be similar – a circumstance which obviates the necessity of 'return' wires for electric telegraphs. Two theories, perhaps equally plausible, and equally consistent with certain recognized laws, have been propounded to account for this interesting phenomenon. The one implies that the current is a foreign element – something superadded to the wire, and that it must therefore be discharged into the *earth* – the great reservoir of superabundant electricity. The advocates of the other theory maintain that the fluid, starting from the zinc, traverses the long wire, and returns through the intervening ground to the copper plate. Should the question be asked, 'Why should a current transmitted from Edinburgh to London not go elsewhere, rather than return to the precise point whence it started?' the answer given is, that the ground between the two places forms one half of the circuit – being equivalent to a 'return' wire. A current cannot be generated in any battery unless an absolutely unbroken circuit exists – unless we provide a way, however roundabout, whereby the fluid evolved at one pole may return to the other. The battery has been in this case not inaptly / compared to a loaded gun; the completion of the circuit being equivalent to the fall of the trigger. A single pair of plates produces too feeble a current for telegraphic purposes, however, and it is found necessary to multiply the number by arranging a series of zinc and copper alternately in a trough. The combined force thus obtained may be said to be proportioned to the increase in number.

The needle instrument, which is now in operation over probably 25,000 miles of wire in England and Scotland alone, is based on the principle of the deviation of a magnetic needle when subjected to electric influence. If the one end of a telegraphic wire, stretching from Edinburgh, and having its other extremity buried in the *earth* in London, be connected with the *zinc* pole of a battery which has its *copper* one in metallic contact with the ground, a current, originating at the zinc, will flow along the wire to London, plunge there into the ground, and return through the intervening earth between the two cities to the copper. If while this current is flowing, a magnetic needle be placed in close proximity to the wire at any point between the two places, it will swing round from its natural position, and place itself at right angles; thus, instead of pointing northwards, it will point, say, towards the west. Now if we reverse the connections of the battery in Edinburgh, by putting the wire into contact with the copper end, whilst the zinc is connected to the ground, the magnetic needle would still place itself at right angles to the wire; but in this case it would swing round to an opposite direction, and point eastwards. If a Schwiegger's Multiplier, as described by Moigno,[21] be interposed at London, *so that the current will flow round its convolutions before entering the ground*, the magnetic needle placed inside will deviate from its vertical position, say to the *right;* and if the battery connections be reversed in Edinburgh as formerly, it will change to the *left*.

Such an arrangement would be to all intents and purposes an electric telegraph. Any person in Edinburgh, having control over the battery, might transmit at will a series of preconcerted signals, consisting of movements to the right and to the left, intelligible to some one in London. Now if both cities are provided with batteries and with Schwiegger's Multipliers, it is obvious that the communication could be made reciprocal, so that Edinburgh could not only speak to London, but *vice versâ*. Multipliers might also be placed in circuit at any point between the two places, so that correspondence might be carried on simultaneously between twenty different towns – the essential condition being the provision of an unbroken metallic channel throughout the whole length, however numerous the *détours* from the main line of wire. The instruments generally require two wires, and contain two multipliers at the back of the dial. The indicating needle in front of the dial is fixed on the same axis as the magnetic one enveloped in the multiplier, so that the deviations of the one correspond with those of the other. The handles are simply mechanical expedients for bringing the battery power into play; for making and breaking the circuit; or for reversing the direction of the current – in short, for / performing with rapidity and precision what we previously supposed was done by the hand. It is obvious, therefore, that if Edinburgh *sends* a message to London, his handles are moved, but if the *receives* one, his needles alone are influenced.

The alphabet is formed partly by simple, partly by complex deviations. Take the *left*-hand needle:– Two movements to the left indicate A; three, B; once right and left, C; once left and right, D; once right, E; twice, F; three times, G. The following eight letters are formed by the simple movement of the *right*-hand needle, whilst the remaining portion of the alphabet is represented by *combined* movements. The rate of transmission varies greatly, being dependent not merely on the experience of the telegraphist, but on his education and quickness of comprehension. An intelligent operator would find no difficulty in reading forty words per minute, whilst an illiterate railway signalman would find *two* sufficient for *his* comprehension in an equal space of time. This instrument possesses some undoubted advantages over others, but experience has shown that for long lines, one or other of those recording instruments, which remain to be explained, are preferable.

The 'printing' telegraph of Morse, so extensively used throughout America, and which is rapidly superseding every other form on the continent, is based on the principle of electro-magnetism. We have shown how the magnetic virtue can be conferred on a piece of soft iron, or removed at will. If a steel 'pricker' or style attached to the armature of an electro-magnet, having its two horns upwards, be so arranged that a ribbon of paper may pass immediately *above* it, it is obvious that when a current is passed round the magnet, the armature will be attracted, and the 'pricker' will scratch the paper. Now, suppose you are in London, and that by simply depressing a key, like that of a pianoforte, you could cause a current from a battery to flow along a wire to Edinburgh, so that it would pass round the wire of an electro-magnet placed there, – it is obvious that you would cause the armature to be attracted, and the paper, if any, to be scratched. Depress the key for an instant, and you leave a small scratch, resembling that of a pinpoint; depress it a little longer, and a longer scratch is left. You have here the exact *modus operandi*. A ribbon of paper is unwound by mechanism, and during this process a series of dots and dashes are scratched on it, which are translated by the telegraphist. The alphabet, as given in a recent work, runs as follows:

A	B	C	D	E	F	G	H	I	
•—	—•••	—•—•	—••	•	••—•	— —•	••••	••	&c.

It will be observed that this alphabet, which reminds us of the celebrated *A* and *B* cypher of Lord Bacon,[22] is based on two primary characters. The instrument could produce only a long line, or a series of dots, and the result is a character unsurpassed in the history of cryptography for its simplicity and ingenuity. Another interesting circumstance in connection with this alphabet is its universality. Being as intelligible to the continental / telegraphist as to the English one, a message in English may be rendered with the greatest accuracy in St. Petersburg, although the Russian operator may know no language but his own.

The 'printing' instrument of Bain, in use on some English lines, is based on that principle of electro-chemical decomposition which Sir Humphry Davy[23] and Ritter[24] so successfully elucidated. If a piece of paper, dipped in an acidulated solution of yellow prussiate of potash, be brought into connection with the *zinc* end of a battery, a steel point conveying a current from the *copper* end will leave a deep blue mark, so long as the circuit is complete. A ribbon of paper so saturated, and resembling a roll of cotton tape, is unwound by mechanism, whilst the alphabet is also formed by dots and dashes. The *modus operandi* of this instrument resembles that of Morse so closely, that the only essential difference lies in the fact of the paper being chemically prepared.

A valuable adjunct to the last two machines deserves special mention. We allude to the 'Relay.' A current may be too weak to influence a large magnet, or to decompose a chemical solution *directly*, yet it may be adequate to the task of influencing a small magnet, or a needle, in such a way as to bring fresh *local* battery power into play sufficient for the required purpose. Contrivances of this kind, termed 'relays,' are also peculiarly valuable on long lines. A battery in London may be incapable of producing intelligible signals in Copenhagen, but it may possess sufficient power to work a 'relay' placed in Hamburg, and so arranged that, bringing fresh power into operation, it repeats with the utmost accuracy the signals transmitted from London; re-impelling the message to Copenhagen as rapidly and correctly as if the London current had traversed the whole length, and thus performing efficiently by mechanical means what would otherwise be inefficiently done by the human hand.

Other kinds of instruments might be deemed worthy of a detailed description, such as those in which the letters are printed in Roman capitals, or represented by an indicator revolving on a circular dial; but as they are seldom used, being peculiarly liable to derangement – and more remarkable for ingenuity than for utility – we shall content ourselves with a simple statement of the fact, that in such cases, the object is attained by the liberation of mechanism through the influence of an electro-magnet: much in the same manner, indeed, as those bells which, occasionally appended to the 'needle' instrument, we often hear ringing at railway stations.

The wire, stretched on poles, which conveys the current to its destination, is generally made of iron which has been previously subjected to the process termed *galvanization*, by being raised to a high temperature and drawn through a bath of melted zinc. The sole object of this amalgamation is the prevention of oxidation, or rust. In such cases, however, the bare wire must be supported by *insulators*, made of earthenware, porcelain, or glass; which, in virtue of their non-conductibility, serve to keep the fluid to its legitimate channel, – the great object of insulation being the prevention of any escape to the ground, through / moisture or other causes. Underground wires, and those which are stretched in damp tunnels, are generally made of copper, invested with one or two coatings of gutta percha.[25]

Another interesting branch of our subject is that of submarine telegraphy. Although, from an early period, it was obvious to those who were conversant with electrical science that an insulated wire could convey a current under water as easily as on the land, still it was not until the introduction of gutta percha as an element in the construction of telegraphs, that subaqueous communication was recognized as *un fait accompli*. A perfect non-conductor, and apparently possessed of the requisite homogeneous, plastic, and pliant properties, no substance seemed better adapted for such purposes, and in the first great trial to which it was subjected in September 1850 between France and England, the result was highly satisfactory. As the feeble experimental rope submerged on that occasion snapped, however, within a few days, submarine communication may be said to date only from October 1851, when a strong one was successfully deposited. In manufacturing a cable, the conducting medium – generally a copper wire – receives three distinct coatings of gutta percha, with a view to the prevention of leakage; it is then surrounded by one or two coatings of hemp or tow soaked in pitch, and is finally surrounded by a sheathing of galvanized iron wires, twisted longitudinally, so that it may acquire the requisite strength, protection, and flexibility.

The failure of the last effort to establish trans-Atlantic communication may be attributed to certain mechanical and engineering defects, which are not likely to operate in any future attempt. Difficulties of a much more serious nature remain, however, to be encountered. Long submarine cables are found to be practically elongated Leyden jars. The conducting wire is analogous to the internal coating, the outer metallic sheathing to the external one. The wire must, therefore, be regularly discharged of the superfluous fluid before it can be used for its legitimate purpose. It has also been found that long lines running parallel to the equator, are peculiarly susceptible of the disturbing influences of induced currents of terrestrial magnetism. Judging from such circumstances, and the results of recent experiment, we think that it would be scarcely possible to transmit more than three or four brief messages per hour by one wire to Newfoundland. There can be no doubt, however, as to the ultimate success of the Atlantic scheme, in a mechanical and engineering point of view, if the necessary conditions are scrupulously fulfilled.

In endeavouring to explain our subject, we have been influenced by a desire to illustrate essential principles rather than subsidiary details. The modifications of the battery are endless, but the fundamental principle of chemical decomposition and chemical affinity is in every case the same. The instrument may assume forms which appear widely different from those which we have selected as types, but each and all will generally be found to be based on one or other of those great physical laws which we have endeavoured to illustrate. /

It is unnecessary to enter into any details as to the manifold purposes to which the electric telegraph is now applied. Already it has become an indispensable agent of civilized society – materially influencing the political, social, and commercial relations of every country in Europe. And from whatever point of view we regard it, we cannot but feel convinced that science, in this her most brilliant achievement, has placed in our hands an instrument which adds another link to that chain of causes which is slowly, silently, and imperceptibly bridging over the chasms which separate nation from nation and race from race; and whose influence on the future of civilization it is impossible to estimate. Its frail tendrils have not only penetrated into every corner of Europe – into remote lands whose religious systems and social institutions exist now as they existed at a time when our ancestors were mere barbarians, but it conveys its own significant lesson to the Indian in his wigwam, to the Hottentot in his kraal,[26] and to the Arab in the desert.

In conclusion: What is electricity? Science has hitherto failed to answer the question satisfactorily. Some hold that it is a *state* or *condition of matter;* others, that it is an independent substance, an impalpable, imponderable, and highly elastic fluid. The nomenclature of the science is, therefore grounded, in some measure, on hypothesis. *Fluid, current, positive, negative*, are simply the convenient terms of convenient theories. We talk of electricity 'traversing a wire;' but an opinion has long been gaining ground that it merely influences the molecular arrangement of the conductor: that, instead of propagating itself by a series of pulsations, it simply causes every component particle to assume certain electrical conditions. We talk of 'positive' and 'negative,' as if there were two distinct currents, one of which is more powerful than the other; whilst in reality this dual force is co-existent, co-active, and mutually dependent, just as if there were only one which, under certain conditions, is capable of producing diametrically opposite results. This uncertainty is by no means confined to electrical science.

We produce light and heat; we throw a stone into the air with an absolute conviction that it will fall to the ground. There are laws of light and of heat, and there is a law of gravitation. But a law implies something – a force, an agency; and what are those forces or agencies? We talk proudly of 'man's dominion over nature,' of 'scanning the heavens,' of 'taming the lightning,' but we can see little beyond the shows of things. The shadow is there, but the substance eludes our grasp. Like the physiognomist, we may indeed decipher something of Nature from the aspect of her countenance, but we cannot see the workings of her inmost heart. The greatest philosopher among us is still, as in the days of Newton, like a child standing on the seashore. The illimitable ocean lies outstretched before him. Now and then she casts a pearl at his feet. But her richest treasures lie far down in those unfathomable depths which mortal hand can never reach, and mortal eye can never pierce. /

'Electricity as a Light-Producer', *Chambers Journal* (1877)

'Electricity as a Light-Producer', *Chambers Journal*, 721 (20 October 1877), pp. 667–9.

ELECTRICITY AS A LIGHT-PRODUCER.

IT has long been the opinion of scientific people that in electricity we have a power the development of which is only at present in its infancy. The marvellous details of our telegraphic system constantly remind us that there is a mysterious fluid round about us which can to a certain extent be made subservient and obedient to the will of man. This familiarity with that which would a few centuries ago have been stigmatised as the outcome of sorcery, has led the ignorant to place a blind belief in its powers. The subtle fluid has in fact taken the place of the necromancer's wand, and is believed by many to be capable of anything or everything. The electrician is thus credited with much that does not of right belong to his domain, and the wildest speculations are occasionally indulged in as to what next he will do for us. That electricity will prove of far more extended use than the present state of knowledge allows, we all have vague anticipations, and among these is the reasonable hope that it will some day supersede coal-gas as a means of artificial illumination. We propose, by a brief review of the present position of electrical research, to point out how far such a hope is justified by facts.

Sir Humphry Davy[1] was the first to discover that when the terminal wires of a powerful electric battery were furnished with carbon-points and brought into such a position that they almost touched, the space between them became bridged over with a dazzling arc of light. The excessive cost of producing this light (owing to the rapid consumption of the metal-plates and acids which together form the battery-power) rendered it for a long time almost inapplicable to any other purpose than that of lecture-room demonstration. But it was evident to all that a means of illumination so nearly approaching in its intensity the light of the sun, would, if practicable, be of immense value to society at large. Apart from its cost, there were many other hindrances to its ready adoption. The incandescent carbon-points – which we may here remark are cut from a hard form of gas-coke – were found to waste away unequally. Some plan had therefore to be hit upon of not only replacing them at certain intervals, but also, in view of this inequality of consumption, of preserving their relative distance the one from the other; otherwise the light they gave became intermittent and irregular. These difficulties were met by employing clock-work as a regulator, and more recently by a train of wheelwork and magnets set in motion by the current itself. These arrangements naturally led to complications, which required the constant supervision of skilled operators, and the coveted light was necessarily confined to uses of a special nature where the question of cost and trouble was unimportant.

The use of the battery for the electric light has for some years been almost entirely superseded by the magneto-electric machine. The construction of this machine is based upon Faraday's discovery,[2] that when a piece of soft iron inclosed in a coil of metal wire is caused to pass by the poles of a magnet, an electric current is produced in the wire. The common form of this machine consists of a number of such iron cores so arranged upon a revolving cylinder that in continual succession they fly past a number of stationary horse-shoe magnets placed in a frame round its circumference. By a piece of mechanism called a commutator, the various small streams of electricity thus induced are collected together into one powerful current. This invention forms one of the most advanced steps in the history of the electric light. But although it produces electricity without the consumption of metal involved in the battery system, another element of cost comes into view in the expense of the steam-power necessary to work it; besides which the original outlay is considerable.

In the year 1853 a Company was formed at Paris for producing (by the aid of some large magneto-electric machines) gas for combustion, by the decomposition of water. The Company failed to produce gas, and what was perhaps more to the annoyance of the subscribers, they failed also to shew any dividends, and the expensive machines were voted impostors. However, an Englishman, Mr Holms,[3] succeeded in turning them to better account, and eventually produced by their aid a light of great power. Mr Wilde of Manchester[4] was another worker in the same field; and improved machines were soon introduced to public notice by both gentlemen. A few years after, the South Foreland and Dungeness lighthouses were provided with experimental lights. (The first-named headland had previously been furnished with an oxyhydrogen or lime light,[5] a source of illumination which is also open to the same objections of requiring constant attention and renewal.)

It is a matter of surprise to most visitors to the South Foreland lighthouse to find that a small factory and staff of men are necessary to keep the electric apparatus in working order. The extent of the establishment is partly explained by the fact that, in case of a breakdown of any part of the apparatus, everything is kept in duplicate. Hence there are two ten horse-power steam-engines, and a double set of magneto-electric machines, although only half that number are in actual use at one time. The old oil-lamps are also kept ready, in view of the improbable event of both sets of electrical apparatus going wrong.

Although lighthouses were the first places to which electrical illumination was applied, there are many other purposes for which that species of light is invaluable. One of the chief of these is its use in submarine operations. Unlike other lights, being quite independent of atmospheric air or any kind of gas for its support, and merely requiring an attachment of a couple of gutta-percha-covered wires[6] for its connection with the source of electricity (which may be at a considerable distance from the place of combustion), it is specially applicable to the use of divers. The importance of a means of brilliantly lighting the work of those engaged in clearing wreck or laying the foundations of subaqueous structures cannot be over-estimated. There is another service too in which we may hope some day to see it commonly employed: we mean as a source of light to our miners. For this purpose, the burner could be placed in a thick glass globe hermetically closed;[7] / in fact the globe might even be exhausted of air, for experiments prove that the light is in several respects improved when burnt in a vacuum! The danger of fire-damp explosion would by this means be almost altogether obviated; for unless the glass were broken (and abundant means suggest themselves for protecting it), no communication could be made between the light and the gas-laden air of the mine. As a means of night-signalling, the electric light can also be profitably applied. This can be done by an alphabet of flashes of varying duration; the readiness with which the light can be extinguished and rekindled by the mere touch of a wire, rendering it peculiarly adapted for such a purpose; while the distance at which it can be seen is perhaps only limited by the convexity of the earth. Several of Her Majesty's ships are now being fitted with the electric light, which is to serve both for signalling purposes, and as a precautionary measure against the attack of torpedo-boats. For military field operations a brilliant light is often useful; and an electrical apparatus is in actual use by one of the belligerents in the present war.[8] In this case, the light is doubtless worked by an electric battery, as a steam-engine is hardly a convenient addition to the impedimenta of a moving column.

Having called our readers' attention to the several special public uses for which the electric light is available, we may now consider how far it can serve us for the more common wants of every-day life. In its crude state as we have described it, governed by such a touchy thing as clock-work, it could not possibly compete with gas for ordinary purposes. But one or two improvements have within the last few months been made, which have led many to hope that the day is not far distant when the light will become common in our streets, if not in our houses.

These improvements are two in number. The one is a plan whereby the electric current can be subdivided so as to serve a number of different lights, and the other is an improvement in the arrangement of the burner. The first-mentioned invention seems most certainly to bring the system more on a par with gas-lighting, only that wires take the place of pipes. But the second offers features of a more novel character. The carbons, instead of being placed point to point, one above the other, as in the old system, are put side by side and made into a kind of candle. The carbons therefore represent a double wick; while the portion of the candle usually made of tallow is made of kaolin, a form of white clay used in the manufacture of porcelain. The points are thus kept at a fixed distance apart; and as they burn, they vitrify the kaolin between them, which both checks their waste and adds, by its incandescence, to the light produced. The old difficulty of keeping the carbons apart by the aid of clock-work, therefore disappears. The invention of this 'electric candle' is due to a Russian engineer, M. Jablochkoff.[9] Another plan which is also credited to the same inventor is that of doing away with the carbon-points altogether, and substituting for them a thin plate of kaolin. The light produced is said to be softer, steadier, and more constant than that obtained by any previous method. Successful experiments with M. Jablochkoff's invention both in France and England have shewn it to be readily applicable to many purposes. It was lately tried at the West India Docks, London, where its power of illuminating large areas for the purpose (among others) of unloading ships by night, was fully demonstrated. Moreover, its portability is such that it can be carried into the depths of a ship's hold. We may mention as a result of these experiments, that the various gas companies' shares have been depreciated to a considerable extent.

Meanwhile, improvements in the magneto-electric machine have not been wanting; Siemens[10] in England and Gramme[11] in France have succeeded in obtaining intense currents from machines far less bulky than those of the old pattern. But still steam-power is required to set them in motion, and until this is obviated, we cannot expect that the electric light can become really available for more general use. The inventors claim that their method of illumination is, for the amount of light obtained, far cheaper than any other known, pleading that one burner is equal to one hundred gas-lights. But we must remember that for ordinary purposes this amount of light is far beyond our needs. In factories where steam-power is already available, and where the light would supersede a large number of gas-burners, it can of course be employed with profit. Indeed we learn that at several large workshops in different parts of France the light is in actual use with the best results. Some of the railway stations both there and in Belgium are also making arrangements for its immediate adoption.

The problem, however, which has now to be solved is, whether the light can be made available for domestic purposes. We fear that the necessary motive-power presents an insuperable objection; for although, as we have explained, one engine will feed a certain number of lights, it will bear no comparison in this respect with the capabilities of a small gas-holder. Besides which, a man would have far more difficulty and expense in starting a steam-engine in his back-garden than he would have (as is commonly done in country districts) in founding a small gas-factory for the supply of his premises. Without losing sight of the benefits which coal-gas has given us, we may hope that it is not the last and best kind of artificial illumination open to us. It blackens our ceilings and walls; it spoils our books and pictures, besides robbing our dwellings of oxygen, and giving us instead a close and unhealthy atmosphere. The combustion of electricity is on the other hand, as we have already shewn, *independent of any supply of air*; and instead of vitiating the atmosphere, it adds to it a supply of that sea-side luxury ozone, which may truly be said to be 'recommended by the faculty.'[12] Besides these advantages, it can be used without any sensible rise of temperature. Another great advantage which its use secures is its actinic[13] qualities, which would enable artists and all whose work depends upon a correct appreciation of colours, to be independent of daylight.

In conclusion, we may say that, beyond the special uses for the electric light which we have enumerated, and for which it has by experience been found practicable, we see no likelihood of its more general adoption until two requisites are discovered. The one is a substance that will, without wasting away and requiring constant renewal, act as an incandescent burner; and the / other is a cheap and ready method of obtaining the electric fluid. For the former we know not where to look, for even the hardest diamond disappears under contact with the electric poles. But with regard to the latter, we cannot help thinking how, many years ago, Franklin[14] succeeded by the aid of a kite-string in drawing electricity from the clouds. Is it too much to hope that other philosophers may discover some means not only of obtaining the luminous fluid from the same source, but of storing it up for the benefit of all?

'The Prime Minister on Electricity', *Saturday Review* (1889)

'The Prime Minister on Electricity', *Saturday Review*, 68:1776 (9 November 1889), pp. 520–1.

THE PRIME MINISTER ON ELECTRICITY.

A SPECIAL interest is always attached to the utterances and writings of eminent statesmen on subjects not directly connected with their public duties. We know beforehand the general relations which the working of their minds has to the problems of current polities. We can guess whither the drift of any speeches they may make will tend. We can anticipate their sharpness or their dreariness, their liveliness or their stupidity. We have previously measured their long-windedness, and meted out their dulness. Their truthfulness, or the reverse, is already weighed in the balance of our anticipations. But when a statesman departs from the beaten track of making or contradicting political statements, / he opens, as it were, a window into the ark of his mind, and we all struggle to raise our eyes to the porthole, and to get a glimpse of the machinery within. We are lucky when the interior is illuminated by electricity. For, although we have had, from our youth upwards, quite the average amount of admiration for Homer and his works, and although we have diligently peered into every chink that has ever been opened to us in Mr. Gladstone's mental ark, we never were able to see anything very clearly.[1]

The engines always seemed to be very compound,[2] and the steering-gear erratic. But these strange phenomena may have been illusions, owing to the fact that every porthole was fitted with a perpetually revolving kaleidoscope in automatic connexion with the rudder.

Lord Salisbury[3] has not often come forward in the character of a man of speculative mind. His excursions into the electrical future of the world will, therefore, interest us the more. And it is characteristic of his eminently practical mind that, in doing so, he dwelt on a development of electrical science which is at first sight excessively unsensational – the subdivision of energy, and its transmission over moderate spaces. But, while Mr. Gladstone was suggesting a philanthropic scheme of legislation, by which an allotment garden[4] was to be brought to every cottage door, ignoring as usual the main practical difficulty in the way of its realization, that cottages are usually in streets and streets usually in towns, the Prime Minister was pointing out that the subdivision and transmission of electrical energy might, in the future, benefit the artisan more than all the philanthropic legislation in the world. What he claims is, that it may enable the artisan, his wife, and his children to carry on in their own homes many of the industries which are now carried on in factories; and so enable them to 'sustain that unity, that integrity of the family, upon which rest the moral hopes of our race and the strength of the community to which we belong.'[5] But the picture of the altered life is not only morally hopeful, it is æsthetically hopeful; although this is the very last aspect of the question which is likely to have weight with him. And it would be a queer nemesis if the art-socialistic school[6] were forestalled in most of their highest aims, not by legislation, but by a series of scientific inventions suggested by a Tory Prime Minister.

It may be worth while to fill in the outlines of the hopeful picture with a little detail. In the first place, it is evident, and the language of the prophecy has taken this into account, that there are many industries to which subdivision of energy is inapplicable. In all cases, for instance, where the object to be laboured on is not portable, as in the case of a ship, or an iron girder, or a carpet, the labour must come to the mountain, and not the mountain to the labour. And this applies to all cases where the object laboured on has to undergo a rapid succession of processes, as in the case of the manufacture of paper or chemicals. But, apart from these industries, there are many others in which the workmen and women only congregate together because the energy which they use cannot at present be obtained in their own dwellings. Turnery, cabinet-making, instrument-manufacture, cutlery, book-binding, pottery, are all, to some extent, instances in point. There will, therefore, be a very large number to benefit by the change when it comes.

The practicability of the scheme is also well worth considering. It is, of course, a matter of pounds, shillings, and pence. Lord Salisbury is not a man to suggest the possibility of an industrial change on a large scale founded on charity. But, besides being an enemy to all attempts to interfere with the natural working of economic laws, he is an electrician. And when we use this word, we do not merely mean to imply that he is a man who has read one or two popular text-books on electricity, and bought some nicely polished machines, which will give pleasant shocks to his friends, but one who has published the results of original research to the satisfaction of his scientific brethren, and who has also carried out in his own person (when out of office) the duties of an electrical engineer. He can, therefore, speak on this subject with an authority very different from that of the Hawarden lecturer[7] on jam, who has, we venture to say, wielded the axe[8] more often than the spade, and who has not, to the best of our knowledge, passed an apprenticeship in the still-room. His opinion, therefore, that the present condition of electrical science foreshadows such an industrial change should be accepted as being of great weight, especially as it met with acquiescence in the assembly of experts which he was addressing. The economic elements of the question seem to favour his view at no distant date. Let us glance at some of the changes which will be produced in the industries to which the new state of things will apply.

At present a large part of the capital sunk in any manufacture where labour is congregated in considerable quantities has been spent in the erection of buildings and machinery. Under the contemplated system the buildings required will be few or none. The machinery, as far as the original sources of energy are concerned, will be the property of the local electrical supply Company, who will sell so much energy to each artisan direct. This supply of energy, conveyed in the form of electricity by underground mains, will be measured at its entrance to each workman's rooms by an electrical meter. This portion of capital, therefore, which is now supplied by the firm, will in the future be supplied by the electrical lighting Company – a transference on no small scale. Whether the cost of the motors and other machinery necessary for the conversion of electrical into mechanical energy in each dwelling will be ultimately borne by the employer or the artisan remains to be seen. At present the supply of energy, and not its conversion, is the important point. Even with the most perfect systems of transmission and subdivision that can be looked forward to, there is likely to be a greater loss of energy between the source and the points of expenditure than is the case in a compact factory at present. On the other hand, there are some economies. The electrical source of energy is, by hypothesis, large enough to supply the wants of a manufacturing district. Unlike centralization in national government, centralization in boilers and engines is in itself economical. Unused electrical energy has also a pleasant way of getting stored up, and also of putting out (like a horse) extra strength when required. And, finally, we shall probably be enabled to use the forces of rivers and tides at a cheaper rate than the force due to the combustion of coal.

Such details as these, and no doubt many others, were in Lord Salisbury's mind when he made his general prophecy. But his remarks on the past effects of electricity (and, indeed, other forces brought under control by men of science) were no less interesting. And in these he was supported by experts who have special knowledge both of the civil and military results of its application to their own experiences.

A. L. Steavenson, 'The Manufacture of Coke in the Newcastle and Durham Districts' (1859–60)

A. L. Steavenson, 'The Manufacture of Coke in the Newcastle and Durham Districts', *Transactions of the North of England Institute of Mining Engineers*, 8 (1859–60), pp. 109–35.

ON
THE MANUFACTURE OF COKE
IN THE
NEWCASTLE AND DURHAM DISTRICTS.

BY MR. A. L. STEAVENSON.[1]

THE importance of *coke* to the *iron* and *coal* trades is too obvious to require any great proof at my hands, and I will, therefore, only summarily dwell upon it.

Iron Trade during 1858.* – The produce of the iron-works supplied with coke from the Great Northern Coal-field was –

	Pig Metal. Tons.
Northumberland.............	45,312
Durham.....................	265,184
Yorkshire (North Riding)......	189,320
Total	499,816

Taking, therefore, *one* ton of metal as requiring 1.75 tons of coke, equals for *the iron manufacture* 874,678 tons of coke. And from the same coal-field (during that year, which was one of considerable depression) there was –

* Hunt's Mining Record[2] (1858), pp. 83–4.

	Tons.
Sent Coastwise	17,819
Exported Foreign	207,103
Sent by Rail south of Leeds	168,745
For use on Railways, Local Consumption, Landsale, and Locomotives	641,611
Distributed by the Newcastle and Carlisle Railway	2,039
Total	1,911,995

We thus see that, during a year in which the trade was below an / average, very little short of 2,000,000 tons of coke were made from the Northern Coal-field alone, the principal consumption being in the manufacture of iron.

During 1859, Mr. Hoyle*[3] takes the average number of blast furnaces in full work in Northumberland, Durham, and Cleveland, at *sixty-eight*, yielding a total of 620,000 tons of metal. Then 620,000 tons x 1.75 tons = 1,085,000 tons of coke; showing an increase of 25 per cent. on 1858.

I approximate the number of furnaces in Great Britain, in which *coke is used*, to be 411, the annual requirements of each being at

14,000 tons = total	5,574,000
Foundries use a large quantity every ton of metal 'brought down,' requiring about 200 lbs. of coke,† giving a total of about	293,526
Total annual quantity in the production of iron in Great Britain	6,047,526

It seems more than probable that, if coke had not been available, this large quantity of metal would not have been produced, and thus the great demand for raw coal in the refineries and rolling mills would have been, at all events, very much less.

Raw coal, to the extent of about one ton, is required in the manufacture of a ton of iron, in addition to the coke already considered. In the hot blast furnaces of some districts, coal is used; but certainly much of the 'small' of soft, bituminous coal seams would be unavailable if not prepared to stand the weight of material and the blast by previous coking. Seams have thereby become valuable which would otherwise have been untouched for many years.

To produce coke nearly twice the quantity of raw material is required, which has a stimulating and beneficial effect, whilst it creates a branch of manufacture for the advantageous investment of capital, and a considerable field for the employment of skilled labour. The effect of the use of coke upon other trades has (by re-action) been generally beneficial, and the railway and shipping traffic much influenced.

* See Mr. R. Hoyle's Annual Statement on the Iron Trade, for 1859.

† Dr. Ure's 'Dictionary of Arts,'[4] &c.

From the consideration of the foregoing facts, it is apparent that the slightest improvement in the mode of manufacture, either in quantity or quality, is a matter of considerable interest to the community at large, as well as those more immediately concerned in the production, and I / have thus felt encouraged in bringing before the members of the Institution this paper, which has been drawn up with a view to assist others who, like myself, have the management of ovens,* without any recognised data to work by, so that improvement or deficiency may be estimated, and that by the discussion of points of practice, bad habits, sanctioned by custom, may be seen and avoided when brought into prominence. And that by ascertaining causes, and rightly understanding the elements of success, we may make good our progress and be enabled to form definite expectations of future achievements.

The introduction or invention of coke was not the actual motor in the rapid and immense development of the iron trade, however necessary it may have been to its existence as a commercial manufacture. The iron trade was ready to burst into action as soon as the necessary fuel was forthcoming; railways contemporaneously sprang up, demanding something more durable than wood, or wood charcoal, and capable of yielding a brighter and more concentrated heat (free from the volatile fuliginous[6] products) than was afforded by raw coal. This want the manufacture of coke supplied, so that the demand has during late years been rapidly increasing, particularly in these districts.

In 1619, Dud Dudley[7] attempted to use raw coal in Worcestershire (for the iron manufacture), but failed, owing to the opposition of other ironmasters; this, I dare say, is well known, and I merely mention the fact of his having taken out a patent for the process for thirty-one years, to show that at that date coke for iron manufacture was not then in use. By 1686 coke was known as a fuel, Dr. Plot† says, 'It is fit for most other uses, but for smelting, fining, and refining of iron, it cannot be brought to do, though attempted by the most curious and skilful artists.' In 1734 Swedenborg,‡ a very able mineralogist, speaking on this subject, says, it had not been brought to perfection in his day. 1765 is the earliest period at which I can find *coke ovens* on record. M. Jars§ says, 'There are nine kilns at Newcastle, upon the edge of the river, to destroy the sulphur contained in the coal, and to reduce it to what is called 'cinders and coaks.' The principal use of the cinders is to heat the malting kilns; it is also used by a silversmith. I have seen

* The only printed form or specification (which I have heard of,) for the guidance of coke burners or workmen, being one prepared by Mr. J. Marley, at Woodifield, in 1847.[5]

† Dr. Plot's[8] 'History of Staffordshire, 1686.'

‡ See Regnum Subterraneum, by Swedenborg, Mineralogist to Charles XII. of Spain,[9] 1734.

§ Voyages Metallurgiques, ou Recherches et Observations sur les Mines et Forges de Fer, &c., en Allemagne, Swede, Norwege, Angleterre, and Ecosse, par feu M. Jars,[10] d' l' Academie Royale des Sciences, Paris, 1774. ... /

a *manuscript* upon 'The art of Working Coal Mines,' in which the first attempts in this manufacture were given as of very ancient date, being made in England.

1788. – At this period several attempts had been made to reduce iron ore with 'coaked coal.'*

1800, or about the early part of the century, a few ovens were to be seen on the Cockfield Fell, on the outcrop of the Brockwell Seam, about half a mile north of Harperly Hall, and in various other country places, mostly in the hands of the owners of small landsale[11] pits, who had no market for the small coal, and coked it from necessity. The late Lord Dundonald[12] had some ovens near Newcastle for making mineral tar, but not being able to get quit of the ammonia his patent was not successful, the residue of this process being coke.

1827. – The Birtley Iron Works, established about this period, and the Lemington, which are the oldest smelting works of modern times, were supplied with the Pontop Colliery Hutton Seam coke.

About 1845 or 1846 the coke trade of the North of England may be said to have first obtained a standing, coke having been chiefly produced on the river Tyne, viz., the Garesfield and Wylam coke, made from the Busty Bank or Harvey and Brockwell Seams.

The Coking District of the North of England has already been described by Mr. T.Y. Hall.†[13] He says, 'This district, from the Etherley Seams on the south, to about half a mile north of the Tyne at Wylam, is nearly twenty-three miles in extent. It is irregular in form, and averages about nine miles in width. It may be taken as averaging 20 miles by 8 = 160 square miles.' The Brockwell and Harvey or Busty Bank Seams of coal being soft, bituminous, and unusually free from impurities, are well adapted for making first-class coke.

The manufacture of coke, which is the subject of my paper, requires great consideration. Its importance has been recognized since the first attempts by 'heap burning;'[14] and so long as the requirements of the blast furnace, locomotive, and foundry continue unsatisfied with raw coal, the practical and economical production of coke will afford occasion of improvement, as the foregoing statements render evident.

The raw material with which we have to deal is shown, by various analyses, to be composed, on an average, of

Carbon.		Hydrogen.		Nitrogen.		Sulphur.		Oxygen.		Ash.		Total.
84.92	+	4.53	+	0.96	+	0.65	+	6.66	+	2.28	=	100.00

The object we have to attain is to drive off, by heat, every constituent except the carbon: the ash will, of course, remain. The process of *burning in mounds* originated in the old charcoal meilers[15] and mounds. Where still practised,

* See Dr. Ure's "Arts and Manufactures."

† See his paper on ' The Extent and Probable Duration of the Northern Coal Field,' to which a map, showing the coking coal field is attached. – Vol. II., 'Transactions' of this Institute./

the coal is placed upon a flat surface, prepared of puddle clay; the larger pieces are arranged regularly, inclining to each other, placed on the sharpest angle, so that as small a surface as possible touches the ground. By this means spaces are reserved for the admission of air, and for the swelling of the heated coals. In building a pile, a number of holes are made, extending along the hearth, and terminating in vertical shafts in the centre. The heap is ignited by putting burning fuel into these vents, which are then stopped by pieces of coal, to prevent the fire ascending; and cause it to extend along the bottom, where the draught is freest. The combustion gradually rises, and bursts forth on all sides. Soon after the smoke has ceased, the fire is covered up with the dust and ashes of former burnings, beginning at the base, and gradually heaping it up to the top. From 40 to 100 tons are generally coked in this way. The per centage of coke yielded by this process is not large; 31.25 I have seen given as the produce, by good authority. Wales and Shropshire have been the principle districts where this system has been carried on. In Wales it is still to some extent practised.

The patent COKE KILNS** have a sound concrete bottom, about eighteen inches thick, to guard against the access of air. In these – the external walls being built of stone, slag, or common brick, lined with fire-brick – by an arrangement of flues in the side walls, and of large coals at the bottom when loaded, a powerful draught is created in the vertical flues, so that the atmospheric air is drawn *down* through the top of the kiln to the seat of combustion beneath. A fifty-ton kiln is filled to the depth of four feet six inches, and covered with a layer of dead ashes two or three inches thick. The fire is applied at the horizontal bottom flues, and the process gradually *ascends*. No smoke rises from the top surface of the kiln, which is cool during the whole process. Such are now in use at some of the largest works in South Wales, and, I have / reason to believe, give satisfaction, more particularly for the purposes of iron manufacture.

The *common round oven* came gradually into use; at first the coke was drawn in a heated state, and afterwards cooled by water, thrown on by buckets; but this has been long discontinued – an improved method of cooling with water, thrown on by pipes and hose, obtaining preference; the only drawback from the latter method of cooling being the contact of water with the hot bricks.

Supposing we have, them, as good circular oven loaded ... (carefully levelled three or four times during loading), that is, up to within a few inches of the top of the door, and the door plastered with 'daub,' so as only to admit sufficient air through vent holes left at the top, the heat of the walls and dome from the previous charge is sufficient to renew or continue the process.† The coals soon begin to emit aqueous and sulphurous vapours, then follows a thick black smoke and reddish flame all around the sides. This sudden combustion is termed 'strik-

* Patented by Messrs. Rogers & Mackworth, 1856; F. Morton, C.E, manager under the patent, Liverpool.

† New ovens require to be fired until they attain the requisite heat, and are not in proper working order until after three or four loads.

ing,' and the damper, previously closed, must be opened. At this stage of the process the gases are particularly offensive; a low red heat gradually prevails, the admission of air being increased; this induces increased heat, and in a few hours openings extend downwards, enabling the volatile matters below the surface to pass off, and, by their ignition, to generate additional heat for carrying on the process. In about twelve hours, a clear bright flame prevails over the entire surface, which increases almost to a white heat. Coking, which is the volatilization and combustion of the gaseous constituents, goes on, basaltiform columns being formed, which allow the gases to rise as the heat descends, and it is now that stones and dirt are particularly hurtful, acting as mechanical obstructions.

Latterly, as the process ceases, we have a clear bright flame, which dies off gradually, lingering longest over the centre of the oven, owing to the smallest coal lodging there; *i.e.*, when loaded from the top, in cases where it had not been properly levelled, and at the side farthest from the door, owing to the previous want of atmospheric oxygen. From the time the combustion begins to slacken, the admission of air should be reduced so as to save the coke. The late Mr. Mackworth*[16] estimated that forty cubic feet of air were required for every pound of coal coked.

When all flame has ceased, the sooner the oven is drawn the better, for it will continue to draw air in spite of every precaution: the red hot coke wastes, loses heat, and becomes inferior as a fuel. So long as any hydrogen remains, the atmospheric oxygen, by natural preference, combines with the gas; but after exhaustion of the hydrogen, it seizes the hot carbon, and a pale blue flame of (C O), carbonic oxide,[17] may be seen issuing from the oven top, if not closed.

To save the coke, especially near the inlet at the door, and in ovens where proximity to a stack of chimney causes a sharp draught, I have covered the coals as soon as loaded with the small refuse coke; this answers extremely well. Mons. Ebelman[18] collected the gases at three different periods, their analyses affording the following results: – [19]

	After 2 hours.	7 hours.	14 hours.	Mean.
'†C O_2	10.13	9.60	13.06	10.93
C O	4.17	3.91	2.19	3.42
$C_4 H_4$	1.44	1.66	0.40	1.17
H	6.28	3.67	1.10	3.68
N	77.98	81.16	83.25	80.80
	100.00	100.00	100.00	100.00
Oxygen to 100 vols. of Nitrogen.	15.70	14.20	17.00	15.60

The relation, then, between the coal and escaping gases is as follows: –

* See his Lecture on Coke to the Bristol Mining School. /

† Ronalds and Richardson's 'Chemical Technology,' [20] presented to the Library of this Institute by Dr.Richardson. /

	Coal.	Coke left.	Gas.
Carbon	89.27 ..	67.00 . ..	23.68
Hydrogen	4.85 ..	....	4.85
Oxygen and Nitrogen	4.47 ..	....	4.47
Ashes	1.41 ..	....	
	100.00 =	67.00	+ 33.00

The relation of the carbon to the hydrogen is as 23.68 : 4.85 or 1 to 0.205 by weight, while the relation in the gas, according to the mean of the above analyses, is 1 to 064 by weight, from which we may infer two-thirds of the hydrogen of the coal are consumed during the carbonization. There is a very small quantity of tar produced in consequence of the high temperature of the ovens, which also accounts for the small quantity of carbureted hydrogen[21] found among the permanent gases. The mean quantity of oxygen, 15.63, for 100 of nitrogen, shows that 10.63 must have combined with the hydrogen and passed off as aqueous vapour, as 16.16 parts must have been introduced for every 100 of nitrogen.

These data farther prove that two-thirds of the whole heat which is lost is sensible, and, of course, necessitates that it should be rendered available on the spot, as it cannot be conveyed to any great distance, and more especially as the gases do not contain much combustible matter.

The heat necessary for coking is also evidently partly produced by the combustion of the products of distillation, and partly by a portion of the residual coke.'

The hydrogen (which the previous analyses of coal show is in proportion of about four and a half per cent.) is the principal element by the combustion of which the process is carried on, but it cannot be separated or volatilized without taking in combination a considerable portion of carbon, yielding the two hydrocarbon gases, carburretted and bi-carburretted hydrogen,[22] the proportion of the latter being generally estimated at about ten per cent. Having a due admixture of air the products should be aqueous vapour and carbonic acid,[23] with, of course, the uncombined nitrogen. If, in practice, we allow, *through the insufficiency of air supplied*, a portion of the oxygen of the $C\ O_2$ to be abstracted, we shall get, with additional loss of carbon, two volumes of carbonic oxide, which necessarily pass off only half consumed in a gaseous though invisible state. /

The *efficiency* of *coke* as a fuel, in comparison with *coal*, is more a question to be considered by the consumer than the producer; but the question of relative utility is so intimately associated, that they cannot well be separated. The heating power of coke is evidently that of the / original coal, minus the power of the expelled combustible constituents. I have heard it said, and have read assertions, that coke was possessed of a heating power as great as the original coal from which it was produced; but when it is considered that nearly one-seventh, by weight, of valuable gas has been taken from it, it must be acknowledged that, if the powers of coal have not been found greater than the residuary coke, the deficiency has been owing to faulty experiment.

Messrs. Armstrong, Longridge, and Richardson* showed that the economic effect of one pound of coal is greater when no smoke is made, to the extent of from seventeen to twenty-two per cent. (*i.e.*, when all the gaseous and carbonaceous products are properly consumed.)

One great advantage which coke has is, that it is chemically purer than coal, the sulphur being much reduced. The following may be taken as a sample of coke of an average quality:–

Carbon	89.00
Silicious[25] matter	7.50
Fe. O. Oxide of iron	3.30
Sulphur	0.20
	100.00

Its superiority to coal consists in its capacity for a *complete and centralised heat, at once* combining with the oxygen necessary for its combustion, and not, as with coal, liable to loss of heat from the absorption incident to the expulsion of the volatile constituents (excepting, perhaps, the fixed oxygen to which I have already alluded).

In a paper read before the Society of Arts†† it is stated that the result of experiments made with great care was as follows:– With two engines, one burning Welsh coal, and fitted with Mr. Beattie's apparatus;[26] the other burning coke, made from Ramsay's coking coal (Newcastle), the average of two days' work was –

	lbs. per Mile.
Consumption of coal	20.36
„ „ coke	24.37

The loads being practically equal.

Mr. Fothergill reduces the coal to a coke value of 13.57 lbs., which shows a saving of 10.80 lbs. per mile, and he considers the durability of tubes and fire boxes to be settled in favour of coal. /

In experiments made by the same gentleman,‡ on behalf of the East Lancashire, and Lancashire and Yorkshire Companies, between Manchester and Blackpool, 39 cwts. of Wigan *coal* performed an amount of duty usually requiring 36 cwts. of *coke*. And in another case, under circumstances equally favourable to each, 39 cwts. of coal equalled 40 cwts. of coke.

* See their 'Report on the Use of the Steam Coals of the Hartley District.'[24]

† By Mr. B. Fothergill, 'On the Relative Value of Coke and Coal in Locomotive Engines.'

‡ Extract[27] from the 'Times,' Sept. 10, and 'Colliery Guardian,' Sept. 18, 1858.

In these experiments, the Wigan coal was costing 5s. 3d. per ton, and the coke used from 11s. to 11s. 6d., the saving to the above companies being estimated at £30,000 per annum. The above results are now very much disputed.

Dr. Ure gives the heating power of 1 lb. of coke to 1 lb. of coal as 65 to 60.

The special feature in the smelting capacity of coke is the *immediate* intense heat which it generates. It is a hard, porous material, like charcoal, offering a very large surface to the action of the oxygen, the only difference being in point of purity. Great care, and the judicious application of purifying agents, will afford the ironmaster a fuel (in coke) second only to charcoal,* 'for the gaseous portion of the COALS used in the blast furnace exercises a deteriorating effect on the quality of the iron produced.' It has been estimated that one cubic inch of beechwood charcoal presents a surface of *one hundred square feet*. The advantages of coke are of a similar nature: the closer the pores the harder the coke, and the stronger the blast can be applied, giving a better effect.

At present coke-made iron will not sell for more than half the price of charcoal iron. In this we see an ample field for improvement.

The Lorn and Ulverstone Furnace Company[29] have,† for forty years , been the only manufacturers of charcoal iron, producing not more than 1500 tons per annum, and selling at £8 10s. to £9 per ton.

To avoid the necessity for coke in the blast furnace, the use of the hot blast was invented by Neilson, in 1829.[30] This affects a considerable saving in fuel, but the quality of iron is not generally so good.

Charred coal, as a substitute for charcoal, used in the fineries,[31] is described by Mr. E Rogers.[32]‡ The structure is analogous to charcoal – free from sulphur, and adapted to the manufacture of tin plates. The material in question 'is made on the floor of an ordinary coke oven, while red hot, after the drawing the charge of coke.' Small coal, to / the depth of four inches, is spread over the bottom, and drawn after about an hour and a half.

The consequent commercial value of coke is, that it supplies a necessity, for in it we have a good, clean, and powerful fuel, which, at the present day, the exhaustion of the old charcoal sources, and the impurities of the raw coal, render of immense importance, and which must increase until chemical or mechanical experience enables us to use coal.

Viewed as an article of commerce, there is to be considered:–

Cost of production, which includes *Capital* – this I have estimated on the basis of a plant of 200 *ovens*, the cost per oven§ being as follows:–

* T. S. Prideaux, 'On the Economy of Fuel.'[28]

† For this and other information I am indebted to Mr. Roper, of the Lorn Furnaces.

‡ See the 'Proceedings' of the South Wales Institute, Vol. I., No. 1.

§ See Appendix [not included here].

	£	s.	d.
Building and materials, 10½ feet oven	23	19	7
With flues and chimneys	4	0	7
Laying on necessary water supply	1	8	11
Gangways and turn-tables	1	3	10
Working gear	0	5	4
Total outlay per oven	30	18	3

In these calculations the cost of fire-brick goods I have taken low, being generally manufactured on the colliery.

For the cost of working charges, current expenses, and upholding of the plant, see Appendix.

The market value of coke varies with the state of the iron trade, at least it generally does so. Many thousand acres of bituminous coals have been increased in present value at least one-half, and this is mainly attributable to the rapid development of the manufacture of iron in these districts. The smelting fuel being almost all coke. The following facts will illustrate this.

In 1769* the English smelted iron by the 'coaks'.

In 1796 the *wood charcoal process* was almost entirely given up, fifty-three blast furnaces were in activity, fired with coke, which furnished 48,000 tons of pig metal, and there was made by charcoal 13,000 tons, making a total of 61,000 tons of pig metal.

		Tons.
1806,	made solely by coke	170,000
1820,	ditto	400,000
1826,	ditto	600,000
1845,	ditto	1,250,000
1851,	ditto	2,500,000
1858,	ditto	3,456,064

Since the introduction of the hot blast in 1827 a considerable proportion of raw coal has been used in the furnaces, but the addition of the consumption of locomotives has maintained an equal if not increased demand for coke.

There are not any special statistics of the coke trade, which compels me to estimate as near as possible.

Coke used in the iron trade	4,032,070
Exported	227,552
Railways, &c.	641,611
	4,901,233

Say 5,000,000 tons produced annually in Great Britain, which, at 300 tons per oven per annum equals 16,666 ovens. The number of hands employed in the coke trade of the kingdom being about 4,000.

* 'Voyages Metallurgiques,' par M. Jars. /

During 1858, in Durham and Northumberland alone, there were manufactured about 2,000,000, and 1,600 hands engaged; the capital embarked in the coke trade of Great Britain being about £500,000, which yields something like *ten per cent.* annually.

After a statement of such vast interests involved in this manufacture, any change in the use of coke will at once appear a serious question. But the fact seems to be, that our present chemical knowledge enables us to do what would have proved futile if attempted by our immediate predecessors, although there is still a wide field for improvement. We have seen the rise of an important branch of manufacture, as much from the requirements of the arts as from the possession of a commercial drug, leading apparently to an immense waste, amounting to nearly one-half of what has been justly called our strength, viz., our coal. And we see now a traffic in its full vigour (however temporarily depressed), which further chemical knowledge may hereafter supersede, making coal applicable to the purposes for which coke is now used, without its requiring to be first submitted to the coking process. /

'Mineral Kingdom: Iron', *Penny Magazine* (1834)

'Mineral Kingdom. – Section XXIV. Iron – No. III', *Penny Magazine of the Society for the Diffusion of Useful Knowledge*, 3:162 (11 October 1834), pp. 396–7.

MINERAL KINGDOM. – SECTION XXIV.
IRON. – NO. III.

Method of obtaining the Metal, from Clay-Ironstone. – This ore has, as we have said, nothing metallic in its appearance; and no one unacquainted with chemistry would suspect that a bar of iron could be extracted from it, any more than they would conceive that a handful of the red earthy matter which we call rust could be forged into a metal. That rust is metallic iron combined with oxygen gas and carbonic acid gas[1], which it has absorbed from the atmosphere; and, in like manner, the metal is concealed in the ironstone in a state of combination with oxygen gas and carbonic acid gas. To separate it from these and the other foreign ingredients which enter into the composition of the ore constitutes the operation called *smelting* (a term derived from a German word signifying 'to melt'), which consists in bringing the clay-ironstone in contact, under a very powerful heat, with other substances, which, having a stronger attraction for oxygen and carbonic acid than iron has, destroy the combination, and set the iron free.

The ore, when taken from the mine, is broken into small pieces about the size of an egg, and is then subjected to the process of *roasting*, which is performed by making a long oblong pile of the broken ore, with intervening layers of small coal, forming a heap about thirty feet long, fifteen feet broad, and five feet high, – sloping at the top like the ridge of a house. There is a thick layer of coal at the bottom, which is kindled when the pile is completed; the whole is gradually ignited, and then left to burn for five or six days, and, when cool, the ore is ready for the smelting-furnace. The roasted ore has changed its colour from grey to red, brown, or blackish-brown; has parted with its carbonic acid gas, as well as the sulphur, and other inflammable substances it may have contained, and has lost from twenty to thirty per cent. of its weight.

The furnace is usually a square pyramidal tower of strong masonry, or brick-work, from forty to fifty feet high...

When first kindled, the fire is made at the bottom of the interior cavity, which is gradually filled with a mixture of ore, coke, and limestone, in the proportions of four of coke, rather more than three of ore, and one of limestone. The heat is urged by compressed air being forced through tubes in the sides into the cavity, by means of powerful bellows, worked by a steam-engine. The mixture is in a highly heated state in the higher part of the furnace, and gradually sinks to that part where the heat, urged by the blast, is most intense, and then it becomes in a state of semi-fusion. Here the more complete decomposition takes place; and the mass being now fluid, the metal, by its greater specific gravity, sinks to the bottom, where it is allowed to run out, from time to time, by opening an aperture left for the purpose. This is *cast-iron*, and the ore yields on an average about thirty per cent. of it. It is conducted into moulds, made with dry sand, on the ground, near the orifice, for the various things made of cast-iron, – from vast beams, wheels, and cylinders of steam-engines, to the smallest articles of domestic use; or it is conducted into moulds for the bars of *pig-iron*, – the form in which cast-iron is sold as a raw material. The term 'pig-iron,' like many others in the arts, was given by the workmen, and, as may be supposed, it has not a very profound or refined etymology. The metal is run off into a main channel which they call the *sow*, and the bars at right angles to it they liken to pigs sucking the teats of the sow. As the ore sinks down, a fresh supply is poured in at the top of the furnace, which is kept / constantly going, and is never allowed to cool unless for the purpose of repair, or when it is *blown out*, as it is termed, by a stoppage of the works.

It will be observed that the coal is not used as it comes from the pit, but is first brought to the state of coke, or mineral charcoal, which is done by a process very similar to that employed for making charcoal from wood; – the coal being brought to a red heat, in heaps so covered as to prevent free exposure to the air, and thus the bitumen is driven off, leaving a cinder behind like that which remains in the retorts used at the gasworks. The coke serves not only as a fuel for producing the heat, but performs other important functions, for it attracts the oxygen from the ore, and enters into combination with the iron, in the state of pure carbon.

The purpose of adding the limestone is to facilitate the melting of the ore, the lime acting the part of a *flux*, as it is termed, from *fluxus,* a Latin word, signifying a flowing or streaming. There are certain mineral substances which, singly, will resist the action of the most violent heat, but, when mixed together, become fusible at comparatively low temperatures. Thus silica, or the earth of flints, is infusible in a very intense heat, but on the addition of a portion of the mineral alkali soda, it melts readily at a low heat and forms glass. The limestone acts upon the earths of flint and clay, which enter into the composition of the ore, in the same way as the soda acts in making glass from sand, and thus a fluid is obtained;

and as the particles in the liquid mixture have free motion, the heavier ones, that is, the iron, sink to the bottom, and the lighter earthy matter rises to the top, and floats on the surface of the melted iron, forming what is called 'slag.' Any one passing by an iron–work must have noticed the heaps of glassy-looking matter, of various colours, thrown aside as rubbish, and which is often used for mending the roads in the neighbourhood; – this is the slag.

Simple as the above process of smelting may seem to be, great skill is required in conducting it, in order to obtain the greatest amount of metal and the best quality of iron which the particular ore is capable of affording. Clay-ironstone, as it was shown in the last section,[2] is very various in quality, both as regards the quantity of iron it contains and the foreign ingredients with which that is mixed, and the process to which it is to be subjected in the smelting-furnace must be varied accordingly. What that is to be is determined by a series of trials, at first on the small scale, which is called an *assaying* of the ore, from the French verb *essayer*, 'to make trial of.' If the quantity of earthy matter exceeds fifteen per cent. the ore cannot be advantageously smelted by itself, and it is mixed with ore of a richer quality. Such a mixture is often advantageous on other accounts, for an ore that is difficult to melt by itself is fused with comparative ease when mixed with an ore of a different quality. The nature of the limestone is also a material consideration; for the effect of limestone as a flux depends not only on its own composition, which within certain limits is variable, but also on that of the ore with which it is to be mixed. Nothing but actual trial can determine what proportion of any particular limestone is best adapted to act as a flux upon any particular clay-ironstone.

Two hundred years ago all the iron ore of this country was smelted with wood-charcoal, but the consumption of wood was so enormous that the manufacture upon a large scale must have ceased had not a method been discovered of using coal instead by converting it into coke. As hard wood makes the best charcoal, so is a pit-coal which yields a compact, hard, heavy coke the best for the smelting-furnace, because a coke of that kind stands the blast best. It is very important also to select a coal as free as possible from sulphur in any shape.

We have mentioned that the heat of the furnace is urged by a blast of condensed air thrown in by means of a steam-engine. An improvement has lately been introduced at the Clyde Iron Works, which promises to be of immense advantage by materially reducing the cost of the smelting. This consists in sending in a blast of *hot*, instead of cold, air.[3] When a blast of cold air is thrown in, a great part of the heat of the furnace is absorbed by the cold air, and therefore a large amount of the fuel is wasted. Now it has been found by experiment that the coal necessary to heat the air before it is thrown into the furnace is very considerably less than that which is required to afford the coke necessary to heat it after it is thrown in. Some successful experiments have also been made for smelting with the coal, and thus saving the waste of converting it into coke.

Cast-iron, or pig-iron, or crude-iron, for it is known by all these names, is not a pure substance, but contains usually about one forty-third part of its weight of carbon, which it obtains from the coke, or charcoal, in the process of smelting. The presence of carbon in its composition may be easily shown by dropping a little diluted muriatic acid[4] on polished cast-iron, when the acid dissolves a portion of the iron, and a film of black carbon is left behind, because it is not soluble in the acid. The quantity of carbon depends a good deal upon the quality of the fuel; and if cast-iron be exposed in a melted state for a length of time to charcoal, and free access of oxygen be prevented, the iron will absorb so much carbon as to be converted into plumbago, or that substance commonly called *black-lead*,[5] of which pencils are made, but which has not a particle of lead in its composition. Cast-iron is neither ductile nor malleable, but is, on the contrary, very brittle; and it melts with such facility at a red heat that it cannot be welded, whereas pure iron is one of the most infusible of the metals. It can be fused to such a degree of liquidity that it may be poured into very minute cavities, as we see by those beautiful ornaments, of the most delicate forms, manufactured at Berlin, and at Sain, near Neuwied, on the Rhine.

.../

Edward A. Martin, *The Story of a Piece of Coal* (1896)

Edward A. Martin, *The Story of a Piece of Coal* (London: George Newnes, 1896).

CHAPTER VI.

HOW GAS IS MADE – ILLUMINATING OILS AND BYE-PRODUCTS

The first, and perhaps, most important portion of the apparatus used in gas-making is the series of *retorts* into which the coal is placed, and from which, by the application of heat, the various volatile products distil over. These retorts are huge cast-iron vessels, encased in strong brick-work, usually five in a group, and beneath which a large furnace is kept going until the process is complete. Each retort has an iron exit pipe affixed to it, through which the gases generated by the furnace are carried off. The exit pipes all empty themselves into what is known as the *hydraulic main*, a long horizontal cylinder, and in this the gas begins to deposit a portion of its impurities. The immediate products of distillation are, after steam and air, gas, tar, ammoniacal liquor, sulphur in various forms, and coke, the last being left behind in the retort. In the hydraulic main / some of the tar and ammoniacal liquor already begin to be deposited. The gas passes on to the *condenser*, which consists of a number of U-shaped pipes. Here the impurities are still further condensed out, and are collected in the *tar-pit* / whilst the gas proceeds, still further lightened of its impurities. It may be mentioned that the temperature of the gas in the condenser is reduced to about 60° F., but below this some of the most valuable of the illuminants of coal-gas would commence to be deposited in liquid form, and care has to be taken to prevent a greater lowering of temperature. A mechanical contrivance known as the *exhauster* is next used, by which the gas is, amongst other things, helped forward in its onward movement through the apparatus. The gas then passes to the *washers* or *scrubbers*, a series of tall towers, from which water is allowed to fall as a fine spray, and by means of which large quantities of ammonia, sulphuretted hydrogen,[1] carbonic acid[2] and oxide,[3] and cyanogen compounds,[4] are removed. In the scrubber the water used in keeping the coke, with which it is filled, damp, absorbs these compounds, and the union of the ammonia with certain of them takes / place, resulting in the formation of carbonate of ammonia (smelling salts), sulphide and sulphocyanide of ammonia.

Hitherto the purification of the gas has been brought about by mechanical means, but the gas now enters the *'purifier,'* in which it undergoes a further cleansing, but this time by chemical means. The agent used is either lime or hydrated oxide of iron, and by their means the gas is robbed of its carbonic acid and the greater part of its sulphur compounds. The process is then considered complete, and the gas passes on into the water chamber over which the gas-holder is reared, and in which it rises through the water, / forcing the huge cylinder upward according to the pressure it exerts.

The gas-holder is poised between a number of upright pillars by a series of chains and pulleys, which allow of its easy ascent or descent according as the supply is greater or less than that drawn from it by the gas mains.

When we see the process which is necessary in order to obtain pure gas, we begin to appreciate to what an extent the atmosphere is fouled when many of the products of distillation, which, as far as the production of gas is concerned, may be called impurities, are allowed to escape free without let or hindrance. In these days of strict sanitary inspection it seems strange that the air in the neighbourhood of gas-works is still allowed to become contaminated by the escape of impure compounds from the various portions of / the gas-making apparatus. Go where one may, the presence of these compounds is at once apparent to the nostrils within a none too limited area around them, and yet their deleterious effects can be almost reduced to a minimum by the use of proper purifying agents, and by a scientific oversight of the whole apparatus. It certainly behoves all sanitary authorities to look well after any gas-works situated within their districts.

Now let us see what these first five products of distillation actually are.

Firstly, house-gas. Everybody knows what house-gas is. It cannot, however, be stated to be any one gas in particular, since it is a mechanical mixture of at least three different gases, and often contains small quantities of others.

A very large proportion consists of what is known as marsh-gas, or light carburetted hydrogen. This occurs occluded or locked up in the pores of the coal, and often oozes out into the galleries of coal-mines, where it is known as fire-damp (German *dampf*, vapour). It is disengaged wherever vegetable matter has fallen and has become decayed. If it were thence collected, together with an admixture of ten times its volume of air, a miniature coal-mine explosion could be produced by the introduction of a match into the mixture. Alone, however, it burns with a feebly luminous flame, although to its presence our house-gas owes a great portion of its heating power. Marsh-gas is the first of the series of hydrocarbons known chemically as the *paraffins*, and is an extremely light substance, / being little more than half the weight of an equal bulk of air. It is composed of four atoms of hydrogen to one of carbon (CH_4).

Marsh-gas, together with hydrogen and the monoxide of carbon, the last of which burns with the dull blue flame often seen at the surface of fires, particularly coke and charcoal fires, form about 87 per cent. of the whole volume of house-gas, and are none of them anything but poor illuminants.

The illuminating power of house-gas depends on the presence therein of olefiant gas *(ethylene),* or, as it is sometimes termed, heavy carburetted hydrogen. This is the first of the series of hydro-carbons known as the *olefines*, and is composed of two atoms of carbon to every four atoms of hydrogen (C_2H_4). Others of the olefines are present in minute quantities. These assist in increasing the illuminosity, which is sometimes greatly enhanced, too, by the presence of a small quantity of benzene vapour. These illuminants, however, constitute but about 6 per cent. of the whole.

Added to these, there are four other usual constituents which in no way increase the value of gas, but which rather detract from it. They are consequently as far as possible removed as impurities in the process of gas-making. These are nitrogen, carbonic acid gas, and the destructive sulphur compounds, sulphuretted hydrogen and carbon bisulphide vapour. It is to the last two to which are to be attributed the injurious effects which the burning of gas has upon pictures, books, and also the tarnishing which metal fittings / suffer where gas is burnt, since they give rise to the formation of oil of vitriol (sulphuric acid), which is being incessantly poured into the air. Of course the amount so given off is little as compared with that which escapes from a coal fire, but, fortunately for the inmates of the room, in this case the greater quantity goes up the chimney; this, however, is but a method of postponing the evil day, until the atmosphere becomes so laden with impurities that what proceeds at first up the chimney will finally again make its way back through the doors and windows. A recent official report tells us that, in the town of St Helen's alone, sufficient sulphur escapes annually into the atmosphere to finally produce 110,580 tons of sulphuric acid, and a computation has been made that every square mile of land in London is deluged annually with 180 tons of the same vegetation-denuding acid. It is a matter for wonder that any green thing continues to exist in such places at all.

The chief constituents of coal-gas are, therefore, briefly as follows:–

(1) Hydrogen,
(2) Marsh-gas (carburetted hydrogen or fire-damp),
(3) Carbon monoxide,
(4) Olefiant gas (ethylene, or heavy carburetted hydrogen), with other olefines,

(5) Nitrogen,
(6) Carbonic acid gas,
(7) Sulphuretted hydrogen,
(8) Carbon bisulphide (vapour), /

the last four being regarded as impurities, which are removed as far as possible in the manufacture.

In the process of distillation of the coal, we have seen that various other important substances are brought into existence. The final residue of coke, which is impregnated with the sulphur which has not been volatilised in the form of sulphurous gases, we need scarcely more than mention here. But the gas-tar and the ammoniacal liquor are two important products which demand something more than our casual attention. At one time regarded by gas engineers as unfortunately necessary nuisances in the manufacture of gas, they have both become so valuable on account of materials which can be obtained from them, that they enable gas itself to be sold now at less than half its original price. The waste of former generations is being utilised in this, and an instance is recorded in which tar, which was known to have been lying useless at the bottom of a canal for years, has been purchased by a gas engineer for distilling purposes. It has been estimated that about 590,000 tons of coal-tar are distilled annually.

Tar in its primitive condition has been used, as every one is aware, for painting or tarring a variety of objects, such as barges and palings, in fact, as a kind of protection to the object covered from the ravages of insects or worms, or to prevent corrosion when applied to metal piers. But it is worthy of a better purpose, and is capable of yielding far more useful and interesting substances than even the most imaginative individual could have dreamed of fifty years ago. /

In the process of distillation, the tar, after standing in tanks for some time, in order that any ammoniacal liquor which may be present may rise to the surface and be drawn off, is pumped into large stills, where a moderate amount of heat is applied to it. The result is that some of the more volatile products pass over and are collected in a receiver. These first products are known as *first light oils*, or *crude coal-naphtha*, and to this naphtha all the numerous natural naphthas which have been discovered in various portions of the world, and to which have been applied numerous local names, bear a very close resemblance. Such an one, for instance, was that small but famous spring at Riddings, in Derbyshire, from which the late Mr Young – Paraffin Young[5] – obtained his well-known paraffin oil, which gave the initial impetus to what has since developed into a trade of immense proportions in every quarter of the globe.

After a time the crude coal-naphtha ceases to flow over, and the heat is increased. The result is that a fresh series of products, known as *medium oils*, passes over, and these oils are again collected and kept separate from the previous series. These in turn cease to flow, when, by a further increase of heat, what are known as the *heavy oils* finally pass over, and when the last of these, *green grease*, as it is called, distils over, pitch alone is left in the still. Pitch is used to a large extent in the preparation of artificial asphalte, and also of a fuel known as 'briquettes.'

The products thus obtained at the various stages of the process are themselves subjected / to further distillation, and by the exercise of great care, requiring the most delicate and accurate treatment, a large variety of oils is obtained, and these are retailed under many and various fanciful names.

One of the most important and best known products of the fractional distillation of crude coal-naphtha is that known as *benzene*, or benzole, (C_6H_6). This, in its unrefined condition, is a light spirit which distils over at a point somewhat below the boiling point of water, but a delicate process of rectification[6] is necessary to produce the pure spirit. Other products of the same light oils are toluene[7] and xylene.[8]

Benzene of a certain quality is of course a very familiar and useful household supplement. It is sometimes known and sold as *benzene collas*,[9] and is used for removing grease from clothing, cleaning kid gloves, &c. If pure it is in reality a most dangerous spirit, being very inflammable; it is also extremely volatile, so much so that, if an uncorked bottle be left in a warm room where there is a fire or other light near, its vapour will probably ignite. Should the vapour become mixed with air before ignition, it becomes a most dangerous explosive, and it will thus be seen how necessary it is to handle the article in household use in a most cautious manner. Being highly volatile, a considerable degree of cold is experienced if a drop be placed on the hand and allowed to evaporate.

Benzene, which is only a compound of carbon and hydrogen, was first discovered by Faraday[10] in 1825; it is now obtained in large quantities / from coal-tar, not so much for use as benzene as for its conversion, in the first place, by the action of nitric acid, into *nitro-benzole*, a liquid having an odour like the oil of bitter almonds, and which is much used by perfumers under the name of *essence de mirbane*; and, in the second place, for the production from this nitro-benzole of the far-famed *aniline*. After the distillation of benzene from the crude coal-naphtha is completed, the chief impurities in the residue are charred and deposited by the action of strong sulphuric acid. By further distillation a lighter oil is given off, often known as *artificial turpentine oil*, which is used as a solvent for varnishes and lackers.[11] This is very familiar to the costermonger fraternity as the oil which is burned in the flaring lamps which illuminate the New Cut or the Elephant and Castle[12] on Saturday and other market nights.

By distillation of the *heavy oils*, carbolic acid and commercial *anthracene* are produced, and by a treatment of the residue, a white and crystalline substance known as *naphthalin* ($C_{10}H_8$) is finally obtained.

Thus, by the continued operation of the chemical process known as fractional distillation of the immediate products of coal-tar, these various series of useful oils are prepared. /

Aniline has been previously referred ... to as having been prepared from nitrobenzole, or *essence de mirbane*, and its preparation, by treating this substance with iron-filings and acetic acid, was one of the early triumphs of the chemists who undertook the search after the unknown contained in gas-tar. It had previously been obtained from oils distilled from bones. The importance of the substance lies in the fact that, by the action of various chemical reagents, a series of colouring matters of very great richness are formed, and these are the well-known *aniline dyes.*

As early as 1836, it was discovered that aniline, when heated with chloride of lime, acquired a beautiful blue tint. This discovery led to no immediate practical result, and it was not until twenty-one years after that a further discovery was made, which may indeed be said to have achieved a world-wide reputation. It was found that, by adding bichromate of potash to a solution of aniline and sulphuric acid, a powder was obtained from which the dye was afterwards extracted, which is known as *mauve.* Since that time dyes in all shades and colours have been obtained from the same source. *Magenta* was the next dye to make its appearance, and in the fickle history of fashion, probably no colours have had such extraordinary runs of popularity as / those of mauve and magenta. Every conceivable colour was obtained in due course from the same source, and chemists began to suspect that, in the course of time, the colouring matter of dyer's madder, which was known as *alizarin*, would also be obtained therefrom. Hitherto this had been obtained from the root of the madder-plant, but by dint of careful and well-reasoned research, it was obtained by Dr Groebe,[13] from a solid crystalline coal-tar product, known as *anthracene*, ($C_{12}H_{14}$). This artificial alizarin yields colours which are purer than those of natural madder, and being derived from what was originally regarded as a waste product, its cost of production is considerably cheaper.

We have endeavoured thus far to deal with (1) gas, and (2) tar, the two principal products in the distillation of coal. We have yet to say a few words concerning the useful ammoniacal liquor, and the final residue in the retorts, *i.e.*, coke.

The ammoniacal liquor which has been passing over during distillation of the coal, and which has been collecting in the hydraulic main and in other parts of the gas-making apparatus, is set aside to be treated to a variety of chemical reactions, in order to wrench from it its useful constituents. Amongst these, of course, *ammonia* stands in the first rank, the others being comparatively unimportant. In order to obtain this, the liquor is first of all neutralised by being treated with a quantity of acid, which converts the principal constituent of the liquor, viz., carbonate of ammonia (smelling salts), into either sulphate / of ammonia, or chloride of ammonia, familiarly known as sal-ammoniac,[14] according as sulphuric acid or hydrochloric acid is the acid used. Thus carbonate of ammonia with sulphuric acid will give sulphate of ammonia, but carbonate of ammonia with hydrochloric acid will give sal-ammoniac (chloride of ammonia). By a further treatment of these with lime, or, as it is chemically known, oxide of calcium, ammonia is set free, whilst chloride of lime (the well-known disinfectant), or sulphate of lime (gypsum, or 'plaster of Paris'), is the result.

Thus:

Sulphate of ammonia + lime = plaster of Paris + ammonia.

or,

Sal-ammoniac + lime = chloride of lime + ammonia.

Ammonia itself is a most powerful gas, and acts rapidly upon the eyes. It has a stimulating effect upon the nerves. It is not a chemical element, being composed of three parts of hydrogen by weight to one of nitrogen, both of which elements alone are very harmless, and, the latter indeed, very necessary to human life. Ammonia is fatal to life, producing great irritation of the lungs.

It has also been called 'hartshorn,' being obtained by destructive distillation of horn and bone. The name 'ammonia' is said to have been derived from the fact that it was first obtained by the Arabs near the temple of Jupiter Ammon, in Lybia,[15] North Africa, from the excrement of camels, in the form of sal-ammoniac. There are always traces of it in the atmosphere, / especially in the vicinity of large towns and manufactories where large quantities of coal are burned.

Coke, if properly prepared, should consist of pure carbon. Good coal should yield as much as 80 per cent. of coke, but owing to the unsatisfactory manner of its production, this proportion is seldom yielded, whilst the coke which is familiar to householders, being the residue left in the retorts after gas-making, usually contains so large a proportion of sulphur as to make its combustion almost offensive. No doubt the result of its unsatisfactory preparation has been that it has failed to make its way into households as it should have done, but there is also another objection to its use, namely, the fact that, owing to the quantity of oxygen required in its combustion, it gives rise to feelings of suffocation where insufficient ventilation of the room is provided.

Large quantities of coke are, however, consumed in the feeding of furnace fires, and in the heating of boilers of locomotives, as well as in metallurgical operations; and in order to supply the demand, large quantities of coal are 'coked,' a process by which the volatile products are completely combusted, pure coke remaining behind. This process is therefore the direct opposite to that of 'distillation,' by which the volatile products are carefully collected and re-distilled.

The sulphurous impurities which are always present in the coal, and which are, to a certain extent, retained in coke made at the gas-works, / themselves have a value, which in these utilitarian days is not long likely to escape the attention of capitalists. In coal, bands of bright shining iron pyrites[16] are constantly seen, even in the homely scuttle, and when coal is washed, as it is in some places, the removal of the pyrites increases the value of the coal, whilst it has a value of its own.

The conversion of the sulphur which escapes from our chimneys into sulphuretted hydrogen, and then into sulphuric acid, or oil of vitriol, has already been referred to, and we can only hope that in these days when every available source of wealth is being looked up, and when there threatens to remain nothing which shall in the future be known as 'waste,' that the atmosphere will be spared being longer the receptacle for the unowned and execrated brimstone[17] of millions of fires and furnaces. /

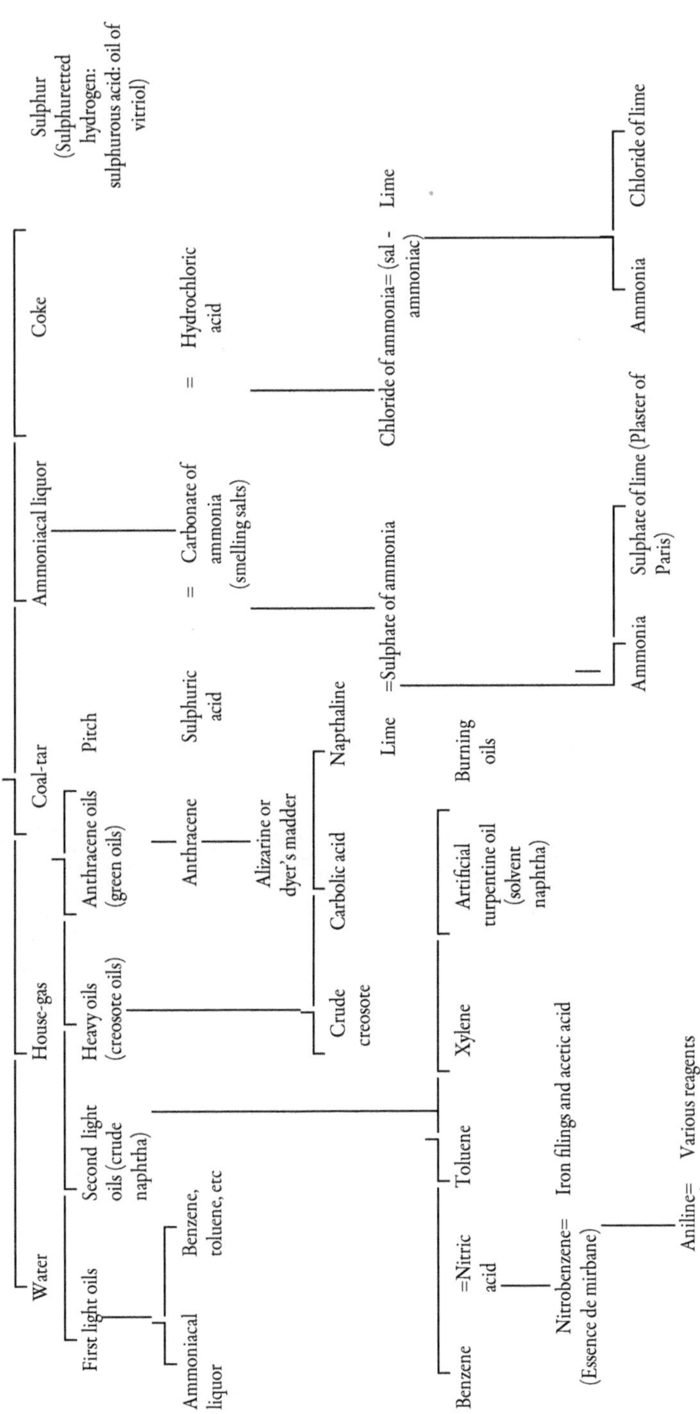
COAL
Water
House-gas
Coal-tar
Ammoniacal liquor
Coke
Sulphur (Sulphuretted hydrogen: sulphurous acid: oil of vitriol)
First light oils
Second light oils (crude naphtha)
Heavy oils (creosote oils)
Anthracene oils (green oils)
Pitch
Ammoniacal liquor
Benzene, toluene, etc
Anthracene
Sulphuric acid
=
Carbonate of ammonia (smelling salts)
=
Hydrochloric acid
Alizarine or dyer's madder
Crude creosote
Carbolic acid
Napthaline
Lime
=Sulphate of ammonia
Chloride of ammonia= (sal - ammoniac)
Lime
Benzene
Toluene
Xylene
Artificial turpentine oil (solvent naphtha)
Burning oils
=Nitric acid
Nitrobenzene= (Essence de mirbane)
Iron filings and acetic acid
Aniline=
Various reagents
Aniline dyes
Ammonia
Sulphate of lime (Plaster of Paris)
Ammonia
Chloride of lime

'Some Account of Coal Tar and its Properties', *Tradesman, or Commercial Magazine* (1809)

W.,[1] 'Some Account of Coal Tar and its Properties', *Tradesman, or Commercial Magazine*, 2:12 (June 1809), pp. 484–6.

SOME ACCOUNT OF COAL TAR AND ITS PROPERTIES.

TO THE EDITOR OF THE TRADESMAN, OR COMMERCIAL MAGAZINE.

SIR, *North Shields, Northumberland*, 10*th April*, 1809.

I HAVE observed the inquiry of your Correspondent, P. page 343, who wishes to be informed about coal tar; of that article there are two extensive manufactories up the river Tyne, one at St. Peter's quay, nearly midway between Newcastle and this place, conducted by Messrs. Row, Humble, and King; the second is near to a place called Paradise, about four miles above Newcastle; and more might have been erected but for corporation trammels.

About twenty years ago, a patent was granted to Lord Dundonald,[2] for making tar from coals; it had been in speculation for / many years before that, but he was the first who offered it to the public as an article of commerce; and I believe the coal tar works at Paradise were particularly *under the protection* of his Lordship; I think he was one of the earliest proprietors.

This tar has been found to answer many useful purposes, being an admirable coating for wood, or other work exposed to the weather; but on account of its being peculiarly subtle,[3] must be carefully kept away from articles of provision, to which it communicates a most unpleasant bituminous flavour. Your Correspondent is perfectly right in his conjectures about its use for ships; it is particularly valuable to them in long voyages in warm climates, where the remora or sucking fish,[4] by striking the ship, often proves fatal to both men and vessels. It is said that ships payed over[5] with this tar, are rendered proof against the perforations or even adhesions of that animal. The advantage of coal tar is not confined however to the ships in the foreign trade; whoever has observed the timber and planks of the pillars at Rochester bridge, and the wharfs and break waters of the fortifications at Sheerness, &c. &c. will see the destructive effects of the sea worms. Against these, coal tar and pitch have been found by experience to be great preservatives as well as against the decay of the timber. To render the effect of this tar still more certain and durable, instruments were contrived for puncturing or indenting the main timbers of a ship, after such have been properly seasoned, for the more expeditious reception of vegetable or mineral tar, prior to her being covere in[6] with planking.

Your's, W.

.../ /

'Colour in the Coal-Scuttle', *Leisure Hour* (1863)

'Colour in the Coal-Scuttle', *Leisure Hour*, 598 (June 1863), pp. 373–5.

COLOUR IN THE COAL-SCUTTLE.

It appears to be one of the special privileges of the thinkers and workers of the nineteenth century to convert to the benefit of man, substances hitherto considered useless and even hurtful. The great Robert Boyle,[1] the illustrious founder of the Royal Society, in an 'Essay on Man's great Ignorance of the Uses of Natural Things,' commences with the proposition, 'that there are very few of the works of nature that have been sufficiently considered, and are thoroughly known.' Had he lived until the present day, he would have found that what was true of the seventeenth century was still more true of the present age. Every day convinces us more and more, that a waste product simply means one whose properties 'have not been sufficiently considered and not thoroughly known;' and perhaps no series of so-called waste products illustrates this fact more fully than those occurring in the manufacture of coal gas.

Coal, chemically considered, is now one of the most important of our minerals. Whether we look at the immense number of useful materials which by chemical treatment it is capable of yielding, or the vast amount of light it has thrown on obscure points of chemical science during the investigation of the properties of those products, it still remains the most valuable and interesting substance, both to the practical manufacturer and to the chemical philosopher, that has ever been bestowed on man.

During the conversion of coal into gas for illuminating purposes, four distinct substances are produced. First come the gaseous products, which, when purified form ordinary gas; secondly, certain watery products called gas liquors; thirdly, tar, which is a mixture of more or less volatile oils holding pitch in solution; and lastly, coke. For many years the gas and the coke were the only utilized products, the gas-liquors being used to pollute any unfortunate river that happened to be in the vicinity, and the tar being almost given away, to serve as a cheap paint for protecting rough iron and woodwork from the action of the weather. With the gas-liquor, which is now a highly valuable material, we must reluctantly part company, the tar being the product concerned in the transformation of coal into colour. Who would have dreamed, ten years ago, that the black, evil-smelling substance, that we hastily passed in the street, holding our breath the while, for fear of inhaling its loathsome vapour, would produce delicious scents, vying with the rose and violet in delicacy of odour, and colours that rival in brilliancy of hue the lovely tints of these queens of the garden? Yet so it is; and to the chemist it is a matter of but little surprise, for he knows that coal-tar is a very complex substance, composed of some hundreds of different compounds possessing the most distinct and opposite properties. The major portion of these we must pass unnoticed, and confine our attention to the crude coal oil obtained from the tar by steam distillation. This crude oil, by several processes of purification and re-distillation, ultimately yields two substances with which we have to deal – carbolic acid and benzol.[2] With carbolic acid most of us are unhappily acquainted, having used it in the impure form of creosote for toothache. Benzol we also know as 'benzine collas.'[3] The property it possesses of dissolving fats and oils, renders it available for the extraction of grease from our clothes; its great volatility causing it to leave no unpleasant smell behind, as in the case of turpentine and other grease solvents. Carbolic acid, when united with lime, forms one of the most powerful disinfectants known. Its antiseptic properties are no less valuable, the preservation of meat by the process of smoking being due to the small quantities of carbolic acid contained in wood smoke. By treatment with nitric acid it forms picric acid, a beautiful substance, crystallizing in light yellow plates, like sliced topazes. It is one of the most intensely bitter compounds known, and has been used by certain fraudulent brewers in the manufacture of bitter ales. It has also been employed in medicines as an antiperiodic[4] in lieu of quinine; but, from its great affinity for animal matter, it dyed the skin of the patients a bright yellow, inflicting on them an artificial jaundice, somewhat difficult to get rid of. This intense affinity for animal substances has rendered it most valuable as a dye for silk and woollen fabrics. The lovely sulphur and canary yellow silks, which were so fashionable in our ball-rooms a few seasons back, owed their colour to this dye. They may be readily distinguished from other shades of yellow, by masticating a few shreds of the material, when, if dyed with picric acid, the bitter taste of that substance will soon render itself apparent. And here we may notice a peculiar fact, that nearly all the coal-tar colours show a great liking for animal substances, fixing themselves to silk and wool with great pertinacity, and manifesting little or no willingness to unite with vegetable fibres, such as cotton or flax, without the interposition of an animal or mineral mordant.

To be rendered available as a source of colour, benzol, the second and most important of the coal-tar products, undergoes a series of transformations. The first of these is its conversion into nitro-benzol. Benzol is readily attacked by fuming nitric acid, which unites with it, forming a liquid of a deep red colour. On the addition of water this liquid deposits a heavy yellow oil, which is nitro-benzol, or the artificial oil of bitter almonds of commerce. This curious oily liquid has the odour and flavour of bitter almonds, and differs from the natural oil in not being poisonous when used in small quantities. It is employed in confectionary, as a substitute for its vegetable prototype, which often contains sufficient prussic acid[5] to render a dish of almond custard a very questionable aliment. Perfumers use it to scent cheap almond soap; but it has lately fallen somewhat into disuse, from the fact of the commercial quality retaining a certain tarry substance that is liable to leave an unpleasant odour on the hands. The second step towards colour is the formation of aniline from nitro-benzol, by the abstraction of certain proportions of oxygen, and the addition of hydrogen. The most unscientific of our readers knows that hydrogen has a great affinity for oxygen, seizing hold of it whenever an opportunity offers, and forming water. The method by which the desired transformation is performed is by the elimination of hydrogen from any substance in the presence of nitro-benzol. Acetic acid and iron filings are therefore mixed with nitro-benzol in a capacious retort, and heat is applied to the mixture. The nascent hydrogen immediately begins to act on the latter substance, one portion abstracting the oxygen, and the other uniting with the deoxidized nitro-benzol, which distils over in the form of aniline. Aniline forms, as it were, the foundation-stone of the aniline dyes, and as such deserves a little consideration. It is a colourless, limpid fluid, having an agreeable wine-like odour, and acrid burning taste. / It belongs to the class of bodies called artificial bases by chemists; that is to say, it is capable of forming salts with the different acids. Thus we have the sulphate, nitrate, and acetate of aniline, corresponding to the sulphates, nitrates, and acetates of potash, soda, iron, silver, etc. It was discovered some forty years ago amongst the products of the decomposition of indigo, and later in very small quantities in coal-tar oil. It is, chemically speaking, a very interesting body, and the researches into its properties have done more for the advancement of chemical science than almost any others with which we are acquainted. A few years ago half a pound of it was thought to be a marvellously large specimen; but, since the discovery of the aniline dyes, it is manufactured by the ton, at a few shillings a pound. The various reactions of aniline with different chemical substances always induced chemists to think that it might some day yield a valuable dye; but its scientific peculiarities were always so interesting, that they led the theoretical philosopher away from its possible economic value. It was not until Mr. W. H. Perkin, a pupil of Dr. Hofmann's,[6] had experimented upon it with a view to the formation of artificial quinine, that any great step was taken. For this purpose he endeavoured to oxidize the sulphate of aniline with a certain oxidizing salt, bichromate of potash, but instead of obtaining the desired result, the mixture only produced a dirty black precipitate. A true chemist is, however, never discouraged, no matter how he may be deceived in his expectations. Instead of losing his temper and throwing the dirty black mess down the sink, Mr. Perkin set to work to investigate its properties, and, in doing so, found it to contain a magnificent dyeing material, capable of giving to silk and wool the beautiful colour popularly called 'mauve,' from a French word signifying 'mallow,' the tint of whose petals this dye closely resembles. The process for obtaining it is simple. Sulphate of aniline is first made by mixing certain proportions of aniline and sulphuric acid. Equal portions of the solutions of sulphate of aniline and bichromate of potash are then mixed, and allowed to stand until the whole of the black precipitate is thrown down. The precipitate is washed, dried, and digested in coal-tar naphtha, until the whole of the resinous portion is dissolved out. The remainder is dried, and digested in spirits of wine,[7] which dissolves the dye, leaving behind a mass of carbonic residue that may be used for printing ink. The alcoholic solution contains the dye, and may be evaporated until the colouring matter remains behind as a dark bronze paste, with purple and green reflections.

Mr. Perkin's discovery immediately put experimental chemists on the alert to torture the different compounds of aniline with other oxidizing agents, and the Patent Office was besieged by would-be patentees of processes for the conversion of aniline into all the colours of the rainbow. Many of these were worthless, and others were infringements of Mr. Perkin's patent. The only ones which have lasted are those for the production of magenta red, by the action of arsenic acid and other gently oxidizing agents on aniline. This process, which is carried out on an enormous scale by Messrs. Simpson, Manle, and Nicholson, consists in treating aniline with certain proportions of arsenic acid. The red dye formed, which is known to the public by the name of 'magenta,' has been thoroughly investigated by Dr. Hofmann, who finds it to be a true base, like soda, iron, or aniline, and capable of forming salts of a very magnificent description.

Those of our readers who visited the International Exhibition[8] will recollect the splendid crowns formed of the acetate of rosaniline,[9] in the chemical department of the eastern annexe. These gorgeous objects consisted of wire frameworks covered with aggregations of pyramidical crystals, which reflected the splendid golden green metallic lustre seen in the wings of rosebeetles. The base itself, when not united to any acid, is, singularly enough, perfectly colourless. It forms salts with most of the acids, which give crystals almost as magnificent as the acetate. From it may be formed, by a process not yet made public, another base named chrysaniline, (from *chrusos*, Gr. gold,) which affords a very magnificent golden yellow dye.

By using bichloride of tin with aniline, a splendid blue is obtained; by substituting chlorate of potash, emerald green is formed; and we should only puzzle and weary our readers if we were to describe the vast number of processes for manufacturing every conceivable colour from this wonderful substance aniline.

There are other coal-tar products besides aniline, which have been transformed into colour in the laboratory, but the results they have yielded are either fugitive or incomparable in brilliancy to those obtained from aniline. Besides which, as nearly every colour is now obtained from this source, it would be useless to seek for novel modes of manufacture from new and less available materials.

The coal-tar dyes are all easy of application, and their colorific properties are very powerful, a mere atom dissolved in water or alcohol being sufficient to dye several pounds of silk or wool. They have not as yet been satisfactorily applied to dyeing cotton and linen, although, by the use of certain mordants they have been printed on muslins and calicoes in a very permanent manner. Their permanence on animal fibres received a most convincing test at the International Exhibition. In Mr. Perkin's case hung several specimens of silk and wool, which remained exposed to the fiercest rays of the sun for more than six months. Before removing them, it was naturally expected that the side turned to the light would have faded; but on examination, the sharpest eyes could detect no difference between the sheltered and exposed portions of the fabrics.

To turn from science to commerce, let us look at the trade value of these dyes to England. Hitherto, our principle dye-stuffs have been imported. We have obtained madder from Holland and France, indigo from India, cochineal from South America, lichens, turmeric, and arnotto[10] from other countries; but now we may reverse all this. In one of the most plentiful of our waste products we find the source of the three primary colours, by the admixture of which we may obtain almost any desired tint. We may therefore, without assuming the character of prophets, safely predict that in a few years England will be the principal colour-exporting nation of the world.[11] Coal will thus add one more element to England's greatness, in addition to those already proceeding from our underground treasuries.

While we are on the subject of colour, let us say a parting word to our female friends, on the prevailing mania for scarlet. There is hardly a garment worn by ladies that is not made of scarlet material. Regent Street[12] at three o'clock is red hot. The attention of the man of musical tastes, at a fashionable concert, is distracted and nullified by the ruddy blaze around him, and he feels a relief almost akin to ecstacy when some lady with finer tastes than her sisters passes him clothed in cool mauve. Even in our churches and homes are our eyeballs seared with this blazing colour. Scarlet, we allow, is a magnificent colour; but abuse it, and the eye becomes distressed. It is like using too much condiment in place of wholesome food. Spring has come, and nature is bursting out / with her glorious greens, violets, blues, and greys, but with very little scarlet. True, summer, with his gorgeous tints, uses this colour; but sparingly. A touch here and there in the golden corn – a speck or two amongst the purple clover – a broken mass of dots, relieved and kept down by the bright green of the cherry trees, are examples of the sparing way in which nature uses scarlet. Let our ladies, then, follow nature, and give up the abuse of this brazen, bull-baiting colour. The chemist has given them mauve, magenta, azuline, emeraldine, and a hundred other delicate colours with names as pretty as their hues. Let them use them with taste and judgment, and Regent Street will once more be a flowerbed – the concert-room a rainbow.

'Saccharin', *Colliery Guardian* (1886)

'Saccharin', *Colliery Guardian*, 20 August 1886, p. 304

SACCHARIN.

In his recent lectures at the Royal Institution on this subject, Professor Sir Henry Roscoe, M.P.,[1] said that Goethe in his early years – about 1741 – described a visit he paid to a 'burning hill,' near which he met an old philosopher engaged in collecting therefrom oils, resin and tar; the labours of that philosopher were not successful. Times have changed since then, for now some branches of the coal-tar industries may be valued at millions sterling per annum, and keep thousands of men in employment. All organic compounds may be referred to certain hydrocarbons or 'skeletons'; two great classes of such compounds are known as paraffinoids[2] and benzoids,[3] for from these hydrocarbons they can be built up by synthesis. In rock oils is the world's largest supply of almost natural paraffinoids, but these cannot be used in the colour industries; the largest supply of the benzoid hydrocarbons may be obtained from coal, of which 10 millions of tons are consumed annually in the blast furnaces of this country. Recently, methods have been adopted to collect the oils from these sources, but so far the endeavour to collect the benzoid hydro-carbons from such sources has been made but in few instances. The gasworks of the country have to be resorted to for benzoids, which might be extracted from coal in special ovens, and the coke be afterwards left for the use of the ironmasters. The coal from the same pit, but dug out at different levels, will yield slightly different oils. The paraffinoid oils are not easily oxidised; when nitric acid is poured upon petroleum spirit it scarcely alters it at all, but when nitric acid is poured into coal naphtha, red fumes are given off, so the benzoid oil is more acted upon. In 1825 Faraday[4] prepared benzene – the starting point of the benzoid hydrocarbons – and he did so in the laboratory of the Royal Institution. In 1848 large quantities of it were made for the first time, under Hofmann's direction, [5] and the next step was the production of aniline, from which the aniline colours are obtained. In one manufactory in Manchester 500 tons weight of aniline are used every year, yet this substance at first, like benzene, remained for years but a chemical curiosity. The coal tar dye industry was started by Perkin's mauve. Cheap wagon grease gradually rose in price till it sold at 1s. per pound for the making of artificial alizarine, a colouring matter which is now manufactured to the value of more than £2,000,000 annually; this industry has nearly driven the madder plant out of cultivation, and naphthol scarlet has nearly extinguished the cultivation of the cochineal insect in the Canaries. Indigo can now be built up by synthesis, and it is artificially manufactured to some extent. The colours derived from 1 lb. of coal will dye a full shade:– (1) Magenta, a piece of flannel, 8 in. by 27 in.; (2) yellow, a piece of flannel, 60 in. by 27 in.; (3) orange, a piece of flannel, 1.93 in. by 27 in.; (4) turkey red, calico, 4 in. by 27 in. Benzoic aldehyde is largely used for flavouring; oil of bitter almonds contains it in large proportion. One ton of Lancashire coal distilled in gas retorts yields an average of:– (1) Coal gas, 10,000 cubic feet; (2) ammonia liquor, 5 per cent., 20 – 23 gallons = 30 lb.; (3) coal tar, 12 gallons, or 139.2 lb.; (4) coke, 13 cwt. 12 gallons of coal tar yield:– (1) Benzene, 1.1 lb.; aniline, 1.1 lb.; (2) toluene, 0.9 lb.; toluidine, 0.77 lb.; (3) phenol, 1.5 lb.; aurine, 1.2 lb.; (4) solvent naphtha, 2.4 lb.; (5) naphthalene, 6.3 lb.; naphthol, 4.75 lb.; naphtha, yellow, 9.5 lb.; (6) creosote, 17 lb.; (7) heavy oils, 14 lb.; (8) anthracene, 0.46 lb.; alizarin, 20 per cent., 2.25 lb.; (9) pitch, 69.6 lb. The colours derived from 1 ton of coal will dye a full shade:– (1) Magenta, 500 yards of flannel 27 in. wide; (2) naphthol yellow, 3,800 yards 27 in. wide; (3) aurin, 120 yards 27 in. wide (orange); alizarin, 225 yards, 27 in. wide calico, Turkey red. Perkin discovered mauve when he was trying to artificially manufacture alkaloid like quinine, but of late certain products have been made by chemists from coal tar derivatives, which products possess febrifuge[6] qualities of value. One of these was discovered in 1881 by Otto Fischer, of Munich;[7] it is not quinine, but it possesses qualities of analogous characters; one advantage is that it does not produce upon the patient the unpleasant effects of large doses of quinine. A dose of 30 grains of it is found to lower the temperature of patients afflicted with typhus fever 3 degs. upon an average. Thallene is also a febrifuge; it has been used with some success in the treatment of yellow fever. Coal tar perfumes are now in more or less general use, including the artificial perfume of the Tonka bean, of the sweet woodruff, and of a variety of sweet grasses. The perfume of 'new-mown hay' – as it is marked in the shops – really comes from coal tar; cumarin is really the active principle of this scent, and of that of the Tonka bean. Vanillin, the active principle of vanilla, is now made from coal tar, and by mixing some of the coal-tar perfumes with oil of bitter almonds, a scent is obtained resembling that of white heliotrope. Mr. Rimmel[8] had forwarded him some of this perfume, and by means of the spray distributor before them he had the pleasure of scenting the theatre of the institution therewith. These coal tar artificial perfumes, he continued, are gradually driving out the industries of extracting the natural perfumes from the plant. About 150 tons of nitro-benzene are used annually for the perfuming of cheap soaps. Of all the marvellous productions from coal tar, the next one bears the palm, namely, saccharin. Saccharin is a white crystalline body artificially prepared from coal tar (toluene) and possessing an intensely sweet taste. It was discovered by Dr. Fahlberg.[9] It is not a sugar, does not produce any appreciable physiological effect on the human body; does not act as a food, but only as a flavour, and passes away unchanged. It contains carbon, oxygen, hydrogen, sulphur and nitrogen, and its chemical name is orthobenzoyl sulphonic imide; its sweetening power is 280 times that of cane sugar. Only within the last few months has saccharin been made in quantity, although it was discovered in 1879, and for some purposes it may prove to be of very great service. As yet it is a little too soon to say whether its consumption will prove injurious, because although it and many other hydrocarbons do not act as poisons, in long course of time those other hydrocarbons have an effect, more especially upon the liver. Large quantities of saccharin have been given to dogs, and one dog had as much of it daily as was equivalent in sweetening power to a pound of sugar, but it did him no harm. There are human diseases, during the course of which sugar must not be taken. In such cases the use of saccharin may prove to be advantageous. Sir Henry Roscoe sweetened some cups of tea with saccharin, and invited the listeners to come to the table and taste the same. He likewise produced some bons-bons and some Swedish punch, flavoured with orthobenzoyl sulphonic amide. – *English Mechanic.* /

THE NUISANCES OF COAL

This section documents the contemporary understanding of the injuries involved in producing and using coal. The section opens with an apocalyptic description of the 'Black Country' as it appeared to an imagined traveller from London to Holyhead in 1822 (p. 187). The traveller would have been on his or her way to Dublin and the account appeared in a London quarterly, so one has to discount the description somewhat for the shock of the unfamiliar. Nevertheless, it is striking that as early as 1822, when British coal output was still less than 30 million tons, and output in the west Midlands still less than a third of what it would become by the end of the century, the industry had transformed a whole district to a hell on earth.[1]

The hell described is one of 'sulphureous vapours', the scarring of the earth, houses so affected by subsidence as to seem to defy the laws of gravity, and noise: a grating, roaring and a trembling of the earth. This section treats the subsidence and the scarring of the earth with pit heaps, soot and ashes, and the pollution of the air and water, though nothing more is said about the noise of the industrial areas. This must have sounded like a cacophony to those reared in rural areas in which mechanical sources of noise were almost absent. The history of noise has been an unexamined topic.

Subsidence was little understood in the nineteenth century. Buddle in 'On Subsidences Produced by Working Beds of Coal' (pp. 189–92) admits that the 'extent of settlement, as shown on the surface, from working coal, depends upon so many contingencies, that it cannot be subjected to any calculation' (p. 190) although he is clearly able to form judgements. However, in two significant respects, viz., whether the subsidence is limited in area to the area excavated or extends more widely, and whether the subsidence is immediate or may be postponed and if so for how long, he is (in the first case) wrong or (in the second case) unable to state an opinion. These aspects mattered since ignorance and confusion on them enabled coal owners to escape liability for surface damages. Coal owners could and did claim that their workings could not have caused the subsidence since their workings did not lie vertically below the subsidence or that they could not be liable because they had ceased working the area years before.[2] The legal aspects are noticed in Volume 2 of this set (pp. 227–58). The question of the area affected by subsidence is that treated by Joseph Dickinson in 'On Subsidence to the Surface Caused by Colliery Workings' (pp. 193–8). Twenty years later than Buddle's piece, it argues that subsidence is generally not merely vertical and therefore affects a wider area than that excavated. It was not, however, until the early years of the twentieth century that significant research was undertaken on the problem in either Britain or elsewhere.[3]

The scarring of the earth with pit heaps was not merely an aesthetic outrage on the good, green earth but in some cases, such as the one described in 'A Burning Pit-Heap: Alleged Extraordinary Effects' (pp. 199–200), a further source of air pollution.[4] This is not to say the aesthetic effects were deemed unimportant at the time. As Alderman House commented at the end of the report 'however salubrious these places might be, he found that people who could help it did not care to reside near a pit-heap'.

There were also less obvious costs, for example habitat loss. A contributor to the *Transactions* of the Tyneside Naturalists' Field Club contributed this note on one of the marine algae or seaweeds, *Sphacelaria Filicina*:

> In a pool overhung by lofty rocks, south of Seaham harbour. Very rare. I have gathered this beautiful plant on two occasions (1859 and 1860), but it does not seem to extend beyond the limits of a very small pool on a ledge of rock completely overhung and darkened by the cliff above.[5]

To which is attached the following note:

> Since writing this notice, I have visited the locality alluded to (October, 1860), and though the tide prevented my reaching the pool in which the Sphacelaria used to grow, I can have little doubt that if it be not now extinct, it will very soon become so. The Marchioness of Londonderry has 'shot' on to the beach, within a few yards of the spot, a huge heap of coal dust and rubbish from the blast furnaces in course of erection on the cliff above. This once beautiful piece of coast scenery is now a hideous tract of 'burning marl,' and the sea literally a sea of ink. Among the numerous interesting victims may also be noted *Asplenium marinum*, which, not long ago, grew here in considerable abundance, but is now totally destroyed by the smoke and dust from the burning rubbish.[6]

The next two items concern soot and chimney sweeps. 'An Account of the Proceedings of the Society for Superseding the Necessity of Climbing Boys' by Sydney Smith (pp. 201–5) became a well-known campaign piece; the next item (pp. 207–10) indicates that the horrors so satirically and so eloquently described by Smith still continued more than half a century later. It has become unfashionable to dwell on such aspects of the Victorian era and there is a danger that the plight of the chimney sweeps, once so well known, will be forgotten. The last substantial study is now thirty years old.[7] The one good reason for lightening the emphasis on their ordeals is that it distracts from the obnoxious and loathsome working conditions suffered, without prospect of legislative intervention, by many industrial workers whose duties involved tending furnaces, boilers and coal-powered machinery. Frank McKenna is one of the very few to have offered a detailed description of what was involved, in this case in the process of 'engine disposal' at a railway locomotive depot. The firebars were removed from the grate in the firebox. An engineman equipped with a long iron rake positioned himself in the maintenance pit underneath the locomotive. A colleague stood on the footplate. The damper door was opened, exposing the floor of the ashpan underneath the firebox.

> The business end of the rake lanced into the ashpan and then all hell was let loose. Into the ashpan were pushed great chunks of heavy clinker, live coals, showers of sparks and clouds of choking white ash. As the evil mixture thudded into the ashpan from above, the raker-out dragged it forward frantically into the metal skip positioned below the ashpan. Foul perspiration streamed from the raker-out, across his back, between his legs, and water gushed from his eyes. There was no escape from the heat, the dust, the smoke or the sparks. The men worked like maniacs, the one above pushing, the one below pulling, the rakes snaking and reddening like creatures demented. This was an inferno even Dante could not describe.[8]

In contrast with this neglect of soot and ashes, air pollution is now at last receiving some attention, as noticed in the Introduction to these three volumes.[9] The texts gathered here demonstrate that there was considerable concern over the issue in late Victorian society. This concern was not confined to the middle or upper classes. A correspondent to the *Penny Magazine* of 1836 writing on the 'Manners of the Northern Coal Miners' wrote:

> Some, too [among the miners], delight in cultivating the rarer specimens of flowers and plants, in situations where the atmosphere of the colliery, which is very injurious to vegetable life, will admit of this; and they are frequently members of the neighbouring Horticultural and Botanical Societies; but the number who find pleasure in such a delightful study as the rearing of flowers is very limited indeed. I am afraid that this pursuit can never be carried on to any great extent in the immediate neighbourhood of a colliery, which is singularly unfavourable to the propagation of vegetable life. In these ungenial regions, 'where smoke and dust bedim the golden day,' the huge volumes of dense smoke continually issuing from the tall chimneys, and borne away in slow dismal pageantry on the wings of the passing breeze, render the atmosphere impure and unhealthy, the effects of which are very visible on the surrounding vegetation; all vegetable life, to a considerable distance from the scene of operations, exhibiting a blighted appearance, and never that freshness of green which pervades it in more salubrious situations.[10]

Rollo Russell's text not only documents the formation of the smoke-laden fogs, later known as 'smogs', in London but attempts one of the first estimates of the economic cost of pollution. Scientific research on the question also began in this era.[11] 'The Smoke Question' (pp. 221–2) is an abstract of one of the earliest pieces of scientific research on what was later known as 'acid rain'. It demonstrates that our environmental concerns are not as modern as we might think. Finally, this collection of texts on smoke pollution includes a vision of the future written in 1914. It looks forward to 2014 and imagines the reaction of a time traveller arriving in London: 'One of the first things which astonished him was the clear air, and then the sight of the blue sky which he had so seldom seen in London before' (p. 223).

River pollution was an issue that divided the classes. It often seemed as if the landed classes were only interested in the issue in so far as it affected their fishing, still an upper-class preserve at this time. The Fisheries Preservation Association, with an address in Portman Square, London, and His Grace the Duke of Northumberland as its President, was not an organization of 'the people'. As late as 1923 *The Times* reported:

> It is pointed out that one of the principal obstacles which has hindered and discouraged the champions of the inland fisheries has been the mistaken idea, amounting to a deep-rooted prejudice, that all measures for the regulation and development of inland fisheries were designed merely to secure the interests of the sportsman.[12]

The tendency of discussions of river pollution to be diverted from issues of public health and popular recreation to the effects on the health of salmon and trout in rivers where the right to fish had become private property understandably alienated the working and professional classes. Manufacturing interests were, of course, reluctant to accept additional controls and regulation. These class divisions help us to understand why the repeated initiatives on river pollution originated in the House of Lords and were defeated in the House of Commons, a history referred to in the first part of V. B. Barrington-Kennett's 'River Pollution by Refuse from Manufactories and Mines Together with Some Remedies Proposed' (pp. 227–35).

The second part of 'River Pollution' consists of a long disquisition on the problem by Charles Neve Cresswell (*c.* 1829–1908), a barrister specializing in drainage and sewage and thus acquainted with conflicts over the issue as part of his daily life. He first offers a 'common sense' analysis of differences over the issue: some people are ignorant or stupid; others are well-disposed but do nothing; others are ill-disposed and cannot be persuaded to change their ways, etc. But in the course of this he describes the key economic issue, already hinted at by the author of the main text, Vincent Barrington Kennett-Barrington. This is the 'free-rider' problem: all may be willing to contribute to some improvement if others do so but the attempts of some to avoid making a contribution and take a 'free ride' undermine the project and it collapses. The problem was clearly understood at the time and Kennett-Barrington quotes the remarks of the 1873 House of Lords Select Committee in explanation:

> Most of those large manufacturers are quite prepared to face the expense and trouble, provided they know what they have to do; but they naturally refuse to go to expense in purifying their waste liquors, unless their neighbours will do something in the same direction.

The conventional remedy for such problems is state intervention; mechanisms based on mutual monitoring by an organization based in civil society are also feasible, especially where the number of interested parties is small. Mechanisms of social control may also be effective in some communities, even where the number of interested parties is large. Action by an individual is clearly ineffective, as Neve's anecdote, given in the second part of the text, illustrated. Neve remembered one man who said

> that he thought he was bound as a public duty to set an example to his neighbours, and he therefore set to work to prevent the pollution of the river which flowed past his works ... [N]one of his neighbours were compelled to do likewise; and after a few years, having gone to considerable expense in doing his best to keep the stream pure, he had seen that those above and below were polluting it the same as ever (p. 233).

Actions by individual local authorities along the course of a river fail in the same way, as Neve goes on to exemplify.

Ideological objections to state intervention were of importance in allowing the continuation of the obvious social inefficiencies caused by river pollution. Robert Rawlinson (1810–98), one of the Commissioners on the first Royal Commission on River Pollution declared in 1866:

> although a foul river was an intolerable nuisance, yet it must be remembered that it was an advance in civilization (hear, hear) ... The discharge of effete matter into running water was a very great improvement on the ash-midden and the cesspool crowded in upon the cottage. (Hear.) ... The Royal Commission ... commenced their labours on the 15th of this month ... They might rest perfectly satisfied that Parliament would not enact any compulsory measure which should destroy trade or which should be burdensome or injurious to the community, but that they would carry such a measure as should be for the benefit of the whole people, and, if possible, to the injury of none. (Loud applause.)[13]

Rawlinson's concept of 'the community' and 'the people' appears to exclude those injured or offended by the pollution of rivers. Such attitudes were by no means universal but even those who did not share them were forced to acknowledge them. Thus Frank Buckland, addressing a sympathetic audience in 1878, and particularly concerned with rivers as a source of fresh fish for food, dwelt on the 'evils' of river pollution, remarking:

> It was most lamentable to think that at the present time, when there were so many mouths to be fed, manufacturers and mineowners, who form a relatively small proportion of Her Majesty's subjects, should be allowed to inflict directly and indirectly such a vast evil on the public in general. These individuals and companies for the most part reaped no inconsiderable profits from their industrial operations, but ... treated with indifference the welfare of the public.[14]

But even after identifying the 'vast evil' perpetrated in the pursuit of profit, Buckland felt it necessary to say that 'He did not wish ... by any means to put down or in any way interfere with the commercial industries, either of manufactories or mines'. Similarly, Hector Maclean Wilson, a medical man and the author of 'The Pollution of Streams by Spent Gas-Liquors from Coke Ovens; And the Methods Adopted for its Prevention' (pp. 237–9) detailing the hideous pollution caused by discharges from coke ovens, felt it obligatory to acknowledge 'that these pollutions are the result of the necessary development of one of the most important trades in the West Riding of Yorkshire'. Progress towards reform of the law and its enforcement was hobbled by such self-defeating protestations until after the First World War. In 1919 *The Times* carried a report headlined 'Salmon Fisheries in Jeopardy: State Control Demanded', a headline that could not have appeared even ten years before.[15]

Notes

1. The description was echoed in a further account a few years later: 'South Staffordshire at Night', *Penny Magazine*, 12:697 (11 February 1843), pp. 53–5.
2. The following findings were reported by Villot in the *Annales des Mines*, series 8, 16 (1889), pp. 421–6 and plate X under the title 'La propagation latéral des Mouvements d'Effrondrement dans les Mines' and abstracted by 'M. W. B.' in the *Transactions of the North of England Institute of Mining and Mechanical Engineers*, 39 (1889–90), p. 150: '[H]eavy falls, produced by the robbing and removal of pillars 33 feet square [10 m square], in a seven-foot [2 metre] seam of coal, lying at a depth of 1,060 feet [325 m], were felt, and damage caused to houses, etc., in villages situated at distances of 2,600 yards, 3,500 yards, 4,000 yards, and 7,900 yards [2,400, 3,200, 3,700 and 7,300 m, respectively], situated on coal measures. No effects were produced at distances of 3,000 yards and 3,700 [yards; 2800 and 3400 m, respectively] where the villages were situated on older rocks forming the margins of the coal-field or basin.'
3. The British engineers were kept up to date with continental research by the publication of abstracts. See, for example: L. L. B., 'Surface and Underground Subsidence in Coal-Mining', *Transactions of the North of England Institute of Mining and Mechanical Engineers*, 59 (1908–9), p. 91 (an abstract of the 'thoroughly exhaustive' memoir by R. Hausse, 'Von dem Niedergehen des Gebirges beim Kohlenbergbau und den damit zusammenhängenden Boden- und Gebäudesenkungen', *Zeitschrift für das Berg-, Hütten- und Salinen-wesen im preussischen Staate*, 55 (1907), pp. 324–446; A. R. L., 'Subsidences in Upper Silesian Coal-Mines', *Transactions of the North of England Institute of Mining and Mechanical Engineers*, 62 (1911–12), p. 28. British research from this period included the theoretically ambitious H. W. G. Halbaum, 'The Great Planes of Strain in the Absolute Roof of Mines' and 'Discussion', *Transactions of the North of England Insti-*

tute of Mining and Mechanical Engineers, 56 (1905–6), pp. 103–39; W. Hay, 'Damage to Surface Buildings caused by Underground Workings [and Discussion]', *Transactions of the Institute of Mining Engineers*, 36 (1908–9), pp. 427–36 and plates XVIII–XX and 'Discussion', ibid., 37 (1908–9), pp. 354–5; and further 'Discussion', ibid., p. 37 (1908–9), pp. 647–8; J. Piggford, 'Notes of Subsidences caused by Coal-Working at Teversal and Pleasley Collieries', *Transactions of the Institute of Mining Engineers*, 38 (1909–10), pp. 129–31 and 'Discussion', ibid., p. 39 (1909–10) pp. 137–44.

4. Henry Mayhew noted burning pit-heaps as a normal feature of the northern coalfields commenting that 'This catastrophe is rather encouraged than checked by the coal owners – seeing that, with the exception of comparatively rare cases, small coal is of little value, and that it is very desirable to keep down the size of the pit heap' (Our Special Correspondent [i.e. Henry Mayhew] 'Labour and the Poor: The Manufacturing Districts: The Coalfield of Northumberland and Durham – What a Coal Pit Is', *Morning Chronicle* [London], 20 December 1849).
5. It appeared in the first photographically illustrated book, by Anna Atkins (1797–1871), *Photographs of British Algae: Cyanotype Impressions*, 8 parts in 3 vols ([London?]: publisher unknown, 1843–53), vol. 1, pt 1, plate 62 on f. 71. A selection of the exquisite and mesmerising plates, not including that illustrating *S. Filicina*, is available on the website of the British Library at http://www.bl.uk (accessed 16 April 2011); that illustrating *S. Filicina* is available on the web site of the Detroit Institute of Arts at http://www.dia.org (accessed 16 April 2011).
6. G. S. Brady, 'A Catalogue of the Marine Algæ of Northumberland and Durham', *Transactions of the Tyneside Naturalists' Field Club*, 4 (1858–60), pp. 266–318 and plate XV. By 'extinct' Brady meant 'extinct from the area'; it is still extant.
7. K. H. Strange, *Climbing Boys: A Study of Sweeps' Apprentices 1773–1875* (London: Allison & Busby, 1982). B. Cullingford, *Chimneys and Chimney Sweeps* (Princes Risborough: Shire, 2003) is also useful, not least for its illustrations.
8. F. McKenna, *The Railway Workers 1840–1970* (London: Faber and Faber, 1980), p. 92. McKenna began his working life as an engine cleaner in 1946 and progressed to become a fireman and then an engine driver with British Railways. Between 1956 and 1969 he was a lay officer of the Associated Society of Locomotive Engineers and Firemen, the drivers' trade union. His account of 'engine disposal' appears to be based on personal experience and thus relates to the 1940s or 50s. It is unlikely that the process was any less unpleasant in the Victorian period.
9. As well as Stephen Mosley's work, noticed in the Introduction to these three volumes, see also: D. Stradling and P. Thorsheim, 'The Smoke of Great Cities: British and American Efforts to Control Air Pollution, 1860–1914', *Environmental History*, 4 (1999), pp. 6–31; B. Luckin, '"The Heart and Home of Horror": The Great London Fogs of the Late Nineteenth Century', *Social History*, 28 (2003), pp. 31–48.
10. A Correspondent, 'Manners of the Northern Coal Miners', *Penny Magazine* (25 June 1836), pp. 242–4 at pp. 243–4.
11. Two studies by Julius Berend Cohen (1859–1935), a chemist, mark the birth of modern research: *The Character and Extent of Air Pollution in Leeds: A Lecture Delivered before the Leeds Philosophical Society on March 3rd, 1896* (Leeds: Goodall and Suddick, Printers, 1896) and, with Arthur G. Ruston, *Smoke: A Study of Town Air* (London: Arnold, 1912); a second edition was published in 1925.
12. 'Pollution of Inland Fisheries: Report for 1919–21', *The Times*, 19 May 1923, p. 7c. The views reported were those of the Ministry of Agriculture in its *Report on Salmon and*

Freshwater Fisheries for the Years 1919–21. At this time, 'sportsman' denoted a person able, because of their wealth, to devote themselves to hunting, shooting, fishing, mountaineering, motor-racing, etc. without the distraction of earning a living.

13. Rawlinson was addressing the Social Science Congress, meeting in Manchester, the centre of antagonism to state intervention in economic affairs, on 5 October; his reference to the 15th of 'this month' is a slip. 'Effete' here means 'spent' or 'worn out' (*OED*) ('Social Science Congress', *The Times*, 6 October 1866, p. 12a).
14. 'The Sanitary Institute of Great Britain', *The Times*, 6 July 1878, p. 13f.
15. 28 February 1919, p. 5f. See also: 'Our Rivers and Salmon: Evils of Pollution: Call for Effective Control', *The Times*, 14 June 1920, p. 9b.

‘[A Description of the Staffordshire Collieries]’, *Knight’s Quarterly Magazine* (1822)

‘[A Description of the Staffordshire Collieries]’, *Knight’s Quarterly Magazine* (1822), as quoted *in extenso*, in ‘Birmingham’, *Monthly Supplement of The Penny Magazine of the Society for the Diffusion of Useful Knowledge* (31 December 1835), p. 47.

Many of my readers must recollect crossing, in the route from London to Holyhead, a miserable tract of country commencing a few miles beyond Birmingham and continuing to Wolverhampton. If the volumes of sulphureous vapour which I shall not compliment with the name of smoke, permitted them at intervals to ‘view the dismal situation waste and wild,’[1] they would observe the surface of the desert around them scarred and broken, as if it had just reposed from the heaving of an earthquake. Now and then they would shudder as they passed the mouth of a deserted mine left without any guard but the wariness of the passenger. Sometimes they would see a feeble and lambent flame, (called by the miners the wild fire,) issue from chaps[2] in the parched earth. It is self-kindled by a process familiar to that chemist, and feeds on gas evolved by the refuse of the coal that has been left in immense caverns, hollowed by the labours of ages, over which the carriage of the unconscious traveller rolls for many miles. They would be struck also with the sight of houses from which the treacherous foundations have gradually shrunk, leaving them in such a state of obliquity with the horizon, as if they stood only to evince the contempt of themselves and their inhabitants for the laws of gravitation.

If the traveller, in addition to these attacks on his organs of smell and of vision, has nerve to inspect more closely the tremendous operations which are going on around him as far as the eye can reach, he must learn to endure the grating of harsh wheels, the roaring of the enormous bellows which, set in motion by the power of steam, urge the fires of the smelting furnace till they glow with almost the bright brilliance of the noon-day sun. He must learn to care little for the sparks which fly from the half-molten iron, under the action of the forge, in torrents of burning rain, while the earth literally trembles beneath the strokes of a mightier hammer than Thor himself ever wielded against giants. /

John Buddle, 'On Subsidences Produced by Working Beds of Coal' (1839)

John Buddle, 'On Subsidences Produced by Working Beds of Coal', *Transactions of the Geological Society of London*, 6 (1841), pp. 165–8.

On Subsidences produced by working Beds of Coal In a Letter to C. Lyell, Esq., F.G.S., from JOHN BUDDLE,[1] ESQ., F.G.S.

[Read November 6th, 1839.]

SUBSIDENCE of the surface invariably follows the working of the subjacent coal, when sufficient pillars are not left to support the overlying mass. The extent of such subsidence is governed by the following circumstances :

1st. The depth of the seams of coal below the surface.
2nd. The thickness of the seam or seams.
3rd. The nature of the strata between the surface and the seams of coal.
4th. Whether the pillars of coal are wholly or partially worked.

If the depth from the surface does not exceed twenty-five or thirty fathoms, and sandstones form the predominant strata, then the subsidence is nearly, if not fully, equal to the thickness of the seam of coal which has been taken out; but should *metal-stone*[2] or shale form the predominant strata, the subsidence is less. This rule I consider to hold good in all cases, let the depth from the surface be what it may; that is to say, the subsidence is always greater under a sandstone than under a metal-stone cover.*

Whenever a lower seam is worked after an upper one has been removed, and the surface lowered in the manner above stated, a *second set,* or lowering, takes place. I have known this to occur three successive times, as will afterwards be shown; and that it might not, under certain conditions of the stratification, take place an indefinite number of times, I am not prepared to say.

* Cover means the *whole* thickness of the strata between the seam and the surface.

The thickness of the coal removed affects the degree of subsidence; but I am not enabled to state in what proportion it operates, not having had an opportunity of making correct observations on this point.

The degree of subsidence, however, does not depend so much on the thickness of the coal as on the effectual removal of it, technically called 'Clean Working.' If a considerable portion of the coal should be left, although by no means adequate to the support of the superincumbent strata, it yet retards the subsidence and prevents the downward pressure of the mass from exerting that degree of force and momentum which it would otherwise do; besides, the small portions of coal which have been left occupy a certain part of the excavation when crushed down.

These observations apply more particularly to the Newcastle system of working, or 'short work,' where rectangular pillars are left, in the first instance, and afterwards removed.

In the working of those pillars, *stooks*, or blocks of coal of considerable strength, are frequently left as props to protect the colliers from the exfoliations of the roof. In this case, a subsidence of the strata above invariably takes place ; but its extent in the *first instance* is governed by the degree of resistance which those stooks of coal present to the downward pressure of the mass. When the sinking of the strata is retarded or stopped in this manner, before the excavation whence the coal has been extracted is entirely filled, the place is said to be 'half or three quarters, etc. crept.' A large tract of a coal-mine not unfrequently remains for several years in this state, without almost any perceptible change taking place; yet in course of time, from the exfoliation of the coal in those 'stooks,' and the operation of the atmosphere, a further subsidence, called a *second creep,* takes place, and generally continues until the excavation is completely closed.

In the Yorkshire system of 'long work,' where the coal is all taken out in the first instance, except small temporary pillars, in addition to which wooden props, together with a sort of stone pillaring called 'gobbing,' are placed for the protection of the colliers, the subsidence of the strata immediately follows the removal of the coal, and the excavation is completely filled, so that no second settlement or *set* takes place.

I have already observed, that the extent of settlement, as shown on the surface, from working coal, depends upon so many contingencies, that it cannot be subjected to any calculation. It rarely happens that the perpendicular depth of a sinking of the surface above coal-workings can be accurately ascertained, as fixed land-marks[3] are seldom attended to in such cases. Railways, or reservoirs of water, however, occasionally afford the means of ascertaining, with tolerable accuracy, the extent to which the surface has subsided by the working out of the coal.

From the formation of a pond of water upwards of three feet deep on a level surface, from underneath which a six-feet seam of coal had been worked at the depth of 100 fathoms, about one-fourth part of the seam having been left in *stooks*, as already described, I ascertained that the subsidence of the surface at its greatest depression had been rather more than three feet. In this case the sandstone strata predominated.

The next case which I have had an opportunity of observing with tolerable accuracy is a more interesting one, as it shows three distinct periods of subsidence, as three seams of coal were successively worked away below. The tract of ground alluded to is of a quadrangular figure, of about twenty-three acres in area, and is crossed by a railway near its eastern or narrowest end. It is in the Marquis of Londonderry's Pensher Colliery,[4] in the county of Durham.

The tract in question contains the following five seams of coal—see Section :

	Thickness		Depth below the Surface
	Ft.	In.	Fathoms.
1st. — The Three-quarter Seam	1	8	54½
This seam is not deemed workable at present.			
2. — The Five-quarter Seam	3	6	62
3. — The High Main ditto	6	3	73
4. — The Maudlin ditto	5	0	83½
5. — The Hutton ditto	3	8	107

The three latter beds have been removed, and caused the subsidence of the surface about to be described, and the Five-quarter is now in course of working.

No. 3. The High-main seam was the first which was wrought in the pillars, and was finished in 1829, when a settlement in the surface was noticed. This was immediately discovered by the lowering of the railway, which required to be raised to its original level.

No. 4. The Maudlin seam was next wrought in the pillars and finished in 1831, when a second settlement of the surface took place, and the railway had again to be raised.

No. 5. was then worked in the pillars and finished in 1833, when a third settlement of the surface took place, which required the railway to be again raised to its original level.

The working of No. 2. commenced two years ago, but is not yet finished. When the pillars are all worked out, I have no doubt that another settlement of the surface will take place.

The extent of each settlement was not measured, but I have lately ascertained that the whole amount of the settlement of the surface by the three *'mine-quakes'* was five feet six inches,—the aggregate thickness of the three seams which have been worked out being fourteen feet eleven inches. This appears to be but a small degree of subsidence, considering the thickness of the coal which has been taken away. But as the railway, which is the gauge-line,[5] passes near to one end of the excavated tract, it may not be supposed to pass over the line of the greatest depression. Indeed, on looking at the ground over the centre of the excavated tract, it appears to be much more depressed; but as there are no land-marks by which to ascertain the fact, I preferred taking the line of the railway, which gives the true result in that part.

The metal-stone strata also considerably exceed in thickness the beds of sandstone, and operate to make the depression less than that noticed in the former instance.

In the present working of No. 2. (the five-quarter seam) the effects of the fractures occasioned by the former excavating of the lower seams are clearly discernible. Innumerable cracks pass through the coal and pavement, as well as through the roof-stone, in a vertical direction, but they are perfectly close,[6] except round the margin of the settlement. Here a breaking and bending of the seam, pavement and roof-stone have taken place. The cracks in the pavement are frequently open, forming considerable fissures; the coal is splintered and the roof- stone is shattered. This is not, however, the case in the interior of the settlement; on the contrary, the cracks are quite close, and the pavement is as level and smooth as if it had never been disturbed. The cracks in the coal pass through the seam without having injured, splintered, or triturated[7] it on the sides of the cracks, as is generally the case with the natural *backs*.[8] The only alteration produced has been to render the coal more tough and *woody,* as the colliers call it, in working than it was before these fractures took place. This effect may be attributed to the escape of the gas by the cracks; and it sometimes takes place from other causes, when the coal is said to be *winded* by the colliers.

The smoothness of the pavement in the interior of the subsided tract is due, probably, to the pressure of the superincumbent mass, which is partially, if not completely, detached from the surrounding strata, and its line of pressure is directly downwards.

I would here observe, that I never noticed any tendency to a sliding or sideway movement in any subsidence of strata occasioned by the working of coal, except the slight obliquity occasioned by the off-break at the sides of the settlement, as already described.

The facts here stated fully confirm, in my humble opinion, the hypothesis adduced in your 'Elements,' (p. 122);[9] and when our pigmy operations can produce such palpable and analogous phænomena —what stupendous effects upon the surface of the globe may we not imagine the grand excavator of nature —the volcano— capable of producing!

Second creeps, or subsidences of the surface, sometimes occur from water being suddenly let off from old colliery-workings, after having been a long time pent up in them.

JOHN BUDDLE.

Walls End, Newcastle-upon-Tyne,

August 22nd, 1839.

Joseph Dickinson, 'On Subsidence to the Surface Caused by Colliery Workings' (1859)

Joseph Dickinson,[1] 'On Subsidence to the Surface Caused by Colliery Workings', *Transactions of the Manchester Geological Society*, 2 (November 1859), pp. 13–17, and 'Discussion', pp. 17–18.

ON SUBSIDENCE TO THE SURFACE CAUSED BY COLLIERY WORKINGS.

A PAPER BY JOSEPH DICKINSON, F.G.S., PENDLETON, MANCHESTER,
(One of Her Majesty's Inspectors of Coal Mines.)

IN most colliery districts the subject of this paper is of importance. It is especially so in a district like this, where coal is worked under a surface extensively intersected with canals and railways, and covered with houses, and with factories containing machinery which should not be disturbed.

The working out of a seam of coal from underneath any extensive area, without leaving sufficient support, naturally causes subsidence. The area over which, and the depth from which this subsidence extends, is the subject which I now propose to bring before the notice of this society.

It seems to be taken as a common rule by some, that, where the strata lie horizontally, subsidence is vertical only; that is, that the surface subsides only immediately over the part where the coal is worked out; and that, where the strata dip at an angle, subsidence is at right angles only to the dip. /

As a rough rule this, possibly, serves some ordinary purposes; but it certainly is not founded upon a consideration of all the circumstances of the cases. On the contrary, subsidences seem to vary with the kind of strata, and the depth and thickness of the seam of coal that is being worked; the subsidence being greatest where the strata are soft and the coal thick, and the least where the reverse obtains. In South Staffordshire, for instance, where many of the strata are soft, and a seam of coal varying from 8 to 12 yards thick, called the 'thick' or '10-yards coal,' is worked (which affords one of the best opportunities of noticing subsidence), it is clearly found that, in horizontal strata, subsidence extends far beyond the working; and the distance to which it extends beyond is known as the 'draw' or 'pull.' The draw or pull, however, is not confined to soft strata and a thick coal. It is common, to some extent, to every stratum when broken, that the sides being deprived of support naturally moulder down[2] toward the angle of rest. Subsidence should, therefore, in all ordinary cases be expected to extend beyond the actual working underneath. I think I may say, that by most mining engineers the pull or draw is recognised. It also seems to be recognised by the Railways Clauses Consolidation Act,[3] which requires 30 days' notice to be given before workings are allowed within the prescribed distance, or where no distance shall be prescribed, within 40 yards of the property; and if found requisite, workings, except certain communications, may be prohibited within such distances. In very soft strata, and with a thick seam of coal at shallow depths, surface subsidence sometimes extends so far beyond the workings, that instead of the rule referred to being any correct guide, it would, with limitation as to depth, be nearer to conclude that the subsidence may extend to an angle of 45° beyond the working. That is to say, that the surface would subside as far beyond the working as it is deep to the working. This, however, seems to be the extreme. With ordinary strata and thin seams, it seldom extends beyond one-third of the depth.

The slope or hade of faults in ordinary strata is about 1 horizontal to 3 in depth, the slope being generally steeper in hard than in soft strata. With mineral veins, likewise, when the strata traversed are of various degrees of hardness, as in the mountain limestone series of Cumberland, Northumberland, and Durham (where the workings being in the vein, the slope or hade admits of being examined throughout), the slope is found to be flattest in the soft shales, and steepest in the hard siliceous sandstones and limestones. In the shales the slope extends to about 1 horizontal to 1 in depth, and averages about 1 horizontal to 2½ in depth; whilst in the sandstones and limestones the slope is much steeper, being sometimes nearly perpendicular, and averages about 1 horizontal to / 5 in depth. These slopes or hades of faults, and mineral veins, are probably the true angles of rest of the particular strata which they traverse, and are apparently the best indication of the limit of probable subsidence.

To leave support, therefore, only under the part of the surface intended to be left undisturbed would be useless. Indeed, it would, generally, be worse than useless, as support so left tends to form an apex on the surface, and would occasion more than usual disturbance to buildings. A similar effect is also produced, but in a less degree, where pillars of solid or nearly solid coal are left over a certain space, and then smaller pillars, which become crushed, outside. The whole of the pillars, when the weight to be supported is equal over the whole, should be uniform, and capable of withstanding the pressure, or they had better not be left at all.

With strata dipping at an angle, if the subsidence were always at a right angle to the dip, as assumed by the rule referred to, it would follow that when the dip approaches the perpendicular, as it sometimes does, the limit of expected subsidence would extend far beyond probable bounds. The rule must, therefore, evidently be taken with limitations. The subsidence may be, and doubtless sometimes is, at a right angle to the dip – coinciding with the rule; but this happens only with strata of certain hardness, and which lie at a certain dip; and it would not so happen with them were they either harder or softer, or if the dip were either more or less. Up to a certain angle of dip, therefore, in estimating the probable extent of subsidence, additions to a right angle should be made; and when beyond the certain angle, deductions are required.

In no ordinary case that has come under my notice, – no matter how steep the seam may be dipping, – but of course excepting running sand, does the extent of subsidence exceed that which an angle of 45°, set off from a horizontal line, comprises. At that angle, even with very soft strata, the support given by the sides seems to cause the angle of rest to be reached before it would ensue were there no side support. With the 10-yards coal seam alluded to, cracks 3 or 4 inches wide are sometimes observable on the surface of the ground where the coal is being worked upwards of 200 yards deep. With thin seams, also, similar cracks are sometimes observable at shallower depths; and occasionally where the coal is all being worked out at once, by longwork,[4] the approach of the face of work is indicated on the surface by an undulation, causing buildings, especially noticeable in engine chimneys, to lean towards the work as it approaches; and as the working passes on underneath, the surface subsides, and the buildings again resume the original, or nearly the original, position. /

When buildings and other works are scattered over the surface, the quantity of the coal seam which would be wasted if left in pillars, often makes it economical to work out the coal under the buildings, unless they be of more than usual value, and afterwards to level up and repair the damage as the ground becomes consolidated. Where several thin seams are worked, the subsidence may amount to several yards; and it has occasionally caused canal banks to require raising, from time to time, until they have become several yards higher than the surface with which they were originally level.

To avoid unnecessary damage to buildings, when the coal is intended to be worked underneath, various methods are resorted to. One of the most successful is, to previously bind the building together with wood or iron, and keep it so until the coal is removed, and the ground has again become consolidated.

When the buildings are numerous and close together, as in a town, regular pillars are usually left; and where pillars so left are adequate, and the coal is hard and has a hard floor, the strata above remain undisturbed. But if the pillars are inadequate, or the coal soft, or if the coal is hard but has a soft floor into which the pillars sink, then subsidence may ensue; and in such cases more surface damage may be occasioned by leaving pillars than if the whole of the coal were worked out, particularly if in working all out the goaf or gob[5] behind be uniformly packed with rubbish[6] as the working advances.

The proportion of coal requisite to be left, in ordinary cases, when pillars are resorted to, depends on circumstances such as I have alluded to. The proportion for each case should be decided upon its own circumstances. The maximum, unless solid coal be left, seldom if ever exceeds two-thirds of the pillars, which allowing for openings made through the pillars, leaves rather more than one half of the whole. The proportion usually left is, however, about one-half, or a little less than one-half, the pillars being made equal in width with the boards or bays;[7] but the openings between the boards are made through the pillars, which reduces the proportion for pillars to that extent below one-half.

When strata subside, they do so in a mass, or are more or less broken up. If broken, they do not readily pack again into as small a space as they originally occupied. The surface of the ground may not therefore subside as much as the seam worked out is thick. Some of the portion may be distributed in the greater space occupied by the broken strata between the working and the surface. With a 4-feet seam of coal all worked out at a depth of 200 yards, the subsidence to the surface has by some been averaged at 3 feet, and that the proportion decreases as the depth increases, until at 600 yards the subsidence dos not reach the surface. The / subsidence may, however, be slow in reaching from such a depth, but it may become appreciable, and certainly so if the superincumbent strata settle down in a body without being broken.

To those mining engineers whose experience of subsidence from colliery workings has been only of hard strata and thin seams of coal, probably some of these observations – especially those on soft strata and thick coal – may appear extreme. Instances, however, are not wanting where subsidence has occurred when it was supposed proper pillars had been left.

DISCUSSION

Mr. BINNEY[8] moved that the thanks of the Society be given to Mr. Dickinson for his very practical and valuable paper. The full attendance of members showed that they might expect good meetings to hear really practical papers on mining.

He hoped this would be the first of a series of engineering and mining papers to be read before the society this session.

The motion was seconded, and passed unanimously.

The CHAIRMAN[9] invited members to make remarks on the paper, for the results of experience were national wealth. Most of them had had more or less experience of the consequences on the surface of getting coal. He could corroborate the statements of Mr. Dickinson to some extent, although he had not had experience in working thick mines, such as those in South Staffordshire, of 10 or 12 yards, or of seams approaching the perpendicular; in the remarks on which, he coincided with Mr. Dickinson, who had enjoyed extensive opportunities of observation. With regard to subsidence in surface, he could also go with Mr. Dickinson. The Chairman mentioned an instance in proof, as being better than generalities. To the north of Wigan they had a seam of coal about 4½ft. thick, which had been worked to a depth of about 150 yards, causing a subsidence of a canal about 3½ft. Mr. Dickinson had given a practical and valuable suggestion with regard to the necessity of mining engineers leaving sufficient pillars for the support of buildings. For instance, —supposing the mine to be horizontal, and the seam of coal to be within 2 yards of the surface, probably 5 yards left would be sufficient; if 10 yards, more would have to be left; and so on in proportion. If there were 10 or 12 seams, a building would, in point of fact, be supported on the apex of a pyramid extending with the depth.

Mr. A. HEWLETT[10] said his experience confirmed that of Mr. Dickinson. The thickest mine under a town or building, of which / he had had experience, was one near Wigan, the seam of which was 7 or 8 feet thick. After going to a depth of about 180 yards, the North Union Railway, which ran above, settled about 6 feet. There was a large extent of coal, and the roof was very strong, but the floor was very soft. He had noticed that when the roof began to move, it moved very rapidly, and to a great extent; also that the roof 'pulled' to a far greater extent than any other he had seen in the district. In working under buildings with this sort of roof, he had often found it safest to take nearly the whole of the seam away, and support the roof substantially.

Mr. T. LIVESEY[11] mentioned an instance where the whole of a 3ft. 6in. seam had been worked, at a depth of 150 yards, without the house of a weaver, who worked above, sustaining any damage. There was sand upon the mine, and it was probable that the coming in of sand under the house prevented damage. The land and house might have subsided, but it must have been regular and easy. He also knew of two mines being worked under buildings; one with what was supposed to be very sufficient pillars, but after a few months the buildings were broken to pieces; in the other instance, the whole of the coal was got without damage.

Mr. RALPH FLETCHER[12] said he could corroborate this statement. There must be subsidence, but it was gradual.

The CHAIRMAN referred to another point in Mr. Dickinson's paper, which deserved consideration. There might be a roof of solid rock 30 yards or 40 yards thick, but it was not certain that the surface would not subside. The superincumbent weight of earth would press the pillars into the soft strata of earth which often underlay the coal, causing the earth to 'heave;'[13] showing that the surface must have subsided, or the bottom of the mine could not have risen to the top. In such cases, though buildings might not be injured, a canal, or any hydraulic work, would necessarily receive great damage. Mining engineers working in the neighbourhood of docks, canals, or similar works, would do well to bear this in mind.

Mr. BINNEY mentioned an important point in reference to deposits of sand and gravel. He had known a mine of about 4ft. thick worked at a depth of 50 yards, which was covered with about 10 yards of solid brick clay; and to his surprise the 'draw' extended from 25 to 30 yards, demolishing about a dozen houses.

The CHAIRMAN suggested that the cracks in the clay had become filled with thin perpendicular strata of sand, upon which water had acted. In draining stiff clay land, it was necessary to go 5 or 6 feet deep, from the same cause.

The discussion took a conversational turn, and was joined by Mr. Hull, Mr. Knowles,[14] and others. /

'A Burning Pit-Heap: Alleged Extraordinary Effects', *Northern Echo* (1895)

'A Burning Pit-Heap: Alleged Extraordinary Effects', *Northern Echo*, 27 November 1895.

A BURNING PIT-HEAP.

ALLEGED EXTRAORDINARY EFFECTS.

A deputation from Evenwood Parish Council attended Auckland Rural District Council on Tuesday to complain of a burning heap at Railey Fell Colliery, belonging Stobart & Co.[1] – Mr Carrick said the people near the heap were living under very disagreeable conditions from the effects of the combustion. Several people were ill; metal work in houses was tarnished; the stench affected food in the pantry, and made people disinclined, and even unable, to take food. Trees were prematurely stripped of their leaves as the result of the exhalations which had been going on for twelve months. – Councillor Cox bore out the complaints, and suggested water to hasten the end of the evil. The sulphurous effects were very disagreeable. – Councillor Rudman said water had been proved to be an aggravation. – Councillor Stobart, J.P.,[2] suggested a committee, and said they were now burying the 'brasses'[3] elsewhere. The nuisance was originally caused by rain. It was very difficult to deal with a great heap on fire. He moved a committee to visit and report. – Councillor Greener, J.P., who seconded, said this was the first time, to his knowledge, that such a complaint had come before a public body. – Ald. House said the deputation had put their case most moderately, and he could see no utility in a committee. The Inspector should visit, and, from his experience, suggest a remedy. West Auckland had suffered from such a cause.[4] It occasioned distress to people suffering from bronchitis, asthma, &c. – Councillor Cox said the committee was merely a movement to 'kill time.' It was well known these evils could be avoided, and it might be a question whether compensation should not be claimed by aggrieved inhabitants. – Councillor Hendy considered the case had been much exaggerated. As manager, he would be glad to meet a deputation. – Councillor Heslop (colliery manager) believed the heap was a nuisance. – Councillor Todd said this was a serious matter. Burning pit heaps had long been – for fifty or sixty years – known in that county, and it was often said that such fumes were considered of advantage to health by destroying what might be prejudicial. – The Inspector suggested reference to the Medical Officer. – Councillor Burnip held that the public health must take precedence of every other consideration. – Ald. House pointed out that, however salubrious these places might be, he found that people who could help it did not care to reside near a pit-heap. – A committee was appointed to visit the heap and report. /

[Sydney Smith], 'An Account of the Proceedings of the Society for Superseding the Necessity of Climbing Boys' (1818)

[Sydney Smith],[1] '[A Review of] *An Account of the Proceedings of the Society for Superseding the Necessity of Climbing Boys*', *Edinburgh Review* 32 (64) (October 1819), pp. 309–20.

ART[ICLE]. III. [A Review of] *An Account of the Proceedings of the Society for superseding the Necessity of Climbing Boys*[2] (London: Baldwin &c, 1816).

AN excellent and well-arranged dinner is a most pleasing occurrence; and a great triumph of civilized life. It is not only the descending morsel, and the enveloping sauce – but the rank, wealth, wit, and beauty which surround the meats – the learned management of light and heat – the silent and rapid services of the attendants – the smiling and sedulous host, proffering gusts[3] and relishes – the exotic bottles – the embossed plate – the pleasant remarks – the handsome dresses – the cunning artifices in fruit and farina! The hour of dinner, in short, includes every thing of sensual and intellectual gratification which a great nation glories in producing.

In the midst of all this, who knows that the kitchen chimney caught fire half an hour before dinner! – and that a poor little wretch, of six or seven years old, was sent up in the midst of the flames to put it out? We could not, previous to reading this evidence,[4] have formed a conception of the miseries of these poor wretches, or that there should exist, in a civilized country, a class of human beings destined to such extreme and varied distress. We will give a short epitome of what is developed in the evidence before the two Houses of Parliament.

Boys are made chimney-sweepers at the early age of five or six.

Little boys for small flues, is a common phrase in the cards left at the door by itinerant chimney-sweepers. Flues made to ovens and coppers[5] are often less than nine inches square; and it may be easily conceived, how slender the frame of that human body must be, which can force itself through such an aperture.

'What is the age of the youngest boys who have been employed / in this trade, to your knowledge? – About five years of age: I know one now between five and six years old, it is the man's own son in the Strand; now there is another at Somer's Town, I think said he was between four and five, or about five; Jack Hall, a little lad, takes him about. Did you ever know any female children employed? – Yes, I know one now. About two years ago there was a woman told me she had climbed scores of times, and there is one at Paddington[6] now whose father taught her to climb: but I have often heard. talk of them when I was apprentice, in different places. What is the smallest-sized flue you have ever met with in the course of your experience? – About eight inches by nine; these they are always obliged to climb in this posture *(describing it)* keeping the arms up straight; if they slip their arms down, they get jammed in; unless they get their arms close over their head they cannot climb.' *Lords' Minutes*, No. 1. p. 8.[7]

The following is a specimen of the manner in which they are taught this art of climbing chimneys.

[']Do you remember being taught to climb chimneys? – Yes. What did you feel upon the first attempt to climb a chimney? – The first chimney I went up, they told me there was some plumb-pudding[8] and money up at the top of it, and that is the way they enticed me up; and when I got up, I would not let the other boy get from under me to get at it, I thought he would get it; I could not get up, and shoved the pot and half the chimney down into the yard. Did you experience any inconvenience to your knees, or your elbows? – Yes, the skin was off my knees and elbows too, in climbing up the new. chimneys they forced me up. How did they force you up? – When I got up, I cried out about my sore knees. Were you beat or compelled to go up by any violent means? – Yes, when I went to a narrow chimney, if I could not do it, I durst not go home; when I used to come down, my master would well beat me with the brush; and not only my master, but when we used to go with the journeymen, if we could not do it, they used to hit us three or four times with the brush?'[9] *Ibid.* p. 5.

In practising the art of climbing, they are often crippled.

'You talked of the pargetting[10] to chimneys; are many chimneys pargetted? – There used to be more than are now; we used to have to go and sit all a-twist to parge them, according to the floors, to keep the smoke from coming out; then I could not straighten my legs; and that is the reason that many are cripples, – from parging and stopping the holes.' *Ibid.* p. 17.

They are often stuck fast in a chimney, and, after remaining there many hours, are cut out.

'Have you known, in the course of your practice, boys stick in chimneys at all? – Yes, frequently. Did you ever know an instance of a boy being suffocated to death? – No; I do not recollect any one at present, but I have assisted in taking boys out when they have / been nearly exhausted. Did you ever know an instance of its being necessary to break open a chimney to take the boy out? – O yes. *Frequently? – Monthly, I might say;* it is done with a cloak, if possible, that it should not be discovered; a master in general wishes it not to be known, and therefore speaks to the people belonging to the house not to mention it, for it was merely the boy's neglect; they often say it was the boy's neglect. Why do they say that? – The boy's climbing shirt is often very bad; the boy coming down, if the chimney be very narrow, and numbers of them are only nine inches, gets his shirt rumpled underneath him, and he has no power after he is fixed in that way *(with his hand up.)* Does a boy frequently stick in the chimney? – Yes; I have known more instances of that the last twelve-month than before. Do you ever have to break open in the inside of a room? – Yes, I have helped to break through into a kitchen chimney in a dining room.' *Lords' Minutes*, p. 34.

To the same effect is the evidence of John Daniels, (*Minutes*, p. 100), and of James Ludford, (*Lords' Minutes*, p. 147.)

'You have swept the Penitentiary? – I have. Did you ever know a boy stick in any of the Chimneys there? – Yes, I have. Was it one of your boys? – It was. Was there one or two that stuck? – Two of them. How long did they stick there? – Two hours. How were they got out? – They were cut out. Was there any danger while they were in that situation? – It was the core from the pargetting of the chimney, and the rubbish that the labourers had thrown down, that stopped them, and when they got it aside them, they could not pass. They both stuck together? – Yes.' *Lords' Minutes*, p. 147.

One more instance we shall give from the Evidence before the Commons.[11]

'Have you heard of any accidents that have recently happened to climbing boys in the small flues? – Yes; I have *often* met with accidents myself when I was a boy; there was lately one in Mary-le-bone, where the boy *lost his life* in a flue, a boy of the name of Tinsey, (his father was of the same trade); that boy I think was about eleven or twelve years old. Was there a coroner's inquest sat on the body of that boy you mentioned? – Yes, there was; he was an apprentice of a man of the name of Gay. How many accidents do you recollect, which were attended with loss of life to the climbing boys? – I have heard talk of many more than I know of; I never knew of more than three since I have been at the trade, but I have heard talk of many more. Of twenty or thirty? – I cannot say; I have been near losing my own life several times.' *Commons' Report*, p. 53.

We come now to burning little chimney-sweepers. A large party are invited to dinner – a great display is to be made:– and about an hour before dinner, there is an alarm that the kitchen chimney is on fire! It is impossible to put off the distinguished personages who are expected. It gets very late for the soup and fish – the cook is frantic – all eyes are turned upon the sable[12] / consolation of the master chimney sweeper – and up into the midst of the burning chimney is sent one of the miserable little infants of the brush! There is a positive prohibition of this practice, and an enactment of penalties in one of the acts of Parliament which respect chimney sweepers. But what matter acts of Parliament, when the pleasures of genteel people are concerned? Or what is a toasted child, compared to the agonies of the mistress of the house with a deranged dinner?

'Did you ever know a boy get burnt up a chimney? Yes. – Is that usual? Yes, I have been burnt myself, and have got the scars on my legs; a year ago I was up a chimney in Liquor Pond Street;[13] I have been up *more than forty chimneys where I have been burnt*. – Did your master or the journeymen ever direct you to go up a chimney that was on fire? Yes, it is a general case. – Do they compel you to go up a chimney that is on fire? Oh yes, it was the general practice for two of us to stop at home on Sunday to be ready in case of a chimney being a-fire. – You say it is general to compel the boys to go up chimneys on fire? Yes, boys get very ill-treated if they do not go up.' – *Lords' Minutes*, p. 34.

'Were you ever forced up a chimney on fire? Yes, I was forced up one once, and, because I could not do it, I was taken home and well hided with a brush by the journeyman. – Have you frequently been burnt in ascending chimneys on fire? Three times. – Are such hardships as you have described common in the trade with other boys? Yes, they are.' – *Lords' Minutes*, p. 100.

'What is the price for sending a boy up a chimney badly on fire? The price allowed is five shillings, but most of them charge half a guinea.[14] – Is any part of that given to the boy? No, but very often the boy gets half a crown; and then the journeyman has half, and his mistress takes the other part to take care of against Sunday. – Have you never seen water thrown down from the top of a chimney when it is on fire? Yes. – Is not that generally done? Yes; I have seen that done twenty times, and the boy in the chimney; at the time when the boy has hallooed out, "It is so hot I cannot go any further;" and then the expression is, with an oath, "Stop, and I will heave a pail of water down."' – *Lords' Minutes*, p. 39.

Chimney-sweepers are subject to a peculiar sort of cancer,[15] which often brings them to a premature death.

'He appeared perfectly willing to try the machines everywhere? – I must say the man appeared perfectly willing; he had a fear that he and his family would be ruined by them; but I must say of him, that he is very different from other sweeps I have seen; he attends very much to his own business; he was as black as any boy he had got, and unfortunately in the course of conversation he told me he had got a cancer; he was a fine healthy strong looking man; he told me he dreaded having an operation performed, but his father died of the same complaint, and that his father was sweeper to King George the Second.' – *Lords' Minutes*, p. 84. /

'What is the nature of the particular diseases? The diseases that we particularly noticed, to which they were subject, were of a cancerous description. – In what part? The scrotum in particular, &c. – Did you ever hear of cases of that description that were fatal? No, I do not think them as being altogether fatal, unless they will not submit to the operation; they have such a dread of the operation that they will not submit to it, and if they do not let it be perfectly removed they will be liable to the return of it. – To what cause do you attribute that disease? I think it begins from a want of care: the scrotum being in so many folds or crevices, the soot lodges in them and creates an itching, and I conceive that by scratching it and tearing it the soot gets in and creates the irritability; which disease we know[16] by the name of the chimney sweeper's cancer, and is always lectured upon separately as a distinct disease. – Then the Committee understands that the physicians who are entrusted with the care and management of those hospitals think that disease of such common occurrence, that it is necessary to make it a part of surgical education? Most assuredly; I remember Mr Cline and Mr Cooper[17] were particular on that subject. – Without an operation there is no cure? I conceive not; I conceive without the operation it is death; for cancers are of that nature that unless you extirpate them entirely they will never be cured.' – *Commons' Rep.* p. 60, 61. /

'Juvenile Chimney-Sweeps', *Ragged School Union Magazine* (1875)

'Juvenile chimney-sweeps', *Ragged School Union Magazine*[1] (July 1875), pp. 145–8.

JUVENILE CHIMNEY-SWEEPS.

ABOVE half a century has elapsed since Sydney Smith called the attention of the public to the physical and moral evils incident to the employment of children to sweep our chimneys. When his famous article[2] appeared, in 1818, in the *Edinburgh Review*, so startling was the revelation of this form of white slavery, that many regarded the tale of their woes as a violent distortion of facts. But, unhappily, the facts were too bad for any possible exaggeration: and that the custom could have existed so long without the denunciation of Christian philanthropists could only be referred to sheer ignorance of the cruel practices of master sweeps.

As is now the case with acrobats, the victims were selected in extreme youth, for the muscles become so rigid after puberty as to altogether preclude the easy ascent of flues. Not rarely children six years of age were chosen for a task which, if deferred to boyhood, could scarcely have been accomplished. Nor was this all; the trade customs were cruel in the extreme. Thus, for example, it was a common practice for the masters to light straw in the fire-grates, in order to stimulate novices, under the influence of fear, to a quick ascent up the flues. As might have been expected, many poor children were suffocated in the chimneys – and others were so jammed in narrow flues as to be unable to extricate themselves, and too many died through terror. Again, these human machines were subject to a special disease, known by the name of the 'sweep's cancer'[3] – a disease caused by the penetration of soot into the bruised flesh, so that the blood was poisoned. This disorder was not only terrible as regards pain, but it was absolutely incurable. Even if they escaped these evils, they were stunted in size, bow-backed and knock-kneed, and so weak in the limbs as scarcely to be able to bear their own weight.

These and similar facts led to commission after commission being issued by the Crown; but nothing was effectually done to extirpate this crying evil until

Lord Shaftesbury, with his usual energy, took up the subject, and in conjunction with Mr. Fox Maule, afterwards Earl of Dalhousie,[4] carried a Bill through Parliament to abolish boy chimney-sweeping. /

This Act has been so loyally obeyed in London, Glasgow, and other great cities, that few of the rising generation are aware that our flues were formerly swept by *human machines*. But, unhappily, this is not the case in many of the midland and northern counties. The Act is not merely evaded but openly defied; unless we may ascribe such disobedience of the law to ignorance of its existence. But whether householders know or are ignorant of the legislative prohibition of boy chimney-sweeps, the police and the magistracy ought not only to be aware of its existence, but to enforce an Act which, in the words of Lord Shaftesbury, seeks to succour 'the most oppressed, degraded, and tortured creatures on the face of the earth.'

That the words thus used in the House of Lords are not an exaggerated statement of the evils denounced, facts which have recently oozed out in the press too fully prove. For example, at the last Cambridge Assizes a master sweep was tried, not for simple infringement of the law, but for causing the death of a boy whom he sent to sweep the flues of Fulbourne Lunatic Asylum. Two days after the poor child died, it is presumed through swallowing soot and other impure matter, which poisoned his blood.

Cynics have intimated that 'Corporations have no conscience, and that they will do as a body what they would be ashamed to do as individuals.' The civic authorities of Liverpool – one of the richest corporations in England – have unhappily done their best to confirm the truth of this maxim. For, instead of enforcing the law, as they were in duty bound to do, it has come out in evidence that they have permitted their flues to be swept by children. And all this at the risk of the boys being suffocated or blood-poisoned, and in any case with the certainty of indescribable pain being inflicted on the helpless poor.

These and similar facts, which he narrated to the House of Lords on May 11th ult.,[5] have led Lord Shaftesbury to introduce a Bill to further enforce a law which has already proved so beneficial to a helpless class. This Bill provides that tickets are to be issued by the chief officer of police in each police district, authorising persons to carry on the business of chimney-sweeps in the district. These certificates are to be renewed yearly, and are not to be transferable, and any person acting as chimney-sweeper without a certificate will be liable to a fine not exceeding ten shillings for the first offence, and for every subsequent offence to a / fine not exceeding twenty shillings. Any person convicted of an offence under this or any other Act may be deprived of his certificate by the magistrate, or a note of the conviction may be endorsed upon the certificate.

Whether this penalty is sufficient *alone* to meet the enormity of this great social crime has been questioned by many journalists, all of whom have done themselves great honour by their energetic support of Lord Shaftesbury in the matter. They consider that at least imprisonment, if not penal servitude, ought in addition to be inflicted on all those who, in defiance of the law, force boys up flues – in other words, do all they can to expose these hapless children to the danger of suffocation.

We are sorry to find, from the discussion which followed the speech on the second reading of the Bill, that the Government, instead of enforcing the existing Act, through their mouthpiece, Earl Beauchamp,[6] gave a very cold reception, if not a decided opposition to this Bill. In spite of the many cases of cruelty, and even of death, narrated by Lord Shaftesbury, he could only say that 'he believed that much more good would be done by calling public attention to the subject than could be effected by the Legislature.' He also added that 'he did not see how the legislation proposed would conduce to the object desired.' Thus, while the Lord Steward,[7] on the one hand, objected to anything being attempted to crush these crying evils, he, on the other hand, intimated that the Bill did not go far enough. Happily the House of Lords did not understand the force of such imperfect logic as this; and after speeches in its favour by the Bishop of London, Earl Fortescue, and Lord Aberdare,[8] it cordially agreed to the second reading of the Bill, which bids fair to become law this session.

In one of its most trenchant articles,[9] the *Times* of the 12th ult. gave a vigorous support to the Bill. In it, whilst condemning the active opposition of the Government to such a needful measure, it forcibly said:– 'We have not much patience with the condescending compliments with which Lord Beauchamp, on the part of the Government, treated the generous and earnest effort of Lord Shaftesbury. It may be a matter for discussion whether his proposal will be effectual; but either that or some other means must be immediately taken to suppress a national scandal. If Lord Beauchamp's children were liable to be forced up a chimney tomorrow, / he would not be content to wait for the gradual influence of Lord Shaftesbury's speeches, admirable as those speeches are. We may rely upon it, however, that Lord Shaftesbury will not rest till this cruelty has been finally suppressed.'

Well did Lord Shaftesbury say, in a peroration which has been universally admired for its persuasive eloquence, 'I have done what I can, and will ask your lordships to do the same. Surely you will now – I say it with all respect – you will, as a part of the Imperial Parliament, now emphatically declare that your laws are passed to be obeyed and not to be systematically broken; that your beneficent statutes shall not be set aside by high or low, rich or poor; and that as all rule and authority come from above, you will exercise them in the spirit in which you have received them, with regard to the very least as feeling your care, and the greatest as not exempt from your power.'

Though the subject does not bear directly on their special labours, yet nevertheless Ragged School teachers have an indirect interest in the suppression of boy chimney-sweeping. Our labours, for example, have had no slight influence in directing the attention of philanthropists to the evils necessarily incident to overwork and under-feeding of the young; and if there is now a general tendency to prevent poor children entering the labour market at too early an age, as well as to diminish their hours of work, no slight portion of this legislation, as well as the public opinion on which it is based, is due to the facts which Ragged School teachers brought under the public notice. Again, any measure which tends to raise the standard of health of the poorer classes, equally tends to raise their moral tone, and to lessen our special sphere of work, and thus to usher in the time when the religious and physical habits of the masses will be so elevated as to render Ragged Schools no longer necessary. We trust, then, that our readers will do all they can to aid in extirpating a species of labour which 'crushes the life out of young hearts.'

Rollo Russell, *London Fogs* (1880)

Rollo Russell,[1] F.M.S., *London Fogs* (London: Edward Stanford, 1880)].

LONDON FOGS.

It may be a wise doctrine, that no ancient and long-tolerated institution deserves to be condemned without a fair inquiry into the evidence for and against its existence. A London fog, like most disagreeable things and persons, may have its merits, and, doubtless, also its firm partisans, who would be prepared to defend it in a general way before a Royal Commission as a beneficial visitation. But the proofs of its utility, if they exist, must be brought to light, and as yet we have had none. It may be upheld as a nebulous and mysterious witticism, a gigantic piece of national humour, an enormous practical joke, and we cannot dispute the plea that it may be a source of amusement to its passing acquaintance. But those who know it well have had enough of it. It has hitherto been spared, because, like other evils of greater magnitude, its ill effects have not been very startling and sudden, and it was hard to believe that so harmless-looking and quiet a thing could do much mischief. The unseen and little-noticed / causes of death and disease, however, are by far the most fatal. The small germ of typhoid or drain fever slays its thousands every year; but this fact attracts less general attention than the drowning of five hundred by a collision or by a flood. Yet of these the first is the most easily preventable evil. So we have been content to pour the refuse from our domestic fires into the open air, and leave the work of scavenging to unaided natural forces; to disregard 'matter in the wrong place,'[2] so long as it has not killed its hundreds or thousands at a time, and have tolerated something like suffocation, so long as it performed its work slowly, made no unseemly disturbance, and took care not to demand its hecatombs very suddenly and dramatically. And smoke in London has continued probably for many years to shorten the lives of thousands, but only lately has the sudden, palpable rise of the death-rate in an unusually dense and prolonged fog attracted much attention to the depredations of this quiet and despised destroyer. /

1. The following are the chief distinctions between a London and a country fog.

A country fog is white, without smell (unless perhaps a slight odour of ozone), and not disagreeable to breathe. It seldom thickens after the first hour after sunrise. It is pure condensed vapour,* / and therefore clean. The sun appears perfectly white when seen through it.

A London fog is brown, reddish-yellow, or greenish, darkens more than a white fog, has a smoky, or sulphurous smell, is often somewhat dryer than a country fog, and produces, when thick, a choking sensation. Instead of diminishing while the sun rises higher, it often increases in density, and some of the most lowering London fogs occur about midday or late in the afternoon. Sometimes the brown masses rise and interpose a thick curtain at a considerable elevation between earth and sky. A white cloth spread out on the ground rapidly turns dirty, and particles of soot attach themselves to every exposed object.

Haziness, if not fog, prevails in London on nearly every day in the year. London haze is quite a different thing from that which occurs naturally in the country, though at times very similar to it in appearance. It is absent only during part of the night and early morning. Every one who has seen the metropolis in the small hours of a fine morning knows the totally changed and unfamiliar appearance of the town when nothing interrupts the vision. On fine, hot, breezy Sundays in summer, when factories are stopped and fires not so much used for cooking, the clearness is so unusual that prominent objects such as St. Paul's Cathedral and the Albert Hall may be seen from distant suburbs. In the daytime, a sightseer on / Primrose Hill or Hampstead Heath,[4] even if he be a poet, will be fortunate if more than a small number of 'distant spires' reveals itself to his gaze. /

It is certain that private houses, and not factories, are chiefly responsible; for some of the very worst fogs have occurred on Sundays, and Christmas Day, 1879, was nearly dark.

In winter more than a million chimneys breathe forth simultaneously smoke, soot, sulphurous acid, vapour of water, and carbonic acid gas, and the whole town fumes like a vast crater, at the bottom of which its unhappy citizens must

* A small quantity of carbonic acid gas,[3] &c., may be held in solution.

creep and live as best they can. If a moderate breeze blows, the products of combustion are removed to other parts of the atmosphere as fast as they are formed, and no dark fog can exist. But when the air is nearly or completely calm, the case is different. In winter the earth does not become sufficiently warmed by the sun to cause the air near its surface to rise, and / the lowest atmospheric strata gain little heat even in the open country. When a substance not susceptible of evaporation obscures the low-lying fog-cloud even before sunrise, the cloud cannot gain warmth sufficient to dissipate it if the conditions which produced the fog are maintained. These conditions are, usually, the mixture of opposite winds and a clear sky above the fog-bank. /

The fog of the middle of December, 1873, was one of the thickest and most persistent of this century, and deserves to be noticed in some detail; not because it differed from the ordinary London fog, except in intensity, but because the character and effects of these fogs are unusually conspicuous in this instance. I was residing at Richmond Park[5] at the time, but, having occasion to go daily to London, thought it worth while to pass through several districts of the town for the purpose of making observations on this remarkable fog. After about a week of cloudy, misty, and quiet weather, on the night of December 8–9, a hard frost came on, with a scarcely perceptible air from W. The 9th was a very fine day in the country and at the western suburbs, but in London there was a dense black fog all day, and many accidents occurred on the river and in the streets. On December 10 the frost continued. At 8 A.M. the thermometer was 22.[6] The calm continued, only a very light air from W. prevailing near the ground, but higher up from N.E. The smoke of London was drifting over Richmond from the N.E. The barometer remained very high. In London, the weather was the same as that of the day before, and many of the fat cattle exhibited at the Great Show at Islington died of suffocation. It was not possible during a great part of the day to see across a narrow street, and in the evening a choking sensation was felt in breathing. On the 11th, / the barometer stood at 30.62,[7] the thermometer at 22. At Richmond the weather was fine, with mist, a dead calm, then a lower current from W. and S.W., and cirro-cumulus clouds from E.N.E. Foggy in London. On the 12th, barometer steady, thermometer about 32;[8] a thick and damp ground-haze. Not so bad in London. Dead calm, but local currents as follows:– Vauxhall, S.E.; Ludgate Hill, S.E.; Camden Town, N.W.; Richmond, W. Cirro-cumulus were still moving from E. On the 13th, a ground-haze at Richmond, cloudy, and dead calm. No very thick fog in West London. Barometer still about 30.64. On the 14th, very slight drizzle in London about 9 A.M. Dead calm. Current N.W. at Belgrave Square; S.E. in City and at Shoreditch at 10 A.M. Dark yellow fog, rapidly thickening northwards from the City, till at Haggerston pitch-black darkness at 10.15 A.M., the lower air being tolerably clear. About a mile of this darkness like that of night; then gradually lighter towards the west, and at Camden Town fair, at Hampstead pretty clear and cloudy, clouds hanging at an elevation of about 350 feet above the sea. At all stations north and west of Haggerston (on the North London line)[9] a N.W. current. In the afternoon a gentle breeze from W.N.W. Thus ended this long period of calm. The deaths exceeded the weekly average by about 700.

We have, in the above instance, a concurrence / of several conditions favourable to the formation of the worst London fogs, namely:– 1. Perfect calm. 2. High atmospheric pressure, and a dry light air. 3. Great cold. 4. A conflict of currents. It is obvious that great cold favours the development of a dark London fog, for this reason, besides others, that a much larger quantity of coal than usual is burned.

The fog of Christmas Day, 1879, was attended with nocturnal darkness in London. In the country it was remarkably thick throughout the day.

Some of the great fogs of the end of January and beginning of February, 1880, were uncommon in their character and development. On the 27th of January there was a sudden great increase in the intensity of the frost, almost absolute calm prevailed, and the easterly current gave way on the ground to a westerly air, with which it became intimately mixed. The east wind apparently continued at a moderate elevation. In many parts of London the fog was exceedingly dark, being mixed with a great volume of smoke, and the sun was invisible. At Hammersmith, at midday, the sun was just visible, at Richmond shining dimly, and at Willesden very brightly. The fog was not inconveniently thick outside London till the evening, when it greatly increased in density. At Richmond, at 2.45 P.M., the thermometer stood at 22, an extremely low temperature. More or less fog occurred here and there on the following days, and / the sky remained clear above it. On the 30th and 31st an exceedingly light lower current from the south moved over southern England, greatly augmenting the temperature. Radiation, however, was not arrested by clouds, and the ground being chilled to a temperature much below the freezing-point by the previous severe frosts, did not thaw even when the thermometer stood at 45[10] in the open air. Thus, in certain localities, especially those least exposed to sunshine, very dense clouds were formed upon the ground by the reduction of the temperature of this slow warm current below the dew-point.[11] On the 31st, at 10 A.M., a ground fog of extraordinary density, little discoloured by smoke, lay over parts of the south-western district of London. I measured the distance at which objects became visible, and found it to be four and a half yards. In some places the fog did not extend as high as the tops of the houses, and the smoke thus escaped into the upper air. In central London, great darkness accompanied the fog during the morning. This fog differed from most others in being entirely due to the chilling of a single atmospheric current by contact with the earth; and for this reason it extended in its intensity only a few feet above the ground. The day was extremely fine in some of the suburbs. In the evening, with a rapid fall of temperature, the fog returned and caused the greatest difficulty to locomotion. On the 1st of February the atmosphere was less foggy / in most districts, but again became almost impenetrable for traffic in the early morning of the 2nd. On the 4th the fog was again exceedingly thick. The fog had thus lasted eight days, on and off, with very great intensity. They were remarkable for their local character, the shady side of a square being several times plunged in a dense mist, while the opposite side rejoiced in sunshine; one end of Piccadilly in thick darkness, while the other remained bright and clear. The following figures indicate the effect of these thick smoky fogs on health:

Week ending	Weather.	Deaths.		Below or above average.
Jan. 10	.. ..	Total	1754	-76
		From Respiratory Diseases	455	-40
Jan. 17	.. ..	Total	1730	-30
		Respiratory	512	-42
Jan. 24	Great cold ..	Total	1900	+139
		Respiratory	559	+104
Jan. 31	Great cold and fog	Total	2200	+607
		Respiratory	757	+341
Feb. 7.	Great cold, and extremely dense fog	Total	3376	+1657
		Respiratory	1557	+1118

The death-rate thus increased from 27·1 for the week ending January 24 to 48·1 for the week ending February 7, which was the period of thickest fog. The death-rate for this last week in nineteen provincial towns was 26·3. The terrible effect of the fogs continued to show itself in the death-rate for the week ending February 14 as follows:–

Total	2495	..	Above Average	730
From Respiratory Diseases	1020	..	” ”	551

In Richmond and Kingston together, the deaths, / which had been 30 in the week ending January 10, rose to 42 in that ending February 7; in Stratford (east end of London), they rose from 13 to 24, but at Croydon[12] only from 35 to 36. The death-rate at Haggerston, in East London, was about doubled, as it had also been in the foggy week of December 1873. In the week ending February 7, the deaths, from whooping-cough[13] in London were unprecedentedly numerous, namely, 248; and from bronchitis, 1223. Fevers seemed to be little affected. The excess of deaths in London during the three weeks was 2994, and of these probably at least 2000 may be ascribed to the character of the fog alone, and not to the cold. In the foggy week of December 1873, the deaths were more than 700 above the average. Of these probably at least 500 were due to the character of the fog. Such are the results, more fatal than the slaughter of many a great battle, of a want of carefulness in preventing smoke in our domestic fires. It is not only the prize cattle at Islington which perish, but a multitude of human beings, strong and weak. In the fogs of January and February, not only the aged and feeble, and persons affected with bronchitis and lung disease, but the strongest and healthiest, were literally choked to death. Of three young men who were out together in the evening of the worst fog, two immediately fell ill from its effects, and died, and the third had a sharp attack of illness. Thousands of people were thrown so much out / of health that they did not recover for some weeks. In an article of the 'British Medical Journal,'[14] we find the following observations on the mortality of this period:– 'The annual death-rate for the week was 48.1 per 1000 of the estimated population; whereas in the nineteen provincial towns the rate did not exceed 26.3 per 1000. The recent cold was fully as severe in many other parts of the country as in London; it is therefore fair to assume that the exceptionally excessive fatality in the metropolis was due rather to the fog, which was local, than to the cold, which was general.' The increase of mortality on that of the preceding week, which was also high, was 54 per cent. for the whole of London, 32 per cent. in the west groups of districts, and 83 per cent. in the eastern districts. The article then proceeds: 'It is smoke that makes London fogs so mischievous; and bearing in mind the disaster of last week, it is worth inquiring whether something cannot be done to mitigate the main cause of this remarkable mortality.' Now, it is certain that much can be done both to remove the special cause of excessive mortality in London fogs, and to increase the general wholesomeness of the London atmosphere, with little trouble, and considerable pecuniary gain to the community. The death-rate during a few days of dense fog palpably mounts to an extraordinary degree, but every year we have a large number of ordinary London fogs / of less density, which, lasting as they commonly do only one or two days, fail to affect the death-rate sufficiently to be noted as the cause of any small increase above the average which may occur. It would be idle to doubt that bronchitis and lung-diseases are dangerously heightened by moderately thick smoke-fogs, when the thickest fogs produce so great a mortality from those diseases. An excess of 600 deaths in the week elicits comment, but an excess of 60 from this cause, occurring perhaps when the rate is below the average, would hardly be noticed. Besides, fatal effects occur in many cases long after the actual cause of illness has ceased, and these escape notice.

We may infer that numerous deaths occur in the course of the year from smoke-fogs, not unusually thick, producing or increasing diseases of the lungs. Besides these cases, we must reckon a large annual loss of life from the perpetual presence in the London atmosphere of smoke and soot, blocking up the air passages and irritating the mucous membrane so as to lead to consumption,[15] lowering the vital energy, depressing the system both by the impurity of the air breathed and by the deprivation of light, for these influences tell heavily on many constitutions, especially those which happen to be in a weak state of health, as those recovering from fever. /

The evil effects of smoke upon health may be roughly classed as follows: Actual suffocation of healthy persons; aggravation of lung diseases, bronchitis, / and nervous disorders; prostration of convalescents and others from want of fresh air; effects similar to those produced more conspicuously by dust in grinding mills, factories of textile fabrics, etc., by the constant presence of small solid particles in the air, weakening the system and shortening life; effects upon the mind and spirits, resulting frequently in a resort to alcoholic drinks, producing disease; damage to eyesight by want of light and use of gas; accidents by railway, road, and river.

Beyond these bodily hurts, the presence of an overshadowing cloud of smoke produces moral evils which at least deserve some consideration. The population which has hitherto made no serious effort to rid itself of the pollution with which it contaminates the vital breath of heaven suffers seriously for its neglect. They lose, in the first place, that glorious and almost universal privilege of looking upon the clear azure above them, a clear-setting sun or clear-rising moon, the magnificent cloud-castles of summer, the delicate hues and forms of clouds, and the crisp brilliancy of every fine winter morning. They lose, too, all distant prospects, urban or rural, and the pleasant variations of cloud-shadows which delight us in the views of great continental cities, which are not blurred or blotted out by smoke. These things are sermons from nature which humanity has need of. London is indeed hideous to look at, but would be / less hideous without its smoke. What is the meaning of the expression, 'Going to the country for fresh air,' but that Londoners, of whom there are three millions, spend the greater part of their existence in foul air, surely a vast deprivation of a natural blessing? Many a life has been saved by timely removal to country pursuits. It is no joke to those who cannot leave their occupation. Air is to man more than water is to fish; he not only moves in it, but breathes it and lives upon it, and contaminated air deprived of its ozone fails duly to refresh him. If we examine the conditions of various trades, we find that those which are most unwholesome to the body tend also to crush out the wholesome buoyancy of the mind. Even the poorest people in the English country districts have, on the whole, an appearance of contentment and good health and spirits, but among the poor who are natives of London the prevailing expression is one of pallor, discontent, and ill-health, especially among women. Smoke and bad air by no means effect all this; they only contribute to it, with strong drink, overwork, and artificial habits. Natural gaiety can hardly be expected in courts and alleys steeped in grime. Flowers from the country, the spring green of the black funereal trees of parks and squares, the health and spirits of the people, soon fade to one sickly hue. The one thing for which, more than any other, the poor of London express envy of the rich is the power of / going at any time 'to the country.' Schools are allowed one day in the year for 'fresh air' in some suburban fields, and it is said that this one day is remembered like a happy dream by those who pass the other three hundred and sixty-four in a wilderness of bricks and mud. Certainly, existence in the perpetual vapours, often stagnant, of a vast and dismal city can hardly be called life, and the poorest countryman fares better and lives longer than the average born citizen.

Another sad effect of smoke is the hopeless way in which it defeats attempts at cleanliness and neatness among even the most scrupulous of the poor. Wives of labouring men coming from the country find the task of keeping their houses clean too hard for them, and give it up in despair. A forced neglect thus eats into the domestic happiness, and disheartens the spirit of the best of them. Then there is the worry and trouble of smoky chimneys, chimney-sweeping, window-cleaning, renewing and cleaning dirty furniture, dress, &c.; extra washing, and the annoyance of having to keep windows closed for fear of smoke or soot entering, and of window-panes covered with a thick film of dirt. There is no reason why London, if freed from its smoke, should not wear as bright and cheerful an aspect as Paris or Brussels. It would be worth while to paint or whitewash its shabby brick walls, and the streets would soon be enlivened with colours. If our own capital were in general as / clear as it is at 5 o'clock on a summer morning, its people would find that a load of which they were unconscious had been removed, and there would be less talk of weak nerves and bad circulation. If the air could be cleared of smoke, trees and flowers which now perish would thrive; the whole town might be sprinkled with gardens and shrubberies, not black and hideous to look upon; and the streets planted with various trees.

We now come to the question of damage to materials done by smoke, and the financial portion of our subject. The outlay rendered necessary by our unnecessary custom of polluting the atmosphere with unburnt fuel is enormous. Almost everything suffers, from granite quays and columns and the stony surface of the Houses of Parliament to the most delicate satins and silks and coloured fabrics of all kinds. The soot and carbon particles deposited on the stone, being charged with sulphurous and carbonic acid,[16] eat away its substance and make renewals necessary at great cost. The drinking-fountain at the end of Great George Street, Westminster, is an example of the rapid spoiling of works of art. It requires restoration five times as often, at least, as it would need in the country. All monuments, statues, and gilding rapidly lose their brightness and whiteness. Iron rusts far more rapidly than in the country, and other metals quickly oxidise. Galvanized iron and bronze do not endure. In these effects sulphurous and sulphuric / acid, resulting from the combustion of coal, are mainly concerned. Mortar swells and crumbles; many expensive textile fabrics can hardly be exposed to the London air without rapid deterioration; many colours will not remain. Pictures gradually become dingy, and require cleaning; and water-colours and frescoes cannot live long unless well protected. Tapestry, and all fine needlework, soon lose their beauty. The outsides and insides of houses painted white frequently require a fresh coat, and ceilings soon grow black if not frequently whitewashed. Books and engravings rapidly become dirty, and require frequent dusting. Sculpture cannot be exposed to the open air without becoming dirty, and even in houses requires cleaning, which wears it down in course of time. The sitting figures, for instance, on the north side of Burlington House might, but for their European garb, be taken for Zulus. The names of streets and railway stations, names of shops and signboards, advertisements at stations, etc., require frequent renovation. Curtains and blinds soon become dingy. All kinds of apparel, if not dark, become discoloured, and the cost of the necessary extra washing of linen amounts to a vast sum. Gas must be used very frequently earlier than it would be required in the country, and sometimes burnt a great part of a day or all day, and some waste also occurs in the extra use of lamps and candles.

Another extra expense is the additional coal / used beyond what would be burnt if the cloud of smoke did not frequently exclude sunshine in the finest weather. In winter, the very days on which sunshine is warmest in the country, are the darkest in London. It has been ascertained that the sun shines in London with only two-thirds of the power, on an average, with which it shines in the country. The early part of the night, it is true, is a little less cold than in the country, but this does not make up for the loss of the sun's rays.

The proportion of unburnt fuel escaping into the air is worth considering when the total annual consumption of coal in London amounts to about 10,000,000 tons. Dr. Angus Smith[17] considers that in Manchester 1 per cent. is thus lost. I have adopted this estimate for London.

Our imperfect system of heating brings into use a wonderful variety of extremely ugly and expensive cowls and other contrivances for inducing the smoke to go out instead of into our houses.

Lastly, a vast number of people prefer to live at a distance from their offices rather than remain permanently in the foul air of the metropolis, and for this removal from smoke they sacrifice, of course, a portion of their income. If the London atmosphere were cleared of its smoke, it would be quite wholesome enough to satisfy a large number of those who now make the tedious double journey, preferring the suburbs mainly on account of its salubrious air. Obviously there would be / not only a saving in travelling expenses, but an increase in the value of house property in London.

The cost of all these noxious effects can only be estimated in a very general way, but the following list probably presents no exaggerated view of the annual loss to the people of London:–

Extra washing (including extra soap used for all purposes). Dr. Arnott's estimate,[18] some years ago, was much higher, namely, £2,500,000	£1,100,000
Dresses, curtains, carpets, and all textile fabrics damaged and renewed. ..	200,000
Wall-papers replaced; time and labour.	50,000
Houses painted inside or outside, say once in 5 years, instead of once in 25 years, and whitewashing ceilings, &c.	100,000
Restoring gilding, metal-work, shop-fronts, names of streets, advertisements, stations, pictures, works of art, monuments, theatres, &c.	100,000
Slow destruction of stonework, granite, marble, etc., on public and private buildings.	1,000
Extra chimney-sweeping.	20,000
Window-cleaning of public and private buildings, including station-roofs, etc., time of servants included.	50,000
Extra gas, candles, and lamps, used.	40,000
Escape of 1/100th part of fuel into atmosphere.	100,000
Depreciation of house property, loss of time by illness caused by fogs, loss of time and money by travelling of persons who would otherwise live in London.	Not estimated.
TOTAL. .. More than	£1,761,000

It will be observed that the waste of heat by our present uneconomical fireplaces has not been taken into account in the above list. /

C. S., 'The Smoke Question' (1895–6)

C. S.,[1] '[Abstract] The Smoke Question', *Transactions of the North of England Institute of Mining and Mechanical Engineers*, 45 (1895–6), pp. 70–1.

THE SMOKE QUESTION.

Neue Beiträge zur Rauchfrage.[2] *By* MESSRS. VON SCHRÖDER *and* W. SCHMITZ-DUMONT. *Dingler's Polytechnisches Journal*, 1896, *vol.* 300, *pages* 65, 111, *and* 136.

The authors subjected a number of young pines, firs, maples, and lindens to the action of dilute sulphurous acid gas[3] (1/10000 to 1/1000000) daily for some weeks, in order to ascertain the minimum limit of the dilution capable of injuriously affecting vegetation. It was, however, found that in all the experiments the trees sickened, although in some cases the sulphurous acid was no longer perceptible to the senses, the effects produced being practically the same whether with short / periods of exposure to more concentrated gas or with longer exposures to the gas in a state of greater dilution. The leaves or needles, particularly those on the new shoots, turned grey, then reddish brown, and finally dropped off. The percentage of sulphur in the leaves was much higher, being in some instances twice or thrice the amount originally present, from which circumstance, coupled with the fact that where the plants were merely watered round the roots with dilute solutions of sulphurous acid no unfavourable action followed (although the quantity of sulphuric acid absorbed therefrom by the leaves was larger than that resulting from the direct absorption of the gas), it is concluded that the damage is caused by the contact and absorption of the acid gas into the substance of the plant through the leaves alone. It is also believed that this is true in the case of other acid gases, and especially of hydrochloric acid.

Further experiments were carried out to determine whether rain has, as is sometimes asserted, the power to wash out some of the sulphurous acid absorbed by leaves exposed to smoke. The results of these investigations go to show that, in the case of such plants as potatoes, the absorbed acid gas may be fully extracted from the dead leaves by the action of rain but not from those still in a condition of vitality. On the other hand, in the case of resinous or waxy leaves, water is incapable of washing out the acid, even in dead leaves, unless under abnormally favourable conditions, such as are little likely to occur in nature. In fact the authors' conclusions, derived from their work, are to the effect that it is practically impossible for the damage occasioned by smoke to trees, particularly those whose leaves contain wax or resin, to be remedied by the re– extractive action of rain, more especially since any small amount of acid so washed out would be, in districts where smoke constantly prevails, immediately, replaced by the absorption of a further quantity. C.S.

'London of the Future', *British Architect* (1914)

'London of the Future', *British Architect* (23 January 1914), pp. 84–5.

LONDON OF THE FUTURE.

NEARLY 200 guests assembled on Tuesday night at the last of the three dinners of the season, which have been arranged for the members of the London Society[1] and their friends at the Waldorf Hotel. The subject for the evening was 'London of the Future,' and on this topic Sir Aston Webb,[2] the chairman of the executive, delivered a most interesting address for about half an hour. Sir Aston was followed by Sir Jas. Ramsay, Sir Boverton Redwood, Sir Jas. Crichton Browne, Sir Wm. Bull, Sir George Riddell, and Mr. H. H. Statham,[3] whose short speeches were followed with much interest, and occupied the time till nearly eleven o'clock.

Sir Aston's address took the form of a dream which he had during the prosy chat of a pessimist, with whom he had dined. He found himself on a bridge crossing the Thames, but such great changes had taken place, that in his bewilderment he asked an intelligent stranger whom he found near him if that were really London. He was assured it was, but soon found that it was the London of a hundred years hence A. D. 2014. One of the first things which astonished him was the clear air, and then the sight of the blue sky which he had so seldom seen in London before. Asking the meaning of this, he was told the abolition of smoke had at last been brought about, owing to the efforts of the Smoke Abatement Society,[4] and the researches of distinguished scientists, such as Sir Wm. Ramsay.[5] In fact the little open square on the south side, with a statue in the centre, was the memorial of a grateful Government to the efforts of the society and its president, Sir Wm. Richmond,[6] whom the statue represented. The idea of a Government which was grateful for anything surprised the visitor from the year 1914. 'Those men on the river bank, what are they doing?' was the next question. To this was replied, 'Oh, they are fishing.' 'Fishing in the Thames! What do they catch?' 'Oh, salmon, and trout, and other fish which are found in similar great rivers; there is a great salmon weir at the Tower.[']7 This was a staggering surprise, but more was to come. 'How comes that fine embankment all along the south bank of the river, with overhanging warehouses in such picturesque fashion?' said Sir Aston. 'Oh, that came about through the efforts of the London Society a hundred years ago.' 'And these bridges, with shops on either side, which are really streets, how could these expensive structures be erected?' 'That was easy enough,' said the informant. 'It was always laid down by town planners that a road could not afford even one unoccupied frontage, but in these street bridges there are two occupied frontages, and they more than pay for the extra width of the bridge, whilst the general comfort to the public and charm of effect are great acquisitions.' 'Come up on this archway crossing the bridge, and look over the City, said Sir Aston's intelligent companion. On going up he was amazed at much more which he now beheld. He was surprised to find a belt of green grass and trees encircling London.[8] He also noted that all the roofs of the houses on the south side were flat, and that these were made into gardens, which he was informed were really and constantly used and much enjoyed because there was no smoke. Aeroplanes were not allowed to alight anywhere within the London area, though they were used beyond, for chiefly military purposes. Rising up in great bulk from the river front was a great building which raised the question. 'What is the purpose of that magnificent building?' 'That is the Imperial House,' was the reply, 'where we meet to think imperially every three years.' 'Isn't that fine block of buildings the home of the County Council?' was the next question. 'It has now become a Government building, and is used for Government offices,' was replied. 'Politics are no longer allowed to rule the actions of the County Council Government. The Council and the City Corporation are now one united body,[9] and form a supreme authority for London, with head quarters at the Guildhall and the Mansion House, where they sustain the traditions and dignities of the past. The Borough Councils still exist, and do most valuable work.' 'Where are the great railway stations[10] which used to bulk so prominently in the view of London?' was a question which elicited much information as to the way in which the stations were gradually supplanted, by one great northern depot underground to link up all the great northern lines, and one large southern terminus underground for the southern lines, the two being in close communication by an underground railway. The great cost of all this was largely found by better lines of roadway above, with finer and larger building sites which well recouped the railway interests. An amusing reply was made to the question as to what had been done with Regent Street. The gentleman of A.D. 2014 was surprised that a 1914 man dare ask about Regent Street, as it / was at that date utterly spoilt. But when asked if they were doing anything to remedy it, he replied. 'Oh, yes, we are going to entirely rebuild it in an harmonious manner. The leases have fallen in again!' Question after question brought forth information about many things which are now in the melting pot. The London University[11] was still where it now is, and the Imperial Institute[12] building, with added wings, and residential quarters, in Queen's Gate. Great arterial roads led out of London in all directions, with two centre lines of quick traffic divided by lines of trees from the slower traffic at the sides. The housing problem had practically settled itself, partly by better means of transit and partly by housing clerks, etc., in suburban instead of central districts; tramways had long since disappeared, but the House of Lords was stronger than ever. There was a Ministry of Arts,[13] and even Trafalgar Square seemed to have been made worthy of its great opportunities. St. Paul's Cathedral was safe for centuries, for no underground cutting or sewer was permitted near enough to hurt it. Of course, one of the London Society's main objects had been followed in that all interesting old buildings and associations had been carefully preserved.[14] There seemed hardly anything left to ask about, till the intelligent guide suggested a visit to see the sewers, which were now like those in Paris. This seemed to have served as a useful shock to Sir Aston, who woke up to meet the reproaches of his friend on his somnolescence, and a final iteration of the belief that it was impossible to improve London.

Sir Wm. Ramsay made an interesting speech. He spoke of our English way of selecting men for dealing with certain subjects of which they were ignorant, as though it made for impartiality. He had been placed on a committee at the University to deal with architecture, though he knew absolutely nothing about it. In reference to the University, he pointed out that a great pile of buildings spread over 50 or 60 acres of ground did not constitute the necessary embodiment of a university, and the London University did not need it, but only a comparatively small, compact building – not a huge collection of schools and laboratories. In reference to the smoke trouble, he suggested one method of abatement might be to tax domestic fires, or tax everyone who made black smoke. The electric carpet, with a heat of 70 degrees might be considered practicable. The gas fire was far nearer the perfect ideal than the coal fire.

Sir Boverton Redwood looked forward to the possibility of having hot air in the winter, and cold in summer laid on to our houses by municipal enterprise.

Sir J. Crichton Browne spoke of the inspiring effect of a really fine city, such as Edinburgh, on the character of its inhabitants.

Mr. Carmichael Thomas,[15] the chairman of the executive very ably presided at the dinner.

Mr. Solomon J. Solomon, R.A.,[16] said that if the Utopia which had been dreamed for them were to materialise then it was obvious that æsthetic consideration must be included in the law of the land.

V. B. Kennett-Barrington, 'River Pollution by Refuse from Manufactories and Mines Together with Some Remedies Proposed' (1883)

V. B. Kennett-Barrington,[1] 'River Pollution by Refuse from Manufactories and Mines Together with Some Remedies Proposed', in J. P. Weeldon et al., *Fish Papers: A Collection of Papers Presented at Conferences during the International Fisheries Exhibition, London, 1883* (London, William Clowes and Son, 1883).

RIVER POLLUTION BY REFUSE FROM MANUFACTORIES AND MINES, TOGETHER WITH SOME REMEDIES PROPOSED.

THE object of this Paper is to bring before the notice of the public the important question of River Pollution by the manufacturing and mining industries, with the view of securing some abatement of a great, and what is still more serious, an increasing national evil.

The subject is one of special importance to all interested in our inland fisheries; but let me impress upon you the fact, that pollution of rivers is injurious not only to the comfort and well-being of a large mass of our population and to the preservation of fish life, but is also prejudicial to the interests of many manufacturers themselves, owing to the foul condition of the water which has to be used in their industries. Besides there is frequently a waste of valuable materials, which are allowed to run as refuse into the streams.

We must remember that foul water, if only used for power, is often a nuisance; if polluted beyond a certain degree, it is injurious even to dark and coarse goods in the washing and dyeing processes, and quite unfit for fine fabrics unless first purified by the manufacturer before use.

After a few general remarks, I shall quote the evidence of reliable authorities in order to give some idea of the / magnitude of the evil, and then I propose to group the various industries under separate heads, and in every case –

First, to point out shortly the cause and effect of the pollution;
Secondly, to refer in general terms to various means suggested for remedying or mitigating the evil.

These remarks will be followed by a short history of the measures and proceedings relating to river pollution, which have occupied so much of the attention of Her Majesty's Government and of both Houses of Parliament from the year 1862 to the present day. This has been compiled by Mr. William Burchell, after a careful examination of numerous Bills, Acts, and Reports of parliamentary proceedings, and other documents on the subject.[2]

The four chief causes of river pollution are clearly set forth by Dr. Edward Frankland in his evidence before the Select Committee of the House of Lords, 1873.[3] They are as follow, viz.:–

First, Solid rubbish of all kinds, causing the silting up of the rivers.
Secondly, Sewage.
Thirdly, Refuse water from manufactories of various kinds.
Fourthly, Mining refuse 'which spoils completely for fish and also for human use, and for agricultural purposes many rivers in the mining districts.'

The question of sewage, which is a large polluting factor, has been already brought under your notice by the Hon. W. F. B. Massey Mainwaring, Chairman of the Native / Guano Company,[4] and, therefore, my remarks will be mainly confined to the case of pollution from the refuse of our industries.

Those industries are conveniently treated by the Royal Commissioners[5] under various heads; some of these I have grouped, for the purpose of this Paper, in the following order, namely:–

Manufacturing Industries.

1. Calico-print, dye, and bleach works.
2. Chemical works (alkali, soap, and colour).
3. Tanneries.
4. Paper mills.
5. Woollen works.
6. Silk works.
7. Linen and jute works.
8. Starch works.
9. Alcohol distilleries.
10. Paraffin, petroleum, and tar works.
11. Sugar refineries.

Mining Industries.

1. Collieries and coal washing.
2. Iron, lead, copper, zinc, and arsenic mines.
3. Tin mines, baryta mines.
4. China clay works.

Metal Industries.

Iron and steel wire, tin plate, and galvanising works.

The evidence quoted in this Paper will show that in the opinion of leading authorities, the industries, taken as a whole, would *not* in the long run be losers by the enforcement of more stringent provisions against pollution than exist at the present moment.

In some cases an outlay of capital, for a time no doubt / unprofitable, would be necessary; but, on the other hand, in many cases it can be clearly demonstrated that such expenditure would prove immediately, or eventually, profitable to the manufacturers themselves. Indeed, many of them so acknowledged in their evidence before the Royal Commissioners. One firm estimated at £3000 a-year and another at £800 a-year the direct money gain to them if the rivers from which they derived their supply of water were rendered clear and colourless.

It will naturally be asked why, under such circumstances, the manufacturers do not voluntarily apply purifying processes? Amongst others, one reason is that they have not a common or an equal interest.

Take fifty paper-mills on one stream. The first maker at the head of the stream receives his water pure; he uses and pollutes it, and sends it forward so polluted. He at any rate can have no pecuniary inducement to purify the water he uses, unless he can see a clear profit to be realized from the refuse materials extracted, and saved in the process of purification; a result which may be too remote, too uncertain, and too small in his estimation for the trouble and risk. His interest in the prevention of pollution therefore may be reckoned as *nil.* The second paper-maker receives the water so polluted – possibly it may be sufficiently pure or will require but little cleansing for his use. Still he has some interest in its purity, and would be prepared perhaps to meet it by some proportionately small outlay. The third will receive the water with twofold pollutions, and his interest in its purification is proportionately greater – and so on through the whole number of mills.

With such diverse, not to say conflicting interests no wonder some controlling power is required. In the / evidence given before the Select Committee of the House of Lords, in 1873, we read, in reference to the industries at Leeds: 'Most of those large manufacturers are quite prepared to face the expense and trouble, provided they know what they have to do; but they naturally refuse to go to expense in purifying their waste liquors, unless their neighbours will do something in the same direction.'

To show the *practicability* of purifying our rivers, to which I desire to call your special attention, I may refer to the following important passage in the first Report of the Royal Commissioners of 1868,[6] viz.:–

2nd Com., 1st Rep., p. 96.

'Of the many polluting liquids which now poison the rivers of the Mersey and Ribble basins, we feel ourselves justified in stating that there is not one which cannot be either kept out of the streams altogether, or so far purified before admission as to deprive it of its noxious character, and this not only without unduly interfering with manufacturing operations, but even in some instances with a distinct profit to the manufacturer; and even in those cases where a certain amount of expense must be incurred in unremunerative operations, the use of the purified stream will more than recompense this expenditure.'

And again, in the fifth Report, dealing with 'Pollution arising from Mining Operations and Metal Manufactures,' we read:–

2nd Com., 5th Rep., p. 1.

'The remedies for the nuisances which these refuse liquids create have been carefully examined, and, after prolonged inquiry and research, we have been able to report that in every case efficient remedies exist and are available, so that the present use of rivers and running waters for the purpose of carrying off the sewage of towns and populous places, and the refuse arising from industrial processes and manufactures can be prevented without risk to the public health or serious injury to such processes or manufactures.'

The action of some authority, independent of merely local interests, is required to bring about the much desired reform. /

Manufacturing Institutions

Class 10. – *Paraffin, Petroleum, and Tar Works.*

2nd Com., 4th Rep., p. 42.

2nd Com., 4th Rep., p. 69.

The Commissioners report that pollution from these works is, in some parts of Scotland, 'a serious and increasing evil.' They consider that the refuse liquids, which are exceedingly foul, cannot be purified by any practicable means, and add that 'total exclusion from running water is the only remedy for this form of river pollution.'

This is remarkable, and worthy of all attention; it is the / only instance, it is believed, in the diligent researches and voluminous reports of the two Commissions, in which this admission is to be found. It is the exception which proves the rule. The Commissioners, however, shortly afterwards qualify their assertion, by adding: 'Fortunately the volume of the polluting liquids is not large, and a portion of them admits of conversion into a profit, in others at an insignificant loss.'

They conclude with the consolatory remark, that 'an absolute prohibition of all drainage from paraffin and petroleum works into streams would, in our opinion, inflict no serious loss upon these branches of manufacture.' 2nd Com., 4th Rep., p. 70.

I should here desire to call your special attention to the very interesting evidence given in 1873 by Sir Lyon Playfair, M.P.,[7] before the Select Committee of the House of Lords on the River Pollution Bill, p. 11.

'I must confess,' he says, 'to your Lordships, that I myself am a great polluter of streams. I have an interest, as a director, in the largest paraffin works in the kingdom,[8] and I am a polluter of streams under that 10th clause.' [One of the clauses in the Bill then under consideration.] 'I think that if you force us to purify the water which we discharge fouled in this way, before long we shall find efficient modes of doing it. At the present moment we have not efficient modes of doing it, and yet, as one of the largest polluters of water in the kingdom from this very thing, I advocate that you should make me purify the water before I discharge it.'

Their Lordships adopted his disinterested advice, and passed the Bill with that 10th clause, but unfortunately the Bill was sent to the Commons very late in the session, and was dropped.

Remedy. – Although the refuse liquids cannot be purified so as to admit of their being discharged into streams, yet there is a method of disposing of them on the works themselves. Their volume being not large, they can be thrown / into the ashpits of the furnaces, where they will be evaporated by the waste heat. This is the course recommended by Dr. E. Frankland in 1873, in his evidence before the same Select Committee of the Lords.[9] p. 17.

Mining Industries.

There is a great distinction between the refuse water from these industries, and those treated in the former part of this paper, owing to the fact that pollution from mines is entirely inorganic, and nearly always arises from matters in suspension.

The chief causes of pollution are, first, the shooting of solid waste refuse into the watercourses; secondly, the / discharge of water which has been used on the dressing-floors to separate the rocky matter, or 'gangue,' from the metallic portion of the ore after crushing. This water, though it generally passes through several catch-pits, carries with it in suspension a certain quantity of finely-divided metallic matter of a highly poisonous nature. Thirdly, the discharge of polluted water from the underground workings into neighbouring streams by adits or by pumps.

Class 1. – *Collieries and Coal-washing.*

2nd Com., 5th Rep., p. 4. The Commissioners remark 'that the water discharged from coal-mines where iron pyrites abound, is much polluted by sulphate of iron, and is highly injurious to fish.' /

DISCUSSION

Mr. C. N. Cresswell[10]

...

What was the position of the public on this question? One would suppose, from the enormous crowds who visited this Exhibition, that they all took a lively interest in pisciculture – that is the propagation and conservation of fish – and therefore necessarily in the purification of our streams. Yet when they came to pick out individuals from the visitors to the buildings belonging to the Native Guano Company and the Manufacturers' and Millowners' Mutual Aid Association, they were able to detect four or five distinct types of mind and character. The first class / were persons who positively received with surprise the information that there was any pollution going on in the rivers at all; it was a new light breaking upon them when they were told that the rivers of the United Kingdom, with scarcely an exception, were polluted to such an extent that they were neither fit for man nor beast. They received it as a new revelation, and went away wondering that such a state of things could exist. He did not like to be unpleasant, and say that those people were stupid; indeed he was afraid that the great majority of the people of this country were stupid on this subject. There was a very old proverb that even the gods themselves did not know how to deal with stupid people. Another type was the influential country gentleman, the Member of Parliament, Chairman of Quarter Sessions, or of the Local Board of his district. He remembered in particular one important man, who said, with a great deal of candour, that he thought he was bound as a public duty to set an example to his neighbours, and he therefore set to work to prevent the pollution of the river which flowed past his works. He found it to be a very expensive proceeding, but still he was willing to bear that in consideration of his position; none of his neighbours were compelled to do likewise; and after a few years, having gone to considerable expense in doing his best to keep the stream pure, he had seen that those above and below were polluting it the same as ever. There was no use in isolated action like that; compulsion ought to be uniformly brought to bear throughout the country. The gentleman to whom he referred took a great deal of interest in what was said to him by the scientific men connected with the Manufacturers' and Millowners Mutual Aid Association. He seemed impressed by it, and said that he should communicate with them; / indeed it was hoped he would become a subscriber and supporter. Many years ago he was consulted with reference to Leeds, which was suddenly called upon to cleanse the Augean stable, and put its house in order; and the different companies established to promote sewage utilisation and disposal had a fair field and every possible favour, provided they spent their own money, and did not damage the Corporation property. Inasmuch as the Sewage Committee of the Corporation had for its chairman one of the shrewdest and most intelligent men in Yorkshire, they could well understand that Leeds was for two or three years practically cleansed at the expense of the various enterprising companies which abounded in those days. The tanneries, dye-works, woollen factories, &c., at Leeds, had brought about a state of things which was not at all exaggerated in the Paper. He recollected his son being sent down in his professional capacity to superintend a chemical experiment that was going on. He reported that one day the colour of the river[11] was red, another day it was green, a third day it was black, and the fourth it might possibly be yellow, but it never was clear. The colour depended entirely on the caprice of the public, and the fashion of the dye they most affected. There was no difficulty, however, in dealing with it; but Leeds found that, after having obtained at enormous expense an excellent specific for their special difficulty, not a single town above them on the river[12] was called upon to do likewise. As the President of the Sewage Committee said to him, what would be the use of their pouring water as clear as Apollinaris[13] into a river which flowed by them as black as ink? Another great obstacle was the strong impression on the minds of manufacturers that they had a prescriptive right to pollute the rivers. Indeed, in the / old law books it would be found that when a man was charged with the pollution of a river, and an attempt was made to obtain an injunction or to support an indictment, they put in a plea that from time immemorial they had a right to pollute that river, and intended to exercise it. He had heard men of the highest position say: 'My father and grand-father polluted the Aire and Calder river, and I intend to do the same. Why should I be deprived of the right without compensation?' If he were reminded of his duty as a legislator, his reply was: 'That is all very well, but everybody in this country must take care of himself.' Then if it were said: 'How about the poor unfortunate people below who want pure water?' the only reply was: 'If people are foolish enough to go down the river instead of remaining where I am, God help them!' However, the Act of 1876[14] had put an end to that argument, and prescription could no longer be pleaded. There was another very important class of objectors, the scientific objector. He believed Mr. Robert Rawlinson[15] had changed his views very much within the last twenty years, but he had heard him say that it would be a fatal mistake in this country to commence cleansing the rivers by removal of pollution unless it were done all over the country uniformly on a scientific system. For instance, he said, if operations were simply confined to the exclusion of *sewage* from the rivers in Yorkshire and Lancashire, they would no doubt be doing a great good to the country; if at the same time *manufacturing refuse* were excluded, much further good would be done, because the streams would then become what they were intended by Nature to be, the great arteries of the country, supplying food to man and animals; but one should not be done without the other, for if the sewage of / the great towns were allowed to fall into the rivers, the manufacturing refuse must also be allowed to flow in with it; the one neutralised and cancelled the other, and therefore the subject should be dealt with completely or not at all. He believed that to be a perfectly scientific and justifiable observation. Now, having to deal with these four or five classes of objectors, it might be said, How could so grave an obstacle to progress on this question be overcome? There was but one remedy – and that had been admitted by the Society of Arts and other kindred institutions – the intervention of the State, of course through constitutional methods. It seemed to him that to-day, if they were to do anything practical towards effecting that much-desired result, it would be well to arm the Council of the Fisheries Exhibition with something in the form of a resolution, and request their powerful intervention with the Government, whose ear they had. Something should be done, if not in the next session, certainly within the next two sessions, to amend the Acts of Parliament already existing, and to give greater stringency to the provisions already to be found on the statute book. It was true that the Rivers Pollution Prevention Act, after twenty years of gestation, was brought forth in the year 1876, and they thought at first that they had attained the summit of their hopes; but all those hopes had been dashed, and everybody who knew anything about the operation of the Act, or had to advise upon its construction, confessed that it was absolutely inoperative. Mr. Baldwin Latham[16] had pointed out one great defect, and he could point out others. One of the definitions was this – that pollution should not be held to include innocuous discoloration; so that you might make the river all the colours of the rainbow, and that would not be / pollution within the meaning of the Act. It might meet the objection made by Colonel Leach,[17] that it was dangerous to make the water too clear if it was not perfectly pure; but as long as the Act stood as it was at present there need be no fear of that risk; it would always be red, black or green, and nobody would think of drinking it. With regard to that objection, he might fairly say that if they were to abandon all efforts to effect anything like improvement in the purification of rivers until they were able to obtain that which they all wished, namely, perfectly *pure* water, they would have to boil the rivers, which, though nothing was impossible to engineers, would be rather an expensive operation. The Act of Parliament went to some extent in the right direction; it declared that to be a misdemeanour which never was one before – that was something; and if there were any discredit attached to polluting the rivers, as there was to stealing one's neighbour's purse, it would be a good thing; but heretofore everybody sympathised with everybody else, and there was no disgrace whatever attaching to it. If you had an Act of Parliament, you must have power to put it in force; and the real cause of the inefficiency of this Act was that there was no power in the country to enforce it; on the contrary, those authorities which had more to do with it than any one else had a strong interest the other way. The Act said that if you had reason to complain you could take proceedings before the County Court, but through the intervention of the sanitary authority; if they would not do it, you must go to the Local Government Board. The sanitary authorities were the greatest criminals of all; there was hardly one that was not polluting the streams around it.[18] The question was how the Act could be amended. It seemed to him there were two ways of doing it. They hoped next year to have an Act / passed for the conservancy of rivers; and in the Bill originally drawn there was power taken for the Conservancy Board to enforce the provisions of the Rivers Pollution Prevention Act; unfortunately, last year the clause was expunged. They might ask the Government to re-introduce the clause. In the next place they were told that if this Government were able to carry any Bill at all affecting social amelioration, it would be the County Boards Bill; well, three years ago the Society of Arts passed a resolution that the very best possible authority to be armed with the power of enforcing the Rivers Pollution Prevention Act would be the County Board, because they were taken from a larger area, and were not likely to be influenced by personal considerations or petty parochial politics. He believed that County Boards would be the means to which they would eventually have to look to see the Act enforced. He would therefore move the following resolution: 'That, having regard to the great and increasing national evils caused by the pollution of the rivers of the kingdom, the Executive Committee is respectfully requested, through the Chairman of the day, to press upon Her Majesty's Government the urgency of effective legislation in the next session, in order to enforce the prohibitions contained in the Rivers Pollution Prevention Act of 1876.'[19] /

H. Maclean Wilson, 'The Pollution of Streams by Spent Gas-Liquors from Coke-Ovens' (1909–10)

H. Maclean Wilson,[1] 'The Pollution of Streams by Spent Gas-Liquors from Coke-Ovens; and the Methods Adopted for its Prevention', *Transactions of the Institute of Mining Engineers*, 39 (1909–10), pp. 71–82.

THE POLLUTION OF STREAMS BY SPENT GAS-LIQUORS FROM COKE-OVENS; AND THE METHODS ADOPTED FOR ITS PREVENTION.

By Dr. H. MACLEAN WILSON.

The pollution of streams by refuse discharged from stills where ammonia has been recovered from gas-liquor is no new thing. Going no farther back than 1875, the question was then specially considered by those who framed the Public Health Act[2] of that year; but there has of late years been a rapid increase both in the number and in the magnitude of these polluting discharges in connexion with patent coke-ovens, and this has caused the Rivers Board,[3] who are responsible for preventing such pollutions, great trouble and anxiety. On the one hand, they have constantly been receiving complaints that clean trout streams, or streams used for the watering of cattle, have suddenly become grossly polluted and unfit for such purposes, and, on the other, they are aware that these pollutions are the result of the necessary development of one of the most important trades in the West Riding of Yorkshire. Their knowledge of the importance of this development of the coal trade has made the Board chary of putting into force their full legal powers. At first, moreover, there was some difficulty in devising proper methods for the prevention of these pollutions. Now, however, that experience has shown that such liquids can be dealt with at no great cost, so as to prevent them from polluting any streams, the Board feel that the time has come when they must do their utmost to enforce the law. /

It is well known, and it will be readily acknowledged, that the members of the Board have shown every consideration for the interests of the manufacturers with whom they have had to deal; the colliery proprietors of the West Riding have done much in the past to put a stop to all the forms of gross pollution of streams caused by discharges from collieries, and generally have always been willing to adopt any reasonable suggestion in that direction. The result is that pollution of the streams by coal-washing water has nearly become a thing of the past. In the main the measures adopted have resulted in checking the waste of vast quantities of good coal. Similar results will certainly be attained when the discharge of chemical refuse is properly dealt with.

It is not long since patent coke-ovens, with their accompanying works for the recovery of ammonia, were introduced into the West Riding. When the Rivers Board was established in 1893, there were none in existence; since then, and particularly during the last 10 years, the numbers have been constantly increasing, until now there are twenty-four batteries in operation, and others half built or shortly to be erected.

The chief liquid refuse from such works is the spent gas-liquor from the ammonia-stills. This is a light brown liquid of a temperature of about 212° Fahr. (100° Cent.); it is turbid, with particles of spent lime and tarry matters, and has a peculiar, offensive smell. It contains large amounts of acidic and basic tar-oils, noxious sulphur compounds, and considerable amounts of cyanides and sulphocyanides. The amount of oxygen which it absorbs in the permanganate test[4] is exceedingly high, and the hardness (owing to the presence of the lime), partly temporary, but chiefly permanent, is very marked. Most of the lime settles readily, leaving a comparatively clear liquid, the chemical composition of which is somewhat complex.

Appended to the paper is a table containing analyses of this refuse.

The effect of the discharge of such a liquid into a stream is immediate and disastrous. It is poisonous to all fish life; it kills the vegetation and the small insects upon which fish live; it is exceedingly poisonous to cattle; it makes the water of the stream quite unfit for manufacturing purposes; and, in short, it is a poisonous, noxious, and polluting liquid. Unfortunately / for those who have erected these patent coke-ovens in the West Riding, the discharge has been in nearly every case into a small clear stream, and its effects have thus been intensified.

The law relating to this form of pollution is clear and distinct. By common law a riparian owner has the right of receiving the water of a stream in its original state of purity, and can take action to stop the discharge of any polluting matter into the stream, unless the person causing such a discharge has acquired a right by prescription or otherwise.

In the Rivers Pollution Prevention Act of 1876,[5] and the West Riding Rivers Act of 1894, such pollutions are dealt with in the same way as pollutions caused by any other manufacturing process. The Rivers Board must obtain the sanction of the Local Government Board[6] before proceedings can be taken by them, and the Local Government Board have to be satisfied, after due enquiry, that means for rendering the refuse harmless are reasonably practicable and available under all the circumstances of the case, and that no material injury will be inflicted by such proceedings on the interests of the industry.

The Local Government Board have already given their consent to proceedings against one colliery proprietor in the West Riding; but in that case no proceedings have been found necessary, as the measures adopted have resulted in stopping the pollution of the stream affected.

The Public Health Act of 1875[7] is much more drastic. Section 68 says that –

> 'Any person engaged in the manufacture of gas who (1) causes or suffers to be brought, or to flow into any stream, reservoir, aqueduct, pond, or place for water, or into any drain or pipe communicating therewith, any washing or other substance produced in making or supplying gas; or (2) wilfully does any act connected with the making or supplying of gas whereby the water in any such stream, reservoir, aqueduct, pond, or place for water is fouled, shall forfeit for every such offence the sum of two hundred pounds, and after the expiration of twenty-four hours' notice from the local Authority, or the person to whom the water belongs in that behalf, a further sum of twenty pounds for every day during which the offence is continued, or during the continuance of the act whereby the water is fouled.'

Under the Acts of 1876 (Section 7) and 1894 (Section 10), every Sanitary Authority[8] is enjoined to give facilities to enable manufacturers within their district to carry their liquid refuse into the public sewers; but provisos are added which make it an easy matter for any Authority to refuse to receive such refuse as / that under consideration. Section 17 of the Public Health Amendment Act, 1890,[9] also gives Sanitary Authorities such powers as would enable them to refuse to receive this refuse.

In only one case in the West Riding is chemical refuse from coke-ovens taken into a public sewer, and in that case it upsets the treatment of the sewage to such an extent that the Sanitary Authority concerned are at present compelled to remodel and extend their sewage works; therefore it is not likely that in any other case a Sanitary Authority will give the desired facilities. /

KNOWLEDGE: GEOLOGY AND EXPLORATION

This is the first of three sections on the use of knowledge in the discovery and production of coal. They are concerned with knowledge and the supply of coal, rather than with knowledge and the demand for coal. Here we turn to the use of knowledge in the discovery of coal and the main scientific discipline involved which is, of course, geology.

The extracts from John Scafe's *King Coal's Levee* (pp. 247–57) take an unfamiliar form for this context: that of a poem. Quite what distinguishes poetry from prose is, of course, a vexed question. To some, the form of the main text of the item, set in lines and arranged to rhyme, will be conclusive. But to others, the absence of discernible moral content will rob it of poetic status and demote the text from poetry to '(mere) verse' or 'song'. Others, specifying imagination rather than moral content as the key characteristic, will point to Scafe's imaginative personification of the rocks and minerals as sufficient to raise it to the status of poetry. It would be unusual now to point to the subject matter as a feature disqualifying the composition from poetic status; nevertheless nineteenth-century poetry, at least as studied in the schools and universities, rarely took an industrial topic for its subject.[1] Still others will point to the tradition of didactic poetry, the model of which is Virgil's *Georgics*, and suggest that Scafe's composition, though perhaps not as skilful as Virgil's, is of the same kind.

There are indeed parallels between *The Georgics* and *King Coal's Levee* and, as the former was well-known in early nineteenth-century England, it is possible that it was Scafe's inspiration. Here is Virgil on the varieties of trees:

> Old Stakes of Olive Trees in Plants revive; By the same Methods *Paphian* Myrtles live: But nobler Vines by Propagation thrive. From Roots hard Hazles, and from Cyens rise Tall Ash, and taller Oak that mates the Skies: Palm, Poplar, Firr, descending from the Steep Of Hills, to try the dangers of the Deep. The thin-leav'd *Arbute* Hazle, graffs receives, And Planes huge Apples bear, that bore but Leaves. Thus Mastful Beech the bristly Chesnut bears, And the wild Ash is white with blooming Pears. And greedy Swine from grafted Elms are fed, With falling Acorns, that on Oaks are bred.[2]

The parallels with Scafe's composition on the varieties of rocks are clear.

Although it is hoped that Scafe's rhymes will give the reader some relief from the monotony of prose, *King Coal's Levee* is included here not for its poetic qualities but for what it tells us of the state of geological knowledge in the early nineteenth century. One does not expect a poet to have accurate and up-to-date knowledge of geology but it is clear that Scafe went to considerable trouble over the scientific accuracy of his poem, obtaining assistance from the Rev. William Daniel Conybeare and, in the composition of the Notes to the poem, the Rev. William Buckland, two of the most distinguished geologists of the time. What was this knowledge?

It was recognized that there were different kinds of rocks.[3] It was assumed that rocks could be classified, despite the difficulties caused by variations between specimens, and some classes of rocks had been named for a long time, for example 'chalk', 'limestone' and 'pyrites'.[4] It had been noticed that some rocks formed 'beds' or 'strata' since at least the sixteenth century. By the end of the seventeenth century it was understood that these strata often dipped and rose and sometimes formed 'basins' or synclinal structures; it was understood that strata might be folded and faulted. That there is an orderly succession of strata was enunciated by John Whitehurst in his 'General Observations of the Strata in Derbyshire' of 1778 but the impact of this work was slight, possibly because of the dross with which his work on Derbyshire was surrounded.[5]

A small number of fossils, for example ammonites, had been noticed by the sixteenth century but it was not understood that they were organic remains until Robert Hooke reached this conclusion in his *Micrographia* of 1665. A century later, in 1766, D. C. Solander published the first catalogue of British fossils and applied a Linnaean nomenclature to them.

The founding work of modern geology, comparable in status to Adam Smith's *Wealth of Nations* or to Darwin's *Evolution of Species* was James Hutton's *Theory of the Earth, With Proofs and Illustrations*, published in 1795.[6] Hutton described rock formation in terms of a geological cycle. Strata were lifted up from under the oceans and thus came into contact with the atmosphere and the erosive actions of rain, snow and ice. The resulting detritus was carried down rivers back into the ocean where it formed new, 'secondary', sedimentary rocks. During uplift, rocks were split and cracked and through the resulting fissures molten material from the earth's core rose to the surface, cooled and formed 'primitive' (igneous) rocks; rocks affected by the heat of the molten material and the pressure arising from this process were changed in form to become metamorphic rocks. It followed from the theory that 'primary' rocks were relatively old, and 'secondary' rocks were relatively young.

Hutton's book, unlike *The Wealth of Nations* or *The Evolution of Species*, became notorious for its prolixity and tedium. Hutton was fortunate to find in John Playfair a supporter who could write and Playfair's *Illustrations of the*

Huttonian Theory of the Earth of 1802 became an essential supplement, or, one suspects, substitute for Hutton's own work.[7]

Hutton's work became the bedrock of geology and enabled rapid progress to be made thereafter but it did not provide a great deal of help to someone such as John Buddle, asked to report on the prospects for finding coal in southern Scotland in 1806 and whose report is extracted on pp. 259–67. The report illustrates the difficulty of exploration for coal at that time. Buddle's method was to tour the district searching for any place, a mine, a well, a quarry, the cliff formed by the erosion of the rocks on the bank of a river, where the strata might be exposed and to identify the strata by a close examination of the characteristics of the rock. These are then compared with those kinds of rocks thought to be indicative of coal and those kinds of rocks beneath which coal has been seen elsewhere.

It is the absences that make this report particularly interesting. First, Buddle had no geological map of the area. William Smith had begun to produce the first geological maps of England and Wales in the 1790s but focused on the area with which he as most familiar: Bath, Bristol and southern England. His first manuscript sketch map of the geology of England and Wales was made in 1801 or before but a finished map, on a scale of 5 miles to the inch (1:316,800), was not published until 1815.[8] Second, Buddle is unable to consult any existing public record of previous geological investigations of the area, although the people he consults in the area are remarkably free with the information they have. Third, he has no information about the fossil record. Fourth, he makes no use of scientific or chemical apparatus: he uses no microscope, nor chemical reagents to identify the chemical composition of a rock. Fifth, he makes no attempt to quantify the observations of the rocks he finds; thus, the density of a rock is not measured but judged by weighing it in his hand.[9]

The one positive feature in Buddle's procedures was the freedom with which his interlocutors gave him information. This was an advantage which was not peculiar to Buddle. Twenty years after Buddle's report, Robert Bald, an eminent Scottish mine engineer, was asked to report on whether a coal seam continued to the north of the current workings or not. Bald availed himself of 'all the local information I could obtain, from persons who were well acquainted with the under-ground operations of the Collieries' and in particular from Mr John Baird of the Shotts Iron Works which owned the neighbouring colliery. Baird told him the results of a borehole he had driven down from the floor of his colliery; Bald thanked him for his 'great attention and zeal'.[10] This freedom of information declined during the nineteenth century. Increasingly, information about the geological structure of the country came to be seen as private property. Information from borings and from colliery shafts was sometimes made freely available and was preserved and distributed by the mine engineering institutes[11] and the government's Geological Survey but increasingly, information was deposited on terms of confidentiality or not at all.[12] In 1916, Aubrey Strahan, the then-Director of the Geological Survey, admitted that the unwillingness of landowners and companies to release information obtained from borings had become a serious problem.[13] There was no attempt to solve the problem, in so far as coal was concerned, until the nationalization of unworked coal deposits by the 1938 Coal Act. The Act also vested ownership of all plans, sections and records of survey previously owned by those with interests in coal in the Coal Commission established by the Act and limited the right to search for and bore for coal in the Commission.[14]

Scafe's poem was written ten years after Buddle's report. During that time William Smith's geological maps became more widely disseminated and the study of fossils was prosecuted with greater system than had been seen before. The major event was the publication between 1804 and 1811 of James Parkinson's *Organic Remains of a Former World*, now often regarded as the beginning of systematic palaeontology.[15] It was in this period that it was realized that different ensembles of fossils were associated with different strata, opening up the possibility of identifying strata by examining their fossils. When linked with the identification, by means of an understanding of the evolution of species, of earlier and later species this became a method of establishing the ordering of the strata in time. The first written statement of this idea appears to be in an unpublished note by William Smith, jotted down in 1796. He did not state the idea in print until 1815. Nevertheless, he had already been credited with the idea by James Parkinson and his priority has never been challenged. Smith published his *Strata Identified by Organized Fossils* in 1816–19 and his *Stratigraphical System of Organized Fossils* in 1817.[16] The idea was taken up and made more widely known by the Rev. William Conybeare and William Phillips in their 1822 *Outlines of the Geology of England and Wales*.[17]

Scafe was remarkably up to date with these profound developments, although he does not labour them or highlight them. The note to verse 298 remarks:

> It is in beds of Lias, and Lias Clay that we find an immense deposit of organic remains, differing essentially from those of the Mountain Lime; such as *Ammonites, Nautilites*, and *Belemnites*, which occur in numbers truly astonishing.

That the fossil ensemble of the Lias 'differs essentially' from that of the Mountain Lime expresses precisely the prime notion of *Strata Identified by Organized Fossils*.

The later development of geology in relation to the coal industry is addressed in 'The Search for New Fields' (Volume 3, pp. 223–57).

Notes

1. See J. Warburg (ed.) *The Industrial Muse: The Industrial Revolution in English Poetry* (London: Oxford University Press, 1958).
2. 'Virgil's *Georgics*', bk 2, ll. 89–101, in John Dryden, *The Works of Virgil Containing his Pastorals, Georgics and Aeneis* (*London:* Printed for *Jacob Tonson, 1697).*
3. My guide here has been John Challinor's *History of British Geology: A Bibliographical Study* (Newton Abbot: David & Charles, 1971), which is much more useful than its subtitle might suggest. The historiography begins with Archibald Geikie, *The Founders of Geology* (London: Macmillan, 1897) in English and Karl Alfred von Zittel, *Geschichte der Geologie und Paläontologie bis Ende des 19. Jahrhunderts* (Munich: R. Oldenbourg, 1899), translated and abridged by M. M. Ogilvie-Gordon as *History of Geology and Palæontology to the End of the Nineteenth Century* (London: W. Scott, 1901); and continues with H. B. Woodward, *History of Geology* (London: Watts, 1911) and F. D. Adams, *The Birth and Development of the Geological Sciences* (Baltimore, MD: William & Wilkins, 1938). The remainder of the twentieth century was dominated by biographical works: E. Bailey, *Charles Lyell* (London: Nelson, 1962) and the same author's *James Hutton* (Amsterdam: Elsevier, 1967); L. G. Wilson, *Charles Lyell: The Years to 1841* (New Haven, CT: Yale University Press, 1972), N. Rupke, *The Great Chain of History: William Buckland and the English School of Geology* (Oxford: Clarendon Press, 1983; R. A. Stafford, *Scientist of Empire: Sir Roderick Murchison, Scientific Exploration and Victorian Imperialism* (Cambridge: Cambridge University Press, 1989); and D. R. Dean, *James Hutton and the History of Geology* (Ithaca, NY: Cornell University Press, 1992). The leading modern works are the two volumes by François Ellenberger, *Histoire de la géologie. Tome 1: Des anciens à la prmière moitibe du XVIIe siècle* (Paris: Technique at Documentation Lavoisier, 1988), *Tome 2: La grande éclosion et ses prémices 1660–1810* (Paris: Technique at Documentation Lavoisier, 1994) and the two volumes by Martin J. S. Rudwick, *Bursting the Limits of Time: The Reconstruction of Geohistory in the Age of Revolution* (Chicago, IL: University of Chicago Press, 2005) and *Worlds before Adam: The Reconstruction of Geohistory in the Age of Reform* (Chicago, IL: University of Chicago Press, 2008).
4. The names of others were introduced surprisingly late. The first recorded occurrence given by the *OED* for the other rocks named by Scafe in the extracts given here are 1681 for mica, 1652 for granite, 1777 for gneiss, 1668 for sandstone, 1646 for gypsum, and 1567 for selenite.
5. To be found in J. Whitehurst, *Inquiry into the Original State and Formation of the Earth: Deduced from Facts and the Laws of Nature* (London: J. Cooper, Printer, 1778).
6. J. Hutton, *Theory of the Earth, With Proofs and Illustrations*, 2 vols (Edinburgh: Printed for Messrs Cadell, Junior, and Davies, London; and William Creech, Edinburgh, 1795). It had been presaged by an abstract published in 1783 and by a paper, 'Theory of the Earth, Or an Investigation of the Laws Observable in the Composition, Dissolution, and Restoration of Land upon the Globe', published in the *Transactions of the Royal Society of Edinburgh*, 1 (1788), pp. 209–304.
7. J. Playfair, *Illustrations of the Huttonian Theory of the Earth* (Edinburgh: Printed for Cadell and Davies, London, and William Creech, 1802).
8. Challinor, History, p. 84. W. Smith, *A Delineation of the Strata of England and Wales, with a Part of Scotland: Exhibiting the Collieries and Mines, the Marshes and Fen Lands Originally Overflowed by the Sea, and the Varieties of Soil According to the Variations in the Substrata; Illustrated by the Most Descriptive Names* (London: J. Cary, 1815).

9. The standard items of equipment for a field geologist later in the century were described by Archibald Geikie as 'few in number and simple in character': a hammer, a small lens, a 'pocket-knife of hard steel for determining the hardness of rocks and minerals', a magnet and 'a small pocket phial of dilute hydrochloric acid' (to test for the presence of lime). Buddle appears to have had none of this equipment (A. Geikie, *Text-Book of Geology* (London: Macmillan, 1882), p. 176). See also Geikie's *Outlines of Field Geology* (London: Macmillan, 1877).
10. R. Bald, *Report Regarding the Coal Field in the District of Whitburn, in the Counties of Linlithgow and Lanark; With the Details of the Operations which have been Carried on by Boring, and the Result Thereof* (Edinburgh: James Auchie, Printer, [1826]), pp. 4, 6, 8. The John Baird Bald mentions is probably John Baird of Urie (1798–1870), the second son of Alexander Baird and the elder brother of James Baird (1802–76) the coal and iron master for whom see A. Slaven and S. Checkland, *Dictionary of Scottish Business Biography 1860–1960* (Aberdeen: Aberdeen University Press, 1986).
11. For example: *An Account of the Strata of Northumberland & Durham as Proved by Borings & Sinking*, 5 vols and a supplementary volume (Newcastle: North of England Institute of Mining & Mechanical Engineers, 1878–1910); *Sections of Strata of the Coal Measures of Yorkshire. Together with a few Derbyshire Sections: 1902–1913* (Sheffield: Midland Institute of Mining Engineers, 1914).
12. The point emerges in Sir John Smith Flett's history of the Geological Survey, *The First Hundred Years of the Geological Survey of Great Britain* (London: His Majesty's Stationery Office, 1937) despite its resolutely cheerful tone; see pp. 129 and 176–8. Flett (1869–1947) was Director of the Survey between 1920 and 1935.
13. A. Strahan, *The Search for New Coal-Fields in England* (London: William Clowes [for the Royal Institution], [1916]), a paper given at the weekly evening meeting of the Royal Institution of Great Britain, 17 March 1916. Aubrey Strahan (1852–1928) was Director of the Geological Survey between 1914 and 1920.
14. The Coal Act (1 & 2 Geo. 6, c. 52). See P. G. Roberts, *The Coal Act 1938* (London: Wildy & Sons, 1938), pp. 46–7 and 54–5.
15. *Organic Remains of a Former World: An Examination of the Mineralized Remains of the Vegetables and Animals of the Antediluvian World; Generally Termed Extraneous Fossils*, 3 vols (London: J. Robson; J. White, and J. Murray, 1804–11).
16. W. Smith, *Strata Identified by Organized Fossils* (London: W. Arding, 1816–19); W. Smith, *Stratigraphical System of Organized Fossils* (London: Printed for E. Williams, 1817).
17. Rev. W. D. Conybeare and William Phillips, *Outlines of the Geology of England and Wales with an Introductory Compendium of the General Principles of that Science, and Comparative Views of the Structure of Foreign Countries: Part I* (London: William Phillips, 1822).

John Scafe, *King Coal's Levee, or Geological Etiquette. With Explanatory Notes. To which is Added the Council of the Metals* (1819)

John Scafe,[1] *King Coal's Levee, or Geological Etiquette. With Explanatory Notes. To which is added the Council of the Metals*, 2nd edn (Alnwick, 1819).

KING COAL'S LEVEE,
OR
GEOLOGICAL ETIQUETTE.

———

——————come, come; I am a King,
My masters, know you that?

SHAKESPEARE.[2] /

…

HAIL shadowy power and subterranean state!
Still may such pomp around the monarch wait,
Still may the grovelling herd in silent awe
Bend at his throne, and make his nod their law,
And may some minstrel soul in happier vein,
With high-ton'd harp, in louder loftier strain,
Spread through this middle world the glories of his reign!
King COAL, the mighty hero of the mine,
– Sprung from a dingy, but a far-fam'd line,
Who, fathoms deep, in peace our earth possest,
Curb'd but in sway by ocean's billowy breast, –
Would hold a Levee: by such gorgeous scene
To please PYRITES,[3] his alluring queen.
Would wield the sceptre sovereign fate decreed,
Enforce obedience, smile the welcome meed,[4]
And prove his pow'r from Vectis to the Tweed.[5]
Forth flew the mandate; earthquakes through the land

Spoke in hoarse tones the monarch's high command:
Air caught the sounds, and in expansion free,
Spread the deep word to Albion's circling sea. /
– Each pond'rous sire, each grave or sprightly dame
Must bow before the prince of smoke and flame;
Must bend their steps, howe'er unus'd to rove,
To greet the dusky King, and his resplendent love.

On ebon throne, with choicest gems enlaid,
Sat the two tenants of earth's darkest shade:
She bright and blithe, and blooming as the spring,
He stern and stately, 'every inch a King.'
From vaulted roof, in glist'ning arches turn'd,
Around the throne the silv'ry gas-lights burn'd;
Rose high in air, with soft ethereal fire,
That left the day no object of desire.
Mirrors of MICA,[6] black, red, green, and white,
Mingling a rich and parti-colour'd light,
Suspensive dwelt those silv'ry suns between,
And pour'd their changeful splendor on the scene.

On either side, at awful distance, stood
The subtle-minded gnomes, a swarthy brood;
The monarch's pages they, – well-train'd to bear
His instant mandates through earth, sea, or air.
Ethereal spirits, – but to visual ray
Now bodied forth, in habits rich and gay:
With tinsel stars upon each velvet dress;
– Conductors of the eye to ugliness!
Each in his hand a staff of office bore,
And grave they stood as mutes beside the dead man's door.

Beneath the queen so costly and so bright,
The maids of honour, rob'd in purest white,
Soft-smiling beauties, cheer'd the dazzled sight.
As in mild summer nights the gazer sees,
When Heaven is fair, and hush'd is every breeze,
The constellation of the Pleiades.[7] /

Behind the throne, triumphant music shed
Its loudest notes around the monarch's head.
The shrill-tongued trumpet, and the deep bassoon,
And cymbal, emblem of the pale-fac'd moon,
From full-blown cheeks, and brawny arms combine
To wake the drowsy echoes of the mine.

Earth shook, – and well it might; for now the throng
In indolent procession mov'd along:
Mov'd, – and around a hollow murmur sent;
Mov'd on, – and star'd, and wonder'd how they went.

What boots[8] it here, in glowing verse to tell
The dire events earth's puppets that befell;
What boots it here, though earth affrighted saw
Another Lisbon[9] yield to nature's law:
Though thousands died, – it but abridg'd the span
That fate allotted to the creature man.

Rocks moving harmless, would indeed be rare!
– Sufficient for our purpose, they were there.
  They met, they marshall'd, all in order due,
Nor master of the ceremonies knew.
No hasty word, no brooding spirit rose,
Spark of hostility, and nurse of foes,
Precedence quick its lucid progress show'd:
– Have mortals always trod this tranquil road?
The rich saloon, the anti-room they pass'd,
And reach'd the spacious presence hall at last.
Duke GRANITE first;[10] – a hoary-headed sire,
Yet blest with symptoms of primæval fire,
That beam'd across the traces of decay,
As vivid tints illume departing day.
Of *solid* parts, of judgment ne'er asleep,
And had through life been reckon'd *very deep*. /
Announc'd by GNEISS,[11] with dignity he came;
King COAL arose, as did his graceful dame;
And welcom'd him, as one in high command,
Who bore the greatest burthen in the land.
There was – as far as our researches go –
No *slight* foundation for their thinking so.
  That GNEISS was but a weather-beaten man,
(And Queen PYRITES smil'd behind her fan)
With shanks so small, and such a thin-sown pate,
He was indeed in *decomposing* state.
– Youth will indulge in levity; but age
Reads the words written on life's fading page:
And most we feel for those who shar'd our way
In joy or grief, from youth's attractive day.
Thence did the duke esteem of sterling price
That lonely man, the weather-beaten GNEISS;
And prov'd at once his master, and his friend,
Determin'd to support him to the end. /

Next came the elder SANDSTONE,[12] jolly fellow!
In good society was ever mellow:
Which spread – as oft it will in such a case –
A rubicund diffusion o'er his face.
He was a staid old toper; one who sat
Firm on his chair, though blind as any bat.
The younger SANDSTONE met no voice of praise,
He had not steer'd his course by virtue's rays,
But truth pronounc'd him – given to *loose* ways.
His brother waited mid the marshall'd throng
For his arrival, and had waited long;
He came not; – and with patience fairly spent
Old SANDSTONE to the presence chamber went.
  Yet some allowance might be justly made,

– We should not be too hasty to upbraid, –
Between the brothers a fair manor lay,
That own'd the great Sir Lawrence LIMESTONE's[13] sway:
Some crown lands also yearly profit pour'd
To aid the splendor of the monarch's board.
Another cause too shall the muse produce,
Alone sufficient to enforce excuse.
His youth was wildly pass'd, – but time will mend
Our early frolics; – all things have their end. /
He had redeem'd his fame in some degree,
And of the married state thought feasibly:
Had to Miss GYPSUM14 due attention shewn,
And trusted soon to call the fair his own;
For she was fair, aye, and an heiress too,
Which might account for such attention due.
But oh! *her* beauty could wake small delight
Compar'd with her sweet cousin SELENITE:[15]
Into whose eyes were one peep only given,
The gazer might be snatch'd, Mohammed-like, to
        Heaven.
But she was born no riches to inherit;
And poor relations have but little merit. /

NOTES.

VERSE.

13. Iron Pyrites,[16] Sulphuret of Iron, or Marcasite, is almost constantly found in Coal, either disseminated in minute grains, or in small nodules, or in thin veins, accompanied by Quartz, or calcareous Spar. It may be known by its weight, its shining metallic lustre, and a strong smell of sulphur when broken.

38. Mica,[17] or Muscovy Glass (so called from being a common substitute for window Glass in the Russian empire) is one of the most abundant mineral substances. Its texture is lamellar, and it occurs in Granite, and the other primitive rocks. It is easily split into thin elastic plates, and, when colourless, is used in enclosing objects for the solar Microscope. It is found also, but more minutely divided, between the natural fissures of slaty Sandstone; and in some, of the finest sort, appears even interspersed through the whole mass.

☞ N.B. That the order of the rock formations and the superposition of the strata might not be broken, many short notes, which in their proper places would have interfered with such an arrangement, have been transferred to the larger / heads, with which they were most immediately connected. It is therefore recommended to the reader to make himself master of the notes, comprising such order, before he proceeds in the text: and, bearing these in memory, it is expected that he will find all the allusions in the text properly elucidated.

84. Granite is the undermost, (that we are acquainted with) and therefore supposed to be the oldest of the *primitive* rocks.[18] It is not stratified; and is a *compound* rock, being an aggregate of Quartz, Felspar, and Mica, in variable proportions. It appears, rising through the stratification of this country, chiefly in Devonshire and Cornwall; but is also seen at Mount Sorrel, near Leicester; at the Malvern Hills, in Worcestershire; and at Shap, Ravenglass, and the back of Skiddaw, in Cumberland. Some Geologists (following the opinion of Dr. Hutton)[19] conceive Granite to be of igneous origin, and to have been protruded from beneath, raising and occasionally disuniting the superincumbent strata.

Quartz, which is above mentioned as a constituent of Granite, in a granular state, composes Sandstone. In a crystallized form it is found on Snowdon, in Wales; and accompanies most metallic veins. Its crystals resemble pure Glass, and are known by the name of *Rock Crystals, Mock Diamonds, Cornish* and *Welch Diamonds*. Compact Quartz is largely disseminated through most rocks in veins and beds; and is so met / with on Skiddaw, in Cumberland. The rounded milk white Pebbles, found on the sea shore, and in gravel, are of Quartz.

Felspar, the other constituent of Granite, will be hereafter mentioned.

90. Gneiss is composed of precisely the same materials as Granite, but is slaty in its structure, owing to the comparatively large quantity of Mica it contains. And from this slaty structure perhaps it arises that the Felspar is very liable to decomposition. It is of very rare occurrence in England, but abounds in the primitive mountains of Scotland and Ireland. /

223. Old red Sandstone is a formation that occupies an important place in the English series, between the Grauwacké[20] and Mountain Lime;[21] attaining on the Beacons of Brecknock the enormous thickness of 2000 feet. It contains strata of red micaceous slaty Sandstone, and of Quartz, Jasper, and other Pebbles; alternating with beds of red Marl, and red Clay, coloured by oxide of Iron. These beds often so closely resemble in colour and substance the strata which compose the new red Sandstone formation that mistakes of one for the other are perpetually taking place. The *old* red Sandstone beds are usually *highly inclined*, like the Grauwacké; those of the *new* are almost always *horizontal*.

Old red Sandstone is extremely unprolific in minerals; containing rarely any shells, and no traces of Gypsum, rock Salt, and sulphate of Strontian,[22] which three last substances occur abundantly in the new red Sandstone formation. It has seldom any valuable deposits of metallic Ore in it.

It occupies an extensive area in the counties of Pembroke, Glamorgan, Monmouth, and Hereford. The red Sandstone and conglomerate beds of the Vale of Exeter, Taunton Dean, and Carlisle; and of the extensive Plains of Cheshire, Salop, and Lancashire, which are by so many writers consigned to the *old* red Sandstone, are component members of the *new*. Between the old and new red Sandstone series is interposed / an enormous mass of strata, constituting *the* Mountain Lime and great Coal formation. The Coal of England occurs, above the Mountain Lime, in strata of solid Coal often many feet thick, alternating with strata of slaty Clay (called Shale), of Iron Stone, and Sandstone; and occupies immense tracts of country in Northumberland, Durham, Yorkshire, Derbyshire, Staffordshire, and S. Wales.

264.[23] Reposing horizontally on the basset edges[24] of the above-mentioned Coal strata (which are usually inclined), we find the new red Sandstone, or new red rock Marl formation.

Of this series the lowest member is the Magnesian Limestone, which will be described under the Limestone family.[25]

The middle region is usually occupied by beds of Conglomerate, and of loose red Sandstone, and Sand; alternating with and covered by a vast thickness of red rock Marl. It is in this formation only that Salt Springs and Rock Salt have hitherto been discovered; viz. in the counties of Worcester, Stafford, Salop, and Chester.

Gypsum occurs in it abundantly in the form of Alabaster, fibrous Gypsum, and Selenite.[26] It furnishes the only Alabaster quarries that exist in England. At Keddleston House, near Derby, are lofty pillars, extremely beautiful, the shafts of which are of Alabaster from the neighbourhood. /

Many sandy strata become consolidated by a calcareous cement, and in this state of union form useful and hard building stone. ...

298.[27] The Limestone of England may be conveniently divided into *seven* distinct kinds.

1. Primitive Limestone, or Statuary Marble; which is of extremely rare occurrence in England, and is only found in small quantity in Devonshire and Anglesea. It abounds in Italy, Switzerland, and Greece; whence it is obtained for the purposes of sculpture. This formation is alluded to in the text under the personification of Lady Marble, mother to Sir Lawrence Limestone. ...
2. Transition Limestone; which has been mentioned in the note on Grauwacké, and in many of its characters is nearly allied to Mountain Lime. On this account, and as being a less important formation, it has no distinct representative in the Poem.
3. Mountain Limestone; which lies next in succession above the old red Sandstone, and abounds in Derbyshire, Somerset, S. Wales, Yorkshire, and Northumberland. The Sir Lawrence Limestone of the Poem is intended as the representative of this formation. Its veins are often charged with valuable stores of Lead. The rock itself often abounds with extensive caverns; as at Castleton, and at the Peak, in Derbyshire: and contains an immense assemblage of organic remains, / such as marine shells, corals and other zoophytes.[28]* Similar remains of different species are found

* Perhaps the most remarkable of the zoophytic remains in the Mountain and other Limestones is the *Encrinus*, so called from the resemblance of some of its species to a lily.[29] It unites to the external form of a flower the mechanism of a numerous series of articulated bones; the whole forming a kind of skeleton, which, from the surprizing number and delicate finish of its parts, surpasses perhaps any thing that can be found in those animals which are usually regarded as belonging to a more perfect and higher class. It appears to have consisted of a root, by which it was attached to the bottom of the sea; and from whence arose a stem many yards long, not constructed (like that of a flower) of one single piece, but composed of many hundred joints, articulating into each other by a beautiful apparatus of grooves and notches; and thus allowing a degree of play which compensates for want of locomotion. Detached joints of this stem form the *Entrochi* and *Asteriæ*[30] so frequent in all Mountain Lime rocks. At the superior extremity of the stem are a series of bones, which, to pursue the analogy, may be considered as representing the calix of a flower; and these again support other series of bones, which form, as it were, the petals. From the interior surface of these petals arise numerous finer filaments, composed also of lesser bones, and bearing a sort of analogy to the stamina of flowers. When the zoophyte was quiescent, the whole of the petals and calix appear to have been closed over the fila-

in all the other succeeding Limestone strata; but Lead, and Copper are worked in no strata more recent than the Mountain Lime; with the partial exception of a little Lead in the Magnesian Limestone.

It is often very compact, admits of a high polish, and is manufactured for ornamental purposes; particularly in Derbyshire. That which is very dark, called there *black Marble*, and quarried at / Bakewell, receives its colour from Bitumen. Lead and other Ores are found in Mountain Limestone in the last named county; and it also furnishes the Lead veins of Cumberland and Durham.

The medicinal waters of Harrowgate,[31] Matlock, and Bristol, are connected with the Mountain Limestone; as those of Bath, and Cheltenham, are with the Lias, which will be hereafter described.

From Mr. Westgarth Forster's excellent 'Section of the Strata'[32] it appears, that in the great Coal Field of Northumberland and Durham, the strata of Mountain Limestone are invariably *under* all the *valuable* seams of Coal; rising from beneath them to the north west, and appearing in succession with other alternating strata on the borders of Cumberland: and this seems also to be the case at Whitehaven, where the Limestone rises in like manner from beneath the Coal, but in an opposite direction: and in South Wales, where the Limestone forms a kind of bason;[33] within which, and conforming to its shape, the Coal seams are situated.

4. Magnesian Limestone, so called from its containing a portion of Magnesia; is of much younger formation than the preceding, and in some degree derivative from it. It is found in the north eastern part of England, extending from near Nottingham, by Wetherby, to Sunderland; and reposing immediately on the Coal / measures.[34] In Gloucestershire, Somerset, and Glamorganshire it contains imbedded in it pebbles and fragments of Mountain Lime, and other older rocks; still retaining the same relative position above the Coal. It is also mixed with a considerable proportion of new red Sandstone, making the lowest member of that formation, and often passing by insensible gradations into it, and into red rock Marl. The quick Lime obtained from it is of a hotter and more acrid quality than from other Limestones; this is supposed to arise from its constituent Magnesia; it is considered therefore more peculiarly adapted to the cultivation of moor lands, from being more active in producing vegetable decomposition. See verse 361. Magnesia sometimes occurs also in beds of the Mountain Lime; which may be recognised by a peculiar glimmering lustre.

5. Lias, or argillaceous Limestone; which is more recent than the preceding, and is abundantly diffused through this country.

It may be described as running across the centre of England, in a direction nearly north east, from Lyme in Dorsetshire to Whitby in Yorkshire. It usually forms an argillaceous soil, from the quantity of Clay that predominates in it: and it contains subordinate beds of Marl. Lias is a marly Limestone, usually blue (darkish lead colour), or white (bluish grey). The white beds generally are the lowest; and both white and blue are disposed in thin slabs, alternating / with bands of Marl and Clay, and occasionally abounding in Iron Pyrites.

---

ments; in which state one of the species exactly resembles a closed lily, whence the name of *Encrinus*, or *Animal Lily* has been given to it, and from it transferred to the whole genus. When roused to action, it appears to have opened its petals, and spread abroad its filaments for the purpose of catching its prey. The stomach of the zoophyte was placed in the centre of the disk of what may be considered as its flower.

Clay is by far the most abundant ingredient in the Lias formation.

White Lias has lately been made use of in the Arts as the material for stone engraving: which was first cultivated in Bavaria, at Munich, where it has since been brought to great perfection, as well as in France. The Flora Monacensis by Schrank and Mayrhoffer, Spix's Craniology,[35] many portraits, maps, &c. have been executed in Lithography, with a degree of beauty that approaches to line engraving. For military purposes it is very useful in multiplying rapidly plans, circular letters, and orders. It has not yet made much progress in England, but is said to be applied in the preparation of forged bank notes. The neighbourhood of Bath and Bristol furnishes white Lias fit for Lithography, but the best comes from Bavaria.

It is in beds of Lias, and Lias Clay that we find an immense deposit of organic remains, differing essentially from those of the Mountain Lime; such as *Ammonites, Nautilites*, and *Belemnites*, which occur in numbers truly astonishing; and with them the remains of tortoises, crocodiles, and a singular reptile of enormous bulk, forming a kind of link between the Dolphin and the Lizard tribe, which has been denominated *Ichthyesaurus*, and is described in the London / Philosophical Transactions for 1814 and 1816, by Sir Everard Home.[36] See verse 373 and 611.

6. Oolite. Interposed between the Lias and Chalk of England is an extensive series of shelly coarse Limestones, all of which occasionally present an admixture of spherical particles resembling the roe of fishes; from which circumstance the name of *Oolite* has been applied to them. One of the lowest beds of this series forms the best building stone in England; and is extensively employed at Bath, and at Ketton in Northamptonshire. When first taken from the quarry it is extremely soft.

Organic remains abound throughout all the beds composing this extensive formation, which stretches north east from Bridport in Dorsetshire, through the midland counties, to the Cleveland Hills in Yorkshire.

Coade's Manufactory of Patent Stone[37] in London, is an imitation of the Bath and Portland Stone for ornamental purposes. See verse 409.

7. Chalk. This name has been applied to a series of beds of snow-white Limestone, attaining a thickness of many hundred feet; varying from the state of Cooper's Chalk to that of a soft building stone; and divided only by irregular and imperfect strata of black Gun Flints, usually disposed in nodules, and occasionally in thin laminæ.

The Chalk district forms an extensive range: / the extreme western point of which is near Honiton in Devonshire; from whence it passes through Wiltshire and Bedfordshire, to Cromer on the coast of Norfolk. It appears again in Lincolnshire, extending to Flamborough Head in Yorkshire. From its western point at Honiton it also bears to the south east, passing through the centre of the Isle of Wight. Another range commences in Berkshire, and extends to the coast between Folkstone and Dover; sending off in its route a branch at Alton, and terminating on the Sussex coast in the picturesque cliffs of Beachy Head. Nodules of Flint are seen deposited in regular layers through the Chalk at the cliffs of Dover and Brighton, and in the quarries throughout the county of Kent; but there is no *mineral* Coal[38] found within many miles of the Chalk formations. Perhaps the nearest will be that in the vicinity of Bristol.

In its passage through Berkshire and Oxfordshire, Chalk forms the range of hills known by the parliamentary name of the *Chiltern Hundreds*.[39]

The lofty cliffs of this formation are subject to repeated falls, from being undermined by the action of the waves. See verse 434. /

Geology has but lately occupied the public attention in this country; and though much has been done within the last few years towards investigating our mineral treasures, yet a very wide field for scrutiny still remains. It were to be wished that the observations of enlightened individuals could be directed to limited districts; and their memoranda be afterwards compared, and united into Mineralogical Histories of the several counties. By which means a great body of information would be produced, not only highly interesting to the naturalist, but highly serviceable to the agriculturist, the miner, and the landed proprietor. /

THE
COUNCIL OF THE METALS

———

Well have ye judg'd, well ended long debate,
————————; and, like to what ye are,
Great things resolved;, ————————

MILTON[40]

But how seldom when many are join'd in debate,
Of the pilots that stand at the helm of a state,
Though professions, like manna, fall softly around,
And the lip sweetly breathes unanimity's sound,
Will sincerity in *every* bosom be found.
To the *letter* they strictly adhere, just to serve
As a mantle, when wide from the *spirit* they swerve.
Now though IRON agreed not to visit the King,[41]
To provide for his sons was a different thing:
With the vote that he gave for the good of the nation,
He had mentally treasur'd this slight reservation. /
So he sent for Jack CLAY, – who was always at hand
When the METALS, rich souls, would his service command, –
And he gave the young fry to that dandy's controul,
To be taught a few airs, and to wait on King COAL:
With an elegant note, that he trusted would clear him.
For he only had promis'd he ne'er would *come near him.*
They went; – and they found the King quaffing his ale,
And enjoying his pipe by the side of old SHALE:
They were rather surpriz'd that old SHALE was his friend,
But bethought them, that kings sometimes love to *unbend.*
CLAY spoke; – and in patience the King heard him out,
Though he scarcely could tell what CLAY's speech was about:
However, he kindly approv'd the connection,
Consigning the brats to his crony's protection.*

* Thin argillaceous[42] strata containing speroidal nodules and flat masses of clayey Iron Stone occur subordinately in many of the Shale beds of the great Coal formation, and at this time supply the principal Iron Foundries of Britain with Ore.

SHALE wove them a bow'r, – that large *palm trees* surrounded, –
And with *ferns* quite gigantic its area bounded. /
A passion for plants had so grappled his soul,
That an old *Hortus siccus*[45] each spare moment stole:
For which he had ransack'd the swamps and the meads,
Till his *Hortus* was richest in *grasses* and *reeds*. /
But a strange antiquarian whim he display'd;
From the simplest of plants his selection was made,
And of structure primeval, like none *we* descry
'Mid the bountiful gifts that the seasons supply; /
Nor confin'd he his search, – for the earth widely knew
From the poles to the tropics the treasures he drew:
Which long in his cabinet hoarded so slily,
As an antient *Herbarium* are priz'd very highly. /
To SHALE then the urchins were duly consign'd,
Who found them at once to his studies inclin'd:
And with him and King COAL in these regular ways
They liv'd snugly enough all the rest of their days.
/

The nodules often contain a vegetable nucleus, from which they derive the outline of their external form. This nucleus is usually a leaf or fragment of some of the plants that occur abundantly in Coal Shale, and which also constitute the entire substance of the Coal itself. The traces of vegetable structure are usually lost in the beds of solid Coal, in consequence of the pressure and chemical changes that have taken place; but the Shale is crouded with lively impressions of vegetables, generally leaves, of which the substance is converted into Coal. In these cases the leaves are separated from each other by a very thin lamina of Shale: but in the absence of such intervening lamina the altered vegetables have become confluent, and their form is generally obliterated. See Parkinson's Organic Remains, vol. I. [43] for an account of the natural process by which all vegetable matter is convertible to Coal.

Perhaps one of the most striking phenomena of Geology is that enormous mass of vegetable matter which has been accumulated, at a very early period in the history of stratification, to compose our Coal beds. In this Island alone many thousand square acres contain beneath them strata of Coal accumulated above each other, sometimes to the number of 40 or 50, and disposed like beds of stone in a quarry, and alternating with strata of Shale and siliceous Sandstone. In both the latter vegetable remains are thickly disseminated, but not in quantity sufficient to be of any use. They also form separate laminæ or strata of vegetables converted to pure Coal varying in thickness from a quarter of an inch to 30 feet and upwards. Coal is seldom / worth working unless its thickness exceeds one foot. The thickest bed of Coal in this country is at Dudley, where there is a stratum (called the *ten yard Coal*) which measures sometimes 12 yards in thickness of solid Coal. Its extraordinary thickness is supposed to arise from the union of three smaller beds, without the interposition of the usual Shale and Sandstones.

The ordinary thickness of good Coal beds is from four to six feet.

The history of the origin of these accumulated masses of vegetable matter, so admirably treasured up for the use of mankind, forms one of the most difficult problems of Geology. We find in them the wreck of various genera of vegetables (many of them apparently tropical, others growing in colder latitudes) confusedly mixed together in the same stratum. They seem at their formation to have been strewed over vast spaces, at the bottom of the then existing ocean in regular strata, alternating with much thicker strata of Shale and Sandstone: the whole of which have since been much disturbed and broken by violent agents, probably acting from beneath.

The nature of the enclosed vegetables is also extremely singular, and is as yet little understood. They seem however to consist entirely of plants of the most / simple structure (monocotyledonous or acotyledonous,)[44] and may be referred principally to reeds, grasses, canes, equisetums, palms, and ferns. Plants of this kind display no trace of that more solid and compound texture which we find in timber trees and the dicotyledonous genera; exhibiting in their interior concentric rings, a central medulla, and medullary radii: whilst the substance of the monocotyledonous plants is disposed in fasciculi of longitudinal fibres, having a central open cavity like a cane or reed. Of modern plants these latter include some of the most elegant tribes, usually having a smooth, delicate, and tapering form, and being graceful in their proportions.

Many species of the fossil ferns seem to have attained the gigantic stature which some species of that genus now arrive at in tropical climates. Many Coal plants resemble in outward form the stems of the cactus tribe, and are covered with an infinite variety of flutings and lozenge-shaped configurations, containing points that apparently formed the bases of their spines or leaflets: but the history of these plants is not yet understood. Perhaps not one of the fossil Coal plants can be proved to be absolutely identical with any now existing. The oldest rock in which we find the remains of solid wood is the Lias, in which are fossil trees of a large size, / that were decidedly dicotyledonous. They occur also in all younger strata, from the Lias upwards; but their identity with any existing species has not yet been established.

John Buddle, 'Search for Coal in a Part of the Counties of Roxburgh and Berwickshire, in July, 1806' (1807)

John Buddle,[1] Jun., *Search for Coal in a Part of the Counties of Roxburgh and Berwickshire, in July, 1806.* (Kelso: Printed by Alexander Ballantyne at the *Kelso Mail* Office, 1807).

BEING requested by several GENTLEMEN of the Counties of ROXBURGH and BERWICKSHIRE,[2] to examine the most likely parts of those Counties for the purpose of making trials for the discovering of COAL; I have in consequence examined, not only such parts of those Counties as are reported to contain COAL, but also such other places, as, an attentive examination of the Strata, might enable me to form such a general opinion of their geological formation, as would enable me to judge more correctly, concerning the object of my more important inquiry. I must, however, beg to be understood, that I have no intention of intruding myself as a Mineralogist, any further than immediately relates to the present investigation of the COAL FORMATION; and I feel great diffidence in describing several of the Stones which I have met with; but having no intention to mislead by too much use of the technical terms of Mineralogy, I have introduced along with them the popular names of the Country.

Although the detail of the Stratification of Quarries, Hills, Ravines, &c. may appear tedious, and of little interest generally, I have, nevertheless, introduced a description of those places, which I have examined, with a plain detail of appearances; presuming the same may be of consequence to the parties interested, and which may enable them to draw their own conclusions unbiassed by any opinion of mine. /

ITINERARY

THROUGH A PART OF

ROXBURGH AND BERWICKSHIRES,

For the purpose of investigating the probability of finding COAL *therein.* /

SPROUSTON QUARRY.

The covering of this quarry is the same kind of sandy and gravelly soil as generally covers the vale of the Tweed.[3] The sand-stone rock of the quarry is not stratified, and appears to be of limited extent; as from the best information I could obtain, it seems to be of an irregular, circular, or oval form, being about 300 yards long, and 200 yards broad, cropping out on every side; from which, I consider it to be a detached mass of sand-stone, reposing upon the same kind of strata as is seen in Mellendean Burn; which opinion is confirmed by the boring, lately made, in the eastern side of the quarry; (a copy of which[4] accompanies this description).

The sand-stone is of a bluish white colour, and close texture, well calculated for building; but has nodules of black argillaceous[5] earth scattered in it; and in the quarry, near the bottom of the sand-stone, large irregular pieces of whin[6] are deposited. The best part of the sand-stone rock is about 20 feet thick. Three veins pass through this quarry, in a north and south direction, which produce no other effect than that of breaking the rock, in an irregular manner, in their respective lines of direction. What renders the examination of this quarry more interesting, is, the discovery of a vein of Coal near its western limit, made some time ago. At present, no part of the vein is to be seen; but Mr Gray, the manager, shewed me the place from which the Coal had been removed, and furnished me with the following description of it:

'The vein of Coal dipped irregularly, in a north-west direction, forming an angle with the horizon of about 45 degrees. Its thickness varied from two to six inches, and its breadth from four inches to two feet.' The specimen of this Coal, which I have seen, is of good quality, being more allied to the pitch, than to the slate Coal. In the under part of this vein, a good deal of pyrites[7] was lodged; and it was interrupted, in some places, by indurated[8] conglomerate clay. In the / distance which this vein was followed, it shewed no tendency either to thicken or grow wider.

Boring in the east part of Sprouston Quarry.

	Fathoms.	*Feet.*	*Inches.*
Bad free-stone[9] - -	0	2	0
Dent[10] - - -	0	4	0
Whin - - -	0	1	0
Blue dent - - -	1	3	0
Hard lime-stone - -	0	1	0
Strong brown clay - -	0	4	0
Blue dent - - -	1	3	0
Very hard whin - -	0	1	6
Brown dent - -	1	0	0
Hard whin - -	0	3	0
Free-stone - - -	0	2	0
Clay mixed with dark blue dent -	0	4	0
Blue dent - - -	0	5	6
Blue free-stone - -	0	4	0
Strong blue dent mixed with iron ore	1	0	0
Strong black dent - -	1	0	0
Hard stone - -	0	4	0
Blue free-stone - -	1	2	0
Hard whin - -	0	3	0
Black dent - -	0	5	0
Whin and dent alternating, the strata, about three or four inches thick,	2	0	0
Hard free-stone - -	2	1	0
Stone extraordinary hard -	1	3	0
Left off in very hard brown stone, and from its weight supposed it to contain iron stone -	0	4	0
Total Depth	21	0	0 /

LONGNEWTON.[11]

In digging a well here, some Coal was found; but as the well was walled before I saw it, I had not an opportunity of examining where the Coal was found; but obtained the following account of it from Mr Oliver; overseer for Mr Scott, of Mertoun:

'The well was first sunk through two feet of gravel; and then into a reddish till[12] and sand, to the depth of nineteen feet; in this red till, several small veins of a lighter hue, ran in various directions, and contained detached fragments of Coal of different qualities, but all of the candle, or slate kind.[13] In the bottom of the well, some pieces of amygdaloid containing steatite[14] were found.' /

DOLPHINSTON HILL.

A trial for Coal was made on this hill, some time ago, by several sinkings, none of which exceeded nine fathoms in depth. The account given of the result of those trials is, that there was a great mixture of Coal Metal, but in such confusion, as to distract the judgment of the colliers employed. The rubbish of the heaps at these sinkings, is a blue dent or metal stone. Had any Coal been in this hill, it must have cropped out in the hill side, towards the Jed.[15] /

From the observations I have made during my Examination of those Places described in the ITINERARY, I shall endeavour to draw conclusions as to what parts of the district, I conceive to be Coal bearing Strata, or Coal Formation, as also those which are not of Coal Formation; but I shall first state what kind of Stratification is considered as favourable to the presence of Coal, and likewise, that which is hostile to it. /

That able Mineralogist, Mr Jameson, in his Mineralogy of the Scottish Isles,[16] informs us, that the following Rocks are indicative of Coal; and his opinion I have generally found correct, so far at least as I have had an opportunity of observing.

1. White argillacious sand-stone.
2. Bituminous shale, shistose[17] clay, and argillacious iron-stone.
3. Sand-stone and lime-stone alternating, particularly if accompanied with bituminous shale.
4. Coal has sometimes been found where sand-stone and basalt alternate, which is frequently the case in the Newcastle Coal district.

In the primitive rocks,[18] Coal is never found, amongst which are granite, porphyry, primitive, lime-stone, micacious shistus,[19] pitch stone,[20] topaz rock,[21] and several other.

And I must add, that I consider red or reddish brown sand-stone as hostile, if not fatal to Coal; although Mr Jameson, in his Mineralogical Survey of Dumfries-shire,[22] asserts that red sand-stone is an 'independent Coal Formation.' I must beg leave to state, that as it is my wish to draw conclusions from facts, I am of a contrary opinion, for I never, in any instance, saw Coal under a confirmed red sand-stone, although I have seen detached pieces embedded in the strata lying above Coal; but I have frequently seen beds or seams of Coal, terminate abruptly against the red sand-stone rock, as if the red sand-stone formed a barrier to the Coal Formation; from which, I consider the presence of red sand-stone as unpropitious to Coal.*

* Since writing the above, I am informed, that in Water-house Colliery, Lancaster, Coal is found under red sand-stone. There is only one stratum of this stone, which is 28 feet

I shall therefore endeavour to define the Sand-stone District of the two Counties, so far as I have examined them; and which seems to be in two divisions, one of which I consider as containing Coal Formations, and the other as having a red Sand-stone Basis. /

REPORT.

From Lennel, ascending the Tweed by Wark, to Carham, and from thence, towards the south-west, by Nottylees, Kerchester, Mellendean Burn, Barbadoes, the south end of Kelso Bridge, and from thence to the whin-stone ridge, which crosses the Tweed, in a south-east direction, at Makerston Mill, may be considered as the southern boundary of the district, which I conceive to be of Coal Formation. The other limits of this district, so far as I have examined, extend from Makerston Mill, in a north-east direction, by way of Stodridge to Cattmoss, and from thence, in a north-east direction, to Lennel Quarry, forming a triangular figure, and including Lord Hume's Western Quarry, Fireburn-mill, Birgham Hill, Sprouston Quarry, Sharpitlaw, Eccles Quarry, Ednam, &c. &c. – How far this Formation may extend towards the north-east of the line from Cattmoss to Lennel, or to the south eastward of the Tweed from Lennel to Carham, I cannot say, not having explored the country in either of these directions, but I take Cattmoss as the extreme northerly point, as the red sand-stone formation commences very near to it.

The western barrier of the sand-stone district in the two Counties, appears to be formed by a mass of whin-stone and porphyry rock, running with many large indentations and interruptions from Harwood Lime Quarries, in a northerly direction, by Ruberslaw, Denham Dean, Menslees, Trony-hill, Newhall Mill, Longnewton, Dryburgh, Black Hill, and thence to Dean-Brae; and I am informed by the Rev. Dr Douglas, to whom I am indebted for much valuable information, that this line continues in a southerly direction, from Harwood Lime Quarries to Greena, with little variation.

The eastern barrier of this district is, as I conjecture also, formed by whinstone and porphyry, stretching nearly in a line from Greena, by the Carter, Roughlynook, Dolphinston, Scraisburgh, and Cessford, to the south-east of Sprouston, and from thence by the line above pointed out as the south-east limits of the district of Coal Formation. I do not know how far it may extend to the north-east, in which direction it seems to diverge or widen. /

Although this district contains a great variety of rocks, and white sand-stone is found in several places, as at Kello Burn, Rutherford Muir, Dryburgh, Trony-hill, Denham Hill, Kilburn, Mossburnford, &c. the red sand-stone predominates;

---

thick. The principal seam of Coal lies 58 fathoms below this red stone, but several strata of grey and white sand-stone, as also blue and black metal stone, or till, lie between them. White sand-stone and grey metal stone, repose upon the red sand-stone.

from which, I consider it as the basis of the district. It is also much intersected by ramifications, as I think, from the great western body of whin, which appear in several places in the shape of dykes, running generally in an east or southeast direction, and seem to be most numerous between Bedrule and the Carter.[23] I am not certain that the red sand-stone division of the district extends further south than an imaginary line drawn from Harwood to the Carter, as at both these places whitish sand-stone and lime-stone are found; from which it is not unlikely, but that the southern Coal Formation of Roxburghshire, commences there.

The country on the western side of the line, pointed out as the limit of the sand-stone district, by Newstead Bank, Quarry Hill, Toftfield Burn, Lindean, and thence by Midlem to Trony-hill, is evidently unfavourable to the presence of Coal, as in all that tract hardly one single Coal Formation is to be found; and the black veins at Newstead Bank, Toftfield Burn, and Lindean, have not, in my mind, the least analogy to Coal, although they have been considered as favourable symptoms.

The only place within the red sand-stone division, of the sand-stone district, in which I have observed Coal Formations, is in Wauchope Burn, at about a quarter of a mile below the junction of its two branches, but it is of a limited extent, being cut off by the whin-stone rock on the south-east and west sides. How far it may extend to the northward is uncertain, but should it continue regular in that direction, it must gain immense depth under Wainburgh Hill.

The Carter, which I consider as lying on the south side of the red sand-stone district, contains Coal on its south side, but what may be the thicknesses, or extent of the seams, I have not had the means of ascertaining. Its north side also exhibits Coal Formations, but does not appear to contain any Seams of Coal; for, had that been the case, their crop must have been discovered in the cleughs,[24] where the torrents have / bared the rock from the summit of the hill to its base, and exhibited a complete section of its strata; so that if any Coal is to be found on the north side of the Carter, it must lie between the bottom of the hill, and the ridge of whin-stone which crosses the Backburn, at about a mile from its junction with the Jed; but I do not think it likely that any Seam of Coal, worth working, is to be found in this situation.

A boring for Coal was made some years ago, in Rule Water, near to Fast Castle,[25] in which, I understand, Coal Formations, and a thin Seam of Coal were found, but why no further search was made, I am not informed. Taking general circumstances into consideration, I am not of opinion, that any workable Seam of Coal is to be found in Bedrule, notwithstanding the circumstances of the boring above stated, as I conceive the basis of that parish to be red sand-stone, upon which the Coal Formation found in the boring rests. I am led to this conclusion from the circumstance of the red sand-stone in Denham Hill Quarry, having a regular and uniform dip towards the south-east, which must necessarily depress it considerably below the level of the boring, near Fast Castle; and on the Jed Water, east of Bedrule, from Dolphinston to its junction with the Ale, is an uninterrupted mass of red sand-stone, varying in colour and texture, but preserving an uniform and gentle dip towards the south-east. Whether this boring might have been deep enough to penetrate the red sand-stone or not, I do not know, but there is little doubt, that had the boring been continued deep enough, it would have reached it.

Coal has been dug for in Dolphinston Hill, but without success; what grounds there could be to lead to the supposition of Coal being there, is not easy to guess, unless it arose from the appearance of some dark coloured dent, near the top of the hill; but the mode adopted to search for it was not the most judicious, as instead of sinking pits on the top of the hill, it would have been more effectual and less expensive to have dug a trench from its summit to its base, or as far as might have been necessary, by which the whole stratification of the hill would have been exposed to view; / and had it contained any Coal, the crop of the seams would have presented themselves.

Search has also been made for Coal on Hunt-hill, and report says, that Coal was found, but of this I could not obtain any distinct account. It is not unlikely that some thin stratum of Coal might be found in digging, but I have no reason to suppose that any seam of consequence was discovered, nor do I see any cause leading to the conclusion, that a workable seam exists in Hunt-hill.

In digging a well at Longnewton, some fragments of Coal were found, which induced the belief that a Seam of Coal was at no great distance; but on investigating the situation in which those pieces of Coal were said to be found, together with the metals cut through in digging the well, I do not consider them in any respect as indicative of the proximity of a Seam of Coal. The well was sunk through, first, gravel two feet thick, second, into reddish till and sand to the depth of nineteen feet, containing veins, in which the fragments of Coal were found, and at the bottom of the well some pieces of amygdaloid were found, but whether in detached pieces, or from a rock, I am not informed. From this, I consider the place where the well is sunk to be of alluvial formation, being the debris of the other strata; that the Coal Veins are formed in the fissures of the till by precipitation, and that the fragments of Coal which they contain have been deposited there by the agency of water, as well as the gravel, &c. This opinion is further supported by the circumstance of the fragments of Coal being smooth, and rounded a little on the sides and angles, which could only arise from attrition. The presence of amygdaloid is also unpropitious to Coal.

The Coal Veins in Stodridge and Sprouston Quarries, and the detached piece of Coal found in Eccles Quarry, are the only *proofs positive* of the existence of Coal, in what I consider to be the Coal Formation, in the division of the sand-stone district, as already described. I do not think that the Coal Veins in

Stodridge and Sprouston lead to any regular Seam, but terminate with the mass of white sand-stone in which they are found, in the horizontal strata below. /

I draw this conclusion from the boring made in Sprouston Quarry, which passed through an alternation of sand-stone, dent, whin, &c. for 24 changes to the depth of 21 fathoms, without meeting with a Seam of Coal. Had any Seam of Coal existed, to which this vein was the *leader*, it would naturally have assumed a horizontal position, near the top of the horizontal strata, bored through, and would, of course, have been discovered by the boring.

I am, nevertheless, of opinion, that that part of the sandstone district, which I have described as containing Coal Formations, may also contain Seams of Coal; but I consider that kind of alternation of the strata, as shewn by the boring at Sprouston, as well as from my own observations in other places, as indicative of thin seams lying at a great depth; indeed, had any Seams of Coal lain near the surface, their crop must have been discovered long before this time. From these circumstances it is evident, that the existence of Coal can only be ascertained by making effectual borings; those which have hitherto been made being quite inadequate to the object of research. I shall therefore endeavour to point out what I conceive to be the most eligible situation for making such borings.

The stratification in the vicinity of Coldstream, and up the Leat River, is exceedingly regular; but the sand-stone strata in Lennel Quarry, as also that between Coldstream Bridge and the town, seem to crop out to the surface; from which, it may be presumed, that the strata which are seen in the banks of the Leat lie underneath, and at a considerable depth below them, as no dyke or vein is visible, which might lead to any other conclusion; and as I consider the stratification in the vicinity of Coldstream to be as favourable to the existence of Coal as any other, or rather more so, I think the most proper situation for an effectual boring to be made, is in the Leat River above the bridge; and at about 80 or 100 yards below the mill, such boring would explore the strata to the greatest depth, at the least expence.

Another boring might be made, with propriety, to the north or north-eastward of the town, as should the crop of any Seam of Coal be concealed under the surface, between / the crop of the free-stone at Lennel Quarry, or that which is seen in the banks of the Tweed below Coldstream, and the proposed place of boring near the mill, such intermediate boring would discover it.

Effectual borings may also be made, with equal propriety, either at Bankhead, near Eccles; on the Eden Water, near Birgham Hill; in Mellendean Burn; or in Fleurs, near to Stodridge; but I think Mellendean the least favourable of those situations, and Eden Water and Fleurs, the best.

Having pointed out what I conceive to be the most proper situations for boring, I shall give an Estimate of the expence of boring, to the depth of 100 fathoms.

JOHN BUDDLE, Jun. /

ESTIMATE for Boring to the depth of One Hundred Fathoms, in the Counties of Roxburgh or Berwick, under the usual risks attendant on such operations, by an English Borer.

	Shillings.	*L.*	*S.*
Boring 5 Fathoms at	6	1	10
5 do. - -	12	3	0
5 do. - -	18	4	10
5 do. - -	24	6	0
5 do. - -	30	7	10
5 do. - -	36	9	0
5 do. - -	42	10	10
5 do. - -	48	12	0
5 do. - -	54	13	10
5 do. - -	60	15	0
5 do. - -	66	16	10
5 do. - -	72	18	0
5 do. - -	78	19	10
5 do. - -	84	21	0
5 do. - -	90	22	10
5 do. - -	96	24	0
5 do. - -	102	25	10
5 do. - -	108	27	0
5 do. - -	114	28	10
5 do. - -	120	30	0
100		315	0
Carriage of the Rods, Tagle Legs[26] and Gin Blocks, Rope, and other Apparatus, and fitting up the same,		100	0
Sharping the Geer,[27] finding Grease, Coals, a Horse to draw the Rods, and sundry other Charges during the Boring,		200	0
Accidents in Boring,		345	0
Extra Expence in Boring through Whin,		140	0
		L.1100 /	

Estimates for Boring to such great depths, cannot in general be offered as accurate from the Stone to be perforated, in some cases being of so hard a nature as hardly to be bored through at all; and the great risk of breaking and losing the Rods in the hole during the Boring, and consequently of frustrating the operation.

FINIS. /

KNOWLEDGE: ENGINEERING

This section turns to the engineering knowledge required to produce coal. No full-scale technical history of coal mining in Britain has ever been published and economists and other interested social scientists have had little to guide them through the complexities of the production process.[1] That the production process was complex is one of the main burdens of this section. Economists and economic historians have tended to assume that because the production process involved picks and shovels it must necessarily have been simple and that because these tools were in constant use for the whole of the nineteenth century and beyond the industry must have been technically stagnant.

A Treatise on the Winning and Working of Collieries (pp. 279–83) and 'On Rock Boring by the Diamond Drill, and Recent Applications of the Process' (pp. 285–8) are both concerned with rock boring, the first major operation in gaining access to the coal. *A Treatise on the Winning and Working of Collieries* by Matthias Dunn describes the process typical of the early and mid-nineteenth century. It was one in which the inadequacies of relatively simple tools had to be compensated with great skill by the Master Borer and his men. The time and skill required, and the high risk of mechanical difficulties and disasters, rendered boring to any depth a significant expense.[2] Costs per fathom increased with increasing depth, as Dunn details, and eventually became prohibitive.[3] 'On Rock Boring', an exposition of the capabilities of his diamond rock drill by Major Frederick Beaumont, a member of a long-established family of coal owners, dates from little more than twenty-five years after Dunn's description but demonstrates a revolution in boring machinery.[4]

The next text (pp. 289–93) concerns the history of explosives. It indicates the complexity of designing an explosive for use in a colliery (in which there might be firedamp and there would certainly be coal dust), which could be controlled so that its destructive power resulted solely in the predictable demolition of volumes of rock or coal; and that could be manufactured, transported and stored safely.[5] To do so required significant research into the chemistry and physics of combustion and explosion.

William Waller's 'On Pumping Water' (pp. 295–6) moves on to the problems of controlling the environment of the mine and the solutions adopted. It is misleading to think of the production process involved in mining coal as one involving only the removal of coal from one place underground to another place on the surface; usually there were three transport processes that had to be attended to, not one. They were the removal of the solid coal, liquid water and gaseous air. These are usually treated under the headings of 'haulage', 'pumping' and 'ventilation'. Often the volumes of liquid and air removed from a colliery dwarfed the volume of coal removed. This text indicates the stupendously large quantities of water raised and the extraordinarily low costs for which this was achieved as early as the 1860s.[6]

Progress in transporting air through the mines was slower. In the early nineteenth century the only effective method of ventilating coal mines was to position a furnace underground, usually at or near the foot of the 'upcast' shaft, and rely on the draught resulting from the movement of the heated air up the shaft to ventilate the mine. A number of other methods had been tried but none achieved marked success. This is the state of things described by Dunn in 1848 in the extract from *A Treatise on the Winning and Working of Collieries* presented on pp. 297–304.[7] His review suggests the frustration of mine engineers at this period: faced with a clear need if the mines were to be rendered safe but with no clear solution.

This sense of frustration will help to explain the heartfelt relief and pleasure which greeted the first tests of Guibal's ventilating fan in the UK in the 1860s ('Description of Guibal's Ventilator, at Elswick Colliery', see pp. 305–9). The idea of using a mechanically rotated fan to ventilate a colliery may seem an obvious one. It had, indeed, been tried before: Dunn's review includes a mechanically operated fan, or pump, based on the rotation of a helix inside a cylinder.[8] Cochrane's account of the operation of the Guibal fan at Elswick, near Newcastle, the first in the country to install the complete system, indicates that a fan is not the simple piece of machinery it may appear to be; not, that is, if one wants to move thousands of cubic metres of air a minute and to do this with equipment that has minimal capital and running costs.

The next text (pp. 311–16) is a remarkable, and classic, account of the explosion in 1878 of the Washburn A Flour Mill in Minneapolis, Minnesota, USA, thought, on its construction, to be the largest flour mill in the world. That a flour mill should explode is strange: a flour mill is not a gasworks, or a gunpowder factory; it is not stuffed with unfamiliar chemicals; it does not generate enormous heat; it does not place materials into highly pressured containers. Peckham's account of his investigation of the cause of the explosion eliminates one possible cause after another. By the end of his account the conclusion that flour dust suspended in the air of the mill is explosive appears inescapable. The brilliance of

Algernon Freire-Marreco (about 1836–82), Professor of Chemistry at Durham University College of Physical Science, who called attention to the explosion, was to realize that the explosion of the flour dust was the rapid oxidation of the 'carbonaceous matter' in the dust; that coal dust was, of course, also 'carbonaceous'; so that if an atmosphere laden with flour dust was explosive so, too, might be an atmosphere laden with coal dust.[9]

This realization explained many features of colliery explosions that had long puzzled the more thoughtful of the industry's engineers and in particular William Galloway (1840–1927). Galloway was educated in Germany, at the University of Giessen and at the Freiburg Bergakademie, as well as in Britain. He became one of HM's Inspectors of Mines firstly in the West of Scotland and then in South Wales. His researches on the role of coal dust in colliery explosions were published in a series of papers in the *Proceedings of the Royal Society* between 1875 and 1887. In the first of these he noted that it was difficult to account for the extent and violence of the explosions that had occurred in mines where 'no large accumulations' of firedamp appeared to exist. In one explosion in France, at the Carpagnac Colliery on 2 November 1874, of which a very detailed account had been published:

> A shot, which blew out the tamping, was fired in one of the working-places, in a seam of bituminous coal, and was accompanied by an explosion which burnt three men so seriously that they died within a week. No firedamp had been detected in this place at any time; but as the floor was covered with very fine, dry coal-dust, and as the shot was fired at the bottom of the face, and would consequently raise a cloud of dust, it was concluded that nothing but the instantaneous combustion of coal-dust, under the influence of the shot, could account for the accident.[10]

Scepticism of his theories among his senior colleagues in the Inspectorate forced his resignation from his post.[11] A gradual accumulation of experimental evidence by himself and others eventually vindicated his position.[12] He was almost certainly responsible for saving more miners' lives than Humphry Davy.

The next three texts (pp. 317–29) are concerned with colliery illumination. This was not usually a major issue in the setting of a mill or factory after the introduction of gaslight in the early nineteenth century. Before this time, as indicated in William Murdock's 'An Account of the Application of the Gas from Coal to Œconomical Purposes' (pp. 105–9), the cost of candles or other illuminants and the cost of tending them could be significant. The issue in the mines was not cost but the technical difficulty of providing light by any device using the light of combustion in an atmosphere that was potentially explosive.

It is often assumed that the problem was solved by the invention of the Davy 'safety lamp' and this was indeed the assumption made by some mining engineers and coal owners, especially in regions where firedamp was unusual. It was not the view, however, of all, especially in areas, like the north-east, where firedamp was a serious problem. As we have already seen in *A Treatise on the Winning and Working of Collieries* (pp. 279–83), Matthias Dunn, for example, allied himself with the view promulgated by the South Shields Committee

> that the naked Davy lamp is without a complete shield, a most dangerous instrument, and has indubitably been productive of those accidents in mines, against which it is still too confidently and generally employed, at the daily imminent risk of producing a like calamity (p. 302).

For engineers such as Dunn, the Davy and other 'safety' lamps needed to be employed with great caution and powerful ventilation had to be the primary solution to the risks posed by firedamp. This divergence of views was the basis for a controversy between 'lampers' and 'ventilationists' which rumbled on for most of the century, only finally subsiding with the introduction of electric light from the 1890s onwards.

'On Safety Lamps for Lighting Coal Mines' (pp. 317–24) provides a review of the history written by Nicholas Wood, perhaps the most eminent of those inclined to rely on the safety lamp. 'Safety Lamps' (pp. 325–6), written thirty years after Wood's paper, by a person clearly closely acquainted with the issue who takes an opposing view.[13] It demonstrates that the issue remained unresolved and raises the question of how and why such an important matter had not been adequately researched, discussed and settled. That such a state of affairs could exist is indicative of the social inefficiency to which we drew attention in the introduction to these three volumes. 'The Coad Electric Miner's Lamp' (pp. 327–9) is a short advocacy piece for an early version of an incandescent lamp, powered by a battery and with some features designed to make it suitable for underground use. The discussion indicates some of the initial problems: the weight of the battery pack, which remains a problem to the present day, the cost, and its inability to act simultaneously as a light source and as a gas detector, a problem eventually 'solved' by disregarding it and keeping 'safety lamps' in use solely as gas detectors. These problems were not solved for a long time. Although fixed electric lighting had been installed in Earnock Colliery in Scotland as early as 1881 and this had been regarded as a success by the mining engineers, the use of portable electric lamps, of the kind exhibited by Coad, was regarded as 'experimental' as late as 1907. the use of portable electric lamps underground was regarded as 'experimental'; by the outbreak of the First World War, however, the use of such lamps was described as 'general'.[14]

'The Telephone in Colliery Workings' (pp. 331–4) concerns the problems of communication in the setting of a mine. In the context of a mill or factory, the only difficulty likely to have been present was that of the noise of the machinery. This was a notorious problem in textile mills:

> You went through the door and you was overwhelmed at the roar of noise, and for about three days that was, all you could hear was the roar in your ears. But after that you became part and parcel of it and you could talk quite normally. Although you didn't realise it, you were doing a lot of lip-reading. It was built into the job.[15]

Before the advent of coalface mechanization, underground work took place in an environment that was, on the whole, remarkably quiet. Indeed, for some – for example boys attending trapdoors on underground passages – it was too quiet, the silence adding to the terror of the mine. It was surface work that was noisy: workers attending the screens used for sorting coal into different sizes and which usually depended for their operation on the vibration of metal griddles created a deafening racket from which there was no respite.

The main communication problem underground was not noise, therefore, but the physical distances, and the difficulties of travelling them, that separated underground workers one from another and from workers above ground. It was this difficulty that Lord Elphinstone sought to solve by installing a telephone in his colliery at Carberry near Inveresk in Scotland in 1880:

> Where so much depends on the efficient drainage of the mine, not only as regards the safety of the 120 men employed in it, but the economical and continuous output, great attention has to be paid to the pumping gear, and several men are engaged in constantly travelling to and fro over the workings inspecting the pumps, and reporting to the men in charge of the engine at the surface. It occurred to Lord Elphinstone that, by fitting up telephones in different parts of the mine, the regular and proper working of the pumps might be discovered at the surface, and the labour of many men dispensed with.

It is interesting to see here the telephone, usually regarded by economic historians as a provider of consumer services, as a piece of labour-saving machinery in a production process. Its use spread only gradually, however, and as late as 1924 the primary communication devices used in collieries were specialized signalling devices, including some closely resembling those used to communicate between signal boxes on railways, which had become statutory requirements under the 1855 Coal Mines Inspection Act.[16]

The next two texts (pp. 335–51) concern underground haulage. This topic was usually divided by mine engineers into 'secondary haulage' which, confusingly, referred to the transport of coal from the face to a main haulage road, and 'primary haulage', which referred to transport along the main haulage roads to the shaft bottom.

'On the Conveyance of Coals Underground in Coal Mines' by Nicholas Wood from 1854–5 draws attention to the difficulties of main-road haulage underground by comparing haulage roads with surface railways, on which he was one of the earliest authorities. He points out the heavy expense of underground haulage and the increasing significance of this as shafts got deeper. Where seams were close to the surface, underground haulage costs could be minimized by sinking frequent shafts; where seams were deep, shafts became a major expense and underground haulage was consequently extended. In short, there was a difficult optimization problem facing mine engineers involving a trade-off between the number of shafts and the length of underground haulage roads which had to be solved in the face of considerable geological uncertainties affecting the costs of sinking shafts and driving roads. The solution to this problem was also be constrained by the extent of the coal leased: a solution involving a single pair of deep shafts and long haulage roads might not be feasible if the area available for lease was small. Despite all the difficulties there was no avoiding the problem and in general it is clear that the shift from shallow to deeper seams as the eighteenth century turned into the nineteenth and the nineteenth into the twentieth, led to greater lengths of underground haulage roads over broader leases. The shafts of 'bell-pits' used to exploit the shallow seams south of Leeds, for example, were typically only a few metres deep and a few tens of metres apart. The shafts of Bullcroft Main and Hatfield Main Collieries which worked neighbouring leases in the eastern and deepest part of the south Yorkshire coalfield were 685 and 846 yards deep (632 and 781 metres, respectively) and 11 km apart.[17]

'Secondary Haulage' by William Galloway refers to transportation from coalface to main haulage road. The main burden of Galloway's paper, published towards the very end of the nineteenth century was the extraordinarily high cost of hauling coal over even short distances from face to haulage road. His most startling evidence is not revealed until he replies to the discussion his paper had provoked. There he presents estimates comparing the cost of main-road haulage with the costs of secondary haulage carried out in a variety of circumstances and by a variety of methods. He thought main-road haulage carried out by the cheapest method, a railway using an endless chain, cost less than 1*d.* per ton mile. To give some perspective one should note that at this time the pit-head price of coal varied from perhaps 5*s.* 0*d.* to 6*s.* 5*d.* per ton.[18] In contrast, using boys, known as 'putters', to push single waggons of coal from working places to a collecting siding on the main haulage might cost 2*s.* 2*d.* per ton mile, over twenty-five times as much. Using sledges or barrows to move coal away from the immediate vicinity of the working place might cost over 10*s.* per ton mile, well over a hundred times as much as endless chain haulage on the main roads. The old method of carrying coal on the back of a man or – before 1842 – a woman was, thought Galloway, not only barbaric but extraordinarily costly: almost £1 per ton mile, well over two hundred times the cost of endless chain main-road haulage.[19]

These figures suggest that the almost exclusive focus of the economic history on coal-cutting machinery has been unfortunate. One possible reason for this is hinted at by Galloway himself. Few colliery companies, even at the end of the nineteenth century, had cost accounting practices capable of separately identifying secondary haulage costs from the costs of other underground processes.

Finally, this section returns to the surface. The last two texts (pp. 353–73) offer two contrasting accounts, separated by less than fifty years, of the surface arrangements of British collieries. The first of these texts (p. 353), another extract from Dunn's 1848 *Treatise*, is remarkable for its brevity and for its focus on separating small coal from large, the latter valuable, the former then almost worthless.[20] The considerable length of Edward Wain's 'Colliery Surface Works' (pp. 355–73) from 1894 is one indicator of the advance in thinking about what should happen at the surface of a colliery: there was now much more to say. The other notable features of the piece are the close attention given to costs and to the productivity of capital. The author, over and over again, emphasizes arrangements designed to increase throughput per hour or per day, each of which reduces the average capital cost per ton of coal. While Wain may have been motivated by an engineer's professional concerns with speed and regularity, the effect of the arrangements he describes were to increase productivity, reduce average costs per ton, and raise profits.

This set returns to technical matters in Volume 2 which deals with organization and production. See pp. 125–41 of Volume 2, for the stock of capital employed at collieries, pp. 227–58 for technical change and pp. 143–225 for material relating to local public goods of significance in the production of coal and to methods of transport and distribution. Questions of efficiency are considered in Volume 3 (pp. 107–94), in their aspect as one of the enduring problems of the industry.

Notes

1. The most useful account of the nineteenth-century technical history has remained the *Historical Review of Coal Mining* published by the Fleetway Press for the Mining Association of Great Britain (MAGB) in 1924 to accompany the colliery exhibits at the British Empire Exhibition at Wembley, London between April and October of that year.
2. See also the table of boring costs given by Buddle on p. 267.
3. Such techniques were described as 'old fashioned' and this, 'the British process', to be 'in the evening of its existence' in 'Scotland', *Colliery Guardian*, 3 May 1862, pp. 349–50.
4. For a contemporary account of the sinking of Monkwearmouth Colliery, for a long time the deepest in Britain, see 'The Deepest Mine in Great Britain', *Chambers Edinburgh Journal*, 181 (18 July 1835), p. 199. Costs of sinking coal mines were analysed in detail in 'Essays on Mining Economy: II. – Analysis of the Expenditure of Coal Mines', *Colliery Guardian*, 2 June 1871, pp. 586–8. A useful technical review of the history is given by E. O. Forster Brown, 'The History of Boring and Shaft Sinking', in [MAGB], *Historical Review of Coal Mining* (London: Fleetway Press for the Mining Association of Great Britain, [1924]), pp. 26–41.
5. One issue not addressed by Stuart, the author of 'The Development of Exposives for Coal-Mines' (pp. 289–93) is the dangers to human health presented by the gaseous products of an explosion. See the letter by Henry Hall, one of HM's Inspectors of Mines,

to the Institute of Civil Engineers ('Correspondence', *Institute of Civil Engineers Minutes of the Proceedings*, 61 (1880) pp. 129–30) which notes a case where the fumes produced by 'Tonite', used in the sinking of a pit had proved 'fatal to life'. Suspicions that the fumes generated by the explosion of Roburite, an explosive composed of a mixture of ammonium nitrate and chlorinated di-nitro-benzol, were dangerous emerged in 1889 and were raised in the House of Commons (House of Commons Debates, *Hansard*, 19 July 1889, vol. 338 col. 842; 'The Use of Roburite in Mines', *Colliery Guardian*, 7 June 1889, p. 815; W. J. Orsman, 'Notes on the Products and Temperature of Detonation of some High Explosives', *Transactions of the North of England Institute of Mining Engineers*, 41 (1891–2), pp. 9–14 and '[Discussion]', pp. 14–18).

6. J. B. Simpson drew attention to the 'great economy' with which water was pumped out of the Cornish mines a few years later and described the 'so satisfactory' results obtained from a Cornish pumping engine installed in a colliery in the Newcastle district ('On the Duty of Cornish and other Pumping Engines for Draining Mines', *Transactions of the North of England Institute of Mining Engineers*', 19 (1869–70), pp. 201–18 and plates XXXVIII–XL and '[Discussion]', pp. 219–21
7. A description of the state of affairs at the time Dunn was writing was also given by Joshua Richardson, 'On the Ventilation of Mines', *Institution of Civil Engineers Minutes of the Proceedings*, 6 (1847), pp. 160–83 and '[Discussion]', pp. 183–212. Dunn was present at the delivery of this paper, remarking that he 'concurred in the general tenor' of it (p. 183).
8. A general review was given by D. P. Morison, 'The Economical Advantages of Mechanical Ventilation', *Transactions of the North of England Institute of Mining Engineers*, 19 (1869–70), pp. 223–32 and plates XLII–XLIII and '[Discussion]', pp. 233–7.
9. While brilliant it was not original. William Galloway, in his paper, 'On the Influence of Coal-Dust in Colliery Explosions', *Proceedings of the Royal Society of London*, 24 (1875–6), pp. 354–72, had noted that 'a mixture of air with several other combustible solids in a finely divided state is explosive at ordinary pressure and temperature, and that some serious explosions have been caused by the accidental ignition of very fine dry flour suspended in the air in confined spaces' (p. 355).
10. Galloway, 'On the Influence of Coal-Dust'. Galloway refers to an account by Pierre Louis Marie Gustave Vital (1848), *Ingénieur des Mines*, but gives no details.
11. J. S. Haldane, 'Health and Safety in British Coal Mines' in [MAGB], *Historical Review of Coal Mining* (London: Fleetway Press for the Mining Association of Great Britain, [1924]), pp. 266–300, at p. 272.
12. Haldane, 'Health and Safety', pp. 272–6. Henry Hall also noted that 'the views advanced were received almost with ridicule' ('Coal-dust', *Transactions of the Federated Institute of Mining Engineers*, 2 (1890–1), pp. 415–21 and '[Discussion]', pp. 422–31). A further review of the history of investigation is given by W. E. Garforth, 'Presidential Address: British Coal-dust Experiments', *Transactions of the Institute of Mining Engineers*, 42 (1911–12), pp. 220–41 and '[Discussion]', pp. 242–5. It was the 'splendid' series of experiments by Garforth, at the experimental station he established at Altofts Colliery in Yorkshire, that finally brought controversy to an end. William Edward Garforth (1846–1921, knighted 1914) was regarded with 'admiration and affection' by his men. See also B. Fraser, *The West Riding Miners and Sir William Garforth* (Stroud: The History Press, 2009).
13. See also the extensive review of the state of the art by A. H. Leech and W. H. Routledge of the Stavely Collieries, Chesterfield, 'Safety Lamps, and Lighting of Mines', *Journal of the British Society of Mining Students*, 6 (1882), pp. 119–65 plates I–XVI.

14. 'The Electric Light at Earnock Colliery', *Colliery Guardian*, 12 August 1881, p. 259; 'Lighting Collieries by Electricity', *Chambers Journal*, 1:31 (2 August 1884), p. 496; L. L. B., 'Electric Safety-Lamp Experiments at Camphausen, Germany. [An abstract of] *Versuche mit tragbaren elektrischen Grubensicherheitslampen auf der Grube Camphausen der Königlichen Berginspektion XI zu Camphausen.* By – Rossenbeck. *Zeitschrift für das Berg-, Hütteen- und Salinen-wesen im preussischen Staate,* 1907, *vol. lv., Abhandlungen, pages 269–282, with 9 figures in the text, Transactions of the North of England Institute of Mining Engineers*', 59 (1908–9), pp. 93–4; R. W. Dron, 'Lighting of Mines', in [MAGB], *Historical Review of Coal Mining* (London: Fleetway Press for the Mining Association of Great Britain, [1924]), pp. 150–69, at p. 168.
15. An anonymous man, born 1920, speaking of the 1930s, quoted in T. Smith and O. Howarth, *Textile Voices: A Century of Mill Life* (Bradford: Bradford Museums, Galleries and Heritage, 2006), pp. 35–7. Victorian mills may have been somewhat quieter or noisier than those of the 1930s but there was no qualitative difference.
16. The Coal Mines Act 1855 (18 & 19 Vict. c. 108). Section IV consisted of 'General Rules to be Observed in Every Coal Mine and Colliery' and included the rule 'Every Working Pit of Shaft shall be provided with some proper Means of signalling from the Bottom of the Shaft to the Surface, and from the Surface to the Bottom of the Shaft' (Sir Andrew Bryan, *The Evolution of Health and Safety in Mines* (Ashire Publishing / A Mine and Quarry Publication, 1975), p. 141. [MAGB], *Historical Review of Coal Mining* ([London]: Fleetway Press for the Mining Association of Great Britain, [1924]), Appendix, p. 22–3 (describing a model of a haulage road signalling system) and pp. 50–1 (describing a shaft signalling system). For the closely allied history of railway signalling systems, see: G. Kichenside, *British Railway Signalling* (London: Ian Allan, 1964) and G. Kichenside and A. Williams, *Two Centuries of Railway Signalling* (Oxford: Sparkford, 1998).
17. A. Hill, *The South Yorkshire Coalfield: A History and Development* (Stroud: Tempus, 2001).
18. R. Church, *The History of the British Coal Industry Volume 3 1830–1913: Victorian Pre-eminence* (Oxford: Clarendon Press, 1986), table 1.11. I have ignored the aberrant data from the small south-west of England fields.
19. Further evidence, relating to practices and costs in the north-east, was presented by T. E. Forster and F. R. Simpson, 'Secondary Haulage: Cost of Putting and Driving', *Transactions of the North of England Institute of Mining Engineers*', 47 (1897–8), pp. 236–9 and '[Discussion]', pp. 240–1.
20. Further descriptions of surface arrangements are given by G. Gilroy, 'Coal Washing Apparatus in use at the Ince Hall Coal and Cannel Company's Collieries at Ince, Near Wigan', *Transactions of the North of England Institute of Mining Engineers*, 15 (1865–6), pp. 61–2 and 'Discussion', pp. 63–6; A. H. Leech, 'Description of Screening Arrangements at Brinslop Hall Collieries', *Transactions of the Manchester Geological Society*, 18 (1885–6), pp. 373–9 and plates I–II; S. Tate, 'Winding, Banking Out, and Screening Plant at East Hetton Colliery', *Transactions of the North of England Institute of Mining and Mechanical Engineers*, 39 (1889–90), pp. 3–5 and plates I–VI and '[Discussion]', pp. 6–9; T. E. Forster and H. Ayton, 'Improved Coal Screening and Cleaning', *Transactions of the North of England Institute of Mining and Mechanical Engineers*, 39 (1889–90), pp. 17–30 and plates I–X and '[Discussion]', pp. 30–2; and J. Rigg, 'Tipping and Screening Coal', *Institute of Civil Engineers Minutes of the Proceedings*, 127 (1897), pp. 163–75 and plate 4. The report of a committee of the Mining Institution of Scotland on 'coal preparation and separation' is detailed in 'The Sorting and Cleaning of Coal', *Colliery Guardian*, 3 January 1890, p. 12.

Matthias Dunn, *A Treatise on the Winning and Working of Collieries* (1848)

Matthias Dunn,[1] *A Treatise on the Winning and Working of Collieries: Including Numerous Statistics and Remarks on Ventilation, and Illustrated by Plans and Engravings. To Which Are Appended a Glossary and Index* (Newcastle-upon-Tyne: The author, 1848).

SECTION VII.

BORING.

Having in the introduction placed before the reader a general idea of the disposition of coal fields, and shewn that many extensive mines of coal are so embedded in alluvial matter, that no correct judgment can be formed of their existence from visible outcrop; it becomes advisable to ascertain the depth, nature, and thickness by boring, for without boring neither the engine power[2] nor other expenditures which may be necessary to attain the desired object, can be estimated. Various new methods have been suggested from time to time in this important branch of Mine Engineering; but I am not aware of any material improvements that have been effected, superior to the system which has been pursued from time immemorial, – viz., by the common cutting chisel and wimble.[3] Therefore, in conformity with the plan of this work, I will proceed to enumerate the principal implements employed in this process, with the mode of using them ... ; and in doing so, I request such of my readers as are well acquainted with these details to excuse prolixity, and to bear in mind that I am writing for all classes of readers, as well as for those of the profession.

IMPLEMENTS USED IN BORING.

1. Brace Head, with short rod attached, is used for lifting and working the rods.
2. Bore Rods of best iron, about one inch square and of different lengths, each rod having a male screw at one end and a female at the other.

3 – 4. Chisels, also fitted with screws, well tempered with steel, with a face of two or two and a half inches, according to the size of / the hole intended to be bored, are generally eighteen inches in length.

5. Wimble, a hollow iron instrument similar to an auger, whose cavity is from eight to ten inches in length, with an opening up one side, with partial overlap, the better to receive and hold the chopped strata.
6. Rest, an instrument whereon the rods rest upon the boring box, whilst screwing and unscrewing.
7. Screw-keys, for screwing and unscrewing the rods.
8. Boring Box of wood, a little larger than the hole, which serves to direct and rest the rods.
9. Topit, for quickly attaching to the rods for lifting, &c.

10 – 11. Right and left handed worm screws.

12. Runner, attached to the winch rope.
13. Boring Frame or Triangles, twenty or thirty feet high, to which are applied jackroll[4] and sheave, for raising and lowering the rods, and for disjointing into convenient lengths.

Besides these, many other small apparatus are used, according to the inventive genius of the borer, to recover the rods in case of breakage – to unscrew them in case of becoming fastened; and in boring through sands or in running strata, sheet or cast iron pipes are applied for the preservation of the boring, sliding within each other like the parts of a telescope.

...

In the ordinary boring, when the rods become inconveniently heavy, a lever of the common description is used; the fulcrum is placed a few inches from the bore rods, at the thick end of the lever, the men working at the other or small end, using it to raise the rods, and allowing them to fall by their own weight, for the purpose of cutting the strata.

The operation of simple boring is to raise the rods, armed with a chisel, a few inches, and then let them fall by their own weight, at the same time turning them gradually round at every stroke, the object of which is to cut away the strata piece by piece, and which process is greatly aided by keeping the hole well moistened with water, if there be not a natural supply. The rods are then drawn up, and unscrewed into convenient lengths, the blunted chisel replaced with the wimble, and so on alternately. When the hole becomes deep, and the rods too heavy to be conveniently lifted by manual labour, a brake or lever is employed as before mentioned, whilst a labourer keeps continually turning them round. A jack roll ... (windlass), horse gin ... , or steam engine, is frequently employed for the more readily raising and lowering the rods, which in deep borings becomes both laborious and critical, as will be seen by the undermentioned scale of ordinary prices by the established borers of the day, viz.:–

1st	five fathoms	–	7s.	per fathom.
2nd	do.	–	14s.	do.
3rd	do.	–	21s.	do.
4th	do.	–	28s.	do.
5th	do.	–	35s.	do.
6th	do.	–	42s.	do.
7th	do.	–	49s.	do.

And so on. Extra charges are made for conveying the rods, fixing the apparatus, or boring through whin[5] or other extraordinary hard metals.

Practised borers can ascertain with the greatest nicety the nature and thickness of the strata bored through, and form a very correct opinion as to the nature of the feeders of water met with in the process. It is moreover justly considered a very onerous and important duty, inasmuch as a false or ignorant account of strata may lead to ruinous expenditure and irretrievable disappointment, which has not unfrequently occurred. The late Mr. Ryan[6] patented an improvement in boring, which had for its object the taking out of the strata in a core similar to the boring of a cheese; but on being tried upon stone, it proved utterly impracticable. As to boring in clay or coal, that operation is generally executed by the wimble. /

The cuttings in the generality of borings are not in the shape of distinct particles, inasmuch as, by the application of water either from the surface or in the bore hole, the cut strata present the appearance of mud and not of distinct particles; – hence the difficulty which will occur for such a composition to find its passage up so narrow an inlet as Mr. Taylor's tube.[7] In boring through coal it might be more applicable, because the particles are more apt to be retained in pieces; but for this purpose either the wimble or a chambered chisel is used, similar to the apparatus for which this patent was obtained. /

Mr. Stott,[8] of Ferry Hill, the principal borer in this part of the country, assures me that he has frequently applied a chambered chisel, chiefly with a view to preserve the particles of coal as much as possible, and to guard against the effects of the inflammable gas, which is frequently so considerable in the first tapping of a seam of coal that it is difficult to retain specimens.

Much therefore depends upon the nature of the strata bored through, as to whether this invention may be made practically useful.

Another method of boring is practised with rods, which are three times the weight of those used in the North of England. A lofty scaffold is raised, whereon the *borer* stands to work the rods, which are lifted by means of a winch with *ungeering*[9] apparatus, the effect of which is, that after the rods are sufficiently elevated they are suddenly let go, and, by their weight and extra strength, cut the strata with increased effect. The height of the scaffold, to which there is a convenient stair, permits the rods to be fitted together in greater lengths than otherwise, thereby adding to their strength, and at the same time diminishing the chance of accident.

Borings have been frequently executed in this part of the country to the depth of 130 fathoms; but where that is intended to be the case, a shaft is generally sunk to an indefinite number of fathoms, in order to expedite the work by unscrewing the rods in greater lengths, or where the bottom of a coal shaft can be made available, the proving of the lower strata is thereby greatly facilitated.

It frequently becomes necessary in mining, to bore holes upwards, which is effected for short distances with great facility by means of the brake or lever, inasmuch as the hole clears itself without the intervention of the wimble.

In boring contracts, exceptions are made with respect to charge in which whin or other exceedingly hard strata intervene. /

It often happens that both hole and rods are lost by the unscrewing of the joints or the rods becoming fastened by the falling in of loose stones, or by projections of the rugged strata at troubles, &c., to avoid which in deep borings the most consummate care and experience are required.

In prosecuting borings through alluvial substances or soft strata, it is proper to secure the bore holes by means of pipes of wood or iron, the hole being enlarged accordingly, and as the power of driving down the pipes is limited, recourse is had to the insertion of one length within the other, upon the principle of a telescope.

So important is the process of boring, and so changeable and uncertain is the disposition of coal fields, that prudent persons do not satisfy themselves with one boring, but by executing a succession of borings to some well ascertained seam, a fair opinion may be formed of the direction and amount of the dip and rise, as also the nature of the roof of the coal. At the same time the intervention of slip dykes often renders such precautions nugatory, and misleads the speculator in regard to the disposition of the beds of coal. It is therefore only common prudence to bore a succession of holes to some upper seam, as it may be safely inferred that the principal seams lie parallel to *it*, whatever their relative depths may be.

Boring is frequently resorted to in coal workings in which a waste[10]... is suspected, the boundaries of which are unascertained.... These borings are necessarily horizontal ...

As soon as a perforation into the waste occurs, the hole ought to be carefully plugged with wood;[11] a new position ...should be taken up twenty or thirty yards back, and new boring drifts at right angles be made right and left until the position of the waste be completely ascertained, and within which lines all the interior workings may be considered safe.

Notwithstanding these precautions, whether from occasional neglect or unforeseen accident, inundations have frequently taken place. Such, indeed, was the case at Heaton colliery, near this town,[12] in the year 1815; for although the drowned waste had been thus ascertained during the course of many hundred yards, yet in an unhappy moment a failure took place in exploring through a fault, and water rushed in, to the destruction of nearly a hundred men and boys, who were entombed in the upper parts of the mine, without the remotest chance of escape, and there the bodies remained for many months.[13]

The omission of boring where wastes were expected to be found, has often led to most disastrous results; for although in many cases both the coal and the superior strata are so open that they indicate the vicinity of a drowned waste, long before the workings are brought in contact with it; yet it is frequently the reverse, in consequence of both coal and stone being so completely water-tight that they exhibit no symptom of water till the communication actually takes place. In collieries, therefore, lying to the dip of drowned wastes of uncertain form and extent, a good system of boring is most necessary; for when once the waste is proved, the water can be gradually let off to the pumping engines, and an opportunity taken to drain it, and thus procure the coal which previously had been left as a barrier of safety. /

Major Beaumont, 'On Rock Boring by the Diamond Drill, and Recent Applications of the Process' (1875)

Major Beaumont,[1] 'On Rock Boring by the Diamond Drill, and Recent Applications of the Process', *Proceedings of the Institution of Mechanical Engineers*, 26 (1875), pp. 92–107 and '[Discussion]', pp. 108–25.

ON ROCK BORING BY THE DIAMOND DRILL, AND RECENT APPLICATIONS OF THE PROCESS.

BY MAJOR BEAUMONT, R.E., M.P., OF LONDON.

In this country important mechanical improvements are slowly accepted; but the principle being right, their progress is always sure. The subject of this paper has been discussed before in public, but the importance of the work done by the Diamond Drill is the reason for its being brought before this Institution. The writer proposes to dwell more particularly on the latest improvements that have been made in the applications of the diamond drill, and on the practical experience that has been obtained as to the best means of utilising the extraordinary properties of the black diamond, called carbonate in this country, and carbonado[2] in Brazil, where it is found.

The diamond is the hardest known substance in nature, its comparison with the other materials next in hardness being described in Ure's Chemical Dictionary[3] as

Diamond	20
Ruby or Corundum	17
Topaz	15
Quartz	10

The writer does not know by what process these figures were arrived at, but assumes that they are little more than guesses based upon the relative facilities with which the different materials can be scratched. Unless hardness means some quality which has no direct reference to durability under abrasion, he thinks that in these figures justice is not done to the diamond. If a well-chosen piece of black diamond or carbonate be brought into contact with solid quartz, the relative hardnesses according to the above table being only as 2 to 1, the quartz would have no chance at all; and the / writer has seen specimens of quartz cut with comparative ease by a steel crown or boring tool set with diamonds, and running at a speed of about 300 rev. per min. He would quite expect a good crown tool to cut 30 ft. or 40 ft. run, before it was rendered useless; and it must be remembered that the diamonds in the crown tool can only be worn away about 1–32nd inch before it is rendered unfit to work, because any further wearing away of the steel in which the diamonds are set would involve the risk of their becoming loose in the setting.

To consider fairly the durability of the two materials, the work done should be looked at in the following manner. The amount of quartz ground up to an impalpable powder in boring 30 ft. depth would amount to 994 cub. in., which represents the contents of that depth of an annular ring 2⅛ in. outside diameter and 1 in. inside diameter, 1 in. being the thickness of the core left untouched. The diamond consumed in doing this work would under ordinarily favourable circumstances be represented by a cube having sides of ¼ in., or 1–64th cub. in. Multiplying 994 by 64 gives 63,616 for the quantity of quartz ground up, as against 1 in the case of the diamond. The writer has also cut solid cores out of glass with a diamond tool. There was necessarily only a small thickness of glass to operate upon, about 2 in., but it could not be seen that any effect was produced on the diamonds; and it appeared quite practicable to drill a deep hole in a material like glass, in which, in consequence of its being homogeneous and having no cracks or flaws, hardness was the only difficulty the diamond drill would have to overcome.

It has frequently been suggested to try to shape the diamond to a cutting edge; but according to the writer's view such suggestions are made under a misconception as to the action of the diamond, which does its work by absolute main force. It is a question not of cutting, but of abrasion, the harder material wearing down the softer one; and any attempt to shape the diamond to a cutting edge would reduce the area subjected to abrasion, and place the diamond in a worse position for doing its work, until its sharp edge had been worn off, which would very soon be the case. This / remark is only intended to apply to the diamond as used for drilling hard rocks. For soft rocks a cutting edge would stand; but such a material would be so easily cut that there would be no advantage in putting the cutting edge on the diamonds.

It appears to be one of the most extraordinary facts in nature that there exists this enormous difference in hardness between the diamond, so completely infinitesimal in bulk, and all other materials. Carbonate is found in connection with the diamond proper, or valuable gem, in the mines of Brazil. It has not as yet been discovered in the diamond diggings of Africa; why, the writer cannot say.

The chemical composition of carbonate and of valuable diamond is stated to be the same, only that the gem is crystallised, while the carbonate is uncrystallised. The writer apprehends it is the fact of its having no stratification which makes the carbonate so valuable for commercial purposes, a bright diamond being more brittle or likely to split; hence, apart from their relative values, for the present purpose the less valuable material is the best. The first carbonate was introduced into Europe as a speculation, and was offered to the diamond cutters at Amsterdam as a material equal in hardness to the diamond dust they were using, and of only a nominal value. Such however was the effect of prejudice, that it was rejected, and at first a hatful of carbonate might have been purchased at *4d.* per carat; but now, depending on its quality, it is worth from 15*s.* to 25*s.* per carat.

In boring into rocks, the hardest known steel is of no use except percussion is used, because, if it is attempted to give a cutting or rubbing action to a steel tool, it is impossible to construct it so that it can work for more than a comparatively short time. Mechanics having only steel at their disposal have been driven therefore to employ percussion in designing machinery for making holes in rocks. It is well known how comparatively difficult it is to give a definite percussive motion and to control it; and how, unless an altogether disproportionate amount of strength be given to the parts, it is impossible to construct a machine to do a great amount of work in striking blows, and yet to be durable. Moreover the work done by the hammer, and its source of power, ought not to be far / apart; or in other words, a series of blows represents work done in a shape in which it is very difficult to transmit it to a distance.

The use of the diamond in this case breaks, as it were, the bottom of Columbus' egg,[4] and many of the difficulties attending machinery for dealing with rocks vanish at once. As an illustration, what a wonderful improvement would be the use of an auger in boring holes in wood, if the only means of drilling that material were hammering a nail in and pulling it out again, or cutting a hole with a gouge and mallet.

The application of the diamond to Mining purposes may be described as the power of making holes in the hardest substance, rapidly, continuously, and without striking blows. For shallow holes, such as those required for ordinary quarry work, shaft sinking, or tunnel driving, the relative advantage of the diamond drill is not so great as it is where holes of a greater depth are required; and the greater the depth, the greater is the advantage of the system: inasmuch as, while difficulties accumulate rapidly with the depth of a hole made by percussion, with the diamond drill they remain the same, and an almost unlimited depth could be drilled without withdrawing the tool, which in the case of deep prospecting holes is a very lengthy operation.

The diamonds are set in a steel crown, as shown in Figs. 18 and 19, Plate 16, and in the specimen exhibited. The crown is kept supplied with water, and is rotated at from 200 to 300 rev. per min., under a pressure varying with the nature of the rock from 300 to 800 lb. Under these circumstances the writer has seen the hard Pennant rock of South Wales cut at the rate of 6 in. per min., a 3 ft. 6 in. hole being put down in 7 min. and a 2 ft. 6 in. in 5 min., and this not as an exhibition, but at the bottom of a shaft in course of construction. /

Donald M. D. Stuart, 'The Development of Explosives for Coal-Mines' (1904–5)

Donald M. D. Stuart,[1] 'The Development of Explosives for Coal-Mines', *Transactions of the North of England Institute of Mining and Mechanical Engineers*, 55 (1904–5), pp. 205–34.

THE DEVELOPMENT OF EXPLOSIVES FOR COAL-MINES.

By DONALD M. D. STUART.

When considering a subject in which the results of experiment and experience have come into conflict, it is useful to recall its past history and trace the sources of disagreement, in order to profit by the teachings of experience; and this is true in an important sense of mining explosives, which affect the best interests of the greatest industry in the kingdom.

Some thirty years ago, gunpowder was without a rival in coal-mining and had enjoyed this position in the previous two centuries. It had proved to be so simple and effective a blasting agent, that the necessity for other substances did not arise; but new explosives were now discovered, and brought into prominence by the Report of the Select Committee upon Explosive Substances[2] appointed by the House of Commons in 1874, and from that time onward the subject has been under constant investigation. These new or modern explosives have claimed the attention of successive Royal Commissions and Mining Institutions. The Royal Commission appointed to inquire into Accidents in Mines, 1879; the Flameless Explosives Committee appointed by The North of England Institute of Mining and Mechanical Engineers, 1888; and the Royal Commission on Explosions from Coal-dust in Mines, 1891,[3] devoted years to the investigation of the subject. The transactions of the Mining Institutions record constant observation and research, and the Departmental Committee[4] appointed, in 1896, by the Principal Secretary of State for the Home Department, to inquire into the Testing of Explosives for Use in Coal-mines, has for the last eight years carried out continuous tests by firing the new explosives in inflammable gaseous mixtures, so as to ascertain which could be fired as blown-out shots without igniting the mixture. These investigations have led to the production of numerous explosives and the development of gunpowder to a high standard of safety and efficiency. /

This evolution arose from the facts that colliery explosions were sometimes caused by blasting, and that in the coal-dust[5] pervading many coal-mines there lay a peril which could be awakened into terrible activity by fire-damp ignited at a shot, and even by the shot itself. The ideal explosive was therefore suggested to be one that, while possessing efficient blasting action, would not ignite fire-damp, nor distil[6] and ignite the educts[7] of coal-dust.

The first stage in the evolution was the introduction of nitro-explosives represented by dynamite, lithofracteur, gun-cotton[8] and other substances that exploded with a rapidity enormously in excess of gunpowder. According to Mr. Is. Trauzl,[9] whose researches were adopted by the Prussian Fire-damp Commission of 1881, a cartridge of grain-gunpowder, 13 inches long, required 0.03 second for complete ignition, but only 0·000,6[10] second was needed to explode a similar cartridge of dynamite. Mr. Trauzl also reported that a grain of confined gunpowder burned off at a speed of 10 millimetres (0.394 inch) per second, with a transmission of the flame from grain to grain of 10 metres (32.80 feet) per second; but unconfined charges of gun-cotton and dynamite detonated with a velocity of 16,500 to 19,500 feet per second.* With these results, the Prussian Commission reported that the enormous rapidity of explosion of high explosives, constituted a fundamental element of safety, reducing the peril of ignition of fire-damp or coal-dust to a minimum, not to say vanishing point; and concluded that the lightning-like rapidity of explosion went far towards limiting, if not excluding, the possibility of ignition of fire-damp by blasting.††

The idea of safety in rapidity of explosion, was a development of Sir Humphrey Davy's researches,[12] in which he found that fire-damp differed materially in combustibility from common inflammable gases, and required exposure to an ignition-temperature for an appreciable time in order to effect its explosion. The question was examined by the French Commission on the Use of Explosives in the Presence of Fire-damp in Mines, and Messrs. E. Mallard and H. Le Chatelier described the phenomenon as 'retardation / of ignition.'‡ When a mixture of

* 'Report of the Prussian Fire-damp Commission,'[11] translated by Dr. P. Phillips Bedson and Mr. L. L. Belinfante, *Trans. Inst. M.E.*, 1893, vol. iv., page 672.

† *Ibid.*, page 672.

‡ *Report of the French Commission on the Use of Explosives in the Presence of Fire-damp in Mines*, translated by Messrs. W. J. Bird and M. Walton Brown, 1890, page 21.[13]

fire-damp and air was raised to a temperature of 1,202° Fahr. (650° Cent.) it was reported that the retardation may amount to 10 seconds; and as the gases of high explosives were produced at an exalted pressure, they would expand and cool below the ignition-point of fire-damp in some thousandths of a second, or a minute fraction of the period of gaseous contact essential to ignition.*

The Royal Commission appointed to Inquire into Accidents in Mines[14] carried out independent investigations, and reported in 1886 that dynamite, gelatine-dynamite, cottonpowder, tonite and potentite[15] would prevent colliery explosions, even by blown-out shots in explosive gaseous atmospheres containing inflammable coal-dust, provided that they were fired in water-cartridges;[16] which, the Royal Commissioners observed, could be done cheaply, simply and without restriction.†

TABLE I. – COLLIERY EXPLOSIONS.

Date.	Colliery.	Explosive Used.
1878	Wester Gartshore	Dynamite
1882	London and South Wales	Dynamite
1884	Naval	Dynamite
1887	National	Gelatine-dynamite, with water-cartridge
1889	Hebburn	Roburite and gelignite
1890	Shelton	Tonite
	Holly Lane	Tonite
	Thorncliffe	Roburite
1891	Apedale	Gelignite, with water-cartridge
1894	Albion	Gelatine-dynamite
1896	Tylorstown	Ammonite

The conclusions of the Prussian, French and British Commissions were not confirmed by practice, and many colliery explosions occurred where high explosives were adopted, both with and without the water-cartridge, some of which are recorded in Table I.

These explosions disclosed the fact that there was a fundamental difference between the conditions of the experiments made for the Commissioners, and the conditions prevalent in the mines; in the former, the explosives proved incapable of causing explosions / of fire-damp or coal-dust, and in the latter they caused explosions of both. This difference in conditions had evidently eluded observation, and collieries that had not suffered explosions by shot-firing for long periods of years while using gun-powder, were now the scenes of explosions while using high explosives substituted with the advice that they would more certainly sustain the record.

* *Ibid.*

† *Final Report*, 1886, page 60.

The disturbing factors that permitted such contrary results to arise between experimental results and practical work, were not adequately considered; and great efforts were made to fasten attention upon the flame of explosives, as the source of gaseous and coal-dust ignitions. The Prussian and British Commissions attached much importance to the presence of flame in a fired explosive, as an indication of danger; and the phrase, 'flameless explosive' was adopted to introduce the nitrate-of-ammonium compounds. An explosive that did not yield flame, was claimed to be innocuous, even if fired in the presence of fire-damp or coal-dust. Both phrase and claim were important, and awakened great interest, insomuch that in 1888 The North of England Institute of Mining and Mechanical Engineers appointed the 'Flameless Explosives Committee' to investigate them. The Committee arranged their experiments to approximate in a measure to the conditions of practical blasting, in angling the line of fire to the axis of the gas-tube, thereby interfering with the velocity at which the products of the explosives were projected through the gaseous mixture; and by means of sight-holes in the side of the gas-tube, direct observations were made of the condition of the products as they issued from the mouth of the cannon and passed through the gaseous mixture. The Committee carried on their investigation for some years, and reported that the high explosives, ammonite, ardeer-powder, bellite, carbonite, roburite and securite[17] produced evident flame, and that the flame from blown-out shots was not prevented by the quantity or length of the stemming.[18]

The phrase, 'flameless explosive' having proved to be untenable, the supporters of these explosives rechristened them 'safety explosives,' and under this title their substitution for gunpowder was vigorously pressed upon owner, agent and manager of mines, in blue books, papers to Mining Institutes, / and journals of the coal-trade, with the assurance that they were the panacea for colliery explosions. The substitution was adopted to but a fractional extent, as in the predominant judgment of owner, agent and manager, gunpowder was the safest, all round and most efficient explosive; and they continued to use it.

The claims of the 'safety explosives' were laid before the Royal Commission on Explosions from Coal-dust in Mines, with an appalling list of explosions alleged to have been caused by gunpowder-shots, and the results of some experiments made with 'safety explosives' and gunpowder, which were claimed to prove that explosions and blasting accidents would almost entirely disappear if gunpowder were prohibited and 'safety explosives' compulsorily substituted. The Royal Commissioners, however, reported that several high explosives 'may be practically safe for all purposes,'* but declined to recommend the universal prohibition of gunpowder, and advised that where its use may be open to ques-

* *Second Report of the Royal Commission on Explosions from Coal-dust in Mines*, 1894, page xxviii.

tion, the Secretary of State for the Home Department should direct certain precautions to be adopted.

The mining industry was not largely influenced by the experiments made with the 'safety explosives,' nor by the claims made for them; long experience with high-grade gunpowder left no doubt that, in practical hands, it was the safest and best explosive; and the 'safety explosives' made very little progress. /

William Waller, 'On Pumping Water' (1866–7)

William Waller,[1] 'On Pumping Water', *Transactions of the North of England Institute of Mining Engineers*, 16 (1866–7), pp. 135–6.

ON PUMPING WATER.

By WILLIAM WALLER.

What should be the cost of raising 1,000 gallons of water 100 feet is a question of vital importance to all parties interested in raising coal. My experience is offered, with the following observations, to supply some answer to this question.

It was stated at the Birmingham Meeting of the British Association[2] that the quantity of water raised over the 125 square miles constituting the South Staffordshire Coal-field, was 50,000,000 gallons per 24 hours (representing ten times the weight of coal raised), at a yearly cost of £125,000, or, deducting five per cent. on the stated capital employed, £500,000, at a cost of £100,000. In endeavouring to ascertain the depth [from which] this quantity was lifted, I have been informed that 128 yards or 384 feet may be taken as the average depth of the pits of the whole field. Assuming this depth to be the average of the lifts, and the quantities raised by each to be equal, pumping on the South Staffordshire Coal-field costs 343 pence per 1,000 gallons raised 100 feet, or, in other words, per million foot pounds. In endeavouring to establish a comparison between this and the Northumberland and Durham District, I have not at command the same details to guide me that I have quoted for South Staffordshire, and, therefore, cannot come to any conclusion on the matter, except, that from observation I should think it would not be below the 343 pence per million foot pounds above given. But as it was stated, at the aforesaid Birmingham Meeting, that fifteen times more water was lifted than coal in this district, and as the coal lifted in 1865 was 25,000,000 tons, there are something like 84,000,000,000 gallons to raise, say the same height, viz., 384 feet, which, at the same rate, would cost £459,200. This sufficiently shows the importance of the matter.

I propose to place beside these data the results obtained under my own observation in waterworks for the supply of towns, where generally the / work is more economically executed. Should any object that these are not parallel cases, I submit that the mining engine, works under more advantageous circumstances, for this reason, that, being necessarily in the first instance sufficient to reduce the water, in keeping it at the reduced level it is working well within its power, and under very economical conditions; whereas, the waterworks engine having to contend with ever varying demands, with extra and intermittent exertion, with increased friction and resistance in restricted pipe area, is under every disadvantage. For the purposes of comparison, however, they may be considered as working under similar circumstances.

The Wolverhampton Waterworks raise water from two wells, and the work done in 1849 was equal to raising 426,000,000 gallons 100 feet high, and the cost (coal 7s. 6d. per ton) £750 per annum, being about 422 pence per million foot pounds.

There are two pumping stations, one at Tettenhall, and one at Goldthorn, the former 140 feet deep, the latter 300 feet deep. The standpipe of the Tettenhall engine is 180 feet high, making a lift of 320 feet. The pumps have plungers 13 inches diameter and 10 feet stroke.

The South Staffordshire Waterworks, in 1859, raised 1,250,000 gallons 450 feet high, at a cost of·22 pence per million foot pounds.

The East London Waterworks Company, in 1849, with 2121½ tons of coal, at 10s. 6d. per ton, raised 2,889,000,000 gallons 100 feet high; and Mr. Wickstead[3] states the total cost of lifting a million foot pounds, taken on the average of several years, with the different engines, to be as under:–

Single-acting Engine, Bolton and Watt		... ...	·543 pence.
Two	do.	do.	·358 „
Two	do.	do.	·333 „
Single-acting Cornish Engine, Harvey & Co.		... ...	·150 „

We see here, from high authority, what a very important difference there is in the duty of the several engines in the same undertaking.

The Southwark and Vauxhall Company, in 1849, with 2920 tons of coal, at 10s. per ton, raised 4,061,000,000 gallons 100 feet high, or 084 pence for coal for lifting a million foot pounds, making the very liberal addition of five-sevenths for labour, repairs, wear and tear, etc. This gives 144 pence per million foot pounds.

The Grand Junction Company,[4] in 1849, with 3170 tons of coal, at 14s. 6d. per ton, raised 2,810,000,000 gallons 100 feet high, or 192 pence for coal alone, for lifting a million foot pounds; adding labour, etc., as before, this gives·276 pence per million foot pounds. /

Matthias Dunn, *A Treatise on the Winning and Working of Collieries* (1848)

Matthias Dunn,[1] *A Treatise on the Winning and Working of Collieries: Including Numerous Statistics and Remarks on Ventilation, and Illustrated by Plans and Engravings. To Which Are appended a Glossary and Index* (Newcastle-upon-Tyne: The author, 1848).

SECTION X.

VENTILATION OF MINES.

In order suitably to conduct the operations of a mine, a good system of ventilation is imperative, which consists of the conveyance of a succession of atmospheric air through the workings, which must be sufficiently powerful, not only to enable the people to respire freely, but also to dilute or carry off the continual product of carburetted hydrogen or carbonic acid gases,[2] which are inseparable from the working of mines.

For a series of years past, this subject has been the continued theme of newspaper controversies and theoretic disquisitions, and it has also been discussed in Parliament, whenever the public mind has been roused to sympathy by sudden explosions, accompanied with loss of life. The merits of the different systems of ventilation, therefore, it is my intention to bring under notice; but I will first / proceed to shew the origin and progress, as well as the amount of perfection to which present practice has obtained in different parts of the kingdom.

The basis of ventilation consists of a spacious upcast and downcast shaft, with adequate air-courses underground; but as the air will not, of its own accord, continue steadily to ascend the upcast shaft, the current must be carried by some artificial means.

The most simple, ancient, and up to the present moment I may say the most practically efficient plan, is *rarefaction*,[3] viz., the placing contiguous to the bottom of the upcast shaft a *lamp* or *furnace* ... to be constantly kept burning, and whose natural effect, both upon the air-current and upon the shaft, is to produce an acceleration to the air, corresponding with the space of the air courses and the magnitude of the furnace, and this is by rarefication of the air.

In very early times, a tube or high chimney was built contiguous to the top of the upcast shaft, into which tube a fire or furnace was occasionally introduced, but experience shewed that it was more efficacious when applied to the shaft itself.

Objections to this application have been found, inasmuch as where the *return air*[4] becoming vitiated with inflammable gas to a dangerous amount, frequent instances have occurred of the said air exploding at the flame of the furnace.

To obviate this objection, it is customary to feed the furnace with fresh and *uncontaminated* air, whilst a separate passage, called a *dumb drift*[5] ... is provided for the general return air of the pit, which passes into the shaft at an outlet considerably superior to that of the furnace air.

It may perhaps be as well here to take a cursory view of the many other devices which have, from time to time, been practised, to produce a lively current, and to avoid the danger of explosion, viz.:– /

1. A continuous *jet of steam*, sent to a considerable depth down the upcast shaft, and there discharged, with a view of increasing the temperature and adding to the velocity of the air current. This device was practised at Hebburn colliery, immediately after the creep[6] of 1811, when the quantity of inflammable air which was then under discharge, prevented the ordinary application of the furnace.

In the year 1835 Mr. Gurney[7] communicated to the Parliamentary Committee,[8] an improved plan of the application of high pressure steam, which was afterwards made the subject of detailed descriptions of his apparatus, to the South Shields committee[9] upon accidents in mines, and which met with the approval of the enlightened members of that committee, although I cannot discover that it has ever been acted upon.

2. *Air pump*. – This exhausting power was also during the same period applied at Hebburn colliery.... It consisted of a square cylinder, constructed of three-inch planks, eight feet long and six feet square, within which a piston was worked by means of a steam engine; it was furnished with four valves, with corresponding side pipes, for the suction and discharge of the air of the mine; thirty strokes per minute, five feet long, was its ordinary speed, by which means it would extract five thousand four hundred cubic feet of air per minute, and which effected a very tolerable substitute for a furnace.

At St. Leonard, upon the Sambre, in Belgium, an air pump was used of the following dimensions:–

	Metre of 37.39 inches.
One cylinder, diameter . .	2.59
Stroke of piston	2.16
Number of strokes per minute	21

This machine would extract two hundred and thirty nine cubic metres of air per minute, and was worked by a steam-engine of twenty horse power.

3. The *hot cylinder* ... was applied in the reopening of a portion of Wallsend colliery, after the derangement by the creep. It consisted of a cylinder ... built into masonry ... and around which were applied heating flues, the intended effect being to produce rarefaction and an increased impulse of the air current, which had to pass through it from the upcast shaft ... ; but the application of fire so nearly connected with air, which might perchance be inflammable, carried with it considerable alarm.

4. The *fan blast*[10] is sometimes employed in Belgium, and also in North Wales, to force a current of air into the mine, by means of wooden or iron pipes; but it is a weak and fanciful resource, especially in collieries producing so little of inflammable air as to be capable of being ventilated by the most simple of the rarifying processes.

5. *Fall of water*[11] – is simple and tolerably efficacious. It is generally had recourse to after explosions, in order to carry down and increase the supply of atmospheric air to the workings, in which the derangement of the air-courses may have rendered the furnace inoperative.

The *spiral* ... is considerably used in Belgium, and is constituted as follows:– The top of the upcast pit, for eight yards in depth and twenty feet in diameter, is formed into a perfect cylinder, into which is introduced an axis twenty feet long, whereon is affixed a spiral[12] of sheet iron fitted closely into the said smoothened shaft, and a steam engine applied to communicate centrifugal motion, with a speed proportionate to the size and power of the machinery; the revolutions of the said axis are generally about three hundred per minute. /

Mr. Gibbons' System. – Before closing this part of the subject, it might be thought invidious were I to omit a proposed invention of Mr. Edward Gibbons,[13] of South Staffordshire, who has already written a treatise upon the subject, and who has succeeded in converting to his opinion not a few theorists and credulous practical miners, and amongst others who bear testimony to his scientific improvements, is Mr. Tremenhere,[14] the government commissioner, whose numerous advantages in the examination of the different systems of mining should have enabled him to be a competent judge. He thus describes Mr. Gibbons' system:– 'Taking advantage of the natural tendency of the gas to ascend, Mr. G.'s plan is to open for it a passage, about two feet square, along the upper part of the stratum of coal, and up the side of the winding shaft, and thence into a chimney from sixty to ninety feet high. The winding shaft thus acts as a downcast shaft for the stream of pure air, and the expense of an upcast shaft is saved, as the air channel of two feet square (or three feet by two) fully answers the purpose. Sometimes a fire is added to the chimney to increase the draft.'

Since none of these various methods have found favour with persons accustomed to the management of the most extensive and difficult collieries, I therefore infer that up to this period, for cheapness and effect, no improvement has taken place in the general principle of *simple rarefaction* produced by an efficient furnace, as there is no difficulty by that means of producing an air current of fifty or sixty thousand cubic feet per minute. /

Having, in the above pages, detailed the systems of ventilation as practical in their most approved state, it may naturally be expected that I should particularise some of those which are self-evidently defective, – that is to say, inadequate both in scientific principle and ordinary practical knowledge.

First, then, I may mention that in a great many collieries we find no ventilating furnace, or if such there be, ten to one but it be either too diminutive, or fitted up so ineffectively that it cannot maintain an air current in an uniform manner.

Until lately, it was quite common to see collieries dependant for their ventilation upon a wooden box of twelve or fourteen inches / square, sometimes led to the engine fire as a substitute for a proper furnace, and sometimes operated upon by a small revolving fanner, worked by a steam engine. There is often a great inattention in the maintenance of the *air ways* in an open and travellable state, but the air is just left to squeeze its way through passages almost impervious to the air, and consequently liable to continual contraction and stoppage by the falling down of the roof. I need hardly express the dangerous consequence of allowing the Davy safety lamps to remain in the hands of the workmen unattended to, or of permitting them to be the proper judges as to when and where they ought to be used, as the more advantageous light of the candle continually tempts them to incur the risk of explosion.

In many of the thick seam collieries, and also in extensive collieries, the quantum of atmospheric air is altogether disproportioned to the space requiring to be ventilated, hence the constant succession of accidents arising from accumulations of gases. In short, where collieries are of minor importance, or in which the working may be let to butties or contractors,[15] the proprietor too often loses sight of the advantage that would accrue both to him and to his people by the employment of some intelligent and scientific manager; hence the fact that life and property are left in the hands of persons inadequately educated and experienced.

Nothing is more common than to hear persons express opinions that practical colliers are the most efficient persons to conduct, economically, a coal mine, forgetting that true *practical science* includes economy, whilst it enables the individual to take that comprehensive view of the whole subject, in which men of a different description will ever be found, in respect to management, to be most ineffective. /

SECTION XIV.

SOUTH SHIELDS COMMITTEE'S REPORT.

The subject of colliery ventilation cannot with any regard to justice, be dismissed without some reference to the valuable records of the South Shields Committee upon accidents in coal mines, that report having been for some time out of print, and as I generally approve of the plan and arrangement, as well as admire the energy, talent, and science, which it displays in every page, I think it advisable to give copious extracts from that valuable document, without the remarks usually appended to printed extracts.

The committee were appointed in the year 1839, after the deplorable explosion at the neighbouring colliery of St. Hilda, by which fifty-two lives were lost. The Secretary of the Society was Mr. James Mather, a gentleman, educated for the medical profession, but who has recently distinguished himself, by his scientific / and literary labours in the cause of humanity, and in the advancement of the commercial and municipal prosperity of his native town.[16]

Very different indeed was the system pursued by this committee to that followed by certain theorists, who have from time to time given to the public an accumulation of unphilosophic and impracticable suggestions. This committee commenced their labours by visiting the most deep and dangerous mines of the district, examining in detail the ventilating process in the shafts, as also in the workings, so as to be conversant with the different plans adopted, in order not only to ventilate but also to remove from the pits the origin of these calamities, – we learn from their report that they had persevered in their investigations and researches to such a degree of perfection, as to set at defiance the criticism of practical viewers, as well as psuedo philosophers, in a word it is my duty here, to bear testimony of their untiring and highly valuable services.

1. SAFETY LAMPS.

The first section of the report is devoted to a description of the different safety lamps, the dates of their invention, and the peculiar qualities belonging to each. The subject is no doubt most important and interesting, but it is not my intention to enter further upon it, than to notice their concluding remarks before they pass on to the more important one of ventilation.

The committee have to report after the most minute investigations and experiments, which they have been able to devote to this branch of their subject, that in their opinion no mere safety lamp however ingenious in its construction, is able to secure fiery mines from explosion, and that a reliance on lamps alone is a fatal error, conducive to those dreadful calamities which they are intended to / prevent. The committee further report that they are of a decided conviction according to the foregoing premises, that the naked Davy lamp is without a complete shield, a most dangerous instrument, and has indubitably been productive of those accidents in mines, against which it is still too confidently and generally employed, at the daily imminent risk of producing a like calamity.

The committee regret to observe that from some erroneous conviction, or other less defensible cause, this mode of securing safety in mines, has been beyond all reasonable bounds relied upon, whilst the far more important and safe system of ventilation has been comparatively neglected.

2. VENTILATION.

The report next adverts to this, the most interesting and important subject of their labours, and in which they have displayed their great tact and sound judgment.

The committee ascertained, that the average velocity of air through the passages of mines in the present system, does not generally exceed three feet per second,[17] in many instances where the mine is dangerous it is considerably less. Three or four collieries are then given in evidence, in respect to their ventilation. The first example, had seventy to seventy-five miles of passages, and only one shaft, 13½ feet diam. for ventilation, drawing of coals, pumping of water, and every other necessary operation between the surface and the works.

The shaft was 850 feet deep, – and divided for 480, into three portions, the downcast, the engine, and upcast shaft, but at that depth the engine shaft air passed into a high seam workings, at that time unemployed, and the pit to the bottom 370 feet, was contracted in its diameter to 10½ feet, divided into two equal parts, one for downcast, the other upcast. /

By the above arrangement, the upper part of the shaft, contains

For upcast – – – – – 36 square feet.*

Three baskets[18] were passing at a time in each shaft, and when in motion were drawn against the downcast current, at the rate of 9½ feet per second, the air having a velocity of only 8½.

* Which in point of fact constitutes the ventilating power, the surplus downcast, not producing any effect.

Each corf in area, 8½ feet, leaving a total downcast of 28½, and upcast 27½ feet area. So that this extensive mine of 400 acres, 850 feet below the surface, contains but a passage of six feet, by five feet square, to supply all exigencies, – being equal to about 29,500 cubic feet of air per minute, supplying the mine of thirty millions of cubic feet of passages, which if it travelled the entire course without being divided, would at that rate take sixteen hours at least. But the air is split into two great columns of ⅔ and ⅓. The whole column, before splitting, moves with a velocity of 435 feet per minute, in an area of 64½ feet, but one-third of this air being separated for a waste section of the mine, the two-thirds consisting of about 19,500 cubic feet, is then carried down to the principle workings. This air losing one-third of its volume in the same area, is decreased in velocity to nearly 300 feet per minute, but as it passes into the *sheths*,[19] or divisions of the workings, and is coursed up and down the boards,[20] it is split into there distinct columns, each of 90 feet area, and there creeps along sluggishly at a rate of 66 feet per minute, or one and one-tenth of a foot per second, through five-sevenths of the entire mine.

The committee upon this subject conclude – that the fault is in the system not in the officers, and men – but the committee are perfectly convinced that with such a small force of ventilation / as can be obtained by the present plan, and as in the north is commonly pursued, (which the instance just detailed demonstrates,) no human foresight or skill in its application can obviate these explosions, while this imperfect ventilation is allowed to continue.

2*d. Example*, – The shaft, which was bratticed,[21] contained an area, – after deducting for space occupied for corves, of one hundred and twenty-two feet – was one thousand feet deep, and the main column was divided into several splits. These splits the committee successively examined, and found to consist as follows:–

	Area.		Feet per second.
1	65	. .	3
2	60	. .	5½
3	60	. .	3 and 1-10th
4 (Boards)	90	. .	1
5	. .	. .	1⅛

Thus reducing the general ventilation considerably lower than one-half of that stated in the evidence of Messrs. Buddle and Wood.

Example, 3rd. – Had a detached upcast shaft of eight feet diameter, with furnace placed in the lowest of four seams, being 700 feet from the surface. In the furnace drift[22] of this colliery, 45 feet area, the air passed with a velocity of 4·3 feet per second = 11,610 cubic feet per minute. The entire upcast of the four mines, fifty and a quarter feet area, consisted of 50,064 cubic feet per minute – each of the seams having its peculiar proportion of air.

In one of the leading passages, having a twenty-eight feet area, the current passed at the rate of six feet per second=10,080 cubic feet per minute, which, on being subdivided in the boards or waste, would not admit a rate of one foot per second, or two-thirds of a mile per hour, and which, in the upper mines, would be less. /

Example, 4th. – Depth, one thousand five hundred and eighty feet, with a single shaft –

	Area	Feet p. sec.	Cubic ft. p. sec.
The air travelling in the chief passage,	36 sq. feet	.....7....	252
" Another passage .	18 do.	..... ·66....	....

The temperature of the mine was eighty Fahrenheit,[23] and is remarkable for the evolution of a very small proportion of gas.

The Committee observe that – Had the gas in this colliery been of the same abundance as in some of the mines already noticed, the very trifling volume of air passed into this mine, on the usual principles of dilution acted on, would, if not improved in a short time, have compelled its relinquishment, by the production of a series of explosions, which would have laid it waste, and deterred the boldest from entering it.

In page thirty-five follows the particulars of a visit to a mine of six hundred feet in depth, working altogether on pillars, with an upcast shaft of eight feet diameter. In proceeding to the workings, they remarked that the air was so weak that it scarcely bent the flame of the lamp from its perpendicular, and was scarcely perceptible to the senses – the air losing its way in progressing to the workings by the imperfectly stopped passages. The object was to get a pressure of air upon the goaves[24] from the men, that the gas might be carried off along with it, but from one cause or other, these workings were continually getting fouled, the gas having to come off the goaves backward.

The Committee are, therefore, obliged, from a strong sense of public duty, to record their conviction derived from personal inspection of many mines, and the fullest official information of many others, *that the system and rate of ventilation of the mines of this extensive coal district, require a great and important change*, for, if / allowed to continue, there is scarcely a single mine amongst them, with one or two rare exceptions, that, in a day or an hour, may not be plunged, by some easy contingency, into a destructive explosion; and that this state of things is produced by too few shafts, to the extent of underground workings, and the consequent slow rate of air which is produced to sweep the passages, rapidly to remove, or fully to dilute the gas. /

William Cochrane, 'Description of Guibal's Ventilator, at Elswick Colliery' (1864–5)

William Cochrane,[1] 'Description of Guibal's Ventilator, at Elswick Colliery', *Transactions of the North of England Institute of Mining Engineers*, 14 (1864–5), pp. 73–81.

DESCRIPTION
OF
GUIBAL'S VENTILATOR, AT ELSWICK COLLIERY.

By WILLIAM COCHRANE.

The ventilation of mines by machinery, though it has been at various times brought before this Institute, and its advantages pointed out in special cases, has not received the full consideration which its importance warrants; and practically the adoption of machinery in this country, instead of the generally adopted furnace system, has made very little progress. The attention of mining engineers has lately been more particularly drawn to this subject, and if a system can be established which will produce the large volumes of air required in the most extensive mines with greater economy and safer action than the furnace, doubtless it will have a claim of preference, for the position of the furnace in the mine itself, the liability to communicate fire to the coal seam or to portions of the shaft, and the most objectionable use of a furnace upcast shaft for the conveyance of either coals or men, also the damage to materials in the shaft, the necessity of slackening the furnace for examination of the drifts, often when by atmospheric variation a contrary step should be adopted for the ventilation of the mine, and, lastly, the waste of fuel – these are objections so serious as must induce the more extended adoption of machinery at the surface, when its merits are as well known in this country as they are abroad. Besides, thinner sections of coal seams are being rapidly brought into operation, and the furnace will be found incompetent to yield the power requisite for satisfactory ventilation, as the cost of providing spacious air-courses becomes too great for the economical working of the seams.[2] In consequence of the much higher resistances with which machine ventilators can cope, and in the case of well constructed fans acting by exhaustion the large volumes of air that / can be put into circulation, the latter seem best qualified to overcome the difficulties mentioned. It is proposed, in this paper, to describe such a fan-ventilating machine, recently erected[3] at the Elswick Colliery near this town, which fulfils many of the desirable conditions, and the results obtained from experiments thereon will serve for comparison with, other systems of ventilation, while they will, it is hoped, provoke discussion on the general subject An accurate comparison of the furnace with the various mechanical ventilators is in the hands of some of our Government Inspectors for investigation, and it would be well if the results they establish could be early published.

The ventilator is upon the principle of an exhausting fan.[4] It consists of eight vanes, each of which is formed of 1 ¼ inch oak cleading,[5] secured by bolts to a pair of bars and angle irons, which are bolted to two cast iron octagonal bosses keyed on the main shaft. These bars being carried past the boss and interlaced, as shown in the accompanying drawing, form a very firm structure, at the same time simple and inexpensive, admitting of a speed of as much as one hundred and fifty or two hundred revolutions per minute, without any danger. This is an important improvement in construction, as it will be seen from Mr. Atkinson's paper[6] upon the Elsecar Fan (Vol. XI. of Proceedings) that its construction rendered a higher speed than sixty revolutions per minute dangerous.

The outside diameter of the vanes is twenty-three feet, the width six feet six and three-quarter inches, and each vane extends about eight feet into the interior of the fan, being inclined at an angle of sixty-seven and a half degrees to a radial line through the apex of the octagonal boss.

The main shaft is driven by a vertical direct-acting engine, with cylinder 23⅝ inches internal diameter, and 19¹¹⁄₁₆ inches stroke, worked at high pressure.

A wall is built on each side of the fan, giving about one inch clearance to the side of the vanes. Outside of one wall the engine is fixed, and in the other an inlet orifice of proper size is left (in the Elswick arrangement it is ten feet diameter), such inlet being connected with the upcast shaft. An arch is carried over the fan, giving about two inches clearance to the vanes, and in continuation of this arch an invert to a point about one-eighth of the circumference below the centre line, at which point the two-inch clearance is increased gradually, expanding the lower curve of the casing till it ends in the sloping side of a chimney formed between the continuation of the side walls of the fan-erection, as / shown on the Plate. A sliding shutter is fitted into cast iron grooved rails for about one-fifth of the circumference, which enables the concentric circle of the top arch to be completed nearly round the fan – that is, giving the two-inch clearance to the vanes. This shutter is worked by a chain passing over sheaves at the top of the chimney and to the outside. For convenience, a manhole-door is left at the foot of the sloping side of the chimney.

The fan being set in motion, the air is drawn through the inlet from the mine, and discharged below the shutter into the chimney, from the top of which it is seen to issue at no great velocity.

This system, called from the inventor the 'Guibal Ventilator,' possesses the following important advantages over other machine ventilators:–

1st. – It is of very simple construction, at the same time very firm, and capable of high speed, as well as of constant working without great wear and tear.

2nd. – The theory and practice of exhausting fans having hitherto been, that there should exist a free discharge all round the circumference, this is the first application to mining ventilation of an exhausting fan which is covered in as described, and in the complete arrangement of which are found the requisite correctives of such a covering, which, without them, would still offer only a very ineffective machine. By the covering the opposing action of winds is prevented, which is a serious check to fans discharging all round the periphery; but the object of chief importance is to prevent the communication of motion by the revolving vanes to the surrounding exterior air, and the formation of currents, which, in an open-running fan, creep along the sides and vanes from the exterior air to supply the partial vacuum caused in the interior by the revolution of the fan. As the demonstration of these facts was well seen in an open-running fan at the Tursdale Colliery, county of Durham, it will be perhaps better to refer to it. A sensible diminution of the ventilating current was perceived with a wind from the N. or S, the direction in which the fan discharged; in one instance, with a high South wind, reducing the air-current one-third of its usual quantity with a calm atmosphere. The air-currents from the exterior at all times could be distinctly seen entering the fan by the drawing in with them of the exhaust steam, which was at that time allowed to discharge from the fan engine at the level of the top of the fan. In consequence of Guibal's system being thoroughly and satisfactorily tested in Belgium, it was resolved to adopt / the covering and chimney to the Tursdale fan, which was done, but only temporarily in wood the joints being made as nearly airtight as possible in the covering, but not in the chimney. The improvement will be seen on comparing the following results:[7]–

	Revolutions per minute.	cubic ft of air per minute.	Water gauges.	Steam pressure at cylinder.	Coal consumed in 24 hours.
Open running– May, 1862	50	22,170	·55	25 lbs.	5 tons
Covered in–Oct., 1862	50	32,930	·90	25 lbs.	4 tons

while the power utilized was found to be increased from 12·69 per cent. when open running, to 26·3 per cent when adapted as above described. The useful effect, though much improved, is still far short of what it should be; but it is thought that the construction of the fan is not good, the vanes being too numerous, and not sufficiently extended towards the centre, allowing them to slide through the air without throwing it off at the circumference.

Thus a heavy loss by the entry of exterior air into the open running fan is evident. On the other hand, with the casing and other appliances of the Guibal system, the space outside the vanes, that is between their extremities and the inside of the casing, presents an aid to the ventilating power, instead of a source of loss. Contrary to what might be expected, and contrary to theory (for the air is thrown off the extremities of the vanes against the casing), a partial vacuum is found in this space, the amount of which, at various speeds, will be seen from the annexed tabulated results of experiments. But the covering in of the fan alone would produce the following disadvantages: – it would check the free discharge of the air, and would communicate to it a high velocity – hence the adaptation of the other parts, viz.: –

3rd. – The shutter and chimney, which are the other new elements in this system, and which are claimed by M. Guibal as essential requirements of a perfect ventilating machine. By means of the shutter enlarging or diminishing the outlet, the volume of air drawn by the fan can be so regulated as to suit the special requirements of the mine, and produce the greatest economical effect. By no known theory can the quantity of air be determined which such a ventilating machine will draw from any particular mine; hence the necessity of experimental trials to determine the best size of outlet and the easy means employed for this purpose. If the outlet be too large, air will be drawn back into the fan, as is the case with open running fans, and in this also if the shutter is imperfectly adjusted. If the outlet be too small, the air cannot get quickly enough / away. In either case, economical effect is lost; and as the circumstances of a mine are never long the same, it seems evident that a machine incapable of such an adjustment must be defective. /

The consumption of coals at one boiler, arranged to work this fan, was for twenty-four hours taken over a fortnight, 2 tons 16 cwts., the average speed of the fan being forty revolutions per minute, day and night. This is found to yield sufficient air for the present workings, the quantity passing through the mine being nearly 40,000 cubic feet per minute. The indicated steam pressure at the boiler is 35 lbs, to the square inch, the water gauge at bank near the inlet is ·70 inches, and underground ·70 inches (at higher speeds there is a greater depression at bank than underground), the seam being very low, the return air-courses are of small area, and the upcast is a 11-feet diameter shaft, used for ventilation only. No engineman is required, one of the firemen being instructed to attend to the requisite oiling of the bearings. In some cases the pumping engine-man might take the engine in charge; the simple arrangement of all the parts offers the least possible risk of any of them getting out of order.

In order to test the capabilities of the ventilator, the experiments above tabulated [omitted here] were made, and it will be seen, from the calculated useful effect, how much superior are the results obtained to those of previous machines of the fan type.

The cost of a fan and engine similar to those at Elswick, is about £400, manufactured in Belgium, including patent royalty; the additional cost of erection (bricks costing 25s. per thousand) was £240, including a connecting drift to the upcast.

There remain yet many interesting and important experiments to be made with this ventilator, but i t has been thought advisable to bring the subject before you without further delay, as though the results are somewhat anomalous and require further investigation for accurate analysis, still the generally satisfactory working of the ventilator is clearly established. It is only fair to add that the fan was constructed specially for the circulation of 50,000 cubic feet of air per minute, with a water gauge of 1.5 inches, which it was guaranteed to yield at 60 revolutions. No.9 experiment, therefore, with a useful effect of 52–40 per cent. of the whole power applied and 67–56 per cent. of the power transmitted to the fan, is the nearest to the conditions for which this machine was proportioned. /

S. F. Peckham, 'On the Explosion of the Flouring Mills at Minneapolis, Minnesota, May 2, 1878, and the Causes of the Same' (1878)

S. F. Peckham, 'On the Explosion of the Flouring Mills at Minneapolis, Minnesota, May 2, 1878, and the Causes of the Same', in A. Freire-Marreco and D. P. Morison,[1] 'An Account of Some Recent Experiments with Coal Dust: Discussion', *Transactions of the North of England Institute of Mining and Mechanical Engineers*, 28 (1878–9) pp. 101–66 at pp. 159–63.

ART. XXXIV. – ON THE EXPLOSION OF THE FLOURING MILLS AT MINNEAPOLIS, MINNESOTA, MAY 2, 1878, AND THE CAUSES OF THE SAME. – BY S. F. PECKHAM.2

As I was sitting at the tea-table on the evening of May 2, I was startled by a noise that sounded as if something as heavy as a barrel of flour had been tipped over on the floor above. A few seconds later the sound was repeated, and we all ran to the door, which commanded a full view of the falls[3] and manufacturing portion of the city. An immense volume of black smoke enveloped the spot where the Washburn A Mill[4] had stood, and a perpendicular column of smoke was projected into the air, above the elevator, at least four hundred feet. The Humboldt and Diamond Mills were directly behind the elevator from the place where I stood. A heavy wind was blowing from a point a little to the east of north, a direction from the Washburn A Mill toward the elevator and the other two mills. In less than two minutes from the time of the first explosion, the elevator, which was 108 feet high, was wrapped in flames from top to bottom. If the structure had been saturated in oil the flames could not have spread much more rapidly. In five minutes flame and smoke were pouring from every window in the Day and Rollins, Zenith and Galaxy Mills, which were between the Washburn A Mill and the river, producing a conflagration which, from ordinary causes, would not have gained such headway in two hours. Six flouring mills, the elevator, a machine shop, blacksmiths' shop, and planing mill, with a number of empty and loaded cars, were in flames in five minutes from the time fire was first observed by any one who survived the disaster.[5]

From my own point of observation, which was about a mile distant, but two distinct explosions were heard; others nearer heard three, the first not as violent as the other two; while those nearer still heard, in addition, a sound which they described as a succession of sharp hisses, resembling the sound of burning gunpowder. Those observers to the windward, whose attention was arrested by the light produced, beyond the distance of half-a-mile, heard only one or two reports, or failed to hear any report at all. From all the testimony in reference to sound it appears that the blow upon the / air was not sufficiently sudden to produce a penetrating sound, but rather a dull, heavy blow, which was not communicated laterally to any great distance.

Burning wheat or flour was smelled for several minutes before the explosion, by persons in such a position that the wind would carry the odour to them. Smoke was also seen issuing from what was known as the exhaust flour-dust spout of the Washburn A Mill for several minutes preceding the explosion.

At the instant the explosion occurred, all observers agreed that the Washburn A Mill was brilliantly illuminated from basement to attic. The illumination was reflected from the water at and around the falls in such a manner as to remind one observer of the effect of a brilliant sunset. Another compared it to the reflection of sunlight from windows when the sun is near the horizon. Still another, who was crossing the lower bridge, had his attention called to what appeared to be a stream of fire, which, as he described it, issued from a basement window and went back again. Immediately thereafter each floor above the basement became brilliantly illuminated, the light appearing simultaneously at all the windows, only an appreciable interval of time intervening as the stories ignited one after the other. Then the windows burst out, the walls cracked between the windows and fell, and the roof was projected into the air, followed by an immense volume of smoke and flame, which ascended to an estimated height of from six to eight hundred feet. As the column of smoke was expanded and borne off upon the wind, brilliant flashes resembling lightning passed to and fro.

Two men, so near the Humboldt Mill that they were nearly buried by the falling rubbish, and on the opposite side from the Washburn A Mill, heard a loud report distinctly while the walls of the Humboldt Mill were still standing, and at the same time were knocked down. Immediately after they saw flames issuing from the basement windows of the Humboldt Mill, and, at the same instant, before they could regain their feet, they experienced a second shock and miraculously escaped being buried beneath the falling walls.

The enormous and sudden displacement of air which followed the explosion, and the tremendous force which was consequently exerted laterally, was shown in the condition of the round-house of the Chicago, Milwaukee, and St.

Paul Railroad,[6] and the broken windows in all directions. The round-house was a wooden structure about forty or fifty feet from the Diamond Mill. The sills were drawn out toward that mill until the building burst, letting a part of the roof fall in and leaving the sides standing at a sharp angle. Ordinary windows, and those of strong plate-glass on Washington Avenue, one-fourth of a mile distant, were projected into the street. Not only the glass but the sash went out bodily, particularly in the lower stories of the buildings. Persons on the river at the water's edge noticed a displacement of the water, producing a wave, estimated to be eighteen inches high, before they heard the report of the explosion.

Whole sheets of the corrugated iron with which the elevator was covered, measuring eight by two feet, but quite thin, were picked up on the east side of the river more than two miles distant, and pieces of six-inch flooring from two to ten feet long were carried to intermediate points.

An examination of the ruins of the several buildings showed that the walls of the Humboldt Mill lay upon those of the Diamond Mill, and those of the Diamond Mill upon those of the west end of the Washburn A Mill, showing that the buildings did not explode simultaneously but successively. The Washburn A Mill evidently exploded / first from fire originating within it, and the high wind prevailing at the time carried the flame into the adjoining mills to the south, and away from the mills next the river. There was enough burning middlings[7] and flour thrown through the broken windows of the latter mills to set them on fire, but they did not explode. Some significance may attach to the fact that the three mills that exploded were all running with more or less open French middlings purifiers,[8] while the three that did not explode had been shut down for several days. There is no question but that the French purifiers project a great deal more dust into the atmosphere of the mills than those that are enclosed, but I have no doubt that in any flouring mill sufficient dust accumulates upon beams and machinery to produce an explosive atmosphere, if from any cause this dust is scattered into the air and flame is communicated to the mixture while the dust is suspended.

There was less than a barrel each of lard oil, lubricating oil, and high-test kerosene in the Washburn A Mill at the time of the explosion.

There is absolutely no proof that any explosive material other than is produced in the manufacture of flour from wheat was in any one of the buildings destroyed, in the cars around them, or in the neighbourhood. The testimony of mill wrights conclusively showed that fire produced by heated bearings is of such extremely rare occurrence in flouring mills as to practically exclude such a cause.* No suspicion of incendiarism has ever been expressed.

* These gentlemen concurred in the statement that the spindle which carries the stone had been known to become welded into the socket in which it revolved, stopping the stone. When asked if the friction produced a welding heat, one replied, 'No, nowhere near it.' It must be an example of perfect contact, producing cohesion.

A slight fire, the effects of which were in nowise serious, occurred in the Washburn A Mill about three months before the explosion. It was discovered from the outside of the mill that smoke was issuing from a spout or conductor that discharged the air that was drawn through between the stones. The object for which the air is drawn through is to cool the stones and to carry off the vapour produced from the wheat by the rise of temperature due to friction. In this case the effects of fire were traced back from the outside of the building to one of the sets of stones on the north side of the mill used for grinding middlings. The effects of flame, however, did not extend beyond the blower which produced the exhaust. This led to the conclusion that the fire did not enter the dust-house, although the smoke must have passed through it. It is supposed that the fire was caused by friction between the stones, they having run dry from one of the causes that may produce dry stones.

In answer to enquiries made of several millers in the Minneapolis Mills, I found them uniformly of the opinion that the meal or flour as it left the stones had a temperature of about 100 degrees Fahrenheit,[9] or less. A number of careful experiments, made with an ordinary chemical thermometer, showed that the wheat enters the stones from the dryers at a temperature of fully 100 degrees Fahrenheit, and that it leaves the stones at 120 to 130 degrees Fahrenheit;[10] the temperature of the ground middlings as it left the stones averaged about 10 degrees higher.

It was also the concurrent testimony of millers and mill-owners that dry stones are of comparatively frequent occurrence, and that they are practically unavoidable. I am convinced that in the Washburn A Mill the frequency of danger from dry stones was considerably increased in consequence of the large number of stones in the mill, and especially from the fact that so few men were employed having the immediate oversight / of the stones. Only two men were employed at the same time for the forty-two run of stone, a number inadequate for that supervision which so important a matter demands, as it is impossible, from the large space occupied by so many stones and the noise incident to their action, that even with the usual signals employed, dry stones should be detected as soon as they become a source of danger.

Obstruction of the feed from any one of a number of accidental causes will produce dry stones. The danger arises from the friction of the stones heating the last portion of the grist that remains between the stones to a temperature sufficient to char it, or convert it into a substance resembling tinder, which would readily ignite from a spark produced by the stones striking together. Another source of danger arises from nails or gravel passing between the stones with the grist, and increasing the friction, producing either a rise of temperature or a train of sparks; perhaps both.

I am aware that numerous instances of dry stones can be cited that have proved perfectly harmless. An instance is on record in which a run of stone ground each other all night with no other result than the complete removal of the grooves which gave the stones a cutting face. On the other hand, cases have occurred in which the grooves became filled with charred wheat of a dark brown colour, packed into them so solidly as to require a mill-pick for its removal. It requires no argument to show that this tinder, thus formed, would become ignited from a train of sparks that would inevitably follow contact of the stones as the grist became compacted or completely removed from between them. It was found by experiment* that masses of flour that had become heated and charred, ignited readily and smouldered, but were inflamed with considerable difficulty; but it should be borne in mind that a number of sets of stones are connected with a common spout or conductor, through which a strong current of air is being continually drawn, and which is filled with a dense cloud of very fine particles of starch (chiefly), heated to a maximum temperature of 140 degrees Fahrenheit. Experiment also proved that the proper mixture of flour-dust and air would not burn explosively, except when brought in contact with flame. White-hot wires and glowing charcoal only burned the particles in contact with them; but it was found that burning pellets of charred wheat and flour would ignite wood, which a strong draught of air readily fanned into a blaze. Under the conditions previously stated, with a draught of air passing through the dry stones strong enough to convey the pellets of smouldering tinder into the common wooden conductor, an explosion becomes possible.

It is urged that these conductors are damp from condensed moisture, and also that a large amount of moisture escapes from the wheat and is conveyed away by the current of air. This loss is no doubt correctly estimated at from five to six per cent. It is, however, chiefly during the first grinding of the raw wheat that this loss is experienced. The middlings is dryer, is ground at a higher temperature and is ground finer, producing more dust. The higher temperature renders the material more inflammable, and at the same time ensures a more complete solution of the vapour in the current of air. Moreover, the first fire in the Washburn A Mill was traced directly to a set of stones which ground nothing but middlings, and all that is known concerning the origin of the fire that produced the explosion confirms the supposition that that fire originated in a set of stones on the opposite side of the mill, which was one of six sets, all of which were used exclusively for grinding middlings, discharging into a common spout or conductor, which communicated directly with the dust-house, in which the dust settled to the / amount of several hundred pounds a day. An explosion in this conductor, communicating flame to the dust-house, would scarcely fail to cause the successive explosions of the dust-house and the different storeys of the mill, the shock of the first explosion being sufficient to throw the dust of the mill into the air.

* Experiments made by Professor L. W. Peck before the coroner's jury.

The opinion expressed by one of the witnesses at the inquest, 'that stones are liable to run dry at any time by accident,' and that 'dry stones can hardly be avoided by any amount of foresight,' appears to be generally entertained by millwrights, millers, and mill owners. Let it be granted that all experience shows that 99 per cent. of dry stones injures nothing but the stones themselves, the one per cent. of residue is burthened with fearful possibilities. If dry stones cannot be prevented in small mills where one miller has charge of perhaps six run of stone, the danger is more than proportionally increased in a mill where one man has charge of twenty run, both with reference to prevention and detection. The problem, therefore, for the consideration of parties immediately interested is, how to prevent or detect dry stones, particularly those used for grinding middlings. This practical problem appears to be fundamental, and one compared with which all others are without much importance. It is true that but few millers are without their experience of minor explosions, or flashes resulting from careless use of lanterns or open lights. Indeed, I have been profoundly impressed with the generally innocent reputation of flouring mills when considered in the light of the immense number of accidents well-known to millers and insurance companies; a number surprisingly large if confined to those occurring in the States of Minnesota and Wisconsin within a few years past. The remedy in such cases is so obvious that the most ordinary care and intelligence is sufficient.

Nicholas Wood 'On Safety Lamps for Lighting Coal Mines' (1852–3)

Nicholas Wood,[1] 'On Safety Lamps for Lighting Coal Mines', *Transactions of the North of England Institute of Mining Engineers*, 1 (1852–3), pp. 3–17].

ON SAFETY LAMPS
FOR LIGHTING COAL MINES.
BY THE PRESIDENT,

NICHOLAS WOOD, ESQ.

IN the year 1813 a society was instituted,[2] of which the late Sir Ralph Milbanke, Bart.,[3] was president, for preventing accidents in coal mines; and in 1814 the society published its first report,[4] which practically consisted of a letter from the late Mr. Buddle,[5] on the various modes employed in the ventilation of collieries, illustrated by plans and sections. I need scarcely say that a copy of this letter must be in the possession of every member of the society;[6] as besides, containing a description of the then methods of ventilation, most valuable suggestions were made by that able and sound practical mining engineer, on ventilation generally, and likewise on what was required to complete the system.

At that period the only light used in coal mines was the candle, which was described as being made of ox or sheep tallow, with a cotton wick, forty-five candles to the pound, ox tallow being considered the best.

And, when the air in the mine became mixed with inflammable gas, or carburetted hydrogen gas, the mode of ascertaining its existence, and the degree of inflammability was described by Mr. Buddle as follows:–

'In the first place the candle, called by the colliers the *low*, is trimmed – that is, the liquid fat is wiped off – the wick snuffed short, and carefully cleansed of red cinders, so that the flame may burn as purely as possible.'

'The candle being thus prepared, is holden between the fingers and thumb of the one hand, and the palm of the other hand is placed between the eye of the observer and the flame, so that nothing but the spire of the flame can be seen, as it gradually towers over the upper margin of / the hand. The observation is generally commenced near the floor of the mine, and the light and hand are gently raised upwards till the true state of the circulating current is ascertained.'

'The first indication of the presence of inflammable air is a slight tinge of blue, a bluish grey colour, shooting up from the top of the spire of the candle, and terminating in a fine extended point. This spire increases in size, and receives a deeper tinge of blue, as it rises through an increased proportion of inflammable gas, till it reaches the firing point. But the experienced collier knows accurately enough all the gradations of *shew* (as it is called) upon the candle, and it is very rarely fired upon excepting in cases of sudden discharges of inflammable gas.'

Mr. BUDDLE then goes on further to state, 'that the shew upon the top of the candle varies very much according to the length of run, or distance which the current of air has passed through,' and that 'the same size of spire which would indicate danger in a current which had passed only one mile might be perfectly harmless in a current that had run five or six miles.' That 'the air course for a short distance beyond, a small discharge of fire damp may be highly inflammable; but by passing a few yards further it becomes so diluted as to be perfectly harmless.' And 'that long experience and attentive observation are consequently necessary to obtain a thorough practical knowledge of the art.'

Such was in 1814 the general mode of lighting coal mines, and the above graphic, and correct description of the mode of ascertaining the presence, and of dealing with the existence of inflammable gas, exhibits the delicate, ticklish, and extremely dangerous method of encountering such an insidious enemy.

When from cases of extreme discharge of gas, or in pillar working, the current of air brought to bear upon the enemy was not sufficient to dilute the gas, so as to reduce it below the inflammable point; then the *steel mill* was resorted to.

The steel mill was an instrument well known in the profession, and consisted of a wheel of steel of about 6 inches in diameter turned rapidly round by a wheel and pinion, a dexterous practitioner, then, by applying a piece of flint to the periphery of the wheel a continuous succession of sparks was elicited, and this produced certainly, at best, a precarious, rather uncertain, but certainly a sufficient light to enable the workman to perform some descriptions of work, and at least to travel pretty well through the workings.

This light, however, required one operator with the *mill* to produce a light for one workman, and hence, as may be supposed, in cases where / the mine could not be cleared of gas to such an extent as that candles could with safety be used; the expense was such that the coal could not be worked at all. And hence, very little pillar working in mines discharging inflammable gas could be practised. Looking at the immense extent of the mines in this district, which was thus rendered incapable of being worked, an extent which was daily, and constantly increasing, in the ratio of the quantity of whole coal excavated in those mines which contained gas. It need scarcely be stated then, that a powerful and accumulating incentive existed, to obtain some mode of lighting mines, to enable such a valuable property to be recovered, and brought into profitable and useful productiveness. Added to this also was the prevailing opinion, that the occurrence of frequent accidents, notwithstanding all the 'experience and thoroughly practical knowledge,' alluded to by Mr. Buddle, of the persons in charge of the mines, required some mode of lighting mines liable to be suddenly rendered inflammable, which would not in such cases explode the gas.

Some rather severe accidents which occurred about the year 1814, directed public attention, and still more that of the scientific world more strongly to the subject; Dr. Clanny,[7] to whom the mining interest owes a debt of gratitude, was the first to produce a Lamp by which a light could be used in an inflammable mixture of gas with impunity. The insulation of the flame by this Lamp was by means of water, and though the first Lamp which was produced, it was too complicated and cumbrous for general use.

In the autumn of the year 1815, however, circumstances occurred which accomplished the object required, and which has been productive of consequences in coal mining of the utmost importance to humanity and to the mining and commercial interests of the country generally. At the same time, and in distant localities, the late Mr. George Stephenson and the late Sir Humphrey Davy both produced lamps[8] which insulated lights in inflammable mixtures of fire-damp without exploding the gas externally.

It is not my wish, neither indeed is it necessary to arouse the then much debated question, as to which of those gentlemen the mining interests are indebted for the first discovery of this invention. Enquiries then made, and subsequent investigations have, in my mind, satisfactorily established, that both those gentlemen were original discoverers; and that it was one of those, not indeed only cases in science where two persons in distant localities, without communication with each other, stumbled upon, or made the same discovery at the same time, and as in this case, / arrived at the same results by very different processes of reasoning and deduction.

Having been privy to the whole process by which my lamented friend Mr. Stephenson arrived at his discovery, it may not be out of place, neither is it, I trust, an inappropriate opportunity, to give a short detail of the circumstances by which that gentleman arrived at such a valuable discovery.

Mr. Stephenson had observed, that when the fire-damp was accidentally exploded in narrow drifts or passages, a tangible and considerable time elapsed between the instant of explosion at one end, and the arrival of the inflamed gas at the other – that in fact the explosion passed along the drift or passage at a defined velocity – and, reasoning upon this fact, he supposed that such velocity would be dependent upon the area of the drift and that it was possible to arrest the flame; and he thought if motion could be imparted to the current of air in such a drift in a contrary direction and of a greater velocity than that at which the explosion passed – the explosion could be arrested or prevented from passing along the drift. He had also observed, that when blowers of gas were ignited, and lighted candles were placed to windward of such blowers, the flame of the blowers were extinguished by the burnt air of the candles.

He then conceived, as he himself stated at the time, 'that if a lamp could be made to contain the burnt air above the flame, and to permit the fire-damp to come in below in a small quantity, to be burnt as it came in, the burnt air would prevent the passing of explosion upwards; and the velocity of the current from below would also prevent it passing downwards.'

A lamp was accordingly made of tin, with a hole in the bottom, for the admission of air to the interior of the lamp, and a top perforated with holes. There was also a slide in the bottom to diminish the size of the hole at pleasure. This lamp was tried in inflammable mixtures, and the area of the hole was diminished until the aperture did not pass the flame. It was, however found, that when so diminished, the least quantity of gas in the air put out the lamp. To remedy this, three tubes were used, when it was found that a greater aggregate quantity of air could be admitted into the lamp without passing the flame – and subsequently a lamp with plates perforated with small holes, for the admission of air, was used, which it was found did not pass the flame. At this period of the investigation the reason why the flame did not pass through the apertures was not known. Although it was clear from the number of holes, that the theory of the velocity of the air passing through such / perforations into the lamp did not act in preventing the flame from passing outwards. All this time the burnt air passed through perforations in the top of the lamp.

Mr. Stephenson had now arrived at the discovery that apertures of a certain area did not pass the flame of fire-damp, and had thus discovered the true principles of a safety lamp. Sir H. Davy at about the same time communicated to the Rev. W. Hodgson,[9] of Newcastle, that he had 'discovered that explosive mixtures of mine damp will not pass through small apertures or tubes, and that if a lamp or lanthorn[10] be made airtight on the sides, and furnished with apertures to admit the air, it will not communicate flame to the outward atmosphere,'[11] and he subsequently found that 'iron wire gauze, composed of wires from one-fortieth to one-sixtieth of an inch in diameter, and containing twenty-eight wires, or 784 apertures to the inch, was safe under all circumstances.'[12]

The process by which Sir H. Davy arrived at the above conclusion, is given by himself in a small work 'On the Safety Lamp for Coal Mines with some Researches on Flame,'[13] which explaining the principles on which the safe insulation of the light is accomplished, is interesting. Sir H. Humphrey states – 'I found that it (the fire damp) required to be mixed with large quantities of atmospheric air, to produce explosion; even when mixed with three or nearly four times its bulk of air, it burnt quietly, and extinguished a taper. When mixed with between five and six times its volume of air, it exploded feebly – it exploded with more energy when mixed with seven or eight times its volume of air; and mixtures of fire damp and air retained their explosive power when the proportions were one of gas to fourteen of air; when the air was in larger quantity, the flame of a taper was merely enlarged in the mixture, an effect which was still perceived in thirty parts of air to one of gas.'[14]

'I found fire-damp much less combustible than other inflammable gases. It was not exploded or fired by red-hot charcoal, or red hot iron; it required iron to be white hot, and itself in brilliant combustion for its inflammation. The heat produced by it in combustion was likewise much less than that of most other inflammable gases.'[15]

'On mixing 1 part of carbonic acid or fixed air[16] with 7 parts of an explosive mixture of fire-damp, or 1 part of azote[17] with 6 parts, their powers of exploding were destroyed.'[18]

'In exploding a mixture in a glass tube of one-fourth of an inch in diameter, and a foot long, more than a second[19] was required before the flame reached from one end to the other, and that metallic tubes prevented explosion better than gas tubes.'[20] /

'In reasoning upon the various phenomena,' says Sir Humphrey,[21] 'it occurred to me – as a considerable heat was required for the inflammation of the fire-damp, and as it produced in burning comparatively a small degree of heat; that the effect of carbonic acid and azote, and of the surfaces of the small tubes in preventing its explosion, depended upon their cooling powers; upon their lowering the temperature of the exploding mixture so much that it was no longer sufficient for its continuous inflammation.'[22]

'This idea, which was confirmed by various obvious considerations, led to an immediate result – the possibility of constructing a lamp, in which the cooling powers of the azote, or carbonic acid formed by combustion, or the cooling powers of the apertures through which the air entered or made it exit – should prevent the communication of explosion.'[23]

It is curious to observe the minute difference of circumstances under which those gentlemen arrived at the same result, Mr. Stephenson had observed that candles placed to windward of a blower, extinguished the flame by the azotic air produced by the combustion of the candles. Sir H. Davy, found by applying azotic, and carbonic acid gas to fire damp in a state of inflammability, they extinguished the flame; and hence, both conceived the notion that the burnt air of the flame within, would, in its passage out of the lamp, as one of the causes, prevent the explosion from passing outwards. Then comes the difference: Mr.

Stephenson thought, that by admitting small quantities of air through the bottom, the velocity of the current would prevent the passage of the flame outwards, (and this, be it observed, was a fact which Sir H. Davy also discovered, for he had found that in a glass tube, 12 inches long, it required a second before the flame passed from one end to the other); and hence, his lamp was fed first by one hole with a slide, next with three tubes, and ultimately by small perforated holes. Sir H. Davy, on the other hand, finding that the fire-damp required a very high temperature for its explosion, conceived the idea of applying radiating surfaces, through which the flame would have to pass from the interior of the lamp, and by these to reduce its temperature, below that which was required for its continuous inflammation.

Ultimately, iron wire gauze was used by Sir H. Davy, as possessing the greatest radiating or cooling surface, and Mr. Stephenson used small perforated holes, for the admission of the air into his lamp, these small holes acting as radiating surfaces, to reduce the temperature of the flame, as well as in accordance with the principles on which his lamp was originally constructed. /

As previously stated, Sir H. Davy found that iron wire gauze of 1-40th to 1-60th of an inch diameter, with 28 wires, or 784 apertures to the square inch, was perfectly safe; and up to this time the lamp bearing his name has been so constructed.

Mr. Stephenson's lamp has been much improved, and the lamp which is now in use, comprises a glass cylinder covered by a cylinder of wire gauze, and instead of the air passing through a perforated plate, it passes through the meshes of the wire gauze. This lamp differs from the Davy lamp inasmuch as in the latter, the air has access through the entire meshes of the wire gauze on all sides, consequently, when immersed in an inflammable mixture, the whole cylinder becomes filled with flame, and if it is continued in such mixture, the wire becomes red hot. Whereas in the Stephenson lamp, the air being only admitted through a few meshes of the gauze within the glass cylinder, the latter preventing the entry of any air or gas from the sides; consequently, a very small portion of gas is permitted to enter, and therefore, the interior of the lamp never being filled with flame, no injury can arise to the wires of the gauze. The small quantity of air or gas entering is, however, productive of another result, viz:– When mixed with gas, there not being a sufficiency of atmospheric air for the combustion of the oil, and not a sufficiency of inflammable gas to support the requisite temperature for its inflammation, the light is extinguished. In the Davy lamp there is a sufficient body of gas to keep up the requisite temperature, and when the lamp is kept in an inflammable mixture, the gas continues burning entirely independent of the combustion of the oil, the wire becomes red hot, radiating the heat sufficient to keep the temperature of the wires below that required for the passage of the flame through the meshes, but still sufficiently high to support the combustion of the gas. There is, however, no acceleration or accumulation of intensity of heat, the wires keep at a dull red heat, if kept in a still atmosphere, and the lamp continues to burn with safety as regards the transmission of the flame through the meshes of the wire gauze.

These are the principles of the two lamps, and I have been a little more minute in the explanation of them, as most of the modern lamps are modifications of one, or the other, or of both; either admitting the air within the lamp unrestrictedly through the meshes of the gauze, allowing continuous inflammation to go on within the lamp, and relying for protection from the radiating property of the gauze as in Sir H. Davy's lamp; or restricting or diminishing the quantity of air admitted into the lamp, as in the Stephenson lamp, and allowing it to go out when immersed / in an inflammable mixture, when the atmosphere does not contain sufficient oxygen, to support the combustion of the oil.

There has, however, recently been a new element brought into operation, which has an important bearing on the construction and safety of these lamps, viz: that of producing a better or more powerful light than the Davy Lamp, and which has led to the rejection of the use of wire gauze as an insulating medium, or the cover of wire gauze over the glass cylinder on the sides of the lamps, and to the employment of glass cylinders alone, to insulate the flame on the sides, the air in all these cases being admitted within and passing out of the interior of the lamp through wire gauze. The principle of insulation, for the passage and exit of the air, is therefore the same as in the Davy lamp, viz: the radiation of the gauze, but then we have only the cylinder of glass, as a protection between the flame of the lamp and the external air. The most extensively used lamp of this description is the Clanny lamp, the construction of this lamp being that of a glass cylinder for the purposes of light, and a wire gauze top.

The Museler Lamp[24] is a lamp most extensively used in Belgium, and does not differ much from that of Clanny, having a glass cylinder for the light, and a gauze top; but in this lamp there is a copper chimney to carry off the smoke from the wick of the burner, and to force the air entering through the wire gauze downwards between the copper chimney and the glass cylinder upon the flame of the burner, the air being admitted through the gauze at the top.

The Boty Lamp[25] is another modification of this principle, having a glass cylinder with a wire gauze top, but in this the air is admitted through a ring of perforated copper at the bottom of the lamp. In other respects it does not much differ from the Museler Lamp.

The Eloin Lamp[26] has also a glass cylinder; the air is admitted through wire gauze near the bottom of the lamp, and is thrown against the burner by a thin copper cap. No other air enters the lamp than that at the bottom through the gauze, consequently it is easily extinguished. Instead of having a cylinder of gauze for the top, this lamp has a copper or brass top, so that the only entry for air is at the bottom, the exit for the vitiated air being at the top through wire gauze. This lamp has not been much used. It has an argand burner,[27] or flat wick.

There are a variety of lamps constructed on this principle, viz., that of obtaining increased light by the use of glass cylinders, all of course of larger diameter than the wire gauze cylinder of the Davy.

Dr. Glover's Lamp[28] has a double cylinder of glass, the air being admitted from the top between the two cylinders, and passing downwards, / enters within the inner cylinder at the bottom of the lamp, through wire gauze, or apertures, and so passes to the burner. The two cylinders are for protection in case of accidents, and the air being passed between the cylinders, operates in keeping them cool. The top of the lamp is wire gauze.

....

I shall now proceed to examine how far the Davy and other lamps can be depended on in practice for safety in lighting mines abounding in inflammable gas.

It is well known to the profession that the safety of the Davy Lamp has been questioned very generally, and more particularly by persons having no experience in its use. Dr. Priara,[29] in 1833, made some experiments to prove its insecurity, but these experiments were made with coal gas, which being essentially different in its inflammability from the firedamp in mines, could not be considered conclusive; and though the object was to prove the superiority of Upton and Roberts' Lamp, yet even comparatively the experiments were of little value, as the only result found with regard to Upton and Roberts' Lamp was, that when immersed in the inflammable mixture it went out.

The South Shields Committee[30] came to the conclusion 'that the Davy Lamp was absolutely unsafe;' 'that the Davy Lamp has been found, by experiment and in practice, to explode the external gas by the passage of the flame through the gauze,' and that 'no doubt can remain that it has been the cause of some of the hitherto unaccountable accidents which have occurred.'

Mr. Darlington,[31] in his evidence before the Committee in 1852, says:– 'I can state from my own practical knowledge of the Davy Lamp, and from the opinions of miners who have for years worked with the Davy Lamp, that it is not a safe instrument in an explosive mixture under a strong current;' and again, 'I have in a mine passed the explosive mixture, but not with a cool clean lamp; it has been at a red heat;' and in answer to the question, 'Is it not the fact that dust will fly off in sparks or scintillas, and that one spark would create an explosion?' Mr Darlington says, 'There are very numerous instances of accidents taking place that we could attribute to nothing else.'[32]

The committee of 1852 state their 'concurrence in the opinion expressed directly or indirectly by the committees of 1835 and 1849,[33] and / also with that so strongly expressed by the South Shields Committee, that where a proper degree of ventilation does not exist in a mine, the Davy Lamp or any modification of it must be considered rather as a lure to danger than as a perfect security.'[34] /

T. S. J., 'Safety Lamps' (1882)

T. S. J,[1] 'Safety Lamps' [Letter], *Colliery Guardian*, 16 June 1882, p. 943.

SAFETY LAMPS.

To the Editor of the Colliery Guardian.

Sir, – As the question of safety lamps for coalmining is becoming more and more important, and many interesting and useful experiments have been made to test the efficiency or otherwise of the various so-called safety lamps used in coalmining, perhaps it may not be considered out of place to make a few remarks thereon. In the first place, it has been definitely proved that the Davy lamp is not a safety lamp in the true sense of the word when exposed to a mixture of air and gas travelling at the rate of 6 ft. per second,[2] and I think it has been conclusively proved by the evidence of eminent mining engineers, such as Mr. Higson, in his evidence given in connection with the Abram Colliery,[3] that under what we may term ordinary velocities, if rendered explosive by admixture with firedamp, the Davy becomes an unsafe light to have in a mine. It is quite evident the Davy lamp is unfit for mines giving off firedamp, and the question at once comes to the front, What lamp should we use in fiery mines? It has been suggested the Mueseler[4] which gives a good light and is steady in strong velocities of air currents. Those are certainly two good and essential qualifications for a safety lamp, but when we come to the vital question – viz., that of safety, we find, according to *Report of Experiments of Mines Commissioners in South Wales5* that 'attention was particularly drawn to the Mueseler lamp, which exploded time after time, irrespective of the make. The experiments proved that this lamp is very dangerous, owing to its supposed security. In its present form it is very little safer than the Davy, and certainly not so much to be relied on.' If the above be a correct view of the results of the experiments with Mueseler it looks very much like a complete condemnation of it as a real safety lamp, as I understand the principal weakness in connection with the construction of the ordinary Mueseler is the size of the orifice at the top of the inner chimney and the construction thereof. The attention of the mining community has already been drawn to the fact of the flame tailing out at the top of the chimney into the gauze by experts such as Mr. W. E. Teale[6] and other gentlemen. I myself noticed the afore-named fact in a coalmine a few days ago, in walking along an incline. There was passing 21,630 cubic feet per minute at a velocity of 560 ft. per minute, and (with what you might term, a fair ordinary light on the Mueseler) when the lamp was stationary a small tongue of flame played around the top of the chimney, thus truly rendering it, as regards safety, no better than the ordinary Davy. This was a Mueseler lamp standing 8 in. high, and weighing 2 lb. 11 oz.[7] I understand Mr. Teale has taken means to prevent an occurrence of this kind with the Protector Mueseler; I, and no doubt many of your readers, would be glad to know the comparative results in connection with the two. We know that in ordinary coal-getting the miner who uses the Mueseler will naturally go in for a maximum of light for his own personal advantage, consequently with the ordinary Mueseler we, I may say, get practically no advantage over the common Davy. Except in the matter of light, at the present time mining authorities will naturally hesitate before investing large sums of money in the purchase of lamps until there is some further satisfactory evidence as to the proper lamp to introduce. I know that in Lancashire there have been already large quantities of Mueselers purchased for coal-mines, and with the object of dispensing with the Davy, and introducing a supposed safety lamp. Myself with many of your readers would be glad to know which is really the best class of safety lamps to use for mines giving off firedamp, such as in the Wigan district.

...

—Yours, &c.,

near Wigan, June 10, 1882. T. S. J.

Assistant C. C. M.

Henry White, 'The Coad Electric Miner's Lamp' (1892–3)

Henry White,[1] 'The Coad Electric Miner's Lamp', *Transactions of the North of England Institute of Mining and Mechanical Engineers*, 42 (1892–3), pp. 29–30, and 'Discussion', pp. 30–1.

THE COAD ELECTRIC MINER'S LAMP.

By HENRY WHITE.

During the last few weeks the writer has several times tried the Coad[2] electric safety-lamps underground, at the Walker colliery, and being highly pleased with the improved light thought that a description of the lamp might be sufficiently interesting to lay before the members of this Institute.

The No. 1 electric lamp gives a light much superior to that of an ordinary safety-lamp, and no doubt would enable work to be done more efficiently underground.

The No. 3 electric lamp should prove very useful for an official,[3] in travelling and examining high places, timber, or loftings;[4] also the rails, joints, lead, gradient, etc., of engine-planes and inclines and working-places generally. It might also be very usefully applied at off-takes,[5] landings, bank-heads,[6] stables,[7] etc.; and at the bottom and top of staples[8] where coals are drawn and safety-lamps are now in use. The writer considers it much superior to the ordinary safety-lamp for use in examining ropes, pulleys, stone, etc., in upcast shafts, staples, etc.

Experimentally it was found that with the ordinary tin-can Davy lamp a piece of white paper 6 inches square could only be seen about 10 yards off, whilst with the No. 3 electric lamp it could be seen at a distance of 40 yards.

This electric lamp reduces the use and generation of electricity down to the level of an ordinary oil lamp, and the light is given at considerably less cost, as one candle-power is given for 10 hours at the cost of one penny.

The battery is a primary single-fluid one, made of ebonite cells,[9] with platinum connexions, which do not corrode in use, the usual fault and trouble with most batteries. No scientific knowledge of electricity is required in its use. To charge the battery the cover is removed, and the cells filled with the fluid; then the zinc plates are dropped in their places when they immediately connect and the cover put on again.

The small incandescent lamp is held on a flexible or yielding support which allows the lamp to be pushed on one side, to prevent it being broken on meeting with a blow; immediately this takes place the circuit of the current is broken, and the lamp goes out; the sparking caused by this / and the making contact takes place in a sealed chamber, into which no gas can enter. When any pressure that pushes the lamp on one side is removed the lamp comes back to its normal position, and is at once automatically relighted. The lamp is further protected by a stout glass envelope or cover.

The weight of the lamp shown in Fig. 1 [not reproduced here], when fully charged, is 4 lbs. 2 ozs., and that of the lamp shown in Fig. 3 [not reproduced here], 5 lbs. 6 ozs.[10]

One charge of 10 ounces[11] of the improved bichromate-of-potash fluid will give ten hours' light.

The consumption of zinc is: for the three-cell lamp, ¾ ounce per ten hours; and for the four-cell, 1 ounce[12] for the same time.

Mr. G. B. Forster[13] asked if there was any apparatus connected with the lamp to indicate the presence of gas?

Mr. Coad (the inventor of the lamp) said there was not; he had not thought there was any necessity for it. Could not a man smell the gas?[14]

Mr. Forster – Perhaps, but not in time to prevent suffocation.

Mr. W. C. Blackett[15] asked if the makers of the lamp were prepared to maintain it at the cost named, of 1d. per candle-power per 10 hours?

Mr. Coad said they did not undertake this, it could be a matter for arrangement.

Mr. Blackett also asked if the fluid could be bought in the open market? / / /

Mr. Coad said that arrangements could be made for colliery owners to make their own.

Mr. BLACKETT – Free of royalty?

Mr. COAD could not say that.

The PRESIDENT proposed a vote of thanks to Mr. White for bringing this electric lamp before their notice; it was very interesting and might be found very useful.

The motion was agreed to.

Mr. WHITE acknowledged the vote of thanks and said he had found the lamp very useful. /

'The Telephone in Colliery Workings', *Colliery Guardian* (1880)

'The Telephone in Colliery Workings', *Colliery Guardian*, 16 April 1880, p. 623.

THE TELEPHONE IN COLLIERY WORKINGS.

On the invitation of Lord Elphinstone, of Carberry Tower,[1] a large number of gentlemen visited on the 8th inst.[2] Carberry Colliery, near Inveresk, in order to inspect the operation of the telephone as an important auxiliary in mining operations. Carberry Colliery is leased by Messrs. Deans and Moore, who sunk the pit about twelve years ago. The coal worked is the great seam, nine feet thick, of the Lothian coal basin, and the jewel coal, which is a lower seam, and five and a-half feet thick. The workings below are very extensive, and stretch in numerous galleries for a mile east and west, with a breadth of nearly a thousand yards. The mineral lies at a very considerable angle, and the workings follow the dip. The upcast and downcast shaft is sunk on the very edge of the seam at the southern side, and galleries are driven north, east and west. The shaft is 75 fathoms in depth, but the coal takes a rapid dip northwards at the rate of 1 in 3, so that at the bottom of the 'dooks'[3] the depth is 210 fathoms. There are three of these main dooks – one for pumping and the others for bringing the coal to the bottom of the shaft by means of an engine working an endless rope. For the purpose of draining the mine there are three pumps – one placed 300 yards from the bottom, another 600 yards, and a third at the foot of the dook, 900 yards from the shaft. The winding engine is 24-in. cylinder and 5 ft. stroke; the winding drum is 10 in. in diameter at the centre, and tapered out to 13 ft. at the edges. The 'dook' engines for drawing up and lowering the bogies[4] in the dook workings are 22 in. cylinders, coupled with two 12 ft. drums. The bogies are drawn by steel ropes direct from the surface engines. There is a winding engine below for the drawing of the coals up the dooks by means of an endless rope. This engine is 5 ft. stroke and 22 in. cylinder, and the steam for working it is conveyed by pipes from the surface furnaces. The engine delivers a tub of 8 cwt. of coal every three-quarters of a minute, night and day. The drainage of the mine is accomplished by means of four pumping engines. There is first a Cornish engine[5] driving 12 in. pumps and delivering 300 gallons a minute from the bottom of the shaft to the surface. The second engine pumps 200 gallons per minute, from a spot 300 yards down the dook, to the bottom of the shaft; a third pumps the water from the end of the works up to No. 2; and the fourth is employed as an auxiliary engine. The ventilation is considered very perfect, being worked by Waddell's 16-ft. fans, and 30,000 cubic feet of pure air are by this means passed through the mine per minute – a quantity which could be almost doubled if necessary. Where so much depends on the efficient drainage of the mine, not only as regards the safety of the 120 men employed in it, but the economical and continuous output, great attention has to be paid to the pumping gear, and several men are engaged in constantly travelling to and fro over the workings inspecting the pumps, and reporting to the men in charge of the engine at the surface. It occurred to Lord Elphinstone that, by fitting up telephones in different parts of the mine, the regular and proper working of the pumps might be discovered at the surface, and the labour of many men dispensed with. After consultation with Messrs. Deans and Moore, the lessees of the colliery, some time ago, it was acknowledged that no form of telephone had been invented which was adapted, in all its details, to the purpose in view. His Lordship happened lately, on a visit to London, to see in operation the Gower-Bell telephone, manufactured by the General Telephone Agency Company Limited, and it occurred to him that it might be adapted to colliery purposes. Accordingly he invited the company to make experiments at Carberry Colliery, which they have done; and, although some working details have not yet been perfected by Mr. Charlton Wollaston, C.E.,[6] who has had charge of the experiments, there is no doubt left in the minds of those most interested that what was desiderated will speedily be supplied, and collieries rendered safer, while the operations will be conducted more economically. Among the gentlemen who responded to Lord Elphinstone's invitation to witness the experiments were Lord Shand; Messrs.[7] Allan Carter, C.E.; David Landale, M.E.; John Morrison, colliery manager Newbattle; R. Clark, colliery [manager], Arniston; Kitto, colliery manager, Prestongrange; Grieve, colliery manager, Tranent; Deans and Moore, and Moore, jun., Carberry; R. T. Moore, M.E., and A. G. Moore, M.E. Rutherglen; James W. Stewart. C.E., Edinburgh; Todd, of Springfield; C. Stewart, Sweethorpe; W. J. Dundas, W.S.; James Hope, Belmont; and Thos. Proudfoot, Pinkiehill; Provost Keir; Dr. Thomson, Musselburgh; and Dr. Young, Portobello.[8] Wires had been laid from the joiner's shop near the pithead at Carberry Colliery down the shaft into the galleries of the great seam and the dooks, and telephones fitted at both ends. These telephones were what are known as the loud-speaking Gower-Bell telephones. They consist of a combination of Hughes' microphone and Bell's telephone improved by Gower. The company assembled in the joiners' shop, and were entertained to a lecture on the telephone by Mr. Wollaston, who described the history of all the sound-transmitting instruments, their mechanism, and the principles of their action. He dwelt on the peculiarity of the telephones which had been fitted up at Carberry Colliery – dissected them, so to speak, for the information of this audience, and showed how they could be used, not only for the purpose intended at that particular work, but in recording the failure or otherwise of the ventilation of mines, in sinking pits or wells, in enabling exploring parties after explosions in mines to communicate instantaneously with the surface, or in enabling divers to converse with each other under or those above water. After the lecture the party descended the pit to the great seam, and proceeding along one of the spacious galleries, came to a handsome dining room, brilliantly illuminated with wax candles burning in silver candelabra. The room, draped with canvas, and decorated with hothouse plants, presented a unique appearance when it was remembered that it was at least 600 feet below the level of the ground, and 200 feet below the level of the Firth of Forth. A sumptuous luncheon was served – Lord Elphinstone being in the chair, and Mr. Deans, of Messrs. Deans and Moore, officiating as croupier.[9] The noble chairman proposed 'The health of her Gracious Majesty,' remarking that a peculiar interest attached to the toast, not only because of the place in which it was drunk, but from the fact that three years ago two of her Majesty's sons had visited and explored the same mine. The toast was enthusiastically pledged, and thereafter the galleries seemed 'full of noises, sounds, and sweet airs, that give delight.'[10] It was the strains of the National Anthem, and other melodies, conveyed by telephone from the joiners' shop, where a band was stationed. The music was most distinct, and the effect charming. Lord Shand proposed 'The health of Lord Elphinstone.' (Applause.) He congratulated the guests on an experience which he was sure they had never before had – the partaking of luncheon in such a spacious dining-hall and at such a distance from the earth's surface and sea level. It was remarkable that science and skill had enabled miners to carry on their operations so admirably and well, and that Messrs. Deans and Moore could give them so beautifully ventilated and so safe a room as they were now in. It said a great deal for the skill which they all knew Messrs. Deans and Moore were possessed of, and for scientific progress. (Applause.) They all knew the deep interest Lord Elphinstone took in the advancement of scientific enterprise. His invention with reference to the electric light, which was in progress, would, he hoped, prove a very great success. (Applause.) And there was not one at the table who did not wish him every success in the exertions he was making to complete the new invention – the experiments which they had that day witnessed. Lord Elphinstone had not only done a great service to coalmasters, but to coalminers generally, in drawing attention in a practical way to the advantages which were to be derived from the use of the telephone in connection with mineral workings. He believed that, on the mere question of profitable working in mineral operations, the telephone must be useful, for they had seen, that, instead of men requiring to come down into the bowels of the earth and traverse great distances from one level to another, they could hear at the surface in a single moment precisely what was doing even at the furthermost end of the pit. (Applause.) But perhaps that was a comparatively low view to take of the instrument, for the believed that it would be ultimately made very useful in the saving of human life. (Applause.) And thus it became a matter of great consequence to thousands of our mining population, who depended for their daily bread on the safety of such mines as that in which they now were. (Applause.) It was remarkable to be told that an exploring party proceeding into dangerous mines could communicate step by step with the surface, detailing their experience, asking for assistance, or enabling them to be withdrawn instantly from danger. (Applause.) He hoped that Scotland would be in the front in adopting the telephone in mineral workings, to the profit of those who were engaged in them, and to the safety and comfort of the mining population. (Applause.) And he trusted that Lord Elphinstone's enterprising tenants, Messrs. Deans and Moore, would be long remembered as having the credit of having introduced the first telephone in Carberry pit (Applause.) Lord Elphinstone, in responding to the toast, said he felt flattered to think that the good wishes of his friends pursued him into the lower regions. (Laughter and applause.) After detailing the reasons which induced him and Messrs. Deans and Moore to try the experiments, he said that he had no doubt Mr. Wollaston would construct instruments that would not only tell at the surface how the pumps were working, but if even a screw or a nut was loose. (Applause.) He proposed the health of Mr. Wollaston, who briefly acknowledged the compliment. The health of the tenants of the coalfield – Messrs. Deans and Moore – was proposed by Mr. Todd, Springfield, and acknowledged by Mr. Deans. After a number of interesting experiments were made with the telephone in communicating with the pit-head, the party were conducted over the workings of the mine and down through the 'dooks' by Messrs. Deans and Moore, jun. – *Scotsman.*[11]

Nicholas Wood, 'On the Conveyance of Coals Underground in Coal Mines' (1854–5)

Nicholas Wood,[1] 'On the Conveyance of Coals Underground in Coal Mines', *Transactions of the North of England Institute of Mining Engineers*, 3 (1854–5), pp. 239–318.

ON THE CONVEYANCE OF COALS UNDERGROUND IN COAL MINES.

BY NICHOLAS WOOD, ESQ., C.E.,

PRESIDENT OF THE INSTITUTE OF MINING ENGINEERS.

The subject of the conveyance of coal underground in coal mines from its separation in the mine to the bottom of the pits is of great importance to the coal trade. The increased cost, above that of the conveyance of coals, and other minerals, by railways on the surface, demand the attention of every one connected with the management of mines, with a view of ascertaining if such cost can in any manner be lessened.

In the year 1825, I published a practical work on the subject of 'The Establishment and Economy of Railways' on the Surface, which, subsequently, went through another edition, published in 1831,[2] and the great progress which railways, and the motive power employed upon them, since that period has undergone, raises a very important question whether such improvements have been adopted in the conveyance of coals underground, and whether sufficient attention has been paid to the subject or not.

There is, however, a wide difference in the circumstances of the two cases – surface railways can be levelled and made of uniform inclination at comparatively small cost to that by which they can be made underground – the latter is, in fact, entirely tunnelling – more even than that, as in the first formation of a road underground the coal is seldom of sufficient height to allow of horses to travel, or for the use of the requisite carriages: and, consequently, the dimensions of the excavation must be / enlarged even before any attempt is made to make the road of an uniform inclination, or to adapt it to any particular description of motive power.

And when it becomes necessary to level up depressions and to take off undulations, then it is very expensive tunnelling in solid rock; sometimes excessively hard and extremely expensive, but always presenting very much greater cost than a similar process on the surface.

And it must also be borne in mind, that there is this difference between making roads underground and on the surface – that in the latter case, perfect levellings can previously be obtained of all the undulations of the surface, and this before any expenditure at all is incurred, and a line of railway thus fixed upon or adopted, which can be formed at the least possible cost. In underground mining or tunnelling, it is all in the dark, we can only guess at the undulations before us; and, therefore, when a certain direction or course is assumed, and which is expected to produce the requisite degree of inclination, the undulations in the strata, or breaks up and down by dykes, often thwart all our calculations. The perfection of a railway is, we presume, that between two points it should be as level and as straight as possible, if the amount and weight of the traffic is the same in both directions;[3] or, if there is a preponderance of traffic in either direction, then that the inclination should be such as to present the same resistance to the motive power in both directions.

In mining engineering, if the ruling principle laid down be that the road should have a certain inclination, either that it should be just water-level, or such an inclination as that the water will just flow from the workings to the pumping shaft, or that it should be such an inclination as that the resistance to the load should be equal in both directions; then if there are any undulations in the regularity of the strata, or bed of coal – [and in every mine such undulations are very frequent, and sometimes very considerable] – then it will be found that to preserve the requisite levels the road, instead of being straight, assumes the most tortuous shape; and in cases where the roads are numerous, and where the levels or roads of two or three beds of coal are laid down upon the same map, they assume very much the tortuous appearances of the gyrations of the animalcula[4] exhibited in an oxyhydra lens.[5]

The formation of the roads underground approach more nearly to that of the formation of a canal through a hilly country, with this difference, that in the formation of a canal on the surface, the engineer can make surveys to regulate and guide the line he may take in its formation, whereas, a mining engineer has to form his canal without being able ever to see beyond that part of the road in which he is immediately engaged in forming. The beds of coal, also, are generally from three to four, or five feet in thickness, probably the / average about four feet: and the height required for horses or machinery about six feet when finished. The rock above or below the bed of coal is generally extremely expensive to excavate, and hence any extra quantity of rock to be taken up or blasted down, beyond that which is absolutely necessary, is very expensive. Vertically, the whole space to operate on is about four feet.

The draining of a mine is, likewise, generally an expensive operation. When, therefore, a pit is sunk, and the pumping-apparatus attached, it becomes of great importance that as large an extent of mine should be drained as possible. The first operation, therefore, generally is, to push away right and left, what are called the water-levels of the colliery, viz:– drifts, adits, or levels,[6] with such an inclination only as that the water will just run towards the bottom of the pit, and these are pushed or extended across the whole extent of the royalty, from one extremity to the other, in the water-level line of the strata or bed of coal, by which all the coal on the rise side[7] of the water levels are drained.

These, as before explained, are generally extremely tortuous, if the bed of coal at all undulates. For the purpose of merely water-levels, this is not of very much consequence; but these levels being at the lowest point at which the seam is opened out, they are very often made the main roads also, whereby the coals are brought out to the bottom of the pit.

In the early period of coal mining, and up to a comparatively recent period in the best managed districts, and, indeed, in the present day in those districts where the stimulus given by the improvements of surface railways has not reached, it is found that almost universally the levels which drain the mine are the horse-roads by which the coals are brought out from the workings to the bottom of the shaft. The coals from the rise parts of the mine being brought down to those levels or roads.

Where the mines are extensive, and where the expense of lifting the water is costly, or where they are drained by day levels,[8] the greatest care is taken in making those levels as flat as possible, barely, or just sufficient inclination for the water to find its way to the pumping shaft or adit, and the horse-road being either formed on the water-level, or on a road driven parallel thereto; this circumstance operates very materially in determining the description of road by which the coals are brought out, and the kind of motive power to be employed thereon.

In the early period of coal mining likewise, and prior to the introduction of mechanical machinery to pump the water, the coal was drained by adits into the sides of the hills – there it became of great importance to adhere to the water level of the strata in draining the mine, and when, even at a later period, machinery was introduced to drain the mine, this was only able to be performed to a certain extent, – and to the extent to which this drainage could be performed it became of equal importance that, as the miners termed it, 'no level should be lost,' but that the levels should be driven strictly water level; and even at a late, and up to the present period, the same rule holds good, viz:– that the levels should be driven strictly water level, hence the coals having to be brought out towards the entrance to the mine on such a gradient, and the load being consequently all in on direction, the motive power is not equally balanced, but greater in the direction of the load than with the empty carriages. Thus, the main-roads for bringing out the coals to the bottom of the pits or adits, may be said to be the water-levels of the mine, the cross-roads bringing the coals from the rise to those roads, and when the stratification of the mine is sufficiently inclined, or the beds lay at an adequate inclination, then the coals are brought down to the main-levels by self-acting planes,[9] and so to the bottom of the pits.

The earliest attempt, therefore, to work coals no doubt began in digging it out where exposed to the surface, or where the beds cropped out to the surface, by adits or levels driven in the direction of the beds' water level, the same level or adit answering the double purpose of drainage and a road to bring the coals out.

We have no records of how or in what manner the coals were brought out to the surface before the introduction of railways. We know that even within the last thirty years coals were carried out to the surface in Scotland by women who were called 'bearers,' and who carried out very heavy weights of coal in panniers, much the same as the fish is carried by the fisherwomen, and where pits were necessary, steps were placed within the area of the shaft which the women ascended with their load of coals. It is probable also that barrows were at one period extensively used for conveying the coals to the mouth of the adit, or to the bottom of the pits, and that where the floor of the mine was soft, planks were laid down whereon to wheel the barrows and likewise, before the introduction of railways, sledges were used in / which the baskets or corves were placed which contained the coals. In this case, also, where the floor of the mine was soft planks were used. These latter roads were likewise called 'barrow-ways,' / which would indicate they were the same description of road, and used for the same purpose as the roads where barrows were used. To a comparatively recent date sledges were used in the pits on the main roads, and likewise on the surface at the top of the pits to convey the coals from the mouth of the pit to the screens, or to the waggons used to convey the coals to the shipping places.

In those districts where early mining has been practised we find the pits very shallow and very numerous.[10] The earliest working having been by adit as before named, and the powers of drainage being at those periods very inefficient, the pits would necessarily be very shallow, limited to the power of raising the water of the mine. And when the mode of conveyance underground was confined to barrows, numerous pits would be requisite to be sunk to supply the deficient and expensive system of conveyance. As the system of conveyance was improved, even by the introduction of sledges, the necessity for sinking pits would be less; but even up almost to the end of the last century, the number of pits sunk was very numerous; although, perhaps, the question of ventilation may, in some cases, have regulated the frequency of sinking. Horses were, no doubt, used for a long period in the shallow pits for drawing the coals to bank by gins; but the depth to which they could raise the coals was, though limited, very much beyond that of manual labour.

The next process was, probably, the use of water-wheels, wherever such a power could be applied; and hence we find that water-wheels were used at and up to a not very distant period, both for the drainage of the mine and for drawing the coals to bank. And such appears to have been the reluctance to part with an old friend, that long after the introduction of the steam engine, the latter was, in many cases, employed to pump the water up to the requisite height, to be afterwards used in working the water-wheel.

In some of the mountainous districts of Wales, water-wheels are indeed still used; and the use of water has been carried to a much greater extent than it can be carried in this manner, especially in South Wales, by the use of what are called 'Balance Pits,' where water is run into a bucket attached to a rope or chain passing over a pulley at the top of the pit, of a greater weight than that of the coals, or weight to be drawn up the shaft, and which is attached to the other end of the rope or chain. The water descending thus draws the coals up the pit. The water is then emptied at the / bottom, the loaded tub of coals placed over it, and they are then drawn up the pit by another and similar process. The water generally runs out to the surface by adits; but in some cases it has to be lifted either by waterwheels or by steam engines. Coals are thus drawn to bank up pits of a depth of 60 to 80 fathoms.

These observations though not, perhaps, strictly applicable to the subject of this paper, are not entirely irrelevant thereto, as the powers of raising the coal to the surface, and, consequently, the number of openings in a given area, modify and determine, to a considerable extent, the means and the mode applied to convey the coals from the workings to such openings. Hence we find in the early stages of the working of coalmines the roads were made from the adits, and from pit to pit, in the water-level line of the coal, draining and cutting off a strip of coal nearest the surface at the least possible cost and labour. Successive strips were then drained or worked more and more towards the dip of the mine, or at greater depth from the surface, as longer and more expensive adits were driven, or as successive improvements advanced, and more power was applied to lift the water and to raise the coal to bank.

Hence it was then the system to commence the winning and working of the mine at the extreme rise part of the coal-field, with successive drainage, and working deeper and deeper, as more power was obtained. This is most clearly exemplified in the valleys and in the hilly and mountainous coal-fields of Great Britain, and especially in the hills of the extensive coal-fields of South Wales. The successive deeper levels, being almost an index of the development of the continuous advancement in science and in the improvements of machinery.

Now, when we may almost be said to have attained such a degree of perfection in machinery and in engine power to almost, if not quite, command the drainage of the deepest part of any of our coal basins, [as the coal measures being the uppermost beds of the series of rocks on which they repose, the coal does not extend to a very great depth from the surface in the coal / fields of Great Britain], and when we can, consequently, place the draining pit, or drawing shaft, in the deepest, or in any other part of any coal field or royalty; we are, consequently, enabled so far as the number of openings to which the coal is to be conveyed underground extends, to place such openings at that point of the coal-field to which the coal can most advantageously be conveyed. This very circumstance, as the natural effect of such a command of / power involves, however, has been the cause of much deeper openings being made, – more expensive, and, consequently, less in number, and, therefore, requires that the coals should be conveyed a much greater distance underground than heretofore.

While, therefore, in the early stages of coal mining, the openings were never more than a hundred, or two or three hundred yards apart, increasing in distance as improvements of winning, draining, and conveyance of the minerals advanced; and even up to within the last half-century, the pits were never more than half a mile or so distant. And though the ventilation of the mine in some degree regulated the distance, like the other improvements in the science and practice of mining, ventilation was improved in the same ratio and kept pace with the other requisites of more extensive mining operations. Now, at the present time, the distance of the pits or openings from each other in the deep mines, are as many miles as they were hundred yards apart in the early period of coal mining. And we consequently see the necessity and importance of the consideration of the means and economy of conveyance of the coals underground in the present extensive system of mining operations.

Having thus given a general outline of the progress and successive increased means of the conveyance of the coals underground, and having pointed out the difficulties attendant on underground operations as contrasted with similar operations on the surface, I shall now enter into the detail of these different modes practised during the successive periods up to the present time. I shall then investigate the powers of each mode, or the motive power employed, which I shall illustrate, as much as possible, by experiments and diagrams [not reproduced here]; and I shall then endeavour to produce some practical results from the enquiry.

It is unnecessary to enter into the minutia or detail of the conveyance of coals by barrows, or by sledges, or even by the more repugnant mode of carrying the coals on the backs of ladies. All these modes are only matters of history, except where the seams are much inclined, and where sledges are used to convey the coals from the face of the workings to the main roads, which I shall now shortly describe.

On the Continent, viz:– in France, Belgium, and Prussia, where the beds of coal are much inclined to the surface, and where the inclination is such that the coals will not slide down the floor of the mine into the main roads, and in some parts of England and Wales also, in similar situations, sledges are used to convey the coals from the face of / the workings to the main roads, and the coals are either packed upon the sledges, and by them conveyed to the bottom of the pit or emptied into the tubs by which the coals are conveyed along the main roads to the bottom of the pit or to the mouth of the levels.

In these cases the main roads are formed along the water-level course of the coal, and at short distances from each other in the rise of the beds between which the coal is generally taken away by the long wall system,[11] in one process, the entire width between the two roads; or it may be worked by the pillar and wall system,[12] the pillars being generally taken away and brought to the same headway as that by which the whole coal is worked, and as the work proceeds to the rise the coals are brought to the lower levels by self-acting inclined planes. Boys are generally employed for this purpose.

Sledges, as before stated, were also used very extensively in the main roads in the more flat mines of England and Wales to carry the coals, from where worked in the face, to the pit, which were drawn by ponies, and when the beds of coal were thick horses were used. These sledges were dragged along the bottom or thill[13] of the mine where it was hard, but where it was soft deals or planks were laid down, or penning[14] composed of narrow pieces of wood laid across the roads, and these were as before stated, called in the districts of Northumberland and Durham 'barrow-ways.'

In these cases one pony, or one horse, was always employed to drag one basket or corf of coals at a time, and, consequently, as may be presumed, and indeed as was the fact, the expense was considerable; hence the necessity, when the beds of coals were not at a great depth from the surface, of having frequent openings or pits, by which the coals could be drawn to the surface. /

The next step was the employment of wheel carriages, which ran upon timber roads, or railways formed of timber. The carriages had wheels similar to our tram wheels, running upon the flat wooden rails, with a ledge on one side, (similar to the cast iron plate rails), to keep the wheels upon the road. But cylindrical wheels, running on wooden roads, similar to the old ledge wooden railways, were likewise used. The wheels were originally of wood with wooden flanches,[15] but subsequently a flat bar or hoop of iron formed the periphery of the wheel, with a plate of iron to act as the flanch of the wheel.[16]

These wooden rails and railways, have, like similar railways on the surface, now given way to cast or malleable iron railways, either the common tram road[17] or the edge rail; and to carriages with wheels of either cast or wrought iron, suitable for each description of railway.

For a long period, or rather down to a very recent period, tram roads with the tram wheel were universally used in this district, but they have now been, if not quite, almost universally superseded by the edge or round top rail. In some districts of England, Wales, and Scotland, however, the tram road is still in use, a prejudice still existing against the use of the edge rail. In most of the iron works in Wales and Scotland, the underground railways are tram roads, with wheels loose on the axle, and constructed so that when a wheel breaks it can easily be replaced.

Up to a recent period also, in the Northumberland and Durham districts, the coals were drawn to bank by baskets or corves. These were placed upon the sledge (when sledges were used), and brought out to the bottom of the pit, were then attached to the rope, and drawn to bank, leaving the sledge at the bottom of the pit. The corf, or basket, was then placed upon another sledge at bank, and so conveyed to the screens or wagons, and the coals emptied out, the empty corf, or basket, having, in the meantime, been again sent down the pit.

In many of the pits in the Midland districts, in Scotland and in Wales, the coals, especially where they are hard and large, are placed on and packed upon the sledges, or trams, or waggons with iron rings, and are so drawn up the pit, both trams and coals. In these cases, however, it is necessary to have guides in the shafts to prevent the trams, or carriages, from striking the sides of the shaft, and from striking each other in passing at meeting in the shaft. Great weights are generally drawn at a time, and the motion or velocity in drawing the coals to bank[18] is extremely slow, the principle being to bring to bank large weights at a slow speed. The contrary is the practice in the North of England, the pits being generally of a much greater depth. The principle is to draw comparatively smaller weights up the shaft but at great rates of speed. And though this practice is more particularly applicable, perhaps, to a comparatively recent period, it is now customary to draw to bank, at one of the pits in the North of England, as many coals as are drawn to bank at two or three of the pits in the Midland Districts or in Scotland and Wales.

It may, however, be remarked, that in the latter localities, the workings / have not yet penetrated to such great depths as the workings in the Newcastle District have done, the necessity has not, therefore, yet arisen, as a measure of economy in the latter case, to have fewer pits and to bring larger quantities of coals to bank at each pit. Still, however, when the greater expense of conveying coals underground as compared with that of the conveyance of coals on the surface is considered, it will, in some cases, be found to be more economical to have more pits with a less distance to convey the coals underground, than fewer pits and a more extended conveyance underground.

It was, for a long time, deemed inconsistent with the principle and economy of drawing coals at a rapid rate up the shafts in the North of England, to adopt the system of the Midland Districts of drawing the coals along with the tubs or carriages up the pits, especially when combined with greater comparative weights, and with the system of guides or slides.

Ultimately, however, the mode of drawing both the coals and carriages to bank was adopted in this district, and with it, of course, the system of slides in the shafts. And such has been the rapidity of conversion to this system, that, at this time, I do not believe there is a single colliery where this system is not adopted, and the old plan of drawing the coals to bank in baskets or corves is not abandoned.

While baskets or corves were used the system of conveyance of the coals underground was to employ small carriages called trams, usually running on plate rails, but sometimes on round or edge rails. The coals were thus brought out from the face of the workings to the main roads by boys which were called 'putters,' (and here it may be remarked, that even after the tram / or plate, and the edge railways were introduced, these roads were still designated 'barrow-ways,') the corves were then lifted by small cranes from the trams and placed upon larger carriages which were called 'rolleys' the roads being called 'rolley-ways,' by which they were conveyed to the bottom of the shaft.

In some cases, even since the system of drawing the tubs as well as the coals to bank has been adopted, the trams or tubs are placed upon the large carriages or rolleys, which are then more generally called 'wagons' (especially where edge rails are used,) and so conveyed to the bottom of the pit, this system has now, however, almost universally given way to the plan of using the same tram or carriage to convey the coals from the face of the workings to the bottom of the pit, and these are mostly called 'tubs.' /

W. Galloway, 'Secondary Haulage' (1896–7)

W. Galloway,[1] 'Secondary Haulage', *Transactions of the Federated Institute of Mine Engineers*, 12 (1896–7), pp. 257–62 and 'Discussion', pp. 262–78.

SECONDARY HAULAGE.

By W. GALLOWAY.

It is now nearly thirty years since the committee of The North of England Institute of Mining and Mechanical Engineers issued their Report on Underground Haulage.* That report dealt with four systems of haulage: endless-chain; endless-rope, with single tubs moving slowly; endless-rope, with trains moving rapidly; and main-and-tail-rope. It was one of the most valuable contributions that had ever been made to the literature of mining, and it had helped to spread a knowledge of the subject to underground haulage by mechanical means all over the world. The committee dealt only with the subject of conveying large quantities of coal from one point to another at distances of many hundreds of feet apart, and were consequently able to show certain marvellously low costs per mile-ton.

But in every mine a secondary system of haulage was necessary – namely, that which served the purpose of collecting the coal from the working-places into a siding, from which it might be conveniently taken away by one or other of the systems referred to in the committee's report; and conveying the empty waggons, which were brought to the siding, back to, and distributing them amongst, the working-places. This operation was usually carried out by boys, men, ponies, or horses. It involved taking single waggons part of the way, at least; and for this reason, as well as because delays of one kind and another were inevitable, it was necessarily more expensive per ton per unit of distance than the primary haulage on important horse-ways or engine-planes.

* *Trans. N.E. Inst.,* vol. xvii.

If the total cost of haulage in a mine for any given time be divided by the total output of coal for the same period the average cost of haulage is obtained, and the average cost of one mine can be compared with that of another. The comparison is not, however, of any particular value unless the conditions and the distances are alike in both cases. The committee dealt with the question of large quantities and long distances in a very careful and exact manner, and there seemed to be hardly anything left to say on that part of the subject; but, so far as the writer could / gather, the question of collecting and distributing had nowhere received the same kind or degree of attention, although he believed it would be found, on enquiry, that it was deserving of the closest scrutiny.

In the case of long engine-planes or horse roadways, in which a primary system of haulage is carried on, there is a fixed point at each end. The distance between the two points is known, and the cost of haulage per unit of distance can at any time be ascertained by dividing the wages and other expenses by the number of tons conveyed in a given time. In the case of haulage from the faces to a siding, there is only one fixed point, or collecting-siding, and the faces are always moving farther and farther away from it. Moreover, no two faces are, as a rule, at the same distance from the collecting siding. Under these circumstances, it is necessary to ascertain the following particulars before we can arrive at the true cost per ton per unit of distance of the haulage from any particular district of faces to a collecting siding:–

1. The distance of each face from the siding.
2. The number of tons of coal sent away from each face within a given time.
3. The aggregate amount paid for haulage in the district in question during the same period.

The distances may be best ascertained by direct measurement at the commencement and conclusion of the period, or, if it be very short, one measurement will suffice. The quantity of coal sent away from each face within the period, as well as the wages paid for haulage in the district, may be taken from the pay book, and the period itself should obviously be made to coincide with one or more ordinary pays. Where horses or ponies are employed, the cost of feeding them, providing harness, renewals, grooming, etc., should all be taken into account.

In the year 1894, while No. 1 pit of the Llanbradach collieries, near Cardiff, was being opened up in the little rock coal-seam, the writer ascertained the cost of haulage twice in this way – viz., for the weeks ending January 27th and September 22nd. The seam of coal is on the average about 3 feet thick, and in the course of driving the principal headings about 3 feet of floor is cut to make a height of 6 feet. Consequently, there was from one-third to one-half as much rubbish as coal hauled during the periods under consideration. The haulage was done exclusively by means of small self-contained semi-portable engines worked by compressed air, designed originally by the author, and made for him by Messrs. Thornewill & Warham, of Burton-upon-Trent, who also designed the valve-gear. Each / engine has two drums, 2 feet in diameter by 10 inches wide between the cheeks, and can be used as a tail-rope engine when required. Some of the ropes were ⅜ inch and some ½ inch in diameter. Each mine-waggon weighs about 12 cwts. when empty, and carries on an average 2 tons of coal. The general inclination of the seam is about 1 in 24. Between the two dates named, two of the fore-winning headings were driven through downthrow faults of 15 and 20 feet respectively, with gradients of 1 in 4 and 1 in 5, to explore the seam on the other side, and two other headings were going to the dip. The workings were also divided into a number of small detached districts just outside the shaft-bottom pillar (1,200 feet square), and they were enlarging gradually as the headings extended further and further away from the shaft. The whole of the workings were carried on by a double-shift, so that each small engine required two sets of attendants. The situation at the time the costs were taken was, therefore, by no means an ideal one. /

The following are the results obtained on charging the whole of the wages against the coal hauled:–

For the week ending January 27th, 1894 –

Number of yard-tons	727,500
Output of coal	2,025 tons.
Average distance for one ton	359 yards.
Wages paid for hauling	£23 11s 11d.

Wages cost for 359 yards = 2·796d. per ton.

For the week ending September 22nd, 1894 –

Number of yard-tons	1,715,487
Output of coal	2,981 tons.
Average distance for one ton	575 yards.
Wages paid for hauling	£45 0s. 4d.

Wages cost for 575 yards = 3·642d. per ton.

A rough-and-ready way of arriving at the cost of secondary haulage per ton of coal where horses are employed to transport the coal from the faces to collecting-sidings, is to divide the average output per day by the number of horses at work in the mine, so as to ascertain the average number of tons per horse per day. The writer has done this for a very large number of mines in South Wales, and has found that the number of tons per horse varies from a minimum of 8, except in the second case mentioned hereafter, to a maximum of 25 tons. This quantity is in addition to the rubbish brought out to the collecting-siding and sent to the surface or carried from one part of the workings to another. In a considerable number of cases where primary haulage by mechanical means is employed, the writer has found that the average number of tons of coal transported from the faces to the collecting-sidings, in addition to the rubbish hauled by the same horses, does not exceed 10 tons per horse.

Take an instance of a colliery of the first magnitude in South Wales with an output of 345,000 tons a year of large and small coal, with mechanical haulage on the main headings, a thick seam of coal, a good roof, no faults, and very moderate gradients. The following is the exact cost of secondary haulage for one year:–

	£	d. Per Ton.
Wages	9,364	6·51
Feeding horses	2,753	1·91
Harness	402	0·28
Amortization of horses	390	0·27
Totals	£12,909	8·97

In another instance in which the proprietors of a colliery instructed the writer to make an exhaustive examination into the costs, he found / that the cost of hauling coal and rubbish by means of horses from the faces to a collecting-siding at an average distance of about 500 yards amounted to rather over 1s. 3d. per ton of coal. The quantity of rubbish handled amounted to about one-third of the gross output. Many of the roadways were situated to the dip of the collecting-siding, but the gradients were not severe. However startling these figures may appear to be, the writer is aware that they are by no means abnormally high.

In instances which have come under the notice of the writer, he has found that the cost of collecting and distributing by means of workmen partly in level roadways, partly in rise roadways with gradients which require considerable effort to push the empty tubs up to the faces, and extending to an average distance of 200 to 300 yards, amounts to about 1d. per ton per 60 yards. It stands to reason that the longer the distance the less is the cost per ton per unit of distance, as there are fewer stoppages and delays.

The question is a vital one for many collieries. Notwithstanding its importance, however, it is generally most difficult to ascertain the cost of secondary haulage. The various items which are chargeable to this service are usually mixed up in the cost-sheets and pay-books with other things with which they have no connexion from the point of view now under consideration: for instance, some of the wages are charged amongst those of men who work on the surface; some amongst those who work underground; horse-feeding and harness are included with stores; in some cases part of this service is carried out by the colliers, and no account is taken of this indirect cost in estimating the total cost; in other cases men or boys are specially paid to do part of the work while horses or ponies do the remainder.

Thus it happens that when one enquires what is the cost of secondary haulage at any given colliery, he is met with the answer that the colliers do it for nothing (there could be no greater fallacy); or that no one can form any idea; or the costs of primary and secondary haulage are mixed up in such a way that the one cannot be separated from the other; or /

part of the cost is given and the remainder is omitted. These statements are not what they ought to be. The services should be kept perfectly distinct, thus:–

1. From faces to collecting-sidings.
2. From collecting-sidings to pit-bottom.
3. Winding, including cost of hitchers, banksmen, enginemen, proportion of steam and stores, repairs and renewals.
4. Screening, including all wages paid for handling the coal, screening, picking, and loading the wagons.

The writer hopes that some of the members of the Institution will follow his example and face the problem by giving the true costs of secondary haulage for the whole of the workings of a pit and not merely for one or more favourable districts. Opinions and guesses are obviously apt to be deceptive, and should therefore be carefully avoided in dealing with a problem of this kind which is susceptible of an exact solution.

[Discussion]

Mr. W. Galloway, replying to the discussion, said...

The following table illustrated the difference between the cost of secondary and primary haulage:–

SYNOPSIS OF THE COST OF CONVEYING MINERALS BY VARIOUS AGENTS IN MINES.

	System.	Agents.	Unit of Weight. Lbs.	Day's Work. Yard-tons.	Cost per Day. £ s. d.	Cost per Ton-mile. s. d.
	1. – IN OR NEAR THE WORKING-PLACES.					
a	Carrying on the back	Man	120	330	0 3 8	19 6·60
b	Wheelbarrow	"	200	540	0 3 8	11 11.40
c	Sledge	"	200	600	0 3 8	10 9.00
	2. – SECONDARY HAULAGE. CONVEYING SINGLE WAGGONS FROM THE WORKING-PLACES TO A COLLECTING-SIDING.					
d	Hand-putters	Boy	550	1,610	0 2 0	2 2.30
e	Horse-putters	Man and horse	2,800	6,864	0 6 6	1 8.00
f	Pony-putters	Lad and pony	896	5,577	0 4 5·5	1 4.879
g	Hand-putters	Man	896	5,252	0 3 8	1 2.740
h	Small-engines	Lad and boy	4,480	15,721	0 9 9·6	1 1.056
	3. – PRIMARY HAULAGE. CONVEYING TRAINS OR AN UNINTERRUPTED SUCCESSION OF SINGLE WAGGONS FROM A COLLECTING-SIDING TO THE BOTTOM OF THE SHAFT.					
k	Horses	Man and horse	—	105,600	0 6 6	0 1·300
l	Endless rope	Engine & men	—	376,107	2 0 4	0 2·267
m	" "	" "	—	354,048	1 5 5	0 1·520
n	Tail rope	" "	—	1,015,308	3 8 1	0 1·417
o	Endless chain	" "	—	626,439	1 7 0	0 0·911

The quantities in *a, b, c,* and *d* systems are taken from the *Cours d' Exploitation des Mines,* Prof. Haton de la Goupilliere;[2] *k* is from Callon's *Lectures on Mining,*[3] and is reckoned at 8 tons, carried 7½ / miles per day on a very good road at least 1,000 yards long; *e* is the more favourable of the two examples of horse-haulage in South Wales, mentioned above; *f* and *g* are on the authority of Mr. H. F. Bulman,[4] and are calculated for a distance of 581 yards, so as to be comparable with *h*, which is the Llanbradach example (hand-putters are, of course, inapplicable, except under very favourable conditions); *l* to *o* are some of the examples given in the Report on the Haulage of Coal published by the North of England Institute of Mining and Mechanical Engineers in 1869; but the cost of maintaining roadways and waggons has been excluded, as it did not appear in any of the other examples. In the five examples taken from French authors, the wages of men and boys and the cost of a horse had been assimilated to the corresponding wages and cost in this country.

As regards the dimensions and capacity of mine-waggons, he would quote the following criticism of Mr. R. Broja,[5] a German mining engineer:–

While in the salt-mines of Germany with plenty of room underground, and in the coal-mines of Upper Silesia, in seams of 6 to 25 feet thick, we are satisfied to continue to use mine-waggons with a capacity of ½ ton, the ordinary capacity of the waggons used in the Pennsylvanian anthracite mines is from 2½ to 3 tons. Capable American mining engineers who are acquainted with German mines find it inexplicable that larger waggons, with their undeniable advantages, have not been introduced into these mines years ago. By the choice of the more advantageous large waggons the whole anthracite mining industry of Pennsylvania has attained its singular and magnificent development*...

[as shown by its increased output:] 15,650,000 tons in 1870, and 58,126,345 tons in 1895.†

* *Der Steinkohlen Bergbau in den Vereinigten Staaten von Nord-America,* 1894, page 21.

† *The Mineral Industry,* 1895, page 125. /

Matthias Dunn, *A Treatise on the Winning and Working of Collieries* (1848)

Matthias Dunn,[1] *A Treatise on the Winning and Working of Collieries: Including Numerous Statistics and Remarks on Ventilation, and Illustrated by Plans and Engravings. To Which Are appended a Glossary and Index* (The Author, Newcastle-upon-Tyne, 1848).

SECTION VIII

Whilst the preparation is going on underground, the top of the pit must also be prepared for the dispatch of business, and according to the north country fashion of the present day, must be provided with spacious *skreens*[2] – apparatus for weighing the coals in the colliers' / tubs, as well as coal waggons. The top of the shaft, for a considerable distance round, must be covered with plates of iron, and all appendages completed for the rapid conveyance of the tubs to and from the shaft's mouth. Many collieries also require an apparatus for the re-skreening of the small coal. Where shafts are sufficiently roomy, it is common to see two tubs alongside each other, in the same cage, but when much contracted, one tub above the other, the departments of the cage being kept quite distinct.

The formation of these screens is varied according to the views of the artificer or the peculiar requirements of the coal ... but in general they are erected sixteen to twenty feet in height, fitted up with bars of iron half an inch apart, with convenient slope, so as to enable the coals to slide easily into the waggons below. To guard against breakage, stoppers are hung at intervals to interrupt the coals in their descent on to the platform below, or into the wagons[.]

The small coal which passes through the skreen bars is either delivered into waggons for immediate sale, or accumulated in heaps, or hoisted up and reskreened, into rough, small, and dust, by the apparatus before mentioned, which consists of a skreen highly elevated, the small coals being drawn up an inclined plane by a chain movement from the winding engine. /

Edward Brownfield Wain, 'Colliery Surface Works' (1894)

Edward Brownfield Wain,[1] 'Colliery Surface Works', Institution of Civil Engineers, *Minutes of the Proceedings*, 1894, pp. 123–45].

11 December, 1894.
SIR ROBERT RAWLINSON, K.C.B, President,
in the Chair.

———

(*Paper No. 2838.*)
'Colliery Surface-Works.'
By EDWARD BROWNFIELD WAIN, Assoc. M. Inst. C.E.

ALTHOUGH the details of underground works are necessarily of primary importance in the successful working of coal, the surface-arrangements constitute an important part of colliery establishments. If convenient arrangements are made to facilitate the loading and preparation of the material for market, considerable economy in working may be effected. By careful attention to the details of the plant, it is possible to reduce the expenditure upon labour at the surface to about one-twelfth of the whole labour-cost. The marked increase in the production of coal in the United Kingdom, in face of burdensome legislation, reduced hours of labour and difficulties consequent upon the greater depth at which the mineral is wrought, is largely due to improved mechanical appliances.

The North Staffordshire coal-field, to which this Paper chiefly refers, furnishes a good example of the development of mining-operations. Although there may be mining-districts in which there are more varied objects of interest and collieries better equipped with modern machinery, it is hardly possible to point to any mines that have been worked for a considerable period in which such great improvements have been made of late years. Speaking of this coal-field, Professor Hull[2] observed, 'In the two years extending through 1857–9 the production nearly doubled itself; and since that time it has increased by about three-fourths, while the number of collieries has not proportionately increased; showing the larger scale upon which the mines are now being worked.'* In 1878, the field yielded 4,098,338 tons of coal and / ironstone. The statistics for 1893 show that the annual output of coal and ironstone has been increased to 5,755,357 tons, an increase of upwards of 40 per cent. in twelve years. There is hardly a colliery in the district the plant of which has not been considerably improved during the past twenty years; and there are numerous instances of the development of extensive plants from small beginnings, such as mark the history of coal-mining in many of the older coal-fields, but particularly in the one referred to.

The considerable angle at which the strata occur results in the outcrop of numerous seams of coal and ironstone in close proximity, thirty-four valuable seams coming to the surface within a space of 2½ miles. These conditions were favourable to shallow workings with adits[3] and small pits, in which horse-gins and windlasses were used, and twenty years ago a large portion of the mineral raised came from such workings. As the upper breadths were worked out, it became necessary to put down suitable winding-machinery, and within the last fifteen or sixteen years more important plants have been introduced. A proof of the efficiency of the methods now generally adopted is afforded by the fact that, though the natural difficulties of working are greater than in most other coal-fields where the seams lie at moderate inclinations, yet the average weight of mineral wrought per workman in the North Staffordshire district is higher than the average for the United Kingdom, the relative figures being 302 tons in the former case and 257 tons in the latter.

Under such circumstances it has been difficult to apply general principles in laying out colliery surface-works. As necessity has arisen, extensions and additions have been made, and the work may be described as one of evolution rather than of design. Comparisons made between such works and those laid out recently on modern principles for a definite output, will probably indicate much waste and inconvenience resulting from spasmodic and desultory extensions.

In Fig. 1, Plate 4 [not included here], is shown the general arrangement of the Whitfield colliery, which thirty years ago had an output of little over 200 tons per day and is now raising ten times that quantity. The dark shaded buildings in the Fig. show the nucleus around which the present works have grown. It may be somewhat invidious to compare this with newer plants erected during the last few years; still, as regards convenience and general arrangements, there are many points worthy of notice, to which the Author proposes to direct attention later. In designing colliery plant, it is generally necessary to allow a large margin of strength / to meet the shocks and stresses peculiar to this class of work, and it is not as a rule advisable to introduce mechanical appliances of an intricate character.

* 'The Coal-Fields of Great Britain.' 4th edition. London, 1881, p. 189.

General Arrangements.

It is of the highest importance that the works should be concentrated as far as possible, so as to permit efficient supervision and to reduce the staff of mechanics and general labourers. A good example of this is exhibited by the colliery mentioned, where in 1876 six small and scattered plants were at work on the property, and were raising less than one-half of the material now being obtained from two shafts. As the plant at each shaft requires its staff of engine-men, stokers, pit-banksmen[4] and foremen, it is evident that great economy is effected by reducing the number of such establishments. In the case mentioned, the reduction in surface-charges effected by concentration has amounted to 4·67*d.* per ton.

Railways. – As it is usual to screen the coal direct into the railway-wagons to the various sizes required for sale, the greatest care is required in laying out the sidings so that work may proceed without hindrance; and, where practicable, the railways should be so arranged as to allow a gentle descent for the wagons to and from the screens. Where the nature of the ground will not admit of this, endless ropes working between the rails are of great service. In no case should dead-end sidings be used if a regular output is to be maintained, as the time lost in shunting wagons will cause serious hindrance to the coal-winding. It is also desirable that each quality and size of coal should be delivered on a separate road so as to allow of continuous loading. A good arrangement is shown in Fig. 1, Plate 4 [not included here], where the sidings as laid out at the Whitfield Colliery are indicated. Empty wagons are hauled by locomotive power to the highest point and are left in sidings arranged on the 'gridiron' principle. From this point they are run down as required into the various screen sidings, a separate line being provided for each of the ten classes of coal. When loaded, the trucks are lowered down to the weighing- machine, which is situated at the place to which the lines converge. After being weighed, the trucks are marshalled in sidings below, ready for transit outwards. It will be seen that by this arrangement all locomotive work through the screens is avoided, and that from the time empty wagons are placed in the sidings above the pits until they are taken away loaded by the branch line, no loco-motive-power / is required. It is found that an average gradient of 1 in 30 is suitable for the empty sidings. This may appear to be steeper than is actually necessary, but allowance has to be made for accumulations of coal-dust under the screens and of snow on the rails in winter. In the sidings below the screens, it is found that the loaded wagons run well on a gradient of 1 in 76.

The cost of shunting is by this means reduced to a minimum, that of dealing with 1,800 tons in eight hours being –

	s.	*d.*
Two shunters (youths) lowering empty wagons to screens at 3s.	6	0
Two shunters taking loaded traffic over machine, one at 4s. and one at 3*s.* 4*d.*	7	4
Total	13	4

equivalent to 0·09d. per ton or about 0·5*d.* per ton per mile.

The considerable length of sidings made available is found to be very convenient, allowing an ample supply of empty wagons to be in position above the screens and providing good standing-room for loaded traffic below, so that any temporary hindrance in working the traffic over the main line does not interfere with the working of the pits. Accommodation for upwards of 100 wagons is provided in the storage roads above the screen-sidings. The through lines used by the locomotives to take the wagons into the storage sidings are laid with single-headed steel rails weighing 84 lbs. per yard; the screen sidings are laid with flat-bottomed rails which weigh 50 lbs. per yard.[5]

Workshops. – Well-fitted workshops are necessary for the purpose of maintaining the mechanical appliances used at collieries. The Author is of opinion, however, that it is not advisable to undertake new work of importance in colliery workshops, but to use them simply for the purpose of making such repairs as may be necessary. In districts where there are good engineering works near to the collieries, even a portion of the last-mentioned work may with advantage be sent out; but where there are not facilities for doing it near at hand, it is of the highest importance that all necessary tools and machinery for repairs should be provided at the colliery. A good smithy, with a small steam-hammer, lathe and drilling-machine, should form part of the equipment, and a carpenters' shop and a saw-mill are also required. Where practicable, the workshops should be built on a level with the pit- bank, and light tramways of the same gauge as that of the underground roads should be provided to facilitate the transport of material from the shops to the pit-shaft. A small pick-smithy / for sharpening the miners' tools, and a shop for light repairs to pit-wagons, placed as near to the shaft as possible, will be found useful in most cases. Fig. 2, Plate 4 [not included here], shows the arrangement of the carefully planned workshops[6] erected for the Whitfield colliery, where 2,000 tons of coal are raised daily. The shops include a saw-mill, with an engine driving a circular saw, a carpenters' shop with a joiners' and pattern-makers' shop attached, a fitting shop with two lathes, planing-, shaping-, boring- and screwing- machines, and a smithy with four fires and one 3-cwt. steam-hammer.

The lamp-room, in which the safety-lamps are cleaned and trimmed, is also included in the same range of buildings; that shown in the Fig. being designed to accommodate about 1,600 lamps. Owing to the greasy nature of the work, it is desirable that the fittings should be made of iron throughout, so as to render the building as nearly as possible fire-proof. The lamps may be stored on narrow shelves fixed on the walls near to the places where they have to be given out, each lamp being numbered and the shelves bearing corresponding numbers. The numbering is done so that each workman may have the same lamp from day to day; the number and the user's name are registered in order to assist identification in the event of damage resulting from the careless handling of any lamp. It is important that the lamp-room should be large enough to allow space for the lamp-men to move about with ease when giving out the lamps. It is not unusual for upwards of 1,000 lamps to be passed out in twenty-five minutes, and to prevent delay a sufficient number of issuing-places should be provided. A lamp-cleaning-machine with rotary brushes, of which there are several types in the market, is of great service. In the lamp-room arranged as shown, three men and one boy can give out 900 lamps in twenty minutes. The actual number of lamps in use is 1,500, and the cost is as follows:–

	£	s.	d.	Per lamp per week. d.
Labour for cleaning, trimming and repairs, five boys and two men	5	16	6	0·93
Material – oil,* 72 gallons of colza at 2*s.* 1½ *d.* 36 gallons of petroleum at 5*d.*	8	8	0	1·34
Sundry stores	0	11	6	0·09
Cost of one lamp per week	.	..	.	2·36

Pit-Bank Arrangements.

As the weight of coal carried in pit-wagons rarely exceeds 10 cwt. in English collieries, it is necessary, where large quantities have to be raised, to make such arrangements on the pit-bank as will allow the material to be easily handled. To land an output of 1,000 tons per day will require not less than 2,000 wagons to be brought to the pit-bank in eight hours; and as each one of these has to be taken from the cage, weighed, conveyed to the screen, emptied and returned to the pit, it follows that the arrangements must be such as will allow a continuous train of wagons to be passed. The size of the wagons, and therefore the weight of the coal carried, is generally limited by the height of the seam worked, but 10 cwt. may be taken as their average load in English collieries. In the South Wales coal-field wagons to carry a load of 20 cwt. are admissible on account of the exceptional thickness of the seams there worked. As will be seen by the Table in the Appendix the weight of the coal forms a small portion of the total load raised, so that any reasonable increase in it would not in most cases overtax the engine-power. In seams between 3 feet and 5 feet thick, wagons carrying about 8 cwt., and measuring 4 feet long, 3 feet wide, and 2 feet deep in the body, are generally used, and are as large as can be conveniently handled and loaded in the workings. In the thicker seams, up to 7 feet, larger wagons are used, on an average about 4 feet long, 3 feet wide, and 2 feet 6 inches deep, and carrying about 10 cwt. The weight of such a wagon if strongly built, to resist the rough handling it meets with underground, is not less than 5 cwt., giving a gross weight of 15 cwt.

* Two gallons of oil, 2 parts of pure colza to 1 part of petroleum, fill 166 lamps for ten hours' burning. /

The wagons are generally built of larch or elm boards 1¼ inch to 1½ inch thick, but advantage would result if thin steel plates were more generally used in substitution for the wooden sides and bottom. A pit-wagon of the same outside dimensions as those last mentioned, but with a steel plate bottom 3/16 inch thick instead of 1½ inch larch boards, and plate sides ⅛ inch thick instead of 1¼ inch boards, weighs 6 cwt., and has a capacity of 12 cwt. This would give an increase in the quantity raised of 200 tons per day where 2,000 wagons are used. The chief objection to the use of steel or iron in the construction of pit-wagons has been the greater cost of repairs when wagons meet with such accidents as are frequent in underground workings. The Author has found, however, that steel wagons which are put together with short screw pins instead of rivets are repaired with no greater difficulty / than wooden wagons; and, further, the damaged plates of steel wagons may be straightened and used again, whilst the broken boards of wooden wagons are valueless.

With the use of screw pins in the construction of the steel wagons, it is found better to put a thin liner of hard wood between the plates at the joints, so as to allow a firmer grip to be obtained than when the two hard steel faces are screwed together.

The gross weight should not be increased beyond 18 to 20 cwt., for if this weight is exceeded much delay to the work results if a wagon leaves the rails, especially in inclined seams. Owing to the shifting nature of the ground, it is difficult to maintain the underground tramways in a thoroughly efficient state, and therefore the question of replacing the wagons on the rails is of considerable importance. It is also undesirable in seams producing much small coal to have so large a load as to unduly encumber the screens; for in such cases there is more difficulty in separating the small from the lump coal than when smaller loads are used. With the improved haulage arrangements by means of endless ropes now in general use, the quantity of coal which can be conveyed along the underground passages is largely increased; and in cases where it is found that the output is limited by the quantity raised in the shaft, it will be better to increase that quantity by employing additional winding-power and a greater number of decks on the cage, or even by duplicating the shafts and winding machinery, than to use wagons which are too heavy to be handled conveniently.

The coal is usually brought to the pit-bank in cages with two or more decks, carrying two wagons end-to-end on each deck. If in changing loaded for empty wagons the cage has to be stopped at the pit-bank level to deal with the first deck, and be subsequently lifted for the operation to be performed with the lower deck or decks, much time is occupied; and in order to avoid such delay it is desirable to make arrangements for changing the decks simultaneously.

Where more than two decks have to be changed, the hydraulic arrangement, Fig. 3, Plate 4 [not included here], invented by Mr. George Fowler,[7] and erected by him at the Cinderhill and Hucknall Collieries, Nottinghamshire, and elsewhere, is a most valuable contrivance. It consists of cages moved by hydraulic power, with the same number of decks as the pit-cages, fixed on each side of the pit. One of these is filled with empty trams and is raised into position. The other cage, empty, is also raised to the same level. As soon as the pit-cage reaches the surface, hydraulic-pressure is applied to / pistons which push the empties into the main cage, and at the same time force the loads on to the cage standing ready to receive them on the opposite side, when the main cage is again ready to be lowered down the shaft. While the cage is running in the shaft, the hydraulic cages are lowered, deck by deck, to the pit-bank level, the loaded trucks are removed from the one and a fresh supply of empties is placed in the other, and they are again raised into position to await the return of the main cage. By this means, the time occupied in changing the wagons on any number of pit-cage decks is the same as that required for one deck. Where, however, there are only two decks to be dealt with, the simplest plan is to fix a platform above the pit-bank level, so as to allow both decks to be changed at the same time. The loaded wagons on the upper deck are run down to a balance-cage connected with a similar cage behind the pit, by which two empties are raised. This arrangement has been introduced at several collieries, one of the best examples of it being that at the Harton Colliery, Durham.* Figs. 4 and 5 [not included here] show an arrangement of this kind constructed by the Author a few years ago at a pit where it is required to deal with 1,000 tons, or 2,000 wagons, daily. The balance-cages being fixed out of the sight of the engineman, allow him a clear view of the pit-top. It may be seen that the loaded wagons gravitate from the pit-cage to the balance-cage, which is connected with the cage for the empties by wire-rope ¾ inch in diameter. The difference in height required to allow fall for the empty wagons to, and the loads from, the cage, renders it necessary to use pulleys of different diameters; and the empty cage being on the larger pulley, power is gained to raise the other cage into position again without balance-weights. The actual saving in winding by this arrangement in a pit 420 yards deep is as follows:–

———	When changing Decks separately.	With the Double platform.
Time of winding	40 seconds	40 seconds
Changing wagons	25 "	10 "
Totals	65 "	50 "
Maximum runs per day of eight hours. .	443	576
" weight per day (2 tons per run) . .	886 tons	1,152 tons

This shows an increase of 266 tons per day, or 30·7 per cent. on the smaller weight.

* Trans. Federated Inst. of Mining Engineers, Vol. i. Plate VI., illustrating Messrs. Forster and Ayton's Paper 'On Mechanical Coal-Cleaning.'[8]

The Mines' Regulation Act[9] provides that 'where the amount of wages of any person depends on the amount of mineral gotten' it 'shall be truly weighed at a place as near to the pit-mouth as is reasonably practicable.' As the large majority of miners are paid by weight, it is necessary to weigh each loaded wagon before it is emptied at the screens, and it is usual to place a weighing-machine near to the pit-shaft. This machine should, however, be placed at such a distance from the shaft as to allow standing-room for a full cage-load of wagons between the machine-plate and the cage. Where a large number of wagons has to be rapidly weighed, a self-recording machine should be used. There are several kinds of scales specially adapted for this class of work; the Author has used two Pooley water-balance machines for several years, and has found them to be quick in action and reliable in every way. Between the weighing-machine and the screens it is advisable to allow some little siding-room for the loads, so that any temporary stoppage of the screens, such as that required for changing railway-trucks, will not stop the work of the pit. Where this is done, some means of hauling the wagons to the screen should be provided. Fig. 5 [not included here] shows an arrangement of creeper-chains[10] and gravity-roads to and from the screens, which is calculated to deal with 1,000 tons daily in eight hours. As the loads leave the weighing-machines they are pushed on to a creeper-chain which catches the axles and hauls them up a short incline rising 1 in 10; after reaching the summit they run clear of the chain down an easy incline of 1 in 40 to the tippler, where the coal is emptied into the screen. The tippler, which will be referred to later, is so arranged that the loaded wagons push out those last emptied. When the empties leave the tippler, they are twisted on the turn-plates to a second creeper-chain which hauls them up an incline of 1 in 4, from which they run back to the pit ready for filling the pit-cages again. The creeper-chains run at about 60 feet a minute, and the whole time occupied in weighing, conveying to the tippler, emptying and returning the empty wagon back to the pit, a total distance of about 300 feet, is two minutes.

The cost of labour for banking 1,000 tons per day by this arrangement is as follows:– /

	£	*s.*	*d.*
Two men pushing empty wagons into the cage . . .	0	8	6
Two men taking loads cut and weighing	0	8	0
Two men at the front of the tippler	0	6	8
One man behind the tippler, twisting empty wagons . .	0	4	0
One boy removing and sorting tallies from wagons . .	0	1	6
One man at the balance-cage	0	3	8
One boy filling the empty balance-cage	0	1	6
Total . . .	1	13	10*

Cost per ton, 0·4*d.*

* These figures show the wages paid prior to August, 1894, which have since been reduced 7½ per cent.

Controllers. – For regulating the supply of wagons, Woodworth Controllers, Fig. 6 [not included here], are found to be of great service. This apparatus is designed to control the delivery of wagons on inclined planes without an attendant to block or release them. It can be opened from any distance by the person requiring the wagons, and all the movements are automatic. [Wain then provides a short description of the controllers which is omitted here.]

...

Tipplers. – In order to empty the coal into the screens, some device by which wagons may be easily turned over is required. Figs. 7 and 8 [not included here] show an ordinary back tippler which is largely used for the purpose. The loaded wagon is run into the tippler, which is set in line with the tramway and is carried on two central journals. Stop-forks are fixed on the frame, which catch the axle of the wagon and hold it so that the centre of the load is a little behind the centre of the tippler. When the catches are drawn back, the heavier end sinks and causes a partial revolution of the frame; the wagon, held firmly by the forks over the axle, is turned almost upside down, and is held in that position until the coal has fallen out. When the brake is released, the heavy portion of the wagon, *i.e.,* the wheels and axles, tilt the frame of / the tippler back to its original position, the catch is pushed in and the empty wagon is removed. The tippler-frame may be either circular as shown in the Fig., or a square cage as in the North of England, or even a flat plate with rails and journals attached as in some of the Lancashire collieries. The only detail common to the various patterns is the central bearing on which the frame is carried; this is so fixed that when a loaded wagon is placed in the tippler, the weight of coal above the centre will cause it to revolve to such a point that when emptied the weight of the lower portion will cause its return. The objections to this tippler are – that it is difficult to regulate the speed at which it is revolved, and that the coal has to fall a considerable distance to the screen-plates below, causing in the case of tender coals serious breakage and an increased amount of slack.

Rigg Tippler. – In the Rigg tippler, Figs. 9 and 10 [not included here], the fall of coal from the wagon to the screen is checked by a swinging door, and by a shoot which forms part of the frame of the tippler.

Side Tipplers. – The most suitable plan is, in the Author's opinion, an arrangement by which the coal may be emptied over the side instead of over the end of the wagon. Where this is done, it is somewhat more difficult to arrange the balance of the load. Side tipplers are generally heavy to work by hand, and are consequently not so quick in action as ordinary end tipplers. Where power is available, the difficulty may easily be overcome by fixing small friction-rollers which can be pressed against the circumference of the tippler frame. Figs. 11 and 12 [not included here] show a side tippler with friction-gear designed by the Author, by means of which wagons containing a load of 10 cwt. may be emptied at the rate of six per minute. This tippler is carried on disk-wheels so as to allow a clear road through for the wagons when empty.

Heath-Woodworth Tippler. – This is an end tippler arranged to be driven by power, which, after starting, is automatic in action. A cog-wheel worked by a rope or chain from the screen-engine is placed on the centre axle, but working free. A short rack with teeth of the same pitch as the cog-wheel, and fixed to the side of the tippler frame, is thrown into gear by a lever, and the tippler is steadily revolved, *Figs.* 13 [not included here]. The rack is thrown out of gear automatically when a complete revolution has been made. By means of a modification of the Woodworth Controller, the wagon is held securely in position without the use of forks as in the ordinary end tippler, and this allows a straight run through for the empty wagons. One man can pass 200 to 300 wagons per hour / through this tippler, and the coals are delivered steadily with a minimum of breakage.

Screens. – Sorting, sizing and preparing the mineral for the market are perhaps the most important of colliery surface-operations, but where the surface-works have been at the outset well planned, there are no special difficulties. The apparatus used is generally very simple, except where one seam contains two or more qualities of coal, or where there are bands of dross or stone which have to be removed, in which case hand-picking belts[11] are required. The subject of screening and picking apparatus would, in itself, afford material for a lengthy Paper, and the Author proposes to give only a short description of some of the types of screen in general use. In laying out the heapstead[12] it is important that there should be sufficient height between the pit-banks and screen-siding levels. The height will vary considerably according to the type of screen used and the number of sizes to be made. In practice it is found that with fixed bar-screens, not less than 20 feet is required if the coal is to be separated into three sizes, whilst with jigging screens[13] it is possible to do the same work with 16 feet where no picking belts are required.

Fixed Bar-Screens. – Fixed bar-screens, Fig. 14, Plate 4 [not included here], may be employed with advantage where the quantity to be passed does not exceed 200 to 250 tons per day, and where the seam is fairly strong, and contains only a low percentage of small. The flattest gradient / should not exceed 1 in 3 or thereabouts for the round coal,[14] but it must be steeper for the smaller sizes. Steel bars of taper section are fixed parallel in cast-iron bearers, with distance-pieces to space the bars. As the coal slides down, the smaller particles fall through upon a fixed shoot if two sizes only are to be made, or on a second set of bars of closer mesh if further separation is required. The coal when tipped on such a screen slides down at a high velocity, and in the case of brittle seam a large amount of small[15] is made by breakage on the screen, and further, where the coal to be screened contains much small, the larger pieces carry a good deal of slack with them into the coal-truck. Where the screens are flattened to prevent this, hand-labour has to be employed in raking down, and the cost of screening is greatly increased. Under such conditions it becomes necessary to provide some other means of dealing with the coal, for which purpose there are various types of mechanical screens.

Mechanical Screens. – These may be classed under three heads:– 1st, revolving-barrel screens; 2nd, endless-belt screens, such as the Lührig belt and the Greenwell screen; 3rd, jigging screens, these being the kind in most general use.

Revolving Screen. – The revolving screen is the oldest mechanical screen, and consists of a cage of bars usually set longitudinally and carried on a central axle driven by gearing from a small engine. Where several sizes have to be made, there is a series of inner rings carrying bars of varying mesh, the widest mesh being inside. The screen is set with a fairly steep inclination, say, 1 in 5 to 1 in 6, and the coal to be screened is delivered into the centre of it. Such an appliance cannot be used with advantage for large coal owing to the amount of breakage caused by the large pieces being carried up the sides of the cylinder as it revolves and falling down upon the coal below. Where, however, it is required to separate a quantity of slack into several sizes, as is necessary with many coal-washing machines, the revolving screen is best adapted for the purpose; and it is not uncommon, with a machine of this type, to make five sizes from slack which has been previously screened through bars of 1¼ inch mesh.

Endless-belt Screens. – The Lührig belt consists of a series of short iron bars coupled together to form an open chain of alternate bars and openings of equal width. This is principally used where it is required to chip bands of dross from the coal. In dressing the coal, a certain quantity of small is made, which falls through the open spaces and is conveyed into the proper / receptacle for slack. The Greenwell screen, Fig. 15 [not included here], consists of a series of endless chains carried on grooved drums at both ends of the screen, and driven by gearing from a small engine. The chains travel between fixed bars of varying widths and of A section. The widest bars are at the end of the screen where the coal is tipped, and the space between them and the moving chains is only sufficient to allow the smallest size to pass. The coal is carried forward to a point where the space is increased by the bars becoming narrower, and the next size is there allowed to pass, and so on. The chief advantage of this screen is that it serves as a picking-belt as well as screening the coal. Another advantage is that very little elevation is required; any number of sizes may be made with a pit-bank only about 12 feet above the rail-level. The speed of the chains is about 45 feet per minute, and the gradient is 1 in 30, or even less. The engine-power is small; an engine with a 9-inch cylinder, working at a pressure of 45 lbs. per square inch, easily drives two screens passing 250 tons per day each. Side-tipplers are a necessity with this screen, in order that the coal may be delivered evenly over the surface.

Jigging Screens. – The most difficult conditions in connection with coal-screening present themselves where it is necessary to deal with a large output from a tender seam of which a great portion is small. In order to reduce to a minimum the cost of handling the coal, it is desirable to treat the whole output at one point, as each screen requires its full staff of men and boys, whether passing a large or a small quantity. Neither of the screens described is capable of doing this at an extensive colliery without being duplicated. Where the work occurs under the conditions mentioned, some form of jigging screen will generally be the most suitable; and it is quite possible to deal with an output of 1,000 tons per day with one screen of this type where the seam is fairly free from shale and where not much hand-picking is required. The ordinary pattern of jigging screen consists of one or more iron trays fitted with screen-bars, or strong iron gauze of suitable mesh. The pans are hung so as to allow free movement, and are driven backwards and forwards by rods connected with cranks or eccentrics. Owing to the exceptionally heavy nature of the work, the wear and tear is considerable, and the apparatus must be strongly constructed. It is, however, desirable to make the body of the screen as light as is consistent with strength, so as to reduce the weight of the moving parts. The screens may be driven either from the end or the side. /

The Lyall screen, which is the best type of side-shaken screen, consists of a heavy iron casing with the screen-grids fixed in tiers. It is thoroughly efficient in action, but is most suitable for a strong coal. As the coal passes down over the screen-grids, which are placed at an inclination of about 1 in 4, it is thrown from side to side and the small is thoroughly separated from it. Between 500 tons and 600 tons is the maximum quantity which can be passed daily over one screen of this type. There appears to be too much knocking about, and consequent breakage of the coal, to allow this pattern to be largely used for tender coal. Very strong framing and supports are necessary to resist the side motion. To provide counterbalance, so as to reduce the shock, it is well to work two of these screens from the same line of shafting with cams or cranks set in opposite directions. End-driven jiggers will be generally found most suitable, as the coal may be passed over them with a smoother and more regular motion. The speed at which the screens are driven will depend on the quantity of coal to be passed, the angle of inclination at which the bars or gauze is set, and the throw of the cranks. A short quick movement is generally found most effective, and the Author's experience is that with a throw of 4 inches to 5 inches a speed of about 100 revolutions per minute of the driving-shaft will be sufficient. If the motion is too smooth and even, as would be the case with a greater throw and lower speed, there is danger of the mass of coal passing without being properly separated, as in the case of fixed bar-screens. The same result will follow if the screen is fixed at too high an angle and the coal passes over at too great a velocity. An inclination of 1 in 4 for the moving parts should not be exceeded in any case. Cranks will as a rule be found to be more suitable than eccentric cams, the former giving an intermittent onward movement which effects a better separation than the more regular oscillation given by the latter apparatus. At the same time, it is easier to adjust and take up the wear on the crank-bearing by gib and cotter than it is to adjust the eccentric-straps on the cams.

In constructing the screens, it is advisable to use two pans, set either one over the other or tandem, so that the movements may be counterbalanced. Fig. 16 [not included here] shows a useful end-driven jigger erected by the Author some years ago. This was designed to separate coal containing about 30 per cent. of small into three sizes, *i.e.*, coal over 2-inch × 4-inch mesh, cobbles[16] through 2-inch × 4-inch and over 2-inch × 1-inch mesh, and slack through 2-inch × 1-inch mesh, and to pass 500 to 600 tons per day of eight hours. /

The cost of this jigger was –

	£	*s.*	*d.*	£.	*s.*	*d.*
Timber	31	2	4			
Iron for pans, shafting &c.	21	15	4			
Steel wire grids	3	10	0			
				56	7	8
Labour – making and erecting				20	5	0
Total				76	12	8

These figures do not include the cost of the engine, nor is there any allowance for management or establishment charges.

For passing a larger quantity under less favourable circumstances, where the amount of small is equal to almost 40 per cent. of the whole output, and where it is necessary to deal with the coal at the rate of 1,000 tons per day of eight hours, the Wain shaker-screen, Fig. 17 [not included here], has been designed. In this apparatus, fixed shoots are used to pass the coal to and from the shakers, the pans of which are only about 6 feet square. By this means the weight to be moved is much reduced. A pair of eccentric cams on each side drive double-ended cranks keyed on a shaft which is carried in bearings and is free to vibrate. The upper ends of the pans are coupled to the cranks, the lower ends being carried by hangers. A reciprocating and oscillating movement is secured, which gives a better riddling action to the screen than is obtained in the ordinary jigger and allows the pans to be set at a very low inclination, the upper pan being set at 1 in 14 and the lower at 1 in 6. The power required to drive the screen is small. With this machine 3 tons per minute (equivalent to 1,440 tons per day of eight hours if the screen could be kept continuously at work) are thoroughly screened with a minimum of breakage. Perforated steel plates are used instead of bars or wire grids, and serve for taking the cobbles and slack from the coals – the smooth surface presented by them admitting of a flatter inclination than can be obtained with the usual wire mesh. In the perforated plates the area of screening-surface is reduced. For this reason they are less suitable to the subsequent screening of the fine slack from the cobbles in the lower pan, and wire grids of 2-inch × 1-inch mesh made of wire ¼ inch in diameter are used.

Winding-Appliances.

The head-gear shown in Fig. 4, Plate 4 [not included here], is of the ordinary type of wooden frame used to carry the pit-top, pulleys &c. In some of the newer plants lattice ironwork or rolled girders are being / employed in place of timber, but without any alteration in the general design of the head-gear.

The height from the pit-bank level to the centre of the pulleys varies considerably, but about 50 feet will generally be found sufficient to allow clearance above the cages and tackling-chains. The winding-engines in general use are horizontal coupled engines with plain slide- or Cornish valves, and with the rope-drum mounted direct on the crank-shaft with two ropes, one ascending as the other descends. Compound or condensing engines are rarely employed in modern winding-gear, as the few seconds in which continuous work has to be done, and the variable load, prevent full advantage being gained from those types of engine. In an Appendix particulars are given of the depth and speed of winding at several collieries having large outputs; and it will be seen from these that an average speed exceeding 30 feet per second is attained in most cases. In the case of Walsall Wood, No. 1 pit, which affords one of the best examples of high-speed winding in the Midlands, the maximum speed is reached in eighteen seconds, the first six revolutions being made in 12¾ seconds, the second six in 6½ seconds, and the third six in 5¾ seconds. The total number of revolutions in the run is 25½, of which only 21 are under steam. The time occupied in making the run of 550 yards is forty-four seconds, which gives an average speed throughout the run of 37½ feet per second, the maximum speed being 60 feet per second, or over 40 miles an hour. The maximum possible output for eight hours' winding, with four wagons on each cage, carrying an average load of 13 cwt. of coal, is in this case 1,385 tons, and actually 1,231 tons have been raised in that time. It will be inferred that under such circumstances all complications in the winding-engines must be avoided. With the higher steam-pressures now used, there should be, however, no difficulty in taking advantage of compound working, provided the high- and low-pressure cylinders are both duplicated.

In designing colliery winding-engines, each of the coupled engines is usually made large enough to start the load at any point, as it is possible that one of the engines may be on the dead-centre at the moment of starting; and, with one high- and one low-pressure engine coupled in parallel, there might be some difficulty in adjustment unless there was an arrangement for giving the low-pressure engine some high-pressure steam to start the load if the high-pressure engine was centred – which could only be done by introducing undesirable complications in the valve-gear. If, however, each of the engines were compounded / with high- and low-pressure cylinders fixed tandem, the difficulty might be overcome. Owing to the variable load due to the decreasing weight of the ascending, and the increasing weight of the descending, rope, winding-engines are usually very wasteful in working. The weight of the rope, especially in the case of deep shafts, forms a large portion of the dead load. The weight of the cages and wagons on both ropes is practically the same, and therefore need not be further considered. The weight to be raised is represented by the weight of coal carried in the wagons, and the weight of the rope. In the case of the Sneyd Colliery, No. 2 (Appendix), the weight of the rope is 56 cwt., and that of the coal to be raised 65 cwt. After the moment of starting, the actual unbalanced load, exclusive of friction in guide-rods, &c., is 56 + 65 cwt. = 121 cwt. As the cage is wound up, the weight of the loaded rope is a constantly decreasing, and that of the descending rope an increasing, factor; so that by the time half the run is made the load is

$$(56/2+65) - 28 = 65 \text{ cwt.}$$

From this point, the descending weight is increased until at the termination of the run the actual load is 65–56 = 9 cwt. These extreme variations of load render it difficult to regulate the consumption of steam in relation to the work done.

Various contrivances are introduced to balance the load, but the best and simplest is a plain balance-rope worked with a parallel drum, *Fig. 18* [not included here]. The balance-rope is attached to the under side of each cage and passes round a pulley in the pit-bottom below the level of the point where the cage is loaded. The Author has been working such a balance-rope for several years in a shaft 240 yards deep where there was no pulley,[17] the rope being simply passed round the timber beams which carry the pit-bottom scaffold. For greater depths it is undesirable to dispense with the pulley, which should be set in slides so that its weight will cause / sufficient tension to keep the balance-rope steady in the shaft. In the Koepe system,[18] there is a simple grooved pulley instead of the usual cylindrical drum, and considerable economy in the first cost of engines and ropes is obtained thereby. The single winding-rope is attached to the cage in the usual manner, passed half round the Koepe drum-ring and back to the other cage. There is always a balance-rope with this arrangement, which is especially suitable for high-speed winding with a light load. For heavy loads it is less suitable, as there is a tendency for the rope to slip a little, which causes inaccuracy in the indicator used to show the position of the cage in the shaft. Many winding-engines are now fitted with drums having a spiral groove, the rope starting on the smallest diameter when the cage is leaving the pit-bottom, and with a well-designed drum of this class a perfect balance may be obtained. The drum is, however, costly, and there is some difficulty in adjusting the rope; on the whole, the most reliable arrangement is a plain parallel drum with a balance-rope under the cages. For balance-ropes, old winding-ropes are found preferable to new ropes, as they exhibit less tendency to twist and curl.

The economy of fuel in colliery-work has received too little attention in the past, the boilers being often supplied with inferior coal or slack which has been considered to be unsaleable. The amount of coal consumed in colliery-work is probably not less than 5 per cent. of the total output of the kingdom; and as slack has now become more valuable, colliery engineers are beginning to give greater attention to the questions of compound working, expansion-gear, condensation, and balanced loads. The engines have been, as a rule, designed to admit steam into the cylinder for almost the whole length of the stroke. Although such an arrangement enables the inertia of the load to be more easily overcome in starting, the back-pressure[19] is considerable in the case of engines running at high speeds, and it is by no means uncommon to obtain from engines working at 80 lbs. per square inch diagrams[20] giving a back-pressure of 10 lbs. per square inch. The general practice is now, however, to cut off steam at about four-fifths of the stroke.

Automatic expansion-gear, either thrown into action by the governors after the engine has reached a given speed, or applied by means of worm-gearing, to gradually increase the cut-off[21] during the run, has been adopted in a few instances with moderate success. The best results are, as a rule, obtained by balancing the load as far as possible, and by adopting expansion-gear which can be / thrown into action by the engineman when the requisite speed has been attained. Condensation, as applied to modern winding-engines, can only be said to have reached the experimental stage, but it is probable that independent surface-condensing apparatus, to maintain a steady vacuum, will be largely used in the future in colliery-works.

Briquette-Works.[22]

The general question of the manufacture of briquette-fuel was dealt with at the Institution in the Session 1893–94.[1] Various methods have been suggested for preparing the small form of non-bituminous coal for coking by mixing tar and other bituminous matter with it, or by adding bituminous coal to the small free-burning coal, but none of these plans have hitherto proved successful. Experiments on this subject are rendered difficult by the lack of reliable information as to the constituent parts of coal necessary for the production of coke.

[1] 'The Manufacture of Briquette-Fuel,' by W. Colquhoun. Minutes of Proceedings Inst. C.E., vol. cxviii. p. 191.[23]

So far as the Author has been able to follow the subject, chemical analyses of coking and free-burning coals appear to give identical results. It is probable that the difference is of a physical rather than of a chemical nature; and it is often found that a given seam may change from coking to free-burning coal in a short distance. The North Staffordshire coal-field supplies a notable instance of this change, as the lower seams of the series on the west side of the district give good blast-furnace coke, whilst on the east side the same give coal which cannot be made into coke by any of the ordinary methods. The change takes place in less than 2 miles; no special reasons are known to account for it.

Although small quantities of coke have been made from non-bituminous coals by the addition of pitch in varying proportions in experimental apparatus, the results have not been such as to warrant extensive application of the methods referred to. Coal tar intimately mixed under steam-pressure gave slightly better results, but in no case was the coke produced of such quality as to be suitable for blast-furnace work, being much inferior to coke from even the commoner qualities of bituminous coal. The various forms of mechanical stokers in the market, with suitable blowers, will consume the smallest coal with good results; but they have / not hitherto been adopted to such an extent as to lead to any great demand for 'smudge' or fine small coal.

In some districts, coal-washing apparatus specially adapted for separating slack into various uniform sizes has been adopted and worked with some success; but it appears doubtful whether any real economy is effected by this method of treating the small, when the interest and depreciation of plant* and the cost of washing are considered. In cases where seams contain a high percentage of dirt-partings and dross, some such method of treatment is absolutely necessary to put the slack into a marketable condition. In the course of a recent discussion on coal-washing,† Mr. James S. Dixon, of Glasgow, gave some interesting particulars, from which it appeared that slack, separated to five sizes and washed by the Lührig process, yielded, after taking into account the loss in washing, an average price but little in excess of that of the unwashed material.

One other method of treating the small coal, which in the case of anthracitic and free-burning coal has been uniformly successful, is to mix plastic adhesive matter with it and to form it into solid blocks under pressure.[25] Many cementing-substances have been used, but in the Author's opinion the pitch process is the most satisfactory. A small plant of this kind was erected by him in 1892 (Fig. 19, Plate 4 [not included here]). After considering the various types of machine in the market it was decided to adopt that of Stevens, on account of its being simple and automatic in its working and having no parts liable to break or cause trouble in working under ordinary circumstances.

The plant consists of a main bucket-elevator for lifting the slack to the distributor, where it is mixed with roughly-ground pitch which has been raised by

* A washing-plant to deal with 500 tons per day costs £10,000.

† Trans. Federated Inst. of Mining Engineers, vol. vii. p. 112.[24]

a small bucket-elevator to the same point. The distributor is a fluted roller with unequal openings, working in a cast-iron case. It takes certain portions, which may be varied according to circumstances, of pitch and slack from each of the hoppers. The materials are passed from the distributor into a Carr disintegrator, which reduces the larger particles and at the same time intimately mixes the two components. From the disintegrator the mixture is again elevated and is passed into a pug-mill,[26] into which steam at a pressure of 65 lbs. per square inch is blown by three ¼-inch nozzles. After the material has been sufficiently heated, it is allowed to fall into / the lower pan of the machine where revolving arms carry it into the mould. The pressure is applied by a vertical steam-cylinder, the piston-rod of which is connected with a lever that, when raised, acts on the press-hammer and so forces the die upwards and compresses the plastic mass against a fixed plate above. The die-table, with eight dies, is revolved by a rack-and-pawl[27] arrangement worked by a crank on the pug-mill shaft, and steam is admitted by an eccentric on the same shaft. As the table revolves, the finished block is raised by the die which runs up an inclined slide to the point of delivery, where an arm, also worked by the pug-mill shaft, strikes the block and pushes it clear of the table. As the die-table continues to revolve, the die is drawn down by an inclined slide until it again reaches the filling-point. All the moving parts being actuated from the same shaft, there is little possibility of a break-down. The rack-and-pawl arrangement by which the die-table is revolved allows an interval of rest in each revolution, and during that period the pressure is applied. The blocks thus made are sufficiently firm to be loaded direct into railway wagons for despatch. Particulars of the cost* of working such a plant have been already given by the Author.

Briquette-making appears to be the most profitable method of dealing with the slack of free-burning coals, more particularly when the seam is so free from dirt partings that the material does not need to be washed before passing through the process of its manufacture into block fuel.

…/

* Minutes of Proceedings Inst. C.E., vol. cxviii. p. 248.[28]

APPENDIX

Name of Colliery and Number of Pit.	Depth from Surface.	Load. No. of Wagons on Cage.	Load. Weight of Rope.	Load. Weight of Cages, Wagons and Chains	Load. Effective Load, *i.e.*, Weight of Coal per Run.	Load. Dead Load at Moment of Starting.	Engine. Description.	Engine. Diameter of Cylinder.	Engine. Stroke.		Engine. Steam-Pressure.	Engine. Type and Diameter of Drum.	Time of Winding.	Average Speed of Winding.	Time of Changing Decks.	Maximum possible Output per Day of Eight Hours.	Remarks.
	Yards.		Cwt.	Cwt.	Cwt.	Cwt.		Ins.	Ft.	Ins.	Lbs. per sq. in.		Sec.	Feet per Second.		Tons.	
Sneyd, No. 1	375	2	18	25	24	67	Horizontal coupled	16	4	0	60	Koepe, 10 feet	35	32–1	10	768	Single–deck cage; balance-rope.
Sneyd, No. 2	620	6	56	76	65	197	Ditto	36	6	0	90	Slightly taper, 21 ft. 6 in.	55	33.9	25	1,170	Three-deck cage; decks changed separately; no balance.
Wallsall Wood, No. 1	550	4	30	60	52	142	Ditto	42	6	0	65	Slightly taper, 20 ft. average diameter	44	37–5	10	1,385	Double-deck cage; both decks changed simultaneously; double platform; no balance.
Ditto No. 2	550	2	30	32	26	88	Ditto	21	4	6	65	Koepe, 20 feet	35	47–1	10	832	Single-deck cage; balance-rope.
Whitfield, No. 1	240	4	19	63	30	112	Ditto	24	4	0	65	Parallel, 12 feet	27	26–4	23	864	Double-deck cage; cages changed separately; balance-rope.
Ditto. No. 2	420	4	29	65	40	134	Vertical coupled	36	5	0	65	Parallel, 20 feet	40	31–5	10	1,152	Double-deck cage; cages changed simultaneously; no balance-rope.
Denaby Main.	450	6	46	72	60	178	Horizontal	40	6	0	70	Parallel, 24 feet	50	27–0	10	1,440	Three-deck cages; decks changed simultaneously by a Fowler hydraulic banking-gear. /

KNOWLEDGE: PHYSIOLOGY AND MEDICINE

This section deals with two neglected topics. Neglected, that is, by both the contemporary industry and subsequent historians. The first is the use in the coal mines of animals as a source of energy and power. The second is what one might term the economic study of work and the working conditions of men and boys in the mines. The first has been neglected, one assumes, because horses and ponies were not felt to represent the future of colliery operations. Overwhelmingly, the assumption of mine engineers, as with many ordinary citizens, was that operations currently undertaken by animals and humans would be mechanized. The duty of an engineer was to invent and perfect the machinery that would accomplish this. To study how better to employ human and animal labour was to divert one's energies from this prime task. This view is defensible. Nevertheless there were estimated to be about 200,000 horses working in British mines in 1878 and the question of how best to employ them was not an unimportant one.[1]

The first point to notice about Charles Hunting's essay on the feeding and management of colliery horses (pp. 381–91), therefore is its rarity.[2] As he notes in some introductory words not reproduced here, 'up to the present time', that is, 1882, 'this important subject had not been touched on in the Proceedings', indicating a silence of over twenty-five years. Hunting managed to find only two items where the matter had been discussed before, both in the proceedings of the South Wales Institute of Engineers.[3]

Hunting's recommendations for the care and feeding of colliery horses were based largely on empirical methods of research – trying things out and comparing the results with other trials – guided by some primitive physiological theory. It is notable that when talking of the constituents of a horse's food he does not mention calories, vitamins or minerals; all concepts then unknown or unknown in nutritional applications.

His paper hints at further difficulties of an economic nature. First, collieries appear to have purchased horses on the open market from outside dealers, rather than breeding them 'in-house', but the market appears to have suffered from inefficiencies relating to the difficulty of judging the quality of a horse:[4]

> In numerous instances where the writer has been called in to examine colliery studs, he has found the pit ponies ... with no permanent incisor teeth visible, and when he has stated their age has been told 'that he must be wrong because the pony had been a year and a half in the pit,' but it was true nevertheless.

The same passage suggests that collieries often failed to solve this problem by employing staff capable of accurately assessing equine quality. It was not possible to check the pedigree of a colliery horse in the way that it was for a race-horse or, later, a shire horse; stud books for the breeds usually used in collieries did not exist.[5]

Second, horse breeders seem to have failed to produce a breed of horse specifically adapted for colliery work. Hunting mentions Welsh and Shetland ponies and Welsh Cobs were widely used in south Wales but these breeds had been bred for other purposes.[6] One possible reason for this is that it was not possible to patent a new breed of horse, although this had not prevented the emergence of the Shire horse, for example, and a number of other breeds during the nineteenth century.[7]

The next text, 'The Milroy Lectures on the Hygienic Aspect of the Coalmining Industry in the United Kingdom' (pp. 393–4), is concerned with the working conditions of miners, rather than the horses and ponies with which they worked. The bulk of the contemporary and modern material published on this topic has taken a humanitarian, rather than a scientific, perspective. This was one of the earliest papers to be published concerned with miners' working conditions from a physiological or medical point of view. The economic relevance of such studies is clear: labour productivity will be lower than necessary if working conditions are poor; it is also possible that the well-being of miners might be improved by changes in working conditions even if these are motivated by the pursuit of profit.

'The Milroy Lectures', by Frank Shufflebotham, was not published until 1914. It was preceded by work in France, soon disseminated to Belgium and Britain, which had been precipitated by new regulations concerning standards of ventilation in French mines. In Britain 'the most interesting portion' of the research was that concerning the influence of temperature and humidity on miners' work:

> There are many mines with temperatures attaining, and even exceeding, 95° Fahr. (35° Cent.), in which, with dry air, the men perform an amount of work practically equalling that in mines with lower temperatures. When the hygrometric degree increases, work becomes onerous, even at far lower temperatures. One of 86° Fahr. (30° Cent.), is, however, still too high; and that of 77° Fahr. (25° Cent.) by wet thermometer is the limit compatible with good work. In a place where this temperature is exceeded, ventilation exerts appreciable influence on the organization [of the body], and with air not moving discomfort is experienced; but it ceases with a current of 39½ inches (1 metre) per second. With 86° Fahr. (30° Cent.) in a damp atmosphere, a man, even at rest, is very ill at ease when the air is still, but with a current of 6½ feet (2 metres) per

> second, this temperature is quite supportable, and a greater amount of work can be performed when, with the wet thermometer showing a temperature above 77° Fahr. (25° Cent.), a ventilation at say 9 feet (1 to 5 metres) per second is ensured.[8]

That conditions of work had a detrimental effect on miners' health, going beyond accidents and the specific, recognized, 'industrial diseases' such as nystagmus or 'miners' blindness, took a long time to be recognized, and such recognition as there was remained at the level of anecdote and journalism. Here, for example, are a General Practitioner's (or 'family doctor's') reminiscences published in 1921 during the national lockout of that year:

> The general practitioner's work here [south Wales], at the moment, is at a minimum, and vividly recalls my experience in a neighbouring area in 1908 when the South Wales miners were out on strike for six months. Prior to that strike my average domiciliary visits numbered twenty-five daily; but, during the out-of-work period, it became quite unusual to be called upon to visit more than one patient a day. Most of one's time was taken up in assisting to dole out provisions to the hungry and needy during the mornings, while the rest of the day was spent at football, cricket, etc., in the nearest available fields with scratch teams of miners. Medical work at that time almost registered zero.[9]

Shufflebotham's work presaged a rash of research, much of it carried out under the auspices of the Industrial Fatigue Research Board, produced in the decade immediately after the First World War.[10] That it used the leading scientific techniques of its times suggests that such research had to wait until progress in the natural sciences had reached this point. However, this is misleading. Much research could have been carried out using merely empirical techniques at any point in the previous century, if not earlier. Shufflebotham's paper summarizes research concluding that as temperature and humidity rise 'hard work becomes impracticable'. To reach this did not require the most powerful resources of Edwardian science. Once again, one suspects the fundamental problem to be one of research funding and organization; that is to say, a problem in the provision of public goods.

Notes

1. C. Thompson, *Harnessed: Colliery Horses in Wales* (Cardiff: National Museum of Wales/ Amgueddfa Cymru, 2008), p. 65, citing an RSPCA estimate. Thompson states that the number had decreased to about 70,000 by 1913. The last horses were not retired from National Coal Board collieries until the 1980s.
2. The term 'pit ponies' will be more familiar than 'colliery horses'. While some ponies of perhaps 13 hands were used, the majority of colliery horses, at least in south Wales, were horses, standing around 15 hands high.
3. J. Brogden, 'Inaugural Address', *South Wales Institute of Engineers*, 10 (1876), and Mr Wight 'Paper' and 'Discussion', *South Wales Institute of Engineers*, 12 (1880), pp. 285 and 395. The subsequent literature was equally sparse. There was F. O. Solomon's contribu-

tion ('The Feeding of Horses, with Special Reference to Colliery Studs', *Transactions of the Institute of Mining Engineers*, 19 (1899–1900), pp. 279–93, and 'Discussion', *Transactions of the North of England Institute of Mining Engineers*, 51 (1901–2), pp. 60–5.) W. C. Blackett remarked on the interest shown in Hunting's paper by members of the North of England Institute but waited twenty years before contributing one of his own on 'Underground Stables' (*Transactions of the North of England Institute of Mining Engineers*, 53 (1902–3), pp. 130–4 and plate XIII, and 'Discussion', pp. 134–7) which casts some doubt on the reality of the interest. Blackett's article was followed by Thomas Adamson 'Underground Horses at an Indian Colliery', *Transactions of the Institute of Mining Engineers*, 29 (1904–5), pp. 496–500 and plate XIX, and 'Discussion', pp. 500–1. The only article I have found in the *Colliery Guardian* is 'Colliery Horses' (18 April 1889, p. 551) which estimated the population of colliery horses at about 130,000, stated that treating the topic needed 'no apology', a sure sign that the author felt it did, and discussed the new 'nail-less' horse shoe. From the late 1880s onwards public discussion was, understandably, dominated by animal welfare issues. See, for example, 'Cruelties to pit-horses', *Chambers Journal*, 4 (3 September 1887), p. 576 and 'The treatment of pit horses', *Colliery Guardian*, 21 February 1890, p. 302. The only modern treatment is brief but informative: Thompson, *Harnessed*, pp. 37–41.

4. George Akerlof referred to the market in used cars as an example of a market affected by 'asymmetric information' in his classic article 'The Market for Lemons: Quality Uncertainty and the Market Mechanism', *Quarterly Journal of Economics*, 84 (1970), pp. 488–500. The market in used horses was exactly similar.
5. The absent stud book for colliery horses is another public good the absence of which may have affected the social efficiency of the industry. For a discussion of this and a number of other interesting economic and cultural issues in the history of animal breeding see, M. E. Derry, *Bred for Perfection: Shorthorn Cattle, Collies, and Arabian Horses since 1800* (Baltimore, MD: The Johns Hopkins University Press, 2003). For the history of the Shire horse, a breed of working horse for which a stud book was eventually established, see the wonderful, enormous and deeply eccentric K. Chivers, *The Shire Horse: A History of the Breed, The Society and the Men* (London: J.A. Allen, 1976).
6. Thompson, *Harnessed*, p. 14.
7. F. M. L. Thompson, 'Nineteenth-Century Horse Sense', *Economic History Review*, 2nd series, 29 (1976), pp. 60–81 marks the revival of modern interest in the economic history of the horse in the nineteenth century and was followed by his edited book *Horses in European Economic History: A Preliminary Canter* (Reading: British Agricultural History Society, 1993). R. Moorecolyer, 'Aspects of Horse Breeding and the Supply of Horses in Victorian Britain', *Agricultural History Review*, 43 (1995), pp. 47–60 reviews the main issues as seen by contemporaries, although the reader is left to speculate on the economics of the industry.
8. 'J. W. P.', '[Abstract of] Conditions of Useful Labour in Underground Workings. –By Joseph Libert. *Ann. [Annales des] Mines Belgique*, 1911, vol. xvi., pages 4–10', *Transactions of the North of England Institute of Mining Engineers*, 62 (1911–12), pp. 102–3.) Libert here reviews the research carried out by Jean Paul Langlois of Paris. For 'hygrometric' and 'wet bulb', see notes 3 and 12 on p. 393.
9. 'General Practitioner', 'Some Medical Impressions of the Miners' Strike', *British Medical Journal*, 2:3159 (16 July 1921), p. 94.
10. The Board published fifty-six *Reports* between 1919 and 1929. Contemporary research conducted independently of the board included for example, Frank Bunker Gilbreth,

Fatigue Study: The Elimination of Humanity's Greatest Unnecessary Waste: A First Step in Motion Study (London: G. Routledge, 1919) and P. S. Florence, *Economics of Fatigue and Unrest and the Efficiency of Labour in English and American Industry* (London and New York: H. Holt and Co., 1924).

Charles Hunting, 'The Feeding and Management of Colliery Horses' (1882–3)

Charles Hunting,[1] 'The Feeding and Management of Colliery Horses', *Transactions of the North of England Institute of Mining and Mechanical Engineers*, 32 (1882–3), pp. 61–110.

Economic horse management consists in obtaining the greatest amount of work at the smallest cost; but here, as in every other department, true economy depends upon careful selection and well-judged method. Good food must accompany good work: neither should be disproportionate. It is difficult to say whether too much or too little of either is the worst economy. But good food and good work are not absolute terms capable of mathematical definition. What is excess of work for one horse is not for another: what is excess of food for one horse may be insufficient for another; or, again, the food required by a horse doing moderate work is insufficient for the same horse doing hard work. There is still another difficulty, viz.: that equal weights of food, of equal market value, may differ indefinitely in feeding value. These few statements will show that careful selection of foods, and well-judged method in proportioning them to the work done, are absolutely essential to economic management, and this skill and judgment require some scientific knowledge and some practical experience not always thought necessary in the horse manager of an establishment. The writer's knowledge of the subject has only been obtained by long experience, by freely accepting the work of others, and / by submitting each theory or statement likely to be of value to a practical test. The subject is far from exhausted, but probably any further development must follow the lines laid down in this paper.

Tabular statements of the cost of feeding show absolutely nothing, save by comparison with others, and a comprehensive estimate should include not only the cost of food but the cost of horse-flesh and the amount of work done. By keeping too many horses to do a certain amount of work the bill for feeding can be made to look economical. By stinting the food an appearance of economy may be effected on paper, but the condition of the horses and the duration of their lives would soon dispel the illusion.

Both these explanations have been offered to account for the statements of economy embodied in the annual reports to the various collieries under the writer's charge, tabulated in the Appendix, page 107.

Economic horse management requires care in the conducting of the smallest details. From the purchase of the animal onwards, every step must harmonize and be subservient to the general object – economy.

In the selection of horses and ponies for 'putting' work[2] there is probably less discretion displayed by the managers of many collieries than in any other department. Hundreds of ponies are sold by dealers as three years old which have not lived twelve months, and it is quite common to find four or five in a drove of twenty, both Welsh and Shetland, especially the latter, not more than five or six months old, but which are always sold as two years old, and not one horse-keeper or owner in a hundred can tell by their dentition whether they are five or twenty months, in both cases the ponies having all 'milk' teeth in their mouths. In numerous instances where the writer has been called in to examine colliery studs, he has found the pit ponies, not cobs,[3] with no permanent incisor teeth visible, and when he has stated their age has been told 'that he must be wrong because the pony had been a year and a half in the pit,' but it was true nevertheless. He has seen several hundred ponies in pits, not two years old, that have been underground over a year. Their history is nearly always the same: 'This pony has never done well since he came down; has a poor appetite, and has no life in him; does not work above half his time, and tires before half the shift is over.' The overmen and drivers are always complaining because the new pony cannot draw the work out. The driver, being paid by the 'score,'[4] has little mercy, and so such ponies are generally covered with scars and blemishes from ill-usage; their hocks and knees are twice as large as they ought to be; the poor brute is made to live in painful misery all its life, and the owners lose more than cent. per cent, in the keeping of a useless, or nearly useless, animal. In horses, / the evil, in many colliery studs, is the other way; they are fine, fat, and good-looking, but their teeth show them to be far into their 'teens,' which means about two years' work instead of ten. The rule should be on all collieries that no horse should be bought under five years old nor over seven, and no ponies bought under three years old off. It is necessary that all animals should be examined by competent judges of age and soundness before they are paid for by the colliery.

Pit horses are probably the hardest worked animals in the kingdom, and hard work cannot be economically done by horses unless in condition; yet how very often it is that both horses and ponies are bought one day from a dealer, after being fed with boiled food and bran, and put to excessive work in the pit the next. In addition to the great risk of importing infectious diseases into underground studs, causing the loss of several hundreds of pounds, there is always tenfold more risk of injury to limbs and internal diseases from new horses out of condition than there would be from new horses well up to their work, which risk, in a well-regulated colliery, is always avoided by working all new animals for three or four weeks in the carts and wagons on the surface before going underground. It is very remarkable that such a palpable common-sense matter should be so often overlooked by the managers of collieries. The absurdity and cruelty of this is only exceeded by the still more common practice of working underground animals twenty to forty hours' shifts without their harness being taken off. There is nothing done on a colliery that is more expensive than overworking the pit animals double and treble shift.

Having secured a fair stud properly proportioned to the work, the next duty is to keep them as economically as possible, and this requires that they be kept in condition.

What is this 'condition' which is so necessary? It is that state of the system in which nerve and muscle are braced to their full extent; that state in which the animal's body is capable of performing its greatest amount of work, and in which alone it is capable of sustaining prolonged efforts. If a horse is looked upon simply as a machine for work, this state is the only one in which it can be used economically. With it, the greatest amount of work of which his muscles are capable can be obtained; without it, a certain amount of mechanism is lying idle, *i.e.*, muscular structure, useless for want of tone. This state depends entirely upon a proper balance of food and work: as soon as an animal is overworked this balance is upset, and a state of being is commenced in which economy is no longer attainable.

There are two things necessary to produce condition in horses – work and food; or, rather, hard work and high feeding: the former is never / lacking in collieries, and the latter can easily be attained if cost be no object. A sufficiency of oats and hay, with plenty of work, will produce condition, but at a most extravagant cost; but high feeding can be economically attained, and horses may be kept in the highest condition, at a cost very much below what is usually incurred for animals doing light work.

There are three conditions which render high feeding economical:–

1. – The selection of the cheapest but best food.
2. – Giving that food in a form most favourable to digestion.
3. – The prevention of waste.

The selection of the cheapest and best food is, of course, a matter to be settled in the first place by experiment, as have been the results now given; and in order that these results be accepted, their advantages must be understood. An outline of the rudiments of feeding will be given, ignorance of which reduces even the most extensive and careful practice to blind rule of thumb.

Long before chemistry and physiology rested upon any definite principles, experience had taught that certain foods possessed special feeding values. By the aid of these sciences it is now known not only which foods are most likely to be useful for any given purpose, but why they are useful; and, in fact, they enable the exact comparative value of the various feeding materials to be stated.

Food may be defined as a material which, when taken into an animal body, is capable of being changed and fitted to build up or replace the tissues of the body. Chemistry shows that these tissues consist of nitrogenous, fatty, and saline matters. It also shows that foods present a similar composition; so that, if the proportion of these constituents in any food is known, a fair idea of its feeding value is obtained. But chemistry alone is not reliable, as these constituents are not always in a form capable of being digested; and here physiology is useful, showing what is and what is not digestible, and also indicating how, under certain circumstances, some constituents are more essential than others.

This similarity of composition between animal and vegetable bodies will perhaps be more apparent by a glance at the following Table:–

Composition of	Dry Muscle.	Dry Blood.	Dry Vegetables.
Carbon	51.893	... 51.965	... 53.46
Hydrogen	7.590	... 7.330	... 7.13
Oxygen	19.127	... 19.115	... 23.37
Nitrogen	17.160	... 17.175	... 16.04
Ash or salts ...	4.230	... 4.415	... ...
	100.000	... 100.000	... 100.000

This Table shows very clearly, from a chemical point of view, how closely animal and vegetable substances resemble each other. The body does not, however, appropriate the constituents of plants in the elementary form here given. These ultimate elements are, in the plant, combined in various proximate forms, suitable for the nourishment of the animal.

The following Table shows the comparative composition of animal and vegetable bodies in those more complex forms, and it will be noticed that again the comparison is very similar:–

PROXIMATE CONSTITUENTS OF	
ANIMAL BODIES.	VEGETABLE BODIES.
Water.	Water.
Nitrogenous matter –	Nitrogenous matter –
Fibrine (flesh).	Gluten (oats, maize, &c.)
Casein (milk).	Legumin (beans, peas, &c.)
Albumen (eggs).	
Fatty matters.	Fatty matters –
	Starch, gum, and sugar.
Saline matters –	Saline matters –
Lime.	Lime
Potass	Potass } Ash.
Soda.	Soda }
Iron.	Iron }

In addition to water, the constituents of both animal and vegetable substances may be arranged in three great classes, nitrogenous, fatty, and saline.

The nitrogenous matter of the animal body is found under three forms, varying to a certain extent in their properties, in accordance with their derivation from flesh, milk, or eggs; but these three forms are similar in composition with each other and with the nitrogenous matter derived from plants, and all or any one of them taken into the body of an animal is capable of supplying all the three varieties. The gluten of oats, barley, and maize, or the legumin of beans, peas, and tares, supplies to the herbivora, forms of nitrogenous matter as suitable and as valuable as the flesh, milk, or eggs consumed by the omnivora.

The fatty matters of the body are not derived from the vegetable foods quite so directly as the nitrogenous. Animals make large quantities of fat when fed upon vegetables containing but a very small percentage of this article. The explanation of this is that vegetables, as the Table shows, contain ingredients – starch, gum, and sugar – which do not retain their original properties when taken into the animal's body. These substances undergo chemical changes, which convert the starch and gum into sugar, and, finally, the sugar into fat. /

These two great classes – nitrogenous and fatty matters – which are found in all animal and vegetable bodies, are those which have the most influence in relation to horse feeding, as the flesh or muscle of the horse is derived entirely from the nitrogenous constituents of vegetables, which may be designated as the flesh-forming matter. The fatty matters are derived from the fatty and starchy constituents of the food, and as the ultimate use of fat in the body seems to be its consumption for the production of animal heat, this class may be called the heat-forming matter.

The saline matters of the food directly supply the saline matters of the body, and they are quite as essential as the other two classes, but they are required in smaller quantities, and they exist in more constant proportion in each article than the other two. Of course, the composition of vegetable foods varies, and it is this variation that constitutes the difference in feeding value of each article.

The following Table gives a fairly correct idea of the constituents of a series of foods:–

	Water	Woody Fibre.	Starch, Gum, Sugar, and Fat.	Nitrogenous Matter	Ash or Saline.
Beans or Peas	14.5	10.0	46.0	26.0	3.5
Barley	13.2	13.7	56.8	13.0	3.3
Oats	11.8	20.8	52.0	12.5	3.0
Maize	13.5	5.0	67.8	12.29	1.24
Hay	14.0	34.0	43.0	5.0	5.0
Carrots	85.7	3.0 (Gelatine)	9.0	1.5	0.8
Flesh	74.0	3.0	3.0	20.0	

The large amount of water present in carrots and beef increases the comparative proportions of the other articles, all of which are in a dried state. Again, the column showing the amount of woody fibre is important, as this article is indigestible, and, therefore, almost useless as food.

The most important point, however, in the Table is this, that each substance differs in composition, some containing a large percentage of fatty or starchy matters, others containing a heavier proportion of nitrogenous matter. This theoretically suggests that some foods are most suitable for the production of muscle, others for the production of fat, and experience fully confirms the correctness of this indication. It will be noticed, however, that in every case the Table shows a higher percentage of starchy than nitrogenous matter. This is not because more fat-forming than flesh-forming food is wanted to meet the waste of tissue, but because / a very large quantity of fat, starch, and sugar is applied in the body to keeping up the animal heat. It is, to speak properly, not only required for the renovation of the body, but as fuel for the use of the animal machine. To meet this double demand, it is found that the vegetable foods are always richest in these elements. No better illustration of the truth of these statements can be found than the practical success of the Banting system.[5] That system, founded upon the above data, clearly proves that foods rich in starch, sugar, or fat will increase the fat of the body, but not add to the muscular strength; that lean meat, which is simply equivalent to the albuminous or nitrogenous principles found in vegetables, does not add to the fat of the body, but does supply the waste of muscle. The demand for these different constituents of food differs according to the state of the animal. In very cold climates the rapid loss of animal heat demands an excessive supply of the heat-producing foods: thus the Esquimaux consume enormous quantities of fat. Again, whenever the muscular system of the animal is greatly taxed a demand for the nitrogenous foods exist. Hunters[6] cannot do their work on hay alone, they require oats and beans to supply the flesh-forming matter. The British soldier and workman has hitherto excelled in physical endurance and muscular power as much on account of his meat diet as his national qualities. The late Mr. Brassey[7] found that when he fed his foreign workmen on the same diet as his British navvies the work done by the two approached an equality; previously they had no chance with Englishmen. Flesh, of course, supplies a heavy percentage of nitrogenous matter, but beans and peas supply even a much larger proportion, and their feeding value was well tested in the late Franco-German war, the German soldiers being largely dependent upon peas as an ingredient of their food to meet the waste of muscular tissue. The wonderful endurance of these men is conclusive evidence of the nutritive value of such food.

The value of the foregoing Table is enhanced when qualified by physiological knowledge, which shows that woody fibre is indigestible, and, therefore, an excess of it in any food is evidence of, at least, one disadvantage. It also teaches that a certain bulk of food is necessary to healthy digestion, and that, therefore, it is impossible successfully to feed entirely on those foods which contain the elements of the body in the most compact form. Further, the Table conveys a warning as to the action of different foods upon the digestive organs; thus, linseed, bran, and maize all cause laxness, whilst beans and peas tend to produce constipation. /

Thus, these articles of provender possess very different properties. Some are laxative, others constipative; but, by judiciously mixing them, both these objections may be removed and a most valuable food produced. To keep horses in health, when not hard worked, no mixtures are needed, and there is one grain in which the nutritive elements are so proportionately arranged that it cannot be improved upon, and practice has long adopted it. But to keep hard working horses in condition is a very different thing. Oats alone are not equal to it, nor can any single grain preserve both health and condition. The fact is, either their chemical constitution or their physiological action is defective, and it is only by mixing different articles, and altering their nutritive value, so as to balance physiological action, that a food can be produced which will not derange the functions of the animal, but which will supply all the requirements of the body.

Both chemistry and physiology then suggest that more than one kind of grain is advisable if economy and high condition are required. But the full economy of mixed feeding is only seen when considered with the money value of the different articles of provender in relation to their nutritive constituents, that is, when the feeding value is compared with the cost of the article. When the chemical, physiological, and monetary value of foods are understood, the cheapest and best food can be selected; or rather those articles of food which, when mixed in proper proportions, afford the largest amount of feeding material, at the smallest possible cost, can be recognised. Thus, and thus only, is the highest feeding compatible with the strictest economy.

If, in the feeding of horses, cost were of no importance, so long as health and condition were obtained, a large proportion of the advantages of using mixed food would be lost, as, unquestionably, oats and hay alone are a very good diet for horses not excessively hard worked. Such materials are, however, 30 per cent. – sometimes 50 per cent. – dearer than other provender equally valuable for feeding. Not unfrequently, when advising the use of a larger quantity of peas, barley, or maize, to a proportionate quantity of oats, it has been asked 'whether the change, although the ingredients are cheaper, would make as good food? Look at the Scotch; see what strong, healthy, muscular men they are, and many of them subsist almost entirely on oatmeal.' This argument is easily refuted. In the first place, oats are not oatmeal; they contain 30 to 40 per cent. of husk – indigestible material, equal in feeding value to chopped straw. This husk has to be paid for at the rate of 500 per cent. more than it is worth as food. In every ton of oats are 7 / or 8 cwts. of husk, which costs at the rate of from £8 to £12, whereas it is only worth £1 per ton, the price given at the manufactories. Secondly, although the Scotch labourers, as a class, are fine, big men, they are decidedly inferior in muscle and 'condition' to the pitmen of Durham and Northumberland, who eat daily from 12 to 24 ozs. of flesh food. There is probably in no part of the world a class of men equal in muscular tone and condition to the coal-hewers of Northumberland. The 'pit-heap' of a large colliery, when the men are assembled to go down, is a sight worth seeing for many reasons, but nothing is more striking than the enormous muscular development of limbs, chest, and shoulders displayed by the majority. Change their diet, substituting oatmeal for meat, and a diminished output of coal and a reduction in the size and tone of their muscles would at once be apparent. To hard-worked men oatmeal is no efficient substitute for beef and mutton, and for hard-working horses oats are inefficient as compared with beans and peas. Experience shows this most plainly, and science explains it by showing that beans, peas, and tares are almost identical with beef and mutton in the amount of muscle-forming material contained by each, whereas oats contain nearly 50 per cent. less than either of them. Now, in horses or other animals excessively worked, the consumption of muscle is far in excess of the waste of other tissue, and the blood must be supplied by a correspondingly large amount of flesh-forming material. To fulfil this requirement, food containing a heavy percentage of nitrogenous material must be given, otherwise the digestive organs will not be able to supply the requisite pabulum[8] to the blood. Beans or beef will supply it, oats or potatoes will not, even when an extra amount of them is given; because this entails the consumption of such an immense bulk of material, a large proportion of which is indigestible and non-nitrogenous, and the digestive organs are overpowered and unable to reduce the mass to a state in which all its value may be absorbed. For these reasons, then, the use of oats as a principal article of diet for excessively hard-worked horses is very expensive, if not injurious. Scientific and practical observations are thoroughly in accord as to this fact, the truth of which was forcibly demonstrated at a colliery in Durham, which fell under the observation of the writer some time ago. The output at this place was decreased from fifteen to twenty scores per day through the horses being unable, from want of condition, or from positive debility, to get the work out. These animals were miserably poor, though allowed 168 lbs. of oats and 154 lbs. of hay each per week. The oats were not crushed and the hay was not chopped. The horses were all large; none under 16 hands, many 16.2. / They worked very long hours and took heavy loads, but their appearance was lamentable after many months of such apparently liberal feeding. On September 1st their food was changed to the following:–

	s.	d.
Crushed peas, 35 lbs., at 34s. per qr.	2	4
" barley, 20 lbs., at 28s. "	1	3
" oats, 40 lbs., at 28s. "	3	4
Bran, 14 lbs., at 7 ½d. per stone		7 ½
Hay, 7 stones, at 9d. „	5	3
	12	9 ½

The old plan being:–

	£	s.	d.
Oats, 168 lbs., at 28s. per qr.		14	0
Hay, 11 stones, at 9d. per stone		8	3
	£1	2	3

Showing a difference of over 9s. 5½d. per horse per week. Besides this saving in money, the digestive organs had 56 lbs. less hay and 59 lbs. less corn to digest, or –

	Lbs.		Lbs.
Mixed grain	109	Old oats	168
Hay	98	" hay	154
	207		322

Within three months this stud of horses was in excellent health and condition, drawing out of the pit, with no application of engine power, from twenty to thirty scores more per day than when first attended. There were 149 horses on the colliery, so that a saving of £3,664 3s. 2d. per annum was effected, which alone was a satisfactory result without reckoning the increased work performed and the increased value of the animals, which also amounted to a very considerable sum. The marvellous change effected in this stud is conclusive evidence that oats can no longer usurp the position of being the best food for hard-working horses. If the choice is limited to a single kind of grain, experience has shown that oats are certainly the best, and science explains it by showing that the essential food constituents of oats are in better balanced proportions and in a more digestible state than in any other grain; but there is a degree of work sometimes exacted from horses which oats are not able to meet, but which can be met by means of well selected mixtures of grain. / Not only are these mixtures equal to the task of balancing the excessive waste of the system induced by hard work, but they do so at a less cost than that at which oats fail to preserve the balance. /

APPENDIX.

APPENDIX

Colliery.	Kind of Food.	Quantity of Food.	Approximate average price of Food.	Total Cost.	No. of Horses.	Cost per Horse in 1881.	Kind of Food.	Quantity of Food.	Approximate average price of Food in 1881.	Total Cost.	No. of Horses.	Cost per Horse.	Differ'ence in favour of Mixed Food.	Remarks.
			s. d.	£ s. d.					s. d.	£ s. d.		£ s. d.	£ s. d.	
SOUTH HETTON AND MURTON.	Hay	281t. 10c. 1q.	78 3 per ton	1,101 15 4	281	23 10 7½	Hay	587t. 18c. 2q.	78 3 per ton	2,300 5 0	134	43 12 5½	20 1 10	The price of hay has been only half the average of that in Newcastle market, due to the large stock bought in 1879 and 1880 at low prices. Health of stud has been excellent, which is the more satisfactory seeing that 'influenza fever' has been more prevalent in the North of England than for a quarter of a century.
	Oats	4,922 bolls	6 0¼ per boll	1,484 19 1			Oats	10,452 bolls	6 0¼ per boll	3,146 9 9				
	Peas	1,793 bolls	9 2 per boll	823 7 1			Green land, bran, beans, &c.			399 0 0				
	Beans	1,213 bolls	9 1¾ per boll	554 10 1			Cost in 1849 AT 1881 prices			5,845, 14 9				
	Maize	6,625 bolls	6 9 per boll	2,234 19 11										
	Barley	290¼ bolls	7 3½ per boll	105 15 0										
	Bran	600 stones	0 8¾ pr. stone	22 0 8										
	Linseed	35 stones	2 2½ pr. stone	3 17 11										
	Green food and grass land			281 0 0										
				6,612 5 1										
RYHOPE	Hay	257t. 15c. 0q.	85 0½ per ton	1,096 4 3	307	22 16 0	Hay	170t. 17c. 0q.	85 0 per ton	726 2 3	85	42 8 11	19 12 11	Health and condition have been exceptionally good, and losses lower than any year since 1861. Slight attacks of 'influenza fever' have twice visited the stud, and each time only a few animals were laid off work and no fatal cases occurred. Although grain was dearer than in 1881, by buying in large quantities the cost per horse was only increased by 1s. 7d. during the year.
	Oats	4,752 bolls	6 0¾ per boll	1,439 1 9			Oats	8,122 bolls	6 0¾ per boll	2,461 19 7				
	Beans	752 bolls	9 0 per boll	338 8 0			Bran	7½ tons	5 10½ per cwt.	44 1 3				
	Barley	92 bolls	7 6 per boll	34 10 0			Grass land			373 0 0				
	Peas	1,872 bolls	9 2½ per boll	862 10 4			Linseed	28 stones	2 0 per stone	2 16 0				
	Maize	8,416 bolls	6 8¾ per boll	2,834 9 11			Cost in 1861 at 1881 prices			3,607 19 1				
	Bran	357 cwts.	5.10½ per cwt.	104 19 0										
	Linseed	57 stones	2 0 per stone	5 12 10										
	Green food and grass land			284 0 0										
				6,999 16 1										
HASWELL AND SHOTTON	Hay	133t. 4c. 0q.	80 0 per ton	532 16 0	255	21 18 9¼	Hay	326t. lc. 2q.	80 0 per ton	1,304 6 0	219	28 7 9¼	6 9 0	Health of stud satisfactory 'Influenza fever,' in a mild form, appeared for a short time, but caused no loss. That the saving is less here than at Ryhope is due to the fact that the system of mixed food and cut hay had been partially in use before 1876.
	Oats	5,403 bolls	6 0 per boll	1,620 18 0			Oats	12,085 bolls	6 0 per boll	3,625 10 0				
	Maize	6,576 bolls	6 5½ per boll	2,123 10 0			Barley	170 bolls	8 0 per boll	68 0 0				
	Peas and beans	2,396 bolls	9 2½ per boll	1,103 3 2			Maize	2,088 bolls	6 5½ per boll	674 5 0				
	Barley	148 bolls	8s, for col. farms	66 12 0			Beans	553 bolls	9 2½ per boll	254 12 3				
	Bran	1,208 stones	0 9 per stone	45 6 0			Bran	4,126 stones	0 9 per stone	154 14 6				
	Licensed	42 stones	2 6 per stone	5 5 0			Green food			134 2 0				
	Green food and grass land			96 17 6			Cost in 1876 at 1881 prices			6,215 9 9				
				5,594 7 8										

Colliery.	Kind of Food.	Quantity of Food.	Approximate average price of Food.	Total Cost.	No. of Horses.	Cost per Horse in 1881.	Kind of Food.	Quantity of Food.	Approximate average price of Food in 1881.	Total Cost.	No. of Horses.	Cost per Horse.	Differ'ence in favour of Mixed Food.	Remarks.
			s. d.	£ s. d.					s. d.	£ s. d.		£ s. d.	£ s. d.	
CASTLE EDEN.	Hay	102t. 2c. 0q.	110 0 per ton	561 11 0	120	20 9 4	Hay	151t. 19c. 0q.	110 0 per ton	835 14 6	85	33 0 3½	12 10 11½	Health of stud good; much better than in 1880. 'Influenza fever' did not attack the underground ponies, and only a few new ones had it in a mild form, but no loss occurred. Although food was high in price during the latter part of the year, by buying in large quantities the cost per horse was kept within satisfactory limits.
	Oats	1,155½ bolls	6 6½ per boll	377 18 10			Oats	5,048 bolls	6 6 ½ per boll	1651 2 4				
	Peas and Beans	812½ bolls	9 2½ per boll	374 1 9			Barley	50 bolls	7 0 per boll	17 10 0				
	Maize	2,838½ bolls	6 9¼ per boll	960 19 0			Bran	6 tons	120 0 per ton	36 0 0				
	Bran	43 cwts.	6 0 per cwt.	12 8 0			Green food and pasturage			265 17 6				
	Linseed	20 stones	2 0 per stone	2 0 0			Cost in 1875 at 1881 prices			2,806 4 4				
	Green food and grass land			168 10 6										
				2,457 19 1										

'The Milroy Lectures on the Hygienic Aspect of the Coalmining Industry in the United Kingdom' (1914)

Frank Shufflebotham,[1] 'The Milroy Lectures on the Hygienic Aspect of the Coalmining Industry in the United Kingdom', *British Medical Journal*, 1:2776 (14 March 1914), pp. 588–91.

The Influence of Temperature on the Health of Miners.

The tables of Professor Cadman and Mr. Walley[2] show that the dry-bulb temperature[3] of some of the mines of this country registers 95.5°, 96°, 92°, 97.8°, 88.8° and 87°F.,[4] and the same observers found that the wet-bulb readings in certain mines were 79°, 82.5°, 77°, 79.8°, 82°, 81.5°, and 87° F.[5] in different mines, and I have made observations myself in coal mines where the dry-bulb / reading has registered as much as 90° and the wet bulb over 80° F.[6] It will therefore be seen that in a considerable number of mines in this country the men are working at very high temperatures, and it cannot be denied that these temperatures are not only injurious to the health of the worker, but without doubt they have a considerable effect upon their working capacity. From the experiments of Dr. Fraser Harris[7] at Birmingham University upon the human subject it appears that high temperatures with a high degree of moisture increase the pulse-rate and the body temperature and cause a considerable loss of body weight; the respiration-rate is not changed out of proportion to the increased pulse-rate. Professor Langlois of Paris[8] has shown that in an atmosphere at a temperature exceeding 77° F.[9] (wet bulb) ventilation exercised a considerable influence. At 86° F.[10] (wet bulb) the subject, even when resting, was very uncomfortable, if not inconvenienced; in a non-ventilated atmosphere exceeding 77° (wet bulb), the body temperature rose 1.8° to 2.7° F., and the blood pressure was increased by 18 to 25 c.cm. of mercury.[11] The quantity of water evaporated varied according to the temperature and to the hygrometrical[12] state of the atmosphere.

Haldane,[13] as a result of experiments which he has made upon the effect of working at high wet-bulb temperatures, summarizes the results of his experiments as follows: 'It is clear that in still and warm air what matters to the persons present is neither the temperature of the air nor its relative saturation, nor the absolute percentage of aqueous vapour present, but the temperature shown by the wet-bulb thermometer. If this exceeds a certain point, about 78° F.,[14] continuous hard work becomes impracticable, and beyond 88°[15] it becomes impracticable for ordinary persons even to stay for long periods in such air, although practice may increase to some extent the limit which can be tolerated. In moving air, on the other hand, the limit is extended upwards by several degrees. Men working a rock drill in a hot end or rise in a mine, for instance, have the great advantage that the air is kept in constant motion by the exhaust air from the drill, and that as this exhaust air is very dry, the wet-bulb thermometer at the working place is considerably reduced, even if the rock be wet or damped by a jet or spray of water to prevent dust.'[16] And when giving evidence before a Departmental Committee on the humidity and ventilation in cotton-weaving sheds,[17] Dr. Haldane said that he should propose that 75° F. (wet bulb)[18] be taken as a maximum, and below this temperature there should always be a difference of 2° between the two thermometers; 70° (wet bulb)[19] is the temperature which the Home Office specify as the maximum for a factory, but he considered that in the special conditions in Lancashire weaving sheds, and limiting the 75° to the summer heat – the warmer part of the year – there should be no objection to going to 75°.

Dr. Pembrey,[20] as the result of observations upon himself and medical students and soldiers, was of opinion that 70° F. by the wet bulb should be the maximum, and he pointed out that at lower temperatures work could be done at a faster rate more efficiently and with less fatigue and injury to health, and that the effect of work in a warm moist atmosphere is to increase the temperature, pulse-rate, and loss of moisture out of proportion to the work done.

The question of wet-bulb temperatures in coal mines has become all the more important on account of the spraying by water of coal seams and roadways for the purpose of preventing explosions, and it can be easily understood that in mines of high temperature with an atmosphere saturated with moisture, while the risk of explosions is diminished the working conditions are less favourable both to the health of the miner and to his efficiency as a workman apart from the consideration of explosions.

According to the French mining law any temperature exceeding 77° F. on the wet-bulb thermometer[21] must be considered high.

THE GROWTH OF KNOWLEDGE

This section consists of a single text, the reflections of Thomas Lindsay Galloway on the development of the 'art' of coal mining over the decades previous to 1877 in the different coal mining regions of Europe.

The forces that generate new knowledge remain obscure to economists and economic historians and there is no generally accepted theory of how the knowledge that produces technical change comes about. It is this ignorance that makes Galloway's remarks of interest.

Galloway identifies differences in expertise in mine engineering between the different countries and relates these differences to corresponding differences in colliery conditions. Where mines have been gassy, for example, techniques of mine ventilation have advanced the furthest. In doing so, he advances a version of the 'necessity' hypothesis on the origin of technical advances: 'necessity is the mother of invention'. As a general hypothesis this will not do; it is easy to point to examples of crying necessity where no corresponding invention has been mothered either for unconscionably long periods or at all. But as a particular hypothesis, it is often attractive. It is difficult not to see a link between the grievous colliery explosions of the north-east in the early nineteenth century and the intense activity that culminated in the invention of 'safety lamps', not only by Humphry Davy but also by William Reid Clanny and George Stephenson, both residents of the district. Galloway adds to the hypothesis by pointing to the international diffusion of research and invention. In this way, inventions called forth by necessity in one region may be adopted in others in which necessity has been less pressing or hardly felt.

This is not to argue that Galloway's hypothesis is a sufficient answer to the general problem; it is not. The 'necessity' hypothesis sees only the demand for new invention and ignores the supply. Its treatment of demand is crude. Demand is not limited to 'necessities' but also covers ordinary wants and luxuries. And, finally, one has to ask 'whose demand?' Necessities felt only by the poor and those without political and social voice are likely to go unheeded; demands for novel luxuries pressed by the rich and powerful are satisfied instead.

T. Lindsay Galloway, 'On the Present Condition of Mining in Some of the Principal Coal-Producing Districts of the Continent' (1877–8)

T. Lindsay Galloway,[1] 'On the Present Condition of Mining in Some of the Principal Coal-Producing Districts of the Continent', *Transactions of the North of England Institute of Mining and Mechanical Engineers*, 27 (1877–8), pp. 171–201.

Referring to what has gone before,[2] it cannot fail to be remarked how variously the art of coal-mining has developed itself in its several branches in each country and district. Not only has nearly every coal-field methods of working peculiar to itself, and suited to its own special circumstances, but the progress which has been made in the employment of machinery, and the applications to which it has been turned, have been chiefly determined by certain ruling conditions. It may be observed how the general adoption of rock-drilling apparatus in the North of France and Belgium is to be accounted for by the amount of stone tunneling which is required in the winning of numerous thin and highly-inclined beds of coal, how the great depths to which many of the shafts have attained has proved an incentive to the study of expansive gear for winding engines, and of the best means of counteracting the weight of the ropes, and how the existence of thick water-bearing strata in the same districts has given birth to several inventions, among them that of MM. Kind and Chaudron,[3] for the piercing of such strata; without the use of pumps. Similarly, it may be remarked, why the large outputs of coal, which are obtained at some of the pits of Saarbruck and Upper Silesia, have necessitated the adoption of the best shaft-fittings and means of extraction known in England or America; and how, on the other hand, the very complete systems of coal-washing, which are in use in Westphalia, have been required on account of the great proportion of stone contained in the coal, which has to be got rid of before it is fit for the manufacture of coke.

ENGLISH AND FOREIGN MINES COMPARED.

If there is little to be said upon the subjects of ventilation and underground haulage, it is because no country on the continent can compete with England in these directions. The fiery mines, with the extensive and complicated workings in that country, have created a real necessity for the strictest attention to the subject of ventilation in all its details, and by the efforts of such men as John Buddle and Sir Humphrey Davy a comparative immunity from accidents has been attained, even in the midst of the greatest dangers. England is also the home of mechanical haulage, because, while the flatness and thickness of the seams of coal favoured the introduction of such means of transit, the high price of labour, the desire for large outputs, and the great areas generally worked from each shaft, rendered the adoption of machinery almost imperative. But although special circumstances will usually be found to account for marked progress in any given direction, it often happens that what was necessary in one situation may be usefully / / adopted in others. In this manner all foreign nations have been more or less indebted to the mining experience of England; and those countries are most advanced in the art of mining who have kept themselves abreast of the progress that was being made elsewhere. England also may derive some benefit from a knowledge of the practice of her neighbours and competitors, and the writer will feel gratified if, in attempting to give some account of what is being done upon the continent, anything should have been suggested which may be of use to English mining engineers.

THE ENGINEERING INSTITUTES AND THE EDUCATION OF ENGINEERS AND MINERS

This section consists of three texts concerned with different aspects of research, education and training in mine engineering and practical mining.[1]

The historiography of this topic is still dominated by the perception that the facilities available for training mine engineers in the UK lagged behind those available 'elsewhere'. Where critics are specific, Germany is usually held up as the model; Belgium and France are also mentioned; in the early years of the twentieth century the USA entered the ranks of those put forward as models to emulate.[2] A systematic international comparison has never been carried out however, and the field remains dominated by anecdote and opinion rather than rigorous historical methodologies.

This historiography has its roots in the contemporary comments of mine engineers themselves and in the earliest histories of the topic which were produced by them. The contemporary comments can be traced through the technical and trade journals. In 1870, for example, John Young, Professor of Natural History in the University of Glasgow, prepared a paper for a joint meeting of the North of England Institute and the Institution of Engineers and Shipbuilders in Scotland. It was typical in its perceptions:

> there is no question that as a whole the mineral resources of this country are not administered with that economy so important in dealing with supplies, which by there very nature are terminable, whose exhaustion is a certainty, though the date may be open to controversy.[3]

And also typical in its admission, that the 'evidence in support of my statement it is difficult to give'.[4] All Young could do as refer to 'the censures incidently dropped by inspectors of mines, and by the better-informed iron-masters' and to mention some egregious examples of error and incompetence. Whether such censures were absent from Belgium or Germany or France and whether such examples could not also be supplied from the experience of those countries were questions which Young failed to ask.[5]

Later elements in Young's presentation make one somewhat suspicious of his claims of professional incompetence. Young laments the injury to the mine engineering profession 'wrought by the unchecked multiplication of tradesmen who assume the same style as the accomplished scientific men' among the profession.[6] 'At present', said Young, 'any man can call himself an engineer', and he appealed 'without hesitation' 'for an emphatic declaration that such a state of things should not exist. Your reputation as a profession is at stake'.[7] Here, then, one suspects that anecdotes of error have been mobilized to support changes designed to raise the class position and status of the profession, to close it to the 'tradesman' and the unqualified, and thereby (though, of course, Young was not so vulgar as to mention this) increase the level of the fees and salaries it could charge its clients and employers.

This is not to argue that the organization of education and training in mine engineering in the UK was without fault. As indicated in the introduction to these three volumes, there is good reason to suspect market failures in all markets for these services, largely the consequence of failures in the market for credit and, specifically, the market for loans for educational purposes. There is no reason to expect such failures to be peculiar to the UK and, if present in Britain, they are likely to have been present throughout continental Europe, in the USA and elsewhere. Hence the focus in the literature, contemporary and modern, on intervention in the market first by trade combinations such as the North of England Institute and later by the state. The focus, however, appears to have been on a matter of secondary importance, viz., the supply of training by colleges and universities. In the UK this demonstrates repeated attempts to supply frustrated by a lack of students able or willing to pay the fees and take the time required to study. Roderick and Stephens note, for example, that no students, not one, enrolled for the degree in mine engineering offered by the Department of Mining and Metallurgy at Sheffield University between the first offer of the course in 1907 and 1919.[8] This, and a catalogue of other failures and disappointments, suggests a failure on the demand side of the market, not on the supply side.

The first text is Nicholas Wood's 'Inaugural Address' to the North of England Institute of Mining Engineers (pp. 405–12). Wood makes it clear that the founding of the Institute was motivated by a desire to reduce the toll of accidents in the industry and by an impatience with the process of government enquiry.

> [W]e may hope that to-day we are entering upon an undertaking which may be of essential utility to the important interests entrusted to our charge, and which may be the means of averting some at least of those dreadful and deplorable catastrophes which have too often been felt with such disastrous consequences to the distressed, and to the sufferers by their occurrence.

Wood was neither a great speaker nor a great writer and his thoughts are clumsily expressed; nevertheless, the sentiment is clear. General remarks are followed by an extensive review of investigation into the accidents and disasters of the industry by Parliament. Wood emphasizes the great labours of one enquiry after another and the mouse-like conclusions they produced. Three hundred and sixty pages here! Six hundred and fifteen there! Two hundred and forty-seven pages more! And yet the loss of life continued:

> [T]hese voluminous Reports, those various, and in some instances probably useful or valuable suggestions have lain dormant – or have been placed upon the shelves of the Colliery Offices without notice or attention.

It was not easy for individual coal owners or mining engineers to each, individually, digest and reflect on this mass of evidence and then 'to test some of the suggestions made, or schemes proposed by those Committees, or by Scientific Gentlemen or others'. What was needed was some form of joint action pursued by a joint organization. Hence, the Mining Institute.

Membership of the Institute was of course voluntary. It represented one possible solution to the problem Wood identified. Others, more familiar in the twentieth century would have involved some form of compulsion: a tax to fund a government research institute, or an Act of Parliament authorizing a compulsory industry levy to fund a research institute administered by the trade itself. The compulsion involved in these solutions is a response to the problem presented by those who would choose to avoid the financial and other obligations of institute membership but who would, nevertheless, benefit from the institute's research. To rely on a voluntary membership was to place great reliance on a cooperative culture within the trade.

There is no doubt that such a culture existed, though it was not sufficiently strong to enable solutions to all the 'free rider' problems that existed in the industry. That it existed led to a feature of the industry that became so taken-for-granted that it became difficult for its members to imagine how things might be otherwise. This was the free exchange of technical information. It was quite normal for members of the Institute to present papers describing, for example, the difficulties that had been experienced in installing a new ventilation system and how these had been overcome, to an audience consisting entirely of their commercial competitors. That the information had value did not lead to its treatment as private property. Members went further, often providing access to their collieries for the purpose of investigation and experiment by engineers from companies with whom they were in daily competition for markets. This was an 'invisible college'. Moreover, as the century progressed it transcended national frontiers, including members from Belgium, France, Germany and Russia, as well as from the colonies and dominions.[9]

That this culture emerged was undoubtedly assisted by the history of combination in the trade in the north-east and the close personal relationships that combination had fostered. The history of combination also appears to have engendered a habit of thinking of the interests of the trade as whole rather than of an individual enterprise. The model provided by the Institute of Civil Engineers, founded in 1818, may also have helped in the establishment of the collegial culture that characterized the engineers of the industry. The existence of consulting mine engineers whose corporate allegiances might be widely spread may also have assisted the emergence and maintenance of a collegial culture. It was undoubtedly also aided by the initial focus of the Institute on the reduction of accidents. Nevertheless, it remains remarkable and undoubtedly helped to speed the diffusion of improved technique throughout the industry.

The Institute did not solve all problems however and one area in which it conspicuously failed was in the provision of training facilities for aspirant mining engineers. T. J. Taylor, 'Prospectus of a College of Practical Mining and Manufacturing Science, Proposed to be Established at Newcastle-Upon-Tyne' (pp. 413–19) documents one major attempt dating from shortly after the foundation of the Institute. The proposal failed. There were two difficulties. One was the site of the College; this was not a trivial matter when the journey from say Cardiff to Newcastle could take many, many hours. Those connected with the Institute naturally tended to favour Newcastle; those based elsewhere in the country, just as naturally, did not. The other difficulty was the cost. As with the foundation of the Institute itself, there were broadly two options: to rely on voluntary contributions and to seek authority to impose a compulsory levy. The latter, it was thought, was not feasible. Confidence in the efficacy of the former was lacking. The project collapsed.

The final text (pp. 421–7) presents extracts from a book by Henry Davies called *Coal Mining: A Reader For Primary Schools And Evening Continuation Classes* designed for juvenile readers.[10] It indicates how the training of boys for the mines was, in some areas of the country, a task assumed by local authorities and taken from the shoulders of the colliery companies. Apart from this the main interest of the book is the diversity and nature of the 'syllabus' it offered. On the one hand there are 'scientific' chapters, such as that which gives an elementary account of coalfield geology. Then there are lessons on 'rules for colliers' which indicates an extraordinary degree of penetration of public (state funded) schools by the interests of private capital. On the other hand there is a dramatic story of a mine disaster and rescue, based on true events of thirty years before. Its inclusion invites many different interpretations. Was this an attempt to motivate students by offering the interest and excitement of a dramatic story well told? Or an attempt to inculcate respect for the 'Rules for Colliers' and all the other matters connected with mine safety? Or an attempt to make work in the mine more attractive by making it appear more 'manly'? It is hard to tell.

Notes

1. Church, *History*, offers a brief introduction to this topic at pp. 429–32. The historiographical context is still provided by M. Argles, *South Kensington to Robbins: An Account of English Technical and Scientific Education since 1851* (London: Longmans, 1964); M. Sanderson, *The Universities and British Industry 1850–1970* (London: Routledge and Kegan Paul, 1972); and G. W. Roderick and M. D. Stephens, 'Mining Education 1850–1914', *Irish Journal of Education*, 6 (1972), pp. 105–20.
2. H. Eckfeldt, 'The Education of Mining Engineers in the United States', *Transactions of the Institute of Mining Engineers*, 29 (1904–05), pp. 401–17. Eckfeldt was a professor of mining engineering at Lehigh University, South Bethlehem, Pennsylvania.
3. J. Young, 'On the Education of the Mining Engineer', *Transactions of the North of England Institute of Mining Engineers*, 21 (1871–2), pp. 21–32, and 'Discussion', pp. 32–46, at p. 22. John Young completed a medical training but was also a Fellow of the Geological Society and of the Royal Society of Edinburgh. His comments, as one might expect from this background, are particularly concerned with inefficiencies in exploration and give a highly critical view of the contemporary practices noticed in pp. 259–67 and 279–83 of this volume.
4. Ibid.
5. Later presentations and discussions include: J. H. Merivale, 'The Education of Mining Engineers', *Transactions of the North of England Institute of Mining Engineers*, 62 (1892–9), pp. 483–5 and Appendices; G. B. Walker, 'Presidential Address: The Education of Mining Engineers', *Transactions of the Federated Institute of Mining Engineers*, 12 (1896–7), pp. 132–59 and 'Discussion', pp. 159–66; J. Wertheimer, 'The Training of Industrial Leaders', *Transactions of the Institute of Mining Engineers*, 23 (1901–2), pp. 494–501, and 'Discussion', pp. 501–16; R. A. S. Redmayne, 'The Training of a Mining-Engineer', 24 (1902–3), pp. 243–54; H. Louis, 'The Mining School at Bochum, Westphalia', *Transactions of the Institute of Mining Engineers*, 40 (1910–11), pp. 405–14 and plate X, and 'Discussion', pp. 414–33; R. W. Dron, 'The Training of Mining Engineers', *Transactions of the Institute of Mining Engineers*, 49 (1914–15), pp. 187–200, and 'Discussion', pp. 200–12.
6. Ibid., p. 24.
7. Ibid., pp. 23–4.
8. Roderick and Stephens, 'Mining Education', pp. 111–12, who also draw attention to deficient facilities.
9. Until 1917. In that year the Council of the Institute passed the following bye-law: 'Enemy Alien Members. In the event of a state of war existing between the United Kingdom and any other country or State, all Honorary Members, Members, Associate Members, Associates, or Students, who shall be subjects of such enemy country or State shall forthwith cease to be Honorary Members, Members, Associate Members, Associates, or Students of the Institution, but they may be eligible for re-election after the war in the usual manner' (*Transactions of the North of England Institute of Mining and Mechanical Engineers*, 68 (1917–18), p. 36.
10. A similar item is W. Glover, *First Lessons in Coal Mining: For Use in Primary Schools* (London: Crosby Lockwood and Son, 1906). Glover described himself on the title page of this work as 'Headmaster of the Higher Standards School, Maesteg, Glamorgan', a

'standard' being a school form, or class, or level, so that 'higher standards' means 'older years' not 'better quality'. In the preface the author notes that 'the lessons are modelled on the Syllabus recently issued by the Education Committee of the Glamorgan County Council, who have decided that instruction in subjects appertaining to Coal Mining shall be given in all Schools in Mining Districts within the County' (p. [iii]).

Nicholas Wood, 'Inaugural Address Delivered to the Members of the North of England Institute of Mining Engineers' (1852–3)

Nicholas Wood,[1] 'Inaugural Address Delivered to the Members of the North of England Institute of Mining Engineers and Others Interested in the Prevention of Accidents in Mines, and in the Advancement of Mining Science Generally at Newcastle-on Tyne, Sept. 3rd, 1852', *Transactions of the North of England Institute of Mining Engineers*, 1 (1852 and 1853), pp. 3–23.

INAUGURAL ADDRESS.

GENTLEMEN, –

In delivering the first address to the Society at the commencement of your labours, I must beg to congratulate the members thereof, on the progress which they have made in so short a time, towards the establishment of the Society. – The association together of upwards of eighty members – the appointment of officers – and the subscription of an amount of funds, which however small is still what may be deemed sufficient for a commencement, – all point towards success. Let us not, however, deceive ourselves. We have only cut the first sod, or laid the foundation stone; the whole of the works or the edifice has yet to be reared, the resources developed, and the ultimate objects attained.

While therefore you have done me the honor to select me to preside over your labours and deliberations, bear in mind that it is only by unremitting perseverance – by the continued exercise of our united and combined efforts, that we can be successful. We must each of us act as if we were individually responsible for the success of the Institution; and with such efforts, and actuated by such feelings, there can be no doubt that we shall be successful.

We have, I think (except the Funds of which I shall speak hereafter,) within us all the elements of success; and supported as I have no doubt we shall be in respect of Funds if we act true to ourselves, and to the objects for which we are associated together, we may hope that to-day we are entering upon an undertaking which may be of essential utility to the important interests entrusted to our charge, and which may be the means of averting some at least of those dreadful and deplorable catastrophes which have too often been felt with / such disastrous consequences to the distressed, and to the sufferers by their occurrence: and that it may be the means of raising the profession to a higher standard of intelligence in Literature and Science, than it has hitherto attained.

The object of the Institution is twofold. –

First. – By a union or concentration of professional experience, to endeavour if possible, to devise measures which may avert or alleviate those dreadful calamities, which have so frequently produced such destruction to life and property, and which are always attended with such misery and distress to the Mining population of the District; and –

Secondly. – To establish a Literary Institution more particularly applicable to the theory, art, and practice of Mining, than the Institutions in the locality present, or which are within the reach of the profession in this locality.

While therefore, we propose that the Institution should practically consist of members of the profession of Mining Engineers, and that it should be substantially of a Literary character, we have thought it advisable to extend the range of its objects and labours, and we have consequently opened its doors to the admission of persons interested in the prevention of Accidents in Mines, and in the advancement of Mining Science generally.

We are aware that this admits of a very extensive application, for who is not interested, if for no other object, from feelings of humanity, in the prevention of Accidents in Coal Mines?

Our intention is however, not to employ the terms in so extensive a meaning. We should be very glad to have the support of any individual in so desirable an object, from whatever motives or feelings he may be actuated; but we wish the principles of the Institution to be understood – it is an Institution of practical miners associated together, to endeavour by a combination of practical knowledge – by an interchange of practical experience – and by a united and combined effort, to improve ourselves in the science of our profession, and by acting together as a body, we may be the instruments of preventing as much as practicable, the recurrence of those / dreadful catastrophes to which I have alluded; and at the same time, to raise the art and science of Mining to its highest practicable scale of perfection, in safety, economy, and efficiency.

Our Institution is in the first place, therefore, intimately connected with the interests of all the Proprietors of coal, and all the Lessees of Mines of this district; or what is generally termed, the Coal Owners of the North. Our claims to their support are all powerful. We are associated together for the prevention of

Accidents in Mines. Who so interested in the prevention of Accidents as Coal Owners? Past experience shews that they are never behind the most energetic philanthropist in attention, and care, to the sufferings of the injured, or victims of those dreadful accidents, or in alleviation of the misery and distress of their relatives or families; on this ground alone, we seek to have their support. But we are also associated together for the improvement of the art of Mining scientifically, practically, and economically. The Coal Owner, or worker of the coal is therefore on that account likewise most materially interested in the success of the Institution. And as one of the prominent features of the Institution, is to endeavour to accomplish the best and most perfect mode of abstracting the coal, so as to produce the largest quantity of coal out of a given area of mine, the Proprietor of the coal, as well as the Worker of it,[2] is no less materially interested in the success of the Institution.

Considering, therefore, that we have paramount claims upon the representatives of those interests for support and assistance, we have consequently opened our doors to the admission of gentlemen of both those denominations; and we humbly solicit their support and co-operation in the one or other, or in both of those characters. We should likewise be glad to have numbered amongst our members, or as supporters of the Institution, any literary, scientific, or practical members of other Institutions, professions, or occupations, whose labours, talents, or professional experience, can in any way aid our efforts, in the accomplishment of the objects of the Institution, either in the prevention of accidents, or in perfecting the art of Mining.

With these general observations on the principles upon which the Institution is founded, I shall now proceed to point out more in detail, an outline of the subjects which we shall have to consider – the range and scope of the studies embraced within our Constitution – / and the branches of Science which it is intended to grapple with, so as to accomplish the objects for which the Institution has been established.

And first of all, as to the prevention of Accidents in Mines.

I think it is a source of justifiable gratification to contemplate; the readiness, almost without an exception, with which the Members of the profession have come forward in obedience to the wishes of those benevolent Noblemen and Gentlemen, who thought that the establishment of such an Institution as this, might contribute towards averting those dreadful accidents; and the anxiety which they have evinced in modelling the Institution, so as to accomplish the object in view.

No set of persons certainly can have more powerful motives to associate together for such a purpose than Mining Engineers; feelings of humanity towards those hardy and adventurous class of workmen, who are immured in our mines, and who suffer by such calamities – the heart-rending scenes which those in charge of such works are compelled to witness on such melancholy occasions – and the distressing bereavements which are continually brought to their very doors, appeal with irresistible force to them above all others, to associate together, if by such an association they can in any degree aid in preventing the recurrence of such fearful visitations.

If these considerations, and no others, operated towards the establishment of such an Institution, sufficiently powerful motives to urge us on, exist; and if we succeed – if our efforts, in however slight a degree, contribute to confer additional safety to our mines – the reward – the approbation of our own consciences, that we may have been the cause of even saving the life of one of our fellow creatures – must be a sufficient inducement to force upon us the utmost exertions of which we are capable, in contributing our mite towards the success of such an Institution.

It has been stated, that we are not the proper persons to unite together for such a purpose. – That we are interested persons, and that the proper persons for such an association, are persons entirely unconnected with the Coal Owners, or with the Managers of Mines; I beg most decidedly, but most respectfully, to doubt the soundness of such a doctrine. – The motives of any gentlemen, of whatever class they may be, / or whatever may be their pursuits in life, who unite together, or in any way contribute towards the prevention of those accidents, cannot be too highly appreciated; the Miners – the Coal Owners – and every one engaged in mining, owe them a deep debt of gratitude for any efforts they may make.

It is from those very feelings, emanating from persons themselves daily exposed in the mines, with those who are liable to suffer, being also individually subjected in the exercises of their duties, to the effects of such accidents – witnessing the heart-rending scenes occasioned by such accidents – and from being supposed to be the only persons, through whose assistance any preventive measures can properly be carried out, that we have deemed it incumbent upon us, and that we consider ourselves a proper class of persons to unite together and at least make the attempt, to endeavour to accomplish the desired object.

At the same time I feel assured that I speak the sentiments of every member of the profession, when I say, that we do not for one moment entertain the idea, that the establishment of this Institution should in the least degree render it unnecessary, or that we should interfere in any way whatever with the establishment of any other Institution, for the prevention of accidents in Mines; and particularly with the one proposed to be established in London. On the contrary, every member of the Institute, I am sure, either individually, or in connection with the Institution, would be most happy to co-operate with, assist, or in any way aid the efforts of any other Institution or Society, having for its object, the prevention of accidents in mines: and that it will be one of the leading objects of this Institution, to consider, afford a careful and impartial trial, or carry into effect any suggestion, plan, or measure submitted to them, having for its object, the prevention of those accidents.

I have thought it necessary to trouble you with those remarks, in consequence of allegations having been made, that the object of the establishment of this Society was to stifle enquiry – to interpose difficulties in the establishment of other Societies – or to create obstacles to the introduction or suggestions of measures recommended by such Societies, towards the prevention of accidents in mines. Whereas, our wish is, and it is our desire, and it should be clearly and distinctly understood, that our object is quite the reverse:– that it is our wish to aid, assist, and carry out the views of such associations – to carefully consider any plan which may be submitted to us – bring our united practical knowledge / to bear upon such consideration; and if the measure, or plan, is at all feasible, or exhibits reasonable prospect of being beneficial, or to accomplish the object for which it is proposed, to do our utmost in giving it a fair and impartial trial.

And here it may not be irrelevant to those considerations or without its use in elucidating the objects we have in view, to glance at what has of late years been done towards the prevention of Accidents in Mines, induced by the frequency and serious extent of those Accidents; and to see how far these enquiries have contributed to arrest the fearful visitations.

In the year 1835, a Committee of the House of Commons was appointed, of which Mr. Joseph Pease[3] was Chairman, a Gentleman from being himself an extensive Coal Owner, being in daily communication with his Mines, and being by his talents, application, and sound practical knowledge, every way suitable for that office. The result of the labours of that Committee, which sat hearing Evidence over a period of 19 days, and produced a Blue book of 360 pages,[4] did not lead to any prominent alleviation of such accidents. They reported 'In conclusion your Committee regret that the results of this enquiry have not enabled them to lay before the House any particular plan, by which the Accidents in question may be avoided with certainty, and in consequence no decisive recommendations are offered, – They anticipate great advantages to the public and to humanity, from the circulation of the Valuable Evidence they have collected. – They feel assured that Science will avail itself of the information, if not for the first time obtained, yet now prominently exhibited: and that the parties for whose more immediate advantage, the British Parliament undertook the enquiry, will not hesitate to place a generous construction on the motives and intentions of the Legislature.'[5]

In the year 1839, (resulting from a serious explosion of Fire Damp at St. Hilda Colliery, near South Shields, by which 50 people were killed,) a Committee was appointed of South Shields Gentlemen, of which Mr. Mather was Secretary,[6] and which sat occasionally for 3 years. – The result of that Committee was a

Report of very great value, published in 1843. It has also been republished, as an appendix to the Report of a Committee of the House of Commons, of this year.[7]

The conclusions to which this Committee arrived were rather numerous. – With regard to SAFETY LAMPS, they concluded that 'no / mere Safety Lamp, however ingenious in its construction, is able to secure fiery Mines from explosions; and that a reliance upon it is a fatal error, conducive to those dreadful calamities, which it is intended to prevent.'[8]

With regard to VENTILATION, 'that considering its power, safety, and economy, facility of execution and command, Ventilation by High-pressure Steam is peculiarly fitted for the present condition of Mines, and adapted for them in every stage of their operations. – That it appears one of the most important and valuable suggestions, and if fully and properly applied, preferable as far as relates to its effects on the safety and healthiness of the mine to any invention of modern date.'[9] – The committee recommended the use of Scientific Instruments, some regulation of Infant Labour, Registry of Plans and Sections, Scientific Education of Officers of Mines, and Government Inspection and Jurisdiction.

In 1845, Sir Henry de la Beche,[10] and Dr. Lyon Playfair,[11] were appointed by government to institute an enquiry into the causes of Accidents in Coal Mines, particularly as regarded the noxious and inflammable Gases, the escape of Gas into Mines, and of obviating danger therefrom by proper Ventilation. – The Labours of these Gentlemen were published in 1847,[12] and the general result appears to have been the recommendation of the appointment of Government Inspectors; and to compel the use of Safety Lamps in all fiery collieries.

In 1849, in consequence of the continuance of those accidents, a Committee of the Lords was appointed, of which Lord Wharncliffe was Chairman, a nobleman every way qualified for such a task. This committee sat receiving evidence 18 days, and produced a Blue Book of 615 Pages.[13] – No Legislative measure was recommended to Parliament by this committee. – They contented themselves with reporting the Evidence, with a commentary upon it in their report, directing attention to various parts of the evidence, especially as regarded the appointment of Inspectors, to improvements in Safety Lamps, and of Ventilation generally; and directed particular attention to the precise action and power of the Steam Jet as a Ventilating Agent, compared with that of the ordinary Furnace, hitherto in use.

During the Session in which this Committee sat, an appointment was made by the Government of Professor Phillips and Mr Blackwell,[14] to investigate and Report on the Ventilation of Mines. – These two Gentlemen made separate Reports; – the former of the Mines in / Northumberland and Durham, Derbyshire and Yorkshire; the latter in Lancashire, Staffordshire, Shropshire, and South Wales, &c.

Those Gentlemen produced a valuable mass of Evidence and Investigation, giving the facts as regarded the system and amount of Ventilation at the different Collieries, and in the different Districts. – The conclusion they arrived at may be shortly stated, by saying that they considered superior practical and scientific Knowledge was required in some of the Districts. – 'superior skill, and unsleeping vigilance in the overlooker;'[15] – which they thought would be promoted by the establishment of provincial Mining Schools, and by a systematic Inspection under the authority of Government.

In 1851, Government Inspectors were appointed; unfortunately however accidents still occurred, and in this Year a Committee of the House of Commons was appointed, of which Mr Cayley[16] was chairman. – This committee sat receiving evidence 5 days and published a report[17] of 247 Pages, (including the reprint of the Report of the South Shields Committee.) – This Committee has made various suggestions, some of them of a most startling nature, both as regards the practicability of their adoption, and their utility in accomplishing the objects for which they are recommended: and certainly great doubts exist as to the propriety, as well as the efficiency of several of their suggestions, as regards the Ventilation of the Mines. One of the opinions they express is – 'Your Committee however are unanimously of opinion that the primary object should be to prevent the explosions themselves: and that if human means (as far as known) can avail to prevent them it is by the Steam Jet system as applied by Mr. Forster;[18] although even in such case it might be prudent in a mine especially fiery to add an inexpensive Steam Jet apparatus at the top of the downcast, as a means in reserve in case of explosion from neglect or otherwise; and your Committee are unanimously of opinion that the Steam Jet is the most powerful, and at the same time least expensive method for the Ventilation of Mines.'[19]

Looking at the Evidence produced before those Committees at the various periods – the information elicited by the labors of the scientific Gentlemen employed to report upon the subject – the conclusions, and recommendations which those Committees and Gentlemen have from time to time arrived at or made; and more especially looking at the conclusions and recommendations which the Committee / of this year has made to the Legislature, I need scarcely say how incumbent it is upon the proprietors and managers of Mines to carefully, minutely, and impartially study and consider, such a mass of Evidence, and the important conclusions to which those Gentlemen have arrived at, or measures which they have recommended.

And here I may again perhaps be permitted to state that the Institution which we are now engaged in establishing, is probably the most proper tribunal to enter upon such an investigation.

It has always been felt that individual Collieries, or individual Coal Owners, were not able or capable of undertaking such extensive experiments as would be required to test some of the suggestions made, or schemes proposed by those Committees, or by Scientific Gentlemen or others; and thus on the principle that what was every body's business was nobody's business[20] – these voluminous Reports, those various, and in some instances probably useful or valuable suggestions have lain dormant – or have been placed upon the shelves of the Colliery Offices without notice or attention.

Now however we have no such excuse open to us, being associated together for the express purpose and object of probing, and investigating every thing connected with the subject of Mining; however crude, inapplicable, or even however ridiculous the proposition or plan may be, it is just as incumbent upon us to give it a fair and impartial investigation as if were the most perfect or valuable suggestion.

Acting as a body, every plan brought before us will have at least a careful and impartial investigation, and if we unitedly find that any subject requires practical elucidation, or if in order to enable us to arrive at a satisfactory conclusion, it is necessary that any plan or suggestion should become the subject of experiment, I feel assured we shall be readily met by our employers, to place their pits at our disposal, and enable us to test by practical experiment or experience, any plan, mode, or suggestion, which may be offered to our notice on so important a subject, – provided we are unitedly of opinion that such experiments or trials can in any way conduce to lessen the number of accidents in Mines, or tend to advance the Science and economy of mining.

T. J. Taylor, 'Prospectus of a College of Practical Mining and Manufacturing Science' (1855–6)

T. J. Taylor,[1] 'Prospectus of a College of Practical Mining and Manufacturing Science, Proposed to be Established at Newcastle-Upon-Tyne', *Transactions of the North of England Institute of Mining Engineers*, 4 (1855–6), pp. 23–33.

PROSPECTUS OF A COLLEGE OF PRACTICAL MINING AND MANUFACTURING SCIENCE, PROPOSED TO BE ESTABLISHED AT NEWCASTLE-UPON-TYNE.

Names of the Committee appointed (with power to add to their numbers) by a General Meeting of Representatives of the Coal Mining Interests of Great Britain, held in London in July last, and by the Coal Trade and Institute of Mining Engineers of the North of England, for the / proposed establishment, at Newcastle-upon-Tyne, of a College, to be entitled the 'British College of Practical Mining and Manufacturing Science':– Nicholas Wood, Hetton Hall, Durham; J. T. Woodhouse, Derby; W. Peace, Wigan; Charles Binns, Chesterfield; G. C. Greenwell, Radstock, Bath; Thomas J. Taylor, Earsdon, Northumberland; I. L. Bell, Mayor of Newcastle; W. G. Armstrong, Jesmond; H. Lee Pattinson, Newcastle; Thos. Sopwith, Allenheads, Northumberland; R. W. Swinburne, South Shields; Robert Plummer, Byker.[2]

It has long been a subject not only of regret but of surprise, that in a country like Great Britain, which for mineral wealth, and the manufactured products of such wealth, is unequalled by any in Europe, a College of Practical Mining Science should still remain a *desideratum*. Nor have inquiries been wanting, from abroad, as to the probability of some such Institution being set on foot, accompanied with intimations that support, as far as a resort to it of pupils may constitute such support, would not be wanting. As a consequence of these first suggestions, the topic has more recently engaged the serious attention of the North of England Institute of Mining Engineers, now consisting of members from all the coal mining districts of England and Wales,[3] by whose request the Council of that body drew up and printed a series of 'Suggestions' on this important subject, in which such general details as were deemed requisite, were gone into. These may be not improperly classed under two principal heads. It was first discussed what locality afforded the greatest number of natural facilities for the establishment of such an Institution, and for its being afterwards efficiently conducted. And in the second place were considered, the branches of science directly or collaterally connected with mining generally, which should be taught by such an Institution. The result of the first inquiry was that, after natural advantages, central position, and local manufacturing and trading pursuits were considered and compared with those of other mining localities, Newcastle-upon-Tyne was decided upon as being, beyond question, possessed of the greatest number of these advantages, and, consequently, a site the most advisable for such a foundation. The result of the second discussion was a programme of the education peculiar to such an establishment, embracing eight distinct branches of teaching, which were deemed to be desirable for the purposes of practical engineering, as applied to mines, whether of lead, copper, tin, iron, or coal, as well as for those branches of science which bear upon the most important manufacturing processes. /

In addition to these more general considerations, others of minor character were gone into and stated; and the whole being printed as a pamphlet, was circulated amongst gentlemen engaged in the coal trade and in iron mining pursuits, so extensively carried on in Northumberland and Durham, and amongst those engaged in the manufactures of which coal, iron, lead, and their products white lead, litharge,[4] colours, coke, artificial alkalies, machinery, &c., &c., are a constituent portion.

The wide distribution of this tract by the Council of the North of England Mining Institute gave the question a practical bearing and consequence, which it had not hitherto nor before attained, and the wished for result of thus directing attention to the subject, was the adoption of a resolution by the Delegates of the British coal and iron mining interests assembled in London, in May, 1854, to the following purport:–

> That this meeting is of opinion that it would be of essential service in the future management of mines, and consequently have a tendency to the prevention of accidents, if a central Mining School, or College, of a practical nature, were established in some convenient and suitable colliery district, with branches therefrom and connected therewith, for the education of mining engineers, or other officers and subordinate persons, to be entrusted with the management and conduct of the mines of this country. And that the Parliamentary Committee, now sitting on Accidents in Mines, be

> solicited to take this subject into their serious consideration, with a view of recommending the Government to afford such aid as they may deem advisable and requisite to establish an institution so necessary and laudable.

In consequence of this suggestion the Committee reported that 'they would urge upon Government to foster by grant in aid, the establishment and maintenance of Mining Schools in the large Mining Districts throughout the Country.'

This resolution having been widely promulgated, together with the printed suggestions of the Council of the North of England Institute of Mining Engineers, led to a further discussion, by the delegates assembled in London, during the following year, by whom the resolution was confirmed, and the site of Newcastle-upon-Tyne named as the most convenient for a foundation of this peculiar nature.

Such is the shape which the question of a central British College of Practical Mining Science has now assumed, and, in compliance with the instructions of their constituents, your Committee now venture to state in detail such further considerations as seem to arise out of the circumstances.

Before proceeding to perform this duty, however, it is necessary to state that, as far as this district is concerned, the proposal to found such / a College has already received the sanction of our great mining interest, the Coal Trade.[5]

On the 6th February of this year, the subject was brought before a General Meeting of the Coal-owners of the Counties of Northumberland and Durham, as a portion of the Annual Report of the General Committee of the Trade. The opinions of the Committee were expressed in the following paragraph:–

> Your Committee now turn, not without gratification, to another topic, which is unquestionably indicative of the advancing state of the trade, this is the Report of the Council of 'The North of England Institute of Mining Engineers,' on the proposed establishment of a College of Practical Mining Science at Newcastle-upon-Tyne, laid before your Committee by that body, and now in the hands of the members of the trade universally. Presuming that the details of this report are known to all present, the Committee can only proceed to impress upon the lessees and lessors also of collieries and mines, the vital importance of giving the proposals, embodied in the document referred to, their best and most favourable consideration. The period has hardly arrived for the Committee to venture a conclusive opinion as to the most eligible mode of raising such funds as may be requisite to erect such an institution on a highly respectable and thoroughly independent foundation, and to secure its permanent utility when so established; but they may express their belief that such support cannot be safely left to spontaneous liberality. It appears to them, on the contrary, desirable that the wealthy and influential interests engaged in the great trades of raising, manipulating, and shipping the coal, iron, and lead, with which these counties abound, in all the forms and combinations which these materials are capable of entering into, or assuming, or are found, together with such friends to the undertaking out of these districts as may be disposed to aid it, should join in procuring either a Charter or an Act of Parliament, of such a nature as would, for a given

> number of years, secure the accruement of the funds necessary to give prosperity to the institution, as well as such permanent pecuniary aids as might in future time be essential to the entire utility and vitality of such an establishment. Your Committee, on the present occasion, deem it their duty to express, generally, their warm approbation of the scheme, as sketched in the Report of the Council of Mining Engineers, and their hope that the great body of the coal trade will add their efforts to promote, by a resolution this day, this great undertaking, for which all opinions seem to concur in pronouncing this locality to be peculiarly adapted by circumstances as well as by nature, but which is, in itself, of national rather than local importance.

The result of this communication and recommendation of the General Committee to the Coal Trade, was the adoption, by the meeting, of the following resolution, passed confirmatory of the convictions of the Committee, and impressing upon the Coal Trade, as a body, the good policy of encouraging the foundation of such a College of Practical Mining and Manufacturing Science:–

> That the Meeting concurs in the Report of the Mining Institute, and in the opinion of the Committee of the Trade, that it is highly desirable to establish a College for the / Advancement of Practical Mining and Manufacturing Science at Newcastle, a locality so well adapted for that purpose, and strongly recommend the Trade to support the same; and the Meeting is further of opinion that the Lessors of Mines and the Mining Interests generally of this and other portions of the Kingdom, as well as the Government, should be applied to for support to such Institution, the object of which appears to the Meeting one of not merely local but of national importance, bearing as it does upon increased skill and economy in production, and also upon the due security of life and property.

Thus, it may now be, without impropriety, assumed that the subject has received the consideration and sanction of the coal and other mining interests of the kingdom at large, as well as of the Northumberland and Durham district, and of those gentlemen in other mining localities who are members of this Institute, and by their acquirements and pursuits qualified to give active and efficient aid to an undertaking of this nature. / /

The entire capital required to be raised, including the purchase of suitable apparatus and endowments for Professors, is estimated at £35,000.[6] Two obvious methods suggest themselves as means of raising and securing the funds necessary for the proposed undertaking. The first of these is to obtain an Act of Parliament, with the assent of all interested, for the levy of a small *per centage*, payable to trustees for this specific purpose, and calculated upon the values or tonnage of the coals, iron, lead, copper, and tin, raised by those who are parties / to the Act; The second is a voluntary subscription, covenanted for in a trust-deed of mutual agreement, to be signed by the parties, and having the force of a legal agreement or bond, vesting the property in trustees. At this stage of the undertaking the Council do not deem it necessary to do more than give a general idea of the trifling amount of *per centage* upon the products enumerated, amply sufficient to raise the sum required; whether this district alone be considered, or the mining interests of the other mining localities of Great Britain be included.

In the valuable Statistical Returns, compiled by Robt. Hunt, Esq.,[7] Keeper of Mining Records, and by him presented to the Library of the North of England Institute of Mining Engineers, are given the totals as well as the detailed particulars of all the coal, iron, tin, lead, copper, and silver raised, or smelted, in the United Kingdom, together with values; the quantities raised or smelted in the several districts being distinguished and stated, together with the greater totals, as follows:–

COAL.

	TONS.	VALUE.
England – Northumberland and Durham	15,420,615	
" Cumberland	887,000	
" Yorkshire	7,260,500	
" Derbyshire	2,406,696	
" Nottinghamshire	813,474	
" Warwickshire	255,000	
" Leicestershire	439,000	
" Staffordshire and Worcestershire	7,500,000	
" Lancashire	9,080,500	
" Cheshire	786,500	
" Shropshire	1,080,000	
" Gloucester, Somerset, and Devon	1,492,366	
North Wales	1,143,000	
South Wales	8,500,000	
Scotland	7,448,000	
Ireland	148,750	
	64,661,401	£14,975,000 (at Pits.)
Tin	5,763	690,000
Copper	13,042	1,229,807
Lead	64,005	1,472,115
Silver, 700,000 ounces		192,500
Iron, (pig)	3,069,838	9,500,000
Zinc		16,500
Arsenic, sulphur ores, and sundry minerals		500,000
		£28,575,922

On coal only, therefore, a tonnage of so small an amount as the 1–90th of a penny per ton (a penny for every 90 tons), would raise a sum of £3,000 a year. Or a payment of twopence-halfpenny in every one hundred pounds value of the mineral produce of the United Kingdom, would raise the like annual amount of £3,000.

But whilst the contribution thus required to raise the requisite funds is of so trifling an amount that it would entail upon a colliery, vending 6,000 tons yearly, a payment of only £2 15s. per annum; yet, considering the difficulty of collection over so wide an area, the possible opposition of particular coal owners to a parliamentary tax, and having regard especially to the circumstance, that the proposed Institution may be expected, not unreasonably, to be self-sustaining, the Committee lean to the opinion, relying upon the great individual interests connected with the mineral produce of the kingdom, that the plan of a subscription would be the preferable one.

To this course they do not yet, however, pledge themselves. Indeed their position is such that they must first feel their way and permit themselves to be governed in a great measure, by future events: expressing, at the same time, their conviction that a project, having for its purpose the establishment of an Institution so directly bearing upon economy in production and upon the preservation of life, cannot be, as it ought not to be, otherwise than eminently successful.

The PRESIDENT,[8] at the termination of the paper, observed that having just heard it read, it was for them to judge whether they should adopt it or not; if they agreed to adopt it the Committee were still willing to receive any recommendation from any member likely to promote the general object in view.

Mr. M. DUNN9 thought they could come to no decision on the subject without an Act of Parliament.

Mr. TAYLOR10 replied, that it would be a very difficult thing to get an Act of Parliament upon which the coal owners of England and Wales would all agree.

Mr. DUNN – But they could not secure a revenue without an Act of Parliament.

Mr. TAYLOR – The numerous pupils would be a source of revenue without it.

The PRESIDENT observed, that as a beginning they only required / £35,000, and he thought it indeed a very extraordinary thing that such a sum could not be raised among the lessors and lessees of collieries, aided by the Corporation of that town and the manufacturing interests in the vicinity, and the other parties interested in the College belonging [to] different parts of the kingdom.

Mr. DUNN – If they agreed upon the voluntary principle, would it not be proper to lay down some rule for receiving subscriptions.

Mr. TAYLOR objected to such a course being adopted, as he felt confident that several parties connected with the Coal Trade would come forward handsomely and subscribe large sums without any dictation as to what they should subscribe.

The PRESIDENT coincided with Mr. Taylor, as he thought it not desirable to lay down any scale of subscription. If parties agreed to a scale beforehand that would alter the matter. At present, after passing the report before them, they might propose a resolution recommending that efforts be made to obtain subscriptions; and if, in a short time, after appealing to certain noblemen and gentleman in the trade they realized £10,000 or more, that in itself would be a good beginning, and set an example to other parties to come forward. The necessity and importance of the College was such, that he could scarcely doubt the most successful results from a well organized plan for securing subscriptions. With their permission he therefore begged to submit the following resolution to their notice:–

> That the prospectus read be approved of and adopted, and that it be printed and circulated; and also that a committee be requested to take such steps as may be requisite to procure subscriptions for the establishment and support of the proposed College.

The PRESIDENT then put the above motion, which was carried unanimously[.]

Henry Davies, *Coal Mining: A Reader For Primary Schools And Evening Classes* (1906)

Henry Davies,[1] *Coal Mining: A Reader For Primary Schools And Evening Continuation Classes*, 2nd edn (Merthyr Tydfil: Educational Publishing Co., 1906).

Lesson 1.
COAL–ITS ORIGIN.

The chemist, by careful examination of a lump of coal, is able to show that it is composed principally of what was once vegetable matter. By comparing its composition with that of grasses, mosses, plants, and trees now growing in our country he will prove that the carbonaceous parts of vegetation to-day found on the surface of the earth are closely allied to the carbon also found in the coal in our fires.

The geologist, too, can easily show that there are clear evidences of ferns, lichens, mosses, and other plants found in the coal beds now buried many hundreds of feet below the earth's surface. These prove beyond doubt that at one time, countless generations ago, what is now coal was once rich vegetation, growing undisturbed by man, near swamps or morasses in the valleys, or on the mountains of our country. Year after year it grew and decayed, until many thousands of rotting roots below formed a rich soil for the growth of fresh plants, which again multiplied, so that dense forests with a thick undergrowth of beautiful creepers and ferns covered the land. This process is now taking place in some parts of Asia and America.

Professor Huxley[2] examined a thin piece of coal under the microscope, and found it to consist largely of small round bodies, and others more or less round, resembling small bags pressed flat. These proved to be the spores and spore cases of lepidodendron and other trees and plants. These spores or seeds must have been produced in large quantities, as bituminous coal is largely made up of them. They are composed mostly of pure bitumen, and are almost exactly the same as the spores of the club moss of the present day. The spores of living club mosses contain so much resinous matter that they are used in making fireworks. It is to these spores, &c., that we owe our blazing and cheerful fires.

An explorer[3] describing the Dismal Swamps of Virginia says: 'From the black water there rose a thick growth and upshooting of black stems of dead trees, mingled with the trunks and branches of others still living, and throwing out the most luxuriant vegetation. The trees were draped with long creepers and shrouds of Spanish moss, which fell from branch to branch, smothering the trees in their clammy embrace, or waving in pendulous folds in the air; cypress, live oak, the logwood, and pine struggled for life in the water, and about their stems floated blocks of timber, on which lay tortoises and enormous frogs. Once a dark body of greater size plunged into a current which marked the course of a river; it was an alligator, many of which came into the swamps at times.'[4]

Hugh Miller,[5] too, standing above black masses of coal which were being brought up from a Scotch coal mine, described the primeval forest, that must at one time have covered what was then the surrounding country, in an interesting manner. He said; 'All round us are the relics of innumerable forms of plant life which flourished and waved luxuriantly in the warm breezes long before Egypt was dreamed of, or Nineveh ever knew Nimrod, or Athens knew Theseus or Athene, or Rome knew Romulus, or, to begin aright, Adam knew Eve. Every tree and plant whose ruins are here compressed into these beds of coal was green and was wood centuries and centuries before Eden had her first rose and Eve had her first walk amid the beautiful flowers. The age of the Pyramids of Ghizeh is nothing compared with this great pyramid of coal. Long, long before that pyramid rose above the sands these seams of coal were packed up close, arranged and ready for human discovery and future use.'[6]

In order to grow from an acorn into an oak tree, or from a tiny seed into a sturdy plant, or eventually into myriads of blades of grass, it was necessary that the seed should have food, and this food the Creator had prepared for it in the atmosphere and surrounding soil. But before the food could become properly changed so as to form a part of the plant itself, power to absorb the right food was necessary. This was supplied by the energy in the heat of the sun. So the little plant stored up heat and sunlight, abstracted from the air and other foods taken from the soil.

By great movements, subsidences and upheavals, which took place in the earth's crust, the parts of the land where the vegetation had been growing for many hundreds of years became covered over by water, or the vegetable matter drifted down to huge lakes, and there became covered by water. Then sand, mud, silt and large boulders again hid the whole of the soft, humid, semi-fluid mixture of bark, leaves, plants, and trunks of trees, and for hundreds and thousands of years it was compressed by the overlying, hardening strata which were being formed, until what was once bright green leaves and sturdy trees became reduced, owing to great pressure and chemical changes, to a black, mineralised substance only a few inches thick. The little sunbeams, which once danced freely amongst the grasses, the bushes, and the fruit, were now 'bottled up' to be some day used to drive, by their combined strength, great steam ships on the ocean, or locomotives on our railways, to smelt the precious ores and to illumine the crowded streets.

Knowing these facts, the intelligent young miner placed alone at the coal face will easily be able to realise fully the beautiful truth contained in the words of an American writer[7] when he said: 'Nature *will* be reported. All things are engaged in writing their history. The planet, the pebble, goes attended by its shadow; the rolling rock leaves its scratches on the mountain; the river its channel in the soil; the animal its bones in the stratum; the fern and leaf their modest epitaph in the coal. The falling drop makes its sculpture in the sand or the stone. Not a foot steps into the snow, or along the ground, but prints in characters more or less lasting a map of its march. Every act of the man inscribes itself in the memories of his fellows and in his own manners and face. The air is full of sounds; the sky of tokens; the ground is all memoranda and signatures; and every object covered over with hints, which speak to the intelligent.'

LESSON 15.
RULES FOR COLLIERS

Amongst the rules which should be attended to by colliers are the following: –

1. Except for a proper purpose, no person shall go into any other than his working place, under any pretence whatever, and in no case shall he go into old workings except by order of an officer of the district.
2. He shall not pass through or beyond any cross of timbers put thus – ×, which in all cases means danger, without leave or order of the Fireman,[8] or other superior officer.
3. He shall on first entering his working place satisfy himself that it has been examined, and found safe, by observing whether the date has been marked with chalk on the face of his working place, and if it has not, he shall not commence to work therein, but shall return immediately to the Lamp Station, and report to the Fireman and to a superior officer, and wait directions from one of them before returning to such working place.

4. He shall strictly observe the directions of the Overman and Fireman, so as to ensure the safety of his working place, and shall at the commencement of each shift, before he begins to work therein, and at proper intervals during his shift while working therein, carefully examine the face, roof, and sides of his working place to satisfy himself that the same is safe.
5. If upon any such examination by a collier of his working place, any danger, want of repair or unsafeness is found, he shall cease all operations therein until such danger is removed, or such want of repair, or unsafeness is made good; and he shall immediately proceed to remove such danger, and make such repair good.
6. He shall keep his workplace safe for working therein, set all timber necessary, and place such props and sprags[9] as are necessary.
7. He shall take care to leave his working place at the close of every day's work in good order, and in a condition fit to be able to resume his labour therein in safety.
8. He must on no account leave in his working place any rubbish, small coal or slack, which shall prevent access to the face of the coal, or interrupt the free ventilation to the face of his working place. And he shall constantly maintain a free opening for the purpose of ventilation between the waste or gob, and the face of the coal and rib in his working place.
9. Every person receiving a lamp from a Fireman, or other person appointed for the purpose, after it is securely locked[10] in his presence carefully, shall examine the lamp to see that it is clean and in proper repair and is properly locked.
10. No person to whom a safety lamp is entrusted, or who has charge or possession of one, shall interfere in any way whatever with it, beyond the necessary trimming of the wick by the pricker,[11] except to put it out.
11. Every person should be careful so to hang his lamp as to avoid risk of it being struck be a tool.[12]
12. No shot shall be fired except by the shotman.[13]

LESSON 22
THE FLOODED MINE
(BY CHARLES WILKINS.)[14]

Many years have passed since the Tynewydd catastrophe[15] in the Rhondda Valley, but its history is as endurable as that of Alma or Balaclava,[16] and well deserves being recounted here. The No. 3 seam of New Cymmer Pit, becoming full of water, became, by its proximity to the Tynewydd Pit, a source of danger, as the men there employed were working close to the boundary. It is stated that the day before the accident one of the Tynewydd men said that they were nearing water, and it is alleged that an approach was made so near that only a slight barrier existed in the pit between the men and an immense body of water. Suddenly, on Wednesday, April 11th, 1877, this barrier is supposed to have given way just as the men were leaving work, for forth into the workings came a torrent so strong and foam-crested that the workers thought the sea was actually upon them, and fled for their lives. Happily most of the men had reached the surface, and only fourteen remained to do battle with the resistless enemy.

Five of these escaped for a little while in one direction, and five in another, but the other four were overwhelmed and lost.

The first five men, led by an elderly collier named Thomas Morgan, ran into what is known as the 'rise' – workings above the ordinary level – and, the air being driven in before them by the rush and weight of the water, they found themselves, though hemmed in, yet in comparative safety.

In this condition, and knowing that a relief party would certainly try to reach them, they plied their mandrils[17] vigorously on the sides of the stalls, until a responsive noise was made by the searchers, and then, their whereabouts being known, a strenuous effort was made by them to cut themselves out.

In one night eight yards of coal were cut through, and as the searchers worked with equal ardour they came on Thursday morning, the day after the irruption, close to one another. When only a thin barrier remained, Morgan's son, eager to get out, rushed at the place and made an opening with a chisel; but so great was the rush of compressed air, that this unfortunate young collier was taken up, just as the March wind takes a seared leaf from the ground, and hurled with immense violence against the opening. So great was the force that death was instantaneous, and some difficulty was experienced in getting the body out of the hole. The other four men were rescued and brought to bank.

Poor Morgan's was an awful death. In the moment of release, just as the hard-fought battle had been won, struck down, battered and slain! That dead man, as he was brought to bank,[18] was a picture on which no eye could look unmoved. The dust of labour was on that youthful head, the furrowed lines of fatigue were upon cheek and brow; even the hand that had wielded the mandril in the wild effort to escape was still clenched.

When the others had been brought up and taken home, and were sufficiently recovered to converse with their friends, one of them related a touching incident, more illustrative than anything that had occurred in the ten days of anxiety, of the deep-seated religious feeling of the colliers. The incident was as follows: –

After their race for life with the torrent foaming at their feet, and threatening every moment to overwhelm them, they rushed, as stated, into the heading from which they were rescued. Then, finding themselves on dry ground and seemingly safe, they, moved by a common impulse, knelt down and prayed, and then in concert, sang a well-known and much-admired Welsh hymn which is translated as follows –

In the deep and mighty waters
No one there can hold my head
But my only Saviour, Jesus,
Who was slaughtered in my stead.
Friend He is in Jordan's river,
Holds above the waves my head,
With His smile I'll go rejoicing
Through the regions of the dead.

One of the colliers stated that he would believe to his dying day that the waters seemed to subside as they sang.[19]

As soon as these men were saved, renewed efforts were made in search of the remaining five. While a determined band of men were searching in the mine, others rigged up pumps, and brought every effort to bear in reducing the water: and on Friday the explorers heard, for the first time, knocking proceeding from Thomas Morgan's stall, where it was conjectured, and as it turned out rightly, the remaining five men were imprisoned.

The sounds of those far-off knocks, heard in the deep cave of the earth and in the watches of the night, were described by the one who first heard them as thrilling in the extreme, solemnly touching – they came like voices from the grave; yet, even as they thrilled to the very soul, they roused and inspired to renewed efforts. There was no halting then.

The officials having a thorough knowledge of the whole mine, and the exact position of the place where the men were, it was soon seen by measurement of the place that 38 yards of solid coal intervened between the men and the explorers, and in the other direction access was completely cut off by so vast a body of water that it was not inaptly called an underground ocean.

To drain this away in time, or cut away the great barrier of coal which lay between – which should it be? In this dilemma it was decided to obtain the aid of experienced divers, and on Saturday Frank Davies and Thomas Purvis, from the firm of Siebe and Gorman, London, came down, accompanied by Garnish, David Adams, and his son James Adams, and descended the workings.

The distance to be traversed was 257 yards, the drift was full of water to the roof, and the peril of the adventure was beyond question. The preparations in the subterranean world, on the edge of the black flowing water, which seemed to sway about as if rejoicing over its triumphs and the captives it held in its grim embrace, were such as no one had ever seen before. Even the experienced diver who first entered the water appeared to have a misgiving of the result, for he said to one standing near;

'Did you know George Smith,[20] the Assyrian explorer?' adding, 'I dived with him just before his last expedition.'

The tone was ominous, but, closing his helmet, the brave fellow waded away and disappeared.

He was followed by the second diver, and the most intense anxiety was caused as the man who held the line called out at intervals, 'Fifty feet,' 'Eighty feet,' 'One hundred feet,' 'Two hundred feet.'

Every cry awoke a responsive echo from the hearts of the lookers-on, and when 'Five hundred feet' was called, and this was known to be within 250 feet of the stall where the five colliers were, men looked at one another rejoicing, and already began to anticipate the recovery of the lot.

But then a dead silence; the line was no longer paid out, and after a brief interval the man in charge disheartened all by saying, 'They are coming back.' The trial was then a failure, and blank dismay settled on every visage.

Soon a bubbling and hissing noise was heard in the distance, and first one diver appeared and then another, and Frank, coming to the surface, and taking off his helmet, and after he had stumbled exhausted to the ground, said:

'We have done our best, and I am very sorry we have been unsuccessful. We found it was impossible to get on further owing to pieces of wood in the water, the broken road, mud, and the strength of the swell.'

Still, unsuccessful as the effort was, no praise could be too great for the daring exhibited. Men applauded even as they sorrowed.

[In the next Lesson, the story is continued and the men are rescued by relays of miners hewing through the coal. As the five entombed men were brought out through the coal, the author comments: 'The grave giving up its dead, the solitary shrouded form rising from its trance, was nothing compared with that procession of five'.]

EDITORIAL NOTES

'The Collieries', *Penny Magazine*

1. *tutelary saint of Durham*: a tutelary saint is a guardian saint, that of Durham is St Cuthbert (about AD 635–87), associated with Durham since his body, believed to be incorruptible, was transferred there in 995 and re-buried in a costly shrine.
2. *Pope Pius II*: Aeneas Sylvius, or Silvius, Piccolomini (1405–64), Pope Pius II 1458–64. He was sent to Scotland in 1435 by Cardinal Albergati, legate to Pope Eugene IV, on a mission to Scotland, the purpose of which remains unclear. His account of his sojourn in Scotland is in Book II of his *Commentaries*, first published in 1584 but based on a manuscript written in the year of Pius's death. A recent translation is now available: Pius II, *Commentaries: Volume I: Books I–II*, ed. M. Meserve and M. Simonetta (Cambridge, MA: Harvard University Press, 2003).
3. *Camden*: William Camden (1555–1623) was an antiquary and historian. His *Britannia* (i.e. *Britannia siue Florentissimorum regnorum, Angliæ, Scotiæ, Hiberniæ, et insularum adiacentium ex intima antiquitate chorographica descriptio* (Londin: Radulphum Newbery, 1586) was a history of the ancient inhabitants of Britain written in an elegant Latin. The first English version was published in 1610. Subsequent editions were considerably expanded and contained substantial topographical material.
4. *commoditie*: convenience.
5. *Messrs. Conybeare and Phillips*: Rev. W. D. Conybeare and William Phillips, *Outlines of the Geology of England and Wales with an Introductory Compendium of the General Principles of that Science, and Comparative Views of the Structure of Foreign Countries: Part I* (London: William Phillips, 1822). No further parts were published. William Daniel Conybeare (1787–1857) was one of the first to realize that different and successive ensembles of fossils were associated with successive strata. He took Phillips's 1815 *Outline of Mineralogy and Geology* and substantially improved it. He was the first to name the Carboniferous formation (*ODNB*).
6. *Crossfell*: or Cross Fell, in Cumberland, now Cumbria. The highest point of the Pennines, rising to 893 m (2,930 feet). Early geological maps showed the coal measures extending across the whole of the Lake District with an eastern margin in the Lune Valley above which the Pennines rise sharply to the peaks of Cross Fell and Great and Little Dun Fell.
7. *Mineral Kingdom*: The references are to articles titled 'Mineral Kingdom', Sections 15 to 21 (Section 16 is mistakenly also labelled Section 15), all subtitled 'Coal', appearing in the issues given in the text which appeared in 1833 on 26 October (pp. 410–11), 2 November (pp. 427–8), 23 November (pp. 450–2), 7 December (pp. 476–8), 14 December (pp. 483–5), 21 December (pp. 491–2) and 28 December (pp. 501–3) respectively.

8. *a somewhat painful sensation*: Pain in strong light is a symptom of miners' nystagmus, sometimes known as 'miners' blindness', a formerly widespread, disabling, occupational disease of the eye caused by working for prolonged periods in low light levels, for example those produced by the Davy safety-lamp. Early writers reported that victims complained of being 'dazzled', later writers that they were often 'photophobic'. The defining symptom is rapid, uncontrollable oscillation of the eye. Swollen eyelids and a 'diminutive appearance' of the eye are not recognized symptoms of the disease. The condition was not noticed by medical scientists until Decondé of Liège reported it in 1861 in the *Annales d'Oculistique* of Belgium. In 1907 it became a scheduled and therefore compensable industrial disease under the 1906 Workmen's Compensation Act although agreement was not reached on its aetiology until the publication of the Medical Research Council's Miners' Nystagmus Committee's *First Report* in 1922 (London: HMSO, 1922). The fullest contemporary account from the pre-war period is T. Lister Llewellyn, 'The Causes and Prevention of Miners' Nystagmus', *Proceedings of the Royal Society of London Series B Containing Papers of a Biological Character*, 85 (1912), pp. 10–27.
9. *door-stead*: A place for a door; a doorway, from door and stead, a place.
10. *herbwaters*: a medicinal infusion.
11. *eight-day clock*: a clock that needs winding only once every eight days, in practice once a week; superior to the cheaper thirty-hour clocks which would have been wound every day. *Oak-table*: as opposed to a cheaper one made from 'deal' or pine.
12. *A few books*: A Bible would have been found in all but the poorest households at this time; a *Pilgrim's Progress* would not have been unusual; a 'few' books would have been relatively uncommon (Altick, *Common Reader*, pp. 246, 255). Together these items suggest a relatively comfortable standard of living for a working-class household.
13. *cuddy ... propriety*: That asses were allowed indoors in 'respectable' households, despite the author's censure, is indicated by the following anecdote told by Samuel Smiles. He recounts a visit with Robert Stephenson to his 'old home and haunts at Killingworth' where he quotes him as saying 'And this humble clay-floored cottage you see here, is where my grandfather lived till the close of his life. Many a time I have ridden straight into the house, mounted on my cuddy, and called upon grandfather to admire his points.' (S. Smiles, *Lives of the Engineers: The Locomotive: George and Robert Stephenson* (1862; London: John Murray, 1879), ch. iv, p. 55).
14. *so early as seven*: The article was written before the 1842 Mines Act prohibiting the employment of boys under ten came into force, on 1 March 1843.
15. *Colonel Breddyl*: That is Lieut.-Col. Thomas Richmond Gale Braddyll (1776–1862) son of a prominent landed family of Ulverston, Lancashire, and an owner of ironworks in that area. He formed the South Hetton Coal Company which sank South Hetton Colliery in County Durham in 1831–3. He was declared bankrupt in 1847. There is a portrait of him as a boy with his mother and father by Sir Joshua Reynolds, *The Braddyll Family*, 1789, in the Fitzwilliam Museum, Cambridge. (Fordyce, *History of Coal, Coke*, *s.v.* South Hetton Colliery; Burke's *Landed Gentry*, 9th edn (1898), *s.v.* Braddyll of Highhead; Haswell History Group, 'Thomas Braddyll and Haswell Colliery' at http://www.haswell-history.co.uk/braddyll.html (accessed 18 January 2011).
16. *rarefication*: the process of making the air less dense so that it rises up the shaft.
17. *Eppleton Jane Pit*: one of the three pits forming the Eppleton Colliery of the Hetton Coal Company, near Hetton-le-Hole, a village about 9 km north-east of the City of Durham.
18. *'blue metal, very mild'*: 'Indurated argillaceous shale, of a blueish purple colour, resembling that of blue slates' (Greenwell, *Glossary*). Indurated: here, a substance that has been

hardened by geological forces, e.g. pressure; argillaceous: clayey; 'mild' possibly used here in its chemical sense to mean 'not caustic' in, for example, the contrast between 'caustic lime' often known as 'quicklime', CaO, and 'mild lime', also known as 'carbonate of lime' and calcium carbonate, CaCo3.

19. *black swad*: a layer of stone or worthless coal at the bottom of a seam.
20. *splinty coal*: Splint is 'Coarse grey-looking coal. It burns to white ashes; it is suitable for burning lime, and the better sorts are well adapted to steam purposes' (Greenwell, *Glossary*).
21. *thill*: 'The floor of a seam of coal' (Greenwell, *Glossary*).
22. *'bord'*: The author here describes the 'bord and pillar' or 'board and pillar' method of working also known as 'pillar and stall' (Durham), 'bord and wall', or 'stoop and room' (Scotland). A system of working coal in which the coal was extracted in two stages. In the first stage the area to be worked was divided up into square or rectangular pillars by driving roadways through the coal. The roadways were the 'bords', 'boards' or 'walls.' Subsequently, the pillars themselves were worked. A plan of the workings thus resembled a chessboard.
23. *London chaldron*: a measurement of volume, approximately equivalent to 3,135 lb.
24. *Plot*: Robert Plot (bapt. 1640, d. 1696), author of *The Natural History of Staffordshire* (Oxford: Printed at the Theatre, 1686) was a naturalist and antiquary, impressively learned and fascinated by the new sciences. He was simultaneously Keeper of the Ashmolean Museum and professor of chemistry in the University of Oxford (*ODNB*).
25. *women have been relieved*: The author gives the impression that no women were then employed underground. It was the fact that women were still employed underground that was 'unsuspected' before the *Report* of the Children's Employment Commission in 1842, not the employment of children.
26. *teemed*: To teem a corve or wagon, etc. is to empty it.
27. *Wallsend*: A town on the north bank of the Tyne about 9 km downstream from Newcastle which became synonymous with the best quality coal as here described. At a later date the name became a valuable trade description or 'brand name'.
28. *dead small*: 'dead' being here simply an intensifier, 'very small'.
29. *Colquhoun*: Patrick Colquhoun (1745–1820) was a magistrate and the founder of the Thames Police. His 'treatise' was *A Treatise on the Commerce and Police of the River Thames: Containing an Historical View of the Trade of the Port of London and Suggesting Means for Preventing the Depredations Thereon by a Legislative System of River Police: With an Account of the Functions of the Various Magistrates and Corporations Exercising Jurisdiction on the River and a General View of the Penal and Remedial Statutes Connected with the Subject* (London: J. Mawman, 1800).

Practical Economy: Or, The Application of Modern Discoveries to the Purposes of Domestic Life

1. *caloric*: a hypothetical substance supposed to account for heat. Thus a hot material was supposed to be full of caloric; a cold substance to be empty of it, much in the same way that we might describe a fully charged battery as 'full' of electricity and a dead one as 'empty' of it. The hypothesis of the existence of caloric was introduced by Antoine-Laurent Lavoisier (1743–94). Lavoisier's enormous prestige undoubtedly contributed to the longevity of the caloric hypothesis. For a modern account in English of his place in the history of science see A. L. Donovan, *Antoine Lavoisier: Science, Administration,*

and Revolution (Cambridge: Cambridge University Press, 1996) and for a more specialized account, R. Fox, *The Caloric Theory of Gases: From Lavoisier to Regnault* (Oxford: Clarendon Press, 1971).

2. *bituminous ... Cannel*: 'A clear and free-burning variety of coal, or a flaming coal of a fuliginous [sooty] character' (Gresley, *Glossary*). The modern definition is based on the carbon content of the coal and contrasts bituminous coals (45–85 per cent carbon) with sub-bituminous coals (35–45 per cent carbon) and lignite (25–35 per cent) on the one hand and with anthracite (86–97 per cent) on the other. *Cannel*: 'A coal rich in hydrogen, produces much gas, and has a hard, dense structure. This word is derived from *Canwyl*, meaning a candle, from the readiness with which it lights and gives off a steady flame (Gresley, *Glossary*). The *OED* is dubious of the etymology offered by Gresley but admits it was widely believed and can offer no other.
3. caput mortuum: '"The dead head". A term used in chemistry, meaning the residuum of a substance that has been acted upon by heat. By punsters the term has been applied to a blockhead' (Riley, *Latin Quotations*). For once, the former meaning is the one meant.
4. *Count Rumford*: Sir Benjamin Thompson, Count Rumford in the nobility of the Holy Roman Empire (1753–1814), natural philosopher, philanthropist and soldier. Born in Massachusetts but a royalist, he sailed for England in 1776. Carried out researches on gunpowder on which he published an article in the *Philosophical Transactions* of the Royal Society in 1781. Subsequently elected a Fellow. Fought for King George in the American colonies 1781–3; knighted 1784. Secured a position at the court of Elector Karl Theodor of Bavaria and examined the problems of feeding and clothing the Bavarian army which led him to investigate the differences in the insulating properties of various textiles. In 1790 confined the beggars of Munich to workhouses; the problems of caring for them at minimum cost led to his researches into nutrition, cooking and heating. Created Count Rumford 1792. Conducted experiments on heat later held to have proved the theory that heat is a 'mode of motion' and disproved the theory that it was a substance, viz., Antoine Lavoisier's 'caloric'. Prevented the occupation and the sacking of Munich by the French and Austrian armies and preserved Bavarian neutrality by a brilliant feat of diplomacy in 1796. Returned to London, 1798, where he became one of the prime movers in the establishment of the Royal Institution, chartered in 1800. (*ODNB*; J. Tyndall, *Heat Considered as a Mode of Motion: Being a Course of Twelve Lectures Delivered at the Royal Institution . . . 1862* (London: Longman, Green, Longman, Roberts and Green, 1863); the standard biography is S. C. Brown, *Benjamin Thompson, Count Rumford* (Cambridge MA: The MIT Press, 1979)).
5. *Mr Kurten*: not identified.

'On Warming and Ventilating', *Quarterly Review*

1. *Neil Arnott*: Neil Arnott (1788–1874) surgeon, physician and public health reformer. Published the *Elements of Physics* in 1827. FRS, 1838. Awarded the Rumford Medal of the Royal Society in 1854 for, inter-alia, the design of the Arnott Stove, a smoke-consuming and fuel-saving grate, described in an article in the *Journal of the Society of Arts*. Subsequently published *On the Smokeless Fire-Place, Chimney-Valves, and Other Means, Old and New, of Obtaining Healthful Warmth and Ventilation* (London: Longman, Brown, Green, and Longmans, 1855) (*ODNB*).
2. *Charles Tomlinson*: Probably Charles Tomlinson (1808–97), science writer, the author of popular books on an immense range of scientific and technical subjects from *The*

Natural History of Common Salt (1850) to *The Tempest: An Account of the Origin and Phenomena of Wind* (1861) (*ODNB*).

3. *Francis Lloyd*: Unknown except as the author of this publication.
4. *T. Hudson Turner*: Thomas Hudson Turner (1815–52), medieval historian. The history noticed here, eventually completed by John Henry Parker and extended to four volumes, was his chief work (*ODNB*).
5. *Cowper* William Cowper (1731–1800), poet. *The Task* (1785) was his most well-known poem and enjoyed great popularity. It evoked the pleasures of a retired domesticity as in the passage quoted here. The line 'the cups / That cheer but not inebriate' became a cliché of the Victorian temperance movement. *Birkett Forster*: That is, Myles Birkett, or Birket, Foster (1825–99) a once popular and highly regarded engraver, water colourist and book illustrator. His landscapes emphasized rural tranquility in a manner now often criticized as sentimental but which ideally complemented Cowper's poem.
6. *carbonic acid gas*: In this context, carbon dioxide, CO2, the product of respiration which, though not normally classified as a poison, will, if present in the air in high proportions, cause fires to be extinguished and death by suffocation. The term was also used in the nineteenth century to refer to the solution of carbon dioxide in water, H2CO3, and the term is now reserved for this solution.
7. listed: from list, a border or edging, specifically here an edging of cloth or other fabric designed to exclude draughts (*OED*).
8. pabulum vitæ: food of life.
9. *Gauger*: Nicolas Gauger (*c.* 1680–1730) the author of *La Mecanique du Feu: ou L'Art d'en Augmenter les Effets, & d'en Diminuer la Dépense ... le Traité de Nouvelles Cheminées Ordinaires, & Qui ne Sont Point Sujettes à Fumer, &c.* (Paris: Jacques Estienne, 1713) translated as *Fires improv'd: being a New Method of Building Chimneys, so as to Prevent their Smoaking: in which a Small Fire, shall Warm a Room Better than a Much Larger Made the Common Way. With the Manner of Altering such Chimneys as are Already Built, so that they shall Perform the same Effects. Illustrated with Cuts. Written in French, by Monsieur Gauger: Made English and improved, by J. T. Desaguliers, M. A. F. R. S. By whom is added, the manner of making Coal-Fires, as useful this New-Way, as the Wood-Fires propos'd by the French author, Explain'd by an Additional Plate. The Whole being Suited to the Capacity of the Meanest Work-Man* (London: printed for J. Senex, 1715).
10. *Dr. Franklin*: Benjamin Franklin (1706–90), founding father of the USA and polymath. His researches into and designs for improved fireplaces and stoves were published as *An Account of the New Invented Pennsylvanian Fire-places: Wherein Their Construction and Manner of Operation is Particularly Explained; Their Advantages Above Every Other Method of Warming Rooms Demonstrated; And All Objections that Have Been Raised Against the Use of Them, Answered and Obviated. With Directions for Putting them Up, and For Using Them to the Best Advantage. And a Copper-plate, in Which the Several Parts of the Machine are Exactly Laid Down, from a Scale of Equal Parts* (Philadelphia, PA: B. Franklin, 1744) and in his *Philosophical Papers: First Printed in the Second Volume of the Transactions by a Philosophical Society, held at Philadelphia, for Promoting Useful Knowledge. Containing a Letter on Smoky Chimnies, with Miscellaneous Observations; and, a Description of a New Stove for Burning of Pit-Coal, and Consuming All its Smoke. Illustrated by Two Copper-Plates. Written by the Late B. Franklin, LL.D.* (London: Printed for C. Dilly, 1791). His role in the improvement of domestic fires and stoves is discussed by Priscilla J. Brewer, *From Fireplace to Cookstove: Technology and the Domestic Ideal in America* (Syracuse, NY: Syracuse University Press, 2000).

11. *untempered*: unmoderated; here unwarmed, cold (*OED*).
12. *Count Rumford*: see note 5 to *Practical Economy*, above.
13. *Essay*: that is: *Count Rumford's Experimental Essays, Political, Economical, and Philosophical: Essay IV. Of Chimney Fire-Places, with Proposals for Improving Them, to Save Fuel; to Render Dwelling-Houses more Comfortable and Salubrious, and, Effectually to Prevent Chimnies from Smoking* (London: printed for T. Cadell jun. and W. Davies, 1796).

Practical Economy: Or, The Application of Modern Discoveries to the Purposes of Domestic Life

1. *Empress*: Persephone, usually described as the 'dread Queen', rather than the Empress, of Pluto, the ruler of the Underworld or Hades.
2. *three-headed dog*. Cerberus.
3. *secrets of this prison house*: a variation on the Ghost's lines in Hamlet I.v: 'But that I am forbid / To tell the secrets of my prison-house, / I could a tale unfold whose lightest word / Would harrow up thy soul.'
4. *Rumford* See note 5 to the previous extract from *Practical Economy*, above.
5. *caloric*: See note 2 to the previous extract from *Practical Economy*, above.
6. *broils … refection*: The author makes a laboured contrast between two kinds of broils, one being grilled cuts of meat intended for 'alimentary refection,' i.e. eating, and another being confused disturbances, tumults or turmoils; quarrels (*OED*).

Armstrong, 'Centenary of the Steam Engine of Watt'

1. *Sir William Armstrong*: William George Armstrong (1810–1900), engineer and armaments manufacturer. A solicitor in early life; became an engineer in 1847 and founded the Elswick Works on the Tyne. By the 1890s the Elswick Works employed 13,000 men and was one of the largest engineering works in the UK. Knighted 1859; created Baron Armstrong, 1887 (*ODNB*).
2. *Watt*: James Watt (1736–1819), the engineer and scientist. The most well-known biography remains that by Samuel Smiles *Lives of Boulton and Watt: Principally from the Original Soho Mss., Comprising also a History of Invention and Introduction of the Steam Engine* (London: John Murray, 1865) later incorporated in to the *Lives of the Engineers*. Twentieth-century biographies include Henry W. Dickinson and R. Jenkins, *James Watt and the Steam Engine* (Oxford: Clarendon Press, 1927) and E. Robinson and A. E. Musson, *James Watt and the Steam Revolution* (London: Adams & Dart, 1969).
3. *Newcomen Engine*: invented by Thomas Newcomen (bapt. 1664–1729) in 1712. It was a pumping engine. Motion was imparted to a pump by a piston moving in a cylinder. The piston was first pushed up by steam. Cold water was then injected into the cylinder, condensing the steam and forming a partial vacuum; atmospheric pressure then pushed the cylinder down again. The cycle was then repeated. Newcomen engines dominated the tin-mining industry of Cornwall and mines of lead and coal elsewhere in Britain. Watt recognized that alternately heating up and cooling down the cylinder and its piston was a waste of energy. He invented an engine with two cylinders in both of which the piston was impelled by steam: one cylinder imparted motion on the up-stroke, as in Newcomen's engine, and another impelled motion on the down-stroke. This is usually known as Boulton and Watt's engine in recognition of Matthew Boulton's manufactur-

ing expertise and innovation, without which Watt's invention would have remained a mechanical toy.

4. *Dr. Roebuck*: John Roebuck (bapt. 1718 d. 1794), ironmaster. Trained and briefly practised as a physician. Involved in a variety of industrial ventures from the 1740s; entered into an association and then a partnership with James Watt from 1765; sold his share in Watts's patent to Matthew Boulton in 1773 (*ODNB*).
5. *Boulton* Matthew Boulton (1728–1809), manufacturer (*ODNB*).
6. *Parallel Motion* The steam in the cylinder pushed a piston vertically upwards. This acted on a beam pivoted about its centre, the other end of which therefore pushed downwards on the piston of the pump. The design problem which the parallel motion solved was that each end of the pivoted beam described an arc while the motions of the pistons were (parallel) straight lines. See R. L. Hills, *Power from Steam: A History of the Stationary Steam Engine* (Cambridge: Cambridge University Press, 1989), pp. 68–9.
7. *Ball Governor* The well-known device which used centrifugal force acting on a pair of spinning balls to regulate the pressure of a boiler.
8. *a steam ship of such gigantic size*: The *SS Great Eastern* designed by Isambard Kingdom Brunel and launched in 1858 was employed in two attempts to lay the Atlantic telegraph. The first, unsuccessful, attempt in 1865 involved 2,300 nautical miles of cable producing a burden of 25,000 tons. The second in 1866 was successful. The cable was inaugurated with a message from Queen Victoria from Osborne House in the Isle of Wight to President Andrew Johnson of the United States in Washington on 30 July 1866 (C. Bright, *Submarine Telegraphs Their History, Construction, and Working: Founded in Part on Wünshendorff's 'Traité de Télégraphie Sous – Marine' and Compiled from Authoritative and Exclusive Sources* (London: Crosby Lockwood and Son, 1898).
9. *First … then … and finally* An example of the sequential accumulation of knowledge noted in the Introduction to this volume.

The Engineer, 'Report to the Metropolitan Board of Works'

1. *The Metropolitan Board of Works*: The Metropolitan Board of Works (MBW) was established by the 1855 Metropolis Management Act which is the '18th & 19th Victoria cap. 120' mentioned in the title. Its remit included sewerage, drainage, paving, cleansing, lighting, street naming and house numbering. The Board's Engineer was Sir Joseph William Bazalgette (1819–91). He was in practice as a consulting engineer from 1842. Appointed Assistant Surveyor to the Second Metropolitan Commission of Sewers for London, 1849, and Engineer, 1852. Engineer to the MBW, 1856–89 when the MBW was replaced by the London County Council. His great achievement was the completion of the Main Drainage of London as described in this Appendix. Knighted 1874. His name drifted into obscurity after his death but has been illuminated by Stephen Halliday's *The Great Stink of London: Sir Joseph Bazalgette and the Cleansing of the Victorian Metropolis* (Stroud: Sutton, 1999).
2. *Lieutenant-Colonel Sir J. M. Hogg*: James Macnaghten McGarel Hogg (1823–90), soldier and administrator. Retired from the Army, 1859. MP (Conservative) for Bath, 1865–8, Truro, 1871–85, and Hornsey, 1885–7. Succeeded to his father's baronetcy 1876; created Baron Magheramorne, 1887. Chairman, Metropolitan Board of Works, 1870–89. His reputation 'permanently stained' by the scandals engulfing the Board in its final years according to the *ODNB*.
3. *penstock*: a sluice or floodgate (*OED*).

4. *Cornish boiler*: A variety of flued boiler. Flued boilers mark an intermediate stage between unstructured boilers, no different in principle from a domestic kettle, and the highly structured multi-tube fire-tube or water-tube boilers typical of locomotive boilers and introduced in the Stephenson's *Rocket* of 1829. The Cornish boiler was in the form of a long cylinder with the furnace located in a large-diameter flue running through the centre of the boiler. Exhaust gases were then led around the boiler shell. It was introduced by Richard Trevithick at the Dolcoath tin mine in Cornwall in 1812. A clear and concise explanation is given by W. A. Tuplin, *The Steam Locomotive: Its Form and Function* (Bradford-on-Avon: Moonraker Press, 1974).
5. *The engine-house*: The engine house at 124 Grosvenor Road, SW1, became a listed building (a building that has been placed on the UK Statutory List of Buildings of Special Architectural or Historic Interest and which may not be demolished or altered without special permission from the local planning authority) in 1970 and other buildings on the site, including the chimney, have been Listed since. See the photographs available on the 'Images of England' website of English Heritage, an agency of the UK central government, at http://www.imagesofengland.org.uk/ (accessed 18 February 2011).
6. *William Newton, Esq*: William Newton (1822–76), engineer, trade unionist and journalist. The representative of Mile End Vestry on the Metropolitan Board of Works, 1862–76 and eventually its chair. (*DLB II*). Remembered for his remarkable eloquence according to the *ODNB*.
7. *Sir J. W. Bazalgette, C.B*: See note 1, above.
8. *Mr. Thomas Lovick*: Thomas Lovick (*c.* 1824–93). An engineer of obscurity; little more is known of him than the details available from census and vital registration records.

'Steam Communication with India', *Penny Magazine*

1. *Judda*: Jeddah; the main port for Mecca.
2. *Cosseir*: or Kosseir or Kossein a seaport described by contemporaries as in 'Upper Egypt', or in the modern Republic of Sudan; a popular route for pilgrims journeying to Mecca.
3. *Lord William Bentinck*: Lord William Henry Cavendish-Bentinck (1774–1839), second son of the third Duke of Portland, soldier, diplomat and Governor-General of India 1828–35. A reformer in India, Thomas Babington Macaulay wrote of him that he was one 'Who infused into Oriental despotism the spirit of British freedom: / Who never forgot that the end of government is the happiness of the governed: / etc.' (*ODNB*).
4. *Mr. Waghorn*: Thomas Waghorm (1800–50), described as a 'naval officer and self-publicist' by the *ODNB*. Involved in a number of schemes, regarded by many as wild and fantastical, to establish steam shipping routes between India and Britain.
5. *janissaries*: Or 'janizaries'. An escort of Turkish soldiers (*OED*).
6. *Mocha*: Or Mokha, a fortified port on the Red Sea described by contemporaries as being in Yemen, Arabia; the principal port on the Red Sea before the development of Aden by the British. The main export was, of course, coffee.
7. *Mr. Rowland Hill*: (1795–1879). The revered inventor of the 'Penny Post', that is, a public postage system based on a uniform tariff regardless of distance and significantly cheaper than previous methods. The number of inland letters rose from 75 million in 1837 to 360 million in 1842, two years after the introduction of the system. Knighted 1860.
8. *the three Presidencies*: 'British India', that is those parts of India that were ruled directly, was divided into the three Presidencies of Bengal, Bombay and Madras.
9. *Surat*: an Indian city about 240 km north of Bombay.

10. *dâk*: an Anglo-Indian term meaning 'post or transport by relays of men or horses stationed at intervals' (*OED*).
11. *Halifax*: Halifax, Nova Scotia; an immense harbour.
12. *Socotra*: or Socotara, an island of about 2,500 sq km in the Indian Ocean near the entrance of the Gulf of Aden; ruled by the Sultan of Keshin who became a British feudatory in 1876; the island was formally annexed in 1886.
13. *Pacha:* Pasha.

'The Manchester and Liverpool Rail-Road', *Penny Magazine*

1. *Wood on Rail-roads*: Nicholas Wood, *A Practical Treatise on Rail-roads, and Interior Communication in General: With Original Experiments, and Tables of the Comparative Value of Canals and Railroads* (London: printed for Knight and Lacey, 1825); second and third editions appeared in 1831 and 1838. Nicholas Wood (1795–1865) was one of the most eminent civil and mining engineers of his day. An early associate and lasting friend of George Stephenson with whom he worked at Killingworth Colliery, Northumberland from 1811; one of the three judges at the Rainhill locomotive trials in 1829 at which the Stephenson's *Rocket* was triumphant; a partner in the Hetton Coal Company and manager of their collieries in Co. Durham from *c.* 1844 and the first President of the North of England Institute of Mining Engineers from 1852 (*ODNB).*
2. *Gordon's ... Locomotion*: Alexander Gordon, *An Historical and Practical Treatise upon Elemental Locomotion, by Means of Steam Carriages on Common Roads: Showing the Commercial, Political, and Moral Advantages, the Means by which an Elementary Power is Obtained, the Rise, Progress, and Description of Steam Carriages, the Roads upon which they May be Made to Travel, the Ways and Means for their General Introduction: Illustrated by Plates, and Embodying the Report of, and Almost the Whole Evidence before the Select Committee of the House of Commons: With an Appendix* (London: Printed for B. Steuart, 1832). Alexander Gordon (1802–68) a civil engineer mainly known for this treatise and his construction and management of lighthouses on colonial shores. There is an obituary of him in the *Minutes of the Proceedings* of the Institution of Civil Engineers, 30 (January 1870), pp. 435–6.
3. *Mr. Telford's Report*: Thomas Telford (1757–1834), civil engineer, one of the pre-eminent engineers of the canal age, was born in Dumfriesshire, Scotland, the son of a shepherd. Designed the improvements to the London to Holyhead Road, the suspension bridge over the Menai Straights on the route to Holyhead and Ireland, St Katharine's Docks in London and the harbour works of Dundee and Aberdeen. The subject of numerous Victorian biographies including one in Samuel Smiles's *Lives of the Engineers*. The leading modern biography remains L. T. C. Rolt, *Thomas Telford* (London: Longmans, Green, 1958). Telford's *Report* was the *Report of Thomas Telford, Esq. On the Roads from London to Holyhead, and from London to Liverpool* (London: Shaw, 1829).
4. *acclivities*: upward slopes; an acclivity is the opposite of a declivity (*OED*).
5. *Milne's Practical View ... of the Steam-engine*: J. Milne, *A Practical View of the Steam Engine: Illustrated by Engravings of the Largest Machine in Scotland Constructed by Messrs. Claud Girdwood, & Co. for the Coal Mines of Sir John Hope, of Craighall, Bart.: With an Account of a Mercurial Statical Dynamometer...* (Edinburgh: printed by A. Balfour and Co. for John Boyd, 1830). The author may have been John Milne (1802–after 1882) known mainly as a harbour engineer and who was active in Edinburgh during 1822–42 (*BDoCE II*). Sir John Hope (1794–1858) was a grandson of John, second Earl

of Hopetoun (1704–1781); the Earl's family had been coalowners in Lanarkshire since the time of Sir James Hope (1614–61) (*Burke's Peerage* 99th edn *s.v.* Hope of Craighall, Linlithgow; *ODNB*).

6. *Dupin*: Baron Charles Dupin, *Force Commerciale de la Grande-Bretagne*, 2 vols (Paris: Bachelier, 1824), vol. 1, p. 149 in this edition where Dupin writes of 'cent lieues' or 100 leagues. Pierre-Charles-François, Baron Dupin (1784–1873) was a French naval engineer, mathematician and politician.
7. *general merchandize and passengers*: that is, it was a public railway in the sense that it offered to convey members of the public and their goods, as opposed to a private railway which conveyed goods for its owners only.
8. *Booth's Account ... Railway*: H. Booth, *An Account of the Liverpool and Manchester Railway: Comprising a History of the Parliamentary Proceedings, Preparatory to the Passing of the Act, a Description of the Railway, in an Excursion from Liverpool to Manchester, and a Popular Illustration of the Mechanical Principles Applicable to Railways. Also, an Abstract of the Expenditure from the Commencement of the Undertaking, with Observations on the Same* (Liverpool: Wales & Baines, 1830). Henry Booth (1788–1869) was a promoter and then Secretary and Treasurer of the Railway (*ODNB*).
9. *permanent road*: Or permanent way, as opposed to the temporary roads laid down to assist construction.
10. *Companion to the Almanac*: The *British Almanac* was published by the Society for the Diffusion of Useful Knowledge from 1828. The *Companion to the Almanac* was a yearbook also published by the Society and often bound with the Almanac itself, with the full title in 1833 of *The Companion to the Almanac; Or Year-Book of General Information for 1833. Containing, Information Connected with the Calendar, and Explanations of The Celestial Changes, and the Natural Phenomena of the Year, &c.; General Information on the Subjects of Chronology, Geography, Statistics, &c. The Legislation, Statistics, and Public Improvements of Great Britain; A Chronicle of Events for 1832; Together with a List of the New House of Commons.*
11. *Mr. Booth*: Henry Booth, noticed above as Secretary and Treasurer of the Liverpool and Manchester Railway, also conceived the idea of a multi-tubular boiler and passed it on to George Stephenson. The multi-tubular boiler was one of the innovations of George and Robert Stephenson's locomotive the *Rocket* built for the Rainhill trials. Gases from the firebox are led along copper tubes through the boiler to the smoke-box thus substantially increasing the heating area and reducing the turbulence in the water. The idea had been pursued by a number of engineers prior to this but not successfully implemented. See Smiles, *Lives of the Engineers: George & Robert Stephenson*, ch. XI, p. 253.
12. *Mr Huskisson ... terminated his life*: William Huskisson (1770–1830) studied medicine in Paris and took part in the storming of the Bastille. Entered Parliament in 1796. President of the Board of Trade, 1823; Secretary of State for the Colonies, 1827; Foreign Secretary, 1828. It is tempting to treat his death on such an occasion as symbolic of the costs of 'progress' but this may be to over-interpret a meaningless accident.

'A Day at a Cotton Factory', *Penny Magazine*

1. *Dr. Aikin:* John Aikin, *A Description of the Country from Thirty to Forty Miles Round Manchester* (London: Printed for John Stockdale, Piccadilly, 1795). John Aikin (1747–1822) trained as a doctor but is now best remembered as the writer of this work which caught Manchester in the early stages of its industrialization (*ODNB*).

2. *Arkwright's inventions*: Richard Arkwright (1732–92). His inventions were the spinning frame later known as the water frame after it was powered by motion taken from water mills, patented in 1769, and his carding engine, patented in 1775. With these inventions Arkwright mechanized all the major processes in the production of cotton yarn.
3. *Leland*: John Leland (*c.* 1503–52) the antiquary who undertook a number of journeys through England and Wales in the six years from about 1539 resulting in the work eventually published as *The Itinerary of John Leland the Antiquary. Publish'd from the Original MS. in the Bodleian Library by Thomas Hearne M.A.*, **9 vols** (Oxford: Printed at the Theater for the Publisher, 1710–12). In this edition the quoted text is in vol. 7 at p. 41.
4. *the first Sir Robert Peel*: Sir Robert Peel (1750–1830). Entered into partnership with William Yates at Bury in 1773. Married his partner's daughter in 1783 and accumulated a large fortune. Entered Parliament 1790. Created baronet 1800. Sir Robert Peel (1788– 1850), second baronet, was his eldest son. He was Home Secretary 1822–7 and 1828–30; Prime Minister 1834–5 and 1841–6 during which period the 1842 Mines Act, the 1844 Factory Act and the repeal of the Corn Laws were carried. Died after a riding accident, paralleling Huskisson's (see note 13 to previous text) fate twenty years earlier.
5. *John Kay:* John Kay (1704–80 or 1781), inventor. His 'fly' or 'flying' shuttle was patented in 1733 and was used initially in the woollen industry but was adapted for use in the cotton industry from the 1750s being in general use by about 1780 (*ODNB*).
6. *Robert Kay*: Robert Kay (1728–1802), as the text states, son of John Kay, who developed his father's invention so that it could be used in the weaving of various patterned fabrics (*ODNB*).
7. *Whitehead*: possibly David Whitehead (1790–1865), cotton manufacturer, although he was associated with Rawtenstall, not Bury (*ODNB*).
8. *Richard Arkwright*: see note 3, above.
9. *whose son*: also Richard Arkwright (1755–1843). At his death, in April 1843 shortly before the publication of this text, it emerged that he was the largest holder of government stocks in England and he was believed to have been the richest commoner in the country (*ODNB*).
10. *Crompton*: Samuel Crompton (1753–1827), the inventor of the spinning mule 'so called because it combined the rollers of Richard Arkwright's water frame with the moving carriage of James Hargreaves's jenny' (*ODNB*).
11. *Hargreaves*: James Hargreaves (bapt. 1721 d. 1778). A 'jenny' is an engine or machine, especially one taking the place of a woman, as here; cf. 'jack' in its various meanings as a contrivance or instrument, especially one taking the place of a man (*OED*).
12. *Dr. J. P. Kay*: Sir James Phillips Kay-Shuttleworth (1804–77), born John Phillips Kay. Trained in medicine at Edinburgh and gained his MD in 1827; set up in practice in Manchester, 1828; published *The Moral and Physical Condition of the Working Classes Employed in the Cotton Manufacture in Manchester*, in 1832, 2nd edn enlarged (London: James Ridgway, 1832). He was later appointed Secretary to the Committee of the [Privy] Council on Education and it is as an educationist that he is now chiefly remembered. He added the name Shuttleworth to Kay on his marriage to Janet Shuttleworth in 1842; he was knighted in 1849 (*ODNB*).
13. *Mr. Thomas Ashton of Hyde*: Thomas Ashton (1775–1845), cotton manufacturer and philanthropist (*ODNB s.v.* his son, also Thomas Ashton (1818–98)).
14. *Mr Orrell's factory*: Travis Brook Mills. Mr Orrell was Alfred Orrell (*c.* 1816–49) a cotton manufacturer, JP and Mayor of Stockport. The Mills passed into the ownership of Robert M'Clure and Sons soon after Orrell's death.

15. *Dr. Ure, Mr. Baines, Mr Guest*: Andrew Ure (1778–1857) trained in medicine at Glasgow University; he was the author of *The Philosophy of Manufactures: or, An Exposition of the Scientific, Moral, and Commercial Economy of the Factory System of Great Britain* (London: Charles Knight, 1835), a eulogy of the factory system and a work which attracted scathing criticism from Marx in *Capital*; Edward Baines (1800–90) worked as a journalist on his father's newspaper, the *Leeds Mercury*, and published his *History of the Cotton Manufacture in Great Britain: With a Notice of its Early History in the East, and in All the Quarters of the Globe; A Description of the Great Mechanical Inventions which have Caused its Unexampled Extension in Britain; And a View of the Present State of the Manufacture, and the Condition of the Classes Engaged in its Several Departments* (London: Fisher, Fisher, and Jackson, 1835); Richard Guest, of whom little is known, published *The British Cotton Manufactures: And a Reply to an Article on the Spinning Machinery Contained in a Recent Number of the Edinburgh Review* (Manchester: Printed by Henry Smith, ... sold by E. Thomson & Sons, ... and W. & W. Clarke, ... and London: Longman, Rees, & Co., 1828).
16. *Mr. Roberts*: Richard Roberts (1789–1864), a resourceful engineer many of whose inventions sought to combine engineering precision with mass production. Son of a shoemaker; apprenticed to Henry Maudslay (1771–1831) renowned for the precision of his machine-tools; in business on his own account from 1816; formed a partnership with Thomas Sharp in 1823 leading to the firm of Sharp and Roberts, later well-known as locomotive designers and manufacturers. The design of the self-acting, or automatic, mule was first patented in 1825 but not made a success until an improved model was produced in 1830. Later, in 1847, designed a Jacquard-controlled punching machine for use on iron plates which has been identified as the first digitally controlled machine tool. Died in poverty (*ODNB*).
17. *some months back*: 'A Day at a Rope and Sailcloth Factory', *Penny Magazine of the Society for the Diffusion of Useful Knowledge* (26 November 1842), pp. 465–72.

Murdock, 'An Account of the Application of the Gas from Coal to Œconomical Purposes'

1. *William Murdock* ... for that year: Murdock was awarded the Rumford Medal for this paper. The Medal had been instituted in 1800 and was presented by the Royal Society 'to the author of the most important discovery or useful improvement ... in any part of Europe during the preceding two years on Heat and Light'.
2. *Philips and Lee*: George Augustus Lee (1761–1826). The *ODNB* explains that in 1792 he became 'managing partner in the Chapel Street mill of the Salford Engine Twist Company owned by George and John Philips, Peter Atherton, and Charles Wood. Atherton and Wood left the company and by 1807 it had become known as Philips and Lee'. The mill was one of the largest in Salford and Manchester and was technologically advanced but Lee was not a 'model' employer, imposing some of the longest working hours in the district. Hence, one presumes, his interest in lighting was not philanthropic but as an aid to exploitation.
3. *by me*: William Murdock (1754–1839) was without fame in his own life time despite his pioneering role in the use of coal-gas for illumination. He was the first to demonstrate the use of coal-gas as an indoor illuminant which he did in his house in Redruth, Cornwall, in 1792 where he was supervising pumping engines for his employers, Messrs Boulton &

Watt. He conducted further experiments on gas at the Neath Abbey Ironworks in south Wales in 1795 and 1796. He was recalled to Birmingham by his employers in 1799 and his activities concerning gas lighting there are described in the present paper. He subsequently fell into obscurity, remembered only by those with a professional interest in coal and gas lighting a fact lamented by the *Colliery Guardian* in a leading article published near the centenary of his death (*Colliery Guardian*, 140 (1940), p. 153).

4. *comparison of shadows*: This is the method which Rumford used in the construction of his photometer. It was based on the then-known fact that the intensity of light diminished in proportion to the square of the distance from its source. Therefore, one light source could be compared to another, standard, source by adjusting its distance from an object until the shadow cast by it was equal in intensity to the shadow cast by the standard. The standard became known as 'one candle power'. Lieutenant General Sir Benjamin Thompson, Count of Rumford, F. R. S., 'An Account of a Method of Measuring the Comparative Intensities of the Light Emitted by Luminous Bodies', Philosophical Transactions of the Royal Society of London, 84 (1794), pp. 67–106, See S. C. Brown, *Benjamin Thompson, Count Rumford* (Cambridge, MA: The MIT Press, 1979), pp. 129–32.
5. *mould candles*: 'a candle made in a mould, as distinct from one made by dipping a wick in melted tallow or wax' (*OED*).
6. *175 grs*: 175 grains, i.e. about 11 g.
7. *Argand Lamp*: Aimé Argand (1755–1803), a Swiss, generally regarded as the inventor of the lamp that bears his name, although the French patent was taken out jointly by Argand and Langé of Paris who had also claimed to be the originator. The lamp was an oil lamp. Argand's innovations were to shape the wick as a ring, increasing the burning surface and enabling complete combustion of the fuel; and to enclose the flame in a glass chimney which steadied it and increased the draught of air through it.
8. *Cannel Coal*: See note 3 to *Practical Economy*, above.
9. *ale gallons*: This was written before the introduction of the Imperial Gallon of 277.274 cubic inches (about 4.54 litres) in 1824. The ale gallon was the most widely used of the various measures of liquid volume in use before 1824 and was equivalent to 282 cubic inches or about 4.62 litres. Thus the ale gallon was about 2 per cent bigger than the Imperial gallon.
10. *peace of 1802*: the Peace of Amiens between Britain, France, Holland and Spain.
11. *Lord Dundonald's Tar Ovens*: Archibald Dundonald, ninth Earl of Dundonald, (1749–1831) father of the famous naval commander Thomas Cochrane (1775–1860), the tenth Earl. The ninth Earl was said to have beggared himself over his chemical investigations including those on the distillation of coal. However, Lunge credits him with no significant discoveries, giving the highest accolade in the field to Frederick Accum (1769–1838), the first to improve the product by boiling down coal-tar in closed vessels or stills and the author of the first treatise on the manufacture of coal-gas (George Lunge, *Coal-Tar and Ammonia*, 2nd edn (London: Gurney and Jackson, 1887), p. 189; F. Accum, *Description of the Process of Manufacturing Coal Gas now Employed at the Gas Works in London, Etc.* (London: Thomas Boys, 1819)).
12. *Dr. Clayton in a paper*: Dr Clayton is John Clayton (d. 1725), dean of Kildare and prebendary of St Michan's, Dublin; the paper was communicated by his son Robert Clayton (1695–1758) at this point Bishop of Cork (*ODNB* s.v. Robert Clayton). His paper is 'An Experiment Concerning the Spirit of Coals', *Philosophical Transactions* [of the Royal Society of London], 41 (1739–41), pp. 59–61.

Macadam, *The Sanitary Aspects of Cooking and Heating by Coal Gas*

1. *Stevenson Macadam*: Dr Stevenson Macadam (*c.* 1830–1901) was the author of a successful textbook, *Practical Chemistry* (London and Edinburgh: William and Robert Chambers, 1865), with further editions in 1866, 1867, 1869, 1871 and 1883 and of a school textbook, *The Chemistry of Common Things* (London, Edinburgh and New York: T. Nelson and Sons, 1866). He declared himself to be a lecturer at the Medical School, Surgeon's Hall and at the School of Arts in Edinburgh, a Fellow of the Royal Society of Edinburgh and a Fellow of the Chemical Society in these publications; in this, later, publication he also refers to himself as a Consulting Analytical Chemist and a Fellow of the Institute of Chemistry.
2. *the Exhibition*: The Glasgow Gas Exhibition, opened on 28 September 1880.
3. *Kitchener*: 'A cooking-range fitted with various appliances such as ovens, plate-warmers, water-heaters, etc.' (*OED*, which gives the first usage in this sense as 1851).
4. *the Bunsen principle*: Robert Wilhelm Eberhard Bunsen (1811–99), professor of chemistry at Marburg, Breslau and finally, from 1852, Heidelberg universities. Invented the magnesium light, widely used in photography, in 1860. With Gustav Kirchhoff (1824–87) pioneered the study of the emission spectra of heated elements. The Bunsen burner uses the principle of a blowpipe, mixing large quantities of air with the gas before ignition to produce a smokeless flame of low luminosity but high heating power.
5. *340° Fahr.*: 340° Fahrenheit, or about 170° Celsius or gas mark 4, a 'moderate' or 'medium' oven.
6. *400°... 500°*: 400° F. is about 200° Celsius or gas mark 6, a 'moderately hot' oven; 500° F. is about 260° Celsius and is off the temperature scale of modern ovens which goes up to 475° F. or 246° Celsius, gas mark 9 ('very hot').
7. *an ordinary middle-class household*: The 1881 *Census of Scotland* shows Macadam's household (himself, his wife and three teenage or adult children) to have been attended by three live-in servants, a relatively large number for a household of this size and composition. It seems likely that his assumptions of what an 'ordinary' middle-class household was like were coloured by his own comfortable circumstances.
8. *brander*: A gridiron (*OED*) presumably so-called because it imparts marks like the branding marks on livestock to meat cooked upon it.
9. *carbonic acid ... oily hydrocarbons*: Carbonic acid is carbon dioxide, CO2. Sulphurous acid has the molecular formula H2SO3. Carbonic oxide is carbon monoxide, CO. Acetylene is the explosive producer of bright light, first produced on a commercial scale in 1895, with molecular formula C2H2.
10. *268 grains ... 821 grains*: There are 7,000 grains (gr) in 1 lb avoirdupois. A grain is now defined as exactly 64.79891 mg in the International System of Units. So 268 gr is about 0.6 of an ounce or about 17 g; 821 gr is about 1.9 oz or about 53 g.
11. *osmazome*: 'A name formerly given to that substance or mixture of substances soluble in water and alcohol which gives meat its flavour and smell; (more generally) meat juice or extract' (*OED*).
12. *cannel gas*: Gas obtained from cannel coal. See note 3 to *Practical Economy*, above.

'Electricity and the Electric Telegraph', *Cornhill Magazine*

1. *Leyden* jars: Devices that appear to store static electricity.

2. *approximation*: The action of bringing close; literally, as here, as well as figuratively (*OED*).
3. *An Expeditious Method for Conveying Intelligence*: C. M., 'To the Author of the Scots Magazine', *Scots Magazine* 15 (February 1753), pp. 73–4. For 'C. M.,' see the text, below.
4. *excited glass tube*: A Leyden jar.
5. *'lichtnin'*: lightning.
6. Anglice: Latin: 'in English'.
7. *Reid and Smith, Hume and Robertson*: Thomas Reid (1710–96), natural and moral philosopher; the author of an *Inquiry into the Human Mind, on the Principles of Common Sense* (Dublin: Printed for Alexander Ewing, 1764) which contested the theory of ideas propagated by Descartes, Locke, and Malebranche. Adam Smith (bapt. 1723 d. 1790), the philosopher and political economist. David Hume (1711–76), the philosopher and historian. William Robertson (1721–93), a Scottish historian now largely forgotten but in his time thought to be the equal of Hume and Gibbon (*ODNB*).
8. *a Frenchman, resident in Geneva*: Georges-Louis Le Sage (1724–1803), a physicist and mathematician, was born and died in Geneva and is sometimes accounted a Swiss; his parents were French. He is now mainly remembered for his theory of gravitation.
9. rifacimento: Italian; a reworking.
10. *at any distance*: Arthur Young, *Travels, During the Years 1787, 1788, and 1789. Undertaken More Particularly with a View of Ascertaining the Cultivation, Wealth, Resources, and National Prosperity, of the Kingdom of France* (Bury St Edmund's: printed by J. Rackham; for W. Richardson, Royal-Exchange, London, 1792), p. 65. A fuller quotation seems worthwhile. Young is in Paris and writes:

    In the evening to Mons. Lomond, a very ingenious and inventive mechanic, who has made an improvement of the jenny for spinning cotton. Common machines are said to make too hard a thread for certain fabrics, but this forms is loose and spongy. In electricity he has made a remarkable discovery: you write two or three words on a paper; he takes it with him into a room, and turns a machine inclosed in a cylindrical case, at the top of which is an electrometer, a small fine pith ball; a wire connects with a similar cylinder and electrometer in a distant apartment; and his wife, by remarking the corresponding motions of the ball, writes down the words they indicate: from which it appears that he has formed an alphabet of motions. As the length of the wire makes no difference in the effect, a correspondence might be carried on at any distance: within and without a besieged town, for instance; or for a purpose much more worthy, and a thousand times more harmless, between two lovers prohibited or prevented from any better connection. Whatever the use may be, the invention is beautiful. Mons. Lomond has many other curious machines, all the entire work of his own hands: mechanical invention seems in him a natural propensity. In the evening to the *Comedie Française*.

11. *Cavallo*: Tiberius, or Tiberio, Cavallo (1749–1809) born in Naples but came to England in 1771 and stayed in England for the rest of his life. Published *A Complete Treatise on Electricity in Theory and Practice: With Original Experiments* (London: Printed for Edward and Charles Dilly, 1777); elected a Fellow of the Royal Society in 1779 (*ODNB*).
12. *Mr. Ronalds of Hammersmith*: Sir Francis Ronalds (1788–1873) inventor, meteorologist and bibliographer. In 1823 he published his *Description of an Electric Telegraph and of*

*some other Electrical Apparatus (*London: Printed for R. Hunter, 1823). As a boy Charles Wheatstone saw his experiments. Knighted 1870 (*ODNB*).

13. *Professor Wheatstone*: Sir Charles Wheatstone (1802–75). In 1834 appointed Professor of Experimental Philosophy at King's College, London, where he began experiments to determine the speed of electric currents in copper wire, obtaining a result of 288,000 miles per hour in comparison with the modern estimate of about 186,000 m.p.h. From these experiments he moved on, in conjunction with William Fothergill Cooke (1806–79), the 'Mr. Cooke' of the text, to the construction of a practical telegraph, patented by Cooke and Wheatstone jointly in 1837 (*ODNB*).
14. *'Never...dispute'*: The words were Wheatstone's and were quoted by John Munro (1849–1930) in his *Heroes of the Telegraph* (London: The Religious Tract Society, 1891).
15. *Professor Morse*: Samuel Finley Breese Morse (1791–1872), the US inventor of the single-wire telegraph and the Morse Code. He conceived the former invention in 1832, built an experimental version in 1835 and a practical system in 1844 but did not apply for a patent until 1849.
16. *Mr. Edward Davy*: Edward Davy (1806–85), chemist. He invented a telegraph system using a relay system in which the electric current was augmented by batteries at intervals along the route thus compensating for the normal attenuation of the current with distance. He published his *Outline of a New Plan of Telegraphic Communication in 1836.*
17. *Bain ... 'far north'*: Alexander Bain (1810–77) clockmaker. The son of a crofter. He invented an electric clock patented in 1841, and an experimental 'printing telegraph', patented in 1843 and now sometimes regarded as a precursor to the facsimile machine. The 'chemical telegraph' mentioned in the text's next sentence used the electric current of the telegraph message to make marks on a moving paper tape soaked in a mixture of ammonium nitrate and potassium ferrocyanide. The paper turned blue when a current passed through it. Watten, Bain's birthplace, is a village in Caithness between Wick and Thurso in the far north of Scotland (*ODNB*).
18. *fluid*: Electricity.
19. *Volta*: Count Alessandro Giuseppe Antonio Anastasio Volta (1745–1827) the Italian physicist who, in 1800, invented the electric battery.
20. *Fabroni*: or more usually Fabbroni: Giovanni Valentino Mattia Fabbroni (1752–1822) an Italian naturalist and chemist. One of the earliest to suggest that electrical phenomena had a chemical origin.
21. *Schwiegger's Multiplier ... Moigno*: the name is variously spelled as Schwieger. Schweiger and Schweigger. Moigno is the Abbé Moigno, François-Napoléon-Marie Moigno (1804–84) a French Jesuit physicist and science popularizer. He published a *Traité de Télégraphie Électrique, Renfermant son Histoire, sa Théorie et la Description des Appareils avec les Deux Mémoires de M. Wheatstone sur la Vitesse et la Détermination des Courants d'Électricité, et un Mémoire Inédit d'Ampère sur la Théorie Electro-chimique* (Paris: A. Franck, 1849).
22. A *and* B *cipher of Lord Bacon*: Francis Bacon, first Viscount Saint Albans (1561–1626), the philosopher and politician. His *A* and *B* cypher was partly a method of steganography (a method of hiding a message rather than translating it into a code). The method was in two stages. In the first stage each letter of the plaintext was transformed into a combination of five As or Bs. For example 'a' was transformed to 'AAAAA', 'b' to 'AAAAB', etc. This yields a coded text. In the second stage an innocuous text of the same length as the coded text is found or composed. Each letter of the innocuous text is then transformed one way if it corresponds to an 'A' in the coded text, another way if it corresponds to a 'B';

for example, the transformation might be into upper case for 'A' and lower case for 'B', or Arial font for 'A' and Times New Roman for 'B', etc.

23. *Sir Humphry Davy*: Sir Humphry Davy (1778–1829), the chemist and inventor of the miner's safety lamp. See Volume 2 (pp. 357–9).
24. *Ritter*: Johann Wilhelm Ritter (1776–1810), a German scientist particularly interested in Galvanism.
25. *gutta percha*: Gutta-percha is rubber. It was distinguished by the Victorians from caoutchouc, also known as India-rubber, derived from the south American *Hevea brasiliensis* and other trees. 'Caoutchouc' is thought to derive from a Carib word, 'Cahuchu'. 'Gutta-percha' was derived from trees of the order *Sapotaceæ* native to south-east Asia; the name is Malay in origin.
26. *Hottentot in his kraal*: 'Hottentot' is now regarded as a derogatory term, the people once referred to as such being the Khoikhoi, or Khoi, sometimes spelled Khoekhoe, of south west Africa. A 'kraal' is a village.

'Electricity as a Light-Producer', *Chambers Journal*

1. *Sir Humphry Davy*: Sir Humphry Davy (1778–1829), the chemist and inventor of the miner's safety lamp. See Volume 2, pp. 357–9.
2. *Faraday's discovery*: Michael Faraday (1791–1867), the scientist. The discovery noted here was made by Faraday in 1821; he termed it the phenomenon of electromagnetic rotation and it is the principle behind the electric motor. In 1831 he discovered the principle of electromagnetic induction which led to the development of the magneto which is what is described here; the dynamo, which uses electro magnets rather than the permanent magnets of the magneto, was a later development (*ODNB*).
3. *Mr Holms*: Probably Frederick Hale Holme, Holm or, more usually, Holmes (*c.* 1811–after 1881), a chemist who patented an electric arc light in 1846. Examples were installed in the South Foreland Lighthouse near Dover in 1858; one is preserved in the Science Museum, South Kensington, London. From the early 1860s he is often referred to as 'Professor Holmes' but the title did not necessarily indicate a university appointment at this time and no academic appointment has been traced.
4. *Mr Wilde of Manchester*: Not identified. His machine caused a sensation at the Royal Society Soirée in 1863 one reporter writing

> Justice to this memorable *soirée* we must fail to do; for although we had hoped to have fortified ourselves for our evening duties by an attendance at Mr. Wilde's trial experiments during the day the fascinations of the marvelous flood of light that poured away from the machine so unceasingly and so gloriously was as irresistible in its influence upon ourselves as it was upon the crowd of illustrious men who honoured the president, General Sabine, with their presence. Never have we seen such excitement among men naturally so stately and reserved.
>
> 'The Royal Society Soirée', *The Standard* [London], 4 March 1867, p. 6.

He was also mentioned in a letter to the *Pall Mall Gazette* in 1866 by John Tyndall of the Royal Institution: 'Mr. Wilde, of Manchester, has recently devised an electro-magnetic machine of far greater power than either that of Mr. Holmes or that of M. Berlioz [of Paris]. I have witnessed the splendid performance of Mr. Wilde's machine, which, if it stand the test of continuous working, will supersede all others' (*Pall Mall Gazette*, 21 December 1866).

5. *lime light*: Current usage is almost entirely metaphorical. This, the literal meaning, refers to 'light produced by a blowpipe-flame directed against a block of pure, compressed quicklime. The lime ... becomes brilliantly incandescent.' The candle-power of the light depended on the flame and its fuel. Combinations of oxygen, coal-gas, benzoline and hydrogen were used, often under pressure. The most powerful in use by the end of the nineteenth century used warm oxygen saturated with benzoline giving a light of up to 1,350 candles (*Chambers Encyclopædia*, s.v. Lime-light).
6. *gutta-percha-covered wires*: See note 26 to 'Electricity and the Electric Telegraph', above.
7. *thick glass globe hermetically closed*: The author here clearly anticipates the invention of the incandescent lightbulb usually credited to Joseph Swan and Thomas Edison and patented in 1879–80. However, the idea had occurred to many and had been demonstrated by James Bowman Lindsay in 1835, Warren de la Rue in 1840 and a number of others subsequently.
8. *the present war*: The Russo–Turkish War of 1877–8.
9. *M. Jablochkoff*: Pavel Nikolayevich Yablochkov (1847–94). His 'electric candle' or 'Yablochkov candle', was a form of arc lamp. Yablochkov developed a lighting system complete with dynamos in Paris. In October 1877, the same month the present text was published, the system was used for the first time, to illuminate the Halle Marengo of the Magasins du Louvre in Paris.
10. *Siemens*: Sir (Charles) William Siemens (1823–83), the renowned electrical engineer and metallurgist. His elder brother, Werner, who co-founded the firm Siemens and Halske in Berlin in 1847 had invented a way of insulating telegraph wires with gutta-percha, making the submarine telegraph possible. William invented a 'self-exciting' electric dynamo in which the current for the electromagnets was generated by the dynamo itself, this dispensing with the necessity for permanent magnets. A naturalized British subject from 1859; knighted 1883 (*ODNB*).
11. *Gramme*: Zénobe Théophile Gramme (1826–1901) was a Belgian electrical engineer who invented the 'Gramme machine', a dynamo capable of generating significantly higher voltages than those previously possible. It was the first electrical motor to be successful industrially.
12. *'recommended by the faculty'*: That is the faculty of medicine; doctors.
13. *actinic*: Used of light to mean having the power to cause chemical changes (*OED*); possibly misused here to mean an absence of effect in perception on the colour of objects.
14. *Franklin*: Benjamin Franklin. See note 11 to 'On Warming and Ventilating'. He proposed this, his most famous, experiment in 1750 and he may or may not have carried it out in 1752. It was designed to show that lightning and electricity were identical. It led directly to the invention of lightning conductors to protect buildings from lightning strikes.

'The Prime Minister on Electricity', *Saturday Review*

1. *Mr. Gladstone ... very clearly*: The author is alluding to Gladstone's writings on Homer (*Studies on Homer and the Homeric Age*, 3 vols (Oxford: Oxford University Press, 1858)), formerly largely ignored by his biographers but treated seriously by both Richard Shannon, in *Gladstone*, 2 vols (1982: London: Allen Lane, 1999) and H. C. G. Matthew in *Gladstone*, 2 vols (Oxford: Clarendon Press, 1986 and 1995). It is fully considered by David W. Bebbington, *The Mind of Gladstone: Religion, Homer, and Politics* (Oxford: Oxford University Press, 2004).

2. *very compound*: A compound steam engine uses exhaust steam from one cylinder to power another and sometimes the exhaust steam from that to power a third.
3. *Lord Salisbury*: Salisbury, prime minister in 1885–6, 1886–92 and 1895–1902, electrified his estate at Hatfield, Hertfordshire, in 1887. The works were extensive including not only the lighting of Hatfield House with nearly 2,000 Swan lamps but also the installation of electrically driven machinery on the Home Farm. The water supply to the house was pumped by an electric motor. The electricity was generated by a combination of water-wheels, gas and steam engines ('Electricity at Hatfield', *British Architect*, 27:16 (22 April 1887), p. 313).
4. *allotment garden*: The author appears to refer to the Allotments Act of 1887 which enabled electors or ratepayers to petition their local authority to provide allotments of land to residents for the purposes of growing vegetables, fruit, etc. and directed the authority under certain circumstances to provide it. However, the Bill, published in July 1887, had been introduced by Charles Ritchie, president of the Local Government Board in Salisbury's Conservative administration, and cannot be attributed to Gladstone's philanthropic scheming.
5. *'sustain ... belong'*: The similarity of these hopes for the restoration of home-working bear a striking resemblance to the late twentieth-century expectation that innovations in telecommunications and information technology would lead to an increase in home-working expressed, for example, in I. Barron and R. Curnow, *The Future with Microelectronics: Forecasting the Effects of Information Technology* (London: Frances Pinter, 1979).
6. *art-socialistic school*: Not a usual term but probably referring to figures such as William Morris and other members of the arts and crafts movement which had been founded in 1880.
7. *Hawarden lecturer*: Gladstone, whose wife's family estate was at Hawarden in Flintshire, Wales.
8. *wielded the axe*: Gladstone was celebrated for his favourite recreation: felling trees. One account was given by *The Times* in 1877 ('Mr. Gladstone at Home', *The Times*, 6 August 1877, p. 8c) which describes the felling of an ash tree 'of not less than 15ft. circumference' by Gladstone and his son. Photographs, now in the National Portrait Gallery, London, of the prime minister, axe in hand, just before or just after felling a mighty specimen were taken by William Currey in 1877 (NPG x12503), Elliot and Fry in 1887 (NPG x127433) and Samuel E. Poulton in 1888 (NPG x5983). See also H. C. G. Matthew, *Gladstone 1809–1874* (Oxford: Clarendon Press, 1986) p. 147).

Steavenson, 'The Manufacture of Coke in the Newcastle and Durham Districts'

1. *Mr. A. L. Steavenson*: Addison Langhorne Steavenson (1836–1913), a colliery viewer from 1858, elected into membership of the North of England Institute of Mining Engineers in 1855, initially based at Woodifield Colliery, Crook, County Durham. A member of the Institute's Council from session 1870–1 and Vice-President, sessions 1888–9 and 1901–2. He published a successor to this paper: 'The Experience Afforded in the Manufacture of Coke during the Last Twelve Years' in the *Transactions of the North of England Institute of Mining and Mechanical Engineers*, 22 (1872–3), pp. 3–19 (*DMM*).
2. *Hunt's Mining Record*; Robert Hunt (1807–87), now remembered as a chemist and photographer, was the first Keeper of the Mining Record Office, part of the Geological

Survey, appointed in 1845. Professor of Mechanical Science, Royal School of Mines, from 1851. He pioneered the compilation of statistics of mining, his *Mineral Statistics* first appearing as a separate publication in 1855; elected a Fellow of the Royal Statistical Society the same year (*ODNB*).

3. *Mr. Hoyle*: Mr. Richard Hoyle JP (1811–67). Described as 'an iron merchant of this town [Newcastle on Tyne]' in a report in *The Times* [London], 23 January 1860, p. 4f; the author of *Richard Hoyle's Circular* published in 1864 and possibly other years. An obituary appeared in the *Newcastle Courant*, 27 December 1867, p. 8e.
4. Dr. Ure's 'Dictionary of Arts: For Dr Ure, see note 16 to 'A Day at a Cotton Factory' above. His Dictionary of Arts was the *Dictionary of Arts, Manufactures, and Mines: Containing a Clear Exposition of Their Principles and Practice* (London: Longman, Orme, Brown, Green, & Longmans, 1839) which went through seven editions, those from the fifth of 1860 being largely rewritten by Robert Hunt.
5. *Mr. J. Marley, at Woodifield*: Probably John Marley (1823–91), mining engineer. Elected a member of the North of England Institute of Mining Engineers in 1852; elected to the Council in or before session 1859–60; President, session 1888–89. Woodifield Colliery was the first colliery at which Steavenson worked.
6. *fuliginous*: sooty (*OED*).
7. *Dud Dudley*: Dud Dudley (1600?–84), ironmaster. He was the illegitimate son of Edward Sutton, fifth Baron Dudley (1567–1643); he claimed in his book, *Dud Dudley's Metallum Martis* (1665), to have smelted iron with coal; whether he managed to produce iron of sufficient quality to stand forging and other manufacturing processes is doubtful (*ODNB*).
8. *Dr Plot*: See note 28 to 'The Collieries', above.
9. *Swedenborg ... Charles XII*: Emanuel Swedenborg (1688–1772) scientist and mystic. He was Assessor of the Royal College of Mines, Sweden (1717–47). His *Opera Philosophica et Mineralia* or the *Regnum Minerale* (Leipzig, 1734) in three huge folio volumes published at the expense of the Duke of Brunswick was his principal scientific work. Mystical experiences in 1743–4 led him to believe that he belonged to the Society of Angels and he wrote only theological works thereafter. Regarded as a prophet in the sect that bears his name. *Charles XII. of Spain*: that is, Charles XII of Sweden (1682–1718), reigned 1697–1718. There has never been a Charles XII or Carlos XII of Spain.
10. *M. Jars*: [Antoine-]Gabriel Jars (1728–1808), Gabriel Jars the Elder, French mineralogist. His *Voyages* in three volumes were published by his brother Gabriel Jars the Younger (1732–69) also a mineralogist: *Voyages Métallurgiques, ou Recherches et Observations sur les Mines et Forges de Fer, la Fabrication de l'Acier, celle du Fer-blanc, et Plusieurs Mines de Charbon de Terre, Faites depuis l'Année 1757, jusques et compris 1769, en Allemagne, Swéde, Norwege, Angleterre, et Escosse, Suivies d'un Memoire sur la Circulation de l'Air dans les Mines, et d'une Notice de la Jurisprudence des Mines de Charbon dans le Pays de Liege, la Province de Limbourg et le Comté de Namur*, 3 vols (Lyon: Gabriel Regnault, 1774–81). The first volume includes Jars's account of coal mining and iron smelting in Northumberland, Durham and Cumberland.
11. *landsale*: A 'colliery to which there is no railway, or tramway, or canal' and which therefore had to sell its coal on to carts at the colliery or in sacks for transport on the backs of horses or donkeys (Greenwell, *Glossary*).
12. *Lord Dundonald*: See note 11 to Murdock 'An Account of the Application of the Gas from Coal', above.

13. *Mr. T. Y. Hall*: Thomas Young Hall (1802–70) mining engineer. Entered the pits at an early age. Noticed by John Buddle and trained by him as a colliery viewer; appointed underviewer at North Hetton Colliery when he was twenty-two. Later viewer to Jonathan Backhouse. While continuing with Backhouse, also became mining engineer to the South Hetton Coal Co. Invented the colliery-shaft guided 'cage' which rendered winding significantly safer and more efficient. Entered into partnership with Buddle and A. L. Potter in 1836 forming the Stella Coal Co. (Welford, *Men of Mark 'Twixt Tyne and Tweed*).
14. *'heap burning'*: The practice of 'burning in mounds', described shortly.
15. *meilers*: Stacks of wood for making charcoal, charcoal kilns (*OED*).
16. *Mr. Mackworth*: Herbert Francis Mackworth (1823–58), nephew of Sir Digby Mackworth, fourth Baronet (1789–1852) a veteran of the Peninsular war who played a leading part in putting down the riots in Bristol in 1831. HM Inspector of Mines for various districts from 1851 until his death. His reports demonstrate enterprise, determination and a quiet outrage at the annual toll of deaths and injuries and his inspectorship became a 'sphere of usefulness and philanthropy' (*The Royal Cornwall Gazette* [Truro], 23 July 1858). His paper, *On the Diseases of Miners*, read before the Society of Arts, 4 April 1855, documenting the shortened life expectation of colliers, received widespread attention. His own early death, attributed to overwork, was widely lamented.
17. *carbonic oxide*: That is, carbon monoxide.
18. *Mons. Ebelman*: Not identified.
19. *following results*: CO2 is carbon dioxide; CO is carbon monoxide; C4H4 is butatriene; H is hydrogen; N is nitrogen. Butatriene is a compound sufficiently unusual to raise suspicions that C4H4 is a misprint for C2H4 (ethylene or ethene in the modern nomenclature), a common constituent of coal-gas.
20. *carbureted hydrogen*; Either CH4, light carburetted hydrogen or mono-carburetted hydrogen (marsh gas; fire-damp) or C2H4, heavy carburetted or bi-carburetted hydrogen.
21. *Chemical Technology*: Friedrich Ludwig Knapp, *Chemical Technology: Or, Chemistry, Applied to the Arts and Manufactures*, ed. E. Ronalds and Thomas Richardson, 2 vols (London: Hippolyte Baillićre, 1848).
22. *carburretted and bi-carburretted hydrogen*: Carburetted hydrogen, also known as light carburetted or mono-carburetted hydrogen, is CH4, popularly known as marsh gas or in coal-mine contexts, fire-damp. Bi-carburetted hydrogen, also known as heavy carburetted hydrogen, is C2H4.
23. *carbonic acid*: carbon dioxide, CO2.
24. *Report ... Hartley District*: This is: W. G. Armstrong, James A. Longridge, and Thomas Richardson, *Three Reports on the Use of the Steam Coals of the 'Hartley District' of Northumberland in Marine Boilers* (London: J. Weale, 1858). W. G. Armstrong is the William Armstrong treated in note 1 to 'Centenary of the Steam Engine of Watt', above; James Atkinson Longridge (*c.* 1818–96) was a coal owner, an early member, elected in 1852, of the North of England Institute of Mining Engineers and a member of its Council in sessions 1852–3 and 1853–4; Thomas Richardson (1816–67) was a chemist, the editor with Edmund Ronalds of Friedrich Knapp's *Chemical Technology; or, Chemistry, Applied to the Arts and Manufactures*, 2 vols (London: Hippolyte Baillière, 1848).
25. *Silicious*: Or siliceous; 'containing or consisting of silica; of the nature of silica'; flinty (*OED*).
26. *Mr. Beattie's apparatus*: Joseph Hamilton Beattie (1808–71), Locomotive Superintendent of the London and South Western Railway Co. from 1850 till his death. Designed a locomotive boiler suitable for burning coal in 1853; his 'apparatus' was for burning

coal smokelessly. Benjamin Fothergill was a Manchester consulting engineer; his *Report on the Coal and Coke Burning Engines on the London and South-Western Railway* was published in Manchester in 1856.

27. *Extract*: 'Substitution of Coal for Coke in Railway Locomotives', *The Times*, 10 September 1858, p. 7f.
28. *'On the Economy of Fuel'*: T. S. Prideaux, *On Economy of Fuel, Particularly with Reference to Reverberatory Furnaces for the Manufacture of Iron, and to Steam Boilers* (London: John Weale, 1853).
29. *The Lorn and Ulverstone Furnace Company*: Iron masters from the Furness district of Cumberland, which includes Ulverston, established the Lorn Furnace Co. in Bonawe, on the shores of Loch Etive, a sea loch, in Argyll, Scotland in 1753 to take advantage of plentiful supplies of wood; it used ore imported from Furness. It continued producing charcoal iron until 1876.
30. *Neilson, in 1829*: The Neilson hot blast introduced in 1828–9 by James Beaumont Neilson (1792–1865) economized on fuel despite theoretical objections that the fuel used in heating the blast outside the furnace should be no less than that required to heat a cold blast inside the furnace (*ODNB*).
31. *fineries*: A finery is a 'hearth where cast iron is made malleable, or in which steel is made from pig-iron' (*OED*).
32. *Mr. E. Rogers*: Ebenezer Rogers, 'On the Manufacture of Charcoal and Coke' (Birmingham: M. Billing's Steam-Press Offices, 1857). (An excerpt from the Minutes of Proceedings of the meeting of the Institution of Mechanical Engineers, held at Birmingham, 28 January, 1857).

'Mineral Kingdom: Iron', *Penny Magazine*

1. *carbonic acid gas*: carbon dioxide, CO_2.
2. *in the last section*: 'Mineral Kingdom. – Section XXIII. Iron – No. II', *Penny Magazine of the Society for the Diffusion of Useful Knowledge*, 3:161 (4 October 1834), pp. 387–9.
3. *An improvement ... air*: See note 30 to Steavenson, 'The Manufacture of Coke'.
4. *muriatic acid*: Hydrochloric acid. The term was used by manufacturing chemists and tended to indicate the presence of impurities.
5. *plumbago ... black lead*: Both synonyms for graphite, a mineral composed of carbon together with variable proportions of alumina, silica, lime, iron and other substances.

Martin, *The Story of a Piece of Coal*

1. *sulphuretted hydogen*: Hydrosulphuric acid, H_2S, the well-known producer of the smell of rotten eggs.
2. *carbonic acid*: carbon dioxide, CO_2.
3. *carbonic ... oxide*: carbon monoxide, CO.
4. *cyanogen compounds*: Cyanogen is a compound of carbon and nitrogen, CN, a colourless and poisonous gas; it forms poisonous compounds with metals, known as cyanides, and, with hydrogen, the poisonous hydrocyanic or prussic acid, well known from Victorian melodramas.
5. *Paraffin Young*: James Young (1811–83), chemist and philanthropist. In 1847 Young was contacted by Lyon Playfair who told him of the petroleum spring mentioned in the text at the Riddings Colliery near Alfreton. Young initially thought the petroleum had been

condensed from the coal and this led him to experiment with the distillation of coal. He established a company to produce petroleum from the Boghead coal found near Bathgate, West Lothian, Scotland, the largest sales at first being for lubricants and for paraffin, used in lamps. He launched Young's Paraffin Light and Mineral Oil Company with a capital of £600,000 in 1866 which exploited deposits of oil shales rather than coal and by 1870 had become known as 'Paraffin Young' (*ODNB*).

6. *rectification*: 'The purification or refinement of a substance by distillation, esp. repeated or continuous distillation' (*OED*).
7. *toluene*: as in trinitrotoluene or TNT, first produced by Willbrand in 1863 but not widely used as an explosive until just before the First World War, subsequent to the publication of this book (J. Read, *Explosives* (Harmondsworth: Penguin, 1942), pp. 51–2; G. I. Brown, *The Big Bang: A History of Explosives* (Stroud: Sutton, 1998), p. 153).
8. *xylene*: A solvent, now used in the printing, rubber and leather industries.
9. benzene collas: 'Collas' was a brand name. A newspaper advertisement from the *Penny Illustrated Paper and Illustrated Times* [London], 2 August 1902 urges readers to 'Ask for "Collas". Cleans gloves – Cleans dresses. Removes tar, oil. – Paint, grease. From furniture, – cloth, &c. Do not buy common benzene. See the word Collas on the Label and Cap. Which is the Original. Extra refined. After using, it becomes quite odourless. Benzine Collas. Ask for "Collas" Preparation, and take no other. Sold everywhere, 6d., 1s., and 1s. 6d. per Bottle'.
10. *Faraday*: Michael Faraday (1791–1867), the chemist and physicist, closely associated with Sir Humphry Davy in his early career.
11. *lackers*: Laquers.
12. *New Cut ... Elephant and Castle*: Both areas of London known for their street markets.
13. *Dr Groebe*: more correctly Carl Gräbe (1841–1927) a German chemist. Together with Carl Theodore Liebermann (1842–1914) he synthesized the dye alizarin in 1868; professor of chemistry, University of Königsberg, 1870–77; then at the University of Geneva, 1878–1906.
14. *sal-amoniac*: A solid soluble in water given a variety of uses in Victorian domestic and professional medicine, for example, as an expectorant, diuretic, diaphoretic, etc.
15. *Ammon, in Lybia*: Ammon, or Ammonium, an oasis, now known as Siwa or Siwah; in the Libyan Desert but in the modern state of Egypt.
16. *iron pyrites*: Bisulphide of iron, $FeS2$; hence the author's reference to it in the context of 'sulpurous impurities'.
17. *brimstone*: Sulphur.

'Some Account of Coal Tar and its Properties', *Tradesman, or Commercial Magazine*

1. *W*: unidentified.
2. *Lord Dundonald*: See note 11 to Murdock, 'An Account of the Application of the Gas from Coal', above.
3. *subtle*: here meaning 'of thin consistency ... rarefied; hence, penetrating' (*OED*).
4. *remora or sucking fish*: There are eight species of sucking fish in four genera, including *Echeneis* and *Remora*. The genus *Remora* includes the whalesucker, *Remora australis*, and the common remora, *R. remora*. The view voiced in the text, which derives from Pliny's account of the Battle of Actium, appears to be without foundation; see E. W. Gudger,

'Some Old Time Figures of the Shipholder, *Echeneis* or *Remora*, Holding the Ship', *Isis*, 13:2 (February 1930), pp. 340–52.

5. *payed over*: 'To pay' or 'to pay over' here means to 'smear or cover (a wooden surface or join, esp. the seams of a ship) with pitch, tar, or other substance, so as to make watertight or resistant to damage' (*OED*).
6. *covere in*: a non-standard spelling; 'cover in'.

'Colour in the Coal-Scuttle', *Leisure Hour*

1. *Robert Boyle*: The Hon. Robert Boyle (1627–92), seventh son of the first Earl of Cork, one of the wealthiest men of his times; his son was able to devote his life to science and scholarship. From about 1645 Boyle participated in the association of men of a scientific disposition which later became the Royal Society. The first to state the law, now known as Boyle's Law, that at a given temperature the pressure exerted by a gas varies inversely with its volume. His 'Essay on Man's great Ignorance' is 'Of Mens Great Ignorance of the uses of Natvral Things', first published in *Some Considerations Touching the Usefulnesse of Experimental Naturall Philosophy: Propos'd in a Familiar Discourse to a Friend by Way of Invitation to the Study of It. The Second Tome, Containing the Later Section of the Second Part* (Oxford: Printed by Henry Hall ... for Ric. Davis, 1671).
2. *carbolic acid and benzol*: Carbolic acid is also known as phenol or phenic acid and has molecular formula C6H5OH. Despite its name it is almost pH neutral. It was discovered to arrest fermentation, destroy animal and vegetable parasites and prevent moulding and putrefaction and was early used as an antiseptic and disinfectant. Benzol is a synonym for benzene, the compound C6H6. Other terms easily confused are benzine, a distillate from petroleum, at this time known as a turpentine substitute; benzoyl, a commercial name applied to a mixture of benzene and other substances but also to the compound C7H5O; and benzoline, a name applied indiscriminately to benzine and impure benzene.
3. *benzine collas*: See note 9 to Martin, *The Story of a Piece of Coal*, above.
4. *antiperiodic*: a drug used to treat diseases occurring at regular intervals, a class thought to comprise agues (a term used to refer to any disease characterized by intermittent fever), neuralgia and headaches. The chief anti-periodics were quinine, as mentioned here, and arsenic, used to treat agues, 'remittent fever' and St Vitus's Dance (Sydenham's Chorea, or Chorea Minor), as well as psoriasis and eczema.
5. *prussic acid*: Hydrocyanic acid, HCN, termed 'prussic acid' because it was first obtained from 'Prussian blue', a colouring matter first produced by a paint maker called Diesbach, possibly Johann Jacob Diesbach, in Berlin in the early eighteenth century. Notorious as an instrument of murder and suicide in Victorian England.
6. *Mr. W. H. Perkin, a pupil of Dr. Hofmann's*: William Henry Perkin (1838–1907), chemist. Entered the Royal College of Chemistry as a pupil of its Director, August Wilhelm von Hofmann in 1853 and became Hofmann's assistant in 1855. In 1856 attempted to synthesize quinine and discovered instead a substance which proved to have the property of colouring substances purple; this was the first of the aniline or coal-tar dyes which eventually almost completely supplanted natural dyes. Became a manufacturing chemist in 1858; his new dye was named 'mauve' in 1859; he sold the business in 1873 and thereafter devoted himself to research. Elected an FRS in 1866; awarded the Davy medal in 1889; awarded the Hofmann Medal of the German Chemical Society and knighted, 1906. August Wilhelm von Hofmann (1818–92) the eminent chemist. Began his career as an assistant to Liebig when he began his researches into coal-tar. In 1845, through

the influence of the Prince Consort, became Director of the Royal College of Chemistry in London and remained so when it later merged with the Royal School of Mines. Remained in Britain until 1864; appointed Professor of Chemistry at Berlin, 1865. Received a royal medal for his 'Memoirs on the Molecular Constitution of Organic Bases' in 1854. Credited with the discovery, early in his career, of the nature of aniline, a substance first isolated in 1826 by the distillation of indigo by Otto Unverdorben (1806–73), without which Perkin's discovery would not have been possible.

7. *spirits of wine*: alcohol.
8. *International Exhibition*: Officially, 'The London International Exhibition on Industry and Art', usually referred to as here. Conceived as a successor to the Great Exhibition of 1851, opened 1 May 1862 at South Kensington on the site that now accommodates the Natural History Museum and the Science Museum. The then_recent death of Prince Albert cast a pall over the opening ceremony which was opened on behalf of the mourning Queen by Princess Mary.
9. *acetate of rosaniline*: a red dye, also called aniline red, new red, magenta, solferino, fuchsine, anileine rouge, roseine and azaline; $C_{40}H_{19}N_3$, HO, $C_4H_3O_3$ (E. Waller, 'Coal-tar colours', *Chemical News*, 14 February 1873, pp. 75–6, at p. 75).
10. *arnotto*: Annatto, derived from the pulp surrounding the seeds of *Bixa orellana*, a tree native to Guiana and other parts of Latin America, and used to produce a bright orange colour, largely, because of its poor permanence when used to dye cloth, in butter, cheese and other foodstuffs.
11. *the principal colour-exporting nation of the world*: Instead, the failure of the British industry to compete with the German became one of the first and main events to be cited by those convinced of the 'decline of Britain' thesis. See E. E. Williams, *Made in Germany* (London: Heinemann, 1896).
12. *Regent Street*: The premier shopping street of London at this time. Liberty & Co. opened in 1874. Oxford Street, the modern equivalent, did not overtake it until the early twentieth century with the opening of department stores such as Selfridges & Co in 1909.

'Saccharin', *Colliery Guardian*

1. *Professor Sir Henry Roscoe, M.P.*: Sir Henry Enfield Roscoe (1833–1915), chemist. A pupil of Robert Bunsen at Heidelberg with whom he collaborated on the chemical action of light for many years. Appointed professor of chemistry at Owen's College (the nucleus of the modern University of Manchester) in 1857. Helped to establish a Working Man's College in Manchester and in 1866 initiated the 'Science Lectures for the People', published at 1*d*. which helped bring the works of the most eminent scientists to ordinary people. Elected F. R. S., 1863; served on the Royal Commission on Noxious Vapours of 1876 and the Royal Commission on Technical Instruction of 1881; president of the Chemical Society, 1881; knighted 1884; elected Member of Parliament (Liberal) for South Manchester 1885 and served until 1895; vice chancellor, University of London, 1896–1902; P. C., 1909 (*ODNB*). Roscoe also mentioned 'saccharin' in his opening address to the British Association in 1887, yielding the first mention of the word in *The Times* newspaper; by March 1888 it was being heavily advertised in the same place.
2. *paraffinoids*: The group of hydrocarbons also known as paraffins or saturated hydrocarbons because each atom of carbon is 'saturated' with atoms of hydrogen in the sense that all possible bonds of carbon with hydrogen are present. They include methane, ethane and propane and have the general molecular formula C_nH_{2n+2} where *n* is an integer

1, 2, etc. For example, where *n* = 1, the formula yields CH4 (methane); where *n* = 2 it yields C2H6 (ethane); etc.

3. *benzoids*: Another group of hydrocarbons, also known as the benzoic group, members of the aromatic series because many have an aromatic odour. They include benzene and have the general molecular formula C*n*H2*n*-6 where *n* is an integer ≥ 6. For example, where *n* = 6, the formula yields C6H6 (benzene); where *n* = 7 it yields C7H8 (toluene); where *n* = 8, C8H10 (iso-xylene), etc.
4. *Faraday*: Michael Faraday (1791–1867), the chemist and physicist.
5. *Hoffman's direction*: That is, Hofmann. See note 7 to 'Colour in the Coal-Scuttle'.
6. *febrifuge*: 'A medicine adapted to drive away or to reduce fever; hence, a cooling drink' (*OED*).
7. *Otto Fischer, of Munich*: Otto Fischer (1852–1932), chemist. A pupil of Adolph von Baeyer who synthesized indigo and won the 1905 Nobel Prize in Chemistry. A specialist on dyestuffs. Professor of Chemistry at Erlangen 1885–1925.
8. *Mr. Rimmel*: Eugène Rimmel (1820–87), the French perfumer and founder of the House of Rimmel (*ODNB*).
9. *Dr. Fahlberg*: Constantin Fahlberg (1850–1910), chemist. Born in Tambov, Russia and trained as a chemist in Moscow, Berlin and Leipzig; travelled to the USA in 1874 and discovered the sweet taste of orthobenzoyl sulphonic amide, also known as ortho sulphobenzamide or benzoic sulfimide (C7H5NO3S), later called saccharine, in 1878 when working at Johns Hopkins University, Baltimore.

'[A Description of the Staffordshire Collieries]', *Knight's Quarterly Magazine*

1. *'view ... wild'*: Milton, *Paradise Lost*, Book 1, l. 60 which continues with the pertinent lines 'A Dungeon horrible, on all sides round / As one great Furnace flam'd, yet from those flames / No light, but rather darkness visible'.
2. *chaps*: as in chapped skin; 'an open fissure or crack in a surface' (*OED*).

Buddle, 'On Subsidences Produced by Working Beds of Coal'

1. *JOHN BUDDLE*: John Buddle (1773–1843), colliery viewer or consulting mine engineer. Easily confused with his father (1743–1806), also John Buddle and also a colliery viewer. The younger Buddle was educated by his father and became his assistant at Wallsend Colliery; established his own practice and became a respected viewer in his own right by his father's death. Appointed colliery viewer to the third Marquess of Londonderry in 1819 and to the Bishop of Durham, the county's foremost royalty owner, in 1837. As a mine engineer his main innovations were his 'double' or 'compound' system of ventilation, originated in 1810, when thorough ventilation was the only defence against the explosion of mine gases, and the panel system of working which allowed ventilation to be improved and better control of the roof. He was an early advocate of the Davy lamp, first trialled in 1816 (*ODNB*). The only full length biography, Christine E. Hiskey, *John Buddle (1773–1843): Agent and Entrepreneur in the North-East Coal Trade* (MLitt dissertation, University of Durham, 1978) is unpublished. See Volume 2, pp. 361–4.
2. metal-stone: 'Sandstone and shale mixed' (Gresley, *Glossary*).
3. *fixed land-marks*: fixed in height above sea-level.

4. *Marquis of Londonderry's Pensher Colliery*: Charles William Vane, third Marquess of Londonderry (1778–1854), soldier and coal-owner. Half-brother of the second Marquess, better known as Lord Castlereagh, Foreign Secretary 1812–22. Served with Wellington in the Peninsular War where he acquired a reputation for 'dash' rather than judgement. Ambassador at Vienna 1814–23. In 1819 he married as his second wife Frances Anne Emily, only daughter of Sir Harry Vane-Tempest, baronet, reputed to be the richest heiress in the kingdom, and changed his name from Stewart to Vane. A Conservative without the pragmatism of Wellington; opposed the Reform Bill and subsequently withdrew from politics and diplomacy to concentrate on the development of his wife's coal properties. Pensher Colliery, or more usually Penshaw or Painshaw Colliery, at Penshaw, a village 9 km west-south-west of Sunderland, was first sunk in 1792; Buddle was the viewer at the time this text was published (*DMM*).
5. *the gauge-line*: the standard gauge line as opposed to a narrow gauge colliery track.
6. *close*: closed, as in 'a close mouth catcheth no flies' (*OED*).
7. *triturated*: reduced to fine particles (*OED*).
8. backs: A 'back' is a 'diagonal parting in coal; a description of hitch where the strata are not dislocated'; 'hitch' being an 'abrupt elevation or depression of the strata to the extent of a few inches to the thickness of the working seam of coal'. Like a slip or fault but of lesser extent (Greenwell, *Glossary*).
9. *'Elements,' (p. 122)*: The text is formally a letter to Charles Lyell (1797–1875), the geologist and author of *The Elements of Geology* (London: John Murray, 1838). On p. 122 Lyell argued that uplifts and subsidences caused by natural phenomena, like that of the 'ninety-fathom dyke' in the Newcastle coalfield, a fault in which the strata are displaced by the distance named, would take place not all at once but in a series of movements of a few feet or yards at a time over periods of many years.

Dickinson, 'On Subsidence to the Surface Caused by Colliery Workings'

1. *Joseph Dickinson*: (*c.* 1819–1912). One of the original HM Inspectors of Mines, appointed in 1850; Chief Inspector 1874 to 1892 when he retired. A member of the Royal Commission on Coal of 1866–71.
2. *moulder down*: To cause to crumble (*OED*).
3. *Railway Clauses Consolidation Act*: The Railway Clauses Consolidation Act 1845, 8 & 9 Vict., c. 20. The Act consolidated in one place the numerous and various provisions usually inserted in the acts authorizing the construction of railways. The text quotes clause 72 of the Act, the second of those relating to working mines near railways.
4. *longwork*: Or longwall; a system of working in which the coal is mined from a continuous 'wall' and no pillars of coal are left behind.
5. *goaf or gob*: 'A space from which the coal pillars have been extracted' (Greenwell, *Glossary*). 'Goaf' was the North Country term.
6. *rubbish*: Here, stone, or poor quality coal not worth raising to the surface.
7. *boards or bays*: More usually, 'bords': the masses of coal between the pillars which are removed in the first stage of pillar and bord systems of working, leaving the pillars behind.
8. *Mr. Binney*: Edward William Binney (1812–81), geologist and philanthropist. Despite youthful inclinations towards geology and chemistry, trained as a solicitor and took chambers in Manchester in 1835. Active in founding the Manchester Geological Society in 1838. Elected FRS in 1856 after his work with Joseph Dalton Hooker on the palaeo-

botany of the Coal Measures. President of the Manchester Geological Society 1857–9 and 1866–7. Active in the support of 'scientific men in humble life'. Made his fortune as a partner of 'Paraffin' Young from 1851 to 1864 (for whom see note 5 to Martin, *The Story of a Piece of Coal*) (*ODNB*).

9. *The CHAIRMAN*: William Peace (1811–61). As is perhaps evident from his remarks Peace was not an engineer, but the mineral agent to the Earl of Crawford and Balcarres, a prominent Wigan coal owner. William Peace was the father of William Maskell Peace (1834–92) the Law Clerk to the Mining Association of Great Britain, the national organization of the coal owners, and, as its sole salaried official, its guiding spirit.
10. *Mr. A. HEWLETT*: Alfred Hewlett (1830–1918). A curate's son who trained as a land surveyor. An advantageous marriage led to him becoming a coal owner and eventually, in 1865, the managing director of the Wigan Coal and Iron Company, one of the largest colliery companies in the country. A veteran of Royal Commissions, his evidence to the Royal Commission on Mining Royalties in 1890, revealed the enormous number of leases held by the company. A significant figure in the Mining Association of Great Britain, serving as president in 1873–4 and 1874–5.
11. *Mr. T. LIVESEY*: Thomas Livesey; not otherwise identified.
12. *Mr. RALPH FLETCHER*: (bapt. 1815 d. 1886). Son of Ralph Fletcher (bapt. 1757 d. 1832) the coal owner and much hated magistrate and Orangeman (*ODNB*). A partner with others of the family in John Fletcher and Others, colliery proprietors, from his father's death. Controlled the firm's Atherton collieries near Wigan from 1867–78 by which time the company was known as Fletcher, Burrows and Co.
13. *'heave'*: Rise up, usually in a mining context the lifting of the floor after coal has been excavated (Greenwell, *Glossary*, *s.v.* 'creep').
14. *Mr. Hull, Mr. Knowles*: Edward Hull (1829–1917) the geologist and author of *The Coal-fields of Great Britain* which went through five editions between 1861 and 1905 (*ODNB*); and Andrew Knowles (1829–90), the colliery proprietor.

'A Burning Pit-Heap: Alleged Extraordinary Effects', *Northern Echo*

1. *Stobart & Co.*: Henry Stobart & Co. Ltd, owners of several collieries in or near Bishop Auckland, Cockfield, Etherley and Evenwood all 10 to 20 km south and west of Durham (*DMM*).
2. *Councillor Stobart, J.P.*: The Stobart family were involved in coal mining as viewers, agents, managers and proprietors, from at least the time of William Stobart (fl. 1791–1828), a north country colliery viewer, until nationalization in 1947. Col. Henry Stobart had died in 1866; this member of the family may have been Frank Stobart (1856–1918) for many years agent to the Earl of Durham, or William Stobart (1822–1905) the Managing Partner of the Wearmouth Coal Co.
3. *'brasses'*: iron pyrites, FeS2 (*Greenwell,* Glossary). When exposed to the air the oxidation can produce sufficient heat to cause combustion and this may have been the cause of the pit-heap catching fire. Stobart's comment suggests he was of this opinion.
4. *cause*: possibly a typographical error for 'case'.

[Smith], 'An Account of the Proceedings of the Society for Superseding the Necessity of Climbing Boys'

1. *Sydney Smith*: The article was unsigned but it soon became known that its author was the Rev. Sydney Smith (1771–1845) the celebrated essayist, wit and humourist. The *Edinburgh Review* was started by a group of natural philosophers, literary people and politicians, including Henry Brougham, afterwards Lord Brougham, Francis Jeffrey and Smith himself. The *Review* was first published in 1802 and Smith was its first editor. For the fame of this article, see pp. 207–10. The fame of Smith remained substantial well into mid century despite the fact that his style and his attitudes were very much of the eighteenth century and not at all of the nineteenth. See the account of him in John Timbs, *Lives of Wits and Humourists*, 2 vols (London: Richard Bentley, 1862), vol. 2, pp. 208–82.
2. *An Account ... Climbing Boys*: The publication supposedly here reviewed is *A Short Account of the Proceedings....*
3. *gusts*: 'Pleasing taste[s] or gratifying flavour[s]' (*OED*).
4. *this evidence*: That is: *The Minutes of Evidence taken before the Lords Committee on the Bill for the Better Regulation of Chimney Sweepers and their Apprentices, and for preventing the Employment of Boys in climbing Chimneys* [Ordered to be printed 18 March 1818] (25) of 1818, vol. 95, p. 1ff. The *Report* of the Committee was published as (61) of 1818, vol. 91, p. 233 ff. The *Report* was widely disseminated by, for example, the Society for Superseding the Necessity of Climbing Boys, but the *Minutes* were less well known.
5. *coppers*: Large vessels made of copper or iron designed for boiling food or laundry.
6. *the Strand ... Somer's Town ... Paddington*: A street and districts of London.
7. Lords' Minutes, *No. 1. p. 8*: Smith's quotations are somewhat loose, though not misleading. There is often nothing to indicate that text has been omitted though he sometimes indicates elisions by '&c.'; italicizations are often Smith's.
8. *plumb-pudding*: Plum pudding.
9. *brush*: The question mark is a slip.
10. *pargetting*: To parget is to 'cover or daub with parget or plaster; to plaster (a wall, etc.)' (*OED*). Chimneys were pargetted internally to stop smoke escaping the flue into the house. See for example the advertisement of D. Evans for an 'improved' sweeping machine which could be used with 'the greatest ease without disturbing the bricks, pargetting or plastering within the chimneys' ('Classified Advertising', *The Times*, 11 January 1844, p. 3d).
11. *Evidence before the Commons*: The *Report from the Committee on Employment of Boys in Sweeping of Chimnies: Together with the Minutes of Evidence taken before the Committee and An Appendix* (400) of 1817, vol vi, p. 171.
12. *sable*: Black. An heraldic term, as if the master chimney sweeper were of noble status; also used to refer to black clothing including funeral and mourning clothes, hence mournful.
13. *Liquor Pond Street*: Now part of the Clerkenwell Road, London.
14. *half a guinea*: Ten shillings and sixpence. A lot of money in 1818; equivalent to perhaps four days' pay for an adult builder's labourer.
15. *cancer*: Cancer of the scrotum. See H. J. Butlin, 'Three Lectures on Cancer of the Scrotum in Chimney-Sweeps and Others', *British Medical Journal*, 1 (25 June 1892), pp. 1341–6; 2 (2 July 1892), pp. 1–6; (9 July 1892), pp. 66–71. Butlin showed that the disease was almost unknown in continental Europe and the USA; that the disease was due to the soot which sweeps daily encountered, argued that the almost uniquely British custom of heating houses by burning coal (rather than wood) in open grates (rather

than in stoves) produced quantities of soot unknown elsewhere and that this was partly responsible for the high prevalence of the cancer in Britain; its low prevalence in Belgium, where coal on an open grate was also the usual method of heating houses, was, Butlin argued, due to the protective clothing that the Belgian sweeps wore and their superior habits of personal hygiene.

16. *we know*: The Committee is interviewing Mr Richard Wright, a surgeon.
17. *Mr Cline and Mr Cooper*: Mr Cline is probably the eminent London surgeon Henry Cline (1750–1827), a man eulogized for his patriotism and integrity by his pupil Astley Cooper, the 'Mr Cooper' of the text. Sir Astley Paston Cooper (1768–1841) was possibly the most well-known London surgeon of his day. Like Cline, a man of democratic principles. Created baronet by George IV in 1821 after removing a cyst from His Majesty's scalp (*ODNB*).

'Juvenile Chimney-Sweeps', *Ragged School Union Magazine*

1. Ragged School Union Magazine: The Ragged School Union was formed in 1844 by a group of philanthropists led by Lord Shaftesbury to combine the resources of the charitable schools for destitute children that had been established in London and elsewhere since the late eighteenth century. Its role declined after the 1870 Education Act began the public funding of elementary education. The standard history is by C. J. Montague, *Sixty Years in Waifdom: Or, the Ragged School Movement in English History* (London: Charles Murray, 1904).
2. *his famous article*: An extract is given on pp. 201–5 in this volume.
3. *'sweep's cancer'*: Cancer of the scrotum. See note 15 to [Smith], 'An Account of the Proceedings of the Society for Superseding the Necessity of Climbing Boys', above.
4. *Earl of Dalhousie*: Fox Maule, later Fox Maule-Ramsay, second Baron Panmure and, from 1860, eleventh Earl of Dalhousie (1801–74), Secretary of State for War (1855–8) and thus responsible for the conduct of British operations during the Crimean War. His role then has overshadowed his introduction of the Chimney Sweepers and Chimneys Regulation Act of 1840.
5. *May 11th ult*: A confusing usage of *ult.* or *ultimo*, 'last', normally used with the ordinal alone, for example '11th *ult.*' to mean the 11th of last month; 'May 11th *ult.*' could mean 11 May 1875 or 11 May 1874. Checking *The Times* shows that 11 May 1875 was meant.
6. *Earl Beauchamp*: Frederick Lygon (1830–91), from 1866 the sixth Earl Beauchamp, was a High Churchman and minor Tory politician. At this point he was Lord Steward in Disraeli's administration.
7. *the Lord Steward*: Earl Beauchamp, see the previous note.
8. *Bishop ... Aberdare*: John Jackson (1811–86), Bishop of London from 1869–85, a man of a naturally conservative cast of mind, solid rather than brilliant, best known for his authorship of a book of sermons *The Sinfulness of Little Sins* which went through thirteen editions between 1849 and 1862 (*ODNB* and *The Times* obituary, 7 January 1885); Hugh Fortescue (1818–1905), known as the Hon. Hugh Fortescue until 1841, as Viscount Ebrington until 1859, then as Lord Fortescue until 1861 when he succeeded his father as the third Earl Fortescue, a 'serious whig of religious bent', and a friend and supporter of Edwin Chadwick, the sanitary reformer (*ODNB*); Henry Austin Bruce (1815–95), from 1873 the first Baron Aberdare, a coal royalty owner, Home Secretary 1868–73 under Gladstone and responsible for the passage of the 1872 Mines Regulation Act (*ODNB*).

9. *trenchant articles*: The untitled editorial with the first line 'Lord Shaftesbury yesterday moved the Second', *The Times*, 12 May 1875, p. 11d.

Russell, *London Fogs*

1. *Rollo Russell*: The Hon. R. Russell, FMS was Francis Albert Rollo Russell (1849–1914), the third son of Lord John Russell (1792–1878) and thus an uncle of Bertrand Russell (1872–1970), the philosopher, to whom he became guardian in 1876. From 1888, when he resigned from the Civil Service, he lived at the family home on the outskirts of Richmond Park and pursued the scientific investigations for which he had already become known. Elected Fellow of the Meteorological Society (FMS) in 1868; Vice-President, 1893 and 1894. *London Fogs* was a bestseller and remains his best-known work (*ODNB*).
2. *'matter in the wrong place'*: dirt; a clichéd witticism.
3. *carbonic acid gas*: Carbon dioxide, CO_2.
4. *Primrose Hill or Hampstead Heath*: elevated areas in the north London suburbs once and, in modern times, once again, affording clear views of the taller buildings of London.
5. *Richmond Park*: an ancient royal hunting ground south-west of London; the adjacent settlement was not at this time regarded, as it is now, as a London suburb.
6. *the thermometer was 22*: 22 degrees Fahrenheit; about 6° Celsius below freezing.
7. *the barometer stood at 30.62*: 30.62 inches of mercury (inHg); equivalent to 1037 millibars or mb, the unit of pressure usual among meteorologists; a very high reading.
8. *thermometer about 32*: 32 degrees Fahrenheit; 0° Celsius.
9. *(on the North London line)*: the North London Railway Company's line from its Broad Street terminus; Haggerston is 2½ km north-east of the City of London.
10. *the thermometer stood at 45*: 45 degrees Fahrenheit; about 7° Celsius.
11. *the dew-point*: the temperature at which dew condenses from the air; it varies with air pressure and the quantity of water vapour per unit of volume of the air.
12. *Croydon*: 16 km south of London; at that time in the countryside.
13. *whooping-cough*: pertussis.
14. *an article of the 'British Medical Journal'*: Anon., 'Fog Fatality in London', *The British Medical Journal*, 1 (14 February 1880), p. 254.
15. *consumption*: tuberculosis. The cause is a bacillus, not identified and described until 1882 when Robert Koch did so, but silicosis is known to increase the risk of developing active pulmonary tuberculosis, suggesting that atmospheric pollutants may have a similar effect, as Russell suggests.
16. *with sulphurous and carbonic acid*: a clear reference to what was later called 'acid rain'.
17. *Dr. Angus Smith*: Dr R. Angus Smith, FRS (1817–84), a chemist well known for his researches into urban air and water pollution. He studied in Liebig's laboratory in Giessen from where he gained his doctorate in 1841; elected FRS, 1857; an Inspector of Alkali Works from 1863 to his death, and an Inspector under the Rivers Pollution Prevention Acts from 1876. Active in the Manchester and Salford Sanitary Association and the author of *Air and Rain: The Beginnings of a Chemical Climatology* (London: Longmans, Green and Co., 1872).
18. *Dr. Arnott's estimate*: Dr Neil Arnott (1788–1874). See note 2 to 'On Warming and Ventilating', above.

C. S., 'The Smoke Question'

1. C. S. was the abstracter; his or her full name is unknown.
2. Neue Beiträge zur Rauchfrage: New Contributions on the Smoke Question.
3. *sulphurous acid gas*: At this time the term referred to a gas with the molecular formula SO_2; when this is dissolved in water H_2SO_3 is formed and this is the modern meaning of 'sulphurous acid'.

'London of the Future', *British Architect*

1. *London Society*: founded in 1912 to foster the 'practical improvement' and 'artistic development' of London. It remains active.
2. *Sir Aston Webb*: Sir Aston Webb (1849–1930) architect of imperial London. President of the Architectural Association, 1884; of the Royal Institute of British Architects, 1902–4. Responsible for the new front to Buckingham Palace, the Admiralty Arch, and the offices of the Grand Trunk Railway of Canada, London; the Imperial College of Science and Technology and the Victoria and Albert Museum, South Kensington, London; the Britannia Royal Naval College, Dartmouth; the Victoria Courts and the University, Birmingham. Edited *London of the Future* by members of the London Society (London: T. F. Unwin, 1921), a development of the present text. Knighted 1904; C. V. O., 1911; K. C. V. O., 1914; G. C. V. O., 1925 (*Who Was Who*; *The Times*).
3. *Sir Jas. Ramsay ... Mr. H. H. Statham*: Sir James Ramsay: unidentified, Sir James Ramsay, baronet, of Banff, Scotland (1832–1925) having no known connection with the London Society. Sir Boverton Redwood (1846–1919) was a chemist and an authority on oil. He was appointed a member of Admiral Lord Fisher's Royal Commission on oil fuel for the navy in 1912, on which see Volume 3, pp. 313–16. Knighted 1905; created baronet, 1911. Sir James Crichton Browne or Crichton-Browne (1840–1938), 'the orator of medicine' was a pioneer in the treatment of mental illness. Medical Superintendent of the West Riding Asylum, Wakefield, 1866–75, where he made his name. One of the Lord Chancellor's Visitors in Lunacy, 1875–1922. An energetic pamphleteer, letter-writer and speaker on subjects allied to medicine and 'a kind-hearted man of wide sympathies' (*The Times*, 1 February 1938, p. 16b); FRS, 1883; knighted 1886. Sir William Bull (1863–1931) was a solicitor, a member of the London County Council, 1892–1901, and Conservative Member of Parliament for Hammersmith and later South Hammersmith, 1900–29; an advocate of the Channel Tunnel. Sir George Riddell (1865–1934), originally best known as a golfer, trained as a solicitor and became the London legal agent for the Cardiff *Western Mail*. With others, purchased the *News of the World* newspaper, and increased its circulation tenfold. A friend of Lloyd George. Knighted, 1909; created baronet, 1918, and a peer in 1920 from which time he was known as Lord Riddell. Henry Heathcote Statham (1839–1924) trained as an architect but was best known as a music critic and, from 1883, as editor of the *Builder*, a post he held for twenty-five years.
4. *Smoke Abatement Society*: Various provincial Smoke Abatement Societies existed, for example in Sheffield. The most prominent were undoubtedly those of Manchester and Salford. A Manchester Association for the Prevention of Smoke was formed in 1842; the Manchester and Salford Noxious Vapours Abatement Association (NVAA) was formed in 1876. National societies started later. A Smoke Abatement Committee became active in 1881, soon changing its name to the National Smoke Abatement Institution; it remained active until 1890. Its place was taken by two organizations. The Smoke Abatement League was formed from a group of smoke abatement societies in Manchester,

Bolton, Oldham, Rochdale, and Middleton in 1895 including the NVAA but had to be re-formed in 1909. Its membership now extending to Glasgow and Sheffield, it held its first annual conference in 1910. The Coal Smoke Abatement Society was formed in 1898; it later changed its name to the National Society for Clean Air and Environmental Protection and is now known as Environmental Protection UK.

5. *Sir Wm. Ramsay*: Sir William Ramsay (1852–1916), chemist. Trained in Germany, for a short time under Bunsen at Heidelberg. Professor of Chemistry, University College, London 1887–1913. Discovered argon simultaneously with Rayleigh in 1894 and subsequently neon, krypton and xenon. Discovered helium, an element previously only known from spectrographic investigations of the sun, to be a product of the disintegration of radium. Knighted 1902; Nobel Prize, 1904.
6. *Sir Wm. Richmond*: Sir William Blake Richmond (1843–1921), painter and anti-smoke campaigner. Named after the poet and artist; an admirer of Ruskin whom he succeeded as Slade Professor of Fine Art at Oxford University in 1878; his paintings now largely forgotten except for the portrait of 'Three Daughters of Dean Liddell' also known as 'The Sisters' which includes a portrait of the Alice Liddell who inspired *Alice in Wonderland* (exhibited, British Institution, 1865, now in a private collection). In 1898 he was involved in a successful court case against the East India Produce Co. whose chimney, 100 yards from his house, gave forth smoke he described in court as 'as black as his coat, opaque, and so thick that he could not see through it' ('Police', *The Times*, 14 November 1898, p. 14f) and this appears to have inspired him to establish the Coal Smoke Abatement Society (later the National Smoke Abatement Society) of which he was the first President (*ODNB*).
7. *at the Tower*: Salmon returned to the Thames below London in 1974 after an absence of 150 years.
8. *encircling London*: The idea of a 'green belt' is associated with the name of Sir (Leslie) Patrick Abercrombie (1879–1957) the pioneer town planner and the author of *The Preservation of Rural England* (Liverpool: The University Press of Liverpool, 1926). A green belt was first formally proposed for London by Sir Raymond Unwin (1863–1940) the technical adviser to the Greater London regional planning committee, 1929–33, and was adopted by the London County Council after the Labour Party won control in 1934; its implementation was not complete until 1958.
9. *one united body*: The Corporation of the City of London remains in existence to the present day. A comprehensive local authority for London, the London County Council, was first established in 1889 but excluded the City. The City also remained aloof from the Greater London Council (1965–86).
10. *the great railway stations*: From Paddington Station (in 1914 the London terminus of the Great Western Railway) in the north-west and going clockwise these were Marylebone (Great Central Railway), Euston (London and North Western Railway), St Pancras (Midland Railway), King's Cross (Great Northern Railway), Broad Street (North London Railway), Liverpool Street (Great Eastern Railway), Fenchurch Street (London, Tilbury and Southend Railway), Cannon Street (the South Eastern Railway's City terminus) and the first of the stations to the south of city, London Bridge (London, Brighton & South Coast Railway), Charing Cross (South Eastern & Chatham Railway), Waterloo (London and South Western Railway), Victoria (London, Chatham and Dover Railway). The ring formed by these stations defined what Londoners considered to be central London; everything else was a suburb.
11. *London University*: The design of the University Senate House in Bloomsbury, usually considered the geographical centre of a university which has premises all over London, was not commissioned until 1931.

12. *Imperial Institute*: The Imperial Institute, now known as the Commonwealth Institute, was established in 1887, to promote research for the benefit of the British Empire. From 1893 it was housed in buildings in Exhibition Road, South Kensington, London. Exhibition Road runs parallel to Queen's Gate.
13. *Ministry of Arts*: There has never been a full Ministry of Arts in the UK. Jennie Lee (1904–88) was appointed Minister of State for the Arts on the creation of this office within the Department of Education and Science in 1967 after having had a loosely defined responsibility for the area since 1964. The office has subsequently been relocated to the Cabinet Office (1970–92), the Department of National Heritage (1992–97) and the Department for Culture, Media and Sport from 1997 where it currently remains.
14. *carefully preserved*: The present 'Listing' system with which the preservation of 'interesting old buildings' is managed was introduced under the Town and Country Planning Act of 1947 (10 & 11 Geo VI, c. 51).
15. *Mr. Carmichael Thomas*: William Carmichael Thomas (1856–1942), art editor and, from 1900 to 1917 chairman, of the *Graphic* illustrated newspaper founded by his father William Luson Thomas (1830–1900) in 1869 as a rival to the *Illustrated London News*. Chairman of the Council of the London Society until 1934 (*Who Was Who*).
16. *Mr. Solomon J. Solomon, R.A*: Solomon Joseph Solomon (1860–1927), a skilful but conservative painter. Became an expert in camouflage after 1914 (*ODNB*).

Kennett-Barrington, 'River Pollution by Refuse from Manufactories and Mines Together with Some Remedies Proposed'

1. *V. B. Kennett-Barrington*: Sir Vincent Hunter Barrington Kennett-Barrington (1844–1903) was born Vincent Hunter Kennett, the son of a captain in the East India Company's army and added Barrington, his mother's name, to his own on her death in 1878. He became involved with the Society for Aiding and Ameliorating the Condition of the Sick and Wounded in Time of War, usually known as the National Aid Society, on its formation in 1870. The Society was re-founded as the British Red Cross in 1905. Under these auspices he offered humanitarian assistance to those involved in the Franco–Prussian War of 1870–71, the Carlist War in Spain (1873–5), the Serbo–Turkish War (1876–7), the Turko-Russian War of 1877–8, the Sudan Expedition (1885) and the Serbo–Bulgarian War in the same year. Knighted 1886. He was also an Alderman of London County Council in 1890–1 and chair of the Statistical Committee of the Metropolitan Asylums Board. He died after a ballooning accident. There is a modern life: P. Morris (ed.) *First Aid to the Battlefront: Life and Letters of Sir Kennett-Barrington (1844–1903)* (Stroud: Alan Sutton, 1992) (*ODNB*).
2. *These remarks ... on the subject*: Burchell's 'short history' is omitted from the extracts presented here.
3. *Select Committee ... House of Lords, 1873*: the reference is: *Report from the Select Committee of the House of Lords on the Pollution of Rivers Bill: Together with the Proceedings of the Committee and Minutes of Evidence* (132) 1873, ix, 5.
4. *the Hon. W. F. B. Massey Mainwaring ... Guano Company*: William Frederick Barton Massey-Mainwaring (1845–1907) was born W. F. B. Massey, the fourth son of the third Baron Clarina, an Irish Representative Peer. Assumed the additional name Mainwaring on his marriage. He was Unionist MP for Central Finsbury (London) 1895–1906 (*Burke's Peerage*). 'Native guano' was not guano at all but treated human sewage.

5. *Royal Commissioners*: The first Royal Commission on River Pollution was created in 1865. The Commissioners were Robert Rawlinson (1810–98), later Chief Engineering Inspector of the Local Government Board, for whose career in public service see the *ODNB*; Sir William Thomas Denison (1804–71), the former Governor of the Madras Presidency, a man 'solid rather than brilliant', of 'great industry and unimpeachable integrity' according to the *ODNB*; and John Chalmers Morton (1821–88), a writer on agriculture (*ODNB*). The Commission was re-established in 1868 and consisted of Denison, Morton and Edward Frankland (1825–99), the chemist who discovered the phenomenon of valency (*ODNB*). This, the second Commission, issued six reports, the first five of which are the first to fifth Reports referred to in the text. The full references are: First Commission: *First Report (River Thames)*, 1866, xxxiii, 1; *Second Report (River Lea)*, 1867, xxxiii, 1; *Third Report (Rivers Aire and Calder)*, 1867, xxxiii, 231; Second Commission: *Reports of Commissioners Appointed in 1868 on the Best Means of Preventing the Pollution of Rivers: First Report: Mersey and Ribble Basins*, 1870, xl, 1; *Second Report: The ABC Process of Treating Sewage*, 1870, xl, 449; *Third Report: Pollution arising from the Woollen Manufacture and Processes Connected therewith*, 1871, xxv, 689 and (*Evidence*), 1873, xxxvi, 1; *Fourth Report: Rivers of Scotland*, 1872, xxxiv, 1; *Fifth Report: Pollution arising from Mining Operations and Metal Manufacturers*, 1874, xxxiii, 1; *Sixth Report: Domestic Water Supply of Great Britain*, 1874, xxxiii, 311.
6. *Royal Commissioners of 1868*: The second Royal Commission. See note 5, above.
7. *Sir Lyon Playfair, M.P*: later the first Baron Playfair (1818–98), chemist. Studied at Giessen under Liebig who invited him to undertake the translation of his renowned *Die organische Chemie in ihre Anwendung auf Agriculture und Physiologie* (1840) and worked with Joule on atomic volume and specific gravity. Nominated to the Royal Commission on the State of Large Towns and Populous Districts; his 1845 *Report on the State of Large Towns in Lancashire* made his name widely known. Appointed chemist to the Geological Survey, 1845, where he researched coal-gases; assisted Young in his experiments on paraffin in 1847; appointed Professor of Chemistry at the School of Mines, 1851; Professor of Chemistry Edinburgh University 1858; Liberal MP for Edinburgh and St Andrews Universities 1868–85 and for South Leeds, 1885–92. FRS 1848; knighted 1883; created Baron Playfair of St Andrews, 1892. For half a century a ubiquitous figure on royal commissions and parliamentary enquiries (*ODNB*).
8. *largest paraffin works in the kingdom*: This was likely to have been the works owned by Young's Paraffin Light and Mineral Oil Company. Playfair had been associated with Young from the time of his initial experiments with paraffin in 1847. See note 5 to Martin, 'The Story of a Piece of Coal'.
9. *Select Committee of the Lords*: See note 3, above.
10. *Mr. C. N. Cresswell*: Charles Neve Cresswell (*c.* 1829–1908), a barrister specializing in drainage and sewage. Author of a contribution to J. C. Lory Marsh (ed.) *Handbook of Rural Sanitary Science: Illustrating the Best Means of Securing Health and Preventing Disease* (London: Smith, Elder, & Co., 1876) and before that a lecture on *Woman: Her Legal Rights and Social Duties* (London: Robert Hardwicke, 1869) which he a developed into *Woman and her Work in the World* (London: Hardwicke and Bogue, 1876).
11. *the river*: the River Aire, which flows through the centre of the city. The River Calder, which flows through Halifax and Wakefield, joins the Aire a few kilometres downstream from Leeds at Castleford.
12. *not a single town ... on the river*: Going down stream towards Leeds, the River Aire passes through Gargrave, Skipton, Keighley, Bingley, Saltaire (the site of Salt's Mill) and Shipley, a town immediately north of Bradford. All these towns accommodated woollen mills.

13. *Apollinaris*: Apollinaris Water was a popular mineral water derived from the Apollinaris Spring in the valley of the River Ahr, a tributary of the Rhine. It was named after Saint Apollinaris of Ravenna, a patron saint of wine. The name and the source is now owned by the Coca Cola Corporation.
14. *Act of 1876*: The Rivers Pollution Prevention Act (39 & 40 Vict. c. 75). It failed to establish any adequate machinery for the enforcement of its provisions. It was the Act in force at the time this text was written.
15. *Mr. Robert Rawlinson*: the commissioner on the first Royal Commission of 1865. See note 5, above.
16. *Mr. Baldwin Latham*: Baldwin Latham (1836–1917) was one of the greatest sanitary engineers of his day. Author of *Sanitary Engineering: A Guide to the Construction of Sewerage and House Drainage* (London: E. & F. N. Spon, 1873), a classic of its times (*ODNB*).
17. *Colonel Leach*: not identified.
18. *polluting the streams around it*: by discharging sewage into water courses.
19. *resolution*: The resolution was seconded and carried unanimously.

Maclean Wilson, 'The Pollution of Streams by Spent Gas-Liquors from Coke-Ovens and the Methods Adopted for its Prevention'

1. *Dr. H. Maclean Wilson*: Hector Maclean, or McLean, Wilson (1858–1930) gained his MD from Edinburgh University in 1890. Chief Inspector of the West Riding Rivers Board for twenty-five years and credited with putting that body in the forefront of organizations concerned with water pollution and water treatment. Author of *Cottage Sanitation in Rural Districts*, 2nd edn (London: Royal Agricultural Society of England, 1896) a pamphlet designed for widespread distribution and now known only from its second edition; and with Harry Thornton Calvert, *A Text-Book on Trade Waste Waters: Their Nature and Disposal* (London: Charles Griffin & Co.,1913).
2. *Public Health Act*: 38 & 39 Vict. c. 55.
3. *Rivers Board*: Wilson is referring to the West Riding Board. This was established by the West Riding of Yorkshire County Council, itself formed only in 1888. The council promoted the West Riding of Yorkshire Rivers Act, 1894 (57 & 58 Vict., c. clxvi). Its history has been written by John Sheail, 'The Sustainable Management of Industrial Watercourses: An English Historical Perspective', *Environmental History*, 2:2 (1997) pp. 197–215.
4. *permanganate test*: A test, utilizing potassium permanganate, KMnO4, also known as potassic permanganate in the nineteenth century, for the quantity of organic material in water. The test was discussed by William Allen Miller (1817–70), then President of the Chemical Society, in his paper 'Observations of some Points in the Analysis of Potable Waters', *Journal of the Chemical Society*, 18 (also numbered as vol. 3 of the new series) (1865), pp. 117–32. The test was attributed by Miller to Johan Georg Forchhammer (1794–1865), the Danish mineralogist and chemist, who published a proposal for the test in 1850. A contemporary description for a non-specialist audience is available in Professor Roscoe, FRS, 'The Progress of Sanitary Science', in Professors Huxley, Roscoe, Wilkins, et al., *Science Lectures for the People: Third Series 1871* (Manchester: John Heywood, n.d.), pp. 121–39.
5. *Rivers ... Act of 1876*: 39 & 40 Vict. c. 75.

6. *Local Government Board*: The department of state responsible for public health as well as local government matters; established under the Local Government Board Act 1871 (34 &35 Vict. c. 70).
7. *Public Health Act 1875*: 38 & 39 Vict. c. 55.
8. *Sanitary Authority*: Local government bodies established under the Public Health Act 1875 (38 & 39 Vict. c. 55). In urban areas they were formed from existing local government bodies which were given additional powers. They were abolished by the Local Government Act 1894 (56 & 57 Vict. c. 73) and their powers transferred to the boroughs and the new urban and rural districts.
9. *Public Health Amendment Act, 1890*: The Public Health Acts Amendment Act 1890 (53 & 54 Vict. c. 59).

Scafe, *King Coal's Levee, or Geological Etiquette*

1. *John Scafe*: (1776–1843), junior army officer and poet. Scafe resigned his commission in 1808 on the death of his father and appears then to have lived the life of a Northumberland country gentleman. Apart from his poetry his main achievement was to help to bring the heroism of Grace Darling, who assisted her father in the rescue of the survivors of the wreck of the *Forfarshire* off the Northumbrian coast in 1838, to public attention. According to the Preface of this edition, the first edition of *King Coal's Levee*, published earlier in 1819, 'consisted of a few copies only [in fact, twenty-five], for private distribution' and was only half the size of this the second edition. Scafe acknowledged assistance from the Rev. W. Conybeare (for whom see note 8 to 'The Collieries' in this volume) and, in the composition of the notes to the poem, the Rev. William Buckland (1784–1856), Professor of Mineralogy and Geology at Oxford University. Although the third edition of 1819 was of only 500 copies and the fourth of only 750 it caused a 'sensation' according to the author of Scafe's biography in the *ODNB*.
2. *Shakespeare*: From *King Lear*, IV.vi. The omitted first half of the first line quoted is 'I will be jovial; come, come'.
3. *Pyrites*: See Scafe's note to verse 13.
4. *meed*: A 'deserved accolade, title or epithet' as in Tennyson's Œnone 'Pallas and Aphrodite, claiming each This meed of fairest' (*OED*).
5. *Vectis to the Tweed*: Vectis was the Roman name for the Isle of Wight, off the southern coast of England; the River Tweed forms the boundary between England and Scotland at Berwick-on-Tweed; 'from Vectis to the Tweed' is therefore from the southernmost to the northernmost of England. A note on p. 2 of the text (not included here) cautions that the geology of the poem is that of England and Wales only, not Scotland.
6. *Mica*: See Scafe's note to verse 38.
7. *Pleiades*: the seven daughters of Atlas and Pleione, the daughter of Oceanus: Electra, Maia, Taygete, Alcyone, Calaeno, Sterope and Merope. Transformed into stars after their death.
8. *boots*: To boot is here to be of use, value or profit: 'What doth it avail, in glowing verse to tell?'
9. *Lisbon*: a reference to the Lisbon earthquake of 1 November 1755 and the subsequent fire in which a reputed 50,000 lives were lost and perhaps 85 per cent of the buildings of Lisbon destroyed including almost every major church. Seen by some theologians as a manifestation of the anger of God and by some enlightenment philosophers as a sufficient counter-example to claims for the beneficent ordering of the universe.

10. *Duke GRANITE first*: See Scafe's note to verse 84.
11. *GNEISS*: See Scafe's note to verse 90.
12. *SANDSTONE*: See Scafe's note to verses 223 and 264.
13. *Sir Lawrence LIMESTONE's*: See Scafe's note to verse 298.
14. *Miss GYPSUM*: See Scafe's note to verse 264.
15. *sweet cousin SELENITE*: See Scafe's note to verse 264.
16. *Iron pyrites, FeS2*: 'Everybody must have noticed the bright brass-like particles of *iron pyrites* in coal. This substance has been formed in the course of the decomposition of the woody matter. The vegetable matter and the water which saturates it contain sulphates which in contact with the decaying organic substances are converted into sulphides; these re-act upon the iron also present in the plant or in the water and form the pyrites or iron sulphide.' (Sir T. E. Thorpe 'The Chemistry of Coal', chs V and VI of Sir T. E. Thorpe (ed.) *Coal: Its History and Uses* (London: Macmillan and Co., 1878), pp. 164–223, at p. 197).
17. *Mica*: a group of minerals composed of aluminous silicates, containing potash, soda or other substances, characterized by a perfect cleavage in one direction. The name is derived from the Latin 'micare', to glitter. The variety Scafe terms 'Muscovy Glass' was also known as 'Muscovite'; plates a metre across were found near Lake Baikal and large plates in Scandinavia, hence its widespread use in the Russian Empire. It yields thin laminae which are usually transparent but tinted yellow brown or green. As Scafe indicates, it was used to set objects for the 'solar microscope', that is, a microscope relying on natural light, only, to illuminate the object. It was also used to glaze lanterns and stoves in preference to glass because it does not shatter with sudden changes of temperature (*Chambers*).
18. primitive *rocks*: Scafe is writing before the modern classification of rocks into igneous, sedimentary and metamorphic had been established. The sense of 'primitive' here is 'original', 'without precursor or predecessor' which is a defining property of those rocks now classified as igneous.
19. *Dr Hutton*: James Hutton (1726–97), one of the founders of modern geology. In his *Theory of the Earth* (1785) he described for the first time in clear terms the formation of the rocks. Briefly, rocks uplifted from under the oceans into contact with the atmosphere are eroded by the actions of rain, snow and ice, the debris being carried by rivers back to the oceans where they are compressed to form new (sedimentary) rocks. During uplift, rocks were split and cracked and through the fissures molten material from the earth's core rose to the surface, cooled and formed 'primitive' (igneous) rocks; rocks affected by the heat of the molten material and the pressure arising from this process were changed in form to become the class of rocks known as 'metamorphic'. The only important addition to this conception since Hutton's time has been the theory of plate tectonics which became widely accepted from the mid-1960s.
20. *Grauwacké*: or Grauwacke (the term being German, not French) or greywacke. A sedimentary rock composed of grains of quartz, felspar and slate embedded in a hard matrix variously composed of siliceous, calcareous, argillaceous, or felspathic matter. Usually gray or dark blue but other colours occur. Harder than sandstone.
21. *mountain Lime*; or Mountain Limestone; see Scafe's note on verse 298.
22. *sulphate of Strontian*: sulphate of strontium, a mineral known as Celestine, found in rhombic prisms of great beauty in Sicily.
23. *264*: Line 264 of the poem is not included here but Scafe's notes are included for their value in illuminating the extracts given.
24. *basset edges*: Usually outcropping edges of strata; here inclined strata that would once have formed the surface only to be covered by deposits later forming the new red sandstone.

25. *Limestone family*: See Scafe's note to verse 298.
26. *Selenite*: The name derives from the Greek *Selene*, 'the moon'. A transparent, crystalline form of gypsum. Like mica, capable of being split into thin plates, and said to have been used by the ancients for purposes later performed by glass.
27. *298*: Line 298 of the poem is not included here but Scafe's notes are included for their value in illuminating the extracts given.
28. *zoophytes*: 'animal-plants'. A term introduced by Cuvier to designate numerous species of simple animals which had a resemblance to plants, but later abandoned as too imprecise to be helpful. Some authorities used the term 'phytozoon', or 'plant-like animal', in preference.
29. Encrinus ... *lily*: Encrinites or fossil crinoids also known as stone-lilies; Scafe's description of 'articulated bones' refers to the 'stem'. Despite the popular name, 'sea lilies', of the modern forms and the fact that they are fixed permanently or temporarily to the sea floor, they are now usually described as animals, not plants as Scafe does in the remainder of this note.
30. Entrochi *and* Asteriæ: Entrochus: 'A name sometimes given to the wheel-like plates of which certain crinoids are composed'; Asterias: 'A genus of *Echinoderms*, containing the common Five-rayed Star-fish, with allied species' (*OED*).
31. *Harrowgate*: now Harrogate.
32. *Mr. Westgarth Forster's ... Strata*: Westgarth Forster (1772–1835), north country geologist and mining engineer; succeeded his father as agent for Sir Thomas Blackett (1726–92) and later became agent for Colonel Beaumont (1758–1829). His *Treatise on a Section of the Strata Commencing near Newcastle upon Tyne and Concluding on the West Side of the Mountain of Cross-Fell* (Newcastle: Preston & Heaton, printers, 1809) appeared in the same year as the first geological map of England by William Smith and was regarded as a *tour de force*. It remained the standard work on the geology of the northern counties for the rest of the century, reaching its third edition in 1883.
33. *bason*: basin.
34. *on the Coal measures*: The implications of these observations in the context of Hutton's theory of rock formation would have been clear to contemporaries. Discounting earth movements so violent as to have completely inverted the normal sequence of strata, one implication is that where *mountain* limestone is observed, the coal measures that once lay above it have been eroded away and no coal of Carboniferous age will be found; another is that where *magnesian* limestone is found coal *may* be found underneath it, if it was not itself eroded away before the magnesian limestone was deposited.
35. *The Flora Monacensis ... Craniology*: The *Flora Monaciensis* published in 1811–18 was a treatise by Franz von Paula Schrank (1747–1835), a German botanist, entomologist, and Director of the Munich Botanical Gardens, illustrated with engravings by J. N. Mayrhoffer. Johann Baptist Ritter von Spix (1781–1826), naturalist, is now chiefly remembered for his exploration of the Amazon in 1817–20; the collection of specimens with which he returned is the basis of the collection of the Munich Natural History Museum and Spix's Macaw is named after him. At the time Scafe's poem was published Spix had recently published a work of comparative craniology, the *Cephalogenesis: Seu Capitis Ossei Structura, Formatio et Significatio per Omnes Animalium Classes, Familias, Genera ac Aetates Digesta* (Monachii: F. S. Hübschmannii, 1815) published with eighteen lithographed plates by Mayrhoffer and others.
36. *a kind of link ... Sir Everard Home*: Sir Everard Home (1756–1832), surgeon, plagiarist and vandal, published 'Some Account of the Fossil Remains of an Animal more nearly

Allied to Fishes than any of the other Classes of Animals' in the *Philosophical Transactions of the Royal Society of London*, 104 (1814), pp. 571–7 and a 'Farther Account of the Fossil Remains of an Animal, of which a Description was given to the Society in 1814' in the *Transactions*, 106 (1816), pp. 318–21. The 'animal more nearly allied to fishes' was that now known as the *Ichthyosaurus* ('fish-lizard'). The fossil had been discovered in the cliffs at Lyme Regis in 1811, or possibly earlier, by Joseph and Mary Anning, a fact which Home omitted to mention, and put on public display in London where, as one of the first complete fossil skeletons of any size to be discovered, it created a sensation. Everard Home was a brother-in-law, pupil and finally executor of the will of John Hunter (1728–93) whose collection of anatomical and pathological specimens formed the basis of the Hunterian Museum of the Royal College of Surgeons in London. Home is suspected of publishing much of Hunter's work as his own in the years after Hunter's death and destroyed most of his papers in 1823; hence his modern reputation as a plagiarist and vandal (*ODNB*).

37. Coade's ... *Patent Stone*: Coade Stone is in fact a type of stoneware; that is, a ceramic material rather than one based on cement, which is the basis for most modern types of artificial stone. It was manufactured by Mrs [Eleanor] Coade's Artificial Stone Company from 1769–1833. The most easily accessible example surviving is the Red Lion now sited at the south end of Westminster Bridge, London.
38. *no* mineral *coal*: The Kent Coalfield was not proved until late in the nineteenth century; the first colliery, the Shakespeare Colliery, was at West Hougham, two or three kilometres inland from Shakespeare Cliff in the White (chalk) Cliffs of Dover.
39. Chiltern Hundreds: A 'Hundred' is an ancient sub-division of a county. The Chiltern Hundreds are those of Bodenham, Desborough and Stoke in the chalk of the Chiltern Hills in Berkshire. Their name became associated with Parliament through a constitutional peculiarity, viz., the absence of any provision by which a member of the House of Commons could resign his seat. A member wishing to resign had to disqualify himself from sitting and the means used to achieve this was to apply for and accept the stewardship of the Chiltern Hundreds, classed as an office of profit under the crown and therefore incompatible with membership of the House of Commons, despite the fact that the office is a sinecure without duties or emoluments. The mechanism was first used in 1750; it remains in being.
40. *Milton*: *Paradise Lost*, Book II.
41. *not to visit the King*: King Coal. The Metals (Gold, Silver, Mercury, Copper, Lead, and others personified), have just agreed that 'they would never come near him!' reflecting the geological fact that coal and the metals named are never found together.
42. *argillaceous*: clayey.
43. *Parkinson's Organic Remains*: James Parkinson, *Organic Remains of a Former World: An Examination of the Mineralized Remains of the Vegetables and Animals of the Antediluvian World; Generally Termed Extraneous Fossils*, 3 vols (London: J. Robson; J. White, and J. Murray, 1804–11). James Parkinson (1755–1824) was a radical, the author of *An Address to E. Burke from the Swinish Multitude* (1793) and a surgeon, the author of *An Address on the Shaking Palsy* (1817) on the disease to which he gave his name, as well as the author of this work on fossils, described as 'the outstanding event' in the history of palaeontology (*ODNB*).
44. *monocotyledonous or acotyledonous*: A cotyledon is an embryonic plant leaf; the most familiar examples are the pairs of cotyledons that form the bulk of, and split easily apart in, peas and beans. Acotyledonous plants are without cotyledons; they include algae, funghi, liverworts, mosses, ferns, horsetails and lycopods. Monocotyledons, as the name

implies, have only a single cotyledon; the most familiar examples are the Liliaceæ; the class also includes reeds and grasses.. Peas and beans are dicotyledons (*Chambers*).

45. Hortus siccus: Literally a 'dry garden', usually, as here, a collection of dried plants accumulated for the purposes of study and reference (Riley, *Latin Quotations*).

Buddle, 'Search for Coal in a Part of the Counties of Roxburgh and Berwickshire, in July, 1806'

1. *John Buddle Jun.*: See note 1 to Buddle, 'On Subsidences Produced by Working Beds of Coal'.
2. *Roxburgh and Berwickshire*: The Counties of Roxburgh or Roxburghshire and Berwick or Berwickshire were Scottish counties in south-eastern Scotland bordering Northumberland in England. They were abolished in the Scottish local government reorganization of 1975. The counties were distant from the main coal mining areas of Northumberland to the south and East Lothian or Haddingtonshire to the north, although one colliery, Kerryburn Colliery, just south of the border in Northumberland, was examined by Buddle for this report.
3. *vale of the Tweed*: Buddle's itinerary has taken him to the village of Sprouston in Roxburgshire which lies no more than a field's length from the River Tweed, the main river of the county.
4. *a copy of which*: Buddle refers to the table of strata given below.
5. *argillaceous*: clayey.
6. *whin*: hard stone; 'whin or whinstone ... but the term is usually applied by borers and sinkers to any exceptionally hard rock that emits a sharp sound under the hammer or chisel' (W. E. Nicholson, *A Glossary of Terms Used in the Coal Trade of Northumberland and Durham* (Newcastle, 1888), quoted by Griffiths, *North East Dialect*).
7. *pyrites*: Iron pyrites, FeS2. See note 16 to Scafe, *King Coal's Levee*.
8. *indurated*: Hardened by geological forces such as pressure.
9. *free-stone*: 'Stone that can be sawn in any direction and readily shaped with a chisel, such as fine-grained sandstone or limestone' (*OED*).
10. *Dent*: 'A tough clay or soft claystone' especially 'that found in the joints and fissures of sandstone or other strata' (*OED*).
11. *Longnewton*: A village between Jedburgh and Melrose, again, not far from the Tweed.
12. *till*: 'A term applied to a stiff clay, more or less impervious to water, usually occurring in unstratified deposits, and forming an ungenial subsoil' (*OED*).
13. *of the candle ... kind*: Cannel coal. See note 3 to *Practical Economy*, above.
14. *amygdaloid ... steatite*: amygdaloid is from the Greek for almond; a rock containing almond-shaped nodules (*OED*). *Steatite*: soap-stone.
15. *the Jed*: The river from which Jedburgh takes its name.
16. *Mr Jameson ... Scottish Isles*: Robert Jameson (1774–1854) a noted geologist and natural historian. His *Mineralogy* was the *Mineralogy of the Scottish Isles: With Mineralogical Observations Made in a Tour through Different Parts of the Mainland of Scotland and Dissertations upon Peat and Kelp*, 2 vols (Edinburgh: C. Stewart & Co., printer, 1800).
17. *shistose*: Now 'schistose', meaning laminated, like a schist.
18. *primitive rocks*: See note 18 to Scafe, *King Coal's Levee*, above. Buddle, however, includes limestone, a sedimentary rock, among his examples of 'primitive rocks'.
19. *micacious shistus*: A schist containing much mica.

20. *pitch stone*: 'A dull vitreous rock resembling hardened pitch, formed by partial hydration of obsidian' (*OED*).
21. *topaz rock*: The *OED* offers the following quotation, from the second edition of Richard Kirwan's *Elements of Mineralogy* (London: J. Nichols, printer, 1794–6) at p. 368 of vol. 1: '*Topaz rock* ... presents a compound of topaz, quartz, shorl, and lithomarga, confusedly compacted together'.
22. *Mr Jameson ... Dumfries-shire*; R. Jameson, *A Mineralogical Description of the County of Dumfries* (Edinburgh: Printed at the University Press, 1805).
23. *the Carter*: Carter Fell, on the English side of the Anglo–Scottish border about 17 km from Bedrule. Carter Bar is the mountain pass below Carter Fell on the border between England and Scotland and on the only inland road route between the two countries. Kerryburn Colliery, examined by Buddle, was at the foot of Carter Fell.
24. *cleughs*: narrow ravines (Griffiths, *North East Dialect*).
25. *Fast Castle*: a twelfth-century earthwork motte located close to Bedrule near Jedburgh. Not the spectacular though ruined Fast Castle on the Berwickshire coast.
26. *Tagle Legs*: not traced.
27. *Sharping the Geer*: 'Sharping' was an alternative to 'sharpening'; so possibly 'Sharpening the Gear' (*OED*).

Dunn, *A Treatise on the Winning and Working of Collieries*

1. *Matthias Dunn*: A member of a family of Tyneside coal fitters (brokers arranging sales between coal owners and shippers). His uncle (d. 1825) was also named Matthias which has led to some confusion in the accounts of Matthias Junior's life. Matthias Junior was born about 1789; his father Robert was a colliery viewer. Matthias Junior was apprenticed to Thomas Smith, another colliery viewer, in 1804. He became an assistant to John Buddle, the leading viewer of his day, in 1808 or 1809. He was marked by his experience of recovering the bodies of the seventy-five victims of the flooding of Heaton Colliery in 1815. With his publication of *An Historical, Geological and Descriptive View* in 1844 he became a prominent advocate of government inspection and was appointed as one of the first four HM Inspectors of Mines in 1850 under the Coal Mines Inspection Act of that year. He remained in this post till ill-health forced his retirement in 1866 when he was about seventy-seven years old. He died in 1869. His diary for 1831 -6 has survived; some extracts from it are given by M. Sill, 'The Diary of Matthias Dunn, Colliery Viewer, 1831-1836', *Local Historian*, 16 (1985), pp. 418 -24. A brief biography, on which this note is based, has been written by Winifred Stokes, 'Matthias Dunn, Campaigner for Mining Safety c. 1789-1869', *Durham County Local History Society Bulletin*, 69 (2006), pp. 3 -20.
2. *engine power*: For pumping engines; the boring results allowed an estimate of how wet the strata were and how much pumping capacity would be needed.
3. *wimble*: Dunn defines this shortly.
4. *jackroll*: Dunn's *Treatise* contains a short 'Glossary of Terms' on six unnumbered pages appearing towards the end of the volume after the engraved plates. This gives 'Jack roll, hand win[d]lass'. The *OED* offers a 'winch or windlass turned directly by handles', like the windlass over a common well.
5. *whin*: See note 6 to Buddle, *Search for Coal*, above.

6. *Mr Ryan*: James Ryan (*c.* 1770–1847). Despite Dunn's comments, Ryan's cylindrical trepanning cutter received favourable notices from many sources. He died in poverty (*ODNB*).
7. *Mr. Taylor's tube*: In the section just omitted Dunn describes an invention to improve boring by Mr James Taylor of Furnival's Inn, an address suggesting Taylor was a lawyer. It involved a tube fitted with a one way valve up which, by means which were obscure, the cuttings were supposed to pass to the surface.
8. *Mr Stott*: George Rawling Stott (b. *c.* 1810). Active as a mineral borer from about 1837 to about 1867; a member of the North of England Institute of Mining Engineers from session 1859–60 to session 1862–3. Many of his borings are recorded in *An Account of the Strata of Northumberland & Durham as Proved by Borings & Sinking*, 5 vols A–B, C–E, F–K, L–R, S–T and a Supplementary Volume (Newcastle: North of England Institute of Mining & Mechanical Engineers, 1878, 1881, 1885, 1887, 1894, 1910) (*DMM*).
9. ungeering: 'Disconnecting machinery' according to Dunn's 'Glossary of Terms'. Possibly related to the nautical word 'jeer', often spelled 'geer' or 'jear' in the seventeenth and eighteenth centuries, meaning tackle used to hoist and lower yards.
10. *a waste*: that is, a worked out area of a mine.
11. *plugged with wood*: to prevent an inflow or inundation of gas or water.
12. *this town*: Newcastle-upon-Tyne.
13. *the destruction ... many months*: Dunn was involved in retrieving the bodies, an experience which is reputed to have marked him for life and to have been instrumental in his decision to join the Mines Inspectorate.

Beaumont, 'On Rock Boring by the Diamond Drill, and Recent Applications of the Process'

1. *Major Beaumont, R.E., M.P.*: Frederick Edward Blackett Beaumont (1833–99), officer in the army's Corps of Royal Engineers, inventor and Tory MP for South Durham 1868–80. Son of Edward Blackett Beaumont (1802–78), and grandson of Lt.-Col. Thomas Richard Beaumont (1758–1829) who had married Diana Wentworth (before 1776–1832) (also known as Diana Blackett) the daughter and heir of Sir Thomas Wentworth, fifth and last baronet (1726–92) of Bretton Hall, Yorkshire. She was the heir, through her grandmother, of the Blackett estates in Northumberland, including their coal and collieries and, through her father, of the Wentworth estates in Yorkshire with their coal and ironstone. Although Major Beaumont was not the heir to either of these estates, he was thus a member of a powerful and sprawling family with connections to the coal industry going back to at least the seventeenth century. See *Burke's Landed Gentry* (1898 edn) s.v. Beaumont of Bretton Hall and *Burke's Peerage* (1949 edn) *s.v.* Allendale.
2. *black diamond ... carbonate ... carbonado*: The term 'carbonate' now usually refers to rocks such as limestone, dolomite and siderite the composition of which is dominated by carbonate minerals, themselves dominated by the carbonate ion $CO^{2}3$. [Production: subscript and superscript should appear one on top of the other] Carbonado is now the usual term. Further deposits have been located in the Central African Republic.
3. *Ure's Chemical Dictionary*: By Andrew Ure (1778–1857) the author of *The Philosophy of Manufactures*. The *Chemical Dictionary* was *A Dictionary of Chemistry, on the Basis of Mr. Nicholson's; In which the Principles of the Science are Investigated Anew, and its Appli-*

cation to the Phenomena of Nature, Medicine, Mineralogy, Agriculture, and Manufactures, Detailed (London: Printed for Thomas & George Underwood, et al., 1821).

4. *Columbus' egg*: The story is recounted by Girolamo Benzoni (b. *c.* 1519) in his 1565 *Historia del Mondo Nuovo* which is as follows in the 1857 English translation:

> It will not be out of place to relate what I heard happened in Spain to Columbus, after he had discovered the Indies; although it had been done in ancient times in other ways, but was new then. Columbus being at a party with many noble Spaniards, where, as was customary, the subject of conversation was the Indies: one of them undertook to say: – 'Mr. Christopher, even if you had not found the Indies, we should not have been devoid of a man who would have attempted the same as you did, here in our own country of Spain, as it is full of great men clever in cosmography and literature.' Columbus said nothing in answer to these words, but having desired an egg to be brought to him, he placed it on the table saying: 'Gentlemen, I will lay a wager with any of you, that you will not make this egg stand up [on its end] as I will, naked and without anything at all.' They all tried, and no one succeeded in making it stand up. When the egg came round to the hands of Columbus , by beating it down on the table he fixed it, having thus crushed a little of one end; wherefore all remained confused, understanding what he would have said: that after the deed is done, everyone knows how to do it; that they ought first to have sought for the Indies, and not laugh at him who had sought for it first, while they for some time had been laughing, and wondered at it as an impossibility'.
>
> *History of the New World* trans. and ed. Rear-Admiral W. H. Smyth (London, Hakluyt Society, 1857), p. 17.

(Although Columbus's voyages were funded by Isabella I of Castile, he was, of course, Genoese.) Beaumont takes the meaning of the story to be 'Once you have the key to the lock, all other difficulties vanish', rather than the more usual 'Once the solution is demonstrated, all can see how easy it is'.

Stuart, 'The Development of Explosives for Coal-Mines'

1. *Donald M. D. Stuart*: Donald Mcdonald Douglas Stuart or Stewart (1852–1942) was the son of Moses G. Stewart, a mining engineer himself born in Northumberland but practising in Somerset where Donald was born. Little is known of his life. He was active in the National Association of Colliery Managers in the 1890s. He was the author of *Coal Dust as an Explosive Agent: As Shown by an Examination of the Camerton Explosion* (London, E. and F. N. Spon: 1894), the Camerton collieries being in the Somerset coalfield, and *The Origin and Rationale of Colliery Explosions* (Bristol: John Wright and Co., 1895). The former argued that the explosion was caused by coal dust, a conclusion that convinced the *Athenæum*'s reviewer (no. 3521 (20 April 1895), p. 508) but which caused little stir outside Somerset (*DMM*).
2. *Select Committee upon Explosive Substances*: The *Report from the Select Committee on Explosive Substances: Together with the Proceedings of the Committee, Minutes of Evidence, and Appendix* (243) of session 1874, ix. 1.
3. *Royal Commission ... Coal-dust in Mines, 1891*: The references are to: the *Final Report of Her Majesty's Commissioners Appointed to Inquire into Accidents in Mines and the Possible Means of Preventing their Occurrence or Limiting their Disastrous Consequences;*

Together with Evidence and Appendices (C. 4699) of 1886, xvi 411; A. C. Kayll, *Report of the Proceedings of the Flameless Explosives Committee* [of the North of England Institute of Mining and Mechanical Engineers] (Newcastle: 1896); *First Report of the Royal Commission on Explosions from Coal dust in Mines: With Minutes of Evidence and Appendices* (C. 6543) of session 1890–1, xxii. 555; there was also a *Second Report* (C.7401 and C. 7401–I) of session 1893–4, xxiv, 583, 615.

4. *Departmental Committee*: The Committee produced the *Report of the Departmental Committee Appointed to Inquire into the Testing of Explosives for Use in Coal Mines* (C. 8698) of session 1898, xiii, 589.
5. *coal-dust*: For the role of coal dust in colliery explosions, see Peckham, 'On the Explosion of the Flouring Mills' (pp. 311–16).
6. *distil*: Possibly meant here in the sense of 'to exude' or 'to flow gently' or 'to instil'.
7. *educts*: The *OED* offers 'A body separated by the decomposition of another in which it previously existed as such, in contradistinction to *product*, which denotes a compound not previously existing, but formed during the decomposition' from Henry Watts's *Dictionary of Chemistry* first published in five volumes over 1863–81.
8. *dynamite, lithofracteur, gun-cotton*: Dynamite, in the form originally patented by Nobel in 1865 is a mixture of nitroglycerine and kieselguhr, the latter being a soft, white, porous earth which provides an inert base for the liquid nitroglycerine. Lithofracteur had a more complex composition than dynamite but remained based on nitroglycerine; it was invented by Friedrich Krebs of Germany but its manufacture was prevented in the UK by Nobel's litigation to protect his patent for dynamite. Gun-cotton was first formed by treating cellulose derived from cotton wool with a mixture of hot, concentrated nitric and sulphuric acids to form nitrocellulose or 'gun cotton' (G. I. Brown, *The Big Bang: A History of Explosives* (Stroud: Sutton, 1998)).
9. *Mr. Is. Trauzl*: Isidor Trauzl (1840–1929), the manager of Nobel's Austrian factory and the inventor of an empirical test, the 'Trauzl test', to measure the relative explosive power of different substances. His evidence was relied on by the Prussian Fire-damp Commission, for which see below. For his test, see Read, *Explosives*, p. 63.
10. *0·000,6*: Stuart uses a comma to separate thousandths in the same way as it is used to separate thousands; 0.0006.
11. *Prussian Friendship Commission*: The Commission's work was first noticed in the *Transactions of the North of England Institute* in abstracts of reports of its daily meetings beginning with C. Z. B. [Charles Z. Bunning] 'The Prussian Royal Fire-damp Commission', in 'Abstracts of Foreign Papers', *Transactions of the North of England Institute of Mining and Mechanical Engineers*, 32 (1882–3), p. 64. Its main report was the *Hauptberichte der Preussischen Schlagwetter-Commission* (Berlin: Ernst & Korn, 1887). The translation to which Stuart refers appeared in the *Transactions of the Federated Institute* in several parts: 'First Part', 3 (1891–92), pp. 1105–50; 'Second Part – Continued', 4 (1893), pp. 631–80, and 'Second Part – [Further] Continued', 5 (1893–94), pp. 500–54.
12. *Sir Humphry Davy's researches*: Sir Humphry Davy (1778–1829), the chemist and inventor of the miner's safety lamp. See Volume 2, pp. 353–5. His researches into fire-damp were conducted during his invention of his 'safety-lamp' and were published in the *Philosophical Transactions of the Royal Society of London* as follows: 'On the fire-damp of coal mines, and on methods of lighting the mines so as to prevent its explosion', 106 (1816), pp. 1–22; 'An account of an invention for giving light in explosive mixtures of fire-damp in coal mines, by consuming the fire-damp', 106 (1816), pp. 23–4 and 'Farther experiments on the combustion of explosive mixtures confined by wire-gauze, with some

observations on flame', 106 (1816) pp. 115–19. These papers were gathered together and reprinted as *The Papers of Sir H. Davy, LL.D. F. R. S. V. P. R. I. Communicated to The Royal Society on the Fire-Damp of Coal Mines, and on Methods of Lighting the Mines so as to Prevent its Explosion, &c.* (Newcastle: Printed for Emerson Charnley, 1817).

13. *page 21*: Published as a separate volume by the North of England Institute, Newcastle.
14. *Royal Commission ... Mines*: the *Final Report of Her Majesty's Commissioners Appointed to Inquire into Accidents in Mines and the Possible Means of Preventing their Occurrence or Limiting their Disastrous Consequences; Together with Evidence and Appendices* (C. 4699) of 1886, xvi 411, pp. 55–7.
15. *gelatine-dynamite ... potentite*: Gelatine dynamite was formed from collodion and nitroglycerine by Nobel, patented in 1875 and called 'blasting gelatine'; it forms a solid but unstable mass, like jelly; 'gelignite' was a development of this. 'Cottonpowder' was another name for gun cotton. Tonite was a mixture of gun cotton and barium nitrate; it was used, for example, in the construction of the Manchester Ship Canal, 1885–94, and the Severn Railway Tunnel during 1873–86 (Brown, *Big Bang*). Potentite was a new name, introduced about 1880, for tonite.
16. *water-cartridges*: tin cartridges in the form of a cylinder in which the explosive is held in the centre and surrounded by water.
17. *ammonite ... securite*: trade names. Ardeer powder and Carbonite were based on nitroglycerine; the remainder were based on ammonium nitrate. Ardeer was the desolate place in Ayrshire where Nobel and his partners sited their dynamite factory.
18. *stemming*: the tamping which secures the explosive charge in place.

Waller, 'On Pumping Water'

1. *William Waller*: not identified.
2. *Birmingham ... Association*: The British Association for the Advancement of Science was founded in 1831 through the energies of Sir David Brewster (1781–1868), Sir Roderick Impey Murchison (1792–1871) and others; the first of its annual meetings, which were peripatetic, took place in Oxford in 1832. The Birmingham meeting referred to here, the third in that city, was held in 1865. I have been unable to trace these statements in the published *Report of the Thirty-Fifth Meeting of the British Association for the Advancement of Science: Held at Birmingham in September 1865* (London: John Murray, 1866) or in newspaper reports of the meeting.
3. *Mr Wickstead*: Thomas Wickstead or Wicksteed (1806–71), civil engineer.
4. *The Grand Junction Company*: The Grand Junction Waterworks Company, formed by the Grand Junction Canal Company, not the Grand Junction Railway running from Birmingham northwards towards Liverpool and Manchester and which became part of the London and North Western Railway Company in 1846.

Dunn, *A Treatise on the Winning and Working of Collieries*

1. *Matthias Dunn*: see note 6 to the Introduction to these three volumes.
2. *carburetted hydrogen or carbonic acid gases*: Dunn means 'light carburetted' or 'monocarburetted' hydrogen, or fire-damp, CH4. Carbonic acid gas is carbon dioxide or 'choke-damp', CO2.
3. rarefaction: Dunn's 'Glossary of Terms' gives 'Rarefy, to heat air to produce expansion'.
4. return air: Dunn's 'Glossary of Terms' gives 'Return air, after it has traversed the workings'.

5. dumb drift: Dunn's 'Glossary of Terms' gives 'Drift (dumb), passage allotted to the foul air'.
6. *creep*: a 'heaving or bursting upwards of the floor of a coal mine' (Griffiths, *North East Dialect*).
7. *Mr. Gurney*: Goldsworthy Gurney (1793–1875) inventor of the steam jet, of lime light and the steam carriage. Knighted 1863.
8. *the Parliamentary Committee*: the Select Committee [of the House of Commons] on Accidents in Mines. Gurney's examination by the Committee is documented in its *Report* (603) of session 1835, v. 1.
9. *the South Shields committee*: South Shields is a town on the south bank of the River Tyne, below Newcastle. An explosion at the St Hilda Pit in South Shields in June 1839 led to the loss of fifty-two lives. At a public meeting called to raise funds for the widows and orphans of the disaster James Mather urged the creation of a committee to investigate the causes of explosions in coal mines and to suggest ways of preventing them. The committee was purposely composed of persons having no previous connection with coal mining. Its *Report* was published in 1843. Robert Galloway gives the fullest account of the Committee to remain easily accessible in his *Annals of Coal Mining and the Coal Trade* (London: Colliery Guardian Co. Ltd, 1904), 2nd series, pp. 157–65. See further in this text for Dunn's own account. Galloway concurred with Dunn's view of the value of the Committee's work calling their opinions 'on the whole remarkably correct, sound, sagacious, and practical' (*A History of Coal Mining in Great Britain* (London: Macmillan & Co., 1882), p. 228).
10. fan blast: Dunn's 'Glossary of Terms' gives 'Fan blast, a means of propelling the air current by the revolutions of a machine.'
11. Fall of water: Dunn's 'Glossary of Terms' gives 'Waterfall, stream of water falling down the shaft.'
12. *spiral*: The diagram accompanying this part of the text, not reproduced here, shows a helix.
13. *Mr Edward Gibbons*: not identified.
14. *Mr Tremenhere*: usually 'Tremenheere'. Hugh Seymour Tremenheere (1804–93) was appointed a Home Office Inspector under the 1842 Mines Act and produced a series of reports on the education of colliers' children and the social conditions of the mining districts. The architect of the 1850 Mines Act which introduced the first technically qualified HM Inspectors of Mines. A 'moderate Anglican Whig' in the view of his *ODNB* biographer.
15. *butties or contractors*: See Volume 2, pp. 155–64.
16. *prosperity of his native town*: At the time of the explosion Mather was a wine merchant; he became rapidly aware of the explosion because of the numbers of people calling at his shop for 'restoratives' (Galloway, *Annals*, Second Series, p. 158).
17. *three feet per second*: An air velocity of 3 feet per second through a shaft of 13½ feet diameter implies the passage of about 25,765 cubic feet of air per minute. This rate of ventilation compared to figures of 100,000 to almost 200,000 cubic feet per minute attained in the best pits in the north-east by 1850. By the beginning of the twentieth century, larger collieries required ventilation rates of 400,000 cubic feet per minute and more.
18. *Three baskets*: For raising coal and miners; a 'corf', plural 'corves', was the usual mining term for such baskets in the north-east and is used by Dunn shortly.
19. sheths: Dunn's 'Glossary of Terms' gives: 'Sheth door, or stopping to guide the main air current'.

20. *boards*: more usually 'bords', the areas from which coal has been removed in 'bord and pillar' working. See p. 14.
21. *bratticed*: divided into two or more shafts by wooden partitioning to form separate air-ways or to divide the winding shaft from ventilation shafts, etc.
22. *drift*: Dunn's 'Glossary of Terms' gives 'Drift, passage excavated in the mine.' Usually at this date a connecting tunnel and usually nearer horizontal than vertical.
23. *eighty Fahrenheit*: about 27 degrees Celsius.
24. *goaves*: Dunn's 'Glossary of Terms' gives 'Goaf, a hollow', 'Goaves, plural of goaf' and 'Gob, the part excavated, goaf.' An area of a colliery from which the coal has been removed; also known as the 'waste'.

Cochrane, 'Description of Guibal's Ventilator, at Elswick Colliery'

1. *William Cochrane*: (1837–1903) was a wealthy coal and iron master from Staffordshire. He was the son of Alexander Brodie Cochrane, another west midlands iron master and the owner of Elswick Colliery, located on the north bank of the Tyne about 2 km west of Newcastle, until his death in 1863. William Cochrane wrote the obituary of Guibal for the *Transactions of the North of England Institute of Mining and Mechanical Engineers*, 39 (1889–90), pp. 14–15 from which, and the discussion following, the following details are taken. Théophile Guibal (1814–88) was born in France and studied at the École Centrale des Arts et Manufactures de Paris from 1833 to 1836. His distinction was such that in 1837 he was appointed to a professorial chair at the newly established École des Mines at Mons in Belgium and he is now known as one of the founders of that institution. His ventilating fan was his greatest invention. It was said of him 'He was a man belonging to no nation, but to every country, and his discoveries were invaluable to the whole world.'
2. *working of the seams*: The friction of the air against the roof, floor and sides of a seam is relatively greater where the seams are thin, and greater power is required to push or pull a given quantity of air through narrow passages than through broad tunnels.
3. *recently erected*: The Elswick Colliery was the first in the country to introduce the Guibal fan in its entirety. Earlier, in 1863, a fan at the Tursdale Colliery, Co. Durham, had been modified according to Guibal's ideas, as described below.
4. *exhausting fan*: As opposed to a fan that works by impelling air into a mine.
5. *cleading*: A covering of felt or timber; cladding. From cleed, to clothe (Giffiths, *North East Dialect*).
6. *Mr. Atkinson's paper*: John J. Atkinson, 'On the performance of a ventilating fan at the Hemingfield Pits of the Elsecar Colliery', *Transactions of the North of England Institute of Mining Engineers*, 11 (1861–2), pp. 89–98.
7. *following results*: The results include measurements of water gauges in inches of water, and steam pressures in pounds per square inch (psi). The measurement of pressure in inches of water is analogous to pressure measurements in inches of mercury. Both are 'gauge measures' meaning that the zero point is normal atmospheric pressure. Pressures below the atmospheric are therefore negative; pressures above are positive. An inch of water (inAq) is equal to approximately 0.036 pounds per square inch or 249 pascals at 0°C in SI units.

Peckham, 'On the Explosion of the Flouring Mills at Minneapolis'

1. *A. Freire-Marreco and D. P. Morison*: Algernon Freire-Marreco (about 1836–82) was Professor of Chemistry at Durham University College of Physical Science, Newcastle. Born in South Shields into a shipping family but educated in Portugal from where the family originated. Studied chemistry under Thomas Richardson (1816–67) of Newcastle; Reader in Chemistry at the Newcastle Medical School; appointed Professor of Chemistry at the College of Physical Science on its foundation in 1871. David Pemberton Morison (about 1840–after 1881) was a mining engineer based at Pelton Colliery, Chester-le-Street, Co. Durham during the 1860s. He was a member of the Council of the North East Institute of Mining Engineers in session 1870–1.

   This text was introduced in the report of the discussion of Freire-Marreco and Morison's paper with the following words: 'Mr. NEWALL [a member of the Institute, possibly Robert Stirling Newall (about 1812–89) a manufacturing chemist] said, he saw that Professor Marreco in his paper had referred to explosions in flour mills in America. In the October number of the American journal of "Science and Art" there was a paper which contains a short description of several explosions there. It was exceedingly interesting, and bore very strongly upon the subject of the explosion of small particles of carbonaceous matter.

   The following is a copy of the paper referred to:–'
2. *S. F. PECKHAM*: Stephen Farnum Peckham (1839–1918) was an American chemist and one of the earliest authorities on petroleum. He was Professor of Chemistry at the University of Minnesota, Minneapolis 1873–81. His Report on the *Production, Technology, and Uses of Petroleum and its Products* published as part of the tenth Census of the United States, was the most comprehensive work on its subject to have been published on its appearance in 1885.
3. *falls*: the St Anthony Falls, the only major natural waterfall on the Upper Mississippi and the source of power for the nineteenth-century flour milling industry of Minneapolis.
4. *Washburn A Mill*: built in 1874 by Cadwallader C. Washburn, whose mills later became part of the General Mills corporation, and claimed as the largest flour mill in the world on its opening. The ruins still exist, forming the focal point of the Mill City Museum adjacent to the Mill Ruins Park.
5. *survived the disaster*: Fourteen workers were killed in the explosion; the ensuing fire killed another four people.
6. *round-house ... Railroad*: a depot for railway locomotives arranged with tracks radiating out from a central turntable; usually circular in plan and hence often termed a 'round-house'.
7. *middlings*: a second-best grade of flour in the three-fold grading system used by US millers.
8. *purifiers*: devices used to remove wheat husks from their kernels.
9. *100 degrees Fahrenheit*: about 38 degrees Celsius.
10. *120 to 130 degrees Fahrenheit*: from about 49 to 54 degrees Celsius.

Wood, 'On Safety Lamps for Lighting Coal Mines'

1. *Nicholas Wood*: Nicholas Wood (1795–1865), civil and mining engineer. The son of a tenant farmer of County Durham. Sent to Killingworth Colliery in 1811 to train as a colliery viewer. There he met George Stephenson and they became close associates, working together on Stephenson's safety lamp and steam locomotives. In 1825 published *A Practical Treatise on Rail-Roads, and Interior Communication in General* (London:

Printed for Knight and Lacey, 1825). Gave evidence to both Houses of Parliament on the Liverpool and Manchester Railway Bill in 1827; a judge at the Rainhill locomotive trials in 1829. Became manager of the Hetton Coal Co.'s collieries in 1844 and was a partner in the enterprise. A leading light in the formation of the North of England Institute of Mining Engineers and its first President. The first President, from 1854 till his death, of the coal owners' Mining Association of Great Britain. In character plain, practical, persevering, thorough and even-tempered according to his *ODNB* biographer.

2. *a society was instituted*: the Sunderland Society or the Sunderland Committee. Formed on the initiative of J. J. Wilkinson, a London barrister, it held its first meeting in Sunderland in October 1813 and had a membership drawn almost entirely from the north-east. Its elaborate structure of Patron, Vice-Patrons, President, Secretary, Treasurer and Permanent Committee found a socially appropriate place for the often aristocratic leading royalty owners, the upper middle-class coal owners and the less socially distinguished colliery viewers, church ministers and others; a full membership list is given by Galloway (*Annals*, [1st Series], p. 423–4). It was dissolved after Davy's invention of his lamp, it being assumed that with this invention the object of the Society had been attained.
3. *Sir Ralph Milbanke, Bart.*: Sir Ralph Milbanke (1747–1825), sixth baronet. He married the Hon. Judith Noel in 1777 and succeeded his father in 1798. On the death of his wife's brother, Thomas, the last Viscount Wentworth, in 1815 he and his wife changed their name to Noel and he was from then known as Sir Ralph Noel or Sir Ralph Milbanke Noel. He was a Whig MP for Co. Durham (1790–1812) and enjoyed a reputation as friend of humanity and a foe of slavery. His only child, Anna Isabella, married George, Lord Byron, the poet.
4. *its first report*: *The First Report of a Society for Preventing Accidents in Coal Mines, Comprising a Letter to Sir Ralph Milbanke on the Various Modes Employed in the Ventilation of Collieries, by John Buddle* (Newcastle-upon-Tyne: Printed for the Society by Edward Walker, 1814).
5. *the late Mr. Buddle*: That is, John Buddle, Jr (1773–1843). See note 1 to Buddle, 'On Subsidences Produced by Working Beds of Coal' in this volume.
6. *the society*: Wood means the Institute over which he presided.
7. *Dr. Clanny*: Dr William Reid Clanny (1776–1850), physician and inventor. Trained in medicine at Edinburgh University and practised as a doctor at Bishopwearmouth, a coal-mining area of Co. Durham, from 1803 until his death. Invented several safety lamps; his first in 1813, two years before Davy's, was described in his paper 'On the Means of Procuring a Steady Light in Coal mines without the Danger of Explosion', *Philosophical Transactions of the Royal Society of London*, 103 (1813), pp. 200–5 (*ODNB*).
8. *both produced lamps*: Clanny's, Davy's and Stephenson's safety lamps were each oil lamps. Clanny's surrounded the flame with a short glass cylinder surmounted by a wire gauze chimney; Davy's surrounded the flame with a tall wire gauze cylinder; Stephenson's lamp went through much development but in one version, the 'third lamp' surrounded the flame with a glass and then surrounded the glass with a perforated iron cylinder. They are illustrated in a useful pamphlet published by the National Coal Board, *Mine Gases* (No place: NCB Industrial Training Branch, 1981). See also R. W. Dron, 'Lighting of Mines' in Anon., *Historical Review of Coal Mining* (London: Mining Association of Great Britain [*c.* 1925]).
9. *Rev. W. Hodgson*: a slip for the Rev. John Hodgson (1779–1845), son of a stone mason, curate of Jarrow and Heworth, from 1808, vicar of Hartburn from 1833, and a respected antiquary. Felling Colliery, also known as Brandling Main Colliery, was in his parish

at Heworth and he preached the *Funeral Sermon for the Felling Colliery Sufferers* at Heworth Chapel in August 1812 taking as his texts St John 11:35 ('Jesus wept') and Luke 19:41 ('When he was come near, He beheld the city, and wept over it'). He produced *An Account of the Explosion, which Killed Ninety-two Persons, in Brandling Main Colliery, at Felling, near Newcastle upon Tyne, on May 25, 1812: With a Plan and Description of that Colliery: A Brief Statement of the Fund Raised for the Widows of the Sufferers; ...* [etc.] (Newcastle: Printed by Edward Walker, 1813). Hodgson acted as a guide for Davy during his visit to the district and assisted him in obtaining supplies of fire-damp for his experiments. Hodgson's life was written by James Raine, *A Memoir of John Hodgson*, 2 vols (London: Longman, Brown, Green, Longmans & Roberts, 1857–8).

10. *lanthorn*: a lantern.
11. *'discovered ... atmosphere'*: The quotation is from a letter of 19 October 1815 from Davy to Hodgson which Hodgson quoted in a letter of his own to the *Newcastle Courant* of 26 October 1816. The whole correspondence was later published in Anon., *A Description of the Safety Lamp invented by George Stephenson, and now in Use at Killingworth Colliery: To which is Added, a Collection of Letters Which have Appeared in the Newcastle Papers, with Other Documents relating to the Safety Lamps*, 2nd edn (London, Edinburgh and Newcastle: Baldwin Cradock and Joy; Archibald Constable and Co., and E. Charnley, 1817).
12. *'iron wire gauze ... all circumstances'*: The quotation is from Sir Humphry Davy, *On the Safety Lamp for Coal Miners: With Some Researches on Flame* (London: Printed for R. Hunter, 1818). In the version appearing in *The Collected Works of Sir Humphry Davy, Bart.*, ed. J. Davy (London: Smith, Elder & Co., 1840), it appears in vol. 6, *Miscellaneous Papers and Researches*, p. 14.
13. *'On the Safety Lamp ... Flame'*: see previous note.
14. *'I found ... gas'*: *The Collected Works of Sir Humphry Davy, Bart.*, vol. 6, p. 10. The quotation is somewhat loose but not materially inaccurate.
15. *'I found ... gases'*: *The Collected Works of Sir Humphry Davy, Bart.*, vol. 6, p. 11.
16. *carbonic acid or fixed air*: carbon dioxide.
17. *azote*: nitrogen, a name common among French chemists, from the Greek meaning 'without life'.
18. *'On mixing ... destroyed'*: *The Collected Works of Sir Humphry Davy, Bart.*, vol. 6, p. 11.
19. *more than a second*: Observations such as this, of the speed of an explosion, were later to play an important role in the design of safe explosives. See Read, *Explosives*, p. 58.
20. *'In exploding ... gas tubes'*: *The Collected Works of Sir Humphry Davy, Bart.*, vol. 6, p. 11. Wood omits from the text, following 'to the other': 'and I found that in tubes of one-seventh of an inch in diameter, explosive mixtures could not be fired when they were opened in the atmosphere;'.
21. *Sir Humphrey*: his name was frequently misspelled in this way.
22. *'In reasoning ... continuous inflammation'*: *The Collected Works of Sir Humphry Davy, Bart.*, vol. VI, p. 11.
23. *This idea ... explosion'*: *The Collected Works of Sir Humphry Davy, Bart.*, Vol. VI, pp. 11–12.
24. *The Museler Lamp*: that is the Mueseler Lamp, named after its inventor, Mathieu-Louis Mueseler of Belgium (1799–1866). His lamp, which was distinguished from other designs by the internal chimney as Wood describes, was made compulsory in Belgian mines in 1864. It was particularly commended by the British Royal Commission on Accidents in Mines in 1886.
25. *The Boty Lamp*: a Belgian lamp. Patented 1844; one of four made compulsory for use in Belgian mines in 1851 but superseded by the Mueseler Lamp in 1864.

26. *The Eloin Lamp*: another Belgian lamp, designed by F. Eloin of Namur in 1846. It was described in a notice by S. H. Blackwell, 'On an Improved Miners' Safety Lamp', *Proceedings of the Institution of Mechanical Engineers*, 2 (1851), pp. 23–6.
27. *argand burner*: see note 7 to Murdock, 'An Account of the Application of the Gas from Coal'.
28. *Dr. Glover's Lamp*: patented by Dr Glover and J. Cail in 1851.
29. *Dr Priara*: not identified.
30. *The South Shields Committee*: see note 6 to Dunn, *A Treatise on the Winning and Working of Collieries*.
31. *Mr. Darlington*: James Darlington (vital dates unknown). He described himself to the 1852 Select Committee on Coal Mines as 'part Proprietor of several mines, and principal Manager of Ince Hall Coal and Cannel Works, about the largest colliery in Lancashire' and stated that he had been educated 'entirely with a view to take the management of collieries and mining, as an engineer' (*Report from Select Committee on the Causes and Frequency of Explosions in Coal Mines*, 1852 (509) v. 1, Qq. 900, 903).
32. *'I can state ... nothing else'*: Darlington's answers to Q. 1373, 1379 and 1378 respectively in the Minutes of Evidence attached to the *Report from Select Committee on the Causes and Frequency of Explosions in Coal Mines*, 1852 (509) v. 1. An explosion of fire-damp killed fifty men and boys at the Arley mine of the Ince Hall company in March 1853. Darlington was an advocate of ventilating coal mines by creating a jet of steam at the bottom of the upcast shaft.
33. *committees of 1835 and 1849*: Parliamentary committees, viz., the Select Committee on Accidents in Mines (*Report*, 1835 (603) V. 1) and the Select Committee (House of Lords) on Dangerous Accidents in Coal Mines (*Report*, 1849 (613) VII. 1).
34. *'concurrence ... security'*: *Report from Select Committee on the Causes and Frequency of Explosions in Coal Mines*, 1852 (509) v. 1, at p. vii of the *Report*.

    In the remainder of the paper Wood reports on experiments designed to discover in which circumstances the flame of various safety lamps would pass through the gauze. He concluded that only in extreme and artificial circumstances would it do so and therefore called into question the conclusions of the South Shields Committee and the 1852 Select Committee.

T. S. J., 'Safety Lamps'

1. *T. S. J*, The author, 'T. S. J.', has not been identified.
2. *6 ft. per second*: this is only 4 miles per hour.
3. *Mr. Higson ... Abram Colliery*: John Higson, a Manchester consulting mining engineer. He gave evidence to the inquest on the forty-six men and boys killed by an explosion at Abram Colliery, Lancashire, on 19 December 1881.
4. *the Mueseler*: see note 15 to Wood, 'On Safety Lamps for Lighting Coal Mines'.
5. Report ... South Wales: not traced.
6. *Mr. W. E. Teale*: William E. Teale (about 1843–1912). Inventor of the 'Protector' version of the Mueseler lamp manufactured by the Protector Lamp and Lighting Co. of Worsley, Manchester. It was exhibited at a meeting of the South Staffordshire and East Worcestershire Institute of Mining Engineers in 1871 where its key feature was given to be a mechanism that extinguished the flame when the lamp was opened.
7. *2 lb. 11 oz*: about 1.2 kg.

White, 'The Coad Electric Miner's Lamp'

1. *Henry White*: Henry White was a mining engineer born in 1847 in South Shields. He gained his Manager's Certificate in 1873 and was manager of the Old Thornley, Black Prince and West Thornley Collieries for the Weardale Iron & Coal Co. in the early 1880s and then of the Walker Colliery, a few kilometers east of Newcastle, for the Walker Coal Co. from about 1888 to at least 1902 (*DMM*).
2. *Coad*: unidentified.
3. *an official*: that is, one of the lower grades of underground colliery management.
4. *loftings*: timber placed up against the roof in broken places to prevent falls of loose stone (Greenwell, *Glossary*).
5. *off-takes*: delivery drifts. Greenwell explains: 'Water pumped up a shaft is not usually lifted higher than is necessary; it is delivered into a drift or adit [a tunnel or passage, here sloping slightly downwards from the shaft so that water would flow down it] driven from low ground into the shaft. This is called a delivery or off-take drift.'
6. *bank-heads*: A bank-head is the upper end of an inclined plane used for the underground transport of coal (Gresley, *Glossary*).
7. *stables*: Pit ponies were normally stabled underground.
8. *staples*: shafts, usually short, connecting two different levels in a colliery, away from the main winding and ventilation shafts which normally passed down through all levels.
9. *ebonite cells*: Ebonite, or vulcanite, was vulcanized rubber. Its main use in electrical apparatus was as an insulator. However, the use of ebonite in the Coad lamp is unclear from White's description. The plate accompanying this paper, not reproduced here, shows a platinum-zinc battery, as White's description implies.
10. *4 lbs. 2 ounces ... 5 lbs. 6 ozs*: about 1.9 kg and 2.4 kg, respectively.
11. *10 ounces*: About 0.3 kg.
12. *¾ ounce ... 1 ounce*: about 21 g and 28 g, respectively.
13. *Mr. G. B. Forster*: George Baker Forster (1832–1901), mining engineer. A son of Thomas Emmerson Forster (1802–75), a well-known colliery viewer. Educated at Cambridge, where he read mathematics, but destined for holy orders. He rebelled, however, and followed in his father's footsteps. Appointed viewer at Cowpen Colliery, at Blyth on the Northumberland coast, in 1858. Came to prominence as a result of his efforts to rescue the men entombed in the Hartley Disaster of 1862. During these efforts rescuers were carried out of the pit unconscious from the effects of carbon monoxide poisoning and this was also the cause of death of those entombed. A Vice-chair of the Northumberland Coal-Owners' Association and of the North of England United Coal Trade Association. In his relations with miners, a man of tact and sympathy. President of the North of England Institute, 1881–4 (*DMM*).
14. *Could not a man smell the gas?*: a crass remark. Coad is presumably thinking of town gas which had a distinct odour. However, the main constituent of firedamp, methane, is odourless; though the other gases with which it is mixed may give a smell to firedamp. Carbon monoxide is highly poisonous but odourless; a mine atmosphere depleted of oxygen is dangerous but odourless. Forster's comment in reply, especially in view of his role in the Hartley Disaster, is remarkably mild.
15. *Mr. W. C. Blackett*: William Cuthbert Blackett (1860–1935), later, after his service in the First World War, Col. Blackett. Manager of Kimblesworth Colliery from about 1884 and of Charlaw, Nettlesworth and Sacriston collieries, Co. Durham, from about 1888; 'agent' for these collieries, i.e. a senior manager having charge of a number of collieries,

from about 1890. These collieries were all owned by Charlaw and Sacriston Collieries Co. Ltd of which he eventually became managing director. On the Council of the North of England Institute from about 1896 and later its President. Recipient of a silver medal of the Royal Humane Society (*DMM*).

'The Telephone in Colliery Workings', *Colliery Guardian*

1. *Lord Elphinstone, of Carberry Tower*: William Buller Fullerton Elphinstone, fifteenth Baron Elphinstone, of Elphinstone, Stirlingshire (1828–93). Carberry Tower, Musselburgh, near Edinburgh, was his seat, not part of his title. A Representative Peer for Scotland, 1867–85; a Lord-in-Waiting to Queen Victoria, 1874–80 and 1886–92. Created a Peer of the United Kingdom 1885. His life otherwise unremarkable (Burke's *Peerage*).
2. *the 8th inst*: the 8th instant, meaning the 8th of this month, i.e. 8 April.
3. *'dooks'*: a Scottish term. Underground inclined planes (Gresley, *Glossary*).
4. *bogies*: small trucks or trolleys (Gresley, *Glossary*).
5. *Cornish engine*: A Cornish engine was usually (a) a pumping engine; (b) a beam engine; and (c) one in which the entry of steam to the cylinder was cut off before the piston had completed its stroke thus allowing the steam to work 'expansively'. Which of these properties would have been regarded as definitive is hard to say. See D. B. Barton, *The Cornish Beam Engine: A Survey of its History and Development from before 1800 to the Present Day* (Truro: D. Bradford Barton, 1965).
6. *Mr. Charlton Wollaston, C. E*: Charlton James Wollaston (1820–1915), civil and electrical engineer. He was an engineer to the Submarine Telegraph Company which laid a cable between Calais and Dover in 1851 and was also involved in the laying of a telegraph cable between Cape Town and Graham's Town after 1862. He was present with Alexander Graham Bell when Bell exhibited the telephone to Queen Victoria at Osborne House in 1878.
7. *Messrs*: here in its original usage as the plural of 'Mister'; there is no implication of joint enterprise, as in the name of a firm such as 'Messrs Huntley and Palmer, Biscuit Manufacturers' and as is the case here in the references to Messrs Deans and Moore, the colliery lessees.
8. *Lord Shand ... Dr. Young, Portobello*: The letters after some of these names indicate a Civil Engineer, a Mining Engineer and a Writer to the Signet, the latter being the term for the principal class of solicitors in Scotland, called thus 'from their having been originally clerks in the office of the King's Secretary, it being their duty to prepare all warrants for charters or grants to be passed under either the Great Seal or Privy-seal, such warrants being called from an early period 'signatures,' because they bore the signet of the King' (*Chambers*). Few of the party can be identified. Lord Shand was Alexander Burns Shand, first Baron Shand (1828–1904), a Scottish advocate and judge; he was appointed a Lord of Session with the title Lord Shand in 1872; he was made a Lord of Appeal in Ordinary and was raised to the peerage as Baron Shand of Woodhouse in the County of Dumfries in 1892. Allan Carter, C. E. , may have been William Allan Carter (fl. 1863–92) a civil engineer, architect and painter. Kitto may have been the R. L. M. Kitto, said to be 'of Australia' and a Fellow of the Royal Geographical Society, who in 1873 was reported to have leased with two partners the coal-fields of Sir George Grant Suttee, baronet, of Prestongrange, East Lothian. A. G. Moore was Alexander George Moore who read his paper, 'Notes of a Mining Engineer's Visit to South Africa', to the Philosophical Soci-

ety of Glasgow in 1893. C. Stewart of 'Sweethorpe' was Charles Stewart of Sweethope. James Hope of Belmont was married to the Hon. Gertrude Elphinstone (d. 1894). Provost Keir was Provost of Musselburgh, a 'provost' being similar to the mayor of an English local authority. Newbattle, Arniston, Prestongrange, Tranent, Carberry, Sweethope, Pinkiehill, Musselburgh and Portobello are all in Midlothian or East Lothian, indicating the party was a predominantly local one.

9. *croupier*: here meaning an assistant chairman officiating at a formal dinner.
10. *'full of noises ... delight'*: Shakespeare, *The Tempest*, III.ii,127–8, spoken by Caliban.
11. Scotsman: The article first appeared in the *Scotsman* for the 9 April 1880.

Wood, 'On the Conveyance of Coals Underground in Coal Mines'

1. *Nicholas Wood*: for Nicholas Wood, see note 1 to Wood, 'On Safety Lamps for Lighting Coal Mines', above.
2. *published in 1831*: this was his *Practical Treatise on Rail-Roads, and Interior Communication in General* (London: Printed for Knight and Lacey, 1825). The second edition of 1831 was published in London by Hurst, Chance, and Co.
3. *same in both directions*: If the weight of the traffic is greater in one direction there may be economies of motive power in making the line slope towards the destination of the heaviest traffic.
4. *animalcula*: now animalcules. Any small animal or microscopic organism.
5. *oxyhydra lens*: The term 'oxyhydra' is unknown. A hydrate is a compound containing water. However, the simplest compound of oxygen and water, $H2O2$, or hydrogen peroxide, has been known as such since it was first isolated in 1818. Wood may have intended a 'scientific' term for water itself. However, the 'systematic' chemical and other names that have been proposed for water include 'oxidane', 'hydrogen oxide' and 'dihydrogen monoxide' but not oxyhydra. Nevertheless, the resulting translation of 'oxyhydra lens' as 'water lens' fits the context reasonably well. The term has been attached to a variety of devices. One of the earliest was invented by Stephen Gray (bapt. 1666 d. 1736), the early investigator of electrical phenomena, sometime before 1696. In the words of Benjamin Ward Richardson, Gray 'made a hole in a piece of brass, a very small hole, and he let a drop of water fall into that hole. While the globule of water was thus suspended it became a magnifier. By this lens he declares he could see animalcules in the water itself, the water that formed the lens' ('A first electrician', *Gentleman's Magazine*, 251:1810 (October 1881), pp. 460–80 at p. 463.) A lace-maker's candle stand involved a different device. The candle was surrounded by four glass globes filled with water. The light from the candle passed through the globes, was refracted and emerged as a single, steady beam of concentrated, bright light enabling close work at night such as that involved in engraving or lace-making. In Britain the globes were known as 'flashes' but in the USA as water lenses. A water lens for a camera was patented by Thomas Sutton, the photographer, in about 1859. A lens of a focal length which could be changed by varying the pressure of the water inside it was described in *Engineering* in 1880 and noticed in the *Manchester Times* for 18 September that year.
6. *drifts, adits or levels*: synonyms, as Wood implies. Greenwell gives 'A drift commonly waterlevel, driven into a mine from a hillside, a grove' for 'Adit'; his explanation of 'Drift' suggests the term is more usually used for a passage connecting different parts of a mine or different parts of a seam, rather than for a tunnel driven for drainage purposes. For 'Level' he gives 'A drain cut in the bottom stone to set away or convey water. A pair of

levels is a pair of drifts, driven in the water level direction of the strata for the purpose of winning coal.'

7. *rise side*: Where strata do not rest horizontally they are said to dip. The 'rise side' is the side at a higher level or 'uphill'. The opposite side is the dip side or the side 'down hill'. Alternatively, the dip is the inclination of the strata when viewed in the direction of the fall; the rise is the inclination when viewed in the opposite direction.
8. *day levels*: levels communicating directly with the surface; levels at the end of which daylight can be seen.
9. *self-acting planes*: inclined passages or tunnels where trucks or tubs would run in one direction by themselves under the influence of gravity. Full trucks running downhill might be used to pull empty trucks up hill.
10. *very shallow and very numerous*: Wood's observation is confirmed by modern archaeological studies. See, for example, M. Roe, *Coal Mining in Middleton Park: An Archaeological Investigation by the Middleton Park Community Archaeological Project* (Halifax: Meerstone Archaeological Consultancy, 2008).
11. *long wall system*: a system of working coal in which the coal is extracted in a single stage from a small number of long and continuous faces. By the early twentieth century long wall faces could be a kilometre long and sometimes longer.
12. *pillar and wall system*: Also known as 'pillar and stall', 'bord and pillar' (Durham), 'bord and wall', or 'stoop and room' (Scotland). ('Bords' were often spelled 'boards'.) A system of working coal in which the coal was extracted in two stages. In the first stage the area to be worked was divided up into square or rectangular pillars by driving roadways through the coal (this was 'working in the whole'). The roadways were the 'bords' or 'walls'. Subsequently, the pillars themselves were worked ('working in the broken'). A plan of the workings thus resembled a chess board.
13. *thill*: the floor of the seam.
14. *penning*: the term is otherwise unknown in this sense.
15. *flanches*: flanges.
16. *a plate of iron to act as the flanch of the wheel*: in other words the flange was transferred from wheel to rail; the upright section of the 'L'-section rail acting, instead of the flange of the wheel, to keep the wagon wheel on the road.
17. *tram road*: a railway composed of iron plates with an 'L'-shaped cross section; in contrast to the 'edge rail', now the familiar type of rail, which has a rounded top.
18. *bank*: the surface.

Galloway, 'Secondary Haulage'

1. *W. Galloway*: William Galloway (1840–1927), mining engineer. The eldest son of William Galloway (1801–54), a Paisley coal owner and JP, and Margaret Lindsay; the brother of Robert Lindsay Galloway (1844–1908), the author of the *History of Coal Mining in Great Britain* and Thomas Lindsay Galloway (1852–1921) the mining engineer. William Galloway was educated at the University of Giessen, the Bergakademie at Freiburg and at University College, London. He became one of HM's Inspectors of Mines firstly in the West of Scotland and then in South Wales. He later established a substantial practice as a consulting engineer and this would have enabled him to gather the data presented in this article. He was the first to investigate systematically the role of coal dust in colliery explosions, publishing his results in a series of papers in the *Proceedings of the Royal Society* between 1875 and 1887. Scepticism of his theories among

his senior colleagues in the Inspectorate forced his resignation from his post. A gradual accumulation of experimental evidence by himself and others eventually vindicated his position. He was also one of the first to suggest that the spreading of stone dust in mines would be an effective way of preventing the explosion of atmospheric suspensions of coal dust. Almost certainly responsible for saving more miners' lives than Humphry Davy but never well known among the general public. Knighted 1924.

2. *Prof. Haton de la Goupilliere*: Julien-Napoléon Haton de la Goupillière (1833–1927), mining engineer. His mother was the daughter of General Baron Petit, embraced by Napoleon on his departure for Elba, in a moment that became sacred to his descendants. A mathematician by inclination. His *Cours d'Exploitation des Mines* was published in two volumes in Paris in 1883 by the Libraire des Corps des Ponts et Chaussees et des Mines. Earlier, he had been responsible for a *Rapport* on fire-damp (le grisou) to the Commission d'études des moyen propres à prévenir les explosions de Grisou (Paris: Dunod, 1878). His career was crowned by his Directorship of the École Polytechnique and the Vice-Presidency of the Conseil Général des Mines. Member of the Académie des Sciences from 1884.
3. Lectures on Mining: Jules Pierre Callon (1815–75). His *Lectures* had been translated by William Galloway and Clement le Neve Foster as *Lectures on Mining Delivered at the School of Mines, Paris*, 3 vols (Paris: Dunod, 1876–86).
4. *Mr H. F. Bulman*: Harrison Francis Bulman (1856–1933) was a colliery manager at Byermoor Colliery, Co. Durham, for John Bowes and Partners, and a mine engineer. He was most well known as the co-author with R. A. S. Redmayne of *Colliery Working and Management: Comprising the Duties of a Colliery Manager, the Superintendence & Arrangement of Labour & Wages and the Different Systems of Working Coal Seams* (London: Crosby Lockwood and Son, 1896) which was the foremost text before the First World War, with new editions published in 1906, 1912, 1925 and 1951.
5. *Richard Broja*: Richard Broja or Bröja (1835–1913). *Der Steinkohlenbergbau in den Vereinigten Staaten* was published in Leipzig by A. Felix in 1894.

Dunn, *A Treatise on the Winning and Working of Collieries*

1. *Matthias Dunn*: see note 6 to the Introduction to these three volumes.
2. skreens: Or screens. Dunn's 'Glossary of Terms' gives 'Skreen, apparatus for separating the small coal from the large.' The most basic form is simply a riddle or sieve perforated with holes of a uniform size, say one inch in diameter: as the riddle is shaken, coals less than one inch in diameter fall through and are thus separated from the larger coals. Dunn gives a description of the somewhat different arrangement usual in the north-east at this time shortly. The screens might be combined with apparatus for weighing the coal in each tub, an essential operation if colliers were to be paid according to the amount of coal they sent up, the usual practice.

Wain, 'Colliery Surface Works'

1. *Edward Brownfield Wain*: (1861–1925) colliery engineer and manager. In 1886 he was appointed manager of the Institute and Middle pits of Chatterley-Whitfield Collieries Ltd, the biggest company operating in the North Staffordshire coalfield. Contributed a number of papers to the *Transactions* of the North Staffordshire Institute of Mining and

Mechanical Engineers in the 1890s. Credited with leading the company into its 'golden age'; by 1923 he was the company's General Manager (*DMM*).

2. *Professor Hull*: Edward Hull (1829–1917), geologist. The author of *The Coal-fields of Great Britain: Their History, Structure and Duration: With Notices of the Coal-fields of Other Parts of the World* (London: E. Stanford, 1861) which went through five editions in the next forty-five years and remained the standard compendium of information on the geology of the British coal fields. A 'hard working man of shallow intellect' according to the *ODNB*.
3. *adit*: 'A drift commonly waterlevel, driven into a mine from a hillside, a grove' (Greenwell, *Glossary*) that is, a tunnel driven into mine workings typically from the side of a hill, inclined sufficiently for water to flow along it away from the mine workings to the surface on the hillside.
4. *pit-banksmen*: The pit bank was the area of the surface around the shaft; pit-banksmen were required to load and unload coal tubs from the cage and to supervise the raising and lowering of underground workers.
5. *84 lbs. per yard ... 50 lbs. per yard*: Comparatively heavy rails for industrial railways. Standard rail weights increased through the nineteenth and early twentieth century as the weight of rolling stock rose. By the late 1940s weights for main line railways in Britain had reached 95 lb per yard for 'bull-head' rails and 110 or 131 lb for flat bottomed types. In the USA, the Pennsylvania Railroad was using 152 lb rails at about the same date.
6. *carefully planned workshops*: The figure shows the smithy; fitting shop; workshops for joiners, pattern-makers and carpenters; and a sawmill laid out adjacent to each other in a single building, unlike the higgledy-piggledy arrangement seen at many collieries.
7. *Mr. George Fowler*: George Fowler (*c.* 1840–1921), mining engineer. His membership of the North of England Institute began in session 1860–1 when he gave his address as the Moira Collieries in Leicestershire but by 1869 he had moved to the Nottinghamshire coalfield with which he remained associated for the rest of his life. Judging from the letter he wrote to *The Times* in 1869, a man of robust common sense, forthrightly expressed, at least in his younger years. There, he compared collieries to powder magazines, and asked:
8. What, may I ask, would be done if it were known that houses in various parts of London were filled with gunpowder? Would the authorities pass a decree that passers-by in the streets should carry no light, smoke no cigars, and wear list [cloth] slippers? Would they not rather order the removal of the powder? ... [But in collieries the] rule has been – use safety lamps, fire no powder – in fact, list slippers, and yet more list; prevention rather than cure.
9. When I say that there are many mines in work in which a man dare not for his life's sake carry a naked candle, I say that which no mining engineer can deny (*DMM*).
10. *'On Mechanical Coal-Cleaning'*: that is, T. E. Forster and H. Ayton, 'Improved Coal Screening and Cleaning', *Transactions of the Federated Institute of Mining Engineers*, I, (1889–90), pp. 83–96 and plates I–X.
11. *The Mines' Regulation Act*: The Coal Mines Regulation Act, 1887, 50 & 51 Vict., c. 58.
12. *creeper-chains*: slow-moving chains set between the tracks and provided with a device to catch tubs or trucks from underneath and thereby pull them along.
13. *picking belts*: conveyor belts along which the coal is passed and from which stone was picked by hand.
14. *heapstead*: this sometimes meant the 'entire surface works about a colliery shaft' including the headgear, screens, winding and pumping engines and engine houses, workshops, stores and so on (Gresley, *Glossary*) but sometimes had a more restricted meaning as the

'elevated platform near the shaft above the surface upon which the tubs are landed and run to the screens' under the force of gravity (Griffiths, *North East Dialect*). It is this more restricted meaning which Wain intends here.

15. *jigging screens*: screens which are made to shake or vibrate to expedite the sorting of the coal.
16. *round coal*: coal in large lumps; for much of the nineteenth century considerably more valuable than small coal since it burned better in the grates and furnaces then in use.
17. *small*: small coal.
18. *cobbles*: the usual name for coal of this size.
19. *no pulley*: at the bottom of the shaft.
20. *Koepe system*: named after its inventor Carl Friedrich Koepe (1835–1922), from 1873 the technical director of several mines in the Krupp industrial combine in the Ruhr. In a conventional winding system the winding rope passes from the top of the cage, up the shaft, over the pulley at the top of the head gear and is then attached to a winding drum made to rotate by a winding engine. In shafts of any depth the weight of the winding rope was considerable and the load on the winding engine therefore varied significantly as the cage was would up and down the shaft. In the Koepe winding system, as Wain explains, the rope passes from the top of the cage, over the pulley at the top of the shaft, around the winding drum and then back over a second pulley and down the shaft to the bottom of the cage. The cage is wound up the shaft by rotating the winding drum; friction between the rotating drum-ring and the rope does the rest. The rotating winding drum simultaneously winds rope in from the top of the cage and out to the bottom of the cage, so the length of the rope suspended in the shaft is a constant and the load on the winding engine is therefore the same throughout the ascent of the cage. The 'balance-rope' that Wain mentions shortly is, in the Koepe system, that part of the winding rope under the cage; it 'balances', or equalizes, the load on the winding engine.
21. *back-pressure*: the pressure exerted on the piston on its return stroke by the steam remaining in the cylinder.
22. *diagrams*: indicator diagrams which gave the pressure acting on the piston as the piston moved back and forth along its stroke; used to check the settings of the valve regulating the entry and exit of steam to and from the cylinder. An explanation is given in P. W. B. Semmens and A. J. Goldfinch, *How Steam Locomotives Really Work* (Oxford: Oxford University Press, 2000), pp. 147ff. The history is given by R. L. Hills, *Power from Steam: A History of the Stationary Steam Engine* (Cambridge: Cambridge University Press, 1989), pp. 92–4. A contemporary explanation is given in W. H. Northcott, *The Theory and Action of the Steam Engine (For Practical Men)* (London: Cassell & Co., 1876).
23. *the cut-off*: The point in the piston stroke at which the inlet valve cuts off the admission of steam into the cylinder; an increased cut-off meant an earlier cut-off. From the point at which steam is cut off the steam works expansively; without a cut-off this opportunity for 'expansive working' is wasted and steam consumption is increased. See Semmens and Goldfinch, *How Steam Locomotives Work*, pp. 157ff.
24. *Briquette-Works*: Briquettes were a form of manufactured fuel composed of mixtures of coal-dust and, usually, pitch which were moulded under pressure and heat to form a brick about twice the size of an ordinary building brick, despite the meaning of the original French word (a 'little brick'). Besides pitch various other materials, tar, asphalt, grease, etc., were used to cement the dust into a solid. Despite being manufactured from what were often regarded as waste materials their cost in Britain remained high compared to ordinary coal and they were much more commonly used in France. Briquettes

were normally used for domestic purposes or in manufacturing establishments; their use as a substitute for coke, as Wain discusses here, was practically unknown.

25. *p. 191*: William Colquhoun, 'The Manufacture of Briquette-Fuel', *Minutes of the Proceedings of the Institution of Civil Engineers*, 118 (1894), pp. 191–226.
26. *p. 112*: The reference is in fact to the 'Discussion on Mr. Hogg's Paper on "Coal-Washing at North Motherwell Colliery"', *Transactions of the Federated Institute of Mining Engineers*, 7 (1893–4), pp. 112–14; Dixon's 'particulars' did indeed take up most of the discussion. John Hogg's paper appeared in the *Transactions*, VI (1892–93), pp. 393–6 + Plate XI.
27. *solid blocks under pressure*: That is, briquettes.
28. *pug-mill*: In this context 'pug' is material 'that has been pulverized, thoroughly mixed, and kneaded into a soft, plastic condition without air pockets for brick-making', etc. (*OED*) and a pug-mill is a machine which performs these operations.
29. *rack-and-pawl*: or 'ratchet and pawl'. A device to prevent machinery from running backwards first used on ships' capstans, and on winches and windlasses. In these applications, the pawl was a short, stout piece of wood attached to the capstan, winch, etc., with a hinge. In forward motion, the free end of the pawl rattled freely over the teeth of the ratchet or rack; should the capstan or winch have attempted to run backwards, however, the free end of the pawl would have been caught in the rack and would have brought the capstan or winch to a halt.
30. *p. 248*: Edward B. Wain, '[Letter]', in 'Correspondence on Briquette-Fuel', *Minutes of the Proceedings of the Institution of Civil Engineers*, 118 (1894), pp. 246–51 at pp. 247–9.

Hunting, 'The Feeding and Management of Colliery Horses'

1. *Charles Hunting*: Charles Hunting, JP (1823–99) was 'largely interested in collieries and other commercial undertakings in East Durham' according to his obituarist. He was a 'staunch Liberal', who was 'well known for his kindness and generosity'. A daughter married Robert Brydon, the Agent of the Marquess of Londonderry at Seaham Harbour, suggesting that he moved in upper-middle-class circles (*North Eastern Daily Gazette* [Middlesbrough], 18 September 1899). Besides the present work he also authored a seventy-six-page booklet *On the Feeding and Management of Draught Horses: Food and Work* (Newcastle upon Tyne: A. Reid, 1874).
2. *'putting' work*: pushing tubs of coal underground.
3. *cobs*: A cob is a 'short-legged, stout variety of horse, usually ridden by heavy persons', or a strong pony (*OED*).
4. *'score'*: 'A standard number of tubs or corves of coal at each colliery, upon which hewers' and putters' prices [piece rates] for working are paid, called the score price. It varies in different localities from 20 to 26 tubs. Thus on the Tyne, the score consists of 20; on the Wear, 21; and on the Tees, from 20 to 26 tubs, at different collieries' (Greenwell, *Glossary*).
5. *Banting system*: The dietary regime followed by William Banting (1796/7–1878) which successfully reduced his weight and improved his health. The diet, suggested by his surgeon, William Harvey, eliminated bread, butter, milk, sugar, beer, soup, potatoes and beans, replacing them with meat, fish and dry toast. He published the diet in his pamphlet *A Letter on Corpulence, Addressed to the Public* of 1863. The earliest edition held by the British Library is the second of the same year published by Harrison & Sons of Lon-

don. There were further editions in 1864 and 1875 and 'Banting' became a well-known term for adopting a diet to lose weight (*ODNB*).

6. *Hunters*: horses, not humans.
7. *The late Mr. Brassey*: Thomas Brassey (1805–70), the civil engineering contractor. His success as a contractor brought him great public prominence; it was to Brassey, along with Morton Peto and Edward Ladd Betts, that the government turned when it required the urgent construction of a seven-mile railway between the port of Balaklava and the troops besieging Sebastopol during the Crimean War. His success in this task increased his prominence and the authority with which he pronounced on business and other questions (*ODNB*).
8. *pabulum*: schoolboy Latin: food.

'The Milroy Lectures on the Hygienic Aspect of the Coalmining Industry in the United Kingdom', *British Medical Journal*

1. *Frank Shufflebotham*: (1874–1932) was born in Newcastle-under-Lyme in Staffordshire, an MD of the University of Cambridge and the Medical Referee under the Workmen's Compensation Act for the North Staffordshire District at the time this article was published. Arnold Bennett wrote of him in a letter to Septimus Bennett, his brother (14 June 1917) 'Shuffle (of Newcastle) is a very nice chap, & very brainy. I expect you know him. He is the great poison gas expert in this country [Britain], & is paying a visit to the front to see his hellish devices in operation on Saturday', *Letters of Arnold Bennett: IV Family Letters*, ed. J. Hepburn (Oxford: Oxford University Press, 1986), p. 187).
2. *Professor Cadman and Mr. Walley*: Whalley's name is misspelled in the text. The reference is to Royal Commission on Mines, *Reports of an Enquiry into the Ventilation of Coal Mines and the Methods of Examining for Firedamp, Made on Behalf of the Royal Commission on Mines* (Cd. 4551), 1909, xxxiv,913, made by John Cadman, Professor of Mining in the University of Birmingham, and E. B. Whalley, an Assistant Inspector of Mines. John Cadman (1877–1941) was the son of a Staffordshire mine surveyor, engineer and manager. Studied geology and mining at Armstrong College, Newcastle; then assistant general manager to his father at Silverdale Colliery; HM Inspector of Mines from 1902; showed conspicuous courage in rescue work at the Hamstead Colliery disaster in 1908. Professor of Mining at Birmingham from 1908. Subsequently the leading authority on petroleum geology and mining technology and a member of the 1913 Admiralty commission on fuel oil which paved the way to the naval conversion from coal to oil (*ODNB*). His life thus embodies the transition from an energy regime based on coal to one based on oil.

   The 'tables' are tables of various measurements of temperature, pressure, etc., taken at forty-three collieries. Shufflebotham has clearly taken the worst examples for his paper but the Cadman–Whalley tables show dry bulb temperatures in the 70s Fahrenheit (low 20s Celsius) to have been normal and in the 80s Fahrenheit (high 20s Celsius) not unusual.
3. *dry-bulb temperature*: A dry-bulb temperature is given by a dry-bulb thermometer which is a thermometer of the ordinary type. A wet-bulb thermometer is one where the bulb is covered with a woollen material which is kept wet. Should water evaporate from the woollen material, which is the ordinary case, the latent heat of evaporation will reduce the temperature shown below that shown by a dry-bulb thermometer. Only if the air is saturated will there be no evaporation and the wet-bulb and dry-bulb thermometers will show the

same temperature. In all other circumstances wet-bulb temperatures are lower than dry-bulb temperatures. The wet-bulb thermometer, by adjusting temperature for humidity in this way, therefore gives a better indication of the level of discomfort experienced in given temperatures. In dry and warm air, the wet-bulb temperature will remain relatively low; in humid and warm air it will be relatively high (*Chambers, s.v.* 'Thermometer').

4. *95.5°, 96°, 92°, 97.8°, 88.8° and 87°F.*; in degrees Celsius: 35.3, 35.6, 33.3, 36.6, 31.6 and 30.6, respectively.
5. *79°, 82.5°, 77°, 79.8°, 82°, 81.5°, and 87° F.*: in degrees Celsius: 26.1, 28.1, 25.0, 26.6, 27.8, 27.5, and 30.6, respectively.
6. *as much as 90°... over 80° F.*: As much as 32° Celsius ... over 27° Celsius.
7. *Dr. Fraser Harris*: Dr David Fraser Harris, later David Fraser Fraser-Harris (1867–1937), physiologist and neurologist. The most relevant of many non-specialist publications is his 'Stephen Hales: The pioneer in the hygiene of ventilation', *The Scientific Monthly*, 3:5 (November 1916), pp. 440–54.
8. *Professor Langlois of Paris*: Jean Paul Langlois (1862–1923), Agrégé Professor of Physiology at the Faculté de Medeciné of Paris.
9. *77° F.*: 25° Celsius.
10. *86° F.*: 30° Celsius.
11. *18 to 25 c.cm of mercury*: unclear. The sphygmomanometer, the common apparatus for measuring blood pressure, was introduced by Scipione Riva-Rocci in 1896 and popularized among the medical profession by Harvey Cushing, an American neurosurgeon, in the early years of the twentieth century. This apparatus measured blood pressure, as it continues to be measured, in millimetres (not cubic centimetres) of mercury (mmHg) with a normal range of 110/65 (systolic/diastolic) to 140/90.
12. *hygrometrical*: relating to the degree of humidity.
13. *Haldane*: John Scott Haldane (1860–1936), physiologist. He was a younger brother of Richard Burdon Haldane (1856–1928) later Viscount Haldane, Liberal Secretary of State for War 1905–12, and father of John Burdon Sanderson Haldane (1892–64) the geneticist, popularizer of science and communist. John Scott Haldane was best known for his research for public health purposes on the chemical and bacteriological constituents of air and on the physiology of respiration. He was closely involved in work on the safety of mines. He was the author of a *Report to the Secretary of State for the Home Department on the Causes of Death in Colliery Explosions and Underground Fires, with Special Reference to the Explosions at Tylorstown, Brancepeth, and Micklefield* ((C. 8112), 1896, xviii, 611). He was appointed to the 1906–11 Royal Commission on Mines and in 1912 was appointed Director of the research laboratory established by the Doncaster Coal Owners' Association. Like Shufflebotham (see 'The Milroy Lectures') he became involved in research on poison gas during the First World War. FR S, 1897; President of the Institute of Mining Engineers 1924–8; Companion of Honour, 1928; Copley Medalist, 1934 (*ODNB*).
14. *about 78° F.*: about 26° Celsius.
15. *beyond 88° F.*: beyond 31° Celsius.
16. *'It is clear ... dust.'*: The quotation is from an article of Haldane's in the *Journal of Hygiene*, 4 (October 1905). This had been quoted by the Departmental Committee on Humidity and Ventilation in Cotton Weaving Sheds in their *Report* (Cd. 4484), 1909, xv, 635, p. 8.
17. *Departmental Committee ... sheds*: see the previous note. Haldane's proposals were given in evidence as his answer to Q. 3139 and quoted in the *Report* at p. 8.
18. *75° F. (wet bulb)*: about 24° Celsius (wet bulb).

19. *70° F. (wet bulb)*: about 21° Celsius (wet bulb).
20. *Dr. Pembrey*: Marcus Seymour Pembrey (1868–1934), physiologist. Worked in similar areas to those of J. S. Haldane but focused on the clinical applications. FRS, 1922 (*ODNB*). His opinions given here are taken from the *Report* of the Cotton Weaving Sheds Departmental Committee (see note 17), p. 8.
21. *77° F. on the wet-bulb thermometer*: about 25° Celsius (wet bulb).

Galloway, 'On the Present Condition of Mining in Some of the Principal Coal-Producing Districts of the Continent'

1. *T. Lindsay Galloway*: Thomas Lindsay Galloway (1852–1921) was a mining engineer and colliery manager. He was the fourth or later son of William Galloway, JP (1801–54) a coal owner of Paisley. He was the brother of both Sir William Galloway (1840–1927), the researcher into coal-dust, and Robert Lindsay Galloway (1844–1908), the author of *A History of Coal Mining in Great Britain* (1882). An earlier Thomas Lindsay had been born to the same family in 1842 but died in 1850.
2. *what has gone before*: Galloway has just given an extensive account of the state of coal mining in northern France, Belgium, Germany and Austria after returning from a tour of those countries in November, December and January 1877–8.
3. *MM. Kind and Chaudron*: Inventors of a method of sinking shafts through water-bearing strata lying above dry strata, using cast-iron rings set one above the other to line the shaft and render it water-tight. The method of excavation could be carried out underwater, obviating the need for the heavy pumping of water before the shaft was made water tight. Kind was the first to apply the method, around 1850, but did not overcome all the problems involved until his collaboration with Chaudron. The first accounts given in England were by Herbert Mackworth, 'Improvements in Boring for Minerals, Wells and Shafts: Kind system', *Transactions of the North of England Institute of Mining Engineers*, 2 (1853–4), pp. 57–67 and Warington Smyth, 'On the sinking of Pit-Shafts by Boring Under Water, as Practised by Messrs. Kind and Chaudron', *ibid.*, XX (1870–71), pp. 187–99.

Wood, 'Inaugural Address'

1. *Nicholas Wood*: see note 1 to 'On Safety Lamps for Lighting Coal Mines'. The 'Inaugural Address' was also published as a pamphlet (Durham: William Ainsley, Printer, 1852).
2. *Proprietor ... Worker of it*: Wood means the lessor and lessee, the royalty owner and the colliery owner, not the colliery owner and the working miner. Working miners were effectively excluded from membership by the annual subscription which began at £2 2*s.* 0*d.* for ordinary members, payable in advance, and by the provision in the rules that new members must be proposed by existing members. The Institute was a society for 'gentlemen', only.
3. *Mr. Joseph Pease*: Joseph Pease (1799–1872) a member of the Quaker family of industrialists and the second son of Edward Pease (1767–1858), the promoter of the Stockton and Darlington Railway. MP for South Durham, 1832–41, and the first Quaker to sit in the House of Commons. Often credited with the founding of the town of Middlesbrough. A 'man of great energy, and possessed [of] unusual administrative talent, and ... a graceful and accomplished speaker' according to his obituary in the *Newcastle Courant* of 16 February 1872.

4. *Blue book of 360 pages*: A 'blue book' was a government report, termed thus from the blue paper used to cover such publications. This one was the *Report from the Select Committee on Accidents in Mines*, 1835 (603), v. 1.
5. *'In conclusion ... Legislature'*: the quotation is from page x of the Committee's *Report.*
6. *Mr. Mather was Secretary*: the South Shields Committee; see note 6 to Dunn, *A Treatise on the Winning and Working of Collieries.*
7. *of this year*: the *Report from the Select Committee on [the Causes and Frequency of Explosions in] Coal Mines*, 1852 (509), v. 1 . The South Shields Committee's *Report* was reprinted as Appendix 4, at pp. 155–228.
8. *'no mere Safety Lamp ... prevent'*: This somewhat loose quotation is from p. 173 of the reprint of the South Shields Committee's *Report* attached to the *Report* of the 1852 Committee.
9. *'that considering ... modern date.'*: The first part of this quotation is from p. 187, the second part from p. 208, of the reprint of the South Shields Committee's *Report* attached to the *Report* of the 1852 Committee.
10. *Sir Henry de la Beche*: Sir Henry Thomas de la Beche (1796–1855), geologist. At first a 'gentleman geologist', living on the income from the family's slave plantation in Jamaica. Published his *Geological Manual* (London: Treuttel and Würtz, Treuttel Jun. and Richter) in 1831. Appointed geologist to the Ordnance Survey, 1832; Director, 1835; later Director of the Museum of Practical Geology and Director of the Royal School of Mines. Knighted, 1842; CB, 1848.
11. *Dr. Lyon Playfair*: See note 8 to V. B. Kennett-Barrington, 'River Pollution by Refuse from Manufactories'.
12. *published in 1847*: Sir Henry T. de la Beche, Dr Lyon Playfair and Mr Warington Smyth, *Reports on the Gases and Explosions in Collieries*, [Command Paper] 815, 1847, xvi, 159.
13. *Blue Book of 615 pages*: The *Report from the Select Committee (House of Lords) on Dangerous Accidents in Coal Mines*, 1849 (613) vii. 1.
14. *Professor Phillips and Mr. Blackwell*: John Phillips, Esq., FRS, *Report on the Ventilation of Mines and Collieries* [Command Paper] 1222, 1850, xxiii, 475; J. Kenyon Blackwell, Esq., *Report on Ventilation of Mines 25th March 1850.* [Command Paper] 1214, 1850, xxiii, 443.
15. *'superior skill ... overlooker'*: From p. 46 of Phillips's *Report.*
16. *Mr Cayley*: Edward Stillingfleet Cayley (1801–62), MP for the North Riding of Yorkshire from 1832 till his death. An independent member. 'Over scrupulous and at times crotchety, there was no counting on his vote until the time to give it arrived' complained one obituarist (*The Times*, 27 February 1862, p. 9b).
17. *a report*: The *Report from the Select Committee on the Causes and Frequency of Explosions in Coal Mines*, 1852 (509), v. 1.
18. *Mr Forster*: Thomas Emerson Forster (1802–75), colliery viewer; the father of George Baker Forster (1832–1901) for whom see note 14 to White, 'The Coad Electric Miner's Lamp'; and the grandfather of Thomas Emmerson Forster (1858–1933), colliery company director. Westgarth Forster (for whom see note 32 to Scafe, *King Coal's Levee*) was a cousin of his father. Born in the lead mining district of the upper South Tyne. When he was fifteen apprenticed to one of the owners of Hebburn Colliery where the resident viewer was Matthias Dunn and the head viewer John Buddle. Appointed resident viewer at Walker Colliery on the Tyne near Newcastle when he was little more than twenty years old; two years later took a senior position at Hetton Colliery, Co. Durham. Later, consulting Engineer to the Earl of Lonsdale and to Lord Boyne. President of the North

of England Institute of Mining Engineers, 1866–9. In work, vigorous and indefatigable; in dealing with his workmen, tactful; in dealing with men of rank, respectful but plain and forthright (*DMM*).

19. *'Your Committee ... Ventilation of Mines'*: The first part of quotation, down to 'neglect or otherwise', is from p. vi of the 1852 Select Committee *Report*; the remainder from the analytical index to the same *Report*, on p. 244.
20. *business*: Wood here states succinctly the 'free-rider' problem in the provision of public goods.

Taylor, 'Prospectus of a College of Practical Mining and Manufacturing Science, Proposed to be Established at Newcastle-Upon-Tyne'

1. *T. J. Taylor*: Thomas John Taylor (1810–61), mining engineer. From a family much connected with mining; Hugh Taylor (1817–1900), the coal owner and MP for Tynemouth, was his brother, as was John Taylor, another mining engineer. Hugh Taylor, Sr, his uncle, was chief agent to the Duke of Northumberland (*DMM*).
2. *Nicholas Wood ... Robert Plummer, Byker*: For Nicholas Wood, see note 1 to Wood, 'On Safety Lamps for Lighting Coal Mines'. J. T. Woodhouse (1809–78) was a leading mining engineer in the East Midlands. Orphaned as a child, his guardian, Edward Mammatt, was agent to the Marques of Hastings, a major coal royalty owner in the district, and Woodhouse succeeded to the post in 1835 (*Biographical Dictionary of Civil Engineers*). W. Peace was William Peace (*c.* 1810–61) of Haigh, Lancashire, a mining engineer and colliery viewer; agent to the Earl of Crawford and Balcarres. He was the father of Maskell William Peace (*c.* 1835–92) the Law Clerk and Secretary of the Mining Association of Great Britain from 1866 till his death. Charles Binns (1813–87) found himself lodging with George Stephenson while he was working on the Liverpool and Manchester Railway and became his Secretary; became a partner with George and Robert Stephenson, George Hudson, the 'Railway King', and Carr Glyn, the banker, in the Clay Cross estate; Binns became manager of the Clay Cross Company from 1840–81. G. C. Greenwell was George Clementson Greenwell (1821–1900) who published a volume of poetry in 1839 but became a colliery viewer by 1848; he was one of the founders of the North of England Institute; his *Practical Treatise on Mine Engineering* (Newcastle-upon-Tyne: M. & M. W. Lambert, 1855) was well regarded but he is probably now best known for his *Glossary* (*DMM*). Thomas J. Taylor of Earsdon is the T. J. Taylor just noted. I. L. Bell is Isaac Lowthian Bell (1816–1904) the wealthy industrialist (*ODNB*). For W. G. Armstrong, see note 1 to Armstrong, 'Centenary of the Steam Engine of Watt' in this volume. H. Lee Pattinson was Hugh Lee Pattinson (1796–1858) a metallurgical chemist who discovered an easy and cheap way of desilverizing lead and took the first photograph of the Niagara Falls (*ODNB*). Thomas Sopwith (1803–79) was a civil and mining engineer; he was Chief Agent to the W. B. [Lead] Mines at Allenheads in the north Pennines from 1845–71, owned at the time of his appointment by Thomas Wentworth Beaumont (1792–1848), a member of the Beaumont-Blackett-Wentworth dynasty; Thomas Octave Murdoch Sopwith (1888–1989), the pioneer aircraft engineer whose name will be familiar to readers of the works of W. E. Johns, was his grandson (*Biographical Dictionary of Civil Engineers*). R. W. Swinburne was Robert Walter Swinburne (1803–86), a Newcastle and South Shields glass and soda manufacturer at one time in

partnership with the executors of the will of Nicholas Wood (*DMM*). Robert Plummer (1799–1869) was a member of the firm of B. Plummer, Jun., & Co., coal fitters and merchants, and Secretary to the Newcastle and Gateshead Chamber of Commerce.

3. *all the coal mining districts of England and Wales*: Although it held its meetings in Newcastle, there was no rule restricting membership of the Institute to the north of England or, indeed, to the UK.
4. *litharge*: protoxide of lead, PbO.
5. *the Coal Trade*: The term was widely used, by themselves and others, to refer to the coal owners collectively. It did not include the royalty owners and it did not usually include coal owners outside the north-east. Nor did it include the shipping or retail trades connected with the coal industry. There were, of course, significant overlaps in membership between the Institute and the Trade.
6. *£35,000*: In sections of the proposal omitted here, an estimate of £16,000 for building costs was given, included in the £35,000. This, the proposal accepted, was 'a considerable sum'. Running costs, exclusive of interest on the money sunk in the building, were expected to be about £3,000 a year, to be met from student fees.
7. *Robt. Hunt, Esq.*: See note 2 to Steavenson, 'The Manufacture of Coke'.
8. *The President*: Nicholas Wood (see note 1 to Wood, 'On Safety Lamps for Lighting Coal Mines').
9. *Mr. M. Dunn*: Matthias Dunn, for whom see note 6 to the Introduction to these three volumes.
10. *Mr. Taylor*: The T. J. Taylor making the proposal.

Davies, *Coal Mining: A Reader for Primary Schools And Evening Classes*

1. *Henry Davies*: little known except for what may be gleaned from his books. In this *Reader*, he announces himself as the 'Author of "Mining Machinery," [(Treharris: The Author, 1896)], "[The] Miner's Arithmetic [and Mensuration: With Answers,' (London: Chapman & Hall, 1898)], "Silent Heroisms" [unknown] "Colliery Accidents: Their Cause and Prevention [(Merthyr Tydvil: Educational Publishing Co., 1906)]," Etc.' but he was probably best known as the author of *How to Become a Colliery Manager* (Wigan: Thos. Wall and Sons Ltd, 1906) a crammer's book for those who wished to pass the Home Office examinations that led to certification as an Under-Manager and Manager of a colliery. On the title page of that book he describes himself as 'Director of Mining Instruction under the Glamorgan County Council'.

   At this time educational careers in state sector were usually divided into two periods only, 'elementary' and 'higher', the latter meaning 'post-primary', not 'university'. 'Primary' or 'elementary' schools were those attended until the end of compulsory schooling at thirteen or fourteen years. Use of the term 'secondary school' was unusual until the passing of the 1944 Education Act, the normal term before this, especially from the 1918 Education Act onwards, being a 'continuation school'. Similarly, the 'Continuation Classes' in the book's subtitle are post-primary classes.
2. *Professor Huxley*: Thomas Henry Huxley (1825–95) the biologist and Darwinian controversialist. His examination of coal under the microscope is described in his 1870 essay 'On the Formation of Coal' available in his *Collected Essays: Volume 8: Discourses: Biological and Geological* (London Macmillan, 1893–5), pp. 137–61.

3. *An explorer*: Sir William Howard Russell (1820–1907), the reporter for *The Times*, whose dispatches from the Crimean War caused such a sensation.
4. *'From the black water ... at times'*: The quotation is from Russell's *My Diary North and South*, 2 vols (London: Bradbury and Evans, 1863), vol. 1, p. 127. Davies may have seen the passage in T. E. Thorpe (ed.), *Coal: Its History and Uses* (London: Macmillan and Co., 1878) which also quotes it, at p. 58.
5. *Hugh Miller*: Hugh Miller (1802–56) a self-taught geologist whose career was referred to repeatedly by Samuel Smiles in his *Self-Help*. His autobiography is available in an edition edited by Michael Shortland, *Hugh Miller's Memoir: From Stonemason to Geologist* (Edinburgh: Edinburgh University Press, 1995).
6. *'All round us ... future use'*: source not identified.
7. *an American writer*: Ralph Waldo Emerson (1803–82). The quotation is from his essay on Goethe in his *Representative Men: Seven Lectures* (Boston, MA: Phillips, Sampson and Co., 1850).
8. *the Fireman*: One of the junior officials of the mine.
9. *sprags*: Sprags are short props or supports.
10. *locked*: Opening a safety lamp in a gassy atmosphere could cause an explosion; they were therefore locked before being handed over to the collier.
11. *pricker*: 'A piece of bent wire by which the size of the flame of a safety lamp is regulated, without removing the top of the lamp' (Gresley, *Glossary*).
12. *struck by a tool*: Thereby causing a spark.
13. *shotman*: Also 'shotfirer'; a junior official charged with the responsibility for firing shots of gunpowder and other explosives.
14. *CHARLES WILKINS*: Charles Wilkins (1831–1913) writer of Merthyr Tydfil. He was, according to a report in the *Western Mail* (23 June 1877) a druid, and, less remarkably, according to a later report, a freemason. He published *The History of Merthyr Tydfil* (Merthyr Tydfil: Southey, 1867), *Wales Past and Present* (Merthyr Tydfil: Southey, 1870) and similar works. His most ambitious book, *The History of the Literature of Wales* (Cardiff: Owen and Co., 1884) received reviews questioning his competence in Welsh, Latin and English. His works on industrial topics, including *The South Wales Coal Trade* from which excerpts are presented in Volume 2 (pp. 327–30, 365–73), drew praise. The excerpt presented here was presaged by his eighty-page booklet *Buried Alive! A Narrative of Suffering and Heroism: Being the Tale of the Rhondda Colliers as Related by Themselves* (London: Houlston and Sons, 1877).
15. *Tynewydd catastrophe*: The disaster happened on 11 April 1877 at the Tynewydd Colliery of the Troedyrhiw Coal Company in the Rhondda Valley, Glamorgan, South Wales.
16. *Alma or Balaclava*: Battles in the Crimean War, both fought in 1854.
17. *mandrils*: or mandrels; miners' picks.
18. *to bank*: To the surface.
19. *waters seemed to subside as they say*: The parallel with the parting of the Red Sea (Exodus 14) is only the most obvious of a number of possible Biblical references here. Also recalled are, for example, the waters of Psalm 77 where 'the very deep trembled' before the Lord.
20. *George Smith*: George Smith (1840–76), Assyriologist. It was he who in 1872 discovered among the cuneiform tablets sent to the British Museum from Nineveh the Chaldean or Babylonian account of a deluge that paralleled the Biblical account of Noah's Flood, thus suggesting an alternative way of reading Genesis, as myth not as history, and rendering his name familiar among the general public (*ODNB*).

For Product Safety Concerns and Information please contact our EU representative GPSR@taylorandfrancis.com Taylor & Francis Verlag GmbH, Kaufingerstraße 24, 80331 München, Germany

Batch number: 08158387

Printed by Printforce, the Netherlands